STUDENTS' GUIDE TO

Operations Research

A Companion to
Introduction to Operations Research, Fourth Edition
By Frederick S. Hillier and Gerald J. Lieberman

Paul A. Jensen
University of Texas at Austin

McGraw-Hill Book Company

New York St. Louis San Francisco Auckland Bogotá Caracas
Colorado Springs Hamburg Lisbon London Madrid Mexico Milan
Montreal New Delhi Oklahoma City Panama Paris San Juan
São Paulo Singapore Sydney Tokyo Toronto

To Ruth Ann and Grace Jensen

STUDENTS' GUIDE TO OPERATIONS RESEARCH

Library of Congress Catalog Card Number: 88-62542
ISBN 0-07-028909-3

Contents

Chapter 1
Introduction **1**

The Structure of this Guide 1
The Nature of Operations Research (1.2) 3

Chapter 2
Overview of the Operations Research Modeling Approach **5**

Chapter 3
Introduction to Linear Programming **8**

Modeling (3.1–3.4) 8
Computer Program 19
Problems 23

Chapter 4
Solving Linear Programming Problems: The Simplex Method **28**

Foundations (4.1, 4.2, 5.1) 28
The Algebra of the Simplex Method (4.3) 34
The Simplex Method in the Tabular Form (4.4) 41
Tie Breaking in the Simplex Method (4.5) 45
Adapting to Other Model Forms (4.6) 48
Computer Program 56
Problems 60
Computer Problems 62

Chapter 5
The Theory of the Simplex Method **64**

The Revised Simplex Method (5.2) 64
A Fundamental Insight (5.3) 73
Computer Program 77
Problems 77

Chapter 6
Duality Theory and Sensitivity Analysis **79**

Duality (6.1, 6.3, 6.4) 79
Sensitivity Analysis (6.5, 6.6) 88
Applying Sensitivity Analysis (6.7) 94
Computer Program 100
Problems 103
Computer Problems 106

Chapter 7
Special Types of Linear Programming Problems **107**

The Transportation Problem (7.1) 106
The Simplex Method for the Transportation Problem (7.2) 116
Network Flow Programming 128
Computer Programs 138
Problems 144
Computer Problems 147

Chapter 8
Formulating Linear Programming Models 151

Goal Programming (8.2) 151
Maximizing the Minimum (or Minimizing the Maximum) (8.3) 161
Computer Program 165
Problems 166

Chapter 9
Other Algorithms for Linear Programming 169

The Upper Bound Technique (9.1) 169
The Dual Simplex Method (9.2) 176
Computer Program 180
Problems 182

Chapter 10
Network Analysis, Including PERT-CPM 185

Notation (10.2) 185
The Shortest Route Problem (10.3) 187
The Minimal Spanning Tree Problem (10.4) 191
The Maximal Flow Problem (10.5) 194
Project Planning and Control with PERT-CPM (10.6) 199
Project Planning with Random Activity Times (10.6) 205
Time-Cost Tradeoffs in Project Planning (10.6) 208
Computer Program 211
Problems 213

Chapter 11
Dynamic Programming 216

Notation 219
Deterministic Dynamic Programming (11.3) 218
Probabilistic Dynamic Programming (11.4) 231
Problems 235

Chapter 12
Game Theory 238

Two-Person Zero-Sum Game 238
Problems 247

Chapter 13
Integer Programming 249

Modeling (13.1, 13.2) 249
A Branch-and-Bound Algorithm for Binary Integer Programming (13.5) 258
A Branch-and-Bound Algorithm for Mixed Integer Programming (13.6) 267
Computer Program 275
Problems 280
Computer Problems 281

Chapter 14
Nonlinear Programming 285

Introduction 285
Unconstrained Optimization (14.4, 14.5) 292
Constrained Optimization (14.6) 300
Quadratic Programming (14.7) 303
Separable Programming 305
Sequential Unconstrained Minimization Technique (14.10) 310
Computer Program 312
Problems 313
Computer Problems 314

Chapter 15
Stochastic Processes 317

Markov Chains (15.3) 317
First Passage Times (15.5) 325
Classification of States (15.6) 328
Long-Run Properties (15.7) 333
Computer Program 338
Problems 340
Computer Problems 342

Chapter 16
Queueing Theory 344
Basic Structure of Queueing Models (16.2) 344
Exponential Distributions (16.4) 351
Birth-Death Processes (16.5) 357
Queueing Models with Infinite Queue and Input Source (16.6) 362
Queueing Models with a Finite Queue (16.6) 368
Queueing Models with a Finite Input Source (16.6) 373

Queueing Models with Nonexponential Service Times (16.7)	378
Queueing Networks (16.9)	381
Computer Program	385
Problems	388
Computer Problems	392

Chapter 17
The Application of Queueing Theory **394**

Decision Models (17.1–17.4)	394
Queueing Systems with Travel Times (17.5)	400
Computer Program	406
Problems	406

Chapter 18
Inventory Theory **409**

Components of Inventory Models (18.2)	410
Deterministic - Continous Review - Uniform Demand (18.3)	411
Deterministic - Periodic Review - Production Planning (18.3)	418
Stochastic Models (18.4)	421
Stochastic - Single Period Model - No Setup Cost (18.4)	423
Stochastic - Single Period Model - Setup Cost (18.4)	426
Stochastic - MultiPeriod - No Setup Cost (18.4)	429
Stochastic - Continuous Review - Fixed Delivery Lag (18.4)	431
Problems	435

Chapter 19
Forecasting **439**

Forecasting Techniques (19.4–19.5)	439
Problems	450
Computer Problems	451

Chapter 20
Markovian Decision Processes **452**

Linear Programming Formulation (20.2–20.3)	452
Problems	456
Computer Problem	458

Chapter 21
Reliability **459**
Structure Function of a System (21.2) 460
System Reliability (21.3) 463
Exact System Reliability (21.4) 467
Bounds on System Reliability (21.5) 473
Problems 475

Chapter 22
Decision Analysis **478**
Decision Trees (22.4) 478
Problems 485

Chapter 23
Simulation **488**
Simulation Model for a Queueing System 488
Computer Programs 498
Problems 489
Computer Problems 501

Preface

Introduction to Operations Research by Frederick S. Hillier and Gerald J. Lieberman has been a classic introductory text for much of the history of operations research. I have used the text for many classes of students from the engineering and business schools at the University of Texas at Austin. Thus I am particularly pleased and honored to have the opportunity to write this guide to support students studying from the fourth edition of this excellent book.

The guide does not supplant the text. Although I have included material from every chapter, not all sections are covered. I have selected subjects primarily related to modeling and computational skills, leaving out those that are primarily theoretical and expository. The text provides important links to the general literature of operations research not included in the guide.

Based on extensive experience in teaching the material, I have attempted to present the covered subjects in a manner most conducive to student learning. Each section has identified goals. Sections are generally short enough to be covered in a single sitting. Definitions and results are grouped together in outline form for easy reference and review. Examples are provided for every computational procedure and model type, and student exercises are included immediately after a subject is discussed. Algorithms are presented in a concise and general fashion so that the procedures can be reproduced with hand calculations. For the most part, I have remained consistent with the notation of the text but have occasionally expanded on the notation to provide the greater generality required by the outline format.

The guide expands the scope of the text in terms of implementation of the computational procedures for the microcomputer. The successful package of computer programs, *Microsolve/Operations Research,* revised edition, published by Holden-Day in 1985, includes programs supporting most of the chapters in the guide. Thus I have taken this opportunity to include discussions linking this package to the course material. Student exercises are provided that require the student to use computer programs. Although the computer-related sections are written with reference to *Microsolve,* many of the remarks and also the exercises are appropriate for other computer implementations. I believe this combination of text, guide, and computer programs provides an educational opportunity not formerly available in this field.

The preparation of a publication of this nature must rest on an extensive base of teaching experience in the subject areas. In this respect I must thank my longtime colleagues in the Department of Mechanical Engineering at the University of Texas, J. Wesley Barnes, Charles Beightler, and William Lesso. These men are pioneers in the use of self-paced methods and microcomputers for instruction in operations research as well as participants with me in many lengthy discussions on teaching methodology. This book is being written while I am on research leave from the University of Texas in the Department of Industrieel Beleid at the Katholieke Universiteit van Leuven in Belgium. I must therefore thank officials at the University of Texas for granting the leave, and my colleagues in Leuven, Ludo Gelders and Luc Van Wassenhove, for their support. Thanks are also due to Fredrick Murphy and Wallace Shows from Holden-Day, Inc., who initiated the idea for the guide and encouraged me to complete it. Special thanks go to my family, who saw many hours of our European stay devoted to this task, and to my wife, Margaret, who did a good deal of the final preparation of the manuscript.

Paul A. Jensen

CHAPTER 1

Introduction

The Structure of This Guide

This book, hereafter called the Guide, was written to support studies from the text *Introduction to Operations Research,* 4th Edition, written by Frederick S. Hillier and Gerald J. Lieberman, published by Holden-Day, Inc. in 1986, hereafter called H & L. Each chapter of the Guide has a direct relationship with a chapter from H & L. Except for this introductory chapter all have the same titles and appear in the same order. Although every chapter is included, not every section is represented. The H & L section numbers that relate to a particular Guide section appear in parentheses after the Guide section title. The H & L sections that have been excluded are primarily expository, primarily proofs, or involve advanced material. Some Guide sections are not based on material from H & L, particularly those related to computer programs and sections on network flow programming, which are of special interest to this author. Most of the sections involve a relatively small body of material that can be covered in a single sitting or class.

A special feature of this guide is the inclusion of the sections called "Computer Program." These describe the relation of the text material to the package of programs for the microcomputer, *Microsolve/Operations Research,* Revised Edition, by Paul A. Jensen, published by Holden-Day in 1985, hereafter called *Microsolve.* Versions are available for both the IBM-PC and the Apple II. The sections illustrate the use of the programs with example input data and output reports. Guidelines are provided for presenting a model to the computer.

All the chapters except the first two include a number of examples illustrating the chapter contents and an extensive set of problems with which the student can test his or her skills.

Except for this introduction and the computer program and problem sections, all the Guide sections have a common structure. We think this provides assistance for the student reviewing the material or searching for a particular definition, result, algorithm, or example. The components of the sections are listed below with a brief discussion of each. Not all sections have every component.

Title: Most, but not all, section titles agree with the titles in H & L. The related H & L section numbers appear in parentheses after the titles.

Introduction: A brief statement about the content of the section.

Goals: Every section has one or more goal statements reflecting the author's opinion on the body of knowledge or set of skills to be derived from the section.

Definitions: The principal terms introduced in the section are listed with their definitions. Notation is also defined. Generally notation follows H & L; however, some variations are introduced for consistency and because of the limitations of the author's word processor. Some new notation is occasionally introduced where H & L has not used notation.

Results: The principal results of the section are listed and described in general terms.

Algorithms: The algorithms or computational processes implementing the operations research technique are described in general terms.

Examples: We have attempted to provide at least one example of every result or algorithm described in the section. The examples are carefully presented in full detail.

Modeling: Here special attention is paid to modeling problem situations in the forms required by the operations research technique.

Problems: Every section involving a model formulation or problem-solving skill has exercises that can be worked immediately after studying the material of the section. Answers are provided in the back of the book. Every chapter also has a problem section including exercises from all sections.

Although the H & L text and this Guide cover almost the same material, they are not interchangeable. The text provides much more in the way of supporting discussion, mathematical proofs, and relation to the literature. The Guide provides concise statements of definitions, results, and algorithms, additional examples, additional problems with solutions, and a link to the *Microsolve* package. Together H & L, this Guide, and *Microsolve* provide a collection of materials that should make operations research techniques easier to learn, and more interesting and should give them greater potential for application.

The Nature of Operations Research (1.2)

It is a mark of modern society that decisions must often be made under circumstances characterized by novel conditions, limited resources, conflicting goals, expensive experimentation, complex organizations, uncertainty, and short response time. Operations research (or the practical equivalent, management science) is a field of study explicitly devoted to aiding decision makers under such circumstances. The goal of operations research is to provide procedures for formulating models of decision-making problems, finding solutions to the models that optimize objective measures of merit, and implementing the solutions in an attempt to solve the problems. To this end a number of mathematical techniques have been developed that are exercised primarily with the help of a digital computer. The purpose of the text *Introduction to Operations Research* and this companion Guide is to provide an introduction to these techniques.

GOAL

- To learn specific terms related to the nature of operations research.

DEFINITIONS

Operations: The activities carried out in an organization related to attaining the goals of the organization.

Research: The process of observation characterized by the scientific method. The steps of process include: observing the situation and formulating a problem statement, constructing a mathematical model, hypothesizing that the model represents the situation in important aspects, and verifying the model through experimentation.

Model: An abstract representation of a decision problem related to the operations of the organization. The model is usually stated in mathematical terms and includes a statement of the assumptions used in the formulation of the model.

Systems Approach: An approach to model formulation that attempts to ascertain and include the broad implications of decisions for organizational goals.

Optimal Solution: A solution to the model that optimizes (maximizes or minimizes) some objective measure of merit over all feasible solutions.

Team: A collection of individuals bringing various skills and viewpoints to a problem. Historically operations research has used the team approach in order that the solution not be limited by past experience in a single field. A team also provides the collection of specialized skills that are rarely found in single individuals.

Operations Research Techniques: A collection of general mathematical models, analysis procedures, and optimization algorithms that have been found useful in operations research studies. These include linear programming, integer programming, network programming, nonlinear programming, dynamic programming, statistical analysis, probability theory, queueing theory, stochastic processes, simulation, inventory theory, PERT/CPM, reliability, decision analysis, and others. Some of these fields have been created by operations research professionals while others derive from a variety of disciplines.

CHAPTER 2

Overview of the Operations Research Modeling Approach

An educational program in operations research typically considers the various operations research techniques listed, in part, in the last chapter. Studies range from the theoretical basis of the techniques, through the computa-tional processes that implement the techniques on the computer, to the application of the techniques, typically taught using textbook examples. There is a danger in this approach that the student, and sometimes even the professor, will forget that the operations research technique is only a part of the process of finding a solution to a problem. Practitioners often claim that the solution technique is one of the smaller components of the process. This chapter is included to provide perspective to the study of the techniques of operations research by listing and describing the several steps in the solution of a typical problem.

GOAL

- To learn the components of the typical operations research study.

RESULTS

The steps are listed below with a brief discussion of each. They are not usually followed in strict order from start to finish; rather there are many loops in the process, with experimentation and logic at each step suggesting modifications to decisions made at earlier steps. The process is rarely complete. Problems continue after a solution is proposed and implemented. Parameters and conditions change with time, requiring a constant review of the solution and a continuous repetition of portions of the solution process.

Formulating the Problem For proper analysis the problem must be formulated in a precise way including statement of objectives, constraints on solutions, appropriate assumptions, available data, and alternatives for action. The statement of the problem at this point is usually in verbal and qualitative terms. Since the problem often arises from sources outside the study team, care must be taken to get agreement on the exact character of the problem to be solved from those who perceive it. There is not much value to either a poor solution to the correct problem or a good solution to a problem that has been formulated incorrectly.

Constructing a Mathematical Model In order to use objective methods such as mathematical analysis or optimization approaches, the problem must be translated from verbal qualitative terms to quantitative terms. Such a quantitative statement is called a mathematical model. Although we hope to study the broad implications of the problem using a systems approach, a model cannot include every aspect of a situation. A mathematical model is always an abstraction which is of necessity simpler than the real situation. Elements that are irrelevant or unimportant to the problem are to be ignored, hopefully leaving sufficient detail so that the solution obtained with the model has value with regard to the original problem. The statement of the abstractions taken to obtain the model are called the *assumptions*. It is important to note that assumptions are not necessarily statements of belief, but are descriptions of the abstractions used to obtain the model. The appropriateness of the assumptions can be determined only by subsequent testing of the validity of the model. Models must be both *tractable*, capable of being solved, and *valid*, representative of the original situation. These dual goals are often contradictory and are not always attainable.

Deriving a Solution Here the operations research techniques described in this book and elsewhere can be used to obtain a solution to the mathematical model. The team may also have to invent new techniques specifically adapted to the problem at hand. It is very possible to derive a model that is impossible to solve, requiring a return to the previous step for simplification or perhaps an abandonment of the project if no acceptable, tractable model can be found.

Testing the Model and Solution This step involves determining the validity of the model and the solution obtained. Does it have relevance to the original problem? Have the assumptions used to obtain a tractable model rendered the solution useless? These questions must be answered before the solution is implemented in actual practice. There is a number of ways to do this. The simplest method simply determines whether the solution makes sense to the decision maker. Solutions obtained by operations research studies may not be predictable but they are often not too surprising. Other testing procedures include sensitivity analysis, the use of the model under a variety of conjectured conditions, and the use of the model with historical data.

Establishing Control over the Solution Problems are usually ongoing rather than occurring only once. Solutions are implemented as procedures to be used over and over again in almost an automatic fashion. It is important to establish controls to be sure that the problem doesn't change and make the solution inappropriate.

Implementing the Solution A solution to a problem usually implies changes for some individuals in the organization. Since resistance to change is common, the implementation of solutions is perhaps the most difficult part of a problem-solving exercise. Although not strictly the responsibility of the operations research team, the solution process itself can be designed to simplify the implementation process. The persons who are likely to be affected by the changes caused by a solution should be consulted as part of the solution process and should perhaps even be a part of the problem-solving team.

CHAPTER 3

Introduction to Linear Programming

Modeling (3.1–3.4)

Linear programming means planning with a linear model. Thus, although solving a linear program usually means interfacing with a computer, the term *programming* here does not imply computer programming; rather it implies *planning*. Because planning is such an important topic in our complex world, linear programming has gained wide acceptance as one of the most practical tools of operations research. It gains much of its relevance from modern computers, which allow the solution of problems of enormous size, making possible the modeling and solving of important problems for government and industry.

The linear program is a mathematical model of some realistic situation. The model does not represent the entire situation, but only those aspects relevant to certain decisions that must be made. These decisions are represented in the model by algebraic unknowns called decision variables. The linear programming algorithm can find the optimum solution for the decision variables with respect to the mathematical model. The decision maker must then interpret and implement this result in the real world.

In contrast to models to be introduced in later chapters, the linear program is a deterministic model rather than stochastic; that is, there are no probability distributions describing the parameters of the model. The linear program is linear rather than nonlinear; that is, only linear expressions are included in the mathematical statement of the model. The variables of the linear program are continuous rather than discrete; for instance they cannot be restricted to only integer values. All these alternative assumptions will be considered in later chapters of this book, but at the expense of greatly increased computational difficulties. It is the simple form of the linear programming model that allows the great efficiency of the solution algorithms.

This chapter describes the creation of the linear program, and the next several chapters describe associated theory and algorithms. We use examples as the principal means of presentation; however, the best learning will come from the student's own efforts at setting up and solving problems. A number of problems are provided at the end of the chapter.

GOAL

- Starting from a prose description of a problem situation, be able to create a linear programming model that when solved will yield a valid solution to the original situation.

DEFINITIONS

Decision Variables: The unknowns of the problem whose values are to be determined by the solution of the linear program. The decision variables represent the decisions to be made in the problem situation. In mathematical statements we give the variables such names as $x_1, x_2, x_3, \ldots, x_n$. The number of decision variables is n, and x_j is the value of the jth variable. In models it is often convenient to use other names such as x_{ij} or y_k or $z(i,j)$. In computer models we use names such as FLOW1 or AB to represent specific problem-related quantities.

Linear Function: A function of the decision variables in the form

$$a_1 x_1 + a_2 x_2 + \cdots + a_n x_n$$

where $a_1, a_2, \ldots, a_n$ are numerical coefficients. All functions in a linear programming model are linear.

Objective Function: The measure by which alternative solutions are compared. It evaluates some quantitative criterion of importance to the person responsible for the decision, such as cost, profit, utility, or yield. The general objective function can be written

$$Z = c_1 x_1 + c_2 x_2 + \cdots + c_n x_n = \sum_{j=1}^{n} c_j x_j.$$

Here c_j is the coefficient of the jth decision variable. The measure selected can be either maximized or minimized.

Constraint: A linear inequality or equality defining limitations on decisions. There may be a number of constraints arising from a variety of sources such as limited resources, contractual obligations, or physical laws. The general designation for the number of constraints is m. A typical constraint might be

$$-2x_1 + 12x_2 + 7x_3 \leq 14.$$

A general statement of the constraints of a linear program is

$$\sum_{j=1}^{n} a_{ij} x_j \begin{bmatrix} \leq \\ = \\ \geq \end{bmatrix} b_i \quad \text{for } i = 1 \text{ to } m.$$

One of the three relations shown in the large bracket must be chosen for each constraint. The numbers a_{ij} are the constraint coefficients. The number b_i is the "right side" of the ith constraint.

Simple Upper Bounds: A constraint that places an upper bound on a variable, such as

$$x_j \leq u_j .$$

Some solution algorithms treat this type of constraint differently than the more general type of constraint described above.

Nonnegativity Restriction: Solution algorithms assume that the variables are constrained to be nonnegative;

$$x_j \geq 0, \quad \text{for } j = 1, \ldots, n .$$

If in fact not all variables are required to be nonnegative, special procedures are required to remove the restriction. These are described in Chapter 4.

Linear Programming Model: The combination of the objective function, constraints, simple upper bounds, and nonnegativity restrictions define the complete linear programming model.

Parameters: The collection of coefficients c_j, a_{ij}, b_i, and u_j, for all i and j, are called the parameters of the model. All the parameters must be known for the model to be completely determined.

Feasible Solution: A specification of values for the decision variables that satisfies all the constraints, including upper bound and nonnegativity restrictions.

Optimal Solution: A feasible solution that maximizes or minimizes the objective function. Whether the objective function is maximized or minimized must be clear from the model statement.

Alternative Optimal Solutions: If there is more than one optimal solution (with the same value of Z), the model is said to have alternative optimal solutions.

Model with No Feasible Solution: If there is no specification of values for the decision variables that satisfies all the constraints, the problem is said to have no feasible solution.

Unbounded Model: If there are feasible solutions for which the objective function can achieve arbitrarily large (if maximizing) or arbitrarily small (if minimizing) values, the model is said to be unbounded.

Standard Form for the Model: For some theoretical developments, it is helpful to have a single standard form. All alternative models can be put into this form, although for practical purposes it is rarely necessary to do this. The standard form adopted here is

$$\begin{aligned} \text{Maximize } Z = \quad & c_1x_1 + c_2x_2 + \cdots + c_n x_n \\ & a_{11}x_1 + a_{12}x_2 + \cdots + a_{1n} x_n \le b_1 \\ & a_{21}x_1 + a_{22}x_2 + \cdots + a_{2n} x_n \le b_2 \\ & \vdots \\ & a_{m1}x_1 + a_{m2}x_2 + \cdots + a_{mn}x_n \le b_m \\ & x_1 \ge 0, x_2 \ge 0, \ldots, x_n \ge 0. \end{aligned}$$

EXAMPLES

E3.1. Chemical Processing A company makes three products: x, y, and z. The products are made from three raw materials: A, B, and C. Products x and y are made by a chemical process which mixes all the materials. The mixture must be at least 10% (by weight) material A and at least 5% material B. The remainder of the mixture is material C. The output of the mixture is 10% waste, 70% product x, and 20% product y. This process can treat no more than 10,000 pounds of input material per month.

A different chemical process which mixes only materials B and C makes products y and z. A mixture of 30% (by weight) material B and 70% material C is processed. Of the output, 30% becomes product y, 60% becomes product z. The remaining 10% of the output is material A, which is used in the first mixture.

Product x, for which there is a maximum monthly demand of 5000 pounds, can be sold for $5 per pound. As much as 500 pounds of y can be sold for $11 per pound, while any additional amount can be sold for $8 per pound. Product z can be sold for $10 per pound. At least 1000 pounds of product z must be processed and sold every month.

Materials A, B, and C can be purchased for $4, $3, and $1 per pound, respectively. No more than 5000 pounds of material B can be purchased each month, while the others are unlimited.

The problem is to determine how much of the products x, y, and z to produce and how much A, B, and C to buy during the month. The goal is to maximize profit.

Solution At first glance the analyst might list the decision variables as x, y, z, A, B, and C. In many cases, however, clarity of modeling is served by defining extra variables not immediately apparent from the statement of the problem. The goal in modeling should be clarity rather than minimization of the number of variables and constraints. Computers are powerful enough to allow some excesses in this area.

Each variable and constraint should be assigned a name related to what it represents in the problem. General variables such as x and y should be avoided unless they represent, as in this problem, relevant quantities. The definition of the variables, in prose, should accompany the model presentation.

Since many constraints in the model represent physical conservation of flow, a flow diagram such as Fig. 3.1 is a great help in proper modeling. The circles in the figure are called nodes, and the directed line segments are called arcs. The arcs and nodes of the figure show the flow of materials in this problem and help to identify the variables that will be used.

From the diagram we define the following decision variables. The dimensional units are shown with each decision variable. We use capital letters with no subscripts for variable names because this is the format required by the computer program we will use to find a solution.

VARIABLE DEFINITIONS

Raw Materials

A, B, C: the quantities of raw materials A, B, and C bought (pounds).

Mixture 1

M1: the amount of mixture 1 (pounds).

AM1, BM1, CM1: the quantities of raw materials A, B, and C input to mixture (pounds).

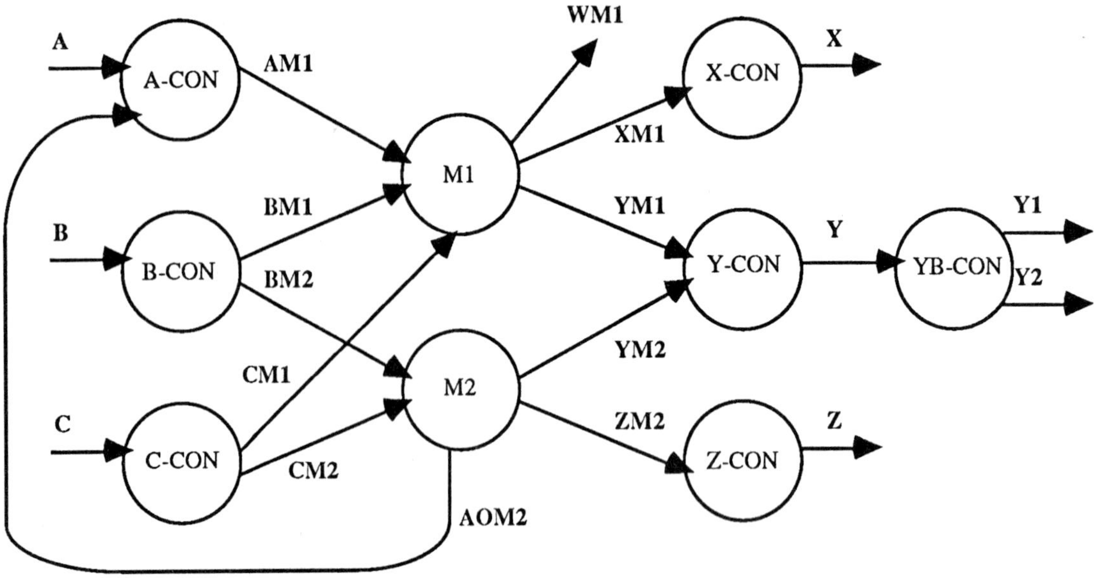

Figure 3.1 Flow Diagram for the Chemical Processing Problem

XM1, YM1: the quantities of products x and y produced by mixture 1 (pounds).

WM1: the quantity of waste produced by mixture 1 (pounds).

Mixture 2

M2: the amount of mixture 2 (pounds).

BM2, CM2: the quantities of raw materials B and C input to mixture 2 (pounds).

YM2, ZM2: the quantities of products y and z produced by mixture 2 (pounds).

AOM2: the quantity of raw material A produced by mixture 2 (pounds).

Finished Product

X, Y, Z: the quantities of products x; y, and z produced (pounds).

Y1: the quantity of product y sold for $11 per pound (pounds).

Y2: the quantity of product y sold for $8 per pound (pounds).

CONSERVATION CONSTRAINTS

Many of the constraints in this model can be taken directly from the flow diagram. These are the conservation of material flow constraints. Conservation simply implies that the total flow entering a node equals the total flow leaving the node. Every node in the figure generates a conservation constraint. Each constraint has been given a name to represent its purpose. Dimensional units are provided for each constraint. Every term of a constraint, together with the constant on the right side, must have the same dimensions.

A-CON (pounds) : Conservation of flow for material A:

$$A + AOM2 = AM1,$$

Since solution algorithms require all variables to be presented on the left side of the relational symbol with only constants on the right, we must rewrite the constraint as

$$A + AOM2 - AM1 = 0. \qquad (1)$$

In a similar fashion we write the remainder of the conservation constraints.

B-CON (pounds): $B - BM1 - BM2 = 0$ (2)

C-CON (pounds): $C - CM1 - CM2 = 0$ (3)

M1-CONI (pounds): $AM1 + BM1 + CM1 = 0.$ (4)

This constraint defines the quantity of the first mix. It implies conservation of flow at the input to the mix. Together with the next constraint, conservation of flow at node M1 is implied. It is unnecessary to write a separate constraint for this purpose.

M1-CONO (pounds): $M1 - WM1 - XM1 - YM1 = 0$ (5)

M2-CONI (pounds): $BM2 + CM2 - M2 = 0$ (6)

M2-CONO (pounds): $M2 - YM2 - ZM2 - AOM2 = 0$ (7)

X-CON (pounds): $XM1 - X = 0$ (8)

Y-CON (pounds):	YM1 + YM2 – Y	= 0	(9)
Z-CON (pounds):	ZM2 – Z	= 0	(10)
YB-CON (pounds):	Y – Y1 – Y2	= 0	(11)

This constraint equates the total Y with the two variables identifying the different revenues associated with the product y.

MIX INPUT CONSTRAINTS

The next constraints define the input component percentages of the two mixtures.

AM1% (pounds): this indicates the percentage of the material A in mixture 1:

$$AM1 \geq 0.1\ M1 \quad \text{or} \quad AM1 - 0.1\ M1 \geq 0 \qquad (12)$$

BM1% (pounds): $BM1 - 0.05\ M1 \geq 0$. (13)

A similar constraint is unnecessary for CM1 because its amount is determined by constraint (4).

BM2% (pounds): $BM2 - 0.3\ M2 = 0$. (14)

A similar constraint is unnecessary for CM2 because its amount is determined by constraint (6).

MIX OUTPUT CONSTRAINTS

The following constraints define the output components of the mixtures.

XM1% (pounds): $XM1 - 0.7\ M1 = 0$ (15)

YM1% (pounds): $YM1 - 0.2\ M1 = 0$ (16)

The amount of WM1 is determined by constraint (5).

YM2% (pounds): $YM2 - 0.3\ M2 = 0$ (17)

ZM2% (pounds): $ZM2 - 0.6\ M2 = 0$ (18)

The amount of AOM2 is determined by constraint (7).

BOUND CONSTRAINTS

Lower bounds of zero on variables, nonnegativity, are handled automatically by the computational process, so these constraints need not be explicitly included in a model entered into the computer. It is traditional, however, to show these constraints as part of the written model. They can be written in a general way as

$$\text{all variables} \geq 0. \qquad (19)$$

Lower bounds that are greater than zero must be entered as explicit constraints.

ZLIM: $Z \geq 1000$. (20)

Many computer programs also handle simple upper bounds in the computational process, so that these need not be explicitly included as constraints. They should be included in the written model.

BNDM1:	$M1 \le 10000$	(21)
BNDY1:	$Y1 \le 500$	(22)
BNDX:	$X \le 5000$	(23)
BMDB:	$B \le 5000.$	(24)

Preparation of the objective function is usually done last after all the variables are known. For the example, the objective is

$$\text{Maximize Profit} = [\text{ Revenue }] - [\text{ Cost }]$$

$$\text{Maximize } Z = 5\,X + 11\,Y1 + 8\,Y2 + 10\,Z - 4\,A - 3\,B - 1\,C. \quad (25)$$

Variables not shown in the objective function have zero coefficients.

This completes the setup of the linear programming model. The traditional way to show the model has the objective function first, followed by the constraints, the simple upper bounds, and finally the nonnegativity restrictions. Actually it is rather difficult to test the model to see if it is correct. Great care should be taken to include all relevant constraints and to create the model in a logical way. One of the simplest ways to test the model is to solve it with a computer program. Very often, simple errors lead to unrealistic answers that are quickly noticed. We will provide an answer for this model in the next chapter.

E3.2. Production Planning A company has a demand for its product projected over the next 6 months as indicated in the table below.

Month	1	2	3	4	5	6
Demand	20	30	60	40	30	20

The demand must be met. There are currently 10 units in inventory. The remainder of the demand must be met by production. If the production in a month is greater than the demand, the excess is carried in inventory at a cost of $40 per unit per month.

Employees make the product at the rate of 1 unit per day per worker. Fifteen are currently employed (at the beginning of the first month). Labor cost is $1000 per month per worker. The company can lay off workers at the beginning of any month at a cost of $600 each. The company can also hire new workers at the beginning of any month at a cost of $900 each. Each employee can work an extra 2 hours (in addition to an 8-hour day) at an overtime rate of 1.5 times the regular wage. The company has a budget of $50,000 per month for all expenses related to this problem.

The problem is to find a policy for hiring and firing workers and the production level for the next 6 months. Set up this problem as a linear program.

Solution Flow diagrams for this problem are shown in Fig. 3.2. There are two diagrams, one for the product and one for labor. Time has been discretized into 1-month intervals, with the beginning of each month represented by a node on each diagram. Arcs that go from one month to the next are inventory arcs. For the product diagram, the flows on these arcs are units of product stored from one month

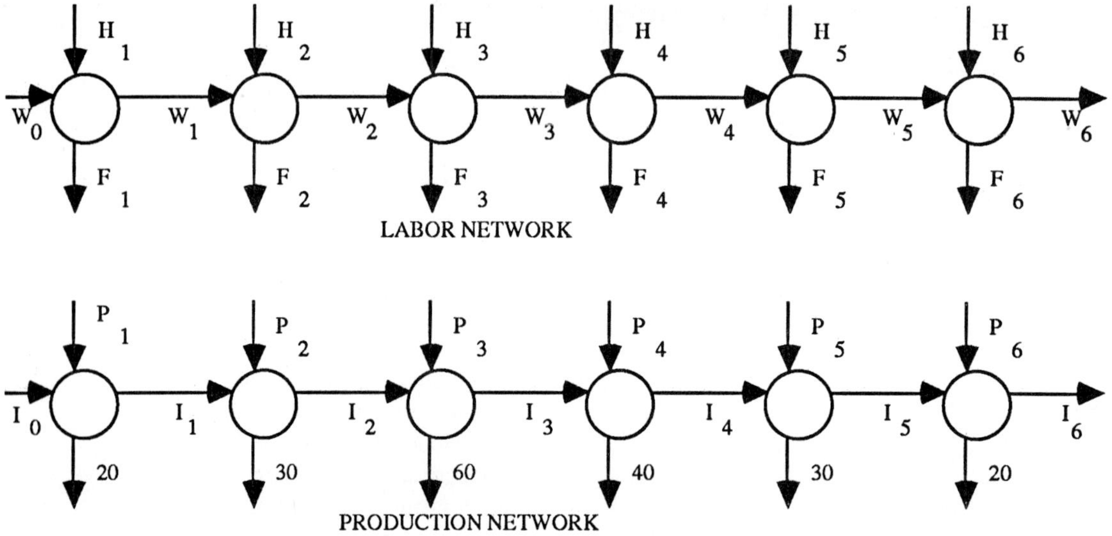

Figure 3.2 **Flow Diagrams for Production Planning**

to the next. For the labor diagram, the flows on the arcs represent workers carried over the month. For products, production provides the inputs and demand provides the outputs. For labor, workers hired provide the inputs while workers fired provide the outputs.

The variables for the model are shown on the figures and listed below. Here we use a more mathematical notation in the statement of the model with subscripts, summations, and general constraints written with variable indices. This type of presentation provides a more compact description of the model but does not reduce the size of the problem or the work required to enter the model data into a computer program. In fact, this representation tends to hide the size of the problem.

VARIABLE DEFINITIONS

In each of the definitions below, t ranges from 1 to 6.

The dimensions of each of the following are units of labor.

W_t: work force during period t.

W_0: the initial work force.

O_t: overtime worked expressed in terms of equivalent full-time workers.

H_t: number of workers hired at the beginning of period t.

F_t: number of workers fired at the beginning of period t.

The dimensions of each of the following are in units of products.

I_t: thc inventory level at the end of period t.

I_0: the initial inventory level.

P_t: the production during period t.

D_t: the demand in period t. These are not variables but parameters given in the table above.

CONSERVATION CONSTRAINTS

Again the conservation of flow constraints can be observed directly from the flow diagrams. Each node contributes one constraint.

WORKt (labor units): $W_{t-1} + H_t - F_t - W_t = 0$ for $t = 1, 2, \ldots, 6$
INVt (product units): $I_{t-1} + P_t - I_t = D_t$ for $t = 1, 2, \ldots, 6$

INITIAL VALUE CONSTRAINTS

WORK0 (labor units): $W_0 = 15$
INV0 (product units): $I_0 = 10$

PRODUCTION CAPACITY CONSTRAINTS

Production is limited by the number of workers, since each worker can produce one unit of product.

CAPt (product units): $W_t + O_t - P_t \geq 0$ for $t = 1, 2, \ldots, 6$.

OVERTIME LIMIT CONSTRAINTS

The maximum number of equivalent overtime workers is 1/4 the number of regular workers.

OVERt (labor units): $O_t - 0.25\, W_t \leq 0$ for $t = 1, 2, \ldots, 6$.

BUDGET CONSTRAINTS

The company cannot spend more than $50,000 each month.

BUDt (dollars): $1000\, W_t + 1500\, O_t + 900\, H_t + 600\, F_t + 40\, I_t \leq 50000$
for $t = 1, 2, \ldots, 6$.

OBJECTIVE FUNCTION

Minimize the total expenditures over the 6 months.

$$\text{MIN: } Z = 1000 \sum_{t=1}^{6} W_t + 1500 \sum_{t=1}^{6} O_t + 900 \sum_{t=1}^{6} H_t + 600 \sum_{t=1}^{6} F_t + 40 \sum_{t=1}^{6} I_t.$$

The model is complete. It has 38 variables and 32 constraints.

MODELING

The examples should point out that simple problem statements give rise to surprisingly large models. These are in fact small models as linear programming goes. Practical examples can have tens of thousands of variables and thousands of constraints. Certainly thousands of variables and hundreds of constraints are not uncommon. Computer programs are available for most mainframe computers that can solve problems of this size.

With so many equality constraints in both models, one might wonder if some variables can be eliminated by substitution. It happens that any equality constraint that can be written with a nonnegative right side and with all but one of the coefficients on the left having negative signs can be solved for the variable with the positive coefficient. That variable can then be replaced in the objective function and constraints, thus eliminating one variable and one constraint. In the chemical processing example, leaving out nonnegativity and simple upper bounds, 16 of the 19 constraints are of this type, which suggests that the problem could be reduced to 5 variables and 3 constraints. This is usually not a wise thing to do, however. A great deal of mathematical manipulation is required, which is subject to error, and it is very difficult to relate the resulting model to the original situation. There is a great sacrifice in model clarity and flexibility to change. If the variables have finite upper bounds, the substitution must also be used for the upper bounds, changing them from simple bounds handled through the computational process to new, more complex, constraints. The savings in constraints will not be realized in this case.

Generally, the rule in modeling for linear programming should be that clarity and flexibility take priority over economy. Most practical models are created to be solved not just once, but many times with varied parameters. For instance, a production planning model may be solved each month as new demand data are estimated. The parameters should be easy to change and not hidden by mathematical manipulations. The variables and constraints should represent easily recognized aspects of the problem, so that executives unfamiliar with the techniques of linear programming can study and change the model.

The difficulty in solving a linear program depends on the number of variables and constraints, with the constraints being much more important than the number of variables (computation time is roughly related to the cube of the number of constraints). Thus, simple substitutions that do not compromise the clarity of the model might well be acceptable. This is especially true for microcomputer codes with limited capacity. For instance, the initial conditions in the production planning example can be easily eliminated from the problem.

Positive, but nonzero, lower bounds can be eliminated from the problem fairly easily, with some loss of clarity, by the following transformation. Assume there is some variable with

$$x_j \geq v_j \text{ and } x_j \leq u_j.$$

Let

$$x'_j = x_j - v_j.$$

or

$$x_j = x'_j + v_j \, .$$

Thus

$$x'_j \geq 0, \text{ and } x'_j \leq u_j - v_j.$$

The variable must be replaced everywhere in the model by its equivalent. Since the equivalent includes a constant, the right sides of the constraints will change. Any constants introduced in the objective function may be dropped.

Computer Program

In this chapter we describe how to create a linear programming model using the *Microsolve* package, while in the next we describe how a solution is obtained and interpreted. To use *Microsolve* for linear programming, choose the first option on the disk menu. The linear model generator will then load from the program disk. The menu for this program is illustrated in Fig. 3.3.

The options on the menu are for the most part self-explanatory. Options 1 and 6 provide for loading and saving data sets from a previously prepared data disk. The student would do well to maintain a disk of data sets, because they are generally difficult to prepare and frequently require modification during the modeling process. Data sets are automatically saved temporarily while a problem is being prepared and solved; however, the temporary models are lost if a new model is created or the computer is turned off.

```
          LINEAR MODEL GENERATOR

 1.  GET MODEL FROM DISK
 2.  ENTER CONSTRAINTS AND OBJECTIVE
 3.  SET UPPER BOUNDS ON VARIABLES
 4.  CHANGE MODEL
 5.  DISPLAY MODEL
 6.  SAVE MODEL ON DATA DISK
 7.  SOLVE LINEAR PROGRAM
 8.  SOLVE 0-1 INTEGER PROGRAM
 9.  ENTER ANOTHER PROBLEM
10.  TURN PRINTER ON
11.  EXIT TO DISK MENU

PROBLEM 'CHEMICAL' IS LOADED
21 VARIABLES AND 19 CONSTRAINTS

OPTION NUMBER:
```

Figure 3.3 **Linear Model Generator Menu**

Option 2 may be used to enter the data for a new model or to change the data for an existing model. The screen display for this option is shown in Fig. 3.4. The constraints and objective function are entered at the bottom of the screen using an algebraic format. The last constraint added is shown at the top of the screen. This reference is helpful when working with a large model. The order in which constraints and variables are entered is arbitrary. Variables and constraints must have names not exceeding five characters in length. The objective function is identified by using the name OBJMAX or OBJMIN in place of the constraint name. The last three letters indicate whether the objective is to be maximized or minimized. A constraint or the objective is entered by typing the name followed by a slash. Then the algebraic expression defining the constraint or objective is entered. A constraint requires that one of the relations “<”, “>”, or “=” then be entered, followed by the right side constant. The relations “<” and “>” represent “≤” and “≥”, respectively. Because of memory limitations, the constraint must remain between the two lines on the screen. If an expression is too long for this space, the constraint (or objective) can be entered in two or more parts, using the same name for both parts. When a name is used a second time, the computer provides the options to replace the existing entry, to extend the existing entry by adding additional terms, or to give a different name to the new entry. This option can be called more than once to change or add to the model.

Models entered in this fashion can be easily changed by simply retyping the constraint or objective or by using the full complement of change capabilities provided by option 4. Option 3 is provided to impose simple upper bounds on the individual variables or on all variables collectively. The model may be displayed on the screen using option 5. If the printer has been turned on using option 10, the display will be sent to the printer rather than to the screen. The model can be solved as either a linear program (option 7) or as an integer (0–1) program (option 8). Option 9 clears memory for the entry of a new problem. Any model resident in the computer memory will be destroyed with this option.

```
LAST ENTRY
_____________________________________________

A-CON / A + AOM2 - AM1 = 0


_____________________________________________

Enter constraint or objective, type STOP to finish
or type HELP for instructions. The expression must
stay within the lines.
EXAMPLE:  CON1/2X1 - X2 + X3 < 12
_____________________________________________

? B-CON / B - BM1 - BM2 = 0


_____________________________________________
```

Figure 3.4 **Constraint and Objective Function Entry for Linear Models**

A few comments on entering models will help the student user of *Microsolve.* Although we are attempting to resolve the most frequently asked questions here, others will undoubtedly arise. One of the advantages of the microcomputer is that trial and error on small problems costs nothing, and we recommend that the student discover other features of the program through experimentation.

- Use constraint and variable names that represent real aspects of the problem. This will help with interpreting solutions and verifying the model.
- Names should start with a letter and be no more than five characters long. Actually longer names can be used but they may be truncated in displays. After the first letter, the name should consist of letter characters or numbers. Some punctuation marks are valid but others are not, so it is safer not to use punctuation marks.
- A constraint or the objective function should be entered as a simple algebraic sum of linear terms. A variable should be mentioned at most once in an expression, and variables with zero coefficients need not be included. Common mathematical devices such as summation signs, parentheses defining terms, and general subscripts cannot be used. Coefficients of "1" need not be entered. Constraints require relations (<, >, or =) and a constant on the right side. The constant may be positive, negative, or zero.
- Variables are stored in the computer in the order in which they appear as the problem is entered. They can be reordered alphabetically with one of the change options, but if some specific nonalphabetic order is to be maintained, one must mention the variable names in the order desired. One possibility is to enter a dummy constraint first with all the variables listed in the desired order and then delete this constraint later. Constraints are also stored in the order entered, although a change option allows them to be rearranged alphabetically by constraint name.
- Variable and constraint names may be changed, but an objective function cannot be renamed as a constraint, nor can a constraint be renamed as the objective function. The objective function can be changed from a maximum to a minimum by changing the name from OBJMAX to OBJMIN. The reverse is also true.
- The constraints and objective can be entered in parts by using the same name for the parts and by choosing the *extend* option. If a variable is mentioned in more than one part, the last coefficient mentioned for that variable is used.
- When the problem is solved, all negative right sides are changed to positive values by multiplying both sides of the constraint by –1 and changing the direction of the inequality relation. A minimization is changed to a maximization by multiplying the objective function by –1. These transformations do not change the optimum solution, but the sign of the

objective function value will change if it has been transformed in this manner.

- For numerical stability, do not use very large numbers or very small numbers in the model. It is always possible to transform a variable or constraint by multiplying it by a constant to obtain this result.

- Do not use too many significant digits in coefficients. In most problems, coefficient values are rarely known with accuracy; hence, excess precision is unnecessary and may be misleading. The model displays provided by the program have a limited number of characters to represent both coefficient and variable name. If the coefficient has too many significant digits, the name will be truncated. A maximum of four significant digits is recommended.

- Do not use redundant equality constraints. If a solution is defined by the intersection of several equalities and one is redundant, the program may indicate that there is no feasible solution because of numerical inaccuracy.

Although the limits of the *Microsolve* linear program (100 variables and 50 constraints for the IBM and 70 variables and 30 constraints for the Apple) will at first seem to be adequate, the student will probably soon discover problems that exceed these limits. There are other programs for the microcomputer and certainly for the mainframe computer that allow larger models, so one option is to seek out and use these programs. To get the most out of *Microsolve,* however, one can use the following measures to reduce the size of the problem.

- Use the simple upper bound capabilities of the program rather than entering the bounds as explicit constraints. The simple upper bounds do not count against the constraint limit.

- Use the transformation noted above to eliminate simple lower bound constraints.

- Seek an alternative formulation of the model. Often the student uses particularly inefficient formulations such as requiring the general variable $x(i, j)$ to be defined for all values of i and j. Many of these variables may be practically or even logically restricted to zero.

- Try to describe the problem as one of the special types of linear programming models discussed in Chapter 7. These models can be much larger.

- Use equality constraints to eliminate variables. This is not generally recommended because of the loss of clarity, but at times great savings can be obtained with little loss. The procedures for doing this are mentioned in the modeling section.

- Use practical considerations to eliminate constraints or variables. Many constraints are loose (a constraint representing a resource that is not used up) and many variables are zero in the optimal solution. These constraints and variables could have been left out without changing the optimum solution. Of course, one cannot be sure which constraints will be loose or which variables will be zero before the solution is found; however, practical arguments can often suggest these conclusions. Chapter 6 will describe post-optimality tests that will indicate whether deleted parts of the model would have any effect if added back. The problem can also be solved repeatedly with different sets of constraints and variables.

- If the problem has natural subdivisions such as the individual time periods in a multiperiod planning model, one can break the problem up and solve it as a collection of smaller problems. The solution obtained is said to be suboptimal, because the collection of optimal solutions to the smaller problems does not in general equal the optimal solution to the complete problem.

Again, the last resort is to seek a program with greater capacity. Especially in the field of linear programming there is a wealth of good codes available to almost every user with access to the mainframe computer.

Problems

These problems are to be "set up" for linear programming. This means that the complete linear programming model is to be written down in a format consistent with the examples given in this chapter. No solution need be determined. Students with access to *Microsolve* should create some of these models using the linear model generator and save them on a data disk. The solution of the linear program and the interpretation of results will be the subject of the next chapter.

P3.1 A company makes two products, called X and Y, from a mix of chemicals. The products are sold by the pound. Up to 1000 pounds of X can be sold for $12 per pound. To sell additional X, the price must be reduced to $9 per pound for sales in excess of 1000 pounds, up to a maximum of 3000 pounds in total sales. Product Y is sold for $18 per pound for any amount up to 2000 pounds. If more than 3000 pounds of X or more than 2000 pounds of Y are produced, the excess must be discarded at a cost of $2 per pound.

After processing the mix, the products are withdrawn in the proportions: 40% is X, 20% is Y, and 40% is a waste product that must be discarded at a cost of $2 per pound. The processing cost of the mix is $1.50 per pound.

The mix is made up of three raw materials identified by the letters A, B, and C. The mix must be at least 45% raw material A and no more than 30% C. Raw material C is free for up to 1500 pounds. Material C costs $4.50 per pound for amounts above 1500. No more than 3000 pounds of material C is available at any price. Material A costs $6 per pound for any amount. There is no limit to the amount of A that can be purchased. Material B costs $3 per pound up to 2500 pounds and $5.50 per pound for additional quantities up to a total of 4000 pounds.

Write the linear programming model which will determine the production and sales plan that will maximize profit.

P3.2 A company wants an aggregate production plan for the next 6 months. Projected orders for the company's product are listed below.

Month	*Demand (units)*	*Production cost ($/unit)*
1	1300	100
2	1400	105
3	1000	110
4	800	115
5	1700	110
6	1900	110

The company must produce over the next 6 months to meet this demand. There are two ways to provide for this variable demand. The production may vary from month to month, or the product may be produced in one month and saved in inventory for some later month's demand. Because of seasonal factors, the cost of production is not constant, as shown in the table.

There is also a cost of changing production levels. If production goes up from one month to the next, there is an additional cost of $2 per unit of change. If production goes down from one month to the next, there is a cost of $1 per unit of change. The current production level is 1000.

The cost of holding an item in inventory for 1 month is $4 per unit per month. Items produced and sold in the same month are not put in inventory. The maximum inventory is 250 units. The initial inventory level is 200 and the final inventory level is to be 100.

Write the linear program that when solved would determine the optimum production quantity for each month.

P3.3 Five products are produced on four machines. The machine requirements in hours per unit are shown for each product in the table below. With the exception of product 4, which does not require machine 1, each unit of product must pass through all four machines. The unit profits for each product are also shown in the table.

	Prod. 1	*Prod. 2*	*Prod. 3*	*Prod. 4*	*Prod. 5*
Machine 1	1.2	1.3	0.7	0.0	0.5
Machine 2	0.7	2.2	1.6	0.5	1.0
Machine 3	0.9	0.7	1.3	1.0	0.8
Machine 4	1.4	2.8	0.5	1.2	0.6
Profit per unit	$18	25	10	12	15

There are four machines of type 1, five of type 2, three of type 3 and seven of type 4. Each machine operates 40 hours per week.

Set up the linear programming model which would determine the optimum weekly production quantities for the products. The goal is to maximize total profit.

P3.4 A government agency has five tasks, but only three contractors bid to perform the tasks. The bids are shown in the table. Set up the linear programming model for the various conditions listed below. In each case the goal is to minimize the agency's total cost.

a. Each contractor can perform as many as two tasks and all the tasks must be done.
b. Each contractor can perform only one task and as many tasks as possible should be done.
c. There is no limit to the number of tasks a contractor can perform and all tasks must be done.

	Task 1	*Task 2*	*Task 3*	*Task 4*	*Task 5*
Contractor 1	65	37	42	29	28
Contractor 2	59	39	50	29	31
Contractor 3	62	46	33	24	31

P3.5 A regional power system has three generating stations: A, B, and C. Each station serves its own local area. Three outlying areas are also served by the system: X, Y, and Z. The power demanded at areas X, Y, and Z is 25 MW (megawatts), 50 MW, and 30 MW, respectively. The maximum generating capacity beyond local requirements and the cost of generation at the three stations is shown in the table.

Generating Station	*Excess capacity (MW)*	*Cost of generation per MW ($)*
A	100	500
B	75	700
C	200	400

Power can be transmitted between any pair of generating stations, but 5% of the amount shipped will be lost. Power can be transmitted from some of the generating stations to the outlying areas, but 10% of the amount shipped is lost. Lines exist from stations A and C to X, from B and C to Y, and from A and B to Z.

a. Set up the linear program to find the optimum power distribution plan from generating stations to outlying areas.
b. Say a generator failure occurs in station A so that it can no longer serve any outlying areas and falls 25 MW short of serving its own area. Set up the

linear program to find the optimum distribution of power in this circumstance.

P3.6 Ten jobs are to be completed by three men during the next week. Each man works a 40-hour week. The times for the men to complete the jobs are shown in the table. The times assume that each job is completed by one man, but the men can also share jobs. The times are then determined proportionally. Thus, if man A does half of job 3 and man C does the other half, the job will require a total time of

$$3 \times 0.5 + 6 \times 0.5 = 4.5.$$

(This assumption is not meant to complicate the problem; rather it is necessary to make linear programming appropriate for this problem.)

Show the linear programming model that will determine the optimum assignment of men to jobs. The goal is to minimize the total time required to complete all the jobs.

	1	*2*	*3*	*4*	*5*	*6*	*7*	*8*	*9*	*10*
Man A	X	7	3	X	X	18	13	6	X	9
Man B	12	5	X	12	4	22	X	17	13	X
Man C	18	X	6	8	10	X	19	X	8	15

P3.7 A company makes two products from four raw materials. In terms of labor requirements, 10 minutes are required per pound of product A and 5 minutes are required per pound of B. There are 400 hours of labor available every month.

The proportional contents of the products in terms of raw materials are shown below. For instance, raw material X must comprise 30% of product A.

Raw Material	*Product A*	*Product B*
W	0.30	0.25
X	0.10	0.10
Y	0.40	0.65
Z	0.20	0.0

The company wants to plan its production for the next two months. Product revenue per pound, maximum sales, and raw material costs for the two months are:

	Revenue per pound ($)		*Maximum Sales (pounds)*		*Cost per pound ($)*			
	A	*B*	*A*	*B*	*W*	*X*	*Y*	*Z*
Month 1	1.00	0.75	1000	2000	0.30	0.15	0.10	0.30
Month 2	1.50	0.90	1500	400	0.40	0.20	0.10	0.30

The company can sell less than the maximum sales in each month but no more. Products produced in the first month can be sold in the second, but 30% of the amount of product A and 10% of the amount of product B saved from one month to the next will be spoiled.

Raw materials can be purchased in month 1 for use in month 2, but the raw material warehouse has a maximum storage capacity of 1000 pounds.

Write the linear program that will determine the optimum product production and sales and the optimum raw material purchases. The goal is to maximize profit.

CHAPTER 4

Solving Linear Programming Problems: The Simplex Method

Foundations (4.1, 4.2, 5.1)

The optimum solution of the linear programming model can be found using an algorithm called the *simplex technique*. This method has been programmed for all major mainframe computers and is probably the most widely used numerical tool of operations research. This chapter describes a simple version of the simplex technique suitable for hand computations. The computer programs implementing the algorithm are very different in many details from the one presented here. All are based on the same principles, however, and the basic understanding one can obtain from this chapter is important for interpreting the results obtained from a computer program, appreciating the computational effort involved in obtaining a solution, and understanding the significance of post-optimality analysis.

GOALS

- Given a model in the standard form, be able to construct the equality form.
- For a model with two structural variables, be able to sketch and interpret the geometric model.
- Be able to identify and compute basic solutions and tell whether they are feasible or infeasible.

DEFINITIONS

Equality Form of the Model: The simplex technique requires that the model be translated into a form with all equalities rather than inequalities. The standard form introduced in the last chapter is shown below together with the equality form. Notice that the objective function has been made into an equation and numbered (0). The inequalities of the standard form have been transformed into equalities by adding a new variable for each inequality. The variables are called "slack variables" and because they are required to be nonnegative, any solution to the equations in the equality form also satisfies the inequalities of the standard form.

The number of equations in the equality form is $m + 1$ (including the objective function equation), and the number of variables is $m + n + 1$ (including the variable Z). In the following discussion we will, however, speak of the set of equations as those which represent the constraints (1) through (m), and the decision variables as all the variables not including Z.

Standard Form

$$
\begin{array}{lllllll}
 & \text{Maximize } Z = & c_1x_1 & + c_2x_2 & + \cdots & + c_n x_n & \\
(1) & \text{Subject to:} & a_{11}x_1 & + a_{12}x_2 & + \cdots & + a_{1n} x_n & \le b_1 \\
(2) & & a_{21}x_1 & + a_{22}x_2 & + \cdots & + a_{2n} x_n & \le b_2 \\
\vdots & & \vdots & & & & \\
(m) & & a_{m1}x_1 & + a_{m2}x_2 & + \cdots & + a_{mn} x_n & \le b_m \\
 & & \multicolumn{5}{l}{x_1 \ge 0, x_2 \ge 0, \ldots, x_n \ge 0.}
\end{array}
$$

Equality Form

$$
\begin{array}{llllllllll}
 & \multicolumn{9}{l}{\text{Maximize } Z} \\
(0) & Z - & c_1 x_1 & - c_2x_2 & - \cdots & - c_n x_n & & & & = 0 \\
(1) & & a_{11} x_1 & + a_{12}x_2 & + \cdots & + a_{1n} x_n & + x_{n+1} & & & = b_1 \\
(2) & & a_{21} x_1 & + a_{22}x_2 & + \cdots & + a_{2n} x_n & & + x_{n+2} & & = b_2 \\
\vdots & & \vdots & & & & & & & \\
(m) & & a_{m1}x_1 & + a_{m2}x_2 & + \cdots & + a_{mn} x_n & & & + x_{n+m} & = b_m \\
 & & \multicolumn{8}{l}{x_1 \ge 0, x_2 \ge 0, \ldots, x_n \ge 0, x_{n+1} \ge 0, x_{n+2} \ge 0, \ldots, x_{n+m} \ge 0.}
\end{array}
$$

Slack Variable: The variable added to an inequality to transform it into an equality. The slack variable for constraint i is x_{n+i}. Later we will also use the notation x_{si} to refer to the slack variable for constraint i.

Structural Variable: A decision variable in the standard form of the model (not a slack variable).

Feasible Solution: A solution to the set of equations (1) through (m) in the equality form such that all variables are nonnegative.

Infeasible Solution: A solution which has at least one variable with a negative value.

Feasible Region: The set of all feasible solutions.

Basic Solution: The solution obtained by setting n of the variables in the equality form to zero (not including Z) and solving for the remaining variables using equations (1) through (m). When n variables are set to zero, m unknown variables remain, and the m equations can be solved for these unknowns. The value of Z can be found from Eq. (0).

Basic Feasible Solution: A basic solution that is feasible. A basic feasible solution corresponds to a feasible corner point of the geometric interpretation of standard form.

Basic Infeasible Solution: A basic solution that is not feasible. This solution corresponds to an infeasible corner point in the geometric interpretation.

Basic Variables: The set of variables not set to zero while determining a particular basic solution.

Nonbasic Variables: The set of variables set to zero while determining a particular basic solution.

Adjacent Basic Solution: A new basic solution obtained by starting from some basic solution and allowing one nonbasic variable to become basic while one basic variable becomes nonbasic. In a geometric interpretation, adjacent basic solutions are connected by a single edge of the feasible region.

Entering Basic Variable: The variable chosen to enter the set of basic variables when moving to an adjacent basic solution.

Leaving Basic Variable: The variable chosen to leave the set of basic variables when moving to an adjacent basic solution.

Optimal Solution: A solution for which the objective function has a value at least as large as any other feasible solution.

RESULTS

Before proceeding with the simplex algorithm, it is important to review some results on which the algorithm is based. Assuming the model has at least one feasible solution and the feasible region is bounded, the following results hold for a linear program.

- There exists at least one optimal solution which is a basic solution.
- There is a finite number of basic solutions.
- If the objective value for a particular basic feasible solution is at least as large as the objective values for all adjacent basic feasible solutions, the particular solution is optimal.

The first result implies that only the basic solutions need to be considered in the search for an optimal solution. The second result shows that since there is a finite number of these, any algorithm that considers one basic solution at a time (and considers each no more than once) will find the optimum in a finite number of trials. The last result can be used to test whether a particular solution is optimal.

EXAMPLE

E4.1 A linear program is shown below in both the standard form and the equality form. Fig. 4.1 shows a geometric interpretation of the problem.

$$\text{Maximize } Z = 2x_1 + 3x_2$$

$$\begin{array}{lrcl}
(1) & -x_1 + x_2 & \leq & 5 \\
(2) & x_1 + 3x_2 & \leq & 35 \\
(3) & x_1 & \leq & 20
\end{array}$$

$$x_1 \geq 0, \quad x_2 \geq 0.$$

Equality Form

Maximize Z

$$\begin{array}{lrcl}
(0) & Z - 2x_1 - 3x_2 & = & 0 \\
(1) & x_1 + x_2 + x_3 & = & 5 \\
(2) & x_1 + 3x_2 + x_4 & = & 35 \\
(3) & x_1 + x_5 & = & 20
\end{array}$$

$$x_1 \geq 0, \quad x_2 \geq 0, \quad x_3 \geq 0, \quad x_4 \geq 0, \quad x_5 \geq 0.$$

Not including Z and Eq. (0), the equality form has five variables and three constraints. A basic solution is found by selecting two of the variables as nonbasic variables. These are set to zero, and the remaining variables are determined by solving the three equations. For instance, select x_4 and x_5 as the nonbasic variables. Setting these to zero, we obtain the equations below. These are easily solved to obtain $x_1 = 20$, $x_2 = 5$, and $x_3 = 20$. This is evidently a basic feasible solution since all the variables are positive. It is identified on Fig. 4.1 as corner point #10.

$$\begin{array}{lrcl}
(1) & -x_1 + x_2 + x_3 & = & 5 \\
(2) & x_1 + 3x_2 & = & 35 \\
(3) & x_1 & = & 20.
\end{array}$$

Although only the structural variables show on the figure, the slack variables also have meaning. The example shows that those slack variables that are zero identify the constraint lines that intersect at the solution. Thus, constraints for slack variables x_4 and x_5 (constraints (2) and (3)) are satisfied exactly by the solution. These constraints are said to be *tight*. Those slack variables that are basic and nonzero identify the constraints that do not intersect at the solution (constraint (1)

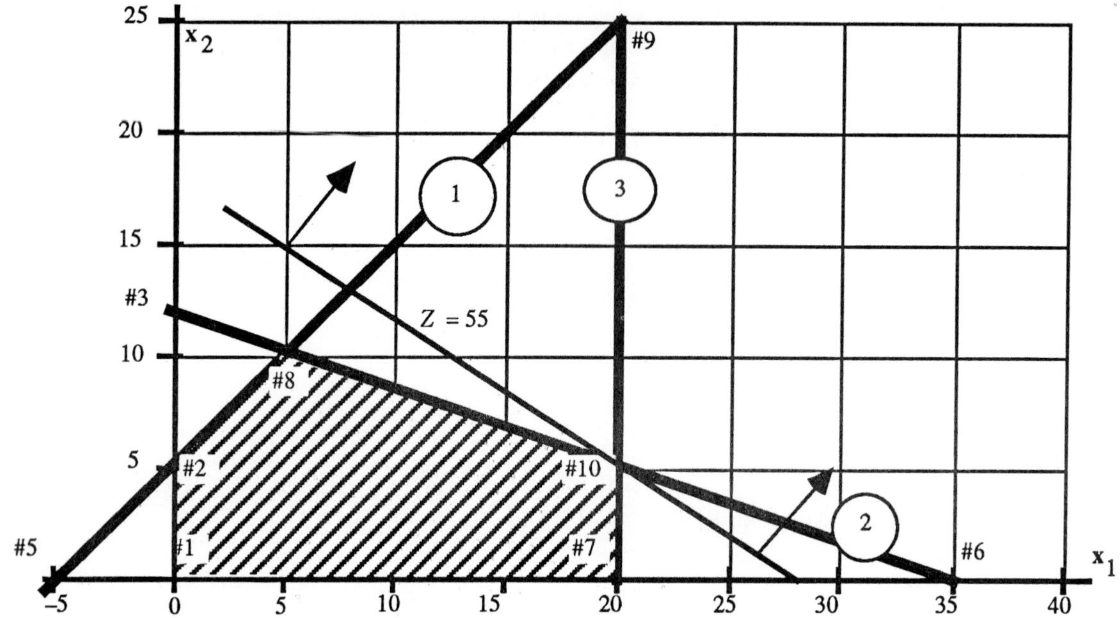

Figure 4.1 Geometric Model of the Example. Note on the creation of the geometric model: The geometric model is drawn using a coordinate system of the two structural variables. A heavy line shows the points at which a constraint is satisfied as an equality. The lines are numbered by the constraint index. The cross-hatched area indicates the feasible region. The line indicated by the arrows shows the set of points for which the objective has the value 55. The arrows show the direction of increasing objective function.

Table 1. **Basic Solutions**

Corner Point	*Nonbasic Variables*	*Basic Variables*	*Solution* $(x_1, \dots, x_5)$	*Feasibility (Yes, No)*	*Objective Value*
#1	(1, 2)	(3, 4, 5)	(0, 0, 5, 35, 20)	Yes	0
#2	(1, 3)	(2, 4, 5)	(0, 5, 0, 20, 20)	Yes	15
#3	(1, 4)	(2, 3, 5)	(0, 11.7, –6.7, 0, 20)	No	—
#4	(1, 5)	(2, 3, 4)	No solution	—	—
#5	(2, 3)	(1, 4, 5)	(–5, 0, 0, 40, 25)	No	—
#6	(2, 4)	(1, 3, 5)	(35, 0, 40, 0, –5)	No	—
#7	(2, 5)	(1, 3, 4)	(20, 0, 25, 15, 0)	Yes	40
#8	(3, 4)	(1, 2, 5)	(5, 10, 0, 0, 10)	Yes	40
#9	(3, 5)	(1, 2, 4)	(20, 25, 0, –60, 0)	No	—
#10	(4, 5)	(1, 2, 3)	(20, 5, 20, 0, 0)	Yes	55

in the example). Such constraints are said to be *loose*. For cases in which a structural variable is nonbasic, the nonnegativity conditions are *tight*, indicating that the structural variable is at zero.

In general if there are m constraints and $n + m$ variables, the number of basic solutions will be bounded by the number of ways to choose m basic variables (or equivalently the n nonbasic variables) from the $n + m$ variables or

$$\frac{(n+m)!}{(m!\,n!)}$$

This is only an upper bound because not all selections of the basic variables may yield a set of equations that has a solution. For the example problem, this bound is computed to be 10. The possibilities are listed in Table 1. A selection of basic variables that does not yield a solution is #4. Review of the table shows that #10, having the largest value of the objective, is the optimum solution.

PROBLEMS

P4.1 For the linear program

$$\begin{array}{llrl} & \text{Maximize } Z = & 5x_1 + 3x_2 & \\ (1) & \text{Subject to:} & 3x_1 + 5x_2 & \leq 15 \\ (2) & & 5x_1 + 2x_2 & \leq 10 \\ (3) & & x_1 + x_2 & \leq 2 \\ (4) & & x_2 & \leq 2.5 \end{array}$$

$$x_1 \geq 0, x_2 \geq 0.$$

a. Show the equality form of the model.

b. What is an upper bound on the number of basic solutions?

c. Sketch the geometric model and identify the corner point solutions. From this representation find the optimum solution.

d. Analytically determine the set of basic solutions by listing all possible selections of the basic variables. Identify which are feasible and which are infeasible. Compute the objective function values for the feasible solutions and select the optimum basic feasible solution.

P4.2 For the linear program

$$\begin{array}{lll} & \text{Maximize } Z = & 8x_1 + 4x_2 + 7x_3 - 3x_4 + 0x_5 + 0x_6 \\ (1) & \text{Subject to:} & 2x_1 - 2x_2 + 3x_3 - 4x_4 - x_5 = 12 \\ (2) & & 3x_1 + 8x_2 - x_3 + 7x_4 + x_6 = 18 \end{array}$$

$$x_1 \geq 0, x_2 \geq 0, x_3 \geq 0, x_4 \geq 0, x_5 \geq 0, x_6 \geq 0.$$

a. What is an upper bound on the number of basic solutions?

b. Analytically determine the set of basic solutions by listing all possible selections of the basic variables. Identify which are feasible and which are infeasible. Compute the objective function values for the feasible solutions and select the optimum basic feasible solution.

The Algebra of the Simplex Method (4.3)

The last section established that at least one optimal solution of a linear program is a basic feasible solution. Further, the optimal solution can be recognized when all adjacent feasible solutions have smaller or equal objective values. This section describes the simplex technique using an algebraic form of the equations. The procedure starts at a given basic solution and iteratively moves from one basic solution to an adjacent one until the optimum is discovered.

GOALS

The student should be able to accomplish the following tasks for an arbitrary linear programming model with a small number of constraints and variables.

- Set up the model for solution by the simplex technique.
- Solve the model using the algebraic form of the equations.

RESULTS

R1. The Simplex Form The algorithm uses the equality form of the model. At each iterative step, the equations (including Eq. (0)) are transformed using linear operations so that the equations have the following characteristics. We call this the simplex form (H & L call this the *proper* form).

With the equations in the simplex form, every basic variable appears with a nonzero coefficient in one and only one equation. In the equation where the basic variable does appear, it has the coefficient 1. Each equation includes only one basic variable.

Since there are $m + 1$ equations, there must $m + 1$ basic variables. The basic variable for Eq. (0) will always be Z. The basic variables for the other equations will change as the algorithm progresses. To illustrate this result, consider again the equality form of Example 4.1, which is in the simplex form. It is labeled Iteration 1 for later reference.

Iteration 1:

Maximize Z

$$
\begin{array}{llcccccl}
E(0) & Z & -2x_1 & -3x_2 & & & & = 0 \\
E(1) & & -x_1 & +x_2 & +x_3 & & & = 5 \\
E(2) & & x_1 & +3x_2 & & +x_4 & & = 35 \\
E(3) & & x_1 & & & & +x_5 & = 20
\end{array}
$$

$$x_1 \ge 0,\ x_2 \ge 0,\ x_3 \ge 0,\ x_4 \ge 0,\ x_5 \ge 0$$

Variable Z appears in Eq. (0) and variables x_3, x_4, and x_5 appear in Equas. (1), (2), and (3), respectively. For a basic solution, the nonbasic variables, x_1 and x_2, have the value zero. It is this particular form of the equations that gives rise to the procedures of the simplex technique. A number of results based on this form are given below.

R2. Basic Solution The values of the basic variables are simply the constant terms (right sides) of the equations they represent. This result is illustrated by the basic solution for the example. The values of the basic variables are

$$Z = 0, x_3 = 5, x_4 = 35, \text{and } x_5 = 20.$$

Nonbasic variables have the value zero.

R3. Meaning of the Coefficients in Equation (0) The negative of the coefficient of a nonbasic variable in Eq. (0) is equal to the increase in Z caused by a unit increase in that variable. To illustrate this result, we rewrite Eq. (0) with only Z on the left side.

$$Z = + 2x_1 + 3x_2 .$$

When the nonbasic variables are zero, we read that Z = 0. But if we allow x_1 to increase to 1, Z will increase by 2. Similarly, if we allow x_2 to increase by 1, Z will increase by 3. This observation leads to yet another result.

R4. Conditions for a Nonoptimal Solution The current basic solution is not optimal if any coefficients in Eq. (0) are negative. If there is a negative coefficient, the objective can be increased by increasing the corresponding nonbasic variable from zero. Evidently for the example problem, the objective will increase if either x_1 or x_2 is increased, so this solution is not optimal. The corollary to this result is listed next.

R5. Conditions for an Optimal Solution If there are no negative coefficients in Eq. (0), the basic solution is optimal. This is important because it provides a stopping rule for the simplex algorithm.

R6. Meaning of the Coefficients in a Constraint Equation The coefficient of a nonbasic variable in a constraint equation (index 1 through *m*) is equal to the decrease in the basic variable of that equation per unit increase in the nonbasic variable. For the example case, this can be seen by rewriting Eq. (1) so that only the basic variable x_3 appears on the left. We first repeat the equation for easy comparison.

$$-x_1 + x_2 + x_3 = 5$$

or

$$x_3 = 5 + x_1 - x_2 .$$

We can see that for each unit increase in x_1, the basic variable x_3 will increase by 1 (the decrease is –1). Thus, the coefficient of x_1 is –1 in Eq. (1). For each unit increase in x_2, the basic variable x_3 will decrease by 1. Thus the coefficient of x_2 is +1 in Eq. (1).

This result is important because it indicates how much a nonbasic variable may increase before the basic variable will decrease to zero. In the example no amount of increase in x_1 will cause x_3 to go to zero. This is indicated by the negative sign of the coefficient of x_1 in Eq. (1). Variable x_2, on the other hand, can increase by 5 to make x_3 become zero. Any larger increase will drive x_3 negative. A general rule can be defined. Let b_i be the right side of equation i and let y_{ij} be the coefficient of nonbasic variable j in equation i. Let δ_{ij} be the amount that x_j can increase in order to drive the basic variable to zero. Then

$$\delta_{ij} = b_i / y_{ij} \quad \text{if } y_{ij} > 0$$
$$\delta_{ij} = \infty \quad \text{if } y_{ij} \leq 0.$$

For the example problem, we observe that $\delta_{11} = \infty$, and $\delta_{12} = 5/1 = 5$.

R7. Changing to an Adjacent Basic Solution To change from one basic feasible solution to an adjacent basic feasible solution, allow some nonbasic variable to increase until one basic variable goes to zero, while all other basic variables remain nonnegative. As a nonbasic variable increases from zero, one or more basic variables will decrease (if none decrease, the solution is said to be unbounded). In order for all basic variables to remain nonnegative, the nonbasic variable can only increase to the smallest value that will drive one basic variable to zero. In general let δ_j be the increase in nonbasic variable j, then

$$\delta_j = \text{Min } \{ (b_i / y_{ij}) \mid y_{ij} > 0 \text{ and } i = 1 \ldots m \}. \tag{1}$$

Let i^* be the value of i for which the minimum is obtained. The basic variable for the constraint i^* becomes zero when x_j increases to δ_j. This is the variable that leaves the basis when variable x_j enters the basis. Variable x_j becomes the basic variable for constraint i^*.

For the example problem if we let x_2 enter the basis,

$$\delta_2 = \text{Min } \{ b_1/y_{12}, b_2/y_{22} \} = \text{Min } \{ 5/1, 35/3 \} = 5.$$

Constraint (3) does not enter the expression because $y_{32} = 0$. The minimum is obtained for constraint (1) so the basic variable for that constraint, x_3, must leave the basis.

R8. Obtaining a New Simplex Form After selecting variables to enter and leave the basis, linear operations can be used to bring the equality form of the model to the simplex form. In particular, let x_j be the variable to enter the basis and let i^* be the constraint determined by the results of R7. Perform the following operations.

1. Divide equation i^* by y_{i^*j}.

2. For every other equation ($i = 0 \ldots m, i \neq i^*$), add the equation to a multiple of the new equation i^* so that the coefficient for x_j is zero.

To illustrate the linear operations on the equations, let E(0), E(1), E(2) and E(3) be the equations before the transformation and E'(0), E'(1), E'(2), and E'(3) be the equations after the transformation. For the example problem, the entering variable is x_2 and $i^* = 1$. Eq. (1) is divided by y_{12}. This number happens to be 1 in this case so the equation does not change.

$$E'(1) = E(1)/y_{12} = -x_1 + x_2 + x_3 = 5 .$$

To eliminate x_2 from Eq. (0), we multiply the new Eq. (1) by 3 and add it to the old Eq. (0).

$$E'(0) = 3E'(1) + E(0)$$

$$\begin{array}{rrrrrl} 3\,[& -x_1 & +x_2 & +x_3 & = & 5\,] \\ +\,[\,Z & -2x_1 & -3x_2 & & = & 0\,] \\ \hline [\,Z & -5x_1 & +\,0x_2 & +\,3x_3 & = & 15\,] \end{array}$$

To eliminate x_2 from Eq. (2), we multiply the new Eq. (1) by –3 and add it to the old Eq. (2).

$$E'(2) = -3E'(1) + E(2) = [\,4x_1 + 0x_2 - 3x_3 + x_4 = 20].$$

Equation (3) does not change, because the coefficient of x_2 is zero.

$$E'(3) = 0\,E'(1) + E(3) = [x_1 + x_5 = 20].$$

The new model in the simplex form can now be written:

Iteration 2

Maximize Z

$$\begin{array}{llrrrrrl} E'(0) & Z & -\,5x_1 & & +\,3x_3 & & & = 15 \\ E'(1) & & -\,x_1 & +\,x_2 & +\,x_3 & & & = 5 \\ E'(2) & & 4x_1 & & -\,3x_3 & +\,x_4 & & = 20 \\ E'(3) & & x_1 & & & & +\,x_5 & = 20 \end{array}$$

$$x_1 \geq 0, \quad x_2 \geq 0, \quad x_3 \geq 0, \quad x_4 \geq 0, \quad x_5 \geq 0.$$

This set of equations has the same set of solutions as the original, but now the equations are written in terms of the basic variables x_2, x_4, and x_5. By allowing x_2 to enter the basis while x_3 leaves, we have moved to an adjacent basic solution. Using the properties observed above, we find that the solution

$$(x_1, x_2, x_3, x_4, x_5) = (\,0, 5, 0, 20, 20) \text{ with } Z = 15$$

can be read directly from the equations. This solution is evidently not optimum, because x_1 has a negative coefficient in Eq. (0).

ALGORITHM

The results listed above allow a more formal statement of the simplex algorithm.

A1. Initialization Step Express the linear program in the equation form. Select some set of basic variables that will yield a feasible solution. Using simple equation operations, transform the equations into the simplex form. When the model has all "less than or equal to" constraints, the slack variables can be selected as the basic variables to obtain the simplex form without transformation. Check this solution for optimality using result R5.

A2. Iterative Step

a. Use result R4 to find a variable that will improve the objective function. The usual rule is to select the variable with the most negative coefficient in Eq. (0), although alternative rules are often used in computer programs. For hand calculations we shall use this "most negative value" rule.

b. Use result R7 to find the variable to the leave the basis.

c. Use result R8 to transform the equations so that they have the simplex form for the new basis.

A3. Optimality Test Check the basic solution for optimality using result R5. If the solution is optimum, stop the algorithm. If it is not, repeat step A2.

EXAMPLE

E4.2 We illustrate the algebraic simplex procedure by continuing with the set of equations labeled Iteration 2. From Eq. (0), we note that this solution is not optimal because x_1 has a negative coefficient. We continue from this point with step A2 of the algorithm.

a. The most negative value rule selects x_1 as the variable to enter the basis.

b. Using R7, we compute the amount x_1 can increase:

$\delta_1 = \text{Min}\ [\ b_2/y_{21}, b_3/y_{31}\ ] = \text{Min}\ [\ 20/4, 20/1\ ] = 5.$

Equation (1) does not enter this computation because $y_{11} < 0$.

This result implies that the basic variable for Eq. (2), x_4, must leave the basis.

c. Performing the linear transformation to obtain the new simplex form yields:

Iteration 3:

Maximize Z

$$
\begin{array}{llrrrr}
E(0) & Z & & -\ 0.75x_3 + 1.25x_4 & & = 40 \\
E(1) & & +x_2 & +\ 0.25x_3 + 0.25x_4 & & = 10 \\
E(2) & +x_1 & & -\ 0.75x_3 + 0.25x_4 & & = 5 \\
E(3) & & & +\ 0.75x_3 - 0.25x_4 & +x_5 & = 15
\end{array}
$$

$$x_1 \geq 0, \quad x_2 \geq 0, \quad x_3 \geq 0, \quad x_4 \geq 0, \quad x_5 \geq 0.$$

The new solution has the basic variables x_1, x_2, and x_5. The basic solution that can be observed from the equations is

$$(x_1, x_2, x_3, x_4, x_5) = (5, 10, 0, 0, 15) \text{ with } Z = 40.$$

Step A3 of the algorithm indicates that this solution is not optimum. Continuing again with the iterative step.

a. The most negative value rule selects x_3 as the variable to enter the basis.

b. Using R7, we compute the amount x_3 can increase

$\delta_3 = \text{Min } [\ b_1/y_{13}, b_3/y_{33}\ ] = \text{Min } [\ 10/0.25, 15/0.75\ ] = 20.$

Equation (2) does not enter this computation because $y_{23} < 0$.

This result implies that the basic variable for Eq. (3), x_5, must leave the basis.

c. Performing the linear transformation to obtain the new simplex form yields:

Iteration 4:

Maximize Z

$$
\begin{array}{llrrrr}
E(0) & Z & & & +\ x_4 & +\ x_5 = 55 \\
E(1) & & & +x_2 & +\ 0.33x_4 & -\ 0.33x_5 = 5 \\
E(2) & & +x_1 & & +\ 0x_4 & +\ x_5 = 20 \\
E(3) & & & +x_3 & -\ 0.33x_4 & +\ 1.33x_5 = 20
\end{array}
$$

$$x_1 \geq 0, \quad x_2 \geq 0, \quad x_3 \geq 0, \quad x_4 \geq 0, \quad x_5 \geq 0.$$

The new solution with basic variables x_1, x_2, and x_3 is

$$(x_1, x_2, x_3, x_4, x_5) = (20, 5, 20, 0, 0) \text{ with } Z = 55.$$

Step A3 of the algorithm indicates that this solution is indeed the optimum. End example.

Several observations can be made from the example. Starting from the value zero, the objective function increased in each iteration, moving to 15 at iteration 2, and then to 40, and finally to 55. The objective will always increase if the variable entering the basis is allowed to increase beyond zero. A case in which this does not happen is called a *degenerate* iteration and will be discussed later.

The basic solutions found can be traced on the geometric model shown in Fig. 4.1 of the last section. Thus at iteration 1, the solution is at corner point #1. As x_2 enters the basis and x_3 leaves at iteration 2, the solution moves to the adjacent corner point, #2, where the value of x_2 is positive but the first constraint is tight. For iteration 3, x_1 enters the basis while x_4 leaves to obtain corner point #8. Here the second constraint has become tight while both original variables are positive. Finally when x_5 enters the basis while x_3 leaves, the solution is at corner point #10, where the first constraint has become loose again, while the third constraint is now tight. The optimality conditions show that all adjacent corner points are inferior to this corner point, indicating that this is indeed the optimum solution. The procedure started at the origin and progressed through a sequence of adjacent corner points until the optimum was found. Not all corner points (or basic solutions) were encountered and the optimum was discovered after a finite number of iterations. This is the essence of the simplex procedure.

The rule for selecting the variable to leave the basis described in result R7 is important. This is illustrated if we violate the rule at iteration 3. With part b of the iterative step we found that the amount x_3 can increase is

$$\delta_3 = \text{Min}\ [\ b_1/y_{13}, b_3/y_{33}\ ] = \text{Min}\ [\ 10/0.25, 15/0.75\ ] = 20.$$

In this case x_5 leaves the basis. If instead we allow x_3 to increase to 40, x_2 will leave the basis. The linear transformation for this basis change provides the form:

Maximize Z

E (0)	Z		$+\ 3x_2$		$+\ 2x_4$		$=$	70
E (1)			$+\ 4x_2$	$+\ x_3$	$+\ x_4$		$=$	40
E (2)		$+\ x_1$	$+\ 3x_2$		$+\ x_4$		$=$	35
E (3)			$-\ 3x_2$		$-\ x_4$	$+\ x_5$	$=$	-20

Violating the rule leads to an infeasible basic solution. In the geometric model of Fig. 4.1, this is corner point #6 outside the feasible region. The rule for selecting the variable to leave the basis guarantees that if the algorithm starts at a basic feasible solution, every subsequent solution will also be feasible.

PROBLEMS

P4.3 For the linear programming model given in P4.1, perform the algebraic simplex method as illustrated in this section. At each step, show the set of equations defining the basic solution and the values of the basic variables and objective function. Show the sequence of basic solutions found on the geometric model.

P4.4 For the linear programming model

$$\begin{aligned} \text{Maximize } Z = \ & 5x_1 - 3x_2 + 4x_3 - x_4 \\ \text{Subject to } \ & 3x_1 + 4x_2 + 3x_3 - 5x_4 \le 13 \\ & 5x_1 - 3x_2 + x_3 + 2x_4 \le 15 \\ & x_1 \ge 0, \ x_2 \ge 0, \ x_3 \ge 0, \ x_4 \ge 0. \end{aligned}$$

a. Show the equality form of this model.

b. Let the basic variables be x_1 and x_3. Use row operations to put the model into the simplex form. Write the basic solution.

c. Starting from this basic solution, use the algebraic simplex technique to obtain the optimum solution.

The Simplex Method in the Tabular Form (4.4)

In order to simplify writing the set of equations at each step of the simplex procedure, a tabular form is introduced that shows only the coefficients of the variables in the equations. The algorithm for the simplex method is also slightly modified to accommodate the tabular form. The method is, however, exactly the same as described in the last section.

GOALS

- Given an algebraic statement of a linear program, be able to solve the model using the tabular form of the equations.
- Given a simplex tableau, be able to tell the meaning of all numbers and terms in the tableau.

DEFINITIONS

Tabular Form: The simplex form, shown in the last section, is a set of equations arranged so that there is one and only one basic variable for each equation. The tabular form shows only the coefficients of the equations with variables identified by column headings. As an example, consider the set of equations identified as Iteration 1 in the last section. The tabular form of the equations is shown below. This display is called the *simplex tableau.*

Iteration 1:

Basic var.	*Eq. no.*	*Coefficient of* Z	x_1	x_2	x_3	x_4	x_5	*Right side*	*Ratio*
Z	0	1	−2	**−3**	0	0	0	0	
x_3	1	**0**	**−1**	**1**	**1**	**0**	**0**	**5**	**5**
x_4	2	0	1	**3**	0	1	0	35	11.67
x_5	3	0	1	**0**	0	0	1	20	—

The first column shows the basic variable associated with each equation and the second lists the equation numbers. The following columns show the coefficients of each variable as they appear in the equations. The column heading shows the name of the variable. The next to last column shows the constants on the right sides of the equations, which must be nonnegative. The final column shows the ratios that are used to determine the variable to leave the basis. We shall often speak of the equations in terms of the rows of the tableau and the variables in terms of the columns. The column for Z is called column (0). Because the equations represented by the tableau will always be in the simplex form, the columns for the basic variables will have a single 1 coefficient in the row for which it is basic, and all other coefficients will be zero.

Pivot Column: The column of the variable selected to enter the basis. In this text we shall use boldface type to show the column. In hand calculations it is common to put a rectangle about the numbers in the column. We have used boldface for column x_2 in the example.

Ratio: The ratio between the number in the "right side" column and the pivot column for those rows in which the pivot column has an entry greater than zero. The ratio for row (0) is not computed. The ratios are shown in the final column of the tableau.

Pivot Row: The row that has the minimum ratio. This is the row whose basic variable leaves the basis. In this text, the pivot row is indicated in boldface. In hand calculations it is circumscribed by a rectangle. Row (1) is indicated for the example, showing that x_3 is leaving the basis. The comparison of ratios is called the ratio test.

Pivot Number: The number at the intersection of the pivot row and pivot column. The number is 1 for this example.

ALGORITHM

A1. Initialization Step Express the linear program in the equation form. Choose some set of basic variables that yield a basic feasible solution. Transform the equations into the simplex form. Create the first simplex tableau using the coefficients from these equations. If row (0) has all nonnegative coefficients, stop with the optimum solution.

A2. Iterative Step

a. Find the column that has the most negative entry in row (0) (we are using the "most negative value" rule here). Let that column be the pivot column.

b. Compute the ratios using the right side and the positive elements of the pivot column. Find the row with the minimum ratio. Let that row be the pivot row.

c. Create a new tableau by the following operations.

Let $\mathbf{y}_i$ be the vector of the i th row the original tableau, and let $\mathbf{y}'_i$ be the ith row in the new tableau. Let p be the index of the pivot row. Let column k be the pivot column and let y_{ik} be the number in the ith row of the pivot column.

The pivot row in the new tableau is

$$\mathbf{y}'_p = \mathbf{y}_p / y_{pk}. \tag{2}$$

The other rows in the new tableau are

$$\mathbf{y}'_i = -y_{ik} * \mathbf{y}'_p + \mathbf{y}_i \quad \text{for } i = 0 \ldots m,\ i \neq p. \tag{3}$$

[These operations eliminate the entering variable from all equations except the pivot row. Thus, the new pivot column will have a single 1 at row p and all other entries will be zero as required by the simplex form.]

A3. Optimality Test If all entries in row (0) are nonnegative, stop with the optimum solution. Otherwise return to step A2.

EXAMPLE

E4.3 We complete the simplex method using the tabular form starting from the tableau above. The next tableau will be

Iteration 2:

Basic var.	*Eq. no.*	*Coefficient of* Z	x_1	x_2	x_3	x_4	x_5	*Right side*	*Ratio*
Z	0	1	− 5	0	3	0	0	15	
x_2	1	0	− 1	1	1	0	0	5	—
x_4	2	0	4	0	− 3	1	0	20	5
x_5	3	0	1	0	0	0	1	20	20

Column 1 is the pivot column and row 2 is the pivot row. The new tableau is

Iteration 3:

Basic var.	*Eq. no.*	*Coefficient of* Z	x_1	x_2	x_3	x_4	x_5	*Right side*	*Ratio*
Z	0	1	0	0	− 0.75	1.25	0	40	
x_2	1	0	0	1	0.25	0.25	0	10	40
x_1	2	0	1	0	− 0.75	0.25	0	5	—
x_5	3	0	0	0	0.75	− 0.25	1	15	20

Column 3 is the pivot column and row 3 is the pivot row. The new tableau is

Iteration 4:

Basic var.	Eq. no.	Coefficient of Z	x_1	x_2	x_3	x_4	x_5	Right side
Z	0	1	0	0	0	1	1	55
x_2	1	0	0	1	0	0.33	– 0.33	5
x_1	2	0	1	0	0	0	1	20
x_3	3	0	0	0	1	– 0.33	1.33	20

This tableau satisfies the optimality conditions because all entries in row (0) are nonnegative.

Review of the algebraic simplex method of the last section reveals that the tableau method has gone through exactly the same steps as the algebraic procedure. They are, in fact, the same method presented in different formats.

The calculations required to move from one tableau to the next comprise the most difficult part of this process. Students will appreciate the computational abilities of the computer after solving a few small problems. If done correctly, the simplex form should be present in all tableaus, the right sides should remain nonnegative, and the objective function should never decrease as the number of the iteration increases. The solution prescribed by the tableau should also satisfy the equations in the original model. If at some iteration one or more of these requirements are violated, a computational or logical error has been made.

PROBLEMS

P4.5 Solve the linear program given in P4.1 with the tabular form of the simplex method. Use the slack variables as the initial basic variables.

P4.6 Solve the linear program given in P4.4 with the tabular form of the simplex method. Use the slack variables as the initial basic variables.

P4.7 The tableau below has been found at an intermediate point of the simplex method. The goal is to maximize the objective. In each of the parts of this question, start from the tableau and perform the suggested pivot operation. Show the complete tableau obtained and comment on any special characteristics it may exhibit. The parts are not cumulative.

Basic var.	Eq. no.	Coefficient of Z	x_1	x_2	x_3	x_4	x_5	Right side
Z	0	1	0	– 2	2	0	– 2	– 2
x_1	1	0	1	1	– 1	0	4	4
x_4	2	0	0	4	1	1	8	8

a. Let x_2 enter the basis and x_1 leave the basis.

b. Let x_2 enter the basis and x_4 leave the basis.

c. Let x_3 enter the basis and x_1 leave the basis.

d. Let x_3 enter the basis and x_4 leave the basis.

e. Let x_5 enter the basis and x_1 leave the basis.

f. Let x_5 enter the basis and x_4 leave the basis.

Tie Breaking in the Simplex Method (4.5)

There are some events that may occur during the performance of the simplex method that provide alternative paths for the algorithm or signal some special characteristic of the problem. These are listed below.

GOAL

- Know the indications, the implications, and how to respond to a tie for the entering variable, a tie for the leaving variable, a degenerate basic solution, alternative optimal solutions, and an unbounded solution.

RESULTS

Tie for the Entering Variable When using the "most negative value" rule for selecting the entering variable, if there is a tie for the most negative value, any one of the tied variables may be chosen arbitrarily. The route to the optimum will be changed, but the simplex method will ultimately find it.

Tie for the Leaving Variable At times the ratio test may show a tie for the row of the leaving variable. The basic variable for any one of the tied rows may be chosen arbitrarily to the leave the basis. The new tableau at the next iteration will show, however, the value of zero for the right sides of each of the tied rows not selected. This means that some of the basic variables have the value zero. This situation is called a *degenerate* solution.

Degenerate Basic Solution This is a basic solution with one or more of the basic variables having the value of zero. If this occurs, the next iteration may show a basis change without an actual change in the solution. Unless special procedures are added, the simplex algorithm may cycle and never stop. Since this rarely occurs in practice, most implementations of the algorithm do not use the special procedures.

Alternative Optimal Solution If the optimal tableau shows one or more nonbasic variables with zero coefficients in row (0), there are alternative optimal solutions. These solutions have different values of the decision variables but the same objective value. An alternative can be found by allowing a variable with the zero coefficient in row (0) to enter the basis. When there are alternative optimums, all linear combinations of the set of optimal solutions are also optimal.

Unbounded Solution When there is a nonbasic variable with a negative coefficient in row (0) and all the other coefficients in that column are nonpositive, then the value of that variable can be increased indefinitely without driving any basic variable to zero. The objective function can then be made arbitrarily large. This condition is called an unbounded solution, and there is no optimum for the model. The algorithm should stop if such an event occurs.

EXAMPLE

E4.4 With a revised version of the model given earlier, take two iterations and note the special characteristics of the solution obtained.

Iteration 1:

Basic var.	Eq. no.	Coefficient of Z	x_1	x_2	x_3	x_4	x_5	Right side	Ratio
Z	0	1	− 3	− 3	0	0	0	0	
x_3	1	**0**	**− 1**	**1**	**1**	**0**	**0**	**5**	5
x_4	2	0	1	**3**	0	1	0	15	5
x_5	3	0	1	**0**	0	0	1	20	—

There is a tie for the entering variable with both x_1 and x_2 candidates. Either could be chosen as the entering variable; however, we choose x_2. A tie also occurs in the ratio test. We have arbitrarily chosen row (1) as the pivot row.

Iteration 2:

Basic var.	Eq. no.	Coefficient of Z	x_1	x_2	x_3	x_4	x_5	Right side	Ratio
Z	0	1	**− 6**	0	3	0	0	15	
x_2	1	0	**− 1**	1	1	0	0	5	—
x_4	2	**0**	**4**	**0**	**− 3**	**1**	**0**	**0**	0
x_5	3	0	**1**	0	0	0	1	20	20

Because of the tie for the leaving variable, a zero appears on the right side for row(2). The current solution is $(x_1, x_2, x_3, x_4, x_5) = (0, 5, 0, 0, 20)$. This is a degenerate solution because the basic variable x_4 has a zero value. Allowing x_1 to enter the basis, observe that the ratio for row (2) is zero. Variable x_4 must leave the basis. Transforming the tableau we obtain.

Iteration 3:

Basic var.	Eq. no.	Coefficient of Z	x_1	x_2	x_3	x_4	x_5	Right side	Ratio
Z	0	1	0	0	**− 1.5**	1.5	0	15	
x_2	1	**0**	**0**	**1**	**0.25**	**0.25**	**0**	**5**	20
x_1	2	0	1	0	**− 0.75**	0.25	0	0	—
x_5	3	0	0	0	**0.75**	− 0.25	1	20	26.7

Although the basis has changed, there is no change in the solution. At the next iteration, the solution will no longer be degenerate.

PROBLEMS

P4.8 For each of the three cases listed, start from the tableau below and let the specified variable enter the basis.

Basic var.	Eq. no.	Z	x_1	x_2	x_3	x_4	x_5	x_6	Right side
Z	0	1	−3	0	0	−3	−2	0	10
x_3	1	0	4	0	1	5	−3	0	4
x_2	2	0	2	1	0	−3	1	0	2
x_6	3	0	1	0	0	2	−2	1	2

(Columns Z through x_6: *Coefficient of*)

a. Let x_1 enter the basis.

b. Let x_4 enter the basis.

c. Let x_5 enter the basis.

Which of the three choices gives the greatest increase in the objective function? Suggest a rule change for the simplex method that will always choose the variable to enter the basis that will give the greatest increase in the objective.

P4.9 Using the tableau of P4.8, if x_1 enters the basis, there is a tie for the variable to leave the basis. Starting from the same tableau let each of the two possibilities enter the basis.

a. Let x_3 leave the basis.

b. Let x_2 leave the basis.

What will the solution be after the basis change in each case?

P4.10 What special characteristic does the tableau below indicate?

Basic var.	Eq. no.	Z	x_1	x_2	x_3	x_4	x_5	x_6	Right side
Z	0	1	−3	2	0	0	−1	0	4
x_3	1	0	2	0	1	0	0	0	13
x_4	2	0	−2	1	0	1	−7	0	7
x_6	3	0	4	2	0	0	−2	1	2

(Columns Z through x_6: *Coefficient of*)

P4.11 For the tableau below, find all alternative optimum solutions.

Basic var.	Eq. no.	Coefficient of Z	x_1	x_2	x_3	x_4	x_5	x_6	Right side
Z	0	1	0	0	0	0	2	4	10
x_3	1	0	4	0	1	5	−3	2	4
x_2	2	0	2	1	0	−3	1	3	2

Adapting to Other Model Forms (4.6)

The simplex method as described to this point is only appropriate for a model with a maximization objective, "less than or equal to" constraints, nonnegative constants on the right side, and nonnegative variables. In this section, the modifications of the method for other forms are listed. These modifications affect only the initial tableau, so the algorithm does not change, however, the interpretation of the solution may change.

GOALS

- Be able to set up a linear program of arbitrary form for solution by the simplex method.
- Be able to use either the big M method or the two phase method for models that include artificial variables.

DEFINITIONS

Equality Constraint (=) A constraint of the form

$$a_{i1} x_1 + a_{i2} x_2 + \ldots + a_{in} x_n = b_i . \tag{4}$$

"Greater Than or Equal to" Constraint (≥) A constraint of the form

$$a_{j1} x_1 + a_{j2} x_2 + \ldots + a_{jn} x_n \geq b_j . \tag{5}$$

We use the index j here to distinguish the constraint from that given in (4).

Surplus Variable (x_{si}): A nonnegative variable subtracted from the "greater than or equal to" constraint to obtain the equality form.

$$a_{j1} x_1 + a_{j2} x_2 + \ldots + a_{jn} x_n - x_{sj} = b_j . \tag{6}$$

Slack Variable (x_{si}): A nonnegative variable added to a "less than or equal to" constraint to obtain the equality form. We have had slack variables before, but we repeat the definition here for completeness. Note that the same notation is used for slack and surplus variables. This is not a problem because at most one of the two types will appear in a constraint.

$$a_{k1} x_1 + a_{k2} x_2 + \ldots + a_{kn} x_n + x_{sk} = b_k . \tag{7}$$

Artificial Variable (x_{ai}): A variable added to the problem for each equality or "greater than or equal to" constraint. It is added to provide a simple initial solution for the simplex technique. If equations of the types shown in (4) and (5) are part of the equality form of the model, artificial variables are added for both types.

$$a_{i1} x_1 + a_{i2} x_2 + \ldots + a_{in} x_n + x_{ai} = b_i \quad (8)$$

$$a_{j1} x_1 + a_{j2} x_2 + \ldots + a_{jn} x_n - x_{sj} + x_{aj} = b_j . \quad (9)$$

When artificial variables are present in the equality form of the model, the artificial variables and the slack variables provide the initial basic solution for the simplex method.

Big M Method: This is a method for defining the objective function when artificial variables are present in the constraints. It is designed so that the artificial variables are forced to a zero value (if possible) by the simplex method. Let the set of constraints having artificial variables be A. The objective function for the big M method is the original objective function minus the sum of artificial variables multiplied by a large positive number (M is the number).

$$\text{Max } Z = c_1 x_1 + c_2 x_2 + \ldots + c_n x_n - \sum_{i \varepsilon A} (M) x_{ai}. \quad (10)$$

The M acts as a penalty for the artificial variables so that they tend to go to zero in the optimum solution. In practical implementations, M must actually be some very large number. This may cause numerical difficulties. For hand calculations, the letter M can be used as a symbol for a large number.

Two-Phase Method: This is an alternative for dealing with the artificial variables. This method defines two objective functions. In phase 1, the objective is to minimize the sum of the artificial variables.

$$\text{Min } Z = \sum_{i \varepsilon A} x_{ai}. \quad (11)$$

At the completion of this phase, if a feasible solution exists, the process will continue with phase 2 using the original objective function.

$$\text{Max } Z = c_1 x_1 + c_2 x_2 + \ldots + c_n x_n. \quad (12)$$

If all artificial variables are not at zero at the end of phase 1, the simplex method should terminate, indicating that no feasible solution exists. This method is almost always used for computer programs because it does not have the numerical problems associated with the big M method.

No Feasible Solution: This is the conclusion one draws when the simplex algorithm terminates with some artificial variables having positive values. This means that there is no combination of the structural variables that will satisfy all the constraints of the model.

RESULTS

To provide a complete algorithm, we describe below several transformations that must be made for nonstandard forms of the linear programming model. These transformations are all made before the iterative part of the simplex procedure begins, and they do not change the remainder of the procedure described in the last section. When transformations are made to the original variables, they must be re-transformed for proper interpretation of the results.

Objective is to Minimize An equivalent maximization problem is obtained by changing the signs of all terms in the objective function. Thus

$$\text{Min } \{c_1 x_1 + c_2 x_2 + \ldots + c_n x_n\} \Leftrightarrow \text{Max } \{-c_1 x_1 - c_2 x_2 - \ldots - c_n x_n\} \quad (13)$$

Lower Bounds on Variables If a variable has a nonzero lower bound such as

$$x_j \geq L_j ,$$

the variable x_j may be replaced everywhere by

$$x_j = x'_j + L_j , \quad (14)$$

and a new model is obtained in which

$$x'_j \geq 0.$$

This transformation is necessary if L_j is negative. It is advisable for computer programs of limited capacity even if L_j is positive because it eliminates a constraint. After the optimum is obtained, the value of the original variable is computed by evaluating Eq. (14) at the optimum solution.

A Constant Term in the Objective Often a model will have a constant term in the objective function. A constant may also appear with the transformations of variables using Eq. (14). A constant cannot affect the values of the variables at the optimum solution, so it may be dropped from the model. The constant should be added back to the objective function value after the optimum solution is found if it is an important aspect of the model.

Unrestricted Variables The simplex method requires that all variables be constrained to be nonnegative. If some model allows one or more variables to be negative, the following transformation of such variables is necesssary.

$$x_j = x'_j - x'' ,$$

where (15)

$$x_j \geq 0, \text{ and } x'' \geq 0.$$

The original variables are evaluated with Eq. (15) after obtaining the optimum. Note that only one additional variable, x'', is required no matter how many negative variables are included in the original model.

Negative Right Sides Consider the model after all transformations of lower bounds have been made using Eq. (14) but before slack or surplus variables have been added. The constraints have been written with all variables on the left and all constants on the right. If a constraint has a negative constant on the right, it must be changed by multiplying both sides of the constraint by –1. If the constraint is an inequality, the direction of the inequality must also be changed in this operation.

Elimination of Nonzero Objective Coefficients for Basic Variables The simplex method requires that the coefficients of all basic variables in row (0) of the tableau be zero. At times this is not true, and corrective measures must be taken. The specific cases of concern are when artificial variables appear in the initial basic solution in both the big M and the two-phase methods, and after phase 1 of the two-phase method. Before the simplex method can begin, these coefficients must be made zero by adding multiples of the constraint rows (1 through m) to the objective function row (0). This will be illustrated in the examples.

EXAMPLES

E4.5 We have created a problem to illustrate several of these results.

$$\begin{aligned} \text{Min} \quad & 3x_1 + 2x_2 \\ \text{Subject to:} \quad & x_1 - x_2 = -11 \\ & -x_1 - 2x_2 \le -10 \\ & x_1 \ge -3 \\ & x_1 \text{ and } x_2 \text{ unrestricted.} \end{aligned}$$

Solve this problem with the big M method.

First, we eliminate the lower bound on x_1 and the unrestricted x_2 by using (14) and (15), respectively.

$$x_1 = x'_1 + L_1 = x'_1 - 3$$
$$x_2 = x'_2 - x''.$$

The model becomes

$$\begin{aligned} \text{Min} \quad & 3(x'_1 - 3) + 2(x'_2 - x'') \\ \text{Subject to:} \quad & (x'_1 - 3) - (x'_2 - x'') = -11 \\ & -(x'_1 - 3) - 2(x'_2 - x'') \le -10 \\ & x'_1 \ge 0,\ x'_2 \ge 0,\ x'' \ge 0. \end{aligned}$$

Eliminating parentheses and moving constants to the right we have

$$\begin{aligned} \text{Min} \quad & 3x'_1 + 2x'_2 - 2x'' - 9 \\ \text{Subject to:} \quad & x'_1 - x'_2 + x'' = -8 \\ & -x'_1 - 2x'_2 + 2x'' \le -13 \\ & x'_1 \ge 0,\ x'_2 \ge 0,\ x'' \ge 0. \end{aligned}$$

Dropping the constant in the objective function, changing the objective to maximization, and multiplying both constraints by –1, we have

$$\begin{array}{llllll} \text{Max} & -3x'_1 & -2x'_2 & +2x'' & & \\ \text{Subject to:} & -x'_1 & +x'_2 & -x'' & = & 8 \\ & +x'_1 & +2x'_2 & -2x'' & \geq & 13 \end{array}$$

$$x'_1 \geq 0, \quad x'_2 \geq 0, \quad x'' \geq 0.$$

Subtracting a surplus variable from the second constraint, adding artificial variables to both constraints, and setting up the objective function for the big M method, we have

$$\begin{array}{llllllll} \text{Max} \quad Z = & -3x'_1 & -2x'_2 & +2x'' & & -Mx_{a1} & -Mx_{a2} & \\ \text{Subject to:} & -x'_1 & +x'_2 & -x'' & & +x_{a1} & & = 8 \\ & +x'_1 & +2x'_2 & -2x'' & -x_{s2} & & +x_{a2} & = 13 \end{array}$$

$$x'_1 \geq 0, x'_2 \geq 0, x'' \geq 0, x_{s2} \geq 0, x_{a1} \geq 0, x_{a2} \geq 0.$$

This is the equality form that is used to create the first tableau.

Basic var.	*Eq. no.*	*Coefficient of* Z	x'_1	x'_2	x''	x_{s2}	x_{a1}	x_{a2}	*Right side*
Z	0	1	3	2	−2	0	M	M	0
x_{a1}	1	0	−1	1	−1	0	1	0	8
x_{a2}	2	0	1	2	−2	−1	0	1	13

Now we must eliminate the coefficients in row (0) for the basic variables by multiplying rows (1) and (2) by $-M$ and adding them to row (0). The result is:

Basic var.	*Eq. no.*	*Coefficient of* Z	x'_1	x'_2	x''	x_{s2}	x_{a1}	x_{a2}	*Right side*
Z	0	1	3	$-3M+2$	$3M-2$	M	0	0	$-21M$
x_{a1}	1	0	−1	1	−1	0	1	0	8
x_{a2}	2	0	1	2	−2	−1	0	1	13

Finally, the tableau is in the simplex form. Note that M explicitly appears in row (0) for hand calculations. It is a symbol for a much larger number than any of the numbers in the tableau. The first iteration of the algorithm begins with x'_2 entering the basis.

After several iterations, the final tableau is:

Basic var.	*Eq. no.*	*Coefficient of* Z	x'_1	x'_2	x''	x_{s2}	x_{a1}	x_{a2}	*Right side*
Z	0	1	5	0	0	0	$M-2$	M	−16
x_{s2}	1	0	−3	0	0	1	2	−1	3
x'_2	2	0	−1	1	−1	0	1	0	8

This is the optimal solution since all coefficients in row (0) are nonnegative. The solution is

$$(x'_1, x'_2, x'', x_{s2}, x_{a1}, x_{a2}) = (0, 8, 0, 3, 0, 0).$$

Since the artificial variables are both zero, the solution is feasible. The solution must be put in terms of the original model:

$$x_1 = x'_1 + L_1 = x'_1 - 3 = 0 - 3 = -3$$
$$x_2 = x'_2 - x'' = 8 - 0 = 8.$$

Since the slack variable is not zero, the inequality constraint of the model is loose. The value of the original objective is 7.

E4.6 Solve the problem given in E4.5 by the two-phase method.

The formulation of the problem is the same until the statement of the objective function. With the two-phase method we have two objective functions.

Phase 1: Min $[x_{a1} + x_{a2}] \Leftrightarrow \text{Max } Z = [-x_{a1} - x_{a2}]$

Phase 2: Max $Z = -3x'_1 - 2x'_2 + 2x''$

Subject to:

$$-x'_1 + x'_2 - x'' + x_{a1} = 8$$
$$+x'_1 + 2x'_2 - 2x'' - x_{s2} + x_{a2} = 13$$
$$x_1 \geq 0,\ x'_2 \geq 0,\ x'' \geq 0, x_{s2} \geq 0,\ x_{a1} \geq 0, x_{a2} \geq 0.$$

The process begins with the solution of the phase 1 problem. The first tableau is:

Phase 1 :

Basic var.	*Eq. no.*	Coefficient of: Z	x'_1	x'_2	x''	x_{s2}	x_{a1}	x_{a2}	*Right side*
Z	0	1	0	0	0	0	1	1	0
x_{a1}	1	0	−1	1	−1	0	1	0	8
x_{a2}	2	0	1	2	−2	−1	0	1	13

Again, we observe that the coefficients of the basic variables are not zero in row (0). The nonzero values are eliminated by simply subtracting rows (1) and (2) from row (0). The revised tableau on which the simplex can begin is shown below.

Phase 1 :

Basic var.	*Eq. no.*	Coefficient of: Z	x'_1	x'_2	x''	x_{s2}	x_{a1}	x_{a2}	*Right side*
Z	0	1	0	−3	3	1	0	0	−21
x_{a1}	1	0	−1	1	−1	0	1	0	8
x_{a2}	2	0	1	2	−2	−1	0	1	13

As for the big M method, x'_2 will enter the basis at the first iteration. At the end of phase 1, the tableau is:

Phase 1 :

Basic var.	*Eq. no.*	Coefficient of: Z	x'_1	x'_2	x''	x_{s2}	x_{a1}	x_{a2}	*Right side*
Z	0	1	0	0	0	0	1	1	0
x_{s2}	1	0	−3	0	0	1	2	−1	3
x'_2	2	0	−1	1	−1	0	1	0	8

Since the value of the objective is zero, all the artificial variables have the value zero and we have found a feasible solution. For subsequent iterations, the columns representing the artificial variables can be dropped from the tableau. To initiate phase 2, we must now substitute the original objective function into the tableau.

Phase 2:

Basic var.	Eq. no.	Coefficient of Z	x'_1	x'_2	x''	x_{s2}	Right side
Z	0	1	3	2	−2	0	0
x_{s2}	1	0	−3	0	0	1	3
x'_2	2	0	−1	1	−1	0	8

We find that a basic variable, x'_2, has a nonzero coefficient in row (0). This is eliminated by multiplying row (2) by −2 and adding it to row (0) to regain the simplex form.

Phase 2:

Basic var.	Eq. no.	Coefficient of Z	x'_1	x'_2	x''	x_{s2}	Right side
Z	0	1	5	0	0	0	−16
x_{s2}	1	0	−3	0	0	1	3
x'_2	2	0	−1	1	−1	0	8

We discover that this tableau is optimum for phase 2. If it were not, we would continue with the simplex method until it terminated with the optimum solution. This is, of course, the same solution that was discovered with the big M method.

PROBLEMS

P4.12 For the linear program given below, construct the initial simplex tableau using the big M method. Be sure the tableau is in the simplex form. Complete the simplex technique to find an optimum for this problem.

$$\text{Min} \quad 7x_1 - 3x_2$$

Subject to:

$$4x_1 + 8x_2 = 30$$
$$-3x_1 + 2x_2 \geq 3$$
$$x_1 \geq 0,\ x_2 \geq 0.$$

P4.13 Solve the problem in P4.12 using the two-phase method.

P4.14 To the problem in P4.12, add the constraint

$$x_1 - x_2 \geq 0.$$

Solve this new problem with the two-phase method.

P4.15 A maximization problem has been solved with the simplex method to obtain the final tableau:

Basic var.	Eq. no.	Coefficient of Z	x_1	x_2	x_3	x_4	x_5	x_6	x_7	x_8	Right side
Z	0	1	2	0	0	0	0	3	6	$-1+M$	37
x_2	1	0	1	1	-1	0	0	11	3	4	2
x_5	2	0	3	0	0	0	1	2	-1	-2	3
x_4	3	0	-1	0	-2	1	0	5	7	1	0

a. What is the optimum solution obtained for this problem?

b. What kind of variable is x_8?

c. What special characteristic does this solution exhibit as indicated by the right side column?

d. What special characteristic does the column for x_3 indicate?

e. Allow x_6 to enter the basis. How does the new solution relate to the solution shown by this tableau?

f. Allow x_1 to enter the basis. How does the new solution relate to the solution shown by this tableau?

P4.16 Consider the problem

Min $x_1 + x_2$

Subject to:

(C1) $x_1 + x_2 \le 10$

(C2) $x_1 + x_2 \ge -10$

(C3) $x_1 - x_2 \le 10$

(C4) $x_1 - x_2 \ge -10$

x_1 and x_2 are unrestricted.

Solve this problem with the simplex method and comment on any special characteristics of the optimum solution. Sketch the feasible region for the problem and show the solution at the various iterations.

P4.17 Drop the constraint (C2) from the problem and solve. Comment on any special characteristics of the optimum solution.

P4.18 Add the simple lower bound constraints $x_1 \ge -5$ and $x_2 \ge -5$ to the model of P4.16. Solve the problem with these constraints explicitly included and comment on any special characteristics of the optimum obtained.

P4.19 Repeat problem 4.18 without the requirement that x_1 and x_2 are unrestricted but use a transformation to eliminate the lower bounds from the constraint set.

Computer Program

Microsolve can be used to solve linear programming models by first choosing the linear programming option on the disk menu, entering the algebraic formulation of the problem with the linear model generator program (or loading a previously prepared data set from a data disk), and selecting the "Solve the Linear Program" option from that program. This option causes the data for the model to be temporarily stored on the program disk, the solution program to be loaded, and the model data to be read again from the disk into the random access memory used by the solution program. The menu of the solution program appears in Fig. 4.2.

The first option on the menu allows the model to be displayed on the screen (or on the printer if option 6 has previously been selected). The display is different from that provided in the linear model generator in that the coefficient matrix is displayed by columns. Each variable is considered in order and all the constraint coefficients for that variable are listed. The numbers presented can be associated with particular constraints by noting the corresponding constraint names at the top of the screen. In addition to this being a useful alternative to the algebraic display for error checking, this format is used because the information describing the model is stored by columns in the computer memory. For a large model it may not be convenient to review the entire display, so options are provided to start the screen display at any given variable and to stop the display by pressing the "Q" key. If the printer has been previously called with option 6, the entire coefficient information is printed from the starting variable without the termination option.

The second option on the menu begins the solution process. Three alternatives are presented for viewing the solution process: watch algorithm details and help make decisions, see solution at each iteration, and see only final solution. The first two options are provided for instructional exercises while the last will usually be

```
        LINEAR PROGRAMMING

     1.  SHOW MODEL
     2.  SOLVE WITH PRIMAL SIMPLEX
     3.  REVIEW SOLUTION
     4.  SENSITIVITY ANALYSIS
     5.  REVISE MODEL
     6.  TURN PRINTER ON
     7.  RETURN TO DISK MENU

     PROBLEM 'CHEMICAL' IS LOADED
     43 VARIABLES AND 19 CONSTRAINTS

     ENTER OPTION NUMBER:
```

Figure 4.2. **Linear Programming Solution Algorithm Menu**

OPTIMUM SOLUTION
BASIC SOLUTION-PHASE 2 - ITER. 25

VAR.	NAME	VALUE	STATUS	VAR.	NAME	VALUE	STATUS
1	A	0	ZERO	22	ART-1	0	ZERO
2	AM1	1547.619	BASIC-4	23	ART-2	0	ZERO
3	AOM2	1547.619	BASIC-1	24	ART-3	0	ZERO
4	B	5000	BOUND	25	ART-4	0	ZERO
5	BM1	357.1428	BASIC-13	26	ART-5	0	ZERO
6	BM2	4642.857	BASIC-6	27	ART-6	0	ZERO
7	C	16071.42	BASIC-3	28	ART-7	0	ZERO
8	CM1	5238.095	BASIC-9	29	ART-8	0	ZERO
9	CM2	10833.33	BASIC-17	30	ART-9	0	ZERO
10	M1	7142.857	BASIC-12	31	ART-10	0	ZERO
11	M2	15476.19	BASIC-7	32	ART-11	0	ZERO
12	WM1	714.2857	BASIC-14	33	SLK-12	833.3333	BASIC-15
13	X	5000	BOUND	34	ART-12	0	ZERO
14	XM1	5000	BASIC-8	35	SLK-13	0	ZERO
15	Y	6071.428	BASIC-11	36	ART-13	0	ZERO
16	Y1	500	BOUND	37	ART-14	0	ZERO
17	Y2	5571.428	BASIC-19	38	ART-15	0	ZERO
18	YM1	1428.571	BASIC-16	39	ART-16	0	ZERO
19	YM2	4642.857	BASIC-5	40	ART-17	0	ZERO
20	Z	9285.714	BASIC-18	41	ART-18	0	ZERO
21	ZM2	9285.714	BASIC-10	42	SLK-19	8.285.714	BASIC-2
				43	ART-19	0	ZERO

OBJECTIVE = 136857.143

***Figure 4.3.* Optimum Linear Programming Solution**

used for larger problems. Fig. 4.3 shows the output format for the final solution using the chemical processing example of Chapter 3. To illustrate the efficiency of the algorithm, this solution required a computation time of 35 seconds on the IBM PC and 90 seconds on the Apple II.

Review of the final solution can tell a great deal about the validity of the model used. Very often an improperly stated model will result in a completely illogical solution such as all zero structural variables. Assuming the results are not immediately inappropriate, a more careful review of the solution should be conducted by plugging the solution back into the original constraints, checking which constraints are tight or loose, or recomputing the objective function with the solution. In addition to checking the model for errors, this will provide insights regarding the importance of the various components of the original problem. In the case of the chemical processing problem, we note that no raw material A is purchased with the entire amount used obtained as a by-product of the second mixture. Students usually will ask how the process gets started when some of the inputs of the process are also outputs from the process. Although of some practical interest, this question is irrelevant to this model because we are describing a steady-state flow process.

We note from the solution that the entire supply of raw material B is used, indicating that the simple upper bound on that variable is limiting the solution. This is particularly indicated by the word BOUND which appears, for example, at the right of row 4 of the display. This means that this variable is not basic but is at its upper bound. The meaning of this is described more completely in Chapter 9 when we discuss the modifications of the simplex technique for simple upper bounds. We also note that the maximum production of X has been reached. One might ask here whether this constraint is really necessary or whether the possibility exists of manufacturing more of product X and disposing of the excess.

The solution shows variables not originally present in the model, specifically the slack and artificial variables that have been added by the computer. These are added in the manner presented in this chapter and do not count against the variable limits of the program. The name SLK is used for both slack and surplus variables. The name ART is used for artificial variables. The number following SLK or ART indicates the constraint number which gives rise to the variable. Note that SLK-12 and SLK-19 are both basic in the optimum solution, indicating that the constraints AM1% and ZLIM are loose constraints. As proper for a feasible solution, the artificial variables are all zero. Some problems may show a very small value for artificial variables at optimality due to round-off errors.

The basic variables are indicated with the word BASIC in the right column. The index that follows indicates the constraint number for which the variable is basic. Nonbasic variables have the word ZERO or BOUND in the right column. Contrary to the procedures of this chapter, a nonbasic variable may be nonzero with a value equal to its upper bound. This modification will be discussed in Chapter 9.

For small problems, the student may want to observe the progress of the simplex algorithm. If the user chooses to see the solution at each iteration, the variables that enter and leave the basis and the values of all the variables will be displayed at each iteration. By choosing to watch the algorithm details and help make decisions, the student will see the displays shown in Fig. 4.4 at each iteration. The display illustrates the small model of E4.1 for the steps taken to move from iteration 1 to the results of iteration 2. The table showing the dual solution in Fig. 4.4a will be described in the next chapter. Fig. 4.4b shows the reduced costs for the nonbasic variables which are the numbers that appear in row (0) of the simplex tableau and provide the information for choosing the variable to enter the basis. The student may select the variable to enter the basis by entering its column number. Pressing the RETURN or ENTER key will allow the computer to make the choice using the "most negative value" rule. Entering "0" for the entering variable will terminate the algorithm. Fig. 4.4c shows the right side of the current tableau under XB(I), the pivot column under ALPHA, and the information required for the ratio test used to select the variable to leave the basis under RATIO. Contrary to the rules of this chapter, numbers are computed for negative entries of the pivot column. This is one of the modifications required to allow for the simple upper bounds. Again the student may select the leaving variable by choosing a row number; however, a wrong selection will make the solution become infeasible.

a. DUAL SOLUTION

ROW	NAME	VALUE
1	C1	3
2	C2	0
3	C3	0

b. COMPUTING REDUCED COSTS

COL.	VAR.	STATUS	D(J)
1	X1	ZERO	–1
3	SLK-1	ZERO	5

MINIMUM OCCURS FOR COLUMN 1
ENTER NUMBER OF PIVOT COLUMN:

c. RATIO TEST

ROW	XB(I)	ALPHA	RATIO
1	5	–1	999994
2	20	4	5
3	20	1	20

MINIMUM RATIO OCCURS FOR ROW 1
ENTER NUMBER OF PIVOT ROW:

d. BASIC SOLUTION-PHASE 2 - ITER 2

VAR.	NAME	VALUE	STATUS
1	X1	5	BASIC-2
2	X2	10	BASIC-1
3	SLK-1	0	ZERO
4	SLK-2	0	ZERO
5	SLK-3	15	BASIC-3

OBJECTIVE = 40

Figure 4.4. **Detailed Iteration Output Display**

Pressing the RETURN or ENTER key will allow the computer to make the correct selection. Fig. 4.4d shows the solution after the pivot operations.

If the printer has been previously turned on using option 6, all the displays are sent to the printer with no opportunity for user interaction. This option is suggested only for small problems. An option is also presented for reviewing the basis inverse at each iteration. This will be discussed more fully in Chapter 5.

Returning to the menu display of Fig. 4.2, option 3 is provided to allow a review the current solution. While solving a problem, the algorithm may be interrupted by pressing Q. The student can use this option to display the current nonoptimum solution. It can also be used to review the optimum solution.

Option 4 provides several opportunities to observe information regarding the sensitivity of the solution to changes in the problem parameters. This important aspect of solution interpretation will be discussed in Chapter 6.

Option 5 runs the linear model generator program so that the model can be revised. In practice linear programming is often an iterative process with certain parameters modified in a trial and error procedure to measure the sensitivity of the results to changes or perhaps to find a preferred value for the parameters. This option provides easy access to the generator program so these changes can be made. No special action is required regarding data sets, as the last model solved is automatically loaded into the generator.

Option 6 controls the information sent to the printer. If the printer has been turned on, screen displays of the model and solution are printed. User interaction is disconnected during printing, so care should be used when selecting the printer option. This option is also used to turn the printer off. Programs always begin with the printer off.

Option 7 returns control to the disk menu so that another program in the

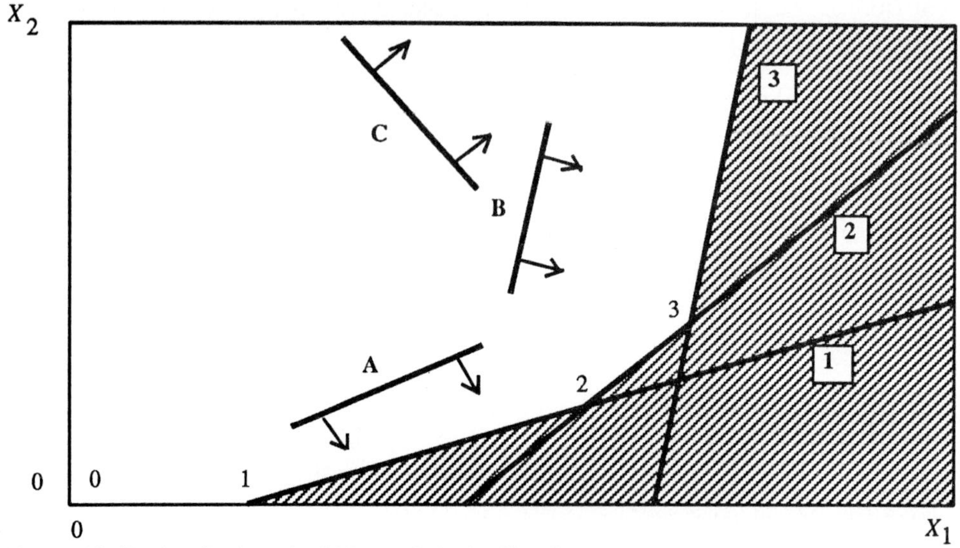

Figure 4.5. **Feasible Region with Different Objective Functions**

PROBLEMS

P4.20 Fig. 4.5 is a graphical presentation of a linear program with two structural variables and three constraints. The constraints are indicated by the large numbers **1, 2,** and **3.** The feasible region is shown in white and the infeasible region is cross hatched. Four feasible corner points are defined by the constraints and the nonnegativity conditions on the variables and are indicated by the small numbers: 0, 1, 2, 3. The objective function line is one of the three lines indicated by the letters **A, B,** and **C.** The arrows represent the direction of increasing objective function. Objective **B** is parallel with constraint **3.** In each case, tell the location of the optimum solution. If more than one optimum exists, characterize all of them.

a. If the objective function is **A** and the goal is to maximize.

b. If the objective function is **B** and the goal is to maximize.

c. If the objective function is **C** and the goal is to maximize.

d. If the objective function is **A** and the goal is to minimize.

e. If the objective function is **B** and the goal is to minimize.

f. If the objective function is **C** and the goal is to minimize.

g. If the objective function is **C** and the goal is to minimize, but the nonnegativity condition on x_1 is dropped.

P4.21 The tableau below is obtained at an intermediate point of the simplex technique

Basic var.	Eq. no.	Coefficient of Z	x_1	x_2	x_3	x_4	x_5	Right side
Z	0	1	0	−2	2	0	−2	16
x_1	1	0	1	1	−1	0	4	4
x_4	2	0	0	4	0	1	8	8

Starting from this tableau in each case, make the following pivots suggested. Show the new tableau and comment on any special characteristics that the solution may exhibit.

a. Let x_2 enter the basis and let x_4 leave the basis.

b. Let x_5 enter the basis and let x_4 leave the basis.

c. Let x_5 enter the basis and let x_1 leave the basis.

P4.22 For the linear programming problem below, set up the first tableau and find the variables that should enter and leave the basis.

a. Use the big M method.

b. Use the two-phase method.

$$\text{Max. } Z = 2x_1 - 3x_2 + x_3 - 4x_4$$

Subject to:

$$\begin{aligned} 2x_1 - x_2 + 3x_3 - 5x_4 &\le 20 \\ x_1 + 2x_2 - x_3 + 4x_4 &\ge 2 \\ x_4 &\le 20 \end{aligned}$$

$$x_j \ge 0 \text{ for } j = 1 \ldots 4.$$

P4.23 Consider again the model of P4.22 and answer the following questions. The artificial variables should not be counted when computing the answers.

a. How many nonbasic variables are there?

b. How many basic variables are there?

c. How many basic solutions are there?

d. Are all the basic solutions feasible? If not, find one that is not feasible.

P4.24 Solve the linear program below to completion. Comment on any characteristics the final solution may possess.

$$\text{Max. } Z = 2x_1 - x_2 + 3x_3 + 5x_4$$

Subject to:

$$\begin{aligned} x_1 - x_2 - 3x_3 \quad &\leq 10 \\ -2x_1 + x_2 \quad - 4x_4 &\leq 5 \\ +5x_3 + 4x_4 &\leq 20 \end{aligned}$$

$$x_j \geq 0 \text{ for } j = 1 \ldots 4.$$

P4.25 Answer the following questions regarding the simplex algorithm.

a. How could you change the algorithm to solve a minimization problem directly without changing it to an equivalent maximization problem?

b. If the algorithm were changed to always choose the variable entering the basis with the negative entry having the smallest absolute value, how would that change the effectiveness of the algorithm?

c. If the algorithm were changed to choose the variable to leave the basis having the greatest ratio, how would that change the effectiveness of the algorithm?

Computer Problems

P4.26 Solve the model given in problem P4.22 with the computer program. Show the sequence of variables entering and leaving the basis. List the basic solutions for each iteration and identify whether they are feasible.

P4.27 Solve the model given in problem P4.24 with the computer program. Show the sequence of variables entering and leaving the basis. List the basic solutions for each iteration and identify whether they are feasible.

P4.28 For the chemical processing example described in E3.1, investigate the effect of the following changes. The changes are not cumulative.

a. Eliminate the upper bound on sales for product X.

b. Eliminate the upper bound on the manufacture of X, but assume any amount produced over 5000 must be discarded at a cost of $1 per pound.

c. Eliminate the restriction on the amount of raw material B that can be purchased.

d. Change the cost of raw material C to $5 per pound.

P4.29 Consider the production planning problem given in E3.2.

a. Solve the problem with the computer program.

b. Using trial and error, determine the overtime rate that makes it uneconomical to use overtime for this plan. How does this affect the production plan?

c. Using the original model, solve the problem with no inventories allowed. How does this affect the labor costs optimum solution?

P4.30 Solve each of the problems given in Chapter 3 with the computer. In each case express the answers in the terms of the original problem in a way that would be understandable to a manager. Explain which constraints are tight and which are loose.

P4.31 When degeneracy is present there is the possibility that the linear programming algorithm may cycle. This is rare in practical problems, but researchers have constructed problems that do cycle. One is presented below. Solve the problem using the "Watch algorithm details" display option and list the basic solutions in the cycle.

$$\text{Max. } Z = 10x_1 - 57x_2 - 9x_3 - 24x_4$$

Subject to:

$$0.5x_1 - 5.5x_2 - 2.5x_3 + 9x_4 \leq 0$$
$$0.5x_1 - 1.5x_2 - 0.5x_3 + x_4 \leq 0$$
$$x_1 \leq 1$$
$$x_j \geq 0 \text{ for } j = 1 \ldots 4.$$

P4.32 Cycling can be eliminated by using revised rules to select the entering and leaving variables. The rules are based on the indices of the variables of the problem. Assume all the variables are designated as x_k, where k is the variable index ranging from 1 to the number of variables in the problem. The rules follow.

> *Rule for selecting the entering variable:* From all the variables having negative reduced costs, select the one with the smallest index to enter the basis.
>
> *Rule for selecting the leaving variable:* Use the standard ratio test to select the leaving variable, but if there is a tie in the ratio test, select from the tied rows the variable having the smallest index.

Run the problem of P4.31 with the "Watch algorithm details" option and manually select the variables to enter and leave the basis using these rules. List the sequence of entering and leaving variables and the sequence of basic solutions. Show the optimum obtained.

* The reference for this method is Bland, Robert C.: "New Finite Pivoting Rules for the Simplex Method," *Mathematics of Operations Research*, **2** (1), 103–107, February 1977.

CHAPTER 5

The Theory of the Simplex Method

The Revised Simplex Method (5.2)

The algorithm implementing the simplex method described in the last chapter is appropriate for instruction because it embodies the essential elements of the technique and can be organized for hand calculations. Computer implementations rarely use the tableau method, however, because it incorporates a number of inefficiencies that would make the method fail for large problems. The principal impediment is the size of the tableau, with its m rows and $m + n$ columns. With 100 constraints and 1000 variables, a fairly small problem, storing the elements of the tableau would require over 100,000 words of computer memory. Computer programs more often use the revised simplex algorithm which does not store the entire tableau, but only the inverse of the basis matrix, which has m rows and m columns, requiring only 10,000 words of memory for the example.

GOALS

- Be able to show the matrix representation of the algebraic model of a linear program.
- Given the basis and basis inverse, be able to calculate the associated basic solution and objective function value.
- Given the basis and basis inverse, be able to construct the tableau used in the tableau implementation of the simplex method.

- Starting from the a given basis (with the associated inverse), be able to find the optimal solution using the revised form of the simplex method.

DEFINITIONS

Matrix Format of the Linear Program:

Maximize $Z = \mathbf{cx}$
Subject to:

$$\mathbf{A\ x} \le \mathbf{b} \text{ and } \mathbf{x} \ge \mathbf{0}.$$

where

$$\mathbf{c} = (c_1, c_2, \ldots, c_n).$$
$$\mathbf{x} = (x_1, x_2, \ldots, x_n)^T.$$
$$\mathbf{b} = (b_1, b_2, \ldots, b_m)^T.$$

(The superscript T indicates transpose.)

$$\mathbf{A} = \begin{bmatrix} a_{11} & a_{12} & \cdots & a_{1n} \\ a_{21} & a_{22} & \cdots & a_{2n} \\ \vdots & \vdots & \cdots & \vdots \\ a_{m1} & a_{m2} & \cdots & a_{mn} \end{bmatrix}$$

Matrix Format of the Equality Form of the Linear Program:

Maximize $Z = \mathbf{cx}$
Subject to:

$$\mathbf{A\ x} + \mathbf{I\ x_s} = \mathbf{b} \text{ and } \mathbf{x} \ge \mathbf{0},\ \mathbf{x_s} \ge \mathbf{0},$$

where $\mathbf{I}$ is an m by m identity matrix, and $\mathbf{x_s}$ is the vector of slack variables,

$$\mathbf{x_s} = (x_{s1}, x_{s2}, \ldots, x_{sm})^T.$$

Basis Matrix (B): A collection of m independent columns selected from **A**.

$$\mathbf{B} = \begin{bmatrix} B_{11} & B_{12} & \cdots & B_{1m} \\ B_{21} & B_{22} & \cdots & B_{2m} \\ \vdots & \vdots & \cdots & \vdots \\ B_{m1} & B_{m2} & \cdots & B_{mm} \end{bmatrix}$$

Basis Inverse: ($\mathbf{B}^{-1}$): The inverse of the basis matrix.

Basic Variables ($\mathbf{x_B}$): The components of the vector ($\mathbf{x}$, $\mathbf{x_s}$) corresponding to the columns selected for the basis matrix.

$$\mathbf{x_B} = (x_{B1}, x_{B2}, \ldots, x_{Bm})^T,$$

where x_{Bi} is the ith basic variable. A *basic solution* is an assignment of values to this vector that statisfies the equality form of the linear program. Nonbasic variables are set to zero for this solution.

Basic Objective Function Coefficients ($\mathbf{c_B}$): The components of the vector ($\mathbf{c}$, $\mathbf{0}$) corresponding to the columns selected for the basis matrix. Here, $\mathbf{0}$ describes the coefficients of the slack variables and consists of m zeros.

$$\mathbf{c_B} = (c_{B1}, c_{B2}, \ldots, c_{Bm}),$$

where c_{Bi} is the objective coefficient for the i th basic variable.

RESULTS

Computing the Basic Solution Given the basis and the basis inverse, the basic solution can be computed by

$$\mathbf{x_B} = \mathbf{B^{-1}b}. \quad (1)$$

The value of the objective is

$$Z = \mathbf{c_B}\,\mathbf{x_B} = \mathbf{c_B}\,\mathbf{B^{-1}b}. \quad (2)$$

Constructing the Current Set of Equations and the Simplex Tableau Given the basis and basis inverse, one can construct the equations in the simplex form using the matrix expression

$$\begin{bmatrix} 1 & \mathbf{c_B B^{-1} A - c} & \mathbf{c_B B^{-1}} \\ 0 & \mathbf{B^{-1}A} & \mathbf{B^{-1}} \end{bmatrix} \begin{bmatrix} Z \\ \mathbf{x} \\ \mathbf{x_S} \end{bmatrix} = \begin{bmatrix} \mathbf{c_B B^{-1} b} \\ \mathbf{B^{-1} b} \end{bmatrix} \quad (3)$$

The coefficients of the tableau come from the matrices of the constants in this expression. The matrix on the right of the equality is the "right side" column. The matrix on the left forms the remainder of the numerical portion of the tableau.

Reduced Cost ($z_j - c_j$) An element of the row (0) of the tableau. The reduced cost for variable j is computed by

$$z_j - c_j = \mathbf{c_B B^{-1} a_j} - c_j, \quad (4)$$

where $\mathbf{a_j}$ is the column for variable j in the original $\mathbf{A}$ matrix.

ALGORITHM: Revised Form of the Simplex

This algorithm will work for a problem in the standard form with positive right sides. Some modification is necessary for problems with nonstandard features such as equality or greater than constraints.

A1. Initialization Step Put the linear programming model in the standard form. Construct the matrices $\mathbf{A}$, $\mathbf{c}$, and $\mathbf{b}$. Let the initial basis consist of the slack variables, so $\mathbf{B} = \mathbf{B^{-1}} = \mathbf{I}$. Also $\mathbf{c_B} = \mathbf{0}$, and $\mathbf{x_B} = \mathbf{b}$. The structural variables are nonbasic with the reduced costs for variable j equal to $-c_j$.

If all reduced costs are nonnegative, stop with the optimum solution.

A2. Iterative Step

a. Choose the nonbasic variable with the most negative reduced cost, x_k, to enter the basis. Let column k of the matrix [**A**, **I**] be the vector $\mathbf{a}_k$. This is the pivot column. The entering variable may be either a structural variable or a slack variable.

b. Compute column k in the current tableau. Let this be the vector $\mathbf{a}'_k$ where

$$\mathbf{a}'_k = \mathbf{B}^{-1}\,\mathbf{a}_k\,. \tag{5}$$

Let a'_{ik} be the ith component of this vector. Find the row, r, for which the minimum ratio is obtained

$$\delta = x_{Br}\,/\,a'_{rk} = \text{Min}\;[\;(x_{Bi}\,/a'_{ik})\mid i = 1\;\ldots\;m,\ \text{and}\ a'_{ik} > 0\;]. \tag{6}$$

If there are no rows which have $a'_{ik} > 0$, the solution is unbounded. Otherwise, the basic variable for the selected row is to leave the basis. Row r is called the pivot row.

c. Compute the new basis inverse by the following operations. Create the vector $\eta = (\eta_1, \eta_2, \ldots, \eta_m)^{\mathrm{T}}$, where

$$\eta_i = \begin{cases} -\,(a'_{ik}\,/\,a'_{rk}), & \text{if } i \neq r \\ (1\,/\,a'_{rk}), & \text{if } i = r\,. \end{cases} \tag{7}$$

Construct the matrix **E**, which is an identity matrix with column r replaced by η.

The new basis inverse is found by multiplying the current basis inverse by **E**.

$$\mathbf{B}^{-1} \Leftarrow \mathbf{E}\;\mathbf{B}^{-1} \quad \text{(the symbol} \Leftarrow \text{means "replaced by.")} \tag{8}$$

Compute the new basic solution and objective function value

$$\mathbf{x_B} = \mathbf{B}^{-1}\mathbf{b}, \quad Z = \mathbf{c_B x_B}.$$

Let $c_{Br} = c_k$ in the vector $\mathbf{c_B}$.

A3. Optimality Test For each nonbasic variable, compute the reduced cost

$$z_j - c_j = \mathbf{c_B B^{-1} a_j} - c_j\,.$$

Note that for slack variables $\mathbf{a_j}$ is a unit vector and c_j is zero.

If the reduced costs of all nonbasic variables are nonnegative, stop with the optimum solution. Otherwise return to step A2.

EXAMPLES

E5.1 Write the equality form of this model in the matrix format.

$$\text{Maximize } Z = 2x_1 + 1.25x_2 + 3x_3$$

Subject to:

$$
\begin{aligned}
&(1) \quad 2x_1 + x_2 + 2x_3 \le 7 \\
&(2) \quad 3x_1 + x_2 \le 6 \\
&(3) \quad x_2 + 6x_3 \le 9
\end{aligned}
$$

$$x_1 \ge 0, x_2 \ge 0, x_3 \ge 0.$$

Setting up the required matrices:

$$\mathbf{c} = [\,2 \quad 1.25 \quad 3\,]$$

$$\mathbf{A} = \begin{bmatrix} 2 & 1 & 2 \\ 3 & 1 & 0 \\ 0 & 1 & 6 \end{bmatrix} \qquad \mathbf{I} = \begin{bmatrix} 1 & 0 & 0 \\ 0 & 1 & 0 \\ 0 & 0 & 1 \end{bmatrix} \qquad \mathbf{b} = \begin{bmatrix} 7 \\ 6 \\ 9 \end{bmatrix}$$

$$\mathbf{x} = \begin{bmatrix} x_1 \\ x_2 \\ x_3 \end{bmatrix} \qquad \mathbf{x_s} = \begin{bmatrix} x_{s1} \\ x_{s2} \\ x_{s3} \end{bmatrix}$$

With these matrices defined, the equality form of the linear program can be written

$$\text{Maximize} \quad Z = \mathbf{cx}$$

Subject to:

$$\mathbf{A\,x} + \mathbf{I\,x_s} = \mathbf{b} \text{ and } \mathbf{x} \ge \mathbf{0}, \mathbf{x_s} \ge \mathbf{0}.$$

E5.2 Using the model in E5.1, let the basic variables be x_1, x_{s2}, and x_3 for constraints (1), (2), and (3), respectively. With this information and the basis inverse given below, compute the basic solution.

The basis, **B**, is made up of the columns of **A** and of **I** corresponding to the basic variables. The basis inverse is found by inverting **B**.

$$\mathbf{B} = \begin{bmatrix} 2 & 0 & 2 \\ 3 & 1 & 0 \\ 0 & 0 & 6 \end{bmatrix} \qquad \mathbf{B}^{-1} = \begin{bmatrix} 0.5 & 0 & -0.166 \\ -1.5 & 1 & 0.5 \\ 0 & 0 & 0.166 \end{bmatrix}$$

$$\mathbf{c_B} = [\,2 \quad 0 \quad 3\,].$$

$$\mathbf{x_B} = \begin{bmatrix} x_1 \\ x_{s2} \\ x_3 \end{bmatrix} = \mathbf{B}^{-1}\mathbf{b} = \begin{bmatrix} 2 \\ 0 \\ 1.5 \end{bmatrix} \qquad Z = \mathbf{c_B}\,\mathbf{x_B} = 8.5.$$

E5.3 Starting from this solution, do one iteration of the revised simplex method. Compute the reduced costs for the nonbasic variables with Eq. 4.

$$c_B B^{-1} a_j - c_j = [1 \quad 0 \quad -0.166\,] \, a_j - c_j \,.$$

$$\begin{aligned}
x_2:&\quad z_2 - c_2 = c_B B^{-1} a_2 - c_2 &&= [1 \;\; 0 \; -0.166] \, a_2 - 1 = -0.083 \\
x_{s1}:&\quad z_{s1} - c_{s1} = c_B B^{-1} a_{s1} &&= [1 \;\; 0 \; -0.166] \, a_{s1} \quad = 1 \\
x_{s3}:&\quad z_{s3} - c_{s3} = c_B B^{-1} a_{s3} &&= [1 \;\; 0 \; -0.166] \, a_{s3} \quad = 0.166.
\end{aligned}$$

The solution is not optimal.

Step A2:

a. Select x_2 to enter the basis, $k = 2$.
b. Find the variable to leave the basis with Eq. 5 and 6.

$$a'_2 = B^{-1} a_2 = \begin{bmatrix} 0.333 \\ 0 \\ 0.166 \end{bmatrix} \qquad \delta = \text{Min} \begin{bmatrix} 2/0.333 \\ — \\ 1.5/0.166 \end{bmatrix} = 6.$$

The basic variable for row (1), x_1, leaves the basis; therefore $r = 1$.

c. Change the basis. Compute η and $\mathbf{E}$ with Eq. 7.

$$\eta = \begin{bmatrix} 1/0.333 \\ 0/0.333 \\ -0.116/0.333 \end{bmatrix} = \begin{bmatrix} 3 \\ 0 \\ -0.5 \end{bmatrix} \qquad \mathbf{E} = \begin{bmatrix} 3 & 0 & 0 \\ 0 & 1 & 0 \\ -0.5 & 0 & 1 \end{bmatrix}$$

Compute new basis inverse with Eq. 8 and solution with Eq. 1 and 2.

$$B^{-1} \Leftarrow E\,B^{-1} = \begin{bmatrix} 1.5 & 0 & -0.5 \\ -1.5 & 1 & 0.5 \\ -0.25 & 0 & 0.25 \end{bmatrix} \qquad x_B = \begin{bmatrix} x_2 \\ x_{s2} \\ x_3 \end{bmatrix} = B^{-1} b = \begin{bmatrix} 6 \\ 0 \\ 0.5 \end{bmatrix}$$

$$c_B = [\,1.25 \quad 0 \quad 3\,], \qquad Z = c_B x_B = 9.$$

Step A.3: Compute the reduced costs.

$$c_B B^{-1} a_j - c_j = [1.125 \quad 0 \quad 0.125] \, a_j - c_j \,.$$

Nonbasic Variable	*Reduced Cost*
x_1	0.25
x_{s1}	1.125
x_{s3}	0.125

The solution is optimal.

E5.4 Using the information from E5.3, construct the final tableau for this problem. The matrices can be rearranged to form the tableau as shown below.

Basic var.	Eq. no.	Z	x_1–x_n	x_{s1}–x_{sm}	Right side
Z	0	1	$c_B B^{-1}A - c$	$c_B B^{-1}$	$c_B B^{-1}b$
x_{B1}–x_{Bm}	1–m	0	$B^{-1}A$	B^{-1}	$B^{-1}b$

Using the matrices determined in E5.3, we have:

Basic var.	Eq. no.	Z	x_1	x_2	x_3	x_{s1}	x_{s2}	x_{s3}	Right side
Z	0	1	0.25	0	0	1.125	0	0.125	9
x_2	1	0	3	1	0	1.5	0	–0.5	6
x_{s2}	2	0	0	0	0	–1.5	1	0.5	0
x_3	3	0	–0.5	0	1	–0.25	0	0.25	0.5

E5.5 Start with the slack variables basis, and do two iterations of the revised simplex algorithm for the problem below.

$$\text{Maximize } Z = 2x_1 + 3x_2$$

Subject to:

(1) $$-x_1 + x_2 \le 5$$

(2) $$x_1 + 3x_2 \le 35$$

(3) $$x_1 \le 20$$

$$x_1 \ge 0, x_2 \ge 0.$$

Setting up the required matrices:

$$\mathbf{c} = [\ 2 \quad 3\ ]$$

$$\mathbf{A} = \begin{bmatrix} -1 & 1 \\ 1 & 3 \\ 1 & 0 \end{bmatrix} \qquad \mathbf{I} = \begin{bmatrix} 1 & 0 & 0 \\ 0 & 1 & 0 \\ 0 & 0 & 1 \end{bmatrix} \qquad \mathbf{b} = \begin{bmatrix} 5 \\ 35 \\ 20 \end{bmatrix}$$

$$\mathbf{x} = \begin{bmatrix} x_1 \\ x_2 \end{bmatrix} \qquad \mathbf{x_s} = \begin{bmatrix} x_{s1} \\ x_{s2} \\ x_{s3} \end{bmatrix}.$$

The initial basic variables are the slack variables so we have:

First Iteration - Step A1:

$$\mathbf{B}^{-1} = \begin{bmatrix} 1 & 0 & 0 \\ 0 & 1 & 0 \\ 0 & 0 & 1 \end{bmatrix} \qquad \mathbf{x_B} = \begin{bmatrix} x_{s1} \\ x_{s2} \\ x_{s3} \end{bmatrix} = \mathbf{B}^{-1}\mathbf{b} = \begin{bmatrix} 5 \\ 35 \\ 20 \end{bmatrix}.$$

Compute the reduced costs with Eq. 4.

$$\mathbf{c_B B^{-1} a_j} - c_j = [0\ \ 0\ \ 0]\ \mathbf{a_j} - c_j\,.$$

Nonbasic Variable	*Reduced Cost*
x_1	-2
x_2	-3

The solution is not optimal.

Step A2:

a. Select x_2 to enter the basis, $k = 2$.
b. Find the variable to leave the basis with Eq. 5 and 6. We use a more convenient tabular form here to show the important information.

Row	*Basic Var.*	*Value*	*a'*	*Ratio*
1	x_{s1}	5	1	5
2	x_{s2}	35	3	11.67
3	x_{s3}	20	0	—

The basic variable from row (1), x_{s1}, leaves the basis; therefore, $r = 1$.
c. Change the basis. Compute η and **E** with Eq. 7.

$$\eta = \begin{bmatrix} 1/1 \\ -3/1 \\ 0/1 \end{bmatrix} = \begin{bmatrix} 1 \\ -3 \\ 0 \end{bmatrix} \qquad \mathbf{E} = \begin{bmatrix} 1 & 0 & 0 \\ -3 & 1 & 0 \\ 0 & 0 & 1 \end{bmatrix}.$$

Compute new basis inverse with Eq. 8 and solution with Eq. 1 and 2.

$$\mathbf{B^{-1}} \Leftarrow \mathbf{EB^{-1}} = \begin{bmatrix} 1 & 0 & 0 \\ -3 & 1 & 0 \\ 0 & 0 & 1 \end{bmatrix} \qquad \mathbf{x_B} = \begin{bmatrix} x_2 \\ x_{s2} \\ x_{s3} \end{bmatrix} = \begin{bmatrix} 5 \\ 20 \\ 20 \end{bmatrix}$$

$$\mathbf{c_B} = [\ 3\ \ 0\ \ 0\ ] \qquad Z = \mathbf{c_B x_B} = 15.$$

Step A3 Compute the reduced costs with Eq. 4.

$$\mathbf{c_B B^{-1} a_j} - c_j = [3\ \ 0\ \ 0]\ \mathbf{a_j} - c_j\,.$$

Nonbasic Variable	*Reduced Cost*
x_1	-5
x_{s1}	+3

The solution is not optimal.

Second Iteration—Step A2:

a. Select x_1 to enter the basis, $k = 1$.
b. Find the variable to leave the basis.

Row	*Basic Var.*	*Value*	$\mathbf{a}'$	*Ratio*
1	x_2	5	–1	—
2	x_{s2}	20	4	5
3	x_{s3}	20	1	20

The basic variable from row (2), x_{s2}, leaves the basis; therefore, $r = 2$.

c. Change the basis. Compute η and **E**.

$$\eta = \begin{bmatrix} 1/4 \\ 1/4 \\ -1/4 \end{bmatrix} = \begin{bmatrix} 0.25 \\ 0.25 \\ -0.25 \end{bmatrix} \qquad \mathbf{E} = \begin{bmatrix} 1 & 0.25 & 0 \\ 0 & 0.25 & 0 \\ 0 & -0.25 & 1 \end{bmatrix}.$$

Compute new basis inverse and solution.

$$\mathbf{B}^{-1} \Leftarrow \mathbf{E}\,\mathbf{B}^{-1} = \begin{bmatrix} 0.25 & 0.25 & 0 \\ -0.75 & 0.25 & 0 \\ 0.75 & -0.25 & 1 \end{bmatrix} \qquad \mathbf{x_B} = \begin{bmatrix} x_2 \\ x_1 \\ x_{s3} \end{bmatrix} = \begin{bmatrix} 10 \\ 5 \\ 15 \end{bmatrix}$$

$$\mathbf{c_B} = [\; 3 \quad 2 \quad 0 \;] \qquad Z = \mathbf{c_B x_B} = 40.$$

Step A3:

$$\mathbf{c_B B^{-1} a_j} - c_j = [-0.75 \;\; 1.25 \;\; 0]\; \mathbf{a_j} - c_j\,.$$

Nonbasic Variable	*Reduced Cost*
x_{s1}	–0.75
x_{s2}	1.25

The solution is not optimal.

PROBLEMS

P5.1 Complete the solution of E5.5 with the revised simplex procedure.

P5.2 Show the matrix format of the equality form of the problem below.

Maximize $Z = x_1 + x_2 + 1.2x_3 + 1.2x_4 + 0.8x_5$

Subject to:

(1) $2x_1 + 2x_3 + x_4 + x_5 \le 12$

(2) $2x_2 + x_3 + 2x_4 + x_5 \le 15$

(3) $x_1 + x_2 + x_5 \le 15$

(4) $5x_1 + 7x_2 + 4x_3 + 5x_4 + 6x_5 \le 6$

(5) $x_1 + x_2 + x_3 + x_4 + x_5 \le 10$

$x_1 \ge 0, x_2 \ge 0, x_3 \ge 0, x_4 \ge 0, x_5 \ge 0.$

A Fundamental Insight (5.3)

Given a linear programming model in the standard form and the final tableau obtained by the simplex method, one can write the final tableau as a function of the rows of the parameters of the original model. This is called a *fundamental insight* because it allows one to investigate how the final tableau changes with changes in the initial parameters. This is very useful for sensitivity analysis.

GOALS

- Given a linear programming model in the standard form and the final simplex tableau, set up the equations which describe the final tableau as a function of the original parameters.
- Investigate the effects on the final tableau of changing the parameters of the original model.

DEFINITIONS

The following definitions relating to simplex tableaus do not include the first column representing Z. That column remains the same in all tableaus.

Initial Row (0) (t): The initial row(0) of the simplex tableau described by the model parameters.

$$\mathbf{t} = [\ -\mathbf{c}\quad \mathbf{0}\quad 0\ ].$$

The first component is a vector consisting of the negative of the n objective function coefficients of the structural variables. The second component is a vector of m zeros, one for each slack variable. The final component is the original value of the objective function.

Initial Rows 1 through *m* (T): The remainder of the initial simplex tableau.

$$\mathbf{T} = [\ \mathbf{A}\quad \mathbf{I}\quad \mathbf{b}\ ].$$

The first component is the m by n matrix of the constraint coefficients for the structural variables. The second component is the m by m identity matrix. The final component is the vector of the original right sides.

Initial Row (*i*) of the Tableau ($\mathbf{t}_i$): Row i of the matrix **T**.

Final Row (0) (t*): Row(0) of the optimal simplex tableau

$$\mathbf{t}^* = [\ \mathbf{z}^*\text{-}\mathbf{c}\quad \mathbf{y}^*\quad Z^*\ ].$$

The first component is a vector of reduced costs for the structural variables. The second component is a vector of reduced costs for the slack variables. The final component is the optimal value of the objective function.

A component of $\mathbf{y}^*$ is y^*_j, representing the reduced cost of the jth slack variable (the slack variable for constraint j).

Final Rows 1 through m ($\mathbf{T}^*$): The remainder of the optimal simplex tableau.

$$\mathbf{T}^* = [\ \mathbf{A}^* \quad \mathbf{S}^* \quad \mathbf{b}^*\ ].$$

The coefficients of this matrix are the equation coefficients adjusted by the linear operations of the simplex method. The first component is the m by n matrix for the structural variables. The second component is the m by m matrix for the slack variables. The final component is the vector of the right sides.

A component of $\mathbf{S}^*$ is s^*_{ij}, representing the coefficient for the jth slack variable in the i th constraint.

Final Row (i) of the Tableau ($\mathbf{t}^*_i$) : Row i of the matrix $\mathbf{T}^*$.

RESULTS

Determination of the Final Tableau The final tableau can be described as a linear combination of the rows of the initial tableau.

$$\mathbf{t}^* = \mathbf{t} + \sum_{j=1}^{m} y^*_j \, \mathbf{t}_j$$

$$\mathbf{t}^*_i = \sum_{j=1}^{m} s^*_{ij} \, \mathbf{t}_j \ .$$

Determination of $\mathbf{y}^*$ *and* $\mathbf{S}^*$ Using the tableau method, $\mathbf{y}^*$ and $\mathbf{S}^*$ appear under the slack variables in the tableau. Using the revised simplex method, they can be computed from the basis inverse.

$$\mathbf{y}^* = \mathbf{c}_B \mathbf{B}^{-1}$$
$$\mathbf{S}^* = \mathbf{B}^{-1}.$$

EXAMPLES

E5.6 If the model of E5.5 were solved to optimality, we would have the following information:

$$\mathbf{B}^{-1} = \begin{bmatrix} 0 & 0.333 & -0.333 \\ 0 & 0 & 1 \\ 1 & -0.333 & 1.333 \end{bmatrix} \qquad \mathbf{x}_B = \begin{bmatrix} x_2 \\ x_1 \\ x_{s1} \end{bmatrix} = \mathbf{B}^{-1}\mathbf{b} = \begin{bmatrix} 5 \\ 20 \\ 20 \end{bmatrix}$$

$$\mathbf{c}_B = [\ 3 \quad 2 \quad 0\ ] \qquad Z = \mathbf{c}_B \mathbf{x}_B = 55.$$

Use these results to create the final simplex tableau.

From the matrices defined in E5.1 we observe

$$\mathbf{y}^* = \mathbf{c}_B\mathbf{B}^{-1} = [\ 0 \quad 1 \quad 1\ ]$$

$$\mathbf{S}^* = \mathbf{B}^{-1} = \begin{bmatrix} 0 & 0.333 & -0.333 \\ 0 & 0 & 1 \\ 1 & -0.333 & 1.333 \end{bmatrix}.$$

Row (0) or the initial tableau is

$$\begin{aligned} \mathbf{t} &= [\ -\mathbf{c} \qquad \mathbf{0} \qquad 0\ ] \\ &= [\ -2 \quad -3 \quad 0 \quad 0 \quad 0 \quad 0\ ]. \end{aligned}$$

The remainder of the initial tableau is

$$\mathbf{T} = [\ \mathbf{A} \qquad \mathbf{I} \qquad \mathbf{b}\ ]$$

$$= \begin{bmatrix} -1 & 1 & 1 & 0 & 0 & 5 \\ 1 & 3 & 0 & 1 & 0 & 35 \\ 1 & 0 & 0 & 0 & 1 & 20 \end{bmatrix}.$$

Now we can compute

$$\mathbf{t}^* = \mathbf{t} + 0^*\mathbf{t}_1 + 1^*\mathbf{t}_2 + 1^*\mathbf{t}_3$$

$$\begin{aligned} \mathbf{t}^* = &\quad (-2 \quad -3 \quad 0 \quad 0 \quad 0 \quad 0\,) \\ &+0^* \ (-1 \quad 1 \quad 1 \quad 0 \quad 0 \quad 5\,) \\ &+1^* \ (\ 1 \quad 3 \quad 0 \quad 1 \quad 0 \quad 35\,) \\ &+1^* \ (\ 1 \quad 0 \quad 0 \quad 0 \quad 1 \quad 20\,) \\ = &\quad (\ 0 \quad 0 \quad 0 \quad 1 \quad 1 \quad 55\,). \end{aligned}$$

$$\mathbf{t}^*_1 = 0^*\,\mathbf{t}_1 + 0.333^*\mathbf{t}_2 - 0.333^*\mathbf{t}_3$$

$$\begin{aligned} &+0^* \ (-1 \quad 1 \quad 1 \quad 0 \quad 0 \quad 5\,) \\ &+0.333^* \ (\ 1 \quad 3 \quad 0 \quad 1 \quad 0 \quad 35\,) \\ &-0.333^* \ (\ 1 \quad 0 \quad 0 \quad 0 \quad 1 \quad 20\,) \\ &= \quad (\ 0 \quad 1 \quad 0 \quad 0.333 \quad -0.333 \quad 5\,). \end{aligned}$$

$$\mathbf{t}^*_2 = 0^*\mathbf{t}_1 + 0^*\mathbf{t}_2 + 1^*\mathbf{t}_3$$

$$\begin{aligned} &+0^* \ (-1 \quad 1 \quad 1 \quad 0 \quad 0 \quad 5\,) \\ &+0^* \ (\ 1 \quad 3 \quad 0 \quad 1 \quad 0 \quad 35\,) \\ &+1^* \ (\ 1 \quad 0 \quad 0 \quad 0 \quad 1 \quad 20\,) \\ = &\quad (\ 1 \quad 0 \quad 0 \quad 0 \quad 1 \quad 20\,). \end{aligned}$$

$$\mathbf{t}^*_3 = 1^*\mathbf{t}_1 - 0.333^*\mathbf{t}_2 + 1.333^*\mathbf{t}_3$$

$$\begin{aligned} &+1^* \ (-1 \quad 1 \quad 1 \quad 0 \quad 0 \quad 5\,) \\ &-0.333^* \ (\ 1 \quad 3 \quad 0 \quad 1 \quad 0 \quad 35\,) \\ &+1.333^* \ (\ 1 \quad 0 \quad 0 \quad 0 \quad 1 \quad 20\,) \\ = &\quad (\ 0 \quad 0 \quad 1 \quad -0.333 \quad 1.333 \quad 20\,). \end{aligned}$$

These results can be combined to obtain the complete final tableau.

	Basic var.	Eq. no.	*Coefficient of* Z	x_1	x_2	x_{s1}	x_{s2}	x_{s3}	Right side
$\mathbf{t}^*$	Z	0	1	0	0	0	1	1	55
$\mathbf{t}^*_1$	x_2	1	0	0	1	0	0333	–0.333	5
$\mathbf{t}^*_2$	x_1	2	0	1	0	0	0	1	20
$\mathbf{t}^*_3$	x_{s1}	3	0	0	0	1	–0333	1.333	20

This application of constructing the final tableau is really not the reason for describing the "fundamental insight." The important applications are related to post optimality analysis as described in the next example.

E5.7 For the example of E5.6 investigate how a change in the right side of the first constraint affects the optimum solution.

The right side of the first constraint is b_1, which before any changes has the value 5. To represent a change in this value, we let $b_1 = 5 + \delta$. We now use the "fundamental insight." Reviewing the equations defining **t*** and **T**, we find that the only equation involving $\mathbf{t}_1$, the first constraint, is $\mathbf{t}^*_3$. All other equations have a zero coefficient for this constraint. Rewriting the defining expression for $\mathbf{t}^*_3$ including the factor δ,

$$\mathbf{t}^*_3 = 1^*\mathbf{t}_1 - 0.333^*\mathbf{t}_2 + 1.333^*\mathbf{t}_3$$

$$\begin{array}{llllllll}
 & +\,1^* & (\,-1 & 1 & 1 & 0 & 0 & 5+\delta\,) \\
 & -\,0.333^*(& 1 & 3 & 0 & 1 & 0 & 35\,) \\
 & +\,1.333^*(& 1 & 0 & 0 & 0 & 1 & 20\,) \\
= & & (\;0 & 0 & 1 & -0.333 & 1.333 & 20+\delta\,).
\end{array}$$

The quantity δ appears only in the right side of the third equation which is the value of the third basic variable, x_{s1}. So

$$x_{s1} = 20 + \delta\,.$$

From this expression, we note that δ can range from –20 to ∞ without causing x_{s1} to become negative. All other variables remain at their current values. In terms of the original parameter, b_1 can range from –15 to ∞ without changing the optimal solution.

PROBLEMS

P5.3 For the problem considered in E5.7, find the ranges over which the values of b_2 and b_3 can vary without causing a basic variable to become negative.

P5.4 For the same problem, let the objective coefficient of x_1 vary by the amount δ_1. Show the top row of the final tableau as a function of δ_1.

P5.5 Suppose the coefficients of x_2 in each of the constraints of E5.5 doubled. How would this change the final tableau?

Computer Program

Microsolve uses an implementation of the revised simplex algorithm to solve linear programming models. Thus, the inverse of the basis is available during the solution process, but the full simplex tableau is not. The student can display the basis inverse at each iteration by choosing the "watch algorithm details and help make decisions" display option. The display will be of manageable size only if the problem is small. All the arrays used by the algorithm are displayed with this option. The display labeled DUAL SOLUTION gives $\mathbf{c_B B^{-1}}$. The table showing the ratio test provides $\mathbf{x_B}$, $\mathbf{a'}_k$ (the column labeled ALPHA) and the ratios. The table used to select the variable to enter the basis shows the reduced costs for the nonbasic variables. The basis inverse, $\mathbf{B^{-1}}$, is an optional display.

PROBLEMS

P5.6 Consider the linear program of P5.2. Set this problem up for solution by the revised simplex method and do one iteration.

P5.7 At some point in the solution procedure of the problem in P5.2, the basis inverse and corresponding basic variables are

$$\mathbf{B^{-1}} = \begin{bmatrix} 0.5 & 0 & 0 & 0 & 0 \\ 0.5 & 1 & 0 & 0 & -2 \\ 0.5 & 0 & 1 & 0 & -1 \\ 1.5 & 0 & 0 & 1 & -7 \\ -0.5 & 0 & 0 & 0 & 1 \end{bmatrix} \qquad \mathbf{x_B} = \begin{bmatrix} x_3 \\ x_{s2} \\ x_{s3} \\ x_{s4} \\ x_2 \end{bmatrix}.$$

Find the basic solution corresponding to this information.

P5.8 Do one iteration of the revised simplex procedure starting from the solution given in P5.7.

P5.9 At optimality, the basis inverse and the corresponding basic variables for problem P5.2 are given below. Construct the simplex tableau showing this optimal solution.

$$\mathbf{B^{-1}} = \begin{bmatrix} 0 & -1 & 0 & 0 & 2 \\ 1 & 2 & 0 & 0 & -4 \\ 1 & 1 & 1 & 0 & -3 \\ 2 & 1 & 0 & 1 & -9 \\ -1 & -1 & 0 & 0 & 3 \end{bmatrix} \qquad \mathbf{x_B} = \begin{bmatrix} x_3 \\ x_4 \\ x_{s3} \\ x_{s4} \\ x_2 \end{bmatrix}.$$

P5.10 The tableau given in E5.4 is the optimum tableau for the problem given in E5.1. Use this information to determine the change in the final tableau for the following changes in the original problem. State whether or not the final tableau retains the simplex form. If it remains in the simplex form indicate if the solution given is dual feasible or primal feasible. The changes are not cumulative.

a. Change the first constraint to

$$x_1 + x_2 + x_3 \leq 10.$$

b. Change the objective coefficient for x_2 from 1.25 to 0.5.

c. Change the objective coefficient for x_1 from 2 to 3.

d. Change the coefficient of x_2 in the third constraint from 1 to 2.

e. Change the right side of the second constraint from 6 to 7.

f. Change the right side of the second constraint from 6 to 5.

g. Increase the right sides of all constraints by 1.

CHAPTER 6

Duality Theory and Sensitivity Analysis

Duality (6.1, 6.3, 6.4)

When a solution is obtained for a linear program with the simplex method, the solution to a second model, called the dual problem, is readily available with very little extra effort. Most students do not appreciate this unexpected gift, but there are several benefits to be gained from studying the dual problem. Often the dual has a practical interpretation that enhances the understanding of the original model. Sometimes the dual is easier to solve than the original model, making it more reasonable to solve the dual to obtain the extra bonus of the answer to the original problem. The dual solution is also useful for post–optimality analysis, which is concerned with the effects of variations in the parameters of the original problem. Duality also has important implications for the theoretical basis of mathematical programming algorithms. In this section the dual problem is defined, the properties that link the original (called the primal) and the dual problems are listed, and the procedure for identifying the dual solution from the tableau is presented.

GOALS

- Given a linear program of arbitrary form, be able to formulate the associated dual model.
- Given the solution to the primal problem, be able to infer properties of the dual solution based on the complementary relations between the solutions of primal and dual problems.

- From the final tableau of the simplex method, be able to identify the optimum solutions of both the primal and dual problems.

DEFINITIONS

Matrix Definition of the Dual Problem: Consider the primal problem in the standard form below. There are no restrictions on the signs of the coefficients. This differs from earlier discussions, which required the right sides to be positive.

$$\begin{aligned} \text{Maximize } Z = \quad & \mathbf{cx} \\ \text{Subject to:} \quad & \mathbf{Ax} \leq \mathbf{b} \\ & \mathbf{x} \geq \mathbf{0}. \end{aligned}$$

The associated dual problem is

$$\begin{aligned} \text{Minimize } y_0 = \quad & \mathbf{yb} \\ \text{Subject to:} \quad & \mathbf{yA} \geq \mathbf{c} \\ & \mathbf{y} \geq \mathbf{0}. \end{aligned}$$

The arrays **c**, **A**, **b**, and **x** have been defined in Chapter 5. The vector **y** is a row vector with m elements. These elements are called the *dual variables*.

Algebraic Definition of the Dual Problem: The algebraic form of the primal problem is shown below. There are no restrictions on the signs of the coefficients.

$$\text{Maximize } Z = c_1 x_1 + c_2 x_2 + \cdots + c_n x_n$$

$$\begin{aligned} (1) \quad & a_{11} x_1 + a_{12} x_2 + \cdots + a_{1n} x_n \leq b_1 \\ (2) \quad & a_{21} x_1 + a_{22} x_2 + \cdots + a_{2n} x_n \leq b_2 \\ & \vdots \\ (m) \quad & a_{m1} x_1 + a_{m2} x_2 + \cdots + a_{mn} x_n \leq b_m \end{aligned}$$

$$x_1 \geq 0, x_2 \geq 0, \ldots, x_n \geq 0.$$

The associated dual problem is

$$\text{Minimize } y_0 = b_1 y_1 + b_2 y_2 + \cdots + b_m y_m$$

$$\begin{aligned} (1) \quad & a_{11} y_1 + a_{21} y_2 + \cdots + a_{m1} y_m \geq c_1 \\ (2) \quad & a_{12} y_1 + a_{22} y_2 + \cdots + a_{m2} y_m \geq c_2 \\ & \vdots \\ (n) \quad & a_{1n} y_1 + a_{2n} y_2 + \cdots + a_{mn} y_m \geq c_n \end{aligned}$$

$$y_1 \geq 0, y_2 \geq 0, \ldots, y_m \geq 0.$$

The constructions of the primal and dual problems lead to the following characteristics. (These will be modified slightly in subsequent definitions.)

- When the primal problem has n variables and m constraints, the dual problem has m variables and n constraints.
- The constraints for the primal are all "less than or equal to," while the constraints for the dual are all "greater than or equal to."
- The objective for the primal is to maximize, while the objective for the dual is to minimize.
- All variables for both problems are restrained to be nonnegative.
- For every primal constraint, there is a dual variable. Associated with primal constraint i is dual variable y_i. The dual objective function coefficient for y_i is the right side of the primal constraint i.
- For every primal variable, there is a dual constraint. Associated with primal variable x_j is dual constraint j. The right side of dual constraint j is the primal objective function coefficient for x_j.
- The number a_{ij} is, in the primal, the coefficient of the jth variable in the ith constraint, while in the dual it is the coefficient of the ith variable in the jth constraint.

Equality Constraints in the Primal: If the standard model above is modified to include one or more equality constraints in the primal, the dual problem must be modified so that the associated dual variables are unrestricted.

Equality Constraint in the Primal ⇔ Unrestricted Variable in the Dual.

For later convenience in interpreting the dual variables, equality constraints should be written with positive right sides.

Unrestricted Variables in the Primal: If the standard model above is modified to include one or more variables in the primal that are unrestricted in sign, the dual problem must be modified so that the associated dual constraints are equalities.

Unrestricted Variable in the Primal ⇔ Equality Constraint in the Dual.

Complementary Solutions for the Standard Form: The simplex tableau obtained while solving the primal problem includes in row (0) a complete solution for the dual problem. The following assumes the primal problem is in the standard form with all positive right sides.

Basic	*Eq.*	Coefficient of									*Right*
var.	*no.*	Z	x_1	$x_2 \cdots$	x_n	x_{s1}	x_{s2}	$\cdots$	x_{sm}		*side*
Z	0	1	y_{s1}	$y_{s2} \cdots$	y_{sn}	y_1	y_2	$\cdots$	y_m		y_0

The solutions for the structural variables of the dual appear in row (0) under the slack variables for the primal problem. The value of y_i is the reduced cost of the slack variable of the ith constraint.

The solution for the surplus variables of the dual constraints appear in row (0) under the structural variables for the primal problem. The value of y_{Sj} is the reduced cost of the structural variable x_j.

The objective function value for the dual, y_0, is the same as for the primal Z.

Complementary Solutions for Nonstandard Forms: When the primal problem includes negative right sides, equality constraints, or unrestricted variables, some modifications are necessary with respect to the rules for obtaining the dual solution.

- Negative Right Side: Here the inequality must be multiplied by (–1) in order to do the simplex method. The tableau then includes a surplus variable rather than a slack. The associated dual variable is still found in row (0) under the surplus variable. The meaning of the dual variable is related, however, to the original statement of the primal constraint, before multiplication by (–1).
- Equality Constraint: Here there is no slack variable for the constraint, but there is an artificial variable. When the big M method is used, the dual variable is found by subtracting M from the number appearing in row (0) for the artificial (note that the dual variable may be negative). When the two–phase method is used, assign the artificials a cost of zero during phase 2. Carry along the artificial variables during phase 2 computations but do not let them enter the basis. The dual variables then appear under the artificials in row (0).
- Unrestricted Primal Variable: In order to deal with this case the simplex method requires a transformation as described in 4.6. The variable is replaced by

  $$x_j = x'_j - x''.$$

  The surplus variable associated with constraint j of the dual problem appears under x'_j in row (0). It may be nonzero for nonoptimal tableaus, but it will always be zero in the final tableau since the dual constraint is an equality.

Computing Dual Variables from the Basis Inverse: Given the basis inverse the dual variables are computed from

$$\mathbf{y} = \mathbf{c}_B\mathbf{B}^{-1}.$$

For a problem in the standard form, this expression gives the dual variables directly. If the problem includes constraint i as a "greater than or equal to" constraint, the sign of the corresponding y_i must be reversed (to become positive) for the dual problem defined here.

RESULTS

Weak Dual Property If **x** is a feasible primal solution and **y** is a feasible dual solution, then the objective function value for the primal solution can be no greater than the objective function value for the dual.

$$\mathbf{cx} \leq \mathbf{yb}.$$

Strong Dual Property If **x*** is an optimal solution to the primal and **y*** is an optimal solution to the dual, their objective function values must be equal.

$$\mathbf{cx}^* = \mathbf{y}^*\mathbf{b}.$$

Complementary Basic Solutions Property Every iteration of the simplex method identifies a basic solution, **x**, for the primal and a solution for the dual, **y**, obtained from row (0) as described above. The solution **y** is basic for the dual problem. If **x** is not optimal for the primal problem, then **y** is not feasible for the dual problem. Their objective function values are equal.

$$\mathbf{cx} = \mathbf{yb}.$$

Complementary Optimal Solutions Property At the final iteration of the simplex method in which the optimal solution of the primal, **x***, is identified, the complementary solution of the dual, **y***, is feasible and also optimal for the dual problem. As described by the Strong Dual Property, the objective function values for these two problems are equal.

Complementary Slackness Property For every iteration of the simplex method, there is a basic primal solution, **x**, and a basic dual solution, **y**. Every primal variable x_j is associated with a dual constraint j. Let y_{sj} be the slack variable for that constraint. Every primal constraint i is associated with a dual variable y_i. Let the slack variable for the primal constraint be x_{si}. This property is described by the following implications.

$$\begin{aligned}
x_j \text{ is basic for the primal} &\Leftrightarrow y_{sj} \text{ is nonbasic for the dual} \\
x_j \text{ is nonbasic for the primal} &\Leftrightarrow y_{sj} \text{ is basic for the dual,} \\
x_{si} \text{ is basic for the primal} &\Leftrightarrow y_i \text{ is nonbasic for the dual,} \\
x_{si} \text{ is nonbasic for the primal} &\Leftrightarrow y_i \text{ is basic for the dual.}
\end{aligned}$$

Symmetry Property For any primal problem and its associated dual problem, all relationships presented above are symmetrical, because the dual of the dual problem is the primal problem.

EXAMPLES

E6.1 Identity the dual problem for the model presented below.

$$\text{Maximize } Z = 2x_1 + 3x_2$$

P(1) $\quad -x_1 + x_2 \le 5$

P(2) $\quad x_1 + 3x_2 \le 35$

P(3) $\quad x_1 \le 20$

$$x_1 \ge 0, \quad x_2 \ge 0$$

Since the problem is in the standard form no preliminary modifications are necessary. The dual problem has three variables and two constraints. Note that the coefficients of the dual constraints are simply the transpose of the coefficients in the primal constraints.

$$\text{Minimize } y_0 = 5y_1 + 35y_2 + 20y_3$$

D(1) $\quad -y_1 + y_2 + y_3 \ge 2$

D(2) $\quad y_1 + 3y_2 \ge 3$

$$y_1 \ge 0, y_2 \ge 0, y_3 \ge 0.$$

E6.2 An intermediate tableau for the primal problem is shown below. Identify the dual solution and show that the primal–dual properties hold.

Iteration 4:

Basic var.	*Eq. no.*	*Z*	x_1	x_2	x_{s1}	x_{s2}	x_{s3}	*Right side*
Z	0	1	<u>–5</u>	<u>0</u>	<u>3</u>	<u>0</u>	<u>0</u>	<u>15</u>
x_2	1	0	–1	1	1	0	0	5
x_{s2}	2	0	4	0	–3	1	0	20
x_{s3}	3	0	1	0	0	0	1	20

From row (0), which is highlighted, we identify the dual variables. The structural dual variables appear under the slack variables. Thus,

$$y_1 = 3, y_2 = 0, y_3 = 0.$$

The surplus variables for the two dual constraints appear under the structural primal variables.

$$y_{s1} = -5, y_{s2} = 0.$$

The objective function value for both the primal and dual problems appears on the right side of row (0).

$$Z = y_0 = 15.$$

From the dual variables, we observe that this is indeed an infeasible solution as required by the complementary basic solutions property. Specifically, the surplus variable for D(1) is negative, so this constraint is not satisfied.

Based on the complementary slackness property we note:

$$\begin{array}{llllll} x_1 & \text{is nonbasic} & (0) & \Leftrightarrow & y_{s1} & \text{is basic} \quad (-5), \\ x_2 & \text{is basic} & (5) & \Leftrightarrow & y_{s2} & \text{is nonbasic} \quad (0), \\ x_{s1} & \text{is nonbasic} & (0) & \Leftrightarrow & y_1 & \text{is basic} \quad (3), \\ x_{s2} & \text{is basic} & (20) & \Leftrightarrow & y_2 & \text{is nonbasic} \quad (0), \\ x_{s3} & \text{is basic} & (20) & \Leftrightarrow & y_3 & \text{is nonbasic} \quad (0). \end{array}$$

E6.3 The final tableau for the primal problem is shown below. Identify the dual solution and show that the primal–dual properties hold.

Basic var.	*Eq. no.*	*Coefficient of* Z	x_1	x_2	x_{s1}	x_{s2}	x_{s3}	*Right side*
Z	0	1	<u>0</u>	<u>0</u>	<u>0</u>	<u>1</u>	<u>1</u>	<u>55</u>
x_2	1	0	0	1	0	0.333	–0.333	5
x_1	2	0	1	0	0	0	1	20
x_{s1}	3	0	0	0	1	–0.333	1.333	20

From row (0), which is highlighted, we identify the dual variables. The structural dual variables appear under the primal slack variables. Thus,

$$y_1 = 0, y_2 = 1, y_3 = 1.$$

The surplus variables for the two dual constraints appear under the structural primal variables.

$$y_{s1} = 0, \ y_{s2} = 0.$$

The objective function value for both the primal and dual problems appears on the right side of row (0).

$$Z = y_0 = 55.$$

From the dual variables, we observe that this is a feasible solution. As suggested by the complementary optimum solutions property, it must also be the optimum solution. Because both surplus variables are zero (nonbasic), both dual constraints are tight at the optimum solution. Because both structural primal variables are basic, this is also apparent from the complementary slackness property.

E6.4 Construct the dual problem for the nonstandard linear program below.

$$\begin{array}{ll} \text{Minimize} & 3x_1 + 2x_2 \\ \text{Subject to:} & x_1 - x_2 = -8 \\ & -x_1 - 2x_2 \leq -13 \\ & x_1 \geq 0 \\ & x_2 \text{ unrestricted.} \end{array}$$

It is very important to put the problem into the standard form first. Attempts to construct the dual without this step almost always fail. We will restate the problem as a maximization with all "less than or equal to" or equality constraints. We multiply the equality constraint by (-1) to make the right side a positive number.

$$\begin{aligned} \text{Maximize} \quad & -3x_1 - 2x_2 \\ \text{Subject to:} \quad & -x_1 + x_2 = 8 \\ & -x_1 - 2x_2 \le -13 \\ & x_1 \ge 0 \\ & x_2 \text{ unrestricted.} \end{aligned}$$

The problem is now in standard form except for the equality constraint and unrestricted variable for which we have provided adjustments. The dual problem is:

$$\begin{aligned} \text{Minimize} \quad & 8y_1 - 13y_2 \\ \text{Subject to:} \quad & -y_1 - y_2 \ge -3 \\ & y_1 - 2y_2 = -2 \\ & y_1 \text{ unrestricted} \\ & y_2 \ge 0. \end{aligned}$$

E6.5 The problem of E6.4 has been solved by the simplex method to obtain the tableau shown below. Find the dual solution.

In order to use the simplex method, the problem was transformed to obtain the following model. Slacks and artificial variables have been added. The modifications are described in E4.5.

$$\begin{aligned} \text{Max } Z = \quad & -3x_1 - 2x'_2 + 2x'' - Mx_{a1} - Mx_{a2} \\ \text{Subject to:} \quad & x_1 + x'_2 - x'' + x_{a1} = 8 \\ & + x_1 + 2x'_2 - 2x'' - x_{s2} + x_{a2} = 13 \\ & x_1 \ge 0,\ x'_2 \ge 0,\ x'' \ge 0,\ x_{s2} \ge 0,\ x_{a1} \ge 0,\ x_{a2} \ge 0. \end{aligned}$$

The final tableau for this problem is shown below.

Iteration 3:

Basic var.	*Eq. no.*	Z	x'_1	x'_2	x''	x_{s2}	x_{a1}	x_{a2}	*Right side*
			Coefficient of						
Z	0	1	5	0	0	0	$M-2$	M	-16
x_{s2}	1	0	-3	0	0	1	2	-1	3
x'_2	2	0	-1	1	-1	0	1	0	8

From row (0), we discover the dual solution. The structural dual variables are

$y_1 = (M - 2) - M = -2$ found under the artificial variable x_{a1}.

$y_2 = 0$ found under the surplus variable x_{s2}.

Under the structural variables of the primal, we find the surplus variables of the dual.

$y_{s1} = 5$ found under x'_1.

$y_{s2} = 0$ found under x'_2.

The value of the dual objective function is $y_0 = -16$.

Substituting these results back into the dual problem will show that the solution is feasible. It is also the optimal solution.

PROBLEMS

P6.1 Set up the dual of this primal linear program.

$$\text{Maximize } Z = 5x_1 - 3x_2 + 4x_3 - x_4$$

Subject to:

$$3x_1 + 4x_2 + 3x_3 - 5x_4 \le 13$$
$$5x_1 - 3x_2 + x_3 + 2x_4 \le 15$$
$$x_j \ge 0 \text{ for } j = 1 \ldots 4.$$

P6.2 The tableau below shows an intermediate solution for the problem of P6.1. Use the information in this tableau to find the primal and dual solutions and to illustrate the various primal–dual relationships.

Basic var.	*Eq. no.*	*Coefficient of* Z	x_1	x_2	x_3	x_4	x_{s1}	x_{s2}	*Right side*
Z	0	1	0	0	−3	3	0	1	15
x_{s1}	1	0	0	5.8	2.4	−6.2	1	−0.6	4
x_1	2	0	1	−0.6	0.2	0.4	0	0.2	3

P6.3 The tableau below shows another intermediate solution for the model of P6.1. Use the information in this tableau to find the primal and dual solutions and to illustrate the various primal–dual relationships.

Basic var.	*Eq. no.*	*Coefficient of* Z	x_1	x_2	x_3	x_4	x_{s1}	x_{s2}	*Right side*
Z	0	1	5.181	1.637	0	0	0.819	1.546	33.82
x_3	1	0	2.818	−0.636	1	0	0.182	0.455	9.18
x_4	2	0	1.091	−1.182	0	1	−0.091	0.273	2.91

P6.4 A linear program together with the optimum tableau is shown below. Write the dual linear program and find its solution from the tableau.

$$\text{Minimize } Z = 3x_1 + 6x_2 + x_3 - x_4$$
Subject to:
$$x_1 + x_2 + x_3 + x_4 = 12$$
$$4x_1 + 5x_2 + x_3 - x_4 \le 15$$
$$x_j \ge 0 \text{ for } j = 1 \ldots 4.$$

Basic var.	*Eq. no.*	Coefficient of: Z	x_1	x_2	x_3	x_4	x_{s1}	x_{s2}	*Right side*
Z	0	1	4	7	2	0	$M+1$	0	12
x_4	1	0	1	1	1	1	1	0	12
x_{s2}	2	0	5	6	2	0	1	1	27

P6.5 Consider the linear programming model below.

a. Show the dual problem.
b. Solve the primal problem using the two–phase method and identify the optimum primal and dual solutions.
c. Solve the dual problem directly using the two–phase method and identify the optimum primal and dual solutions.

$$\text{Minimize } Z = 5x_1 + 3x_2 - x_3$$
Subject to:
$$x_1 - 2x_2 + x_3 \ge 2$$
$$-2x_1 - x_2 - 3x_3 \ge -10$$
$$x_1 + x_2 + x_3 = 5$$
$$x_j \ge 0 \text{ for } j = 1 \ldots 3.$$

Sensitivity Analysis (6.5, 6.6)

The deterministic linear programming model assumes that all numerical coefficients are known and constant. That an assumption is made for modeling purposes does not imply that the assumption is necessarily true. The coefficients of a linear program are frequently difficult to estimate, are capable of modification by management action, and may change with time. It is the responsibility of the analyst to determine whether violations of assumptions severely degrade the quality of the answers determined with the model. *Sensitivity analysis* is the activity by which one studies the effects of changes in the model on the optimum solution. It is thought by some to be one of the most important aspects of an operations research study. It happens that the final linear programming tableau contains information that simplifies sensitivity analysis. It is the purpose of this section to formalize the use of this information for general changes in the model. The next section studies specific types of model changes. These results are based on the fundamental insight studied in Chapter 5.

GOALS

- Be able to write the final tableau as a function of the rows of the initial tableau so that the effect of arbitrary changes of the parameters can be reflected in the final tableau.
- Use the tableau constructed in this manner to predict the effects of changes in model parameters on the optimal solution.
- Starting from a solution revised to reflect model changes, be able to apply the primal simplex method to obtain a new optimum solution.

DEFINITIONS

Primal Simplex Method: A simplex method for which the solution to the primal problem is always feasible, while, for all iterations but the last, the dual solution is infeasible. The primal solution is feasible but not optimal until the final iteration. The simplex method described in the previous chapters is a primal method.

Dual Simplex Method: A simplex method for which the solution to the dual problem is always feasible, while, for all iterations but the last, the primal solution is infeasible. The primal solution is said to be superoptimal (an objective function value larger than the optimal) but not feasible until the final iteration. The algorithm for the dual simplex method will be studied in Chapter 9.

RESULTS

Final Simplex Tableau as Function of the Model Parameters When the initial tableau has the form

Eq. no.	*Z*	*Coefficient of*		*Right side*
		Structural variables	*Slack variables*	
0	1	$-\mathbf{c}$	$\mathbf{0}$	0
$1-m$	0	$\mathbf{A}$	$\mathbf{I}$	$\mathbf{b}$

the final tableau has the form

Eq. no.	*Z*	*Coefficient of*		*Right side*
		Structural variables	*Slack variables*	
0	1	$\mathbf{z}^* - \mathbf{c} = \mathbf{y}^*\mathbf{A} - \mathbf{c}$	$\mathbf{y}^*$	$Z^* = \mathbf{y}^*\mathbf{b}$
$1-m$	0	$\mathbf{A}^* = \mathbf{S}^*\mathbf{A}$	$\mathbf{S}^*$	$\mathbf{b}^* = \mathbf{S}^*\mathbf{b}$

The matrices in these expressions have been defined in Chapter 5. This result is used for sensitivity analysis in the following way.

a. Solve the linear program with the original parameters, **A**, **c**, and **b**. From the final tableau identify the matrix **S*** (the basis inverse) and the vector **y*** (the dual variables). These also can be found from the revised simplex method.

b. Define revised parameters **A**, **c**, and **b** in order to study some sensitivity question. Substitute the revised parameters into the final tableau.

c. If the resulting final tableau does not have the *simplex form*, use row operations to put it in that form.

d. If the resulting tableau is both primal and dual feasible, it shows the new optimum. If the result is primal feasible but dual infeasible, use a primal simplex algorithm starting from this tableau to obtain the new optimum. If the result is primal infeasible but dual feasible, use a dual simplex algorithm starting from this tableau to obtain a new solution. If the result is both primal and dual infeasible, add artificial variables to provide a primal feasible solution for the expanded problem and then use a primal simplex algorithm to find the new optimum.

Note that only the columns changed need be recomputed in the final tableau. Thus, if the right side vector changes, only the new right side vector, **b***, need be computed. If column j of **A** changes, only the new column j of **A*** need be computed. If $\mathbf{a}_j$ is column j of **A** and $\mathbf{a}^*_j$ is column j of **A***, then

$$\mathbf{a}^*_j = \mathbf{S}^*\mathbf{a}_j.$$

Multiple changes may be investigated using the general description of the final tableau shown above.

EXAMPLES

E6.6 The linear program we have considered several times before appears below with the final tableau of the simplex method. Recompute the tableau after each of the changes listed. Comment on the optimality and feasibility of the current basic solution in the revised tableau and indicate the steps that are necessary to obtain a new optimum solution. The changes are not cumulative.

$$\text{Maximize } Z = 2x_1 + 3x_2$$

(1) $-x_1 + x_2 \le 5$

(2) $x_1 + 3x_2 \le 35$

(3) $x_1 \le 20$

$$x_1 > 0, x_2 > 0.$$

Basic var.	Eq. no.	Coefficient of Z	x_1	x_2	x_{s1}	x_{s2}	x_{s3}	Right side
Z	0	1	0	0	0	1	1	55
x_2	1	0	0	1	0	0.333	−0.333	5
x_1	2	0	1	0	0	0	1	20
xs_1	3	0	0	0	1	−0.333	1.333	20

From the tableau we discover the matrices:

$$\mathbf{y^*} = [\,0 \quad 1 \quad 1\,]$$

$$\mathbf{S^*} = \begin{bmatrix} 0 & 0.333 & -0.333 \\ 0 & 0 & 1 \\ 1 & -0.333 & 1.333 \end{bmatrix}.$$

DETERMINE THE EFFECT OF CHANGING THE RIGHT SIDE OF CONSTRAINT (2) TO 20

Since this change affects only a single column, only the right side of the final tableau need be computed.

$$\mathbf{b^*} = \mathbf{S^*b} = \begin{bmatrix} 0 & 0.333 & -0.333 \\ 0 & 0 & 1 \\ 1 & -0.333 & 1.333 \end{bmatrix} \begin{bmatrix} 5 \\ 20 \\ 20 \end{bmatrix} = \begin{bmatrix} 0 \\ 20 \\ 25 \end{bmatrix}.$$

From the new right side, the new basic solution can be written

$$x_2 = 0, x_1 = 20, \text{ and } x_{s1} = 25 \text{ with } Z = 40.$$

This solution is feasible. Since row (0) has not changed except for the right side, the new solution is also optimal for the revised problem. Note that changing the right side of the constraints can only change the feasibility of the solution and not the optimality.

CHANGE THE OBJECTIVE FUNCTION

$$\text{Maximize } Z = 5x_1 - x_2.$$

Here only the top row of the original tableau has changed. To compute the new row(0) for the structural variables of the final tableau,

$$\mathbf{z^* - c = y^*A - c}.$$

Note that only c has changed in this expression. Let the new vector be $\mathbf{c'} = \mathbf{c} + \Delta$.

$$\mathbf{z^* - c' = z^* - (c + \Delta) = (z^* - c) - \Delta}.$$

Therefore, the new elements of row (0) are simply the old elements less the change in the original coefficient. Since $\Delta_1 = 3$ and $\Delta_2 = -4$, the new tableau is:

Basic var.	Eq. no.	Coefficient of Z	x_1	x_2	x_{s1}	x_{s2}	x_{s3}	Right side
Z	0	1	-3	4	0	1	1	55
x_2	1	0	0	1	0	0.333	-0.333	5
x_1	2	0	1	0	0	0	1	20
x_{s1}	3	0	0	0	1	-0.333	1.333	20

This tableau is not in the simplex form because the entries in row (0) for basic variables x_1 and x_2 are not zero. Multiplying Eq. (1) by –4 and multiplying Eq. (2) by 3 and adding the results to row (0), one obtains the simplex form.

Basic var.	Eq. no.	Coefficient of Z	x_1	x_2	x_{s1}	x_{s2}	x_{s3}	Right side
Z	0	1	0	0	0	-0.333	5.333	95
x_2	1	0	0	1	0	0.333	-0.333	5
x_1	2	0	1	0	0	0	1	20
x_{s1}	3	0	0	0	1	-0.333	1.333	20

The current basic solution is not optimal for the changed conditions because there is now a negative number in row (0) of the tableau. Applying the primal simplex to this tableau will eventually lead to a new optimum solution.

CHANGE CONSTRAINT (2)

(2) $$2x_1 + 3x_2 \leq 35$$

Only the column for x_1 has changed. The new number in row (0) is

$$z_1 - c_1 = \mathbf{y}^* \, \mathbf{a}_1 - c_1 = 3 - 2 = 1.$$

To compute the x_1 column in the final tableau for rows 1 to m,

$$\mathbf{a}^*_1 = \mathbf{S}^*\mathbf{a}_1 = \begin{bmatrix} 0 & 0.333 & -0.333 \\ 0 & 0 & 1 \\ 1 & -0.333 & 1.333 \end{bmatrix} \begin{bmatrix} -1 \\ 2 \\ 1 \end{bmatrix} = \begin{bmatrix} 0.333 \\ 1 \\ -0.333 \end{bmatrix}.$$

The revised final tableau is:

Basic var.	Eq. no.	Coefficient of Z	x_1	x_2	x_{s1}	x_{s2}	x_{s3}	Right side
Z	0	1	1	0	0	1	1	55
x_2	1	0	0.333	1	0	0.333	-0.333	5
x_1	2	0	1	0	0	0	1	20
x_{s1}	3	0	-0.333	0	1	-0.333	1.333	20

This tableau is not in the simplex form. We must eliminate by row operations all the nonzero coefficients of x_1 except in Eq. (2). After this is done, the revised tableau in the simplex form is:

Basic var.	*Eq. no.*	*Coefficient of* Z	x_1	x_2	x_{s1}	x_{s2}	x_{s3}	*Right side*
Z	0	1	0	0	0	1	0	35
x_2	1	0	0	1	0	033	–0.66	–1.66
x_1	2	0	1	0	0	0	1	20
x_{s1}	3	0	0	0	1	–033	1.66	26.66

After the changes, the current basic solution is dual feasible (because all entries in row (0) are nonnegative) but not primal feasible (because there are negative values on the right side). The dual simplex method can be used to find the new optimum solution.

CHANGE CONSTRAINT (2)

(2) $$4x_1 + 3x_2 \leq 35$$

In a manner similar to the last example we obtain

$$\mathbf{a}^*_1 = \mathbf{S}^*\mathbf{a}_1 = \begin{bmatrix} 0 & 0.333 & -0.333 \\ 0 & 0 & 1 \\ 1 & -0.333 & 1.333 \end{bmatrix} \begin{bmatrix} -1 \\ 4 \\ 1 \end{bmatrix} = \begin{bmatrix} 1 \\ 1 \\ -1 \end{bmatrix}$$

The new number in row (0) is

$$z_1 - c_1 = \mathbf{y}^*\mathbf{a}_1 - c_1 = 5 - 2 = 3.$$

After incorporating these changes into the final tableau and performing row operations to bring the tableau to the simplex form, we obtain the tableau shown below. This basic solution is neither primal nor dual feasible, so neither the primal nor dual simplex method can be used to reoptimize the problem.

Basic var.	*Eq. no.*	*Coefficient of* Z	x_1	x_2	x_{s1}	x_{s2}	x_{s3}	*Right side*
Z	0	1	0	0	0	1	–2	–5
x_2	1	0	0	1	0	0.333	–1.33	–15
x_1	2	0	1	0	0	0	1	20
x_{s1}	3	0	–1	0	1	–0.333	2.33	40

To find the new solution starting from this tableau, it will be necessary to add an artificial variable. First write Eq. (1) in the algebraic form.

$$x_2 + 0.33x_{s2} - 1.33x_{s3} = -15.$$

Multiplying this equation by –1 and adding an artificial variable x_a we obtain

$$-x_2 - 0.33x_{s2} + 1.33x_{s3} + x_a = 15.$$

This equivalent equation replaces Eq. (1) in the tableau and the artificial variable becomes basic for this row. A big M is assigned to the artificial variable in row (0).

Basic var.	*Eq. no.*	*Coefficient of* Z	x_1	x_2	x_{s1}	x_{s2}	x_{s3}	x_a	*Right side*
Z	0	1	0	0	0	1	–2	M	–5
x_2	1	0	0	–1	0	–0333	+1.33	1	15
x_1	2	0	1	0	0	0	1	0	20
x_{s1}	3	0	–1	0	1	–0333	2.33	0	40

After eliminating M from row (0), the primal simplex procedure can begin again from this tableau in a search for a feasible and optimal solution.

PROBLEMS

The following problems relate to the example of this section. Determine the effect of each change on the optimum tableau and the optimality and feasibility of the solution. Changes are not cumulative.

P6.6 Change the objective function to $-5x_1 + x_2$.

P6.7 Increase all the right sides by 10.

P6.8 Change constraint (3) to $x_1 + x_2 \leq 20$.

P6.9 Change constraint (3) to $2x_1 + x_2 \leq 20$.

Applying Sensitivity Analysis (6.7)

In this section, we review the processes for performing various specific types of sensitivity analyses. In each case, because only a prescribed subset of the model parameters are varied, the analysis is easier than the general procedures described in the last section.

GOALS

- Be able to perform the various types of sensitivity analyses listed below.

  Interpret shadow prices.
  Changes in the right sides of the constraints.
  Changes in the coefficients of a nonbasic variable.
  Introduction of a new variable.
  Changes in the coefficients of a basic variable.
  Introduction of a new constraint.

DEFINITION

Shadow Price: The derivative of the objective function with respect to a change in the right side of a constraint (also called the marginal value of the resource represented by the constraint or the change in the objective function value per unit change in the right side). It is useful for measuring the sensitivity of the objective function value to changes in the right sides of the constraints. For a "less than or equal to" or equality constraint, this is the increase in the objective function value per unit increase in the right side. For a "greater than or equal to" constraint, this is the increase in the objective function value per unit decrease in the right side. It should be remembered that this is a rate of change and that there is a range over which changes of the right side will result in the predicted change in the objective function value. For degenerate solutions, the range may be zero.

RESULTS

Determination of Shadow Prices The shadow price for constraint i is the optimal dual variable y^*_i.

Changes in the Right Sides of Constraints Only the rightmost column of the tableau is changed by variations in **b**, so only primal feasibility can be affected. Row (0), except in the rightmost position, does not change, so the solution remains dual feasible. Let θ_i be the change in b_i and θ be the vector of changes. The rightmost column in the final tableau is given by

$$y^*_0 = \mathbf{y}^*[\,\mathbf{b} + \theta\,]$$
$$\mathbf{b}^* = \mathbf{S}^*[\,\mathbf{b} + \theta\,].$$

If for specific values of θ, elements of $\mathbf{b}^*$ become negative, the current basis is infeasible and a dual simplex method can be used to find the new optimal solution.

Changes in the Coefficients of a Nonbasic Variable Assume x_j is nonbasic in the final tableau. The original objective function coefficient becomes $c_j + \theta_0$, and the constraint coefficients become $\mathbf{a_j} + \theta$, where θ is an m –vector of changes. The dual constraint associated with x_j is

$$\mathbf{y}[\,\mathbf{a_j} + \theta\,] \geq c_j + \theta_0.$$

If this constraint is satisfied for the current optimal dual solution, $\mathbf{y}^*$, the optimal primal solution does not change.

If the constraint is not satisfied, find the new column j in the final tableau:

$$\text{Row (0): } \mathbf{y}^*[\,\mathbf{a_j} + \theta\,] - [c_j + \theta_0\,]$$
$$\text{Rows } (1 - m\,)\text{: } \mathbf{S}^*[\,\mathbf{a_j} + \theta\,].$$

The tableau changes only in the jth column. The new solution is dual infeasible but primal feasible, so a primal method can be applied to find the new optimum.

Introduction of a New Variable Let some new variable x_j be added to the problem after the optimal solution is obtained. It has objective function coefficient c_j and constraint coefficients $\mathbf{a_j}$. The dual constraint associated with x_j is

$$\mathbf{y a_j} \geq c_j\,.$$

If this constraint is satisfied for the current optimal dual solution, $\mathbf{y^*}$, the optimal primal solution does not change with addition of the new variable.

If the constraint is not satisfied, find the new column j in the final tableau:

$$\text{Row (0): } \mathbf{y^* a_j} - c_j$$
$$\text{Rows } (1 - m): \mathbf{S^* a_j}.$$

The tableau changes only with the addition of the new column. The new solution is dual infeasible but primal feasible, so a primal method can be applied to find the optimum.

Changes in the Coefficients of a Basic Variable Assume x_j is basic in the final tableau. Let the original objective function coefficient become $c_j + \theta_0$ and the constraint coefficients become $\mathbf{a_j} + \theta$, where θ is an m –vector of changes. Because x_j is basic, the complementary slackness property requires that the dual constraint associated with x_j be satisfied as an equality.

$$\mathbf{y}[\,\mathbf{a_j} + \theta] = c_j + \theta_0.$$

Since this probably will not be true for the current optimum dual solution, $\mathbf{y^*}$, and since other changes will affect the jth column of the tableau, it is necessary to reconstruct the *jth* column with the general procedures of the last section.

The new column j in the final tableau is

$$\text{Row (0): } \mathbf{y^*}[\,\mathbf{a_j} + \theta] - [c_j + \theta_0\,]$$
$$\text{Rows } (1 - m): \mathbf{S^*}[\,\mathbf{a_j} + \theta].$$

The tableau changes only in the jth column. The changes will cause the tableau to lose the *simplex form.* Row operations are required to regain the form. The new solution may be both dual infeasible and primal infeasible. If this is true, optimality may be regained using artificial variables and a primal simplex method.

Introduction of a New Constraint Let a new constraint be added to the problem after the optimal has been determined by the simplex. The constraint is

$$\mathbf{ax} \leq b$$

where $\mathbf{a}$ is a row vector with n components and b is a constant. If the constraint is satisfied by the current optimal primal solution, $\mathbf{x^*}$, the optimal solution does not change.

If the constraint is not satisfied, add a slack variable, x_s, to obtain the equality form

$$\mathbf{ax} + x_s = b.$$

Add this constraint as the bottom row of the tableau (a new column will also be added for the slack variable). Do row operations to regain the simplex form in the new row. The new slack variable is the basic variable for the new row. The right side of the new row will become negative because of these operations, so a dual simplex procedure must be used to regain optimality.

If the new constraint is an equality or a "greater than or equal to" constraint, an artificial variable must be added. This becomes the basic variable for the new row. In this case, the right sides remain positive, but a big M or two–phase method must be used to drive the artificial variable out of the basis. An artificial variable can also be introduced after adding an inequality constraint to allow the primal simplex method to be used rather than the dual simplex method.

EXAMPLES

E6.7 A primal linear program is shown below, together with the dual problem and the final tableau of the simplex procedure obtained for the solution of the primal. Incorporate each of the changes suggested. If the optimal solution changes, modify the final tableau to incorporate the changes and suggest how a new optimal solution can be obtained. The changes are not cumulative. Note that some of the model variations of the type considered in this section have been illustrated in the example of the last section.

Primal:

Maximize $Z = 2x_1 + 3x_2$

P(1) $-x_1 + x_2 \leq 5$

P(2) $x_1 + 3x_2 \leq 35$

P(3) $x_1 \leq 20$

$x \geq 0, x_2 \geq 0$

Dual:

Minimize $y_0 = 5y_1 + 35y_2 + 20y_3$

D(1) $-y_1 + y_2 + y_3 \geq 2$

D(2) $y_1 + 3y_2 \geq 3$

$y_1 \geq 0,\ y_2 \geq 0,\ y_3 \geq 0.$

Basic var.	*Eq. no.*	*Coefficient of* Z	x_1	x_2	x_{s1}	x_{s2}	x_{s3}	*Right side*
Z	0	1	0	0	0	1	1	55
x_2	1	0	0	1	0	0.333	–0.333	5
x_1	2	0	1	0	0	0	1	20
x_{s1}	3	0	0	0	1	–0.333	1.333	20

From the tableau, we discover the matrices:

$$\mathbf{y}^* = [\,0 \quad 1 \quad 1\,]$$

$$\mathbf{S}^* = \begin{bmatrix} 0 & 0.333 & -0.333 \\ 0 & 0 & 1 \\ 1 & -0.333 & 1.333 \end{bmatrix} \qquad \mathbf{x}^* = \begin{bmatrix} 20 \\ \\ 5 \end{bmatrix}.$$

CHANGE THE RIGHT SIDE OF THE CONSTRAINTS

Let b_2 go to 20 and b_3 go to 26. This change only affects the right side of the final tableau.

$$\mathbf{b}^* = \mathbf{S}^*\,[\,\mathbf{b} + \theta\,] = \begin{bmatrix} 0 & 0.333 & -0.333 \\ 0 & 0 & 1 \\ 1 & -0.333 & 1.333 \end{bmatrix} \begin{bmatrix} 5+0 \\ 35-15 \\ 20+6 \end{bmatrix} = \begin{bmatrix} -2 \\ 26 \\ 33 \end{bmatrix}.$$

The new basic solution has

$$x_2 = -2,\ x_1 = 26, \text{ and } x_{s1} = 33.$$

This solution is not feasible, and a dual simplex method may be used to recover feasibility.

ADD A NEW VARIABLE

Say a new variable, x_3, is added to obtain the model:

Primal:

$$\text{Maximize } Z = 2x_1 \quad 3x_2 \quad +4x_3$$

Subject to:

P(1) $\quad -x_1 + x_2 + 2x_3 \le 5$

P(2) $\quad x_1 + 3x_2 \le 35$

P(3) $\quad x_1 + x_3 \le 20$

$$x_1 \ge 0,\ x_2 \ge 0,\ x_3 \ge 0.$$

The new variable contributes a new constraint to the dual problem.

D(3) $\quad 2y_1 + y_3 \ge 4.$

The current optimal solution $\mathbf{y}^* = [\,0 \quad 1 \quad 1]$ is not feasible for this constraint, so the current solution for the primal is not optimal. It is necessary to reconstruct the tableau with the new variable added.

Row (0): $\mathbf{y}^*\mathbf{a}_j - c_j = [\,0 \quad 1 \quad 1\,]\,\mathbf{a}_j - 4 = -3$

$$\text{Rows } (1 - m): \mathbf{S^* a_j} = \begin{bmatrix} 0 & 0.333 & -0.333 \\ 0 & 0 & 1 \\ 1 & -0.333 & 1.333 \end{bmatrix} \begin{bmatrix} 2 \\ 0 \\ 1 \end{bmatrix} = \begin{bmatrix} -0.333 \\ 1 \\ 3.333 \end{bmatrix}.$$

The new tableau appears below. Optimality can be recovered with a primal simplex method.

Basic var.	*Eq. no.*	*Z*	x_1	x_2	x_3	x_{s1}	x_{s2}	x_{s3}	*Right side*
Z	0	1	0	0	−3	0	1	1	55
x_2	1	0	0	1	−0.333	0	0.333	−0.333	5
x_1	2	0	1	0	1	0	0	1	20
x_{s1}	3	0	0	0	3.333	1	−0.333	1.333	20

ADD A NEW CONSTRAINT

Add the following constraint to the model.

$$x_2 \geq 10.$$

The current optimal solution, $x_1 = 20$ and $x_2 = 5$, does not satisfy this constraint so action must be taken to incorporate it into the tableau. If the constraint were directly added to the tableau, a dual simplex algorithm could be used to recover optimality. We will use, alternatively, an artificial variable, so that the primal method may be used. Adding surplus and artificial variables, we obtain

P(4) $$x_2 - x_{s4} + x_{a4} = 10.$$

Adding this row and a new column for the artificial variable to the tableau,

Basic var.	*Eq. no.*	*Z*	x_1	x_2	x_{s1}	x_{s2}	x_{s3}	x_{s4}	x_{a4}	*Right side*
Z	0	1	0	0	0	1	1	0	*M*	55
x_2	1	0	0	1	0	0.333	−0.333	0	0	5
x_1	2	0	1	0	0	0	1	0	0	20
x_{s1}	3	0	0	0	1	−0.333	1.333	0	0	20
x_{a4}	4	0	0	1	0	0	0	−1	1	10

This tableau is not in the simplex form. Using row operations to correct the form, one obtains

Basic var.	*Eq. no.*	*Z*	x_1	x_2	x_{s1}	x_{s2}	x_{s3}	x_{s4}	x_{a4}	*Right side*
Z	0	1	0	0	0	1 + 0.333*M*	1 − 0.333*M*	*M*	0	55 − 5*M*
x_2	1	0	0	1	0	0.333	−0.333	0	0	5
x_1	2	0	1	0	0	0	1	0	0	20
x_{s1}	3	0	0	0	1	−0.333	1.333	0	0	20
x_{a4}	4	0	0	0	0	−0.333	0.333	−1	1	5

Continued application of the primal simplex will ultimately discover the optimum solution or indicate that the new model does not have a feasible solution.

PROBLEMS

Problems P6.10 through P6.15 relate to the linear program shown below. For P6.11 through P6.15 show the parts of the final tableau that change and indicate the steps that must be taken to find the optimal solution.

$$\text{Maximize } Z = 5x_1 - 3x_2 + 4x_3 - x_4$$

Subject to

$$\text{(P1)} \quad 3x_1 + 4x_2 + 3x_3 - 5x_4 \le 13$$

$$\text{(P2)} \quad 5x_1 - 3x_2 + x_3 + 2x_4 \le 15$$

$$x_j \ge 0 \text{ for } j = 1 \ldots 4 .$$

Optimal Tableau:

Basic var.	*Eq. no.*	Coefficient of: Z	x_1	x_2	x_3	x_4	x_{s1}	x_{s2}	*Right side*
Z	0	1	5.181	1.637	0	0	0.819	1.546	33.82
x_3	1	0	2.818	–0.636	1	0	0.182	0.455	9.18
x_4	2	0	1.091	–1.182	0	1	–0.091	0.273	2.91

P6.10 Estimate the change in the objective function value caused by the following changes.

a. Increase the right side of constraint (P1) from 13 to 14.
b. Decrease the right side of constraint (P2) from 15 to 14.
c. Increase the nonbasic variable x_1 from 0 to 1.

P 6.11 Change the right side vector to $\mathbf{b} = (14, 14)^T$.

P 6.12 Change the coefficients of x_1 in the constraints to $\mathbf{a}_1 = (2, 2)^T$.

P6.13 Add a new variable, x_5, to the problem with $c_5 = 5$ and $\mathbf{a}_5 = (4, 2)^T$.

P6.14 Change c_3 to +2, and make $\mathbf{a}_3 = (3, 3)$.

P6.15 Add the constraint $x_1 + x_2 + x_3 + x_4 \le 10$.

Computer Program

The *Microsolve* linear program has a sensitivity analysis feature which is fairly standard among linear programming codes. After an optimum solution has been obtained, the sensitivity analysis option may be called. Three different displays are available: dual variables, ranges on the objective function coefficients, and ranges on the right sides. In this section, we illustrate these using the Chemical Processing example first considered in E3.1. The optimum solution is shown in Fig. 4.3.

The dual variable display is shown in Fig. 6.1. There is a dual variable for each constraint, so the first two columns show, respectively, the number of the constraint (ROW) and the name of the constraint. The number in the VALUE column is the dual variable associated with the constraint. The general interpretation of a number in this column is the rate of change of the objective function value per unit increase in the right side of the constraint (while holding all other problem parameters constant). Since the problem is linear, there is some range of the right side over which the rate of change remains constant. The range will be provided by the third display of this section. When degeneracy is present, the range may actually be zero.

For a constraint that is loose—that is, not restricting the optimum solution—the dual variable will be zero, indicating that if the right side of the constraint is increased by a small amount the objective function value will not change. This is illustrated in the example by constraints AM1% and ZLIM, both of which are loose at the optimum solution.

For a "less than or equal to" constraint, the dual variable will always be nonnegative, indicating that if the right side of the constraint is increased, the problem will become less constrained and the objective function value will be allowed to increase (or remain the same). Recall that the objective is always stated as a maximization by the program. A decrease in the right side will cause the objective value to decrease at the same rate.

For a "greater than or equal to" constraint, the dual variables will always be nonpositive, indicating that if the right side of the constraint is increased, the problem will become more constrained and the objective function value will decrease. This is a slightly different interpretation than in the text, where the dual

DUAL SOLUTION

ROW	NAME	VALUE	ROW	NAME	VALUE
1	A-CON	−1.0	11	YB-CON	−8.0
2	B-CON	−26.0	12	AM1%	0
3	C-CON	−1.0	13	BM1%	−25.0
4	M1-CONI	−1.0	14	BM2%	−25.0
5	M1-CONO	0	15	XM1%	0.92857
6	M2-CONI	−1.0	16	YM1%	8.0
7	M2-CONO	−1.0	17	YM2%	7.0
8	X-CON	−0.92857	18	ZM2%	9.0
9	Y-CON	−8.0	19	ZLIM	0
10	Z-CON	−10.0			

Figure 6.1 **Dual Solution**

SIMPLE RANGING FOR
OBJECTIVE FUNCTION COEFFICIENTS

VAR.	OBJ. COEF.	TYPE	LOWER RANGE	UPPER RANGE
A	–4.0	ZERO	—	–1.0
AM1	0	BAS-4	–69.0	3.0
AOM2	0	BAS-1	–69.0	171.0
B	–3.0	BOUND	–26	—
BM1	0	BAS-13	–57.0	25
BM2	0	BAS-6	–23.0	57.0
C	–1.0	BAS-3	–4.0	—
CM1	0	BAS-9	–2.948	69.0
CM2	0	BAS-17	–9.857	24.428
M1	0	BAS-12	–2.85	—
M2	0	BAS-7	–6.9	17.099
WM1	0	BAS-14	–28.5	—
X	5.0	BOUND	0.9285	—
XM1	0	BAS-8	-4.071	—
Y	0	BAS-11	–19.0	—
Y1	11.0	BOUND	8.0	—
Y2	8.0	BAS-19	–11.0	11.0
YM1	0	BAS-16	–14.25	—
YM2	0	BAS-5	–23.0	57.0
Z	10.0	BAS-18	–1.5	38.5
ZM2	0	BAS-10	–11.5	28.5

Figure 6.2 **Sensitivity Analysis for Objective Function Coefficients**

variables for all inequality constraints are required to be nonnegative. The two interpretations give the same values but the signs are reversed for "greater than or equal to" constraints. This is illustrated for the example by constraint BM1%.

For equality constraints, the dual variable may assume either sign. Most of the constraints of the example are of this type.

The second sensitivity display is shown in Fig. 6.2. Here there is a line for each variable. The first column shows the variable name and the second shows the objective function coefficient as stated in the model. The third column shows the status of the variable in the optimum solution. ZERO indicates that the variable is nonbasic and has the value zero. BOUND indicates that the variable is nonbasic and has a value equal to its simple upper bound. This is a possibility because the solution program is a bounded variable simplex procedure, as will be described more fully in Chapter 9. If the variable is basic, the word BAS-*i* will appear in this column, indicating the constraint number for which the variable is basic. The last two columns provide the interesting part of this display because they show the range over which the objective function coefficient may change (while holding all other problem parameters constant) while the current solution remains optimal. This is important information because the actual coefficients may be imprecisely known. A large range indicates that the uncertainty may not be too important. A small range indicates that the value may be critical to the determination of the optimum. It should be stressed that the range for a particular change assumes all

SIMPLE RANGING FOR
RIGHT SIDES OF CONSTRAINTS

CONST.	RHS.	LOWER RANGE	UPPER RANGE
A-CON	0	–5238.	833.33
B-CON	0	–15714.	2500
C-CON	0	–16071.	—
M1-CONI	0	–5238.	—
M1-CONO	0	—	714.28
M2-CONI	0	–10833.	—
M2-CONO	0	–5238.	833.33
X-CON	0	–3793.	2000.
Y-CON	0	—	5571.4
Z-CON	0	—	8285.7
YB-CON	0	—	5571.4
AM1%	0	—	833.33
BM1%	0	–357.1	2500.
BM2%	0	–15714.	2500.
XM1%	0	–2000.	625.
YM1%	0	–1428.	714.28
YM2%	0	–4642.	833.33
ZM2%	0	–5238.	833.33
ZLIM	1000	—	9285.7

Figure 6.3 **Sensitivity Analysis for Right Sides**

other parameters are held constant. When dashes appear in a range column the limit is unbounded from below for a lower range, and unbounded from above for an upper range.

The third sensitivity display shows range information for the right sides of the constraints and is illustrated for the example in Fig. 6.3. A line of the display shows the constraint name, the right side defined for the model, and the lower and upper limits of the range over which the right side may be changed (holding all other parameters constant) while the identity of the basic variables in the optimum solution remains constant. When the constraint is loose, such as ZLIM in the example, the right side may be changed over the range without changing the values of the basic variables. When the constraint is "tight," however, changing the right side within the range will not change the identity of the basic variables, but the values of the basic variables will change in a linear fashion over the range. The objective function will also change with the rate given by the dual variables. The example does not provide a good illustration of this, as most of the constraints are conservation of flow or define mixture percentages. Changing the right sides of these constraints does not always have a practical interpretation.

Problems

The model below, with the corresponding optimal tableau, will be used for problems P6.16 to P 6.23. The changes suggested in the problems are not cumulative.

$$\text{Maximize } Z = 2x_1 + x_2 - 3x_3 + 5x_4$$

Subject to:

P(1) $\quad 3x_1 - x_2 + x_3 + 2x_4 \le 8$

P(2) $\quad x_1 + x_2 + 4x_3 - x_4 \le 6$

P(3) $\quad 2x_1 + 3x_2 - x_3 + x_4 \le 10$

P(4) $\quad x_1 + x_3 + x_4 \le 7$

$$x_1 \ge 0,\ x_2 \ge 0,\ x_3 \ge 0,\ x_4 \ge 0.$$

Basic var.	*Eq. no.*	Z	x_1	x_2	x_3	x_4	x_{s1}	x_{s2}	x_{s3}	x_{s4}	*Right side*
Z	0	1	6	0	4	0	2	0	1	0	26
x_4	1	0	11/7	0	2/7	1	3/7	0	1/7	0	34/7
x_{s2}	2	0	17/7	0	33/7	0	4/7	1	–1/7	0	64/7
x_2	3	0	1/7	1	–3/7	0	–1/7	0	2/7	0	12/7
x_{s4}	4	0	–4/7	0	5/7	0	–3/7	0	–1/7	1	15/7

P6.16 Write the dual to the linear program and find the dual solution from the tableau above.

P6.17 Estimate the change in the objective function value caused by the following parameter changes.

a. Increase the right side of constraint (P1) from 8 to 9.
b. Increase the right side of constraint (P2) from 6 to 7.
c. Decrease the right side of constraint (P3) from 10 to 9.
d. Increase the nonbasic variable x_1 from 0 to 1.

P 6.18 Change the right side vector to $\mathbf{b} = (9, 7, 9, 7)^T$.

P 6.19 Change the objective function coefficient of x_3 to +3, and change the coefficient of x_3 in constraint (P2) to 5.

P6.20 Add a new variable, x_5, to the problem with $c_5 = 5$ and $\mathbf{a_5} = (4, 1, -1, 0)^T$.

P6.21 Add a new variable, x_5, to the problem with $c_5 = 6$ and $\mathbf{a_5} = (1, 1, 1, 1)^T$.

P6.22 Add a new constraint to the model

$$x_2 + 2x_3 - 3x_4 \le 6.$$

P6.23 Add a new constraint to the model

$$x_2 + 2x_3 - 3x_4 \ge 6.$$

P6.24 Write the dual problem for the linear program given below. List the entire set of basic solutions for both primal and dual models. Show complementary pairs of primal and dual basic solutions. Specify whether each is feasible, infeasible, or optimal.

$$\text{Maximize } Z = 60x_1 + 48x_2 + 20x_3$$

Subject to:

P(1)	$5x_1 + x_2 + x_3 \leq 48$
P(2)	$2x_1 + 2x_2 + x_3 \leq 24$

$$x_1 \geq 0, \quad x_2 \geq 0, \quad x_3 \geq 0.$$

P6.25 Given the problem below with the sensitivity analysis information given by the computer, answer the following questions.

$$\text{Maximize } Z = 2x_1 - 3x_2 + x_3 - 4x_4$$

Subject to:

C1	$2x_1 - x_2 + 3x_3 - 5x_4 \leq 20$
C2	$x_1 + x_2 - x_3 + x_4 \geq 6$
C3	$x_4 \leq 20$

$$x_1 \geq 0, \quad x_2 \geq 0, \quad x_3 \geq 0, \ x4 > 0.$$

A. DUAL VARIABLES

ROW	NAME	VALUE
1	C1	1
2	C2	0
3	C3	1

B. SIMPLE RANGING FOR OBJECTIVE FUNCTION COEFFICIENTS

VARIABLE	OBJECTIVE COEFFICIENT	TYPE	LOWER RANGE	UPPER RANGE
X1	2	BAS–2	1.6	6
X2	–3	ZERO	—	–1
X3	1	ZERO	—	3
X4	–4	BAS–3	–5	—

C. SIMPLE RANGING FOR RIGHT SIDES OF CONSTRAINTS

CONSTRAINT	RIGHT SIDE	LOWER RANGE	UPPER RANGE
C1	20	–100	—
C2	2	—	80
C3	20	0	—

a. Which constraints are tight and which are loose?
b. What does the first row (regarding X1) of Table B indicate?
c. What does the second row (regarding X2) of Table B indicate?
d. What does the first row (regarding C1) of Table C indicate?
e. What does the first row (regarding C2) of Table C indicate?

Computer Problems

P6.26 Solve the production planning problem described in E3.2 with a computer program. From the sensitivity analysis information identify the constraints that restrict the optimum solution, the inequality limit whose relaxation would most reduce the cost of operation, the monthly demand that is most costly to meet, the objective function coefficient whose estimation requires the most accuracy, and the monthly demand with the smallest sensitivity range relative to the current solution.

P6.27 Solve the problem given in P6.25 with the computer. Test the sensitivity analysis results by actually changing each parameter to values as listed below. Solve the problem with the computer after each change and comment on the results obtained.

a. Change the objective function coefficient of x_1 to 1.7.
b. Change the objective function coefficient of x_1 to 1.5.
c. Change the objective function coefficient of x_1 to 5.5.
d. Change the objective function coefficient of x_1 to 6.5.
e. Change the right side of C1 to –99.
f. Change the right side of C1 to –101.
g. Change the right side of C2 to 79.
h. Change the right side of C2 to 81.

CHAPTER 7

Special Types of Linear Programming Problems

The linear program is a general model that can be used for a wide variety of problem situations. Many linear programming models, however, possess special structures that allow the use of more efficient optimization algorithms. Most of these are variations of the simplex method adapted to the particular model structure. Principal examples are the network flow models, which are considered in this chapter. The first part of the chapter discusses the well-known transportation problem and the adaption of the simplex method used for its solution. The second part of the chapter presents material not in H & L describing the general network flow programming model. This model includes as special cases the transportation problem and a number of other problems important in operations research.

The Transportation Problem (7.1)

This problem can be described in terms of finding an optimum distribution plan for some commodity. Specified supplies of the commoditiy are available at a number of locations called sources. There is a specified demand for the commodity at each of a number of destinations. The transportation cost between each source-destination pair is known. The problem is to find the optimum distribution plan for shipments from sources to destinations that minimizes total shipping cost. A generic description of the problem is shown in Fig. 7.1. The transportation costs are shown in the body of the matrix and the supplies and demands appear along the right and bottom margins.

	DESTINATION				
	D1	D2		DN	SUPPLY
SOURCE S1	C_{11}	C_{12}	. . .	C_{1n}	s_1
S2	C_{21}	C_{22}	. . .	C_{2n}	s_2
⋮	⋮	⋮		⋮	⋮
SM	C_{m1}	C_{m2}	. . .	C_{mn}	s_m
DEMAND	d_1	d_2	. . .	d_n	

Figure 7.1 **Generic Transportation Model**

The transportation model was one of the earliest optimization problems considered by the pioneers of operations research. Solution algorithms have been widely used for solving distribution problems, but there are a number of applications not described as distribution problems. The transportation model often appears as a component of a more difficult decision-making situation such as the facility location problem.

GOALS

- Know the assumptions characterizing the transportation problem.
- Be able to write the linear programming model of the transportation problem.
- Be able to show an equivalent transportation problem when the assumptions are varied as described in the modeling section.

DEFINITIONS

Source: A location at which a supply of the commodity is available. The sources are numbered from 1 to *m*.

Destination: A location at which there is demand for the commodity. The destinations are numbered 1 to *n*.

Supply (s_i): The amount of the commodity available at a source, $i = 1 \ldots m$.

Demand (d_j): The amount of the commodity required at a destination, $j = 1 \ldots n$.

Transportation Cost (c_{ij}): The cost of transporting a single unit of the product from source i to destination j, $i = 1 \ldots m$, $j = 1 \ldots n$. The unit cost is independent of the quantity shipped, so the total cost function is linear.

Balance of Supplies and Demands: The total supply must equal the total demand.

Distribution Variables (x_{ij}): The amount shipped from source i to destination j, for $i = 1$ to m, $j = 1$ to n. These are the decision variables of the problem. The complete solution is called a *distribution policy.*

RESULTS

Linear Programming Model The problem is to find the distribution policy that uses all supplies and satisfies all demands at minimum total cost.

Objective Function: Minimize Cost.

$$\text{Minimize } Z = \sum_{i=1}^{m} \sum_{j=1}^{n} c_{ij} x_{ij}.$$

Subject to: The supply at each source must be used.

PS(i):
$$\sum_{j=1}^{n} x_{ij} = s_i \quad \text{for } i = 1 \ldots m.$$

The demand at each destination must be met.

PD(i):
$$\sum_{i=1}^{m} x_{ij} = d_j \quad \text{for } j = 1 \ldots n.$$

Nonnegativity.

$$x_{ij} \geq 0 \text{ for } i = 1 \ldots m \text{ and } j = 1 \ldots n.$$

Dual Linear Programming Model Taking the dual of the primal model above, we obtain the following linear program.

Let u_i be the dual variable corresponding to the constraint PS(i).

Let v_j be the dual variable corresponding to the constraint PD(j).

Objective Function:

$$\text{Maximize } y_0 = \sum_{i=1}^{m} s_i u_i + \sum_{j=1}^{n} d_j v_j.$$

Subject to:

D(i, j): $u_i + v_j \leq c_{ij}$ for $i = 1 \ldots m$, $j = 1 \ldots n$.

The values of u_i and v_j are unrestricted in sign for all i and j.

Conditions for Optimality Let a basic solution for the primal problem be defined. The number of basic variables for the problem is $m + n - 1$. There are $m + n$ constraints for the primal, but one is redundant.

Let a complementary dual solution be defined. Because of the redundant primal constraint, one of the dual variables in the complementary solution is arbitrary. One is set to zero for the algorithm described later. The complementary slackness conditions require that the dual constraint corresponding to each primal basic variable be tight.

$$u_i + v_j = c_{ij} \quad \text{for every basic variable } x_{ij}.$$

If all the other dual constraints are satisfied for the dual solution, the primal solution is optimal. The condition for the constraints to be satisfied is

$$u_i + v_j \leq c_{ij} \quad \text{for all } x_{ij} \text{ that are nonbasic.}$$

Alternatively one can require the slack variable for all dual constraints to be nonnegative for feasibility.

$$c_{ij} - u_i - v_j \geq 0 \quad \text{for all } x_{ij} \text{ that are nonbasic.}$$

If these conditions are satisfied, the solution is optimal. This result is the foundation for the solution algorithm described in the next section. It is a good example of the use of the duality conditions discussed in Chapter 6.

MODELING

The model of the transportation problem is simply the matrix of costs along with the supplies and demands as shown for the generic problem in Fig. 7.1. The model for a particular situation is complete when a transportation model is defined whose solution can be used to determine the solution for the original situation.

Certain deviations from the strict statement of the transportation model can be handled by "tricks" that transform the problem into an equivalent transportation problem. The solution to the transformed problem can then be interpreted in terms of the original problem. Several of these variants are discussed below.

Total Supply Greater Than Total Demand This case is illustrated by Fig. 7.2a. The modification is to add an extra (dummy) column to the tableau as in Fig. 7.2b, with the demand for the dummy destination equal to the excess supply. A solution will have some positive flow in the added column. This indicates that not all the supply of some source is used. Generally zeros are used for the costs on the extra column, indicating that it doesn't matter which supply is not entirely used. If in fact there is some penalty for not using all of a particular source, that number can used

		DESTINATION D1	D2	D3	SUPPLY
SOURCE	S1	10	20	18	**20**
	S2	8	15	12	**15**
	S3	13	17	19	**15**
DEMAND		**10**	**20**	**16**	

(a)

		DESTINATION D1	D2	D3	DD	SUPPLY
SOURCE	S1	10	20	18	0	**20**
	S2	8	15	12	0	**15**
	S3	13	17	19	0	**15**
DEMAND		**10**	**20**	**16**	**4**	

(b)

Figure 7.2 **Model with Supply Greater than Demand**

in the cell of the dummy column. If a particular source must use all of its supply, a big M (a large positive cost) may be used in its cell.

Minimum Required Shipment from a Source With total supply greater than total demand, it may be required that some sources ship minimum amounts. The supply at a source represents the maximum amount that can be shipped. For instance, say source 1 in Fig. 7.2a must ship at least 5 units. This is handled by providing two rows for each source having a minimum requirement as shown in Fig. 7.3. One source represents the minimum and the other represents any amount above the minimum. Using the cost of M in the dummy column forces the minimum requirement to go to actual destinations rather than the dummy.

		DESTINATION D1	D2	D3	DD	SUPPLY
SOURCE	S1M	10	20	18	M	**5**
	S1E	10	20	18	0	**15**
	S2	8	15	12	0	**15**
	S3	13	17	19	0	**15**
DEMAND		**10**	**20**	**16**	**4**	

Figure 7.3 **Model with Minimum Required Shipment from a Source**

Total Demand Greater Than Total Supply This case requires a dummy source with supply equal to the excess of demand over supply. An example is shown in Fig. 7.4. If the solution uses a cell of the dummy row, the associated destination does not receive the amount demanded.

		DESTINATION D1	D2	D3	SUPPLY
SOURCE	S1	10	20	18	**20**
	S2	8	15	12	**15**
	S3	13	17	19	**15**
	SD	0	0	0	**21**
DEMAND		**20**	**25**	**26**	

Figure 7.4 **Model with Demand Greater than Supply**

Minimum Required Shipments to a Destination With total demand greater than total supply, it may be required that some destinations receive minimum shipments. This is modeled by providing two columns for such destinations. The column representing the minimum will have a big M in the dummy row. The case is illustrated in Fig. 7.5, where destination 2 has a minimum requirement of 20.

Cost of Manufacture and Revenue at Sale Say that in addition to shipping costs, each source has a cost of manufacture and each destination has a revenue at sale, where

$$f_i = \text{cost of manufacture at source } i,$$
$$r_j = \text{revenue at sale at destination } j.$$

These are incorporated into the tableau by revising the cost for cell (i, j):

$$c'_{ij} = c_{ij} + f_i - r_j.$$

Because revenue would be expected to be larger than total cost, this revised cost might be negative, indicating a profit. To illustrate this case we assume again the shipping cost matrix of Fig. 7.2a, but now we assume that there is a cost of 10, 11, and 12 for manufacture at sources S1, S2, and S3, respectively. There is a revenue of 23, 28, and 30 for sale at destinations D1, D2, and D3, respectively. The supplies given represent maximum production at the sources, and the demands are maximum requirements at the destinations. The model as presented in Fig. 7.6 has both a dummy source and a dummy destination. The dummy source is inserted to allow destinations not to accept deliveries, and the dummy destination is inserted to

		DESTINATION				
		D1	D2M	D2E	D3	SUPPLY
SOURCE	S1	10	20	20	18	**20**
	S2	8	15	15	12	**15**
	S3	13	17	17	19	**15**
	SD	0	M	0	0	**21**
DEMAND		**20**	**20**	**5**	**26**	

Figure 7.5 **Model with Minimum Requirements at a Destination**

		DESTINATION D1	D2	D3	DD	SUPPLY
SOURCE	S1	-3	2	-2	0	20
	S2	-4	-2	-7	0	15
	S3	2	-1	1	0	15
	SD	0	0	0	0	46
DEMAND		10	20	16	50	

Figure 7.6 **Model with Cost of Manufacture and Revenue at Sale**

allow sources not to make shipments. The transportation costs have been adjusted to include both manufacturing costs and sales revenues.

Multiperiod Models A production scheduling problem involving more than one period of time can easily be described as a transportation model. Time is an important component only if there is the possibility of using the production of one period to meet the demands of another. Products stored in inventory are the means of allowing production to meet demands of a later period. Products whose delivery is delayed (called backorders) are the means of allowing demand to be met by the production of a later period. Both options imply added cost. Fig. 7.7 shows a general schematic for setting up a two-period problem.

In the Fig. 7.7,

C_T is the matrix of shipping costs,

C_I is a matrix of the cost of holding an item in inventory for one period, and

C_B is a matrix of the cost of one backordered item for one period.

The inventory and backorder matrices may be matrices of constants or may vary with source and destination. If backorders are not allowed, as is often assumed, all the elements of the backorder cost matrix have the value of big M. The model is easily expanded for more than two periods. In general a problem with T periods will have mT rows and nT columns. If the size of the problem is measured as the number of cells in the matrix, the size increases as the square of the number of periods.

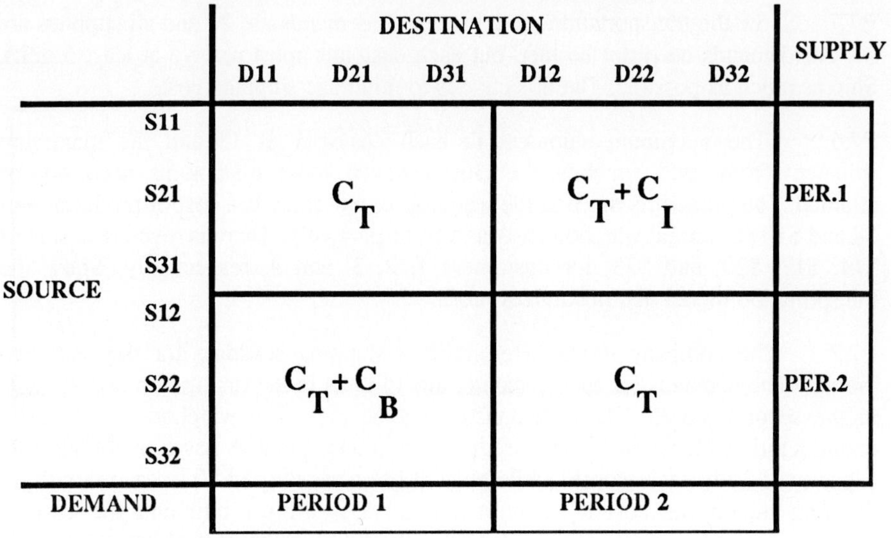

Figure 7.7 A Two-period Model

PROBLEMS

The problems for this section relate to a company with two warehouses and four customers. The transportation costs between warehouses and customers are shown in the table below.

		Customer			
		1	*2*	*3*	*4*
Warehouse	A	10	15	8	13
	B	3	5	7	10

P7.1 Show the linear programming model of this problem when each warehouse has a supply of 30 and each customer has a demand of 15. The objective is to minimize shipping cost. Demand must be satisfied.

P7.2 Show the transportation model of the problem stated in P7.1.

P7.3 Show the transportation model when all demands are 15 and all supplies are 40. All demands must be met, but not all supplies must be shipped. The objective is to minimize shipping cost.

P7.4 Show the transportation model when all demands are 20 and all supplies are 30. All demands need not be met, but ship as much as possible. The objective is to minimize shipping cost.

P7.5 Show the transportation model when all demands are 20 and all supplies are 30. All demands need not be met, but each customer must receive at least 5 units. Ship as much as possible. The objective is to minimize shipping cost.

P7.6 The maximum shipment to each customer is 15 and the maximum shipment from each warehouse is 30; however, these maximums need not be attained. The product is made at the warehouses and there is a cost of production of \$8 and \$10 per unit at warehouses A and B, respectively. There is revenue at sale of \$14, \$17, \$20, and \$23, for customers 1, 2, 3, and 4, respectively. Show the transportation model that maximizes profit.

P7.7 The company needs to establish a shipping schedule for the next two months. The demands for each customer are 15 units in the first month and 20 units in the second month. These demands must be met. The warehouses are really manufacturing plants where the products are made. Plant A has a manufacturing capacity of 30 in each month, while plant B has a capacity of 50 in each month. In the first month the cost of manufacture at A is \$8 per unit and the cost of manufacture at B is \$10 per unit. In the second month the cost of manufacture is \$10 at both plants. Products can be stored at the customer sites from one month to the next at a cost of \$1 per unit. Products cannot be stored at the plants. Shipping costs are as given in the table above except that the shipping company is giving a discount of \$1 per unit on all routes during the first month.

The goal is to minimize total production, shipping, and inventory costs over the two months. Not all production capacity will be utilized by the solution. Show the transportation model that will solve this problem.

P7.8 Modify the solution of P7.7 to allow shortages in the first period to be filled by production in the second period. The backorder cost is \$2 per unit.

The Simplex Method for the Transportation Problem (7.2)

The transportation problem is a linear program, so it can be solved using the simplex method described in earlier chapters. Because of its special structure, however, the simplex method can be considerably simplified. The new method is much more efficient for both hand computations and computer implementation. As will be discussed later in the chapter, the transportation problem is just one of the larger class of network problems, all of which allow special versions of the simplex method.

GOALS

- Be able to apply the northwest corner rule, Vogel's method, and Russell's method for finding an initial basic feasible solution for the transportation problem.
- Starting from a given set of basic cells, be able to solve a transportation problem by hand using the transportation simplex method.

- Be able to interpret the steps of the transportation simplex method in terms of the simplex method for general linear programs.

DEFINITIONS

Transportation Tableau: A tableau format used for hand calculations to solve the transportation problem with the simplex method. The general tableau is shown in Fig. 7.8.

Most of the notation in the tableau has been described in the last section. Each source and destination combination defines a *cell* of the tableau. The general cell for source i and destination j is called cell (i, j). Primal variable x_{ij} is associated with the cell (i, j) while the dual variables u_i and v_j are associated with row i and column j, respectively.

Cycle: A path through cells in the tableau. The cycle starts at one cell, passes through other cells in a sequence of alternating horizontal and vertical moves, and finally returns to the original cell. We will have many illustrations of cycles in the examples.

Basis: A selection of $m + n - 1$ cells from the tableau arranged so that no cycle can be traced through the basic cells. The basic cells are indicated by circles in the tableau.

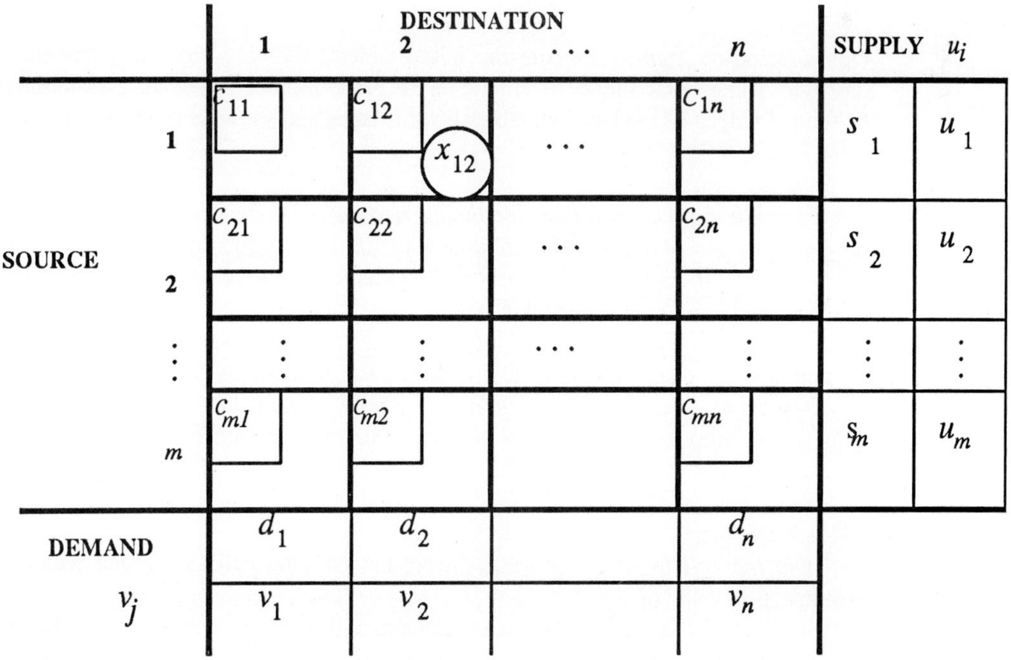

Figure 7.8 **The General Transportation Tableau**

Primal Basic Solution: An assignment of values to the primal variables x_{ij} such that only basic cells have nonzero values and the supplies and demands are satisfied. For a given basis there is a unique assignment. The values are shown within the circles on the tableau.

Complementary Dual Basic Solution: An assignment of values to the dual variables u_i and v_j so that the complementary slackness condition

$$c_{ij} - u_i - v_j = 0$$

is satisfied for all basic cells. One of the dual values is arbitrary and may be set to zero. Once this is selected, the other dual variables are uniquely determined by the location of the basic cells. The dual variables are unrestricted in sign.

Conditions for Optimality: A given basis is optimal if the complementary dual basic solution is feasible. This is checked by computing the slack variables for the dual constraints associated with the nonbasic cells

$$d_{ij} = c_{ij} - u_i - v_j.$$

The values are shown in the nonbasic cells of the tableau. If these values are all nonnegative, the dual solution is feasible and the primal solution is optimal.

ALGORITHMS

SIMPLEX ALGORITHM FOR THE TRANSPORTATION PROBLEM

A1. Initialization Step Prepare the initial tableau showing problem parameters. Start with some basis shown as circles in the basic cells of the tableau. Determine the unique values of the basic variables for this basis and show them in the circles.

A2. Stopping Rule

Compute the dual variables for the current basis. Assign the value of zero for the dual variable of the row or column with the most basic cells. Determine the values of the others to satisfy the complementary slackness condition. Show the values at the boundaries of the tableau.

Compute the dual slack variables for the nonbasic variables. For each nonbasic cell compute the dual slack variable d_{ij} and show it in the body of the cell.

Determine whether the solution is optimal. If all the values of d_{ij} are nonnegative, stop with the optimal solution; otherwise continue with the iterative step.

A3. Iterative Step

Find the cell to enter the basis. Select the entering cell as the one with the most negative value of d_{ij}.

Find the cell to leave the basis. Construct the cycle, which starts with the entering cell, passes through only basic cells, and returns to the entering cell. Show the cycle as a sequence of alternating vertical and horizontal lines connecting pairs of cells on the cycle. Mark the entering cell with a plus (+). Mark the first basic cell on the cycle with a minus (–). Alternatively mark each basic cell on the cycle with (+) or (–) until the entering cell is reached. Find the basic cell marked with a minus having the smallest value of x_{ij}. This is the cell that will leave the basis. If there is a tie, select any one of the tied cells arbitrarily. Let d be the value of the basic variable for the leaving cell.

Change the basic solution. For every cycle cell marked with a plus, increase the basic variable by δ. For every cycle cell marked with a minus, decrease the basic variable by δ. Remove the circle from the leaving cell. Add the circle to the entering cell with the basic variable equal to δ.

Prepare a new tableau. The new tableau should show all problem parameters and the current basis.

Return to step A2.

ALGORITHM TO FIND AN INITIAL BASIC SOLUTION

The simplex algorithm may start from any basic solution. When first encountering a problem, however, some procedure must be used to find the first basic solution. A general algorithm follows. The procedure crosses out rows and columns.

B1. Initialization Step Draw a tableau showing all problem parameters. None of the rows or columns are crossed out.

B2. Iterative Step According to some criterion, select a cell that has not been crossed out. Put a circle in the cell. Assign a value to the basic variable for the cell that will just use up the remaining supply for the row of the cell or the remaining demand for the column of the cell (the smaller of the two). Reduce the remaining supply for the row and the remaining demand for the column by the amount assigned. Cross out the row or column whose supply or demand goes to zero. If both go to zero, cross out only one.

B3. Stopping Rule If only one row or column remains, let all the cells not yet crossed out be basic and assign them all the remaining supply or demand. Stop with the basic solution defined. If more than one row and more than one column remain, go to step B2.

There are alternative possibilities for the selection rule of step B2. They differ with respect to the work required to carry them out and the quality of the initial solution they generate. Generally the methods requiring the greatest effort will yield the best solutions. For hand calculations the effort is often justified. For computer programs it is often true that the simpler methods are more effective because the iterative step of the transportation simplex is so efficient. Several alternatives are described below.

Northwest Corner Rule: The upper left-hand corner of the tableau is called the northwest corner. The rule is to select the uncrossed cell closest to the northwest corner. This is the simplest rule to apply.

Vogel's Method: Compute for each uncrossed row the difference between the smallest cost in the row and the second smallest cost. Do the same for uncrossed columns. Select the row or column with the greatest of the differences. The rule is to choose the uncrossed cell in the selected row or column with the smallest cost.

Russell's Method: Compute for the uncrossed rows and columns

u_i = the value of the largest uncrossed cost in row i.

v_j = the value of the largest uncrossed cost in column j.

For each uncrossed cell compute

$$d_{ij} = c_{ij} - u_i - v_j.$$

The rule is to choose the uncrossed cell with the largest negative value of d_{ij}.

EXAMPLES

E7.1 For the transportation problem given in Fig. 7.9, find the initial feasible solution with the northwest corner rule and use the simplex method to find the optimal solution. Using the northwest corner rule, we find the initial solution given in Fig. 7.10.

Due to the complementary slackness condition, we have for the basic cells

$$u_i + v_j = c_{ij}.$$

One of the dual variables can be assigned arbitrarily to zero. Here we let $u_3 = 0$, because row 3 has the largest number of basic cells. The remainder of the dual

		DESTINATION					SUPP
		1	2	3	4	5	
	1	15	15	16	11	11	15
SOURCE	2	13	11	15	9	6	15
	3	8	12	11	7	8	15
DEMAND		5	10	15	5	10	

Figure 7.9 **Data for the Example**

	DESTINATION 1	2	3	4	5	SUPPLY
SOURCE 1	15 (5)	15 (10)	16	11	11	15
2	13	11 (0)	15 (15)	9	6	15
3	8	12	11 (0)	7 (5)	8 (10)	15
DEMAND	5	10	15	5	10	

Figure 7.10 **Initial Solution by the Northwest Corner Rule (Z = 565)**

	DESTINATION 1	2	3	4	5	SUPPLY	u_i
SOURCE 1	15 (5)	15 (10)	16	11	11	15	8
2	13	11 (0)	15 (15)	9	6	15	4
3	8	12	11 (0)	7 (5)	8 (10)	15	0
DEMAND	5	10	15	5	10		
v_j	7	7	11	7	8		

Figure 7.11 **Determination of the Dual Variables**

variables are uniquely determined by this decision. The dual variables are then assigned in the order given below. This order is not unique, but an order must be followed that allows determination of all dual variables. The operations are generally performed directly on the tableau. Fig. 7.11 shows the complete dual solution.

$$u_3 = 0,$$
$$v_3 = c_{33} - u_3 = 11 - 0 = 11,$$
$$v_4 = c_{34} - u_3 = 7 - 0 = 7,$$

$$v_5 = c_{35} - u_3 = 8 - 0 = 8,$$
$$u_2 = c_{23} - v_3 = 15 - 11 = 4,$$
$$v_2 = c_{22} - u_2 = 11 - 4 = 7,$$
$$u_1 = c_{12} - v_2 = 15 - 7 = 8,$$
$$v_1 = c_{11} - u_1 = 15 - 8 = 7.$$

The next step is to determine dual feasibility. The dual slack variables are computed for each nonbasic cell from the expression

$$d_{ij} = c_{ij} - u_i - v_j.$$

The results of the computation are shown on Fig. 7.12 in the upper right-hand corner of the nonbasic cells. If this quantity is nonnegative for all nonbasic cells, the current basic solution is optimum. Since we find a number of negative values in the cells of the example, the current dual solution is not feasible and the current primal solution is not optimal. Using the most negative value rule, we select x_{25} to enter the basis. If there is a tie for the most negative value, the entering variable can be chosen arbitrarily from the tied cells.

Once a variable is chosen to enter the basis, some basic variable must be chosen to leave. We do this by finding the unique cycle that includes the entering cell and basic cells. The cycle for the present example is shown in Fig. 7.13 with a solid line through cells (2,5), (2,3), (3,3), and (3,5). There is only one cycle for any given entering variable. For hand calculations it is found by observation. The cycle will always include an even number of cells, and each row and column will have exactly two or no cells on the cycle.

		DESTINATION					
		1	2	3	4	5	SUPPL
	1	15 / (5)	15 / (10)	16 / -3	11 / -4	11 / -5	15
SOURCE	2	13 / 2	11 / (0)	15 / (15)	9 / -2	6 / -6	15
	3	8 / 1	12 / 5	11 / (0)	7 / (5)	8 / (10)	15
DEMAND		5	10	15	5	10	
v_j		7	7	11	7	8	

Figure 7.12 **Determination of Dual Feasibility and Primal Optimality**

	DESTINATION 1	2	3	4	5	SUPPLY	u_i
SOURCE 1	15 (5)	15 (10)	16 / -3	11 / -4	11 / -5	15	8
2	13 / 2	11 (0)	15 (15) -	9 / -2	6 / -6 +	15	4
3	8 / 1	12 / 5	11 (0) +	7 (5)	8 (10) -	15	0
DEMAND	5	10	15	5	10		
v_j	7	7	11	7	8		

Figure 7.13 **The Cycle through the Basic Cells**

For x_{25} to enter the basis, the value of the variable must increase. Since the variables for row 2 must always sum to 15, the value of x_{23} must decrease by the same amount. Again we note that the sum of flows in column 3 must remain constant at 15. This implies that x_{33} increases by the amount of decrease of x_{23}. For similar reasons x_{35} must decrease by the amount of increase of x_{33}. Finally we have returned to x_{25}, which is increasing. In general we indicate the direction of change by placing a plus in the cell of the entering variable, and then placing alternatively minus and plus in the basic cells on the cycle. The maximum increase in the value of the entering variable is the minimum of the values of the cells marked with a minus. Let the minimum obtained be δ. For the example this occurs for cell (3,5) with δ equal to 10. That cell is then chosen to leave the basis. If there is a tie for the variable leaving the basis, any one can be chosen. The next solution will then be degenerate (have a basic variable at the zero level).

To find the new basic solution, we add δ. to the values of all cells marked with a plus and subtract δ from all cells marked with a minus. The result is shown in Fig. 7.14.

All the operations of the second iteration are shown on one tableau in Fig. 7.14. The dual variables are assigned. The value of d_{ij} for each cell is computed, and cell (1,4) is selected to enter the basis. The corresponding cycle is shown. There is a tie for the leaving variable, and cell (2,3) is selected to leave the basis. The resulting solution is shown in Fig. 7.15.

Iteration 3 is a degenerate iteration because the value of δ is zero. Cell (3,1) enters the basis, but the leaving variable cell (3,4) has a value of zero. The new solution is shown in Fig. 7.16.

In iteration 4, cell (1,3) enters the basis with δ equal to 5. The resultant solution appears in Fig. 7.17. The d_{ij} of all cells are nonnegative, so the dual solution is feasible and the primal solution is optimal.

SOURCE \ DESTINATION	1	2	3	4	5	SUPPLY	u_i
1	15 (5)	15 (10) -	16 -3	11 -4 +	11 1	15	4
2	13 2	11 (0) +	15 (5) -	9 -2	6 (10)	15	0
3	8 1	12 5	11 (10) +	7 (5) -	8 6	15	-4
DEMAND	5	10	15	5	10		
v_j	11	11	15	11	6		

Figure 7.14 **Iteration 2 of the Simplex Method (Z = 505)**

SOURCE \ DESTINATION	1	2	3	4	5	SUPPLY	u_i
1	15 (5) -	15 (5)	16 1	11 (5) +	11 1	15	0
2	13 2	11 (5)	15 4	9 2	6 (10)	15	-4
3	8 -3 +	12 1	11 (15)	7 (0) -	8 2	15	-4
DEMAND	5	10	15	5	10		
v_j	15	15	15	11	10		

Figure 7.15 **Iteration 3 of the Simplex Method (Z = 485)**

E7.2 Use Vogel's method to find the initial basic feasible solution for the example problem.

When done by hand, Vogel's method is usually performed directly on the tableau, with the selection of basic variables in each iteration accompanied by the crossing out of a row or column and the recomputation of differences and supplies and demands. The tableau becomes so messy, however, that we suggest using the tabular format below together with the transportation matrix. Each row of the table shows the row and column differences, the basic variable assigned, the adjustment

SOURCE \ DESTINATION	1	2	3	4	5	SUPPLY	u_i
1	15 (5) -	15 (5)	16 -2 +	11 (5)	11 1	15	0
2	13 2	11 (5)	15 1	9 2	6 (10)	15	-4
3	8 (0) +	12 4	11 (15) -	7 3	8 5	15	-7
DEMAND	5	10	15	5	10		
v_j	15	15	18	11	10		

Figure 7.16 **Iteration 4 of the Simplex Method (Z = 485)**

SOURCE \ DESTINATION	1	2	3	4	5	SUPPLY	u_i
1	15 2	15 (5)	16 (5)	11 (5)	11 1	15	0
2	13 4	11 (5)	15 3	9 2	6 (10)	15	-4
3	8 (5)	12 2	11 (10)	7 1	8 3	15	-5
DEMAND	5	10	15	5	10		
v_j	13	15	16	11	10		

Figure 7.17 **The Optimal Solution (Z = 475)**

of demands and supplies, and the row or column crossed out. Vogel's method on the example problem yields the optimal solution shown in Fig. 7.17 without additional iterations.

	Row Differences			*Column Differences*						
No.	1	2	3	1	2	3	4	5	*Basic var.*	*Action*
1	0	3	1	5	1	4	2	2	$x_{31} = 5$	$d_1 = 0, s_3 = 10$ Cross out col.1.
2	0	3	1	—	1	4	2	2	$x_{33} = 10$	$d_3 = 5, s_3 = 0$ Cross out row 3.
3	0	3	—	—	4	1	2	5	$x_{25} = 10$	$d_5 = 0, s_2 = 5$ Cross out col. 5.
4	4	2	—	—	4	1	2	—	$x_{14} = 5$	$d_4 = 0, s_1 = 10$. Cross out col. 4.
5	1	4	—	—	4	1	—	—	$x_{22} = 5$	$d_2 = 5, s_2 = 0$. Cross out row 2.
6	Only row 1 remains								$x_{12} = 5$	$d_2 = 0, s_1 = 5$.
7	Only row 1 remains								$x_{13} = 5$	$d_3 = 0, s_1 = 0$.

E7.3 Use Russell's method to find the initial basic feasible solution. Test the solution for optimality. If the solution is not optimal, select the variable to enter the basis.

Again we use the table format with the u_i and the v_j shown for rows and columns.

	Rows (u_i)			*Columns (v_j)*						
No.	1	2	3	1	2	3	4	5	*Basic var.*	*Action*
1	16	15	12	15	15	16	11	11	$x_{25} = 10$	$d_5 = 0, s_2 = 5$ Cross out col. 5.
2	16	15	12	15	15	16	11	—	$x_{22} = 5$	$d_2 = 5, s_2 = 0$ Cross out row 2.
3	16	—	12	15	15	16	11	—	$x_{31} = 5$	$d_1 = 0, s_3 = 10$ Cross out col. 1.
4	16	—	12	—	15	16	11	—	$x_{33} = 10$	$d_3 = 5, s_3 = 0$ Cross out row 3.
5	Only row 1 remains								$x_{12} = 5$	$d_2 = 0, s_1 = 10$.
6	Only row 1 remains								$x_{13} = 5$	$d_3 = 0, s_1 = 5$.
7	Only row 1 remains								$x_{14} = 5$	$d_4 = 0, s_1 = 0$.

Russell's method has also discovered the optimum solution.

E7.4 Start from the basic solution given in Fig. 7.17. For each nonbasic cell, find

a. the marginal change in the objective function if that cell is allowed to enter the basis,
b. the set of cells defined by the cycle for that cell,
c. the increase in the variable for that cell if it were to enter the basis,
d. the total cost of the solution obtained when that cell is allowed to enter the basis. Since the solution of Fig. 7.17 is optimal, all basis changes will result in an increase of the objective function.

The table below shows the required information for each nonbasic variable.

Nonbasic cell	*Marginal cost*	*Cells on cycle*	*Variable change*	*Total cost increase*
(1,1)	2	(1,1), (1,3), (3,3), (3,1)	5	10
(1,5)	1	(1,5), (1,2), (2,2), (2,5)	5	5
(2,1)	4	(2,1), (2,2), (1,2), (1,3), (3,3), (3,1)	5	20
(2,3)	3	(2,3), (2,2), (1,2), (1,3)	5	15
(2,4)	2	(2,4), (2,2), (1,2), (1,4)	5	10
(3,2)	2	(3,2), (3,3), (1,3), (1,2)	5	10
(3,4)	1	(3,4), (3,3), (1,3), (1,4)	5	5
(3,5)	3	(3,5), (3,3), (1,3), (1,2), (2,2), (2,5)	5	15

Note that the cost change is the product of the marginal cost and the change in the basic variables.

PROBLEMS

P7.9 Solve the linear programming model derived in P7.1 with the simplex method for general linear programs.

P7.10 Solve the transportation model derived in P7.2 with the simplex method described in this section. Use the northwest corner rule to find an initial feasible solution.

P7.11 Solve the transportation model derived in P7.2 with the simplex method. Use Vogel's method to find an initial feasible solution.

P7.12 Solve the transportation model derived in P7.2 with the simplex method. Use Russell's method to find an initial feasible solution.

P7.13 Given the transportation model below, use the northwest corner rule to find an initial solution and do one iteration of the simplex method.

		DESTINATION						
		1	2	3	4	5	6	SUPPLY
SOURCE	1	21	12	28	17	9	0	50
	2	15	13	20	M	12	0	60
	3	18	17	22	10	8	0	40
	4	M	2	10	5	0	0	70
	5	33	39	35	27	23	0	30
DEMAND		40	30	50	60	50	20	

P7.14 Given the transportation model of P7.13, use Vogel's method to find an initial solution and do one iteration of the simplex method.

P7.15 Given the transportation model of P7.13, use Russell's method to find an initial solution and do one iteration of the simplex method.

P7.16 Compare the costs of the initial solutions obtained with the three methods and rank the methods on the basis of the quality of the initial solution. Also rank the methods on the basis of the effort required to find the initial solution.

Network Flow Programming

The transportation problem considered in this chapter is a special case of a broader class of problems called network flow programs. These in turn are a special case of the still more general linear program considered earlier. In addition to transportation problems, the class of network flow programming includes such problems as the assignment problem, the shortest path problem, the maximum flow problem, the pure minimum cost flow problem, and the generalized minimum cost flow problem. It is an important class because algorithms exist for the solution of the optimization problem that are many times more efficient than linear programming in the utilization of computer time and space resources. The algorithms are variations of the primal simplex method adapted to take advantage of the special network structure. Because of its importance we have chosen to include this subject in this guide even though it is not included in H & L. The *Microsolve/Operations Research* computer package includes a network flow programming optimization algorithm. In this section we are concerned with modeling rather than solution algorithms.

GOALS

- Know the meaning of the components of a network flow programming model and the assumptions implied by the model.
- Be able to translate a textual description of an appropriate situation into a network flow programming model.

DEFINITIONS

Network Models: The network flow model consists of nodes and arcs, as in Fig. 7.18. In the context of modeling a problem, each node, shown as a circle in the figure, will represent some aspect of the problem such as a physical location, an individual worker, or a point in time. Thus for modeling purposes it is often convenient to assign names to the nodes as in the example problem, where we use the names N1 through N4. Arcs are the directed line segments of the figure. An arc will be identified by the nodes at its ends. Thus one arc in the figure originates at node N1 and terminates at node N3.

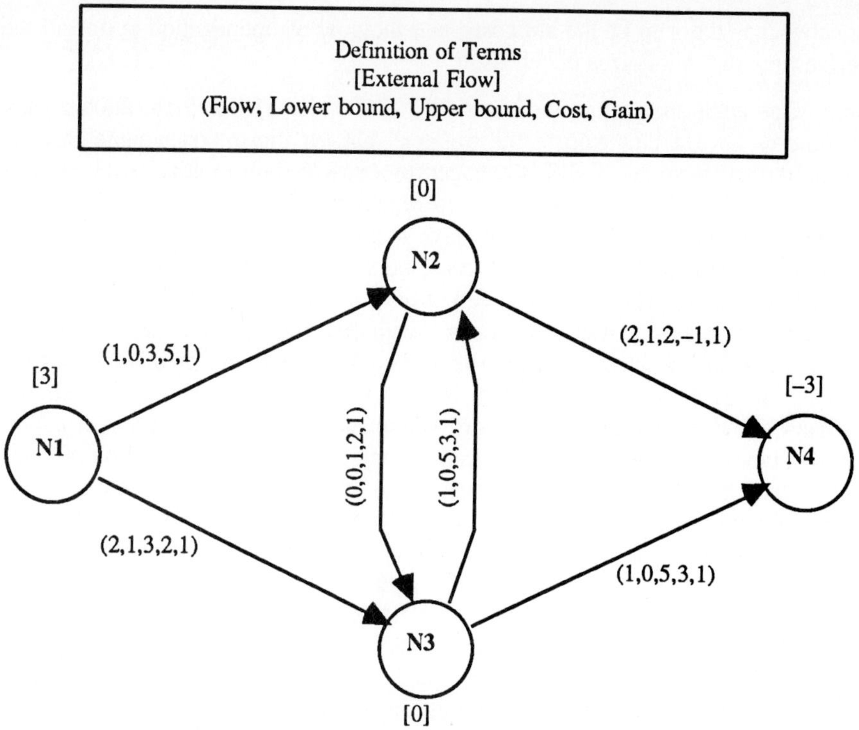

Figure 7.18 **Example Network**

Flow: Flow is associated with the network, entering and leaving at the nodes and passing through the arcs. The network of the figure has three units of flow entering at N1 and leaving at N4. Flows entering or leaving a node from external sources are called external flows and are identified in the figure with square brackets. Flow is conserved at the nodes, implying that the total flow entering a node must equal the total flow leaving the node. Thus the three units of flow entering N1 must pass through the arcs leaving N1. In the figure, flow is the first number in the parentheses adjacent to the arc.

Bounds: Flow is limited in an arc by the lower and upper bounds on flow, shown as the second and third numbers in the parentheses. Thus in the figure the flow on the arc from N1 to N3 must be at least 1 and at most 3. Within the restrictions imposed by conservation of flow for each node and the bounds on flow for each arc, there are usually many feasible flows (a "flow" is an assignment of an arc flow to each arc). The problem of network flow programming is to find a feasible flow, if one exists, and an optimal flow from the set of feasible flows. The lower and upper bounds are parameters of the arc and the flow is the arc variable.

Cost: The criterion for optimality is cost. Associated with each arc is a third parameter (the fourth number in the parentheses), the cost per unit of flow. If a flow x passes through the arc with unit cost c, a cost cx is incurred. The total cost for the network is the sum of the arc costs, and the goal of optimization is to find the feasible flow that minimizes this measure.

Gain: One additional parameter is assigned to the arcs of Fig. 7.18, the arc gain. All the arcs have a unit gain in the example, but for illustration assume that the gain on the arc from N1 to N3 is changed to 0.5. The gain multiplies the flow at the beginning of the arc, leaving N1, to obtain the flow at the end of the arc, entering N3. Thus if 2 units of flow leave node N1 on this arc, only 1 unit will enter N3. In general if a flow x is assigned to an arc, this is the flow at the beginning of the arc. The flow at the end of the arc with gain, g, will be xg.

The gain is a very useful modeling parameter. The network may represent a water distribution problem where the gain models evaporation or other losses (in this case all gains will be less than 1). The network may represent a product distribution and manufacturing network where the gain models a transformation from one type of flow to another. Thus an arc will cause the transformation of labor to products when the gain factor is specified in units of product per unit of labor. An arc gain may be any number except 0, including negative numbers. A gain of 1 indicates that flow is conserved in an arc, neither increased nor decreased. A network in which all arcs have unit gains is called a *pure* network. The optimum solution for a pure network will always have integer flows. If some gains have values other than 1, the network is a *generalized* network. The solution to the generalized network need not have all integer flows.

The arc lower bound, upper bound, and cost all refer to the flow at the beginning of the arc. Thus the flow restrictions and the arc cost are independent of the gain factor. Gain factors do not modify the requirement of conservation of flow at the nodes; however, the gain factors do cause adjustments in the flows that enter nodes.

MODELING

When learning to use network models, it is helpful to recognize several special cases that are usually discussed in introductory texts. These are the transportation, assignment, shortest path, and maximum flow models. The special cases differ primarily in the set of arc parameters that are relevant or the arrangement of nodes and arcs. For instance, for the transportation model only the arc costs are relevant and all arcs originate at one set of nodes and terminate at another. We will describe the special cases in terms of the generalized model defined above and note that for the special cases only a subset of the parameters are relevant. All irrelevant parameters will take on the default values. For the special network models of this section we set the parameter default values as: 0 for the lower bound, M (a large number) for the upper bound, 0 for the cost, and 1 for the gain.

Using the default values for parameters, all the special cases can be solved using algorithms defined for the more general case. There exists, however, a number of algorithms for solving each special case that do not use the irrelevant parameters at all. In this way the special case algorithms are more efficient than the more general ones.

		DESTINATIONS			
		D1	D2	D3	SUPPLY
SOURCES	S1	3	1	M	5
	S2	4	2	4	3
	S3	M	3	3	3
DEMAND		3	3	3	

Figure 7.19 **Matrix Model of a Transportation Problem**

Transportation Problem A typical transportation problem is shown in Fig. 7.19. It deals with sources where a supply of some commodity is available and destinations where the commodity is demanded. The classical statement of the transportation problem uses a matrix with the rows representing sources and columns representing destinations. The algorithms usually proposed in introductory texts for solving the problem are based on the matrix representation. The costs of shipping from sources to destinations are indicated by the entries in the matrix. If shipment is impossible between a given source and destination, a large cost of M is entered. This discourages the algorithm from using such cells. Supplies and demands are shown along the margins of the matrix. One requirement of the model is that total supply must equal total demand. To accomplish this with unbalanced supplies and demands, a dummy source or destination must be added. The example of Fig. 7.19 is unbalanced by having too much supply.

The network model of the transportation problem is shown in Fig. 7.20. Sources are identified as the nodes on the left and destinations on the right. Allowable shipping links are shown as arcs, while disallowed links are not included. Since the network solution algorithms only require that arc information be stored and manipulated, the latter feature represents a savings for the network model over the matrix representation since only existing arcs are stored in the computer for the network while the matrix stores information for every cell. The network model will be much more memory efficient when there are many disallowed links. For most practical problems, a density of 5–10% of allowable cells is typical.

Note that only arc costs are shown in the network model, as these are the only relevant parameters. All other parameters are set to the default values. The network has a special form important in graph theory; it is called a bipartite network since the nodes can be divided into two parts with all arcs going from one part to the other.

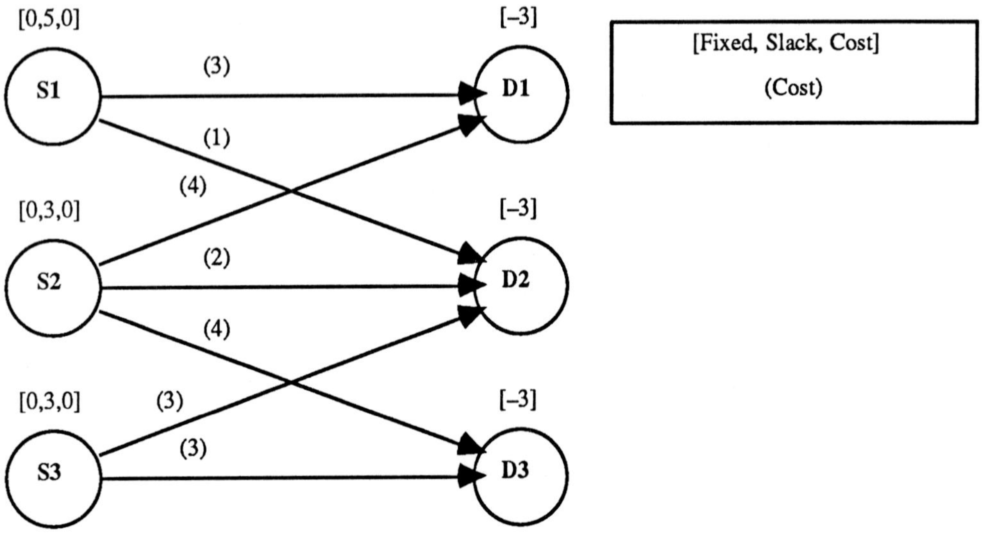

Figure 7.20 **Network Flow Model of the Transportation Problem**

The node external flows are the supplies and demands. On each destination node a demand is a negative fixed external flow, indicating that this amount must leave the network. On the source nodes a new notation is used with three parameters shown. They are

[fixed flow, slack flow, slack cost] .

The fixed flow is the flow that *must* enter or leave, with the sign indicating direction. A nonzero slack flow indicates a variable external flow that *may* enter or leave as determined by the optimization. The magnitude of the slack flow is the maximum of this variable quantity, while the sign indicates whether it enters or leaves. The slack cost is the unit cost associated with the external flow. A positive value indicates a cost and a negative value indicates a revenue. In the example, the slack flows indicate that the source nodes need not send all that is available, but the optimization is to determine what portion of the supply is to be used.

If the supply represented a maximum production at the three sources and a cost of manufacturing were given, this cost would be presented as the slack cost in the model. The use of the slack parameters very often simplifies the modeling task.

Variations of the classical transportation problem are easily handled by modifications of the network model. If links have finite capacity, the arc upper bounds can be made finite. If supplies represent raw materials that are transformed into products at the sources and the demands are in units of product, the gain factors can be used to represent transformation efficiency at each source. If some minimal flow is required in certain links, arc lower bounds can be set to nonzero values.

Assignment Problem A typical assignment problem, presented in the classic manner, is shown in Fig. 7.21. Here there are five machines to be assigned to five

	J1	J2	J3	J4	J5
M1	*M*	8	6	12	1
M2	15	12	7	*M*	10
M3	10	*M*	5	14	*M*
M4	12	*M*	12	16	15
M5	18	17	14	*M*	13

Figure 7.21 **Matrix Model of the Assignment Problem**

jobs. The numbers in the matrix indicate the cost of doing each job with each machine. Jobs with costs of M are disallowed assignments. An assignment algorithm will determine the minimum cost matching of machines to jobs. The network model is in Fig. 7.22. It is very similar to the transportation model, except that the external flows are all +1 or –1. The only relevant parameter for the classical assignment model is arc cost (not shown in the figure for clarity) ; all other parameters should be set to default values. Clearly the assignment network also has the bipartite structure.

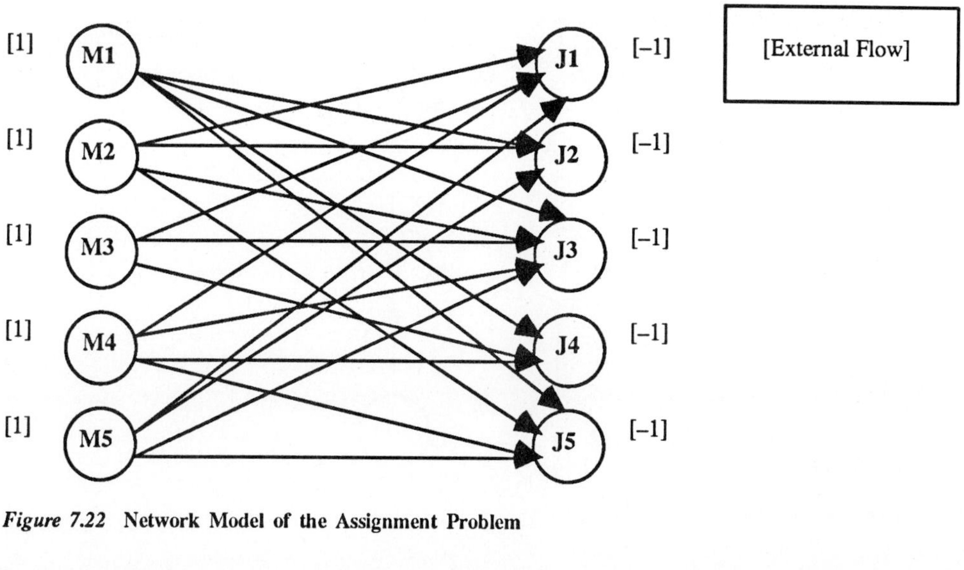

Figure 7.22 **Network Model of the Assignment Problem**

Various changes in the assignment model, such as each machine being capable of two jobs, are easily handled by slight changes in the network model.

Shortest Path Problem This problem uses a general network structure where only the arc cost is relevant. A typical case is shown in Fig. 7.23. The problem is to find the shortest path from some specified node to some other node or perhaps to all other nodes. The latter problem is called the shortest path tree problem because the collection of all shortest paths from a specified node forms a spanning tree. Since it is not much more difficult to find the paths to all nodes than it is to find the path to one node, the shortest path tree problem is usually solved.

The network flow equivalent to the shortest path tree problem is formed by equating arc distance to arc cost, assigning an external flow of $n - 1$ (n is the number of nodes) to the source node, and assigning external flows of -1 to every other node. This is illustrated in Fig. 7.23 for the shortest path tree from node A. When solving this flow problem, the computer will assign flow from the source to each node by the least cost path, since there are no bounds on arc flows. The shortest path tree will consist of those arcs with nonzero flow in the optimum solution. The solution to the example is shown in Fig. 7.24.

For this problem only arc costs are relevant; all other parameters have the default values.

Maximum Flow Problem The maximum flow problem is again structured on a general network; but here the arc capacities, or upper bounds, are the only relevant

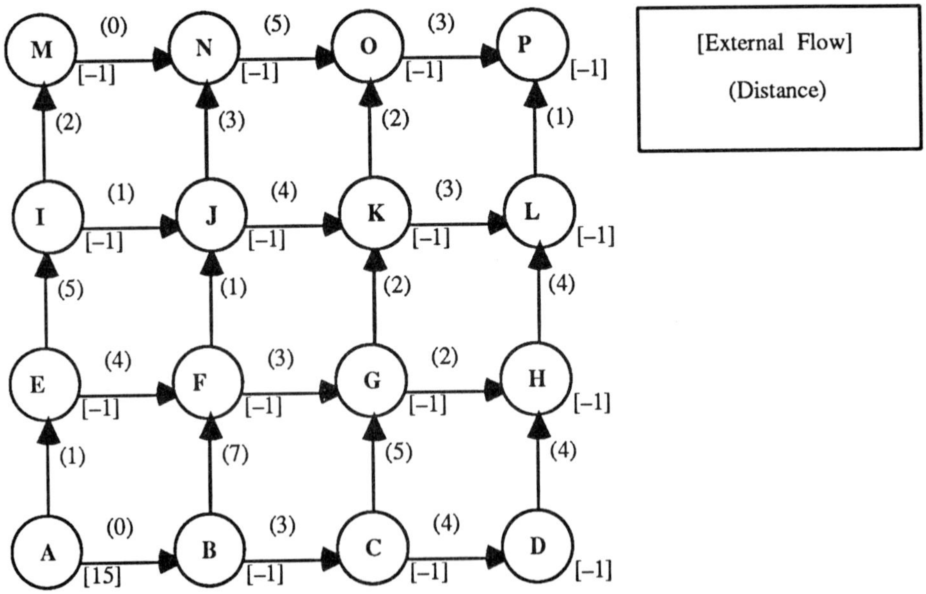

Figure 7.23 **Shortest Path Problem**

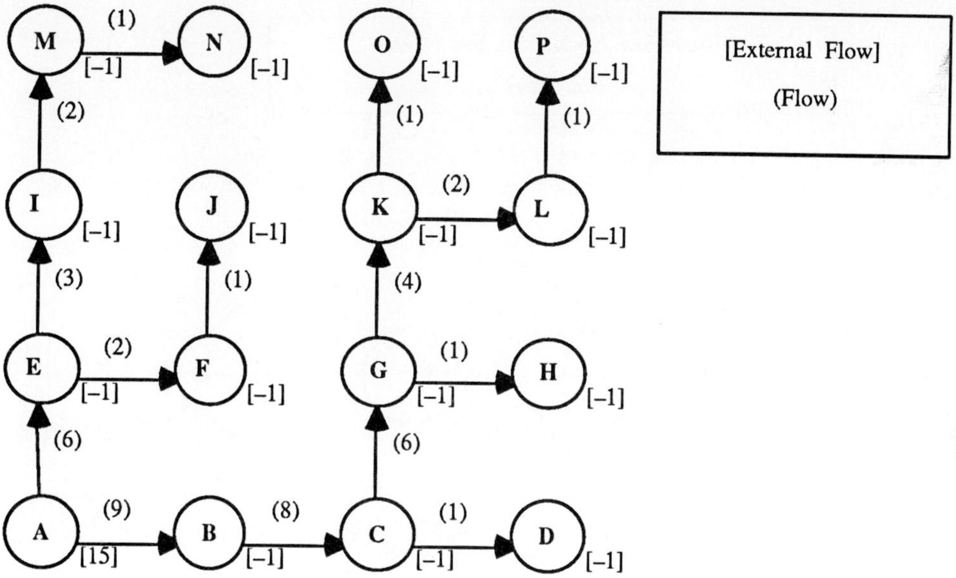

Figure 7.24 **Solution of the Shortest Path Problem**

parameters. The problem is to find the maximum flow possible from some given source node to a given sink node. This clearly can be solved using the general model with parameters set as in Fig. 7.25. All arc costs are zero, but the slack external cost at the sink is set to –1. Since the goal of the algorithm is to minimize cost, the maximum flow possible will flow to the sink node.

For power distribution problems, the maximum flow problem with losses may be important. Here losses are represented by arc gains less than 1.

Other Problems Of course, network flow models are not limited to the special cases. Any problem that can be described using nodes and arcs, where arcs have the parameters of lower bound, upper bound, cost, and gain, and nodes have external flow parameters, can be solved by these techniques. Some caution must be suggested, however, since many problems are "almost" network problems. Unless they can be put into the terms of this chapter they cannot be solved with the algorithms described in this chapter.

Some more general models have been suggested in the literature, such as multicommodity flow models and networks with side constraints. Algorithms for these models are not as efficient as the single-commodity algorithms suggested here, but are, of course, appropriate for a larger class of problems.

EXAMPLES

E7.5 A company has two warehouses and four customers. The shipping costs between warehouses and customers are shown in the table below. If the supply at

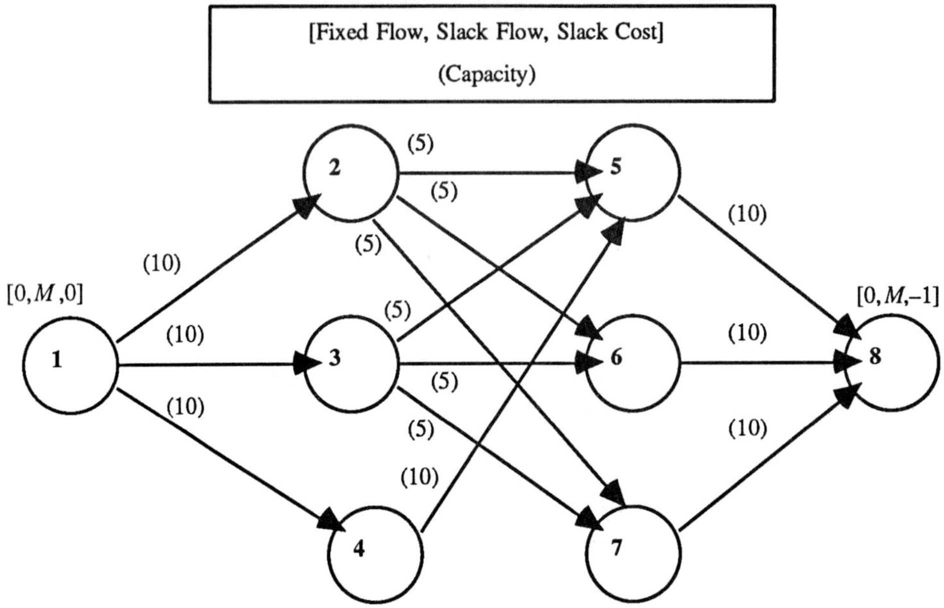

Figure 7.25 **Maximum Flow Problem**

each warehouse is 30 and the demand for each customer is 15, show the network flow model that when solved would determine the optimum shipping pattern.

Shipping Costs between Warehouses and Customers

	Customer			
Warehouse	*D1*	*D2*	*D3*	*D4*
SA	10	15	6	13
SB	3	6	7	10

In this example total supply equals total demand, so all inputs to the network can be fixed external flows. The network model is shown in the Fig. 7.26.

E7.6 Change the problem so demands are now 20 for each customer while supplies remain at 30 for each warehouse. Demands need not be met, but each customer must receive at least 5 units.

The network for this example is the same as in Fig. 7.26, except that the external flows have changed. It is never necessary to add dummy supply nodes or demand nodes as for the transportation matrix model. The only change is on the external flows at the demand nodes. These become

$$[\text{ Fixed flow, slack flow, slack cost }] = [\,-5, -15, 0\,].$$

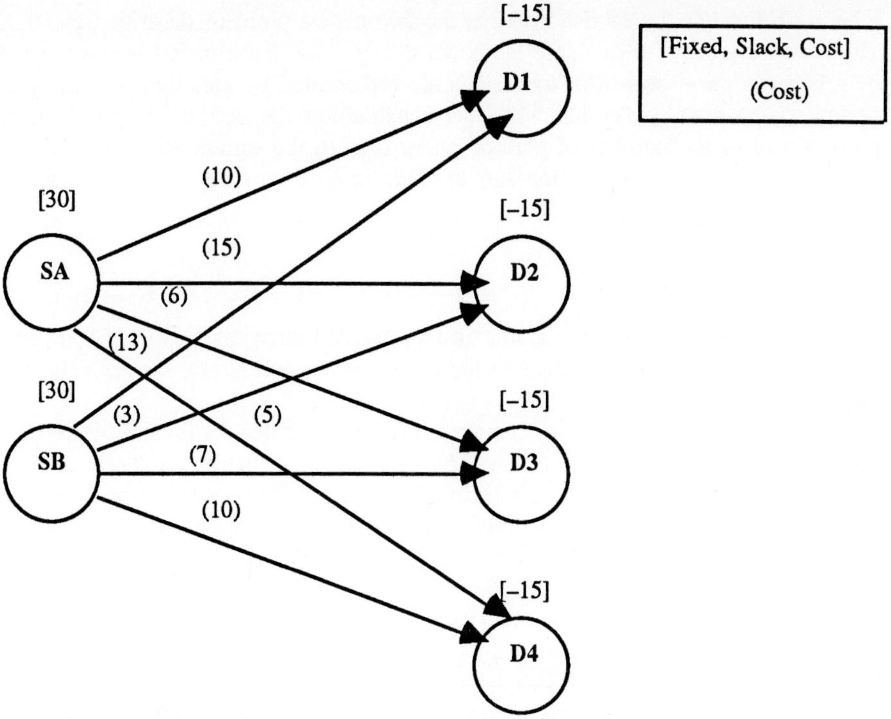

Figure 7.26 **Network Model for E7.5**

This fixed flow forces at least 5 units to be sent to each customer. The slack flow allows as many as 15 more to be shipped (for a maximum total of 20); the slack cost indicates that there is no penalty or reward for shipping the extra amount.

E7.7 Change the problem so that the maximum shipment to each customer is 15 and the maximum shipment from each warehouse is 30; however, these maximums need not be attained. The product is made at the warehouses and there is a cost of production of $8 and $10 per unit at warehouses A and B, respectively. There is a revenue at sale of $12, $14, $16, and $18, respectively, at the four customers. Show the network model that can be used to solve this problem.

Again the arcs of the network model are the same. The external flows of the nodes change to represent flexibility in shipments and receipts.

Node	[	*Fixed,*	*Slack,*	*Cost*	]
SA	[	0,	30,	8	]
SB	[	0,	30,	10	]
D1	[	0,	–15,	–12	]
D2	[	0,	–15,	–14	]
D3	[	0,	–15,	–16	]
D4	[	0,	–15,	–18	]

E7.8 Construct the model to solve the two-period problem described in P7.7. The network model for this case is shown in Fig. 7.27. Each period is represented by a transportation network. Inventories are represented by arcs that go from one period to the next. Note that with this construction the size of the network is proportional to the number of periods rather than to the square of the number of periods as for the transportation model. This is an important advantage for the network model over the transportation model.

PROBLEMS

P7.17 A company has one manufacturing plant and three sales outlets (A, B, and C). Shipping costs from the plant to the outlets A, B, and C are, respectively, $4, $6, and $8.

The company is to plan production, shipping and sales for three periods. The data for the periods are shown below. The plant has the capability to store some of the production of one period for sale in a later period. The storage cost is $1 per unit per period. The maximum storage is 100 units. Set up the network model that will solve this problem.

	Manufacturing data		*Selling price at outlets*			*Max. sales at outlets*		
Period	*Cost/unit*	*Capacity*	*A*	*B*	*C*	*A*	*B*	*C*
1	$8	175 units	$15	$20	$14	50	100	75
2	10	200	18	17	21	75	150	75
3	11	150	15	18	17	20	80	50

Computer Programs

Like linear programming, very excellent programs are available for solving network flow programming problems on mainframe computers. Researchers have developed algorithms to solve the general network flow programming problem and all the special case problems, such as transportation, shortest path, and maximum flow, much more efficiently than the general linear programming algorithms. Models with thousands of arcs and hundreds of nodes are readily solved in computation times of only a few seconds. Much larger models have been solved in a variety of application areas.

Microsolve has very good programs for creating and solving network flow programming problems on a microcomputer. The network generator, which we will discuss first, offers many features that allow the student to easily create moderately large network models for the computer, up to 250 arcs and 50 nodes for the IBM and 150 arcs and 50 nodes on the Apple II. These limits are certainly sufficient for educational exercises and small application problems. The solution algorithm solves the generalized, minimum cost, network flow programming problem, the most general class considered in this chapter. All the other problems that have been mentioned are special cases of this problem, so all can be solved with this computer program.

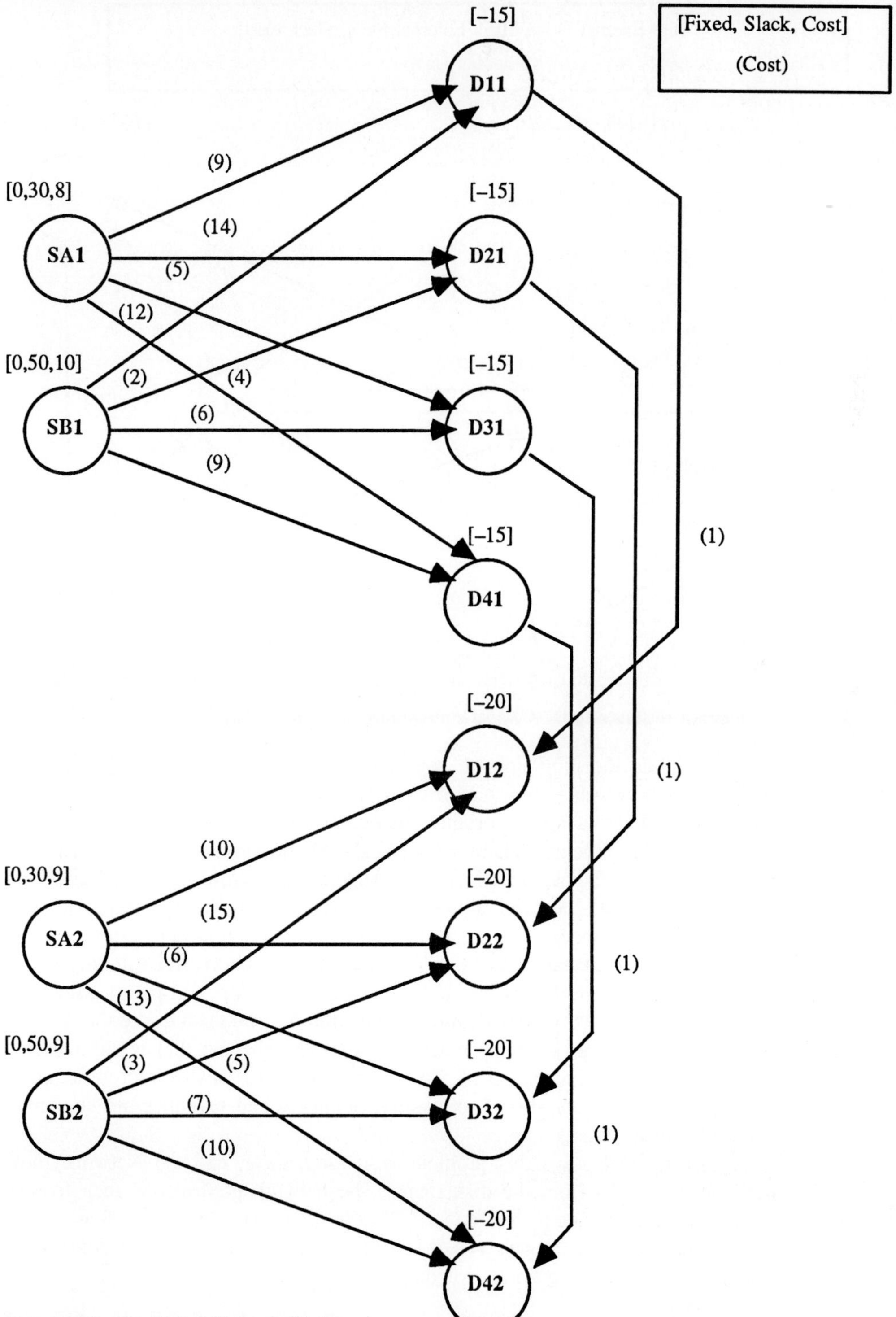

Figure 7.27 **Two-Period Network Model**

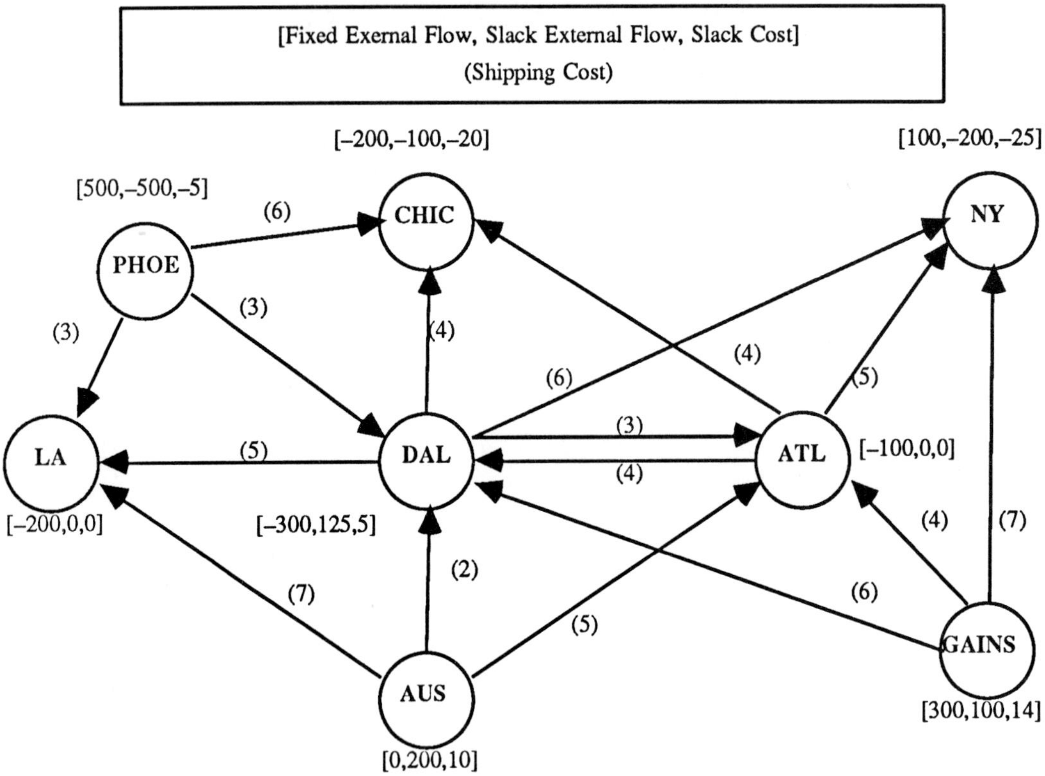

Figure 7.28 **Example Network to Illustrate the Computer Programs**

To illustrate the programs we consider the distribution problem described in Fig. 7.28.

Here we have a single product manufactured at three locations, Austin, Gainesville, and Phoenix. There is demand for the product at the other five locations, Atlanta, Chicago, Dallas, Los Angeles, and New York. A variety of complex supply and demand situations are represented by the external flow parameters on the nodes. The slack costs on the nodes represent either cost of manufacture (+) or revenue at sale (–). The arcs represent alternative shipping routes for the product. Notice that Dallas and Atlanta are transshipment points where the product can be both received and shipped. The numbers on the arcs are the per unit shipping costs. The problem is to find a shipping schedule that maximizes the profit (total revenue less total cost). The network model is always represented as a cost model, so costs are shown as positive numbers and revenues are shown as negative numbers.

To set up and solve this problem with *Microsolve,* call the Network Flow Programming option from the disk menu. The network generator is then loaded, with the menu appearing as in Fig. 7.29. This program has a variety of features for entering and changing models which are described in detail in the *Microsolve* manual. Here we illustrate how the example problem is defined.

NETWORK MODEL GENERATOR

1. SET ENVIRONMENT
2. CREATE NODES
3. ADD ARCS
4. ADD OR CHANGE TRANSPORTATION ARCS
5. SET EXTERNAL FLOWS
6. DISPLAY NETWORK PARAMETERS
7. CHANGE NETWORK
8. READ MODEL FROM DISK
9. SAVE MODEL ON DISK
10. SOLVE PROBLEM
11. SAVE MODEL AS A LINEAR PROGRAM
12. TURN PRINTER ON
13. CLEAR FOR ANOTHER PROBLEM
14. RETURN TO DISK MENU

PROBLEM LOADED IS DISTRIBUTION
8 NODES AND 16 ARCS

ENTER OPTION:

Figure 7.29. **Menu for the Network Generator**

The first step is to use option 1 to set the environment. This option allows us to tell the computer that the only relevant parameter on the arcs is arc cost. The other parameters—lower bound, upper bound, and gain—are set to the default values of 0, 999999, and 1, respectively. This simplifies significantly the problem of entering arc data. The environment can be changed at any time, so various portions of the network may be entered under different environments, but this will not be necessary for the example.

The second step is to use option 2 to define the nodes of the problem. Here the number of nodes is entered as 8 and the names shown on the figure are entered to identify the nodes. It is always useful to give the nodes names to simplify the interpretation of the results and the incorporation of any modifications that may be necessary.

The next step is to add the arcs to the model. This can be done with option 3, which requires the arcs to be entered one at a time with the following data:

starting node, ending node, parameters as required by environment.

For the example, only three items need be entered for each arc since cost is the only parameter. An alternative for entering arc data is option 4. This option presents a transportation matrix so that parameters may be more conveniently entered. First each node must be designated as a source (S), a destination (D), a transshipment node (T), or not to be included in the display (Press Return or Enter). These assignments are not permanent and they may be selected for the user's convenience. For the present model we specify AUS, GAINS, and PHOE as sources, CHIC, NY, and LA as destinations, and DAL and ATL as transshipment nodes. The display of Fig. 7.30 then appears.

```
          A    C    D    L    N
          T    H    A    A    Y
          L    I    L
               C

ATL       ?

AUS

DAL

GAINS

PHOE

ENTER: ARROWS, RETURN, /, OR 'A':
```

Figure 7.30. **Matrix Tableau for the Transportation Structure**

Data can be entered at the question mark. Entering A causes an arc to be formed, and the computer requests the parameter values for the arc. The question mark can be moved around with the arrow keys. The / key moves the mark down and the RETURN key moves the mark up. Using this feature, the arcs can be easily entered.

The next step is to choose option 5 to enter the external flow data. After this operation, the model is complete. The remainder of the options are for modifying the data that have been entered, saving the data on the disk, recalling a previously saved model, or displaying the model currently in memory. Option 11 is particularly useful for problems that are "almost" network models except for some additional constraints that do not fit the network assumptions. Option 11 allows the network model to be saved on a data disk as an equivalent linear program. This model can subsequently be loaded into the linear model generator for treatment as a general linear program. The variables are given the names FI/J, where I and J are the node indices. Conservation of flow constraints and bounds are automatically created for the linear program.

The network generator is very flexible, and any network within the capacity limits of the program can be entered with little difficulty. A general rule for creating network models is that arc parameters should not be too large or too small or have too many significant digits. There are various small and large numbers defined in the computer program that can be confounded by parameters that have excessively large or small values. Almost all problems can be easily transformed to give parameter values within a reasonable range

The problem is solved by selecting option 10. This causes the solution program to be loaded. Its menu appears in Fig. 7.31.

With option 1, one can solve the problem. Various alternatives are available for the computer display including minimum output, continuous output showing the variables that enter and leave the basis at each iteration, and extensive output

1. SOLVE THE NETWORK WITH THE PRIMAL SIMPLEX
2. REVIEW SOLUTION
3. RETURN TO THE NETWORK GENERATOR TO REVISE MODEL
4. TURN PRINTER ON
5. RETURN TO DISK MENU

DISTRIBUTION IS LOADED
9 NODES AND 30 ARCS

ENTER AN OPTION NUMBER:

Figure 7.31. **Network Solution Algorithm Menu**

ARC PARAMETERS AND FLOWS
COST = –1475

ARCS THAT START AT ATL

GO TO	NUMBER	LOWER	UPPER	COST	GAIN	FLOW
CHIC	1	0	999999	4	1	100
DAL	2	0	999999	3	1	0
NY	3	0	999999	5	1	0

ARCS THAT START AT AUS

GO TO	NUMBER	LOWER	UPPER	COST	GAIN	FLOW
ATL	4	0	999999	5	1	0
DAL	5	0	999999	2	1	75
LA	6	0	999999	7	1	0

ARCS THAT START AT CHIC

GO TO	NUMBER	LOWER	UPPER	COST	GAIN	FLOW
SLACK	7	0	100	–20	1	100

.
.
.

ARCS THAT START AT SLACK

GO TO	NUMBER	LOWER	UPPER	COST	GAIN	FLOW
AUS	23	0	200	10	1	75
DAL	24	0	125	5	1	125
GAINS	25	0	100	14	1	0
ATL	26	0	100	99999	1	0
AUS	27	0	0	99999	1	0
CHIC	28	0	200	99999	1	0
DAL	29	0	300	99999	1	0
LA	30	0	200	99999	1	0

Figure 7.32 **Optimum Flow Solution**

showing intermediate results at each iteration. The latter is provided for the student interested in learning the details of the algorithm.

Two conclusions of the solution algorithm are possible: either there is no feasible solution to the problem or the optimum result will be obtained. The optimum result for the example problem is shown in Fig. 7.32 as it appears with the IBM PC version of the program. Because of screen limitations, the Apple II display is slightly different.

The program automatically adds a number of arcs not present in the original model. These include the artificial arcs that are inserted for each node. They can be identified by the large cost on the arcs. They are equivalent to the artificial variables introduced for equality constraints by the linear programming algorithm. An arc is also created for each slack flow. A new node is also added by the program with the name SLACK. All artificial and slack arcs originate or terminate at the SLACK node.

One other set of information is used by the program in the solution process, the node potentials. These correspond to the dual variables of linear programming and are shown in Fig. 7.33. When some arcs have nonzero lower bounds, the fixed external flows, also shown in this display, may be different than those originally entered. The *Microsolve* manual has more information on this.

Option 3 of the menu provides an opportunity to return to the network generator so that the model may be revised. Often the solution process is an iterative one, with network parameters sequentially changed to obtain a measure of the sensitivity of the solution to parameter variations. This is also a useful option when a modeling mistake is discovered.

Problems

Problems P7.18 through P7.25 use the transportation model given below.

NODE PARAMETERS

NODE	NAME	POTENTIAL	EXT. FLOW
1	ATL	11	–100
2	AUS	10	0
3	CHIC	15	–200
4	DAL	12	–300
5	GAINS	7	300
6	LA	12	–200
7	NY	14	100
8	PHOE	9	500
9	SLACK	0	0

Figure 7.33. **Node Potentials and External Flows**

Source	D1	D2	D3	D4	Supplies
	Destination				
S1	10	10	6	15	10
S2	5	15	10	12	15
S3	11	8	7	21	8
Demands	5	3	8	17	

P7.18 Show the basic solution when the basic cells are (S1,D2), (S1,D4), (S2,D1), (S2,D4), (S3,D1), and (S3,D3). Starting with this solution, solve the problem with the transportation simplex method.

P7.19 With the dual variables defined as:

$$u_1 = 0,\ u_2 = -3,\ u_3 = +3, \text{ and}$$
$$v_1 = 8,\ v_2 = 18,\ v_3 = 6,\ v_4 = 15,$$

find the corresponding complementary primal basic solution.

P7.20 With the partial selection of basic cells: (S1,D2), (S1,D4), (S2,D1), (S2,D4), and (S3,D1), what cells are candidates for the last basic cell?

P7.21 Find an initial basic solution using the southwest corner rule, an obvious variation on the northwest corner rule. Starting from this solution, do one iteration of the transportation simplex method.

P7.22 Find an initial basic solution with Vogel's method and do the transportation simplex algorithm to find an optimum solution.

P7.23 Find an initial basic solution with Russell's method and do the transportation simplex algorithm to find an optimum solution.

P7.24 Add another supplier to the problem with a supply of 5 units. The shipping costs to the four destinations are 4, 9, 7, and 13, respectively. Start from the optimum solution obtained without the new supplier and use the transportation simplex method to find a new optimum. Not all supplies need be used.

P7.25 Using the shipping costs originally given and the production and demand data given below, set up the transportation model to find the production schedule that maximizes profit.

Source Information

	Minimum Production	*Maximum Production*	*Cost of Production*
Source 1	10 units	15 units	$10/unit
Source 2	15	15	12
Source 3	0	8	13

Destination Information

	Minimum Sales	*Maximum Sales*	*Revenue at Sale*
Destination 1	5 units	5 units	$20/unit
Destination 2	3	10	25
Destination 3	0	8	22
Destination 4	10	20	30

P7.26 Solve the assignment problem shown below with the transportation simplex. Use any one of the methods for finding an initial solution. If alternative optimum solutions exist, find as many as you can.

	E	F	G	H
A	3	2	14	3
B	21	20	17	5
C	14	14	16	4
D	14	3	14	4

P7.27 A company has three workers. On a particular work day, six jobs are scheduled to be completed. A cost is estimated for each worker and job and is shown in the table below. Set up the transportation model for each of the situations below.

- **a.** Find the minimum cost assignment when each worker can do two jobs.
- **b.** Find an assignment to do as many jobs as possible with minimum cost when each worker can do only one job.
- **c.** Find a minimum cost assignment when each worker can do any number of jobs.

	Job					
Worker	*1*	*2*	*3*	*4*	*5*	*6*
A	3	2	2	6	4	6
B	4	3	7	5	3	3
C	9	9	7	9	7	6

P7.28 A company is planning its aggregate production schedule for the next three months. Units may be produced on regular time or overtime. The relevant costs and capacities are shown in the table below. The demands for each month, which must be met, are also shown. Units produced in a particular month may be sold in that month or kept in inventory until sale in a later month. There is a \$1 cost per unit for items kept in inventory for 1 month, a \$3 cost for items kept for 2 months, and a \$5 cost for items kept for 3 months. Initially there are 15 items in inventory, which have been in storage for 1 month. Sales may be backordered at a cost of \$2 per unit per month. Show the transportation model that when solved would yield the optimum production plan.

	Capacity (units)		*Production cost (\$/unit)*		*Demand*
Month	*Reg. time*	*Overtime*	*Reg. time*	*Overtime*	*(units)*
1	100	20	14	18	60
2	100	10	17	22	80
3	60	20	17	22	140

Computer Problems

P7.29 Solve P7.28 with the computer program.

P7.30 The cost matrix for a transportation problem is shown below together with supplies and demands. Set up and solve this problem as a network flow problem.

	Demander					
Source	*1*	*2*	*3*	*4*	*5*	*Supplies*
1	9	7	5	3	1	15
2	1	2	3	4	5	15
3	5	5	4	3	2	10
4	6	2	5	8	5	11
Demands	10	15	5	8	13	

P7.31 Consider a slight variation of P7.30. A new supplier is added, with a supply of 20 units. The unit shipping costs to demanders are shown below.

	Demander				
	1	*2*	*3*	*4*	*5*
New supplier	4	3	6	5	2

Each demander still has a minimum demand, as shown in the table for P7.30, but each demander can take as many as 10 additional units. Set up and solve the network model that will minimize distribution costs. All supplies must be utilized.

P7.32 The table below shows some of the information for a distribution problem. Supplies, demands, and direct shipping costs from suppliers to demanders are shown. On a second table are shipping costs to and from a terminal that can transship between suppliers and demanders. Additionally, the following restrictions must be met.

- **a.** All demands must be satisfied.
- **b.** Suppliers 1 and 2 can together ship no more than a total of 10 units to demander 5 directly.
- **c.** No shipping link can handle more than 7 units.
- **d.** The transshipment terminal can handle no more than 15 units.

Set up the network flow model and solve.

Direct Unit Shipping Costs

	Demander			
Supplier	*5*	*6*	*7*	*Supplies*
1	5	4	3	15
2	1	2	3	15
3	5	5	4	15
6	1	4	15	
Demands	17	15	20	

From Suppliers to Terminal

Suppliers	*1*	*2*	*3*	*4*
Terminal	2	2	3	3

From Terminal to Demanders

Dem.	*5*	*6*	*7*
	3	1	2

P7.33. A company has two manufacturing plants (A and B) and three sales outlets (I, II, and III). Shipping costs from the plants to the outlets are shown below.

	Outlet		
Plant	*I*	*II*	*III*
A	4	6	8
B	7	4	3

The company is to plan production, shipping and sales for the next two periods. The data for the periods is shown below. The plants can store products produced in one period for sale in the next. The maximum storage at each plant is 50 and the inventory cost is $1 per unit.

Plant Manufacturing Data

	Plant A		*Plant B*	
Period	*Unit cost ($)*	*Capacity*	*Unit cost ($)*	*Capacity*
1	8	175	7	200
2	10	150	8	170

Outlet Demand Data

	Selling price ($)			*Max. sales*		
Period	*I*	*II*	*III*	*I*	*II*	*III*
1	15	20	14	100	200	150
2	18	17	21	150	300	150

Find the solution that maximizes profit using a network flow model.

P7.34 A company makes three products in four plants. Because of differences in labor skills, different times are required to produce the products in the various plants. The time requirements (minutes per unit) are shown in the table below. A dash indicates that the product cannot be made at the plant. The demand for the products is also shown.

Time Requirements

	Plant				
Product	*1*	*2*	*3*	*4*	*Demand*
A	15	12	—	—	70
B	10	—	7	9	80
C	--	20	15	25	40

The total time available in each plant is 25 hours per week. The hourly charge for labor is $10, 12, 9, and 15 for plants 1, 2, 3, and 4, respectively. Not all the time available at a plant need be used. There is no labor charge for time not used.

Show the generalized network model (network with gains) that if solved would determine the minimum cost policy for producing the products in the amount demanded.

P7.35 A developing country has two mines from which fossil fuel can be obtained, labeled S1 and S2, two power plants that burn the fuel to produce electricity, labeled P1 and P2, and three cities that use the electricity, labeled C1, C2, and C3. The government's planning agency wants to determine the optimum plan for producing and delivering the electricity and for mining the fossil fuel for a given period of time. The demand at the cities is 1000 MWH for C1, 500 MWH for C2, and 3000 MWH for C3. Demand is measured in megawatt hours (MWH).

The power must be transmitted from power plants to cities over lines that have some losses. These losses depend on the origin and destination of the power transmitted and are given as a percentage of the power transmitted from the power plant.

Percent Power Loss

	City		
Plant	*C1*	*C2*	*C3*
P1	1	5	2
P2	8	4	9

The power plants burn the fossil fuel to produce electricity. The efficiency of a plant is measured in MWH produced per ton of fuel input. Each plant is limited in terms of the maximum input of fossil fuel allowed during the period. Each plant has a processing cost for the fossil fuel. This data are given in the table below.

Power Plant Data

Plant	*Efficiency (MWH/ton)*	*Max. Input (tons)*	*Processing cost per ton ($/ton)*
P1	1	4000	10
P2	0.9	3000	9

The fossil fuel must be shipped from the mines to the plant. The shipping costs are listed below in dollars per ton.

Shipping Cost ($/ton)

	Plant	
Mine	*P1*	*P2*
S1	6	12
S2	3	8

During the time period covered by the plan, a limited amount may be taken from each mine. For mine S1, 1200 tons may be mined for a cost of $9 per ton, and an additional 1500 tons can be mined for a cost of $12 per ton. For mine S2, 1500 tons can be mined at a cost of $13 per ton, with an additional 2000 tons available for $15 per ton.

Show in detail the network model that could be used to solve this problem. Find the optimum solution.

CHAPTER 8

Formulating Linear Programming Models, Including Goal Programming

In the last several chapters we have dwelt on the theory and algorithms associated with the solution of linear programming models. Here we return again to the formulation of models. Particularly stressed are procedures for dealing with problems with more than one objective.

Goal Programming (8.2)

Most decision-making situations do not have an obvious objective function. In fact, many decisions must be made in the face of competing objectives in an atmosphere of confrontation. Consider the city council making zoning decisions balancing the desires of residents, business persons, developers, and environmentalists; the corporate managers allocating the annual budgets to the several operating divisions; or the academic department head making course assignments to the members of the faculty. The problem of the decision maker is to balance the goals of the competitors in such a way that most are partially satisfied; in other words, to reach a compromise. The administrator is always looking for the perfect compromise, the one that satisfies everyone, but of course this is rarely found. Rather we have committees, commissions, elections, contests, or even chance as ways to arrive at decisions, which at best partially satisfy some of the participants.

To this point in the text, operations research has done little to alleviate this problem, as the optimization models we have discussed allow only one objective. The methods of goal programming, however, describe ways to deal with more than one objective function. This is not a complete answer to the problem, because whenever there are competing goals, a purely objective analysis can rarely yield the "best" decision. There will always be a subjective component of the solution procedure. The methods do provide organized ways of considering more than one goal and often yield compromise solutions that are acceptable to the protagonists.

GOALS

- Given a problem that has more than one objective, reflected by various goals, but that otherwise has the form of a linear program, be able to formulate the model that measures the relative attainment of the goals.
- Understand and be able to apply nonpreemptive goal programming.
- Understand and be able to apply preemptive goal programming.

DEFINITIONS

Objective Function (Z_k): One of several linear functions of the decision variables which evaluates the attainment of some measure of effectiveness.

$$Z_k = c_{1k}x_1 + c_{2k}x_2 + \dots c_{nk}x_n = \sum_{j=1}^{n} c_{jk}x_j \quad \text{for } k = 1, \dots, K .$$

Lower One-Sided Goal: The goal of having a value of "at least" some level for an objective. The goal might be written as a "greater than or equal to" constraint.

$$Z_k = \sum_{j=1}^{n} c_{jk}x_j \geq L_k ,$$

where L_k is the lower goal for the kth objective. For goal programming, however, this is not a firm constraint. The objective function value may fall below L_k if the goal is unobtainable or the "best" solution involves a compromise with other goals.

Upper One-Sided Goal: The goal of having a value of "at most" some level for an objective. The goal might be written as a "less than or equal to" constraint:

$$Z_k = \sum_{j=1}^{n} c_{jk}x_j \leq U_k ,$$

where U_k is the upper goal for the kth objective. Again this is a way to describe the goal and not a firm constraint.

Two-Sided Goal: The goal of having a value "equal to" some level for an objective. The goal might be written as an equality constraint:

$$Z_k = \sum_{j=1}^{n} c_{jk}x_j = G_k .$$

where G_k is the goal for the kth objective.

Usually a particular objective will appear as only one of these three kinds of goals, although it is conceivable that an objective could have both upper and lower goals with the range between them a region of indifference.

Goal Constraint: A constraint to be used in the linear programming model which measures the deviation from the goal.

$$\sum_{j=1}^{n} c_{jk}x_j - y_k^+ + y_k^- = L_k$$

or

$$\sum_{j=1}^{n} c_{jk}x_j - y_k^+ + y_k^- = U_k$$

or

$$\sum_{j=1}^{n} c_{jk}x_j - y_k^+ + y_k^- = G_k ,$$

where y_k^+ is the positive component (the amount the objective is above the goal), and y_k^- is the negative component (the amount the objective is below the goal). Note that all three types of goals are represented by the same type of linear constraint. Each goal constraint has a different pair of component variables.

Penalty Weights (p_k^+ and p_k^-): Constants that measure the per unit penalty for violating constraint k .

p_k^+ is the penalty applied to the positive component.

p_k^- is the penalty applied to the negative component.

The three kinds of goals are associated with the following penalty assignments.

lower one-sided goal: $p_k^- > 0, p_k^+ = 0$

upper one-sided goal: $p_k^- = 0, p_k^+ > 0$

two-sided goal: $p_k^- > 0, p_k^+ > 0.$

Nonpreemptive Goal Programming: Here the goals are considered of comparable importance. The penalties measure the relative importance of the goals and the objective function of the goal programming problem is simply the weighted sum of the deviations from the objectives. The objective is to

$$\text{Minimize } Z = \sum_{k=1}^{K} p_k^+ y_k^+ + p_k^- y_k^- .$$

Since the goals very often will be measured in different dimensions, the penalties play the double duty of transforming all goals to the same dimensional units and showing their relative importance. In this approach, the subjective step is the determination of the weights. Different weights will probably yield different solutions.

Preemptive Goal Programming: Here the goals are divided into sets and each set is given a priority. Thus we have first-priority goals, second-priority goals, and so on. The solution is obtained by first optimizing with respect to the first-priority goals. Then, holding constant the value of the first-priority objective function, the optimum solution is obtained for the second-priority goals. The feasible solution space for this second problem is the set of alternative optima for the first problem. The process continues until all priorities are thus considered. The goals within any set are related with weights as in nonpreemptive goal programming.

Of course the subjective part of this procedure is the division of the goals into priority sets and the selection of penalties within a priority set.

RESULTS

Sequential Procedure for Preemptive Goal Programming The following algorithm solves the preemptive goal programming problem as a sequence of linear programming problems.

A1 Divide the goals into priority sets, $S_1, S_2, \ldots, S_K$. Determine penalty weights relating goals within each set. Set up the constraints of the linear programming model including all the goal constraints. Let $p = 1$.

A2 Let the objective function for the pth priority set be:

$$\text{Minimize } Z_p = \sum_{k \in S_p} p_k^+ y_k^+ + p_k^- y_k^- .$$

Solve the linear program to obtain the solution, **x***, and the optimum objective function value, Z_p^*.

A3 If $p = K$, stop with **x*** the optimum solution. Otherwise add a constraint to the linear program which holds the pth objective function constant:

$$\sum_{k \in S_p} p_k^+ y_k^+ + p_k^- y_k^- = Z_p^* .$$

Increase p by one and go to step *A2*.

Although all goal constraints are included in the linear programming model for step A2, the goals for priority sets greater than p do not affect the solution. These constraints do not change the feasible solution space because the positive and negative component variables allow the goals to assume any values.

The constraint added in step A3 can be included in the tableau with the form

$$\sum_{k \varepsilon S_p} p_k^+ y_k^+ + p_k^- y_k^- + x_{ap} = Z_p^*.$$

Here x_{ap} is an artificial variable which will be the basic variable for the new constraint. When this constraint is added, the objective value is Z_p^*, so the artificial variable is initially zero. The artificial variable should be given a large cost for subsequent priority levels so that the equality constraint remains satisfied. After the constraint is added, row operations are required to bring the tableau to the *simplex* form. The objective function for the pth problem will be

$$\text{Minimize } Z_p = \sum_{k \varepsilon S_p} p_k^+ y_k^+ + p_k^- y_k^- + \sum_{k=1}^{p-1} M x_{ak}.$$

Streamlined Procedure for Preemptive Goal Programming This procedure allows the preemptive problem to be solved with the solution of a single linear programming model. Define a *set* penalty for each set of goals where

M_1 is the penalty for priority set S_1,

M_2 is the penalty for priority set $S_2, \ldots,$

M_K is the penalty for priority set S_K.

The set penalties are ordered such that

$M_1 >> M_2 >> \ldots >> M_K$ (Here >> means "much greater than.")

$M_K = 1.$

Use the objective function

$$\text{Min. } Z = M_1 \sum_{j \varepsilon S_1} p_j^+ y_j^+ + p_j^- y_j^- + M_2 \sum_{j \varepsilon S_2} p_j^+ y_j^+ + p_j^- y_j^- + \ldots$$

$$+ \sum_{j \varepsilon S_K} p_j^+ y_j^+ + p_j^- y_j^-$$

Solve the linear programming problem to obtain the solution **x***. If the set penalties have been chosen correctly this is the optimum solution.

If the method is done by hand, the set-penalty values can be carried symbolically as in the big M method used for artificial variables. If the solution is obtained with a computer program, using large coefficients may result in numerical difficulties. It may also be difficult to choose the penalties so that the priorities are preserved.

EXAMPLES

E8.1 A government agency has the responsibility of moving some toxic industrial waste which is located at five plant sites to three disposal facilities located in isolated parts of the country. The waste is to be transported by truck. There are a number of routes available and the problem is to choose the routes on which to move the waste. The agency also must choose the amount of waste to be delivered to each site. Because these are controversial questions, a public hearing is held. Representatives from a number of groups are present including residents near the disposal sites, residents along the routes, environmentalists, and representatives of the corporation that owns the plants. The corporation must pay the bill for the transportation. After much discussion the following goals become clear.

Residents near the sites : Maximize the amount sent to my site because jobs are proportional to the amount sent.

Residents near the transportation routes : Minimize the amount sent along my route because of the environmental impact of the truck travel.

Environmentalists : Minimize the total environmental impact of the shipments.

Corporation: Minimize the total cost of the shipments.

Early discussions reveal that these goals are entirely incompatible. Each group is in favor of maximizing or minimizing its individual goal. In order to bring order to the procedure, the agency creates a commission with members from each group. The commission has a staff of analysts who collect a variety of data. The transportation costs between plants and disposal sites are shown in Table 8.1 along with the amount of waste produced each month (measured in truckloads). The numbers in the table are in hundreds of dollars, but we will refer to the cost in terms of dollars. With the single objective of minimizing cost, the optimum solution is to send the waste by the least expensive route.

Let x_{ij} = the number of truckloads shipped from plant i to destination j .

The minimum cost solution is then:

$$x_{12} = 20, x_{21} = 10, x_{32} = 15, x_{42} = 17, x_{53} = 22, \text{ with } Z = \$651.$$

Table 8.1. **Cost per Truckload from Plant to Disposal Site**

		Plant				
		1	*2*	*3*	*4*	*5*
Disposal site	1	7	10	10	6	21
	2	4	15	6	3	18
	3	12	17	8	5	15
Waste		20	10	15	17	22

Table 8.2. **Environmental Impact per Truckload (EU)**

		Plant				
		1	*2*	*3*	*4*	*5*
Disposal site	1	50	35	90	60	50
	2	52	30	80	65	80
	3	71	40	110	75	70

The environmentalists and residents along the routes get together and determine the environmental impact for each route as shown in Table 8.2. An entry in the table provides a measure of environmental damage for each load passing through a route. For lack of other names the environmental measure is called EU. The solution that minimizes total EU can again be solved by observation:

$$x_{11} = 20, x_{22} = 10, x_{32} = 15, x_{41} = 17, x_{51} = 22, \text{ with } Z = 4620\text{EU}.$$

This solution disturbs some residents along the routes, since the waste must travel through their neighborhoods.

The residents at the sites cannot agree on individual goals. Each site wants all the deliveries. They do decide that they can live with their respective communities if the solution is fair. A fair solution is one in which each community gets approximately the same deliveries. Neither the solution of the corporation nor the solution of the environmentalists comes close to satisfying this goal.

To resolve the impasse the commission suggests that each group come up with numerical goals. The groups meet and, in the spirit of accommodation, state goals that are somewhat less restrictive than their individual optimums. The goals are:

Corporation : The cost of transportation should be no more than $725.

Environmentalists : The total environmental impact should be no more than 5000EU.

Residents along routes : No route should have more than 15 truckloads.

Residents at sites : The amount delivered at each site must be at least 25 truckloads but no more than 31.

The commission decides to honor the request of the residents along the routes as strict constraints. The other constraints are to be treated as goals in a goal programming model. The complete model is shown below. The notation used is

c_{ij} = the unit transportation cost from plant i to site j

e_{ij} = the unit environmental impact for the route from plant i to site j

s_i = the supply of waste at plant i .

Only the constraints of the model are shown. The objective function will depend on the approach used for goal programming.

GOAL PROGRAMMING MODEL

All waste must be moved:

$$(Si) \qquad \sum_{j=1}^{3} x_{ij} = s_i \qquad i = 1, \ldots, 5.$$

Upper one-sided transportation cost constraint:

$$(G1) \qquad \sum_{i=1}^{5} \sum_{j=1}^{3} c_{ij}x_{ij} - y_1^+ + y_1^- = 725.$$

Upper one-sided environmental constraint:

$$(G2) \qquad \sum_{i=1}^{5} \sum_{j=1}^{3} e_{ij}x_{ij} - y_2^+ + y_2^- = 5000.$$

Lower one-sided goals for sites (Each site must receive at least 25 loads):

$$(G3) \qquad \sum_{i=1}^{5} x_{i1} - y_3^+ + y_3^- = 25.$$

$$(G4) \qquad \sum_{i=1}^{5} x_{i2} - y_4^+ + y_4^- = 25.$$

$$(G5) \qquad \sum_{i=1}^{5} x_{i3} - y_5^+ + y_5^- = 25.$$

Upper one-sided goals for sites (Each site must receive no more than 31 loads):

$$(G6) \qquad \sum_{i=1}^{5} x_{i1} - y_6^+ + y_6^- = 31.$$

$$(G7) \qquad \sum_{i=1}^{5} x_{i2} - y_7^+ + y_7^- = 31.$$

$$(G8) \qquad \sum_{i=1}^{5} x_{i3} - y_8^+ + y_8^- = 31.$$

Nonnegativity and simple upper bounds on the variables (the requirements of the route residents):

$$0 \le x_{ij} \le 15 \quad \text{for } i = 1, \ldots, 5, j = 1, \ldots, 3.$$

For purposes of a sequential analysis we consider G1 and G2 to comprise individual priority sets and group G3, G4, G5, G6, G7, and G8 together to form a third set. The objectives for the three sets are

G1: Minimize $Z = y_1^+$

G2: Minimize $Z = y_2^+$

G3–G8: Minimize $Z = y_3^- + y_4^- + y_5^- + y_6^+ + y_7^+ + y_8^+$.

To gain understanding of the problem, we will solve the goal programming problem with the six possible sequences defined by the sets. The results are shown in Table 8.3.

To illustrate the construction of the table consider run 2. For this sequence of priorities,

$$Z_1 = y_1^+$$
$$Z_2 = y_3^- + y_4^- + y_5^- + y_6^+ + y_7^+ + y_8^+$$
$$Z_3 = y_2^+.$$

For the first iteration of the algorithm, $S_1 = \{G1\}$, and we use the objective

$$\text{Minimize } Z_1 = y_1^+.$$

Solving the linear program we obtain $Z_1 = 0$ and the following nonzero variables.

$x_{11} = 5, x_{12} = 15, x_{21} = 10, x_{32} = 15,$

$x_{41} = 2, x_{42} = 15, x_{51} = 8.83, x_{53} = 13.17,$

$y_2^+ = 38.33, y_3^+ = 0.83, y_4^+ = 20, y_5^- = 11.8, y_6^- = 5.17, y_7^+ = 14, y_8^- = 17.83,$

$Z_1 = 0, Z_2 = 25.8, Z_3 = 38.33.$

For the second iteration, we add a constraint that holds the first priority objective function constant:

$$y_1^+ = 0.$$

Since $S_2 = \{G3, G4, \ldots, G8\}$ the objective function is now

$$\text{Minimize } Z_2 = y_3^- + y_4^- + y_5^- + y_6^+ + y_7^+ + y_8^+.$$

Table 8.3. **Results of Sequential Goal Programming**

						Trips to sites		
Run	S_1	S_2	S_3	*Cost*	*Envir. impact*	*Site 1*	*Site 2*	*Site 3*
1	G1	G2	G3-G8	725	5038	25.8	45	13.2
2	G1	G3-G8	G2	725	5215	21	38	25
3	G2	G1	G3-G8	737	5000	27.8	45	11.3
4	G2	G3-G8	G1	874	5000	31	28.5	24.6
5	G3-G8	G1	G2	743	5200	25	31	28
6	G3-G8	G2	G1	875	5006	31	28	25

The solution of this linear program has $Z_2 = 11$ and nonzero variables

$$x_{11} = 5, x_{12} = 15, x_{21} = 10, x_{32} = 5, x_{33} = 10,$$
$$x_{41} = 2, x_{42} = 15, x_{51} = 4, x_{52} = 3, x_{53} = 15,$$
$$y_2^+ = 465, y_3^- = 4, y_4^+ = 13, y_6^- = 10, y_7^+ = 7, y_8^- = 6,$$
$$Z_1 = 0, Z_2 = 11, Z_3 = 465.$$

This solution improves the second-priority goal as expected.

For the third iteration, we add a second constraint that holds the second-priority objective function constant:

$$y_3^- + y_4^- + y_5^- + y_6^+ + y_7^+ + y_8^+ = 11.$$

Since $S_3 = \{G2\}$ we use the objective

$$\text{Minimize } Z_3 = y_2^+.$$

The solution of this linear program has $Z_3 = 215$ with the solution

$$x_{11} = 5, x_{12} = 15, x_{21} = 10, x_{32} = 15,$$
$$x_{42} = 7, x_{43} = 10, x_{51} = 6, x_{52} = 1, x_{53} = 15,$$
$$y_2^+ = 215, y_3^- = 4, y_4^+ = 13, y_6^- = 10, y_7^+ = 7, y_8^- = 6,$$
$$Z_1 = 0, Z_2 = 11, Z_3 = 215.$$

This solution improves the third-priority goal and is reported in Table 8.3.

Reviewing Table 8.3 the commission might conclude that the solutions identified by runs 1, 2, and 3 are unacceptable because of the wide variability of the number of deliveries to the sites. The solutions found in runs 4 and 6 are better in this respect but seem to be excessively costly. Run 5 gives a reasonable solution for cost and the shipments to the sites are within the desired limits, but the environmental costs are high. Since the corporation and the environmentalists are within approximately the same percentage of their goals, perhaps this solution will be acceptable to all.

One point is clear. Goal programming has not identified the optimum solution. In a multiobjective situation, the final decision must rest on subjective grounds. The method has, however, provided an organized procedure for identifying alternative solutions that perhaps will lead to an acceptable compromise.

PROBLEMS

P8.1 Use the priority ranking shown for run 5 and solve E8.1 using the streamlined procedure. Because of the size of the problem, a computer program must be used.

P8.2 The federal government suggests that a nonpreemptive approach be used to arrive at a solution for E8.1. The objective function is to represent total equivalent cost measured in dollars. The transportation costs enter the objective directly. A federal study has estimated the cost of environmental impact to be \$0.25 per EU. The costs of lost jobs at the sites differ because of economic conditions at the sites. The costs per job below the minimum level at the sites 1, 2, and 3 are, respectively, \$100, \$150, and \$50. Set up and solve this problem.

P8.3 A mutual fund manager has 200 million dollars to invest and five alternative investment opportunities. An investment portfolio is defined by specifying the number of units of each opportunity purchased. Each opportunity has a unit investment cost, which is known with certainty. The annual return for an investment is a random variable. Research has determined the expected value and variance per unit of investment. The expected return and variance of an opportunity is proportional to the number of units invested in the opportunity with the constants of proportionality given in the table below. The total expected return is the sum of the expected returns of the opportunities. Similarly, the total variance is the sum of the variances of the opportunities. Data concerning the problem is given in Table 8.4. Costs and annual returns are given in millions of dollars.

Three goals are determined for the investment portfolio. These are listed below in priority order.

GOAL 1: The annual return must be at least 50.

GOAL 2: The total variance must be no more than 150.

GOAL 3: The amount invested in opportunities 2 and 4 should be equal.

The budget limitation is a firm constraint. A preemptive goal programming approach is to be used.

a. Show the goal constraints that represent the three goals in the linear programming model.
b. Solve the problem by hand, using the sequential procedure.
c. Solve the problem by hand, using the streamlined procedure for goal programming.

Maximizing the Minimum (or Minimizing the Maximum) (8.3)

In a problem where more than one entity must pay the cost or realize the profit, minimizing total cost or maximizing total profit may not be acceptable. A global

Table 8.4. **Unit Data for Investment Opportunities**

	Opportunity				
	1	*2*	*3*	*4*	*5*
Cost	20	60	30	65	30
Expected return	6	15	6	12	5
Variance	36	81	20	8	0

optimum has no concern for fairness, and one entity may be treated poorly in comparison to another in the the global optimum solution. For instance, the optimum locations for fire stations may not be the solution that minimizes total response time, but rather the one that minimizes the maximum response time. One objective for fitting a line to a set of points is to minimize the total deviation between the points and the line. A reasonable alternative objective would be to minimize the maximum deviation. The corporate problem of allocating resources to decentralized divisions could be solved to maximize total profit; however, an alternative goal would be to maximize the minimum profit of the divisions. For problems that are otherwise linear this kind of objective can be modeled with linear programming.

GOAL

- When the objective is to maximize the minimum of a set of linear functions (or minimize the maximum), be able to write the linear program that models this objective.

RESULTS

Maximizing the Minimum: Let the linear functions involved be

$$Z_k = c_{1k}x_1 + c_{2k}x_2 + \dots c_{nk}x_n = \sum_{j=1}^{n} c_{jk}x_j \quad \text{for } k = 1, \dots, K.$$

Let the objective function be to

$$\text{Maximize } Z = \text{Minimum } \{ Z_1, Z_2, \dots, Z_K \}.$$

The linear program for this problem is

Maximize $Z = z$

Subject to

$$(\text{M}k) \qquad \sum_{j=1}^{n} c_{jk}x_j \geq z \quad \text{for } k = 1, \dots, K$$

and all other constraints of the linear problem. Note that K constraints are added to the problem, (M1), (M2), . . . (MK). The constraints force all the linear functions to be greater than the variable z. Furthermore, that variable is to be maximized. For the simplex technique, z must be moved to the left side of the constraints. Since z is in general unrestricted in sign, it may be necessary to replace z by its positive and negative components.

$$z = z^+ - z^-.$$

where $z^+ \geq 0$ and $z^- \geq 0$. This will not be necessary if all $c_{ij} > 0$.

Minimizing the Maximum:
Let the objective be to

$$\text{Minimize } Z = \text{Maximum } \{ Z_1, Z_2, \ldots, Z_K \}.$$

The linear program for this problem is

Minimize $Z = z$
Subject to

$$(\text{M}k) \qquad \sum_{j=1}^{n} c_{jk} x_j \leq z \quad \text{for } k = 1, \ldots, K$$

and all other constraints of the linear problem. The added constraints force all the linear functions to be less than or equal to the variable z that is to be minimized.

EXAMPLES

E8.2 Consider again the problem of E8.1. The commission members have agreed to accept a solution in which the environmental degradation will be limited to 5200 EU, no route will carry more than 15 trucks per month, and all sites will have delivered between 25 and 31 loads. It is further agreed that each plant will pay for the waste shipments originating at the plant. There is some disagreement here because the global solution probably will not be fair in the sense that the plants will not bear equal unit costs for disposing of the waste. The plants are independent profit centers of the corporation, so each has the goal of maximizing profit. The corporation decides to adopt a distribution policy that will minimize the maximum unit cost to be paid by any one of the five plants. Find the optimum solution.

The linear model for this case will have a constraint for the unit cost component of each plant. The unit cost is the total cost divided by the number of units shipped from the plant. For instance, at plant 1 the total cost will be

$$7x_{11} + 4x_{12} + 12x_{13}.$$

Since the total amount shipped is 20 loads, the unit cost is this expression divided by 20.

$$0.35x_{11} + 0.2x_{12} + 0.6x_{13}.$$

In order to minimize the maximum unit cost, the variable z is introduced and the constraint below is defined.

$$0.35x_{11} + 0.2x_{12} + 0.6x_{13} - z \leq 0.$$

A similar constraint is constructed for each plant.

$$(\text{P}i): \qquad \sum_{j=1}^{3} (c_{ij}/s_i)\, x_{ij} - z \leq 0 \qquad \text{for } i = 1, \ldots, 5.$$

The model also includes the other constraints describing the situation. All waste must be moved:

(S*i*): $$\sum_{j=1}^{3} x_{ij} = s_i \quad i = 1, \ldots, 5.$$

Environmental constraint:

(E): $$\sum_{i=1}^{5} \sum_{j=1}^{3} e_{ij} x_{ij} \leq 5200.$$

Site constraints:

(SL*j*): $$\sum_{i=1}^{5} x_{ij} \geq 25 \quad \text{for } j = 1, \ldots, 3.$$

(SU*j*): $$\sum_{i=1}^{5} x_{ij} \leq 31 \quad \text{for } j = 1, \ldots, 3.$$

Nonnegativity and simple upper bounds on the variables (the requirements of the route residents):

$$0 \leq x_{ij} \leq 15 \quad \text{for } i = 1, \ldots, 5, j = 1, \ldots, 3.$$

The objective function has only one term.

$$\text{Minimize } Z = z.$$

The solution to this defines a maximum unit cost of $z = 16.215$ with nonzero variables

$$x_{11} = 13.3, x_{12} = 6.7, x_{21} = 0.8, x_{22} = 1.2, x_{23} = 8\ x_{32} = 15,$$
$$x_{41} = 15, x_{43} = 2, x_{51} = 1.9, x_{52} = 5.1, x_{53} = 15.$$

The total transportation cost of this solution is 829. This result compares to the cost of 743 when the total cost was minimized subject to the same constraints. The attempt to provide a fairer solution has resulted in significantly increased total cost.

E8.3 The officers of the corporation realize that they have erred in the attempt at fairness. The model does not attempt to minimize overall cost of transportation. As an alternative they suggest that the maximum unit cost be limited to 16.5, but that the objective be to minimize total cost.

This modification is simply accomplished by adding the constraint

$$z \leq 16.5$$

and changing the objective function to

$$Z = \sum_{i=1}^{5} \sum_{j=1}^{3} c_{ij}x_{ij} \ .$$

The solution to this problem is much more satisfactory, with a cost of 774.8. The nonzero route flows are

$$x_{11} = 7, x_{12} = 13, x_{21} = 6.4, x_{23} = 3.6\ x_{32} = 15,$$
$$x_{41} = 10.6, x_{43} = 6.4, x_{51} = 4, x_{52} = 3, x_{53} = 15.$$

PROBLEM

P8.4 A company wants a production plan for the next six months. Projected orders for the company's products are listed below with the direct cost of production in each month. The plan must specify the amount to produce in each month to meet the demands. Any amount produced in excess of total demand can be stored in inventory at a cost of $4 per unit per month. Initial and final inventories are 0.

Month	*Demand units*	*Production cost ($/unit)*
1	1300	$100
2	1400	105
3	1000	110
4	800	115
5	1700	110
6	1900	110

In addition to the direct costs of production and inventory, overhead costs must be charged for the maximum production level obtained and the maximum inventory level obtained during the six-month period.

The overhead cost for production = $300*(maximum production level).

The overhead cost for inventory = $100*(maximum level of inventory).

These costs are charged only once during the six-month period.

Set up and solve the linear programming model that determines the minimum cost plan.

Computer Program

The models considered in this chapter can all be solved as linear programs, but because of the added constraints and variables required by the formulations, there are few interesting problems that allow hand solutions. Nonpreemptive goal programming, the streamlined procedure for preemptive goal programming, and the objective of maximizing the minimum all result in a single linear programming model that can be solved by standard procedures.

The sequential procedure for preemptive goal programming requires the solution of two or more linear programming models with added constraints and a modified objective function. Here it is convenient to have easy, interactive access to the model generator program as provided by *Microsolve*. The easiest way to perform the sequential procedure is to include an explicit constraint for the objective function of each priority set. Thus for run 2 of E8.1 we would include the constraints

$$y_1^+ - Z_1 = 0$$
$$y_3^- + y_4^- + y_5^- + y_6^+ + y_7^+ + y_8^+ - Z_2 = 0$$
$$y_2^+ - Z_3 = 0.$$

These constraints do not bind the solution, but they do provide an easy way to evaluate the three objectives described by the model.

For the first run in the sequence, we would adopt the objective function: Minimize $Z = Z_1$.

For the example, the solution to this problem has $Z = 0$. For the next step in the sequence we add the simple constraint $Z_1 = 0$, and change the objective function to: Minimize $Z = Z_2$.

For the example, the solution to this problem has $Z = 11$, so the next step in the sequence has two added constraints: $Z_1 = 0$ and $Z_2 = 11$. The new objective function is: Minimize $Z = Z_3$.

The solution to this problem is the optimum solution to the goal programming problem. These changes are particularly easy to accomplish with the *Microsolve* linear model generator.

At some point in the procedure, insertion of the equality constraint holding the value of a goal constant may cause the solution at the next step to be infeasible. This occurs because there is actually only one feasible solution, however, the numerical inaccuracy with which the goal value is specified in the constraint makes that solution infeasible. In this event, the optimum solution is the last feasible solution found.

Problems

P8.5 Consider the situation described in P8.4. Rather than be concerned about the overhead costs of production and inventory it is decided that the problem will be solved with a goal programming approach. The following goals are adopted.

GOAL 1: The average production cost is to be no more than $109 per unit.

GOAL 2: The maximum monthly production level in the six months is to be 1500 units.

GOAL 3: The maximum monthly inventory level in the six months is to be 100 units.

a. Assuming the priority of the goals is in the order given, use the streamlined procedure to solve this preemptive goal programming problem.

b. Assuming the priority of the goals is in the order given, use the sequential procedure to solve this problem.

c. Assuming the priority of the goals is the reverse of the order given, use the sequential procedure to solve this problem.

P8.6 A problem that arises from game theory is to find the values of the decision variables p_j for $j = 1, \ldots, n$, where a set of m linear functions of the variables are no more than the value of v, called the value of the game. The value of the game is to be maximized. The sum of the decision variables is to equal 1. Solve this problem for the linear functions given below.

$$
\begin{aligned}
&5p_1 + 4p_2 + 3p_3 \\
&3p_1 + 2p_2 + 4p_3 \\
&6p_1 + 2p_2 + 3p_3 \\
&1p_1 + 4p_2 + 5p_3 .
\end{aligned}
$$

P8.7 At Texas O & R University, the various engineering departments are located in buildings along a single street as shown in the map below. Distances shown on the map are in feet from the assumed origin. The dean of engineering wants to locate his office somewhere along the street. All locations are allowed (i.e., the street can be considered as a continuum of possible locations).

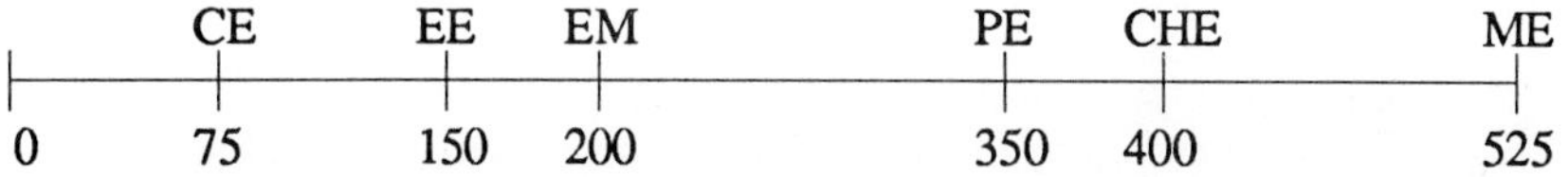

The dean has determined the weekly number of trips by faculty and others between his office and the departments. The trip table is shown below.

Trip Table

Dept.	ME	EE	CE	CHE	PE	EM
Trips	125	160	137	52	76	15

Model as a linear program and solve the problem of locating the dean's office with the following conditions.

a. The goal is to minimize the total distance traveled.
b. The goal is to minimize the maximum distance traveled from any of the departments.
c. The goal is to minimize the total distance traveled, but no department is to be more than 300 feet from the office.

Hint: The location of the dean's office is the decision variable x. The distance from the office to a department is computed by including a constraint for each department of the form below illustrated for the PE department.

$$x + L_{PE} - R_{PE} = 350,$$

where L_{PE} is the distance the dean's office is to the left of PE and R_{PE} is the distance the office is to the right of PE. The distance between the office and PE department is

$$L_{PE} + R_{PE}.$$

P8.8 Model and solve the problem of P8.7 when the departments are on a two-dimensional plane. Now the departments have both x and y coordinates as given in the table below.

Department Locations

Dept.	ME	EE	CE	CHE	PE	EM
x	525	150	75	400	350	200
y	25	50	125	175	300	400

Travel is rectilinear; that is, parallel to the axes of the coordinate system. This implies that the distance between the office and a department is the sum of the absolute distances between their coordinates. For instance, if the dean's office is at location (x,y), the distance to the PE office is

$$|x - 350| + |y - 300|.$$

Model as a linear program and solve the problem of locating the dean's office with the following conditions. (Note: The rectilinear distance measure is the only one that allows a linear programming formulation.)

a. The goal is to minimize the total distance traveled.
b. The goal is to minimize the maximum distance traveled from any of the departments.
c. The goal is to minimize the total distance traveled, but no department is to be more than 400 feet from the office.

P8.9 Solve problem P8.8 with a goal programming approach. Two goals are defined.

GOAL 1: The average distance traveled on any trip is no more than 240 feet.

GOAL 2: The office must be at least 100 feet away from every department.

Find the solution when the priority of the goals corresponds to the order given.

CHAPTER 9

Other Algorithms for Linear Programming

The Upper Bound Technique (9.1)

The computer time and memory required for the solution of a linear program depend heavily on the number of structural constraints of the model. To this point the structural constraints have included all the constraints except nonnegativity. The nonnegativity constraints are handled as part of the computational procedure, so they need not be explicitly represented. In this section we show how a second kind of constraint, those representing simple upper bounds, can be handled computationally and thus deleted from the set of structural constraints. The change requires a somewhat more complicated simplex algorithm, but the slightly increased computational effort is more than compensated for by the savings due to the reduced number of structural constraints.

GOAL

- To be able to solve small problems by hand with the simplex algorithm adapted for simple upper bounds.

DEFINITIONS

Simple Upper Bound: An upper limit to the value that can be attained by a decision variable. Some or all of the variables may be so bounded. The bound may be written in constraint form as

$$x_j \le u_j .$$

Slack and artificial variables are not bounded in this manner.

Complementary Decision Variables: A decision variable j with a simple upper bound can be represented by either x_j or x^*_j, where

$$x^*_j = u_j - x_j .$$

The two variables are said to be complementary to each other and only one will be used in the algorithm at any time. Both variables are bounded by zero and u_j.

$$0 \le x_j \le u_j$$

and

$$0 \le x^*_j \le u_j .$$

ALGORITHM

The algorithm is a variation of the simplex algorithm introduced in Chapter 4. We will describe the approach for the tableau presentation although it can be used with the revised simplex technique. The principal change is in the method used to select the leaving variable and the changes to the tableau caused by replacing a variable with its complement.

A1. Initialization Step Express the linear program in the equation form. Select basic variables that yield a basic feasible solution. If the basic variables have upper bounds, be sure that they have values no greater than these bounds. Transform the equations into the simplex form. Create the first simplex tableau using the coefficients from these equations. If row (0) has all nonnegative coefficients, stop with the optimum solution.

A2. Iterative Step

a. Find the column that has the most negative entry (we are using the "most negative value" rule here). Let that column be the pivot column with the index k.

b. Compute the ratios using the right side and the elements of the pivot column. Let y_{ik} be the element in the ith row of the pivot column and let b'_i be the current right side.

1. If $y_{ik} < 0$ and the basic variable for row (i) has an upper bound u, then let the ratio be $(u - b'_i) / (-y_{ik})$.

2. If $y_{ik} > 0$, then let the ratio be b'_i / y_{ik}.

Find the row with the minimum ratio. If there are no ratios defined by either condition 1 or 2, the solution is unbounded.

If the minimum ratio is greater than or equal to u_k (the upper bound of the entering variable), there is no pivot row. Go to step c3.

Otherwise the pivot row is the row for which the minimum ratio is obtained. Call this row (p).

If the minimum ratio is less than u_k and found with case 1, go to step c1.

If the minimum ratio is less than u_k and found with case 2, go to step c2.

c1. A basic variable has gone to its upper bound. Let j be the index of the basic variable. Replace the basic variable by its complement. To do this in the tableau, reverse the signs in column j (it only has one nonzero element, +1) and subtract u_j from the right side of row (p). Continue with step c2. (If x_j is basic, it will be replaced by x^*_j. If x^*_j is basic it will be replaced by x_j.)

c2. Create a new tableau by the following operations (these are the same as described in Chapter 4).

Let $\mathbf{y}_i$ be the vector of the ith row the original tableau and let $\mathbf{y}'_i$ be the ith row in the new tableau. Let p be the index of the pivot row. Let column k be the pivot column and let y_{ik} be the number in the ith row of the pivot column.

The pivot row in the new tableau is

$$\mathbf{y}'_p = \mathbf{y}_p \,/\, y_{pk}.$$

The other rows in the new tableau are

$$\mathbf{y}'_i = -y_{ik} * \mathbf{y}'_p + \mathbf{y}_i. \quad \text{for } i = 0, \ldots, m, \; i \neq p.$$

Go to step A3.

[These operations eliminate the entering variable from all equations except the pivot row. Thus the new pivot column will have a single 1 at row (p) and all other entries will be zero as required by the simplex form.]

c3. In this case the basis does not change, but the entering variable goes to its opposite bound.

Replace the entering variable by its complement. This is done by first subtracting u_k times the kth column from the right-hand side and then reversing the signs of all the elements in column k. Continue with step A3.

A3. Optimality Test If all entries in row (0) are nonnegative, stop with the optimum solution. Otherwise return to step A2.

Note that if the optimum solution contains any variables complementary to the original variables, the result must be transformed to the original variables.

EXAMPLES

E9.1 Consider the linear programming problem below with simple upper bounds prescribed for its variables. Fig. 9.1 shows the graphical representation of the problem. The circled numbers 1 and 2 show the constraints, and the upper bounds are shown with the dotted lines.

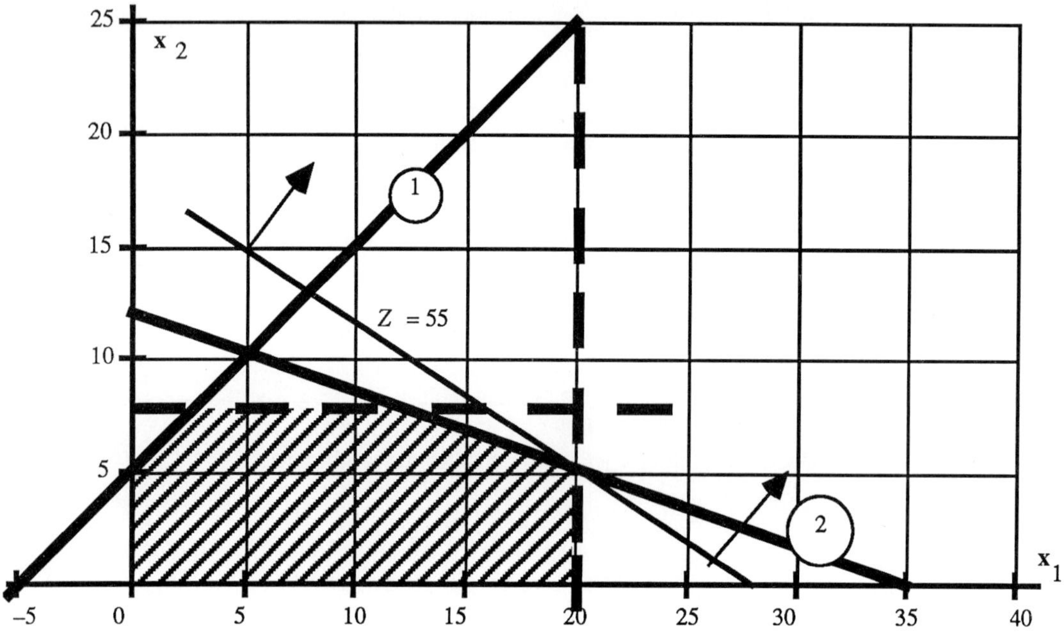

Figure 9.1 **Graphical Representation of a Model with Upper Bounds**

$$\text{Maximize } Z = 2x_1 + 3x_2$$

$$-x_1 + x_2 \leq 5 \quad (1)$$

$$x_1 + 3x_2 \leq 35 \quad (2)$$

$$0 \leq x_1 \leq 20, \; 0 \leq x_2 \leq 8.$$

Equality Form:

Maximize Z

$$Z - 2x_1 - 3x_2 = 0 \quad (0)$$

$$-x_1 + x_2 + x_{s1} = 5 \quad (1)$$

$$x_1 + 3x_2 + x_{s2} = 35 \quad (2)$$

$$x_1 \geq 0, x_2 \geq 0, x_{s1} \geq 0, x_{s2} \geq 0.$$

$$x_1 \leq 20, x_2 \leq 8.$$

Using the slack variables as the initial basis, the first tableau is

Iteration 1:

Basic var.	*Eq. no.*	*Coefficient of* Z	x_1	x_2	x_{s1}	x_{s2}	*Right side*	*Ratio*
Z	0	1	−2	**−3**	0	0	0	
x_{s1}	1	**0**	**−1**	**1**	**1**	**0**	**5**	5
x_{s2}	2	0	1	**3**	0	1	35	11.67

With the most negative value rule, x_2 is chosen to enter the basis. The minimum ratio for the rows is 5, which is less than the upper bound for x_2, so x_{s1} is chosen to leave the basis. The new tableau is

Iteration 2:

Basic var.	Eq. no.	Z	x_1	x_2	x_{s1}	x_{s2}	Right side	Ratio
Z	0	1	**−5**	0	3	0	15	
x_2	1	**0**	**−1**	**1**	**1**	**0**	**5**	(8 − 5)/(1) = 3
x_{s2}	2	0	**4**	0	−3	1	20	5

Column 1 is the pivot column. Since x_2 has an upper bound of 8, the negative coefficient in equation 1 must be considered in determining the ratio. Row (1) contributes the minimum ratio, indicating that x_2 is going to its upper bound. As in step c1 of the algorithm, we must replace x_2 by its complement x^*_2.

Basic var.	Eq. no.	Z	x_1	x^*_2	x_{s1}	x_{s2}	Right side
Z	0	1	−5	0	3	0	15
x^*_2	1	0	−1	−1	1	0	−3
x_{s2}	2	0	4	0	−3	1	20

Now performing row operations to regain the simplex form, we find the new tableau:

Iteration 3:

Basic var.	Eq. no.	Z	x_1	x^*_2	x_{s1}	x_{s2}	Right side	Ratio
Z	0	1	0	5	**−2**	0	30	
x_1	1	0	1	1	**−1**	0	3	(20 − 3)/(1) = 17
x_{s2}	2	**0**	**0**	**−4**	**1**	**1**	**8**	8

Column x_{s1} is the pivot column and row (2) is the pivot row. The new tableau is

Iteration 4:

Basic var.	Eq. no.	Z	x_1	x^*_2	x_{s1}	x_{s2}	Right side	Ratio
Z	0	1	0	**−3**	0	2	46	
x_1	1	**0**	**1**	**−3**	**0**	**1**	**11**	(20 − 11)/(3) = 3
x_{s1}	2	0	0	**−4**	1	1	8	—

Variable x^*_2 must enter the basis. Row (2) shows no ratio because the slack variable is unbounded. Therefore, row (1) has the minimum ratio and x_1 must leave the basis. Since x_1 is going to its upper bound, we must replace it with its complement. Again performing step c1,

Basic var.	Eq. no.	Coefficient of Z	x_1	x^*_2	x_{s1}	x_{s2}	Right side
Z	0	1	0	–3	0	2	46
x_1	1	0	–1	–3	0	1	–9
x_{s1}	2	0	0	–4	1	1	8

Bringing x^*_2 into the basis,

Basic var.	Eq. no.	Coefficient of Z	x^*_1	x^*_2	x_{s1}	x_{s2}	Right side
Z	0	1	1	0	0	1	55
x^*_2	1	0	0.333	1	0	–0.333	3
x_{s1}	2	0	1.333	0	1	–0.333	20

This tableau satisfies the optimality conditions because all entries in row (0) are nonnegative. The final basic solution has x^*_1 nonbasic and x^*_2 basic with value 3. To obtain the values for the original variables, we must compute the complements of these two variables.

$$x_1 = u_1 - x^*_1 = 20 - 0 = 20$$
$$x_2 = u_2 - x^*_2 = 8 - 3 = 5.$$

E9.2 Change the problem above so that the upper bound of x_2 is 4. The graphical representation of this problem is in Fig. 9.2. The first tableau for this case appears below.

Iteration 1:

Basic var.	Eq. no.	Coefficient of Z	x_1	x_2	x_{s1}	x_{s2}	Right side	Ratio
Z	0	1	–2	**–3**	0	0	0	
x_{s1}	1	0	–1	**1**	1	0	5	5
x_{s2}	2	0	1	**3**	0	1	35	11.67

Since the bound on the entering variable is 4, which is less than the minimum ratio, the basis does not change. The tableau will change, as in step c3 of the algorithm, to replace x_2 with its complement. The solution moves to (0,4) on the figure.

Iteration 2:

Basic var.	Eq. no.	Coefficient of Z	x_1	x^*_2	x_{s1}	x_{s2}	Right side	Ratio
Z	0	1	**–2**	3	0	0	12	
x_{s1}	1	0	**–1**	–1	1	0	1	—
x_{s2}	2	0	**1**	–3	0	1	23	23

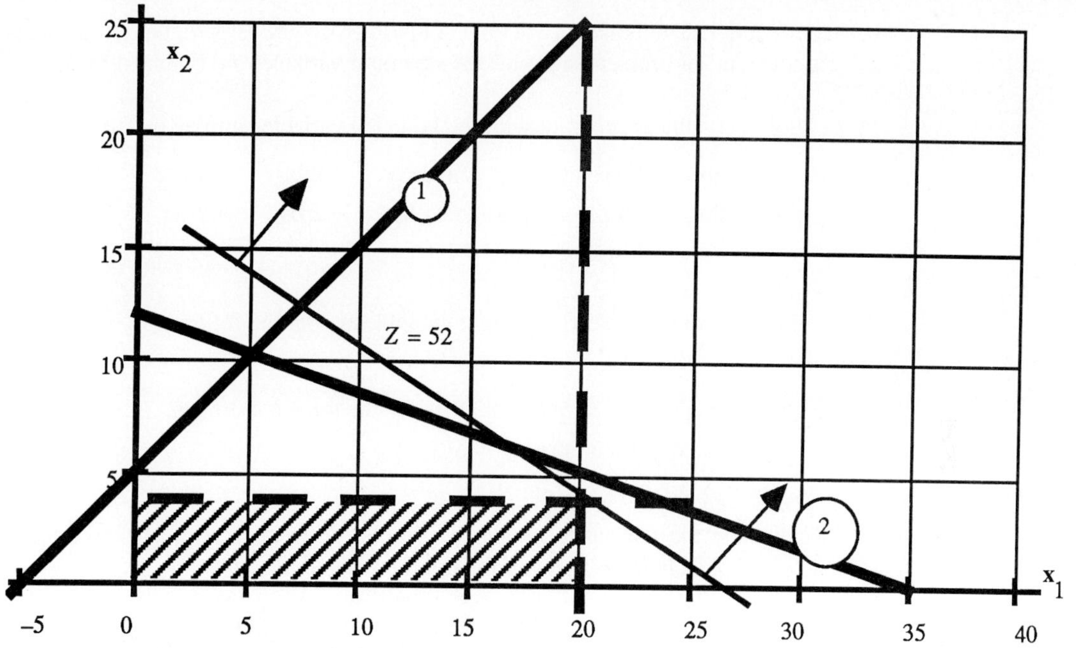

Figure 9.2 **Example with Upper Bound on x_2 Changed to 4**

In this iteration, x_1 must enter the basis. Since the minimum ratio is again greater than the upper bound u_1, the basis does not change, but the complement of x^*_1 replaces x_1. The solution is now (20,4). The new tableau is

Iteration 3:

Basic var.	*Eq. no.*	*Coefficient of* Z	x^*_1	x^*_2	x_{s1}	x_{s2}	*Right side*
Z	0	1	2	3	0	0	52
x_{s1}	1	0	1	–1	1	0	21
x_{s2}	2	0	–1	–3	0	1	3

This is the optimum solution. Since x^*_1 and x^*_2 are nonbasic and therefore at zero, the original variables are

$$x_1 = 20 - 0 = 20 \text{ and } x_2 = 4 - 0 = 4.$$

PROBLEMS

As will be discussed in Chapter 13, linear programming is often used to solve a relaxation of the integer programming model. The problems below represent binary integer programming models in which the requirement that the variables be either 0 or 1 has been replaced with the less restrictive requirement that the variables be between 0 and 1. The bounded variable simplex procedure is particularly useful for solving this kind of problem since all the structural variables are bounded by 1.

P9.1 Solve this linear program with the bounded variable simplex method.

$$\begin{array}{llllllll} \text{Maximize} & 84x_1 & + 48x_2 & + 25x_3 & + 29x_4 & + 128x_5 & \\ \text{Subject to} & 49x_1 & + 30x_2 & + 19x_3 & + 29x_4 & + 91x_5 & \leq 130 \\ & \multicolumn{6}{l}{0 \leq x_j \leq 1 \text{ for } j = 1, \ldots, 5 .} \end{array}$$

P9.2 For the problem below, construct the tableau with the following information:

x_{s1}, x_{s2}, and x_{s3} are the surplus variables for the three constraints,
x_2, x_4, x_{s1}, and x_{s3} are nonbasic,
x_1, x_3, and x_{s2} are basic.

Manipulate the tableau to obtain the simplex form and continue the bounded variable simplex technique to obtain the optimum solution.

$$\begin{array}{llllll} \text{Minimize} & 7x_1 & + 3x_2 & + 6x_3 & + 5x_4 & \\ \text{Subject to} & 2x_1 & + x_2 & + x_3 & + x_4 & \geq 2 \\ & x_1 & + 2x_2 & + 2x_3 & + x_4 & \geq 2.5 \\ & x_1 & + x_2 & + 2x_3 & + 2x_4 & \geq 2.5 \\ & \multicolumn{5}{l}{0 \leq x_j \leq 1 \text{ for } j = 1, 2, 3, 4 .} \end{array}$$

The Dual Simplex Method (9.2)

The primal simplex method we have studied operates on a feasible but nonoptimal solution (a primal feasible solution) and drives it to optimality. The dual simplex method operates on an infeasible but superoptimal solution (a dual feasible solution) and drives it to feasibility. This method is useful for reoptimizing a problem after a constraint has been added or some parameters of the problem have been changed. It is also useful for problems for which a dual feasible solution can be easily found.

GOAL

- To be able to apply the dual simplex method to a simplex tableau in which all the elements of row (0) are nonnegative but one or more of the right sides are negative.

ALGORITHM

The iterative step of the primal simplex method (the one we have studied until now) first selects a variable to enter the basis and then finds the variable that must leave the basis to maintain feasibility. The dual simplex method does the opposite. It first selects a variable to leave the basis and then finds the variable that must enter the basis to maintain optimality. This is the principal operative difference between the two methods.

A1. Initialization Step The procedure usually begins with an optimal tableau created by using the primal simplex method, but with some changes in the problem causing one or more right sides to be negative. A requirement of the method is that all elements of row (0), except the right side, be nonnegative. The tableau must be in the simplex form. If the right side has all nonnegative entries, stop with the optimum feasible solution.

A2. Iterative Step

a. Find the row with the most negative right side. (Actually any row with a negative value will do, but we are using the "most negative value" rule). Let that row be the pivot row with the index p. The basic variable for row p is to leave the basis.

b. For each negative coefficient in row p, compute the negative of the ratio between the number in row (0) and the coefficient in row (p). If there are no negative coefficients, stop, because there is no feasible solution.

Let the column with the minimum ratio be the pivot column. This is the variable to enter the basis. The index of the pivot column is k.

$$-y_{0k} / y_{pk} = \text{Min } \{-y_{0h} / y_{ph} \mid y_{ph} < 0, h = 1, \ldots, n\}$$

c. Create a new tableau by the following operations (these are the same as for the primal method).

Let $\mathbf{y}_i$ be the vector of the ith row of the original tableau and let $\mathbf{y}'_i$ be the ith row in the new tableau. Let p be the index of the pivot row, k the index of the pivot column, and y_{ik} the number in the ith row of the pivot column.

The pivot row in the new tableau is

$$\mathbf{y}'_p = \mathbf{y}_p / y_{pk}.$$

The other rows in the new tableau are

$$\mathbf{y}'_i = -y_{ik} * \mathbf{y}'_p + \mathbf{y}_i \quad \text{for } i = 0, \ldots, m, i \neq p.$$

[These operations eliminate the entering variable from all equations except the pivot row. Thus the new pivot column will have a single 1 at row (p) and all other entries will be zero as required by the simplex form.]

A3. Feasibility Test If all entries on the right side are nonegative, stop with the optimum solution. Otherwise return to step A2.

EXAMPLES

In Chapter 6 we investigated changes in a linear programming model that caused the optimum solution to become infeasible. We repeat here some examples from that chapter and use the dual simplex method to recover optimality. The original problem with the optimal primal simplex tableau is shown below. The variables x_{s1}, x_{s2}, and x_{s3} are the slack variables for the three constraints.

$$\text{Maximize } Z = 2x_1 + 3x_2$$
$$-x_1 + x_2 \le 5 \qquad (1)$$
$$x_1 + 3x_2 \le 35 \qquad (2)$$
$$x_1 \le 20 \qquad (3)$$
$$x_1 \ge 0,\ x_2 \ge 0.$$

Optimal Tableau:

Basic var.	*Eq. no.*	*Coefficient of* Z	x_1	x_2	x_{s1}	x_{s2}	x_{s3}	*Right side*
Z	0	1	0	0	0	1	1	55
x_2	1	0	0	1	0	0.333	–0.333	5
x_1	2	0	1	0	0	0	1	20
x_{s1}	3	0	0	0	1	–0.333	1.333	20

CHANGING THE RIGHT SIDE OF CONSTRAINTS

E9.3 Let b_2 go to 20 and b_3 go to 26.
This change only affects the right side of the final tableau.

Basic var.	*Eq. no.*	*Coefficient of* Z	x_1	x_2	x_{s1}	x_{s2}	x_{s3}	*Right side*
Z	0	1	0	0	0	1	1	46
x_2	1	0	0	1	0	0.333	–0.333	-2
x_1	2	0	1	0	0	0	1	26
x_{s1}	3	0	0	0	1	–0.333	1.333	33

The value of x_2 is negative, as indicated by the right side of row (1), so x_2 must leave the basis. The only negative entry in row (1) is the coefficient for x_{s3}, so this variable must enter the basis. To change the tableau we perform the usual pivot operations. First divide through row (1) by the pivot element (–0.333). Then eliminate each nonzero coefficient in the x_{s3} column by multiplying the pivot row by a constant and adding it to the concerned row. The resultant tableau appears below.

Basic var.	*Eq. no.*	*Coefficient of* Z	x_1	x_2	x_{s1}	x_{s2}	x_{s3}	*Right side*
Z	0	1	0	3	0	2	0	40
x_{s3}	1	0	0	–3	0	–1	1	6
x_1	2	0	1	3	0	1	0	20
x_{s1}	3	0	0	4	1	1	0	25

Since the right sides are all positive, this is a feasible solution, and since the coefficients in row (0) are nonnegative, this must be the optimal solution. In general there is no guarantee that a feasible solution will be obtained in one iteration.

ADD A NEW CONSTRAINT

E9.4. Add the following constraint to the model.

$$x_2 \geq 10.$$

The current optimal solution, $x_1 = 20$ and $x_2 = 5$, does not satisfy this constraint, so action must be taken to incorporate it into the tableau. In Chapter 6 we added both a surplus variable and an artificial variable so that the primal simplex could be used. Here we add only the surplus variable and use the dual simplex method. With the surplus the constraint becomes

P(4) $$x_2 - x_{s4} = 10.$$

Adding the negative of this row to the tableau, together with a new column for the surplus variable,

Basic var.	Eq. no.	Coefficient of Z	x_1	x_2	x_{s1}	x_{s2}	x_{s3}	x_{s4}	Right side
Z	0	1	0	0	0	1	1	0	55
x_2	1	0	0	1	0	0.333	–0.333	0	5
x_1	2	0	1	0	0	0	1	0	20
x_{s1}	3	0	0	0	1	–0.333	1.333	0	20
x_{s4}	4	0	0	–1	0	0	0	1	–10

To regain the simplex form for column x_2, we must add row (1) to row (4). The resulting tableau is

Basic var.	Eq. no.	Coefficient of Z	x_1	x_2	x_{s1}	x_{s2}	x_{s3}	x_{s4}	Right side
Z	0	1	0	0	0	1	1	0	55
x_2	1	0	0	1	0	0.333	–0.333	0	5
x_1	2	0	1	0	0	0	1	0	20
x_{s1}	3	0	0	0	1	–0.333	1.333	0	20
x_{s4}	4	0	0	0	0	0.333	–0.333	1	–5

This solution is superoptimal but not feasible. x_{s4} must leave the basis. Only x_{s3} has a negative coefficient in row (4), so this variable must enter the basis. Performing the usual procedure for changing the tableau we obtain

Basic var.	Eq. no.	Coefficient of Z	x_1	x_2	x_{s1}	x_{s2}	x_{s3}	x_{s4}	Right side
Z	0	1	0	0	0	2	0	3	40
x_2	1	0	0	1	0	0	0	–1	10
x_1	2	0	1	0	0	1	0	3	5
x_{s1}	3	0	0	0	1	1	0	4	0
x_{s3}	4	0	0	0	0	–1	1	–3	15

This solution is both feasible and optimal.

PROBLEMS

P9.3 Solve the problem below with the dual simplex method. Let the initial basis be the surplus variables of the constraints. With this selection, the initial basis is dual feasible and primal infeasible.

$$\begin{array}{llllll} \text{Minimize} & 3x_1 & + 7x_2 & + 4x_3 & + 5x_4 & \\ \text{Subject to} & 2x_1 & + x_2 & + 3x_3 & + 4x_4 & \geq 7 \\ & x_1 & + 2x_2 & + 4x_3 & + 2x_4 & \geq 6 \\ & 3x_1 & + 4x_2 & + x_3 & + x_4 & \geq 5 \\ & \multicolumn{5}{l}{x_j \geq 0 \text{ for } j = 1, 2, 3, 4.} \end{array}$$

P9.4 A linear program is given below along with the optimum tableau.

$$\text{Maximize } Z = 5x_1 - 3x_2 + 4x_3 - x_4$$

Subject to

$$\text{(P1)} \quad 3x_1 + 4x_2 + 3x_3 - 5x_4 \leq 13$$

$$\text{(P2)} \quad 5x_1 - 3x_2 + x_3 + 2x_4 \leq 15$$

$$x_j \geq 0 \text{ for } j = 1, 2, 3, 4.$$

Optimal Tableau:

Basic var.	*Eq. no.*	Z	x_1	x_2	x_3	x_4	x_{s1}	x_{s2}	*Right side*
			Coefficient of						
Z	0	1	5.181	1.637	0	0	0.819	1.546	33.82
x_3	1	0	2.818	−0.636	1	0	0.182	0.455	9.18
x_4	2	0	1.091	−1.182	0	1	−0.091	0.273	2.91

a. Change the right sides to $b = (20,5)^T$. Create the new tableau representing the basic solution. Use the dual simplex method to find the optimal solution.

b. Starting from the tableau given above, add the constraint

$$x_1 + x_2 + x_3 + x_4 \leq 10.$$

Incorporate this constraint into the tableau and use the dual simplex method to find the new optimal solution.

Computer Program

The simplex algorithm of *Microsolve* uses the upper bound technique so that simple upper bounds are handled by the solution procedure and need not be entered as explicit constraints in the model. This results in significant savings in both model size and the computer time required to solve the model.

The upper bound technique has a different implementation in *Microsolve* than described in this chapter. Variables are not complemented when they reach their bound, and they always appear as they were originally defined in the model. A nonbasic variable will be in one of two states, at zero or at its upper bound. The rules of the simplex technique are modified slightly to account for the fact the a variable may enter the basis by either increasing from zero or decreasing from its upper bound. Similarly, a variable may leave the basis by decreasing to zero or increasing to its upper bound. When the entering variable reaches its opposite bound before any basic variable goes to a nonbasic state, the entering variable is also the leaving variable and the basis does not change.

The detailed output of the *Microsolve* linear programming algorithm shows these various possibilities. To illustrate, we will use the problem described in E9.1. Fig. 9.3 shows the computer display at the end of iteration 3 when x_1 and x_{s1} are basic, x_2 is nonbasic at its upper bound, and x_{s2} is nonbasic at zero. This same information is shown as Iteration 4 in E9.1. Note that the computer program maintains the original variable x_2 at a value of 8, while E9.1 has complemented x_2.

In the test to determine the variable to enter the basis, we must recognize that while a variable at the zero level requires a negative reduced cost to enter the basis, a variable at its upper bound requires a positive reduced cost to enter. Thus in Fig. 9.4, we have X2 entering the basis with a positive reduced cost.

To find the variable to leave the basis, we note that the signs of the coefficients in the column for the entering variable have different meanings depending on whether the entering variable is increasing or decreasing. Since X2 is decreasing, a positive sign in the column (shown as ALPHA in the Fig. 9.5) indicates that the basic variable corresponding to the row is increasing. Fig. 9.5 shows that the basic variables for both rows 1 and 2 are increasing as X2 enters the

BASIC SOLUTION - PHASE 2 - ITER. 3

VAR.	NAME	VALUE	STATUS
1	X1	11	BASIC-1
2	X2	8	BOUND
3	SLK-1	8	BASIC-2
4	SLK-2	0	ZERO

OBJECTIVE = 46

Figure 9.3. **Computer Representation of Basic Solution**

COMPUTING REDUCED COSTS

COL.	VAR.	STATUS	D(J)
2	X2	BOUND	3
3	SLK-2	ZERO	2

Figure 9.4. **Computer Display of Reduced Costs**

VARIABLE X2 ENTERING BASIS
BY DECREASING FROM ITS UPPER BOUND.
UPPER BOUND ON X2 IS 8.

ROW	XB(I)	ALPHA	RATIO
1	11	3	3
2	8	4	249997.7

Figure 9.5. **Computer Display of Ratio Test**

BASIC SOLUTION - PHASE 2 - ITER. 4

VAR.	NAME	VALUE	STATUS
1	X1	20	BOUND
2	X2	5	BASIC-1
3	SLK-1	20	BASIC-2
4	SLK-2	0	ZERO

OBJECTIVE = 55

Figure 9.6. **Computer Display of Solution after the Basis Change**

basis. X1 leaves the basis by going to its upper bound. The ratio for row (2) is high because the basic variable for row (2) is a slack variable. Slack variables are given an upper bound of 999999.

After the pivot operation, the new basic solution is shown in Fig. 9.6. This happens to be the optimum solution.

Problems

Data for P9.5–P9.8 The tableau below shows the results of the simplex method at an intermediate iteration. The variables have the following simple upper bounds.

$$x_1 \le 6,\ x_2 \le 8,\ x_3 \le 10,\ x_4 \le 6,\ x_5 \le 1,\ x_6 \le 7.$$

For each case of P9.5 through P9.8, start from the tableau below and perform the operations required. Show the resulting tableau and give the resulting basic solution in terms of the original variables (not complemented).

Basic var.	*Eq. no.*	*Coefficient of* Z	x^*_1	x_2	x_3	x^*_4	x_5	x_6	*Right side*
Z	0	1	0	–2	0	–4	–3	0	20
x_6	1	0	0	4	0	–3	1	1	3
x^*_1	2	0	1	–3	0	2	–1	0	4
x_3	3	0	0	3	1	5	2	0	7

P9.5 Let x^*_4 enter the basis and do one simplex iteration.

P9.6 Let x_2 enter the basis and do one simplex iteration.

P9.7 Let x_5 enter the basis and do one simplex iteration.

P9.8 Start from the tableau above and use the bounded variable simplex technique to find the optimum solution. Use the "most negative value" rule to select the variable to enter the basis at each iteration.

P9.9 An integer program is given below.

$$\text{Maximize } Z = x_1 + x_2$$

Subject to

(P1) $$-11x_1 + 4x_2 - x_3 = 4$$

(P2) $$2x_1 + x_2 + x_4 = 3$$

(P3) $$-6x_1 + 4x_2 + x_5 = 7$$

$$x_j \geq 0 \text{ and integer for } j = 1, 2, 3, 4, 5.$$

One way to solve an integer program is to relax (forget) the integer requirement and solve the resulting linear program. When this is done for the problem above the following tableau is obtained.

Basic var.	*Eq. no.*	*Coefficient of* Z	x_1	x_2	x_3	x_4	x_5	*Right side*
Z	0	1	0	0	0	0.714	0.071	2.64
x_2	1	0	0	1	0	0.428	0.142	2.28
x_1	2	0	1	0	0	0.285	–0.071	0.357
x_3	3	0	0	0	1	–1.42	1.35	1.21

The cutting plane method for integer programming then adds a constraint to the linear program called a "cut." This constraint retains all the integer solutions but makes some of the real solutions to the linear program infeasible. A valid cut for this problem is the constraint

$$3x_4 + x_5 \geq 2.$$

Using a surplus variable x_6, this constraint can be written

$$-3x_4 - x_5 + x_6 = -2.$$

Add this constraint to the tableau, do row operations to regain the simplex form, and perform the dual simplex method to obtain a feasible solution. The variable x_6 is the basic variable for the new row.

P9.10 An integer program is given below.

$$\text{Maximize } Z = -x_1 - x_2$$

Subject to

(P1) $4x_1 + 10x_2 \geq 12$

(P2) $10x_1 + 4x_2 \geq 12$

$x_j \geq 0$ and integer for $j = 1, 2$.

By relaxing the integrality requirement and solving the resulting linear program, the following tableau is obtained. Some of the numbers are shown as fractions.

Basic var.	Eq. no.	Coefficient of Z	x_1	x_2	x_{s1}	x_{s2}	Right side
Z	0	1	0	0	6/84	6/84	–144/84
x_2	1	0	0	1	–10/84	4/84	72/84
x_1	2	0	1	0	4/84	–10/84	72/84

Starting from this tableau, sequentially add the cut constraints:

(C1) $4x_1 + 9x_2 \geq 12$

(C2) $4x_1 + 8x_2 \geq 12$

(C3) $9x_1 + 4x_2 \geq 12$

(C4) $8x_1 + 4x_2 \geq 12$

After each cut is added, solve the resulting tableau with the dual simplex technique. The final solution should have integer values for the variables.

Data for P9.11–P9.13. For each case of the P9.11 through P9.13, start from the tableau below and perform the operations required. Show the resulting tableau and give the resulting basic solution. Comment on the optimality and feasibility of the solution obtained..

Basic var.	Eq. no.	Coefficient of Z	x_1	x_2	x_3	x_4	x_5	x_6	Right side
Z	0	1	0	2	0	4	3	0	20
x_6	1	0	0	6	0	–1	1	1	–3
x_1	2	0	1	3	0	2	–1	0	8
x_3	3	0	0	–3	1	–5	2	0	–7

P9.11 Let row (1) be the pivot row and perform one dual simplex iteration.

P9.12 Let row (3) be the pivot row and perform one dual simplex iteration.

P9.13 Starting from the tableau above, use the "most negative value" rule to select the pivot row. Use the dual simplex method to obtain an optimal, feasible solution.

CHAPTER 10

Network Analysis, Including PERT-CPM

Notation (10.2)

The word "network" is a common term describing the interrelationships between a number of different entities. Thus we have transmission networks, distribution networks, communications networks, project networks, and good-old-boy networks. Networks are popular because they are easy to draw. Thus we have a variety of maps, diagrams, and charts showing the entities (nodes) and their interrelationships (branches) as illustrated in Fig. 10.1. Networks are visual, and the relationships they describe are usually simple, easy to understand, and sometimes capable of manipulation.

There are important characteristics of networks that cannot easily be observed. For instance, the ambulance dispatcher needs to know the least travel time route through a road network, the pipeline designer wants the minimum length layout of pipes, the public works officer must find the maximum flow through the storm sewer system, and the manager must identify the activities on the critical path for a project network. The questions above are examples of, respectively, the shortest route problem, the minimal spanning tree problem, the maximum flow problem, and the project planning problem. The algorithms to solve these problems are each considered in the units of this chapter. In this section we list the general definitions and notation that will be used throughout the chapter.

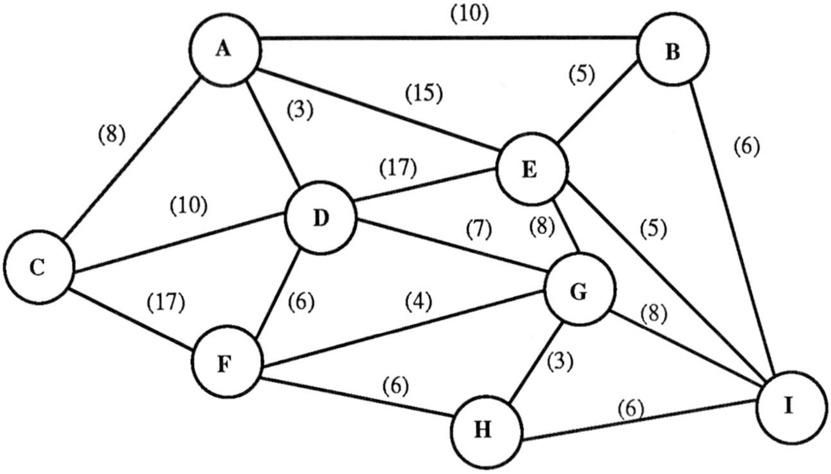

Figure 10.1 **Example Graph or Network**

DEFINITIONS

Node: The circles in the figure identifying the entities that are related. The number of nodes will be n.

Branch: The line segment connecting two nodes showing some relationship between the nodes. Branches will be identified by a node pair. Thus (C,A) is a branch of the figure.

Graph: A collection of nodes and branches.

Branch parameters: The numbers shown in parentheses adjacent to the branch. The meanings of the parameters will differ for various problems. The branches in the figure have only one parameter.

Network: A graph in which there is a flow of some quantity through the branches. Various problems involve different kinds of flow. Conservation of flow at the nodes is a general characteristic of networks.

Chain: A sequence of branches that connect two nodes. The branches (C,A), (A,B), (B,I) form a chain from C to I in the figure.

Cycle: A chain that begins and ends at the same node without repeating any branches. The branches (C,A), (A,D), (D,F), (F,C) form a cycle in the figure.

Spanning Tree: A collection of $(n - 1)$ branches that contain no cycles.

Oriented Branch: A branch that is directed from some node, called the origin, to another node, called the destination. An example is a one-way street in a road network. Oriented branches are identified with an arrowhead showing the orientation.

Oriented Graph: A graph in which all branches are oriented. Graphs in which all branches are oriented are sometimes called networks whether or not flow is a characteristic of the problem.

The following are specifically for flow networks.

Flow Capacity: The maximum flow that can pass through a branch in a given direction.

Source: A node for which all branches touching the node are oriented away from the node.

Sink: A node for which all branches touching the node are oriented towards the node.

The Shortest Route Problem (10.3)

In this section, the parameter on a branch represents its length. The problem is to find the collection of branches (or chain) that comprises the shortest route from a specified node, called the origin, to a second specified node, called the destination. A closely related problem, which we will consider, will find the set of shortest routes from the origin node to all other nodes in the graph. This is called the shortest route tree problem and can be solved with very little additional difficulty. The algorithm in this section is appropriate for graphs in which all branch lengths are nonnegative. It can be used for both oriented and unoriented graphs.

GOAL

- Given a graph with lengths defined for the branches, find the shortest route from some origin node to some destination node.
- Given a graph with lengths defined for the branches, find the shortest route tree for some origin node.

ALGORITHM

Following H & L in Section 10.3, we give below the algorithm for finding the shortest route tree. The algorithm is presented as a set of rules for filling in a table and is illustrated with the example that follows. Some additional notation helps in the discussion.

Branch Length ($d(i, j)$): The length of the branch from node i to node j.

Set of Solved Nodes (S): The set of nodes for which the shortest route has already been determined at some point in the algorithm. The unsolved nodes are the nodes not in S.

Shortest Distance ($\pi(i)$): The length of the shortest route from the origin node to node i in S.

ALGORITHM

A1 Let $n = 1$ and let i_0 be the origin node. Let $S = \{i_0\}$, let $\pi(i_0) = 0$.

A2 Column 1: Show the value of n. At any step, n is the number of nodes in the set S.

Column 2: List the members of S (the solved set) that have at least one branch connected to an unsolved node.

Column 3: For each node listed in column 2, find the closest unsolved node.

Column 4: Let i be the index of the node listed in column 2 and let j be the index of the node listed in column 3. Compute for each case

$$\pi'(j) = \pi(i) + d(i, j).$$

Show these numbers in column 4.

Column 5: Select the smallest number in column 4. Let i be the node in column 2 and j the node in column 3 from which this number was computed. Show node j in column 5.

Column 6: Show the branch (i, j). Add (i, j) to the shortest route tree.

A3 Add node j to S. Let $\pi(j) = \pi'(j)$. If S consists of all nodes, then stop. Otherwise increase n by 1 and repeat step A2.

If it is desired to find the shortest route to a specified destination node, i_n, step A3 is changed to read:

A3 Add node j to S. Let $\pi(j) = \pi'(j)$. If $j = i_n$, then stop. Otherwise increase n by 1 and repeat step A2.

EXAMPLES

E10.1 Find the shortest route from C to I in the graph shown in Fig. 10.1.

1 *n*	*2* *Solved Nodes*	*3* *Closest Unsolved Node*	*4* *Distance to Unsolved Node*	*5* *Node Added to to Solved Set*	*6* *Length of Shortest Route*	*7* *Branch Added to Tree*
1	C	A	8	A	8	(C,A)
2	A	D	11			
	C	D	10	D	10	(C,D)
3	A	B	18			
	C	F	17			
	D	F	16	F	16	(D,F)
4	A	B	18			
	D	G	17			
	F	G	20	G	17	(D,G)

1 *n*	*2* *Solved Nodes*	*3* *Closest Unsolved Node*	*4* *Distance to Unsolved Node*	*5* *Node Added to to Solved Set*	*6* *Length of Shortest Route*	*7* *Branch Added to Tree*
5	A	B	18			
	D	E	27			
	F	H	22			
	G	H	20	B	18	(A,B)
6	A	E	23			
	B	E	23			
	D	E	27			
	F	H	22			
	G	H	20	H	20	(G,H)
7	A	E	23			
	B	E	23			
	D	E	27			
	G	E	25			
	H	I	26	E	23	(A,E)
8	B	I	24			
	E	I	28			
	G	I	25			
	H	I	26	I	24	(B,I)

At the final step, node I has been added to the tree and the shortest route from C to I has been found with length 24. To find the branches on the route one can draw the graph formed by the branches shown in the last column of the chart as illustrated in Fig. 10.2. Observation shows that the path consists of branches (C,A), (A,B), and

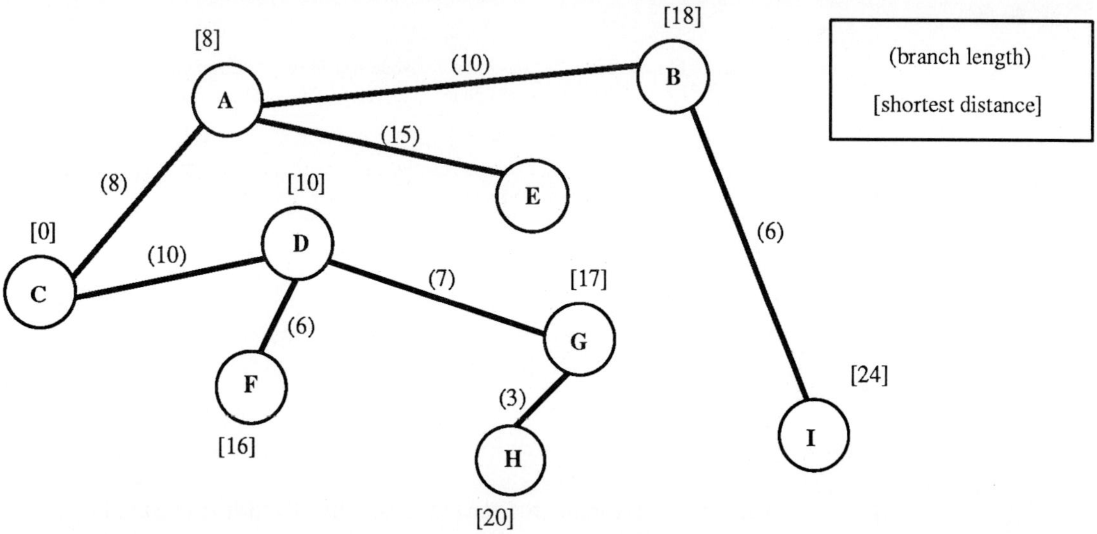

Figure 10.2 **Solution to the Shortest Route Tree Problem**

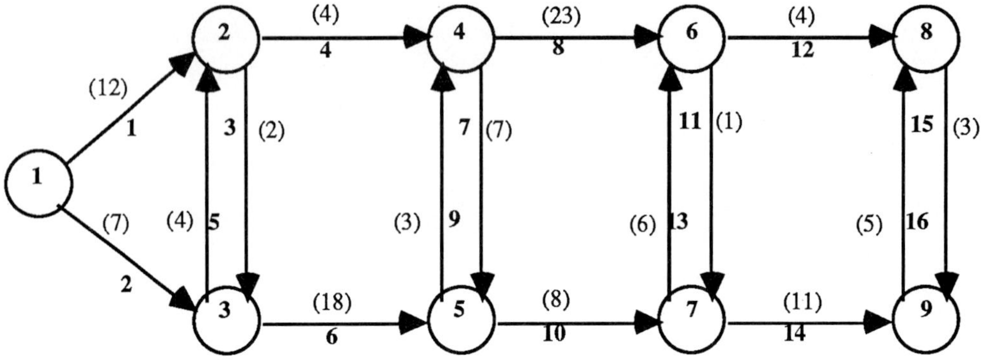

Figure 10.3 **The Oriented Graph for E10.2**

(B,I). Note that the figure defines a spanning tree connecting node C with all other nodes. The tree defines a unique chain from C to each of the other nodes, which in fact is the shortest route to that node. In this case we have discovered the shortest route tree because node I happened to be the one added after all other nodes were already in the tree. The algorithm will generate the shortest route spanning tree if the procedure is stopped only when all the nodes have entered the solved set.

E10.2 The algorithm can be adapted to the oriented graph if the direction of orientation is considered when finding the set of unsolved nodes connected to solved nodes and the lengths of the corresponding branches. Solve the shortest route tree problem for the network of Fig. 10.3 when the origin is node 1. Only the first few steps are shown in the table below for this example.

1 *n*	2 Solved Nodes	3 Closest Un- solved Node	4 Distance to Unsolved Node	5 Node Added to to Solved Set	6 Length of Shortest Route	7 Branch Added to Tree
1	1	3	7	3	7	(1,3)
2	1	2	12			
	3	2	11	2	11	(3,2)
3	3	5	25			
	2	4	15	4	15	(2,4)

PROBLEMS

P10.1 Find the shortest route tree for Fig. 10.1 when node G is the origin node.

P10.2 Find the shortest route tree for Fig. 10.4 when the origin is node L.

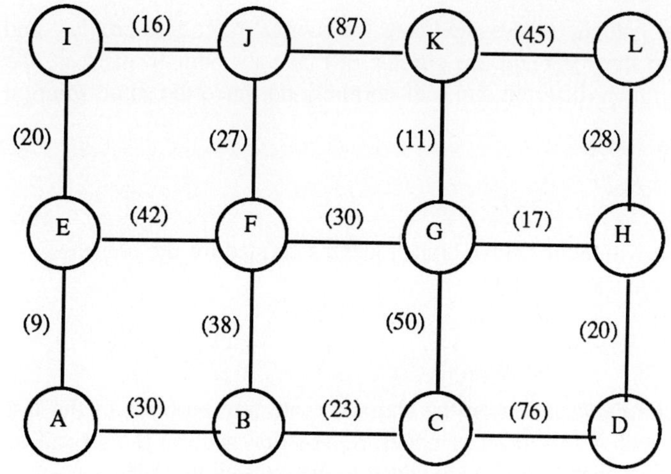

Figure 10.4 **Graph with Lengths on the Branches**

P10.3 Find the shortest route tree from node A using the branch lengths in the table.

	A	B	C	D	E	F
A	—	27	43	16	30	26
B	7	—	16	1	30	25
C	20	13	—	35	5	0
D	21	16	25	—	18	18
E	12	46	27	48	—	5
F	23	5	5	9	5	—

The Minimal Spanning Tree Problem (10.4)

Here the problem is to find a selection of branches that provides a chain between every pair of nodes. The objective is to minimize the total length of the branches selected. The method described in this unit is appropriate only for graphs in which all branches are not oriented and in which all branch lengths are nonnegative. It is not hard to see that the solution must form a spanning tree, thus giving rise to the name of the problem. Although the solutions to the shortest route tree problem and the minimal spanning tree problem are similar in that they both form trees, the problems are in fact much different and will normally not have the same solution for a given graph.

GOAL

- Given a graph with nonnegative branch lengths defined for the branches, find the minimal spanning tree.

ALGORITHM

The algorithm is a simple variation on the shortest route tree problem of the last unit. Again we work with a solved set of nodes, ***S***. The first node in the set can be arbitrarily selected. Subsequently nodes are added to the set with the rule:

> Find the branch (i, j) from a solved node, i, to an unsolved node, j, with the smallest length. Add the branch (i, j) to the tree and the node j to the solved set ***S***.

The process ends when all nodes have been added to the tree. The set of branches added to that point comprises the minimal spanning tree. When ties appear in the selection step they may be resolved arbitrarily.

A more formal algorithm is obtained by changing step 2 of the shortest path algorithm slightly. The rules for column 4 become:

> Column 4: Let i be the index of the node listed in column 2 and let j be the index of the node listed in column 3. Show $d(i, j)$ in column 4.

Following the algorithm with this change will yield the minimal spanning tree.

EXAMPLE

E10.3 Find the minimal spanning tree of the graph of Fig. 10.1. When solving small problems by hand, the graphical minimal spanning tree can be constructed sequentially on paper. At each step, the branch and node that should be added to the tree can be discovered by observation. The solution to this problem is shown in Fig. 10.5. When presenting a solution, always show the sequence in which the branches and nodes were added to the tree so that the procedure of the algorithm may be verified. We have arbitrarily started the algorithm with node C.

The total length of the branches selected is 40, which is the minimum over all spanning trees. The solution is independent of the node selected to start the process. In this case the solution forms a path. This is not true in general.

PROBLEMS

P10.4 Find the minimal spanning tree for the graph of Fig. 10.4.

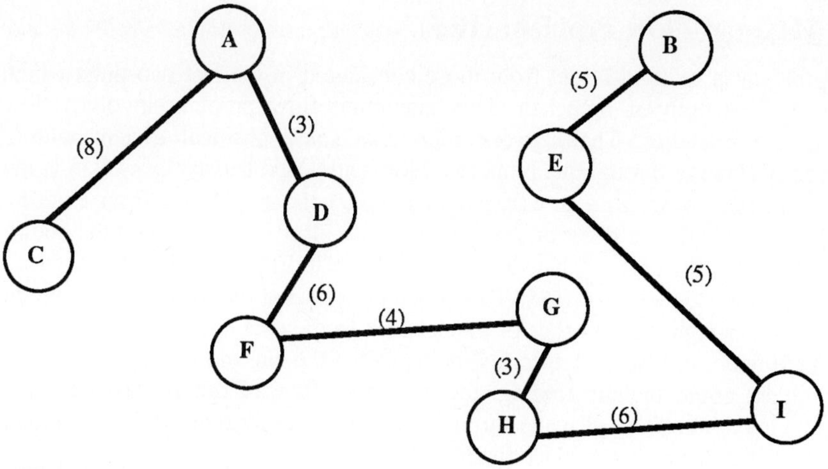

Sequence of Tree Additions

Sequence	1	2	3	4	5	6	7	8	9
Node	C	A	D	F	G	H	I	E	B
Branch	—	(C,A)	(A,D)	(D,F)	(F,G)	(G,H)	(H,I)	(I,E)	(E,B)
Length	—	8	3	6	4	3	6	5	5

Figure 10.5 **The Minimal Spanning Tree for Fig. 10.1**

P10.5 Several offshore oil wells are to be connected by a pipeline to an onshore terminal. Given the distances between the wells shown in Fig. 10.6, find the selection of pipe segments between wells that will minimize the total length of pipe while connecting all wells to the terminal.

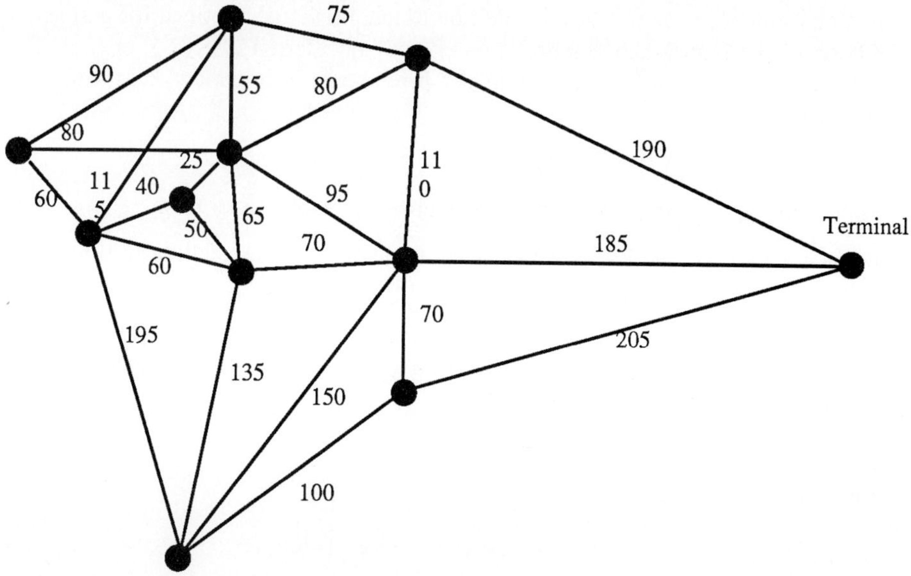

Figure 10.6 **Distances between Oil Wells and Terminal**

The Maximal Flow Problem (10.5)

This problem is quite different from those considered in the last two units which involved the length of branches. This maximum flow problem involves flow through the branches. The network represents some physical system with a commodity flowing through the branches. Flow enters and leaves the system at the nodes. Nodes also act as a transshipment points, collecting flows from entering branches and disbursing flows on leaving branches. Flow is conserved at the nodes. The amount of flow entering a node must also leave it. Each branch in the network has some given capacity for flow. This problem is to find the maximum flow that can be sent through the branches of the network from some specified node, called the source node, to a second specified node, called the sink node. Applications of this problem could include finding: the maximum flow of orders through a job shop, the maximum flow of water through a storm sewer system, or the maximum flow of product through a product distribution system.

GOALS

- Given a network with branch capacities, a specified source, and a specified sink, find the maximal flow that can be sent from the source to the sink through the branches of the network. Also identify the flow on each branch for the maximum flow.
- Given a maximum flow, find a set of branches in the minimal cut.

DEFINITIONS

It is convenient to use notation in addition to that previously defined for graphs. In this notation a branch between nodes i and j may be referred to as (i, j) or (j, i). The order in which the indices appear in the parentheses is important, as it indicates direction.

Source Node (i_0): A specified node that can provide any amount of flow.

Sink Node (i_k): A specified node that can absorb any amount of flow.

Branch Capacity ($c(i, j)$): The capacity (nonnegative) for additional flow from node i to node j in branch (i, j). For a given branch, both $c(i, j)$ and $c(j, i)$ may be positive.

Initial Branch Capacity ($c'(i, j)$): The maximum amount of flow increase from i to j when the flow from i to j is zero.

Branch Flow ($f(i, j)$): The flow from i to j.

Flow Augmenting Path: A chain of branches

$$(i_0, i_1), (i_1, i_2), (i_2, i_3), \ldots, (i_{k-1}, i_k),$$

where i_0 is the source, i_k is the sink and k is the number of branches in the path.

A requirement of the path is that each branch in the path have additional capacity for flow. That is

$$c(i_{n-1}, i_n) > 0 \quad \text{for } 1 \leq n \leq k\,.$$

Flow Change (Δ): The amount that the flow can be increased on a flow augmenting path

$$\Delta = \text{Min}\ \{c(i_{n-1}, i_n) \mid 1 \leq n \leq k\}\,. \tag{1}$$

Minimal Cut: The set of branches that limit the value of the maximal flow.

ALGORITHMS

Algorithm to Find the Maximal Flow

A1 Set $c(i, j) = c'(i, j)$ and $c(j, i) = c'(j, i)$ for each branch.

A2 Find a flow-augmenting path in the graph. If no flow-augmenting path exists, stop with the maximum flow.

A3 Compute the flow change Δ for the path with Eq. (1).

A4 Change the capacities on branches on the flow-augmenting path.
If branch (i, j) is on the path: decrease $c(i, j)$ by Δ and increase $c(j, i)$ by Δ.
If branch (j, i) is on the path: decrease $c(j, i)$ by Δ and increase $c(i, j)$ by Δ.
(Note that the direction the branch appears in the path is important for this step.)
Return to step A2.

To find the branch flows associated with the maximum flow, for each branch (i, j):

If $c'(i, j) - c(i, j) > 0$ then $f(i, j) = c'(i, j) - c(i, j)$ and $f(j, i) = 0$. (2)
If $c'(j, i) - c(j, i) > 0$ then $f(j, i) = c'(j, i) - c(j, i)$ and $f(i, j) = 0$.
Otherwise $f(i, j) = f(j, i) = 0$.

For the maximal flow it must be true that either $f(i, j)$ or $f(j, i)$ is zero.

Algorithm to Find the Minimal Cut

B1 Find the maximal flow. Mark the source node with an x. Do not mark the other nodes.

B2 Find a node marked with a single x. If there are no such nodes stop. The minimal cut is the set of branches that originate at a marked node and terminate at an unmarked node.

B3 Let the node found in step B2 be node i. For each branch, (i, j), originating at node i with $c(i, j) > 0$, mark node j with an x. When all such branches have been considered, mark node i with a second x and go to step B2.

This algorithm can also be used as a formal procedure for finding a flow-augmenting path if step B3 is changed to read

B3 Let the node found in step B2 be node i. For each branch, (i, j), originating at node i with $c(i, j) > 0$, mark node j with an x. If node j is the sink node, stop; there is a flow-augmenting path. It can be found by tracing the unique path from the source node to the sink node passing only through marked nodes. When all such branches have been considered, mark node i with a second x and go to step B2.

EXAMPLES

E10.4 Find the maximal flow from node A to node F through the network of Fig. 10.7. This is an oriented graph in which flow is possible only in the direction of the arrowheads. The numbers in parentheses are the branch capacities for flow in the direction of the arrowheads.

To use the algorithm we must first show it with no orientation, as in Fig. 10.8. Note that there are parentheses at both ends of each branch. For a branch (i, j) the number nearest node i shows $c(i, j)$ and the number nearest node j shows $c(j, i)$. For the oriented graph, flow is possible only in one direction so that we have, for instance, $c(\text{B,E}) = 5$, while $c(\text{E,B}) = 0$. There are many flow-augmenting paths from A to F. We select the path (A,B), (B,E), (E,F). The value Δ for this path is 5. Adjusting the branch capacities according to the algorithm we obtain Fig. 10.9. From Fig. 10.9, we observe the flow-augmenting path (A,C), (C,D), (D,F). Again the value of Δ for this path is 5. Adjusting the capacities, we obtain Fig. 10.10. In Fig. 10.10, there is only one flow augmenting path from A to E, (A,C), (C,E), (E,B), (B,D), (D,F), with Δ of 5. Adjusting the branch capacities results in Fig.

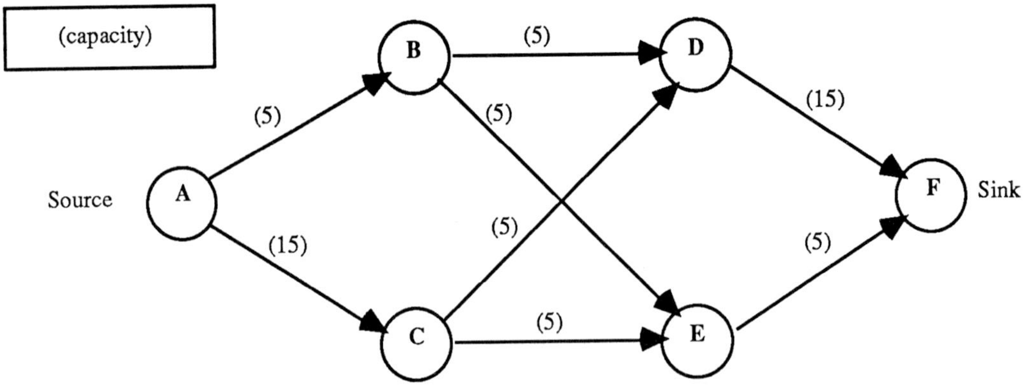

Figure 10.7 **Example Maximal Flow Problem**

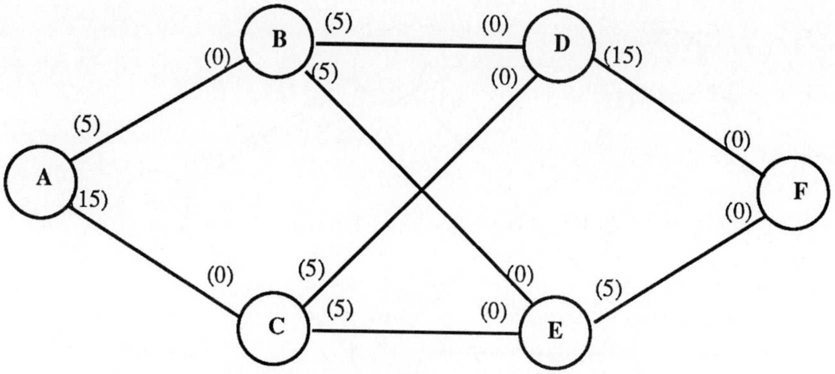

Figure 10.8 **Example in the Form Required by the Algorithm**

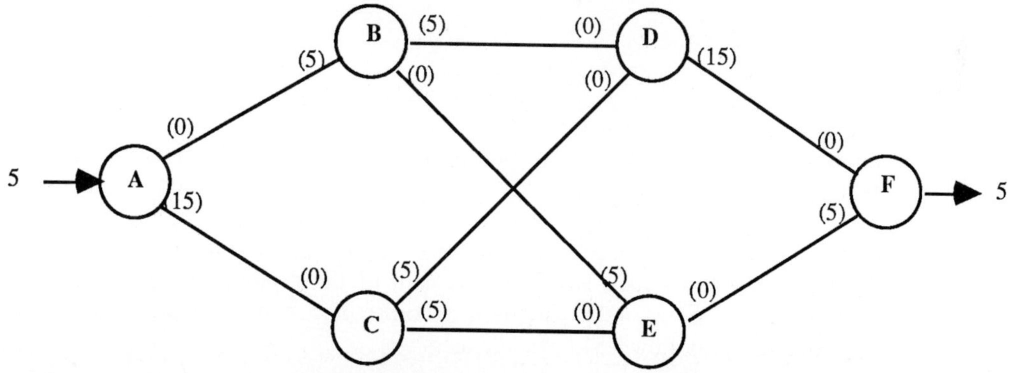

Figure 10.9 **Example after One Flow Augmentation**

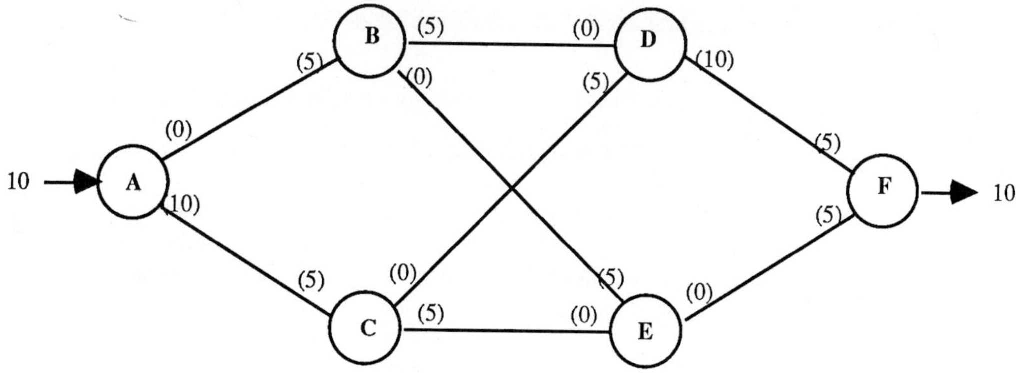

Figure 10.10 **Example after Two Flow Augmentations**

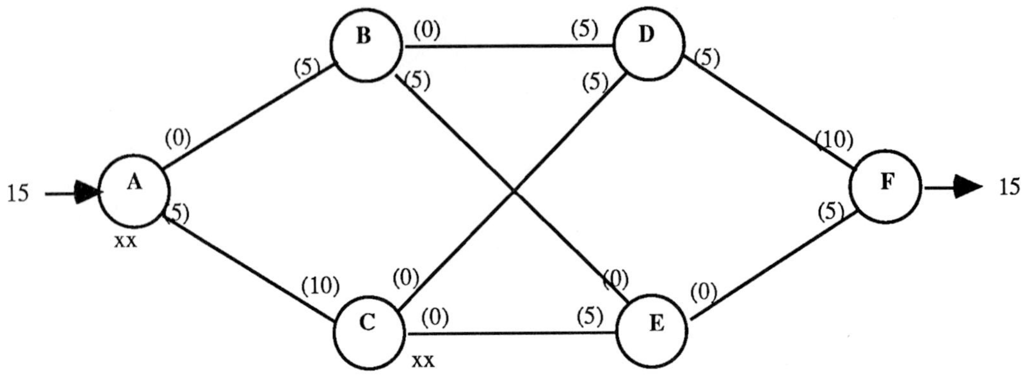

Figure 10.11 **Last Flow Augmentation for the Example Problem**

10.11. Examination of Fig. 10.11 reveals no additional flow-augmenting paths. All are blocked by some branch with zero capacity. The minimal cut is found by the algorithm above. First node A is marked. Node C is marked from node A through branch (A,C) with positive capacity. No other nodes can be marked. The branches on the minimal cut are those that pass from a marked to an unmarked node. (A marked node has xx adjacent to the node.) Thus the branches on the minimal cut are (A,B), (C,D), and (C,E). Note that the sum of the original capacities on these branches is 5 + 5 + 5 = 15. This is in accord with a famous theorem of network analysis, the "Max flow - Min cut" theorem:

> The value of the maximal flow is equal to the sum of the capacities on the minimal cut.

The flows on the branches of the graph can be determined by using Eqs. (2). For instance:

$$c'(A,B) - c(A,B) = 5 - 0 > 0, \text{ therefore } f(A,B) = 5 \text{ and } f(B,A) = 0.$$

The other flows, together with the original capacities of the oriented graph, are shown in Fig. 10.12. From this figure another characteristic of the minimal cut may be seen. The flows on the branches of the minimal cut are equal to the capacities of the branches. Another characteristic not shown by this example is that flows on branches passing from an unmarked to a marked node must be zero.

PROBLEMS

P10.6 Fig. 10.13 shows a maximum flow problem after flow has already been augmented in several iterations. Starting from this solution, augment the flow until the maximum flow is obtained. Show the branch flows for this solution and identify the minimal cut.

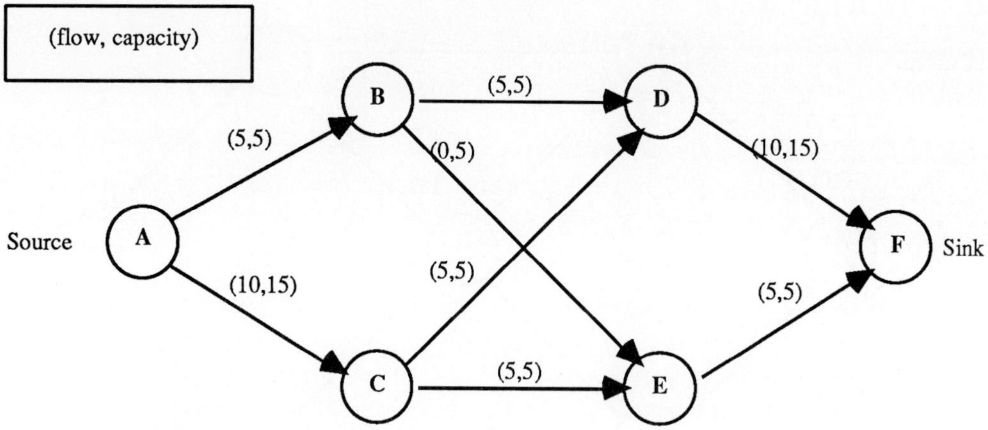

Figure 10.12 **Solution of the Maximal Flow Example**

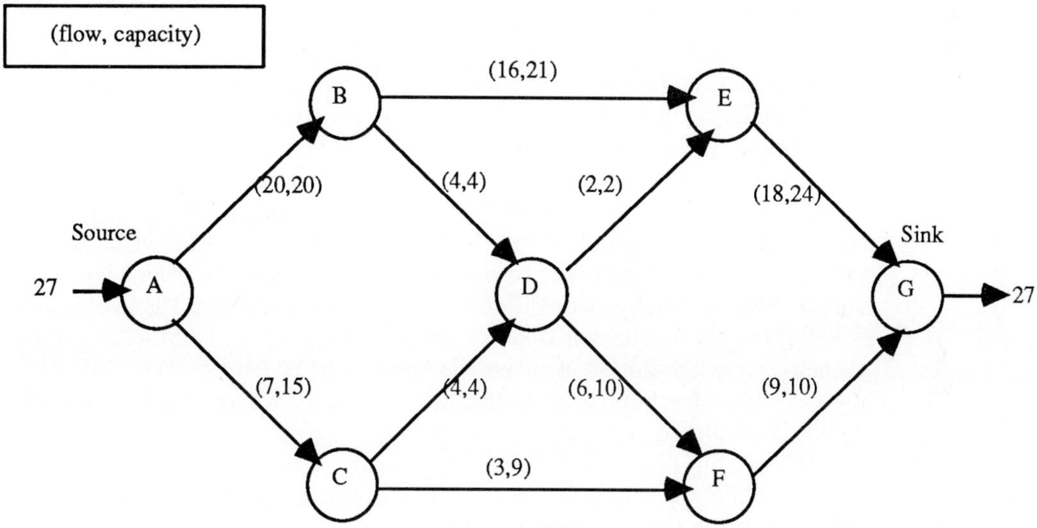

Figure 10.13 **Network for P10.6**

P10.7 Figure 10.14 shows a network with the directional capacities shown on the branches. Starting from this network, augment the flow until the maximum flow is obtained. Show the branch flows and identify the minimal cut.

Project Planning and Control with PERT-CPM (10.6)

Perhaps the most frequently used analytical technique associated with networks is project planning and control. Projects such as constructing a building, designing a new weapon system, or publishing a book typically require large numbers of individual activities, usually performed by different contractors or different entities

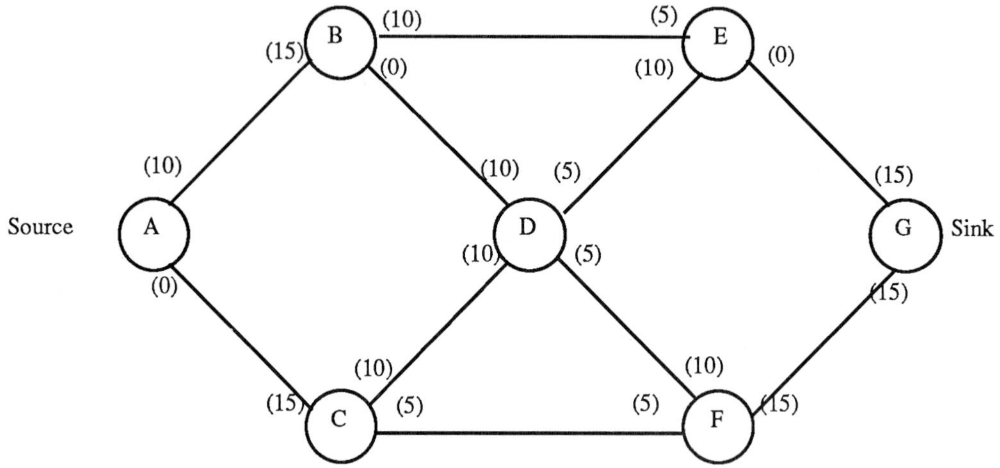

Figure 10.14 **Network for P10.7**

within the same corporation. The management of projects requires careful control of the scheduling of the activities because some activities must be finished before others begin, capital and other resources must be allocated to the projects at the proper times, contracts must be let, and work orders must be released. Questions such as when is the earliest time the project will be completed, which activities are the most critical in terms of meeting a contracted completion date, which activities are behind schedule, and where more money should be spent to meet a completion date can be answered by using PERT-CPM discussed in the unit. The two methods, PERT (Program Evaluation and Review Technique) and CPM (Critical Path Method), were developed at about the same time and have some differences; however, usage has blurred the distinction between them and the joint acronym of the title is often used.

This section determines the project schedule when activity times are deterministic, while the following two sections consider random activity times and tradeoffs between activity times and costs.

GOALS

- Given the activities and events of a project network be able to find the activities that are most critical to the timely completion of a project.
- Be able to compute the earliest and latest times at which activities can be scheduled to begin and finish.

DEFINITIONS

Project Network: A collection of nodes and oriented branches that define the activities and events of a project. the precedence order of the activities is defined by

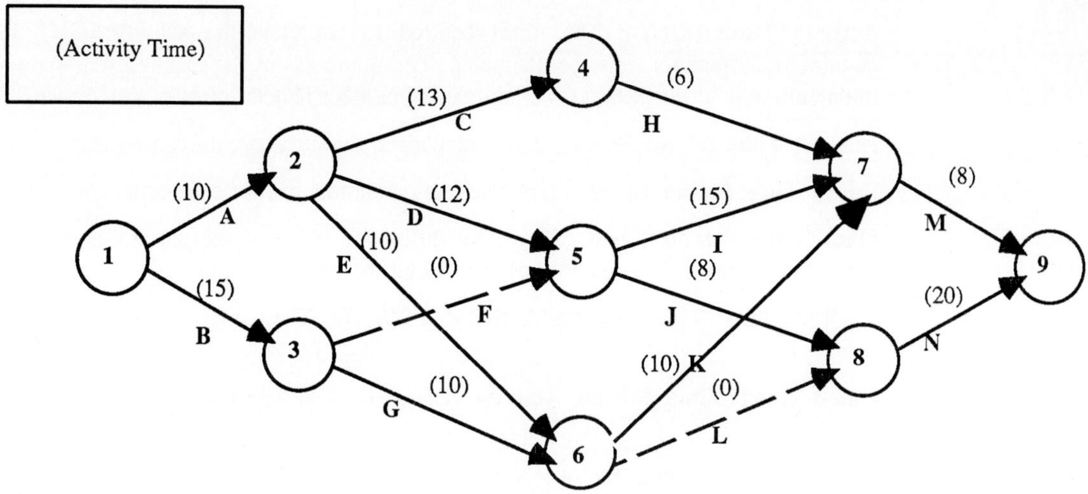

Figure 10.15 **The Example Project Network**

the network. An example that will be used throughout this unit is shown in Fig. 10.15.

Event (Node): A node of the project network representing the point of time when some set of activities is completed and another set of activities may begin. The events are numbered 1 through n (the number of events). They must be numbered so that if there is a directed chain of branches in the network from node i to node j, then $i < j$. Event 1 is the *start* event, which is the node that has only leaving branches, and event n is the *finish* event, which is the node that has only entering branches.

Activity (Branch): An individual component of the project. We have identified activities with letters in the figure. The branch representing an activity originates at one node, i, and terminates at another, j. Thus we can refer to an activity as (i, j). We assume that there is at most one activity between any given pair of nodes.

Precedence Order: The network shows the precedence order of activities (and events). If there is a path in the network (i, j) . . . (i', j'), where activity (i, j) comes before (i', j') then the completion of activity (i, j) must precede the beginning of activity (i', j'). Also event i must precede event j'. The precedence order is a very important part of the description of the project because it places constraints on the scheduling of activities. Because the network describes the precedence order it must be acyclic (have no cycles). Otherwise the completion of an activity would be required to precede its beginning, a logical impossibility.

Dummy Activity: An activity that does not represent a component of a project, but is inserted in the network to establish a precedence that would otherwise be impossible to represent. Activity F is an example in the figure. It establishes that activity B must precede activities I and J. Dummy activities are shown with a dashed branch.

Activity Time ($t(i, j)$): The time required to complete the activity (i, j). In practice, this quantity must be estimated. The numbers for the example are shown in parentheses. In this section, we assume the number is deterministic and known.

Earliest Time for an Event ($E(i)$): The earliest time that event i can occur.

Latest Time for an Event ($L(i)$): The latest time that event i can occur.

Slack Time for an Event ($S(i)$): The difference between the earliest and latest time, which shows the flexibility of scheduling the event.

Earliest Start Time for an Activity ($ES(i, j)$): The earliest time that (i, j) can begin.

Latest Start Time for an Activity ($LS(i, j)$): The latest time that (i, j) can begin.

Earliest Finish Time for an Activity ($EF(i, j)$): The earliest time that (i, j) can end.

Latest Finish Time for an Activity ($LF(i, j)$): The latest time that (i, j) can end.

Slack Time for an Activity ($ST(i, j)$): The difference between the latest and earliest start times (or finish times), representing the flexibility in scheduling the activity.

Immediate Predecessors ($\boldsymbol{P}(i)$): The set of activities that immediately precede event i (whose arcs enter node i).

Immediate Followers ($\boldsymbol{S}(i)$): The set of activities that immediately follow event i (whose arcs leave node i).

Critical Path (C): The set of activities whose delay will delay the completion of the project. These are the activities with zero slack time.

RESULTS

Calculation of the Earliest Time for an Event The earliest time for the occurrence of an event is the greatest of the earliest finish times of all of its immediate predecessors. Thus

$$E(j) = \max_{i} \{E(i) + t(i, j) \mid (i, j) \in \boldsymbol{P}(j)\}.$$

These equations are solved by first setting $E(1)$ to zero and then solving in order for $E(2), E(3), \ldots, E(n)$.

Calculation of the Latest Time for an Event The latest time for the occurrence of an event is the smallest of the latest start times of all of its immediate followers. Thus

$$L(j) = \min_{k} \{L(k) - t(j, k) \mid (j, k) \in S(j)\}.$$

These equations are solved by first setting L(n) = E(n) and then solving in order for L(n – 1), L(n – 2), . . . , L(1).

Calculation of the Slack Time for an Event The slack time for the event is the difference between its latest and earliest times.

$$S(j) = L(j) - E(j) .$$

Calculation of Earliest, Latest, and Slack Times for Activities For activity (i, j),

$$ES(i, j) = E(i)$$
$$EF(i, j) = E(i) + t(i, j)$$
$$LF(i, j) = L(j)$$
$$LS(i, j) = L(j) - t(i, j)$$
$$ST(i, j) = L(j) - [E(i) + t(i, j)] = LS(i, j) - ES(i, j) = LF(i, j) - EF(i, j).$$

EXAMPLE

E10.5 We will compute all results for the example of Fig. 10.15. The first step is to compute the earliest time for each event, as in Table 10.1. Now with the earliest completion time of the project determined as 50, the latest time for each event can be determined as in Table 10.2. Also shown are the event slack times. Finally the important times for activities can be determined as in Table 10.3. It evident from these results that the earliest that the project can be completed is 50 time units from its beginning. The activities (1,2), (2,5), (5,8), and (8,9) are on the critical path. The results of the calculations are reported in Fig. 10.16.

The critical path is actually the path with the greatest activity times from start node to finish node, or the longest path. Although it does not occur for this example, there may be more than one critical path. This will happen if there are two paths with the total time of both equal to the time of the longest path.

The information defined in Table 10.3 can be used to schedule the activities of the project. Starting an activity at any time between its earliest and latest start time will not affect the finish time of the project. Once a project has begun and actual activity times are observed, the results of the analysis can be used as a management tool for reporting and controlling the project.

Table 10.1 **Computation of Earliest Event Times**

Event (j)	*Preceding event* (i)	E(i) + t(i, j)	E(j) = Max [E(i) + t(i, j)]
1	—	—	0
2	1	0 + 10 = 10	10
3	1	0 + 15 = 15	15
4	2	0 + 13 = 23	23
5	2	10 + 12 = 22	
	3	15 + 0 = 14	22
6	2	10 + 10 = 20	
	3	15 + 10 = 25	25
7	4	23 + 6 = 29	
	5	22 + 15 = 37	
	6	25 + 10 = 35	37
8	5	22 + 8 = 30	
	6	25 + 0 = 25	30
9	7	37 + 8 = 38	
	8	38 20 = 50	50

Table 10.2 **Computation of Latest Event Times and Event Slack Times**

Event (j)	*Following event* (k)	L(k) – t(j, k)	L(j) = Min[L(k) – t(j, k)]	Slack time L(j) – E(j)
9	—	—	50	50 – 50 = 0
8	9	50 – 20 = 30	30	30 – 30 = 0
7	9	50 – 8 = 42	42	42 – 37 = 5
6	7	42 – 10 = 32		
	8	30 – 0 = 30	30	30 – 25 = 5
5	7	42 – 15 = 27		
	8	30 – 8 = 22	22	22 – 22 = 0
4	7	42 – 6 = 36	36	36 – 23 = 13
3	5	22 – 0 = 22		
	6	30 – 10 = 20	20	20 – 15 = 5
2	4	36 – 13 = 23		
	5	22 – 12 = 10		
	6	30 – 10 = 20	10	10 – 10 = 0
1	2	10 – 10 = 0		
	3	20 – 15 = 5	0	0 – 0 = 0

Table 10.3 **Computation of Activity Times**

Activity	*Earliest start* (ES)	*Earliest finish* (EF)	*Latest start* (LS)	*Latest finish* (LF)	*Slack time* (ST)
(1,2)	0	10	0	10	0
(1,3)	0	15	5	20	5
(2,4)	10	23	23	36	13
(2,5)	10	22	10	22	0
(2,6)	10	20	20	30	10
(3,5)	15	15	22	22	7
(3,6)	15	25	20	30	5
(4,7)	23	29	36	42	13
(5,7)	22	37	27	42	5
(5,8)	22	30	22	30	0
(6,7)	25	35	32	42	7
(6,8)	25	25	30	30	5
(7,9)	37	45	42	50	5
(8,9)	30	50	30	50	0

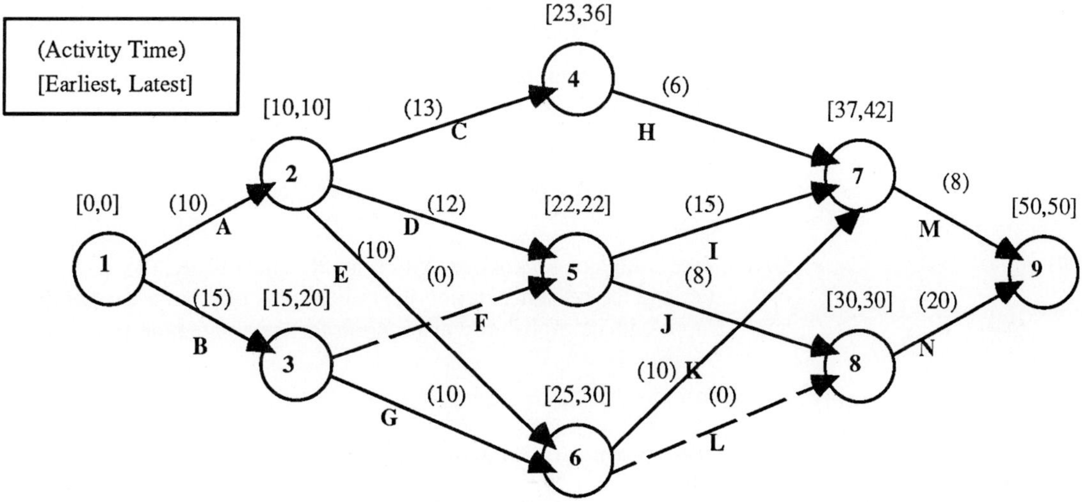

Figure 10.16 **Solution to the Node Equations for the Example**

PROBLEM

P10.8 Identify the critical path and compute all important scheduling times for the network shown in Fig. 10.17.

Project Planning with Random Activity Times (10.6)

In the last section, activity times were assumed known and deterministic. In fact, during the planning of a project, when PERT-CPM is normally employed, the time to perform an activity is sometimes very difficult to estimate. Now we will

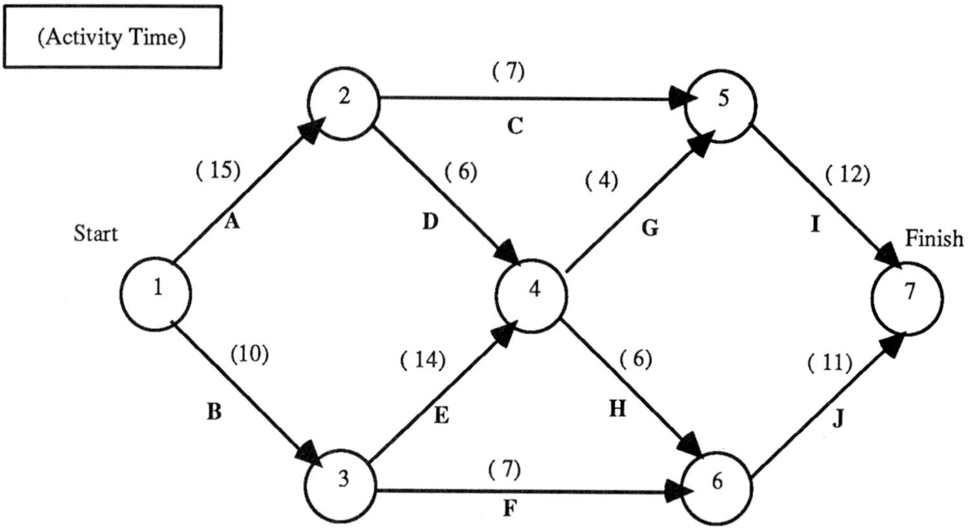

Figure 10.17 **Precedence Network for P10.8**

investigate the alternative assumption that activity times are random variables with known probability distributions. An estimate for the probability distribution of the project completion time is obtained.

GOAL

- Given three estimates for each activity time, the most likely, the optimistic, and the pessimistic, find the critical path of a project network and the approximate probability distribution for the completion time.

DEFINITIONS

Most Likely Estimate ($m(i, j)$): An expert estimate as to the most likely time to complete activity (i, j).

Optimistic Estimate ($a(i, j)$): The least possible time to complete the activity.

Pessimistic Estimate ($b(i, j)$): The greatest possible time to complete the activity.

Beta Distribution: A continuous probability distribution that ranges from a to b with mode m. The completion times of the activities are assumed to have this distribution.

RESULTS

Variance of the Activity Time ($\sigma^2(i, j)$) This is estimated from the range,

$$\sigma^2(i, j) = [(b(i, j) - a(i, j))/6\,]^2 \,. \tag{3}$$

Expected Value of the Activity Time ($t_e(i, j)$) Estimated with the equation

$$t_e(i, j) = (1/3)\ \{2m(i, j) + (1/2)\ [a(i, j) + b(i, j)]\}. \qquad (4)$$

Critical Path (*C*) The activities with zero slack time when the critical path algorithm is applied to the project network using the expected activity times.

Distribution of the Project Completion Time With the assumption that the critical path remains the same over all realizations of the random activity times, the project completion time is approximately normal, with

$$\text{Mean} \quad \mu = \Sigma\ [\ t_e(i, j) \mid (i, j) \in C\ ] \qquad (5)$$
$$\text{Variance}\ \sigma^2 = \Sigma\ [\ \sigma^2(i, j) \mid (i, j) \in C\ ]\ . \qquad (6)$$

EXAMPLE

E10.6 Let the activity times specified in Fig. 10.15 be the most likely time, take the optimistic time as one-half this value, and take the pessimistic time as 1.5 times this value. Find the distribution of the project completion time.

With these assumptions the expected time for each activity is equal to the most likely time, because the most likely time is in the middle of the range. Therefore the critical path is the same as in E10.5. If the most likely time were not in the middle, we would have to compute the expected values and repeat the critical path computations. The activities on the critical path are (1,2), (2,5), (5,8), and (8,9). The variances and expected values are shown in Table 10.4 along with their sum, which determines the parameters of the project completion time distribution. The project completion time has an approximately normal distribution with a mean of 50 and a standard deviation of 4.43 (the square root of the variance). Using this result we can answer probability questions about the project using a normal distribution table.

PROBLEMS

P10.9 Analyze the network of E10.5 if the most likely times are equal to the activity times given in Fig. 10.15, the optimistic times are one-half these values, and the pessimistic times are twice these values.

Table 10.4 **Computation of Project Distribution Parameters**

Activity	(1, 2)	(2, 5)	(5, 8)	(8, 9)	*Sum*
a	5	6	4	10	
m	10	12	8	20	
b	15	18	12	30	
t_e	10	12	8	20	50
σ^2	2.78	4	1.78	11.11	19.67

P10.10 The following estimates are given for the activity times for the network of Figure 10.17. Use this data to calculate the critical path and an estimate of the probability distribution for the project completion time.

Activity	*Optimistic*	*Most likely*	*Pessimistic*
A	8	15	20
B	8	10	15
C	5	7	9
D	3	6	12
E	10	14	25
F	7	7	7
G	3	4	8
H	5	6	10
I	9	12	18
J	8	11	15

Time-Cost Tradeoffs in Project Planning (10.6)

Here we assume that activity times are not fixed but can be controlled by changing the budget allocated to each activity. Additional money means reduced activity time. Thus we obtain an optimization model that sets the activity times to minimize the cost of the project while meeting some prescribed project completion time. With the proper assumptions this is a linear programming model.

GOAL

- Given crash and normal times with the associated crash and normal costs, set up the linear programming model that will determine how much money to allocate to each activity in order to meet a desired completion time for the project.

DEFINITIONS

Crash Time ($d(i, j)$): The minimum time required to complete an activity (i, j).

Normal Time ($D(i, j)$): The normal time (or maximum) time required to complete the activity.

Duration Time ($x(i, j)$): The activity time to be selected that minimizes total cost subject to a constraint on project completion time.

Crash Cost ($C_d(i, j)$): The cost of completing the activity in the crash time.

Normal Cost ($C_D(i, j)$): The cost of completing the activity in the normal time.

Incremental Direct Cost ($C(i, j)$): The cost increase per unit decrease in activity time. It is calculated by

$$C(i, j) = [C_d(i, j) - C_D(i, j)] / [D(i, j) - d(i, j)]. \qquad (7)$$

Cost Intercept ($K(i, j)$): The intercept of the cost curve for zero duration time.

$$K(i, j) = C_d(i, j) + C(i, j) * d(i, j). \quad (8)$$

Earliest Time for Event ($y(i)$): The earliest time for event i. This is a variable quantity which depends on the duration times selected for the activities.

RESULTS

Linear Programming Model for Selecting the Optimum Duration Times

OBJECTIVE FUNCTION

Minimize cost.

Minimize $Z = \sum_{(i,j)} [\, K(i, j) - C(i, j) * x(i, j)\,]$. The sum is over all activities.

This is equivalent to

$$\text{Maximize } Z = \sum_{(i,j)} C(i, j) * x(i, j)\ . \quad (9)$$

BOUNDS ON DECISION VARIBLES

$$x(i, j) \geq d(i, j) \quad \text{for all } (i, j) \quad (10)$$

$$x(i, j) \leq D(i, j) \quad \text{for all } (i, j). \quad (11)$$

PRECEDENCE CONSTRAINTS

The earliest time for an event is the greatest of the completion times of any of its predecessors.

$$y(j) = \text{Max } [\, y(i) + x(i, j) \mid (i, j)\ \varepsilon\ \boldsymbol{P}(j)] \quad \text{for all } j.$$

This is equivalent to the linear constraints

$$y(i) + x(i, j) - y(j) \leq 0 \quad \text{for all } (i, j). \quad (12)$$

MAXIMUM PROJECT COMPLETION TIME CONSTRAINT

$$y(n) \leq T \quad (13)$$

where T is the desired completion time.

The relations (9), (10), (11), (12), and (13) define a linear program that when solved will determine the optimum duration times for all activities.

EXAMPLE

E10.7 Assume the times given in Fig. 10.15 are the normal times for the activities and that the crash times are one-half the normal times. The normal costs are all taken as zero, but the crash costs (which represent the increase over the normal costs) are given in the table below. Set up the linear programming model to find the optimum duration times when the desired completion time is 40.

Activity	*Cost*	*Activity*	*Cost*
(1,2)	100	(4,7)	50
(1,3)	150	(5,7)	50
(2,4)	75	(5,8)	150
(2,5)	100	(6,7)	300
(2,6)	200	(6,8)	0
(3,5)	0	(7,9)	50
(3,6)	100	(8,9)	300

Note that no variables need be defined for the dummy activities; however, constraints of type (12) must be included for all activities, including dummy activities.

OBJECTIVE

$$\begin{aligned}\text{Maximize } Z = {} & 20\, x(1,2) + 20\, x(1,3) + 11.54\, x(2,4) + 16.67\, x(2,5) + 40\, x(2,6) \\ & + 20\, x(3,6) + 16.67\, x(4,7) + 7.67\, x(5,7) + 37.5\, x(5,8) + 150\, x(6,7) \\ & + 25\, x(7,9) + 15\, x(8,9)\,.\end{aligned}$$

PRECEDENCE CONSTRAINTS

$$\begin{array}{ll} y(1) + x(1,2) - y(2) \le 0 & y(4) + x(4,7) - y(7) \le 0 \\ y(1) + x(1,3) - y(3) \le 0 & y(5) + x(5,7) - y(7) \le 0 \\ y(2) + x(2,4) - y(4) \le 0 & y(5) + x(5,8) - y(8) \le 0 \\ y(2) + x(2,5) - y(5) \le 0 & y(6) + x(6,7) - y(7) \le 0 \\ y(2) + x(2,6) - y(6) \le 0 & y(6) \qquad\qquad - y(8) \le 0 \\ y(3) \qquad\qquad - y(5) \le 0 & y(7) + x(7,9) - y(9) \le 0 \\ y(3) + x(3,6) - y(6) \le 0 & y(8) + x(8,9) - y(9) \le 0\,. \end{array}$$

COMPLETION TIME CONSTRAINT

$$y(9) \le 40\,.$$

BOUNDS

$$\begin{array}{ll} 5 \le x(1,2) \le 10 & 3 \le x(4,7) \le 6 \\ 7.5 \le x(1,3) \le 15 & 7.5 \le x(5,7) \le 15 \\ 6.5 \le x(2,4) \le 13 & 4 \le x(5,8) \le 8 \\ 6 \le x(2,5) \le 12 & 5 \le x(6,7) \le 10 \\ 5 \le x(2,6) \le 10 & 4 \le x(7,9) \le 8 \\ 5 \le x(3,6) \le 10 & 10 \le x(8,9) \le 20 \end{array}$$

Solution of this linear program gives the following optimum activity duration times. The cost of this solution is 3746.78. The dual variable for the completion time constraint is 36.67, indicating that the cost of reducing the completion time by one additional time unit is 36.67.

Activity	*Duration*	*Activity*	*Duration*
$x(1,2)^*$	10	$x(4,7)$	6
$x(1,3)^*$	12	$x(5,7)^*$	15
$x(2,4)$	13	$x(5,8)^*$	8
$x(2,5)^*$	7	$x(6,7)^*$	10
$x(2,6)$	10	$x(7,9)^*$	8
$x(3,6)^*$	10	$x(8,9)^*$	15

The activities with an asterisk are on the critical path. The solution of this problem will typically have more than one critical path.

PROBLEMS

P10.11 The times and costs in the table below are given for the network of Fig. 10.17. Set up and solve the linear programming model that will determine the minimum cost assignment of funds to activities to obtain a project completion time of 35.

Activity	*Normal time*	*Normal cost*	*Crash time*	*Crash cost*
A	15	60	10	200
B	10	150	5	275
C	7	90	4	180
D	6	200	4	250
E	14	20	8	150
F	7	500	3	800
G	4	300	4	300
H	6	50	2	80
I	12	180	8	300
J	11	200	7	400

Computer Program

Chapter 7 indicated that a number of network models are special cases of the minimum cost network flow programming model. All the models described in this chapter, with the exception of the minimal spanning tree, can be solved using the *Microsolve* network algorithm. Fortunately, finding the minimal spanning tree is the simplest of the problems considered here, and rather large examples can be easily solved by hand. Alternatively, it is not difficult to write a computer program for this case. In the following we describe how each of the other models can be solved by the network flow programming algorithm in *Microsolve*.

SHORTEST ROUTE PROBLEM

For this problem the branches are equivalent to arcs. If the branches are oriented, the arcs are the same as the branches. If the branches are not oriented, two arcs passing between the same two nodes but in opposite directions must be used to represent a single branch. The length of the branch is represented by the cost of the arc. The other parameters of the arcs are set to the default values (zero for lower bound, a large value for upper bound, and unity for gain). This is done automatically by selecting an environment that specifies that only arc costs are relevant.

If one desires the shortest route from some origin node to some destination node, a fixed external flow of 1 is placed at the origin node and a fixed external flow of –1 is placed on the destination node. All other nodes have zero external flow. On solving this model, the shortest route will be indicated by those arcs that have a flow of unity. All other flows will be zero.

If one desires the shortest route tree from an origin node, a fixed external flow of $n - 1$ is placed at the origin node, and a fixed external flow of –1 is placed on all other nodes. The optimum flow solution will have nonzero flows on all arcs that are members of the tree. This construction is illustrated in Figs. 7.23 and 7.24.

MAXIMUM FLOW PROBLEM

For a network with oriented branches, this problem is represented directly by the arcs of the minimum cost flow model. Here, however, only the arc capacity parameter is relevant, with the other parameters assuming the default values. If the maximum flow problem has unoriented branches with nonzero capacities in both directions, two arcs in opposite directions must represent each branch. Thus if a branch passes from node i to node j with nonzero capacities $c(i, j)$ and $c(j, i)$, then an arc (i, j) must be created with capacity $c(i, j)$, and an arc (j, i) must be created with capacity $c(j, i)$.

A slack external flow of M is placed at the source node with a cost of zero, and a slack external flow of $-M$ is placed at the sink node with a cost of –1. When solving, the algorithm will try to push as much flow as possible from source to sink, thus obtaining the maximum flow. At optimality, the node potentials will indicate the arcs on the minimal cut. An arc on the minimal cut will pass from a node with potential 0 to a node with potential 1. The network model for the maximal flow problem is illustrated in Fig. 7.25.

PERT/CPM CRITICAL PATH DETERMINATION

Although the network algorithm can be used to solve for the critical path and earliest and latest times for the nodes, the process is awkward. Many very good computer codes are available for both the mainframe and microcomputers. The method below describes how *Microsolve* can be used.

The critical path for any project network is the path with the greatest total activity time. To find the longest path with network algorithm, let the cost of each arc be set equal to the negative of the activity time. Then finding the shortest route tree using the START node as the origin node will identify the longest path to the FINISH node (which is also the critical path). The negative of a node potential at optimality is the same as the earliest time for the node in the project network.

To find the latest times for the nodes, reverse all the arcs of the network and use the FINISH node as the origin node. Again find the shortest route tree. The latest time for a node is the project completion time added to the node potential (which is negative).

Of course, the linear programming algorithm of *Microsolve* can be used to determine the optimum time/cost tradeoff for a project network. Because of the limited number of constraints allowed by the program, larger problems can be solved only if the nonzero lower bounds are eliminated by transforming the variables. We have for each activity

$$d(i, j) \leq x(i, j) \leq D(i, j).$$

With the transformation

$$x'(i, j) = x(i, j) - d(i, j),$$

the new variables have the limitations

$$0 \leq x'(i, j) \leq D(i, j) - d(i, j).$$

The nonnegativity restictions and simple upper bounds need not be entered as constraints, thus reducing considerably the size of the problem and the time required to solve it. Of course the original variables must be recovered after the optimum solution is obtained with the transformation.

$$x'(i, j) = x'(i, j) + d(i, j).$$

Problems

P10.12 Using the graph in Fig. 10.18:

a. Find the shortest route tree with origin node A.
b. Find the shortest route tree with origin node C.
c. Find the minimal spanning tree.

P10.13 Using the graph in Fig. 10.19:

a. Sketch the shortest route tree with origin node at the center of the figure.
b. Sketch the minimal spanning tree.

P10.14 Starting from the flows given in Fig. 10.20, perform the maximal flow algorithm until the maximum flow is found. Show the new flows on the arcs and identify the minimal cut.

P10.15 For the graph given in Fig. 10.21:

a. Find the shortest route tree with the origin at node 1.
b. Find the minimal spanning tree.

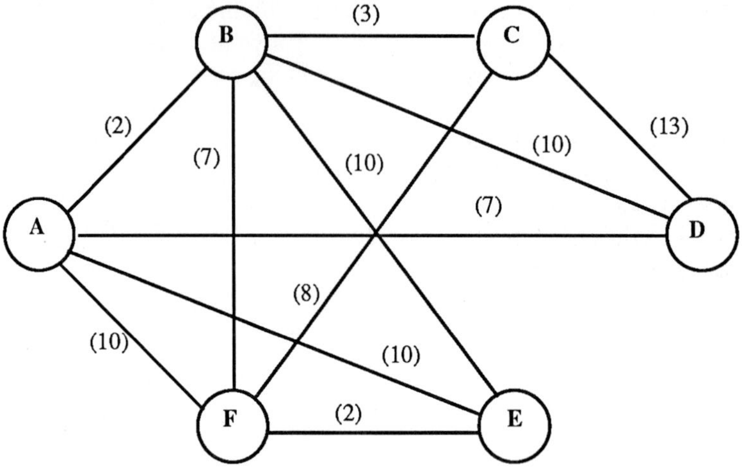

Figure 10.18 **Graph for P10.12**

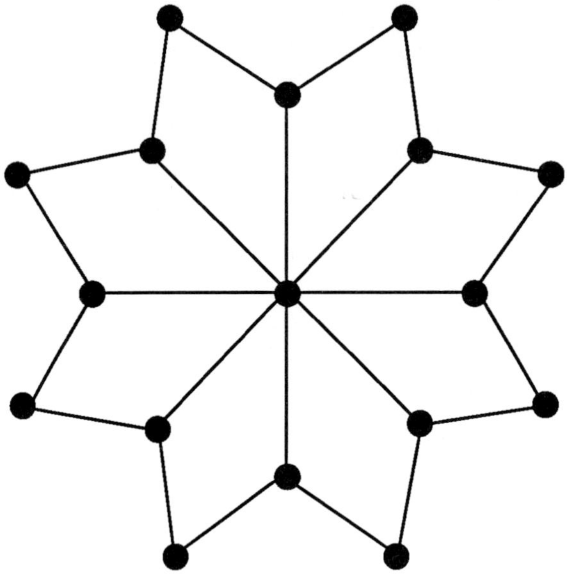

Figure 10.19 **Graph for P10.13**

P10.16 Assuming the branches of Fig. 10.21 are all directed from left to right and that the numbers represent branch lengths find the shortest route tree with node 1 the origin node.

P10.17 Assuming the branches of Fig. 10.21 are all directed from left to right and that the numbers represent branch capacity, find the maximum flow with node 1 the source node and node 9 the sink node. Find the corresponding minimal cut.

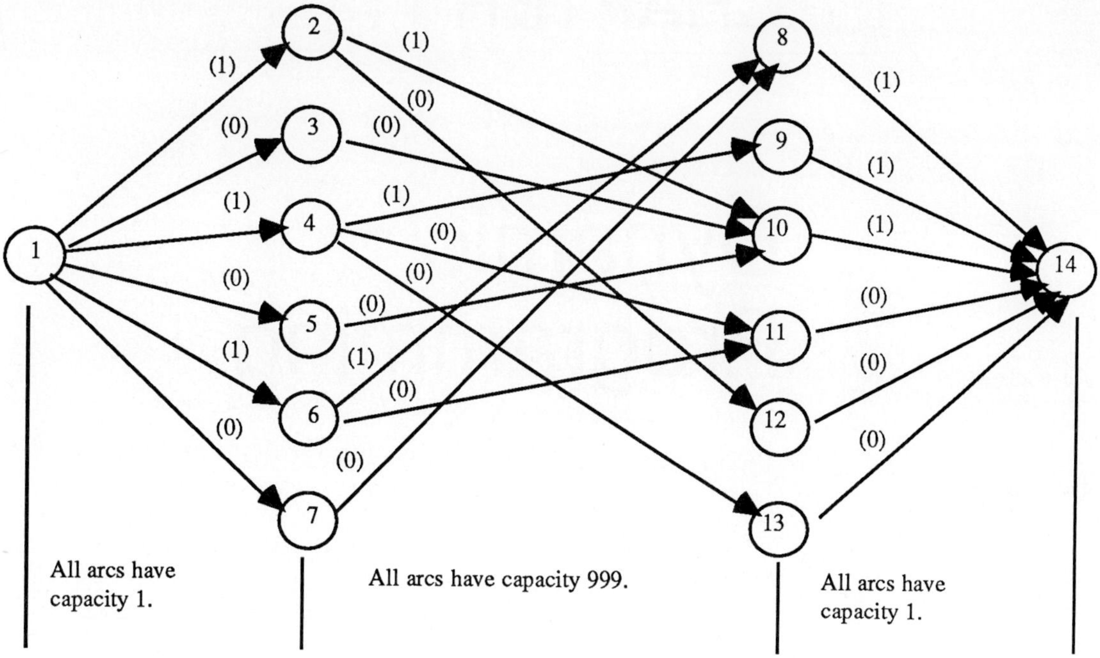

Figure 10.20 **Network for P10.14**

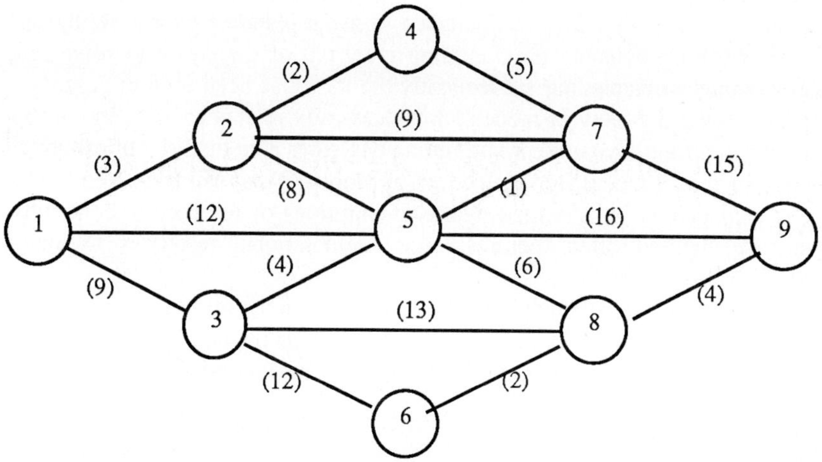

Figure 10.21 **Graph for P10.15 through P10.18**

P10.18 Assuming the branches of Fig. 10.21 are all directed from left to right and that the numbers represent activity times, find the critical path for the project network. Compute all important times related to the activities and events of the network.

CHAPTER 11

Dynamic Programming

Notation

The word "dynamic" implies variation with time and the word "programming" implies planning. Together they can be taken to mean planning over time. Indeed, the original work on dynamic programming grew out of the desire to solve time variable planning problems, but subsequently the term has been used to describe a method for solving a variety of models, not necessarily related to time. In contrast to linear programming, dynamic programming describes a method or philosophy of solution rather than a model format. The set of problems that can be solved by this method is very general, not limited by the assumptions of linearity or continuity. However, the method often requires large computational resources to obtain solutions.

In this section we will attempt to provide a general format for specifying dynamic programming models. In this effort we will go beyond H & L and other introductory texts, which present the subject primarily by example.

MODELING

The dynamic programming model is described with Fig. 11.1. Each box in the figure represents a stage of a sequential decision process. The system begins in some state $\mathbf{s}_1$, called the initial state, for which the decision maker must make decision $\mathbf{x}_1$. Some return R_1 is obtained whose value is based on the state and

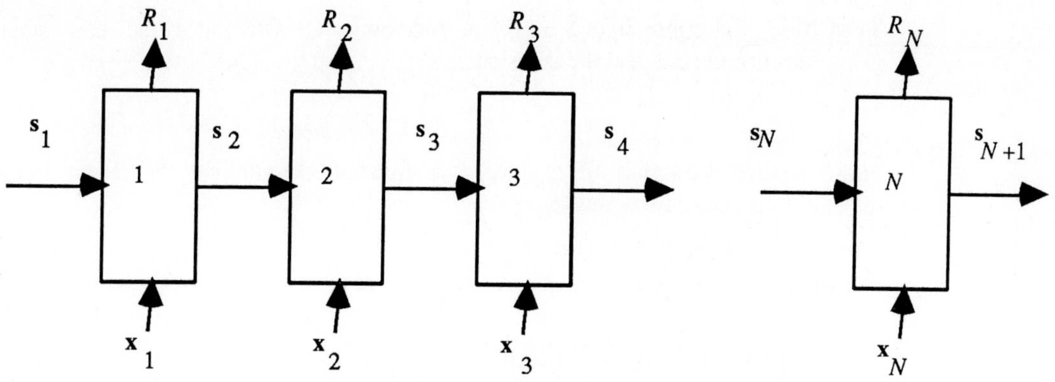

Figure 11.1 **Schematic of the Dynamic Programming Model**

decision. Because of the action implied by the decision, the system moves to a new state $\mathbf{s}_2$. There a second decision $\mathbf{x}_2$, is made, resulting in the return R_2 and moving the system to the next state $\mathbf{s}_3$. The process continues until, for a finite stage problem, the *Nth* decision is made, moving the system to the final state $\mathbf{s}_{N+1}$. For an infinite stage problem, the process never stops with N approaching infinity. Often the indices assigned to the stages indicate discrete points in time justifying the term "dynamic" in our title.

The objective of dynamic programming is to select the sequence of decisions to optimize some function of the stage returns. There are several possible forms of this function; however, for many applications the function is a simple sum.

In this chapter we consider two varieties of dynamic programming: discrete dynamic programming, in which the state variables take on discrete values, and probabilistic dynamic programming, in which the transition from one state to the next is governed by a probability distribution. We do not consider continuous dynamic programming, in which the state variables are defined on the continuum, because this form is rarely practical due to computational difficulties. In this section we present the notation that will be used throughout the remainder of the chapter.

DEFINITIONS

Stage: A discrete point in time or a step in the decision process at which a decision must be made. Stages are indexed 1, 2, . . . , N.

State ($\mathbf{s}_n$): A vector of observable characteristics of the system at stage n which describes the system with sufficient accuracy for a decision to be made.

Initial State ($\mathbf{s}_1$): The state in which the sequence begins.

Final State ($\mathbf{s}_{N+1}$): The state in which the sequence finishes.

Decision ($\mathbf{x}_n$): A vector describing the decision made at stage n.

Transition Function ($t_n(s_n, x_n)$): A function that determines the new state given the current state and the decision.

$$s_{n+1} = t_n(s_n, x_n) .$$

Stage Return Function ($R_n(s_n, x_n)$): A function determining the return from making decision x_n from state s_n .

Objective Function ($Z(R_1, R_2, \ldots, R_N)$): A function defining how the stage returns are to be combined to obtain a measure of effectiveness for the sequence of decisions. Common functions are

$$Z = \text{Min } (R_1 + R_2 + \ldots + R_N) \quad (1)$$
$$Z = \text{Min } (R_1 \times R_2 \times \cdots \times R_N) \text{ with } R_n > 0 \text{ for } n = 1, 2, \ldots, N \quad (2)$$
$$Z = \text{Min } \{\text{Max } (R_1, R_2, \ldots, R_N)\}. \quad (3)$$

Maximization may replace minimization in the cases above.

Principle of Optimality: If the system is in a given state at some stage, the optimum sequence of decisions following the state is independent of the sequence of decisions that was used to reach the state. For dynamic programming to be applicable to a problem, this principle must hold for the states and decisions defined for the problem.

Optimum Value Function ($f_n^*(s_n)$): The value associated with the optimal sequence starting from state s_n in stage n .

Decision Return ($f_n(s_n, x_n)$): The value of making decision x_n from state s_n and then using the optimum sequence starting from state s_{n+1}.

For the case of Eq. (1),

$$f_n(s_n, x_n) = R_n(s_n, x_n) + f_n^*(s_{n+1}). \quad (4)$$

For the case of Eq. (2),

$$f_n(s_n, x_n) = R_n(s_n, x_n) \times f_n^*(s_{n+1}). \quad (5)$$

For the case of Eq. (3),

$$f_n(s_n, x_n) = \text{Max } \{R_n(s_n, x_n), f_n^*(s_{n+1}) \}, \quad (6)$$

where $s_{n+1} = t_n(s_n, x_n)$.

Recursive Relationship: The function determining the optimum value.

$$f_n^*(s_n) = \text{Min } \{ f_n(s_n, x_n) \mid x_n \in \mathbf{X}(s_n) \}$$

Here $\mathbf{X}(s_n)$ is the feasible set of decisions for stage n in state s_n. For this expression to be valid, the principle of optimality must hold for the formulation.

Optimum Policy ($x_n^*(s_n)$): The optimum decision determined by the recursive relationship.

In the following sections we will use this notation to set up and solve problems with dynamic programming.

Deterministic Dynamic Programming (11.3)

The deterministic dynamic programming model assumes that a decision $\mathbf{x}_n$ made from state $\mathbf{s}_n$ will lead to a specific state $\mathbf{s}_{n+1}$ as determined by the transition function. Probabalistic dynamic programming (to be considered in the next section), in comparison, assumes that the new state is unknown but that it has a known probability distribution. The word discrete implies that there is a discrete set of possible states at each stage. We consider the deterministic, discrete problem in this section. We also assume that the number of possible states at each stage is finite, the number of stages is finite, and that there is a finite number of possible decisions at each stage.

GOAL

- Be able to set up a dynamic programming model for a discrete deterministic problem and solve the model to obtain the optimum solution.

ALGORITHM

There are two main steps for solving a problem, solving the recursive equation and recovering the solution. The general recursive equation for a minimization problem with a sum of stage returns is

$$f^*_n(\mathbf{s}_n) = \text{Min } \{R_n(\mathbf{s}_n, \mathbf{x}_n) + f^*_{n+1}(\mathbf{s}_{n+1}) | \ \mathbf{x}_n \ \varepsilon \ \mathbf{X}(\mathbf{s}_n)\} \text{ for } n = 1, 2, \ldots, N.$$

Since f^*_{n+1} appears in the equation for f^*_n, it is apparent that these equations must be solved in the reverse order of the stage indices. Solving the equations in this order is called backward recursion. Further, in order to solve stage N, the value of f^*_{N+1} must be given. In fact to use backward recursion, the function $f^*_{N+1}(\mathbf{s}_{N+1})$ must be given as part of the formulation. After the recursive equation has been solved in order for stages N, $N - 1$, $N - 2$, . . . , 2, 1, one obtains the function $f^*_1(\mathbf{s}_1)$. Usually the initial state is given in the problem formulation so the function need only be computed for a single state.

Solving the equations determines the values of the policy function $\mathbf{x}^*_n(\mathbf{s}_n)$, the decision variables that optimize the recursive equation for each state at each stage. Note that the recursive equation must be solved for every state in every stage. For the discrete, finite problem this is possible because there is only a finite number of states. When the problem is discrete, the optimum is usually obtained by computing the value of the decision return for every feasible decision. This is the computational burden of dynamic programming, because many practical problems require that a great number of states be evaluated at every stage.

The second step of the process involves recovering the optimum solution. The policy function specifies the optimum solution for every state, so given an initial state, $\mathbf{s}_1$, it is easy to find the first member of the optimum sequence of decisions:

$$\mathbf{x}^*_1 = \mathbf{x}^*_1(\mathbf{s}_1).$$

The next state is found with the help of the transition function,

$$\mathbf{s}_2 = t_1(\mathbf{s}_1, \mathbf{x}^*_1).$$

The second decision follows from the policy function

$$\mathbf{x}^*_2 = \mathbf{x}^*_2(\mathbf{s}_2).$$

The recovery process continues in this fashion until the optimum value of $\mathbf{x}^*_N$ is determined. For the deterministic problem, the complete optimum solution can be found starting from any state in any stage.

EXAMPLES

E11.1. Knapsack Problem This is an example of a one-constraint resource allocation problem. Consider the boy scout faced with the problem of selecting items for his knapsack before a long hike. There are a number of items he could take and he has assigned a numerical benefit to each unit of each item. He has put an upper limit on the amount of weight he can carry and each item has a specified weight. The problem is to select the set of items yielding the maximum benefit while keeping within the weight limit. This is a prototype of many problems which arise in more realistic situations and has been the subject of a great deal of study. For example the mathematical programming model of a three item problem is shown below.

$$\begin{aligned} \text{Maximize} \quad & 6x_1 + 8x_2 + 11x_3 \\ \text{Subject to} \quad & 3x_1 + 5x_2 + 7x_3 \le 10 \\ & x_j = 0, 1, 2, \ldots \quad j = 1, 2, 3. \end{aligned}$$

From the model one can see that the scout can take more than one unit of each item and the benefit is a linear function of the number of items brought. The coefficients in the objective function are the per unit benefits of the items, and the coefficients in the constraint are the per unit weights. The weight limitation is 10. The problem cannot be solved by linear programming because of the discrete nature of the items. It can be solved by integer programming. Here we use dynamic programming.

This is not really a sequential decision problem; however, we will order the decisions x_1, x_2, x_3. The ordering is arbitrary for this kind of problem. To formulate the problem for dynamic programming, we must define for each stage: the states, the decisions, the transition function, and the recursive equation. In addition we must define the initial state and provide an optimum value function for the final state.

FORMULATION OF THE KNAPSACK PROBLEM

Stages: Three stages or $N = 3$.

State: s_n = The amount of weight not yet allocated at stage n. $0 \le s_n \le 10$ and integer. The states can be restricted to integer values because all the item weights are integer.

Initial State: $s_1 = 10$.

Final State: $0 \le s_{N+1} \le 10$. Because of the discrete nature of the items, it may not be possible to exhaust the entire weight limitation.

Final State Value: $f^*_{N+1} = 0$ for all s_{N+1}. There is no value for leftover capacity.

Decision: x_n = number of items of type n to bring. The set of feasible decisions at stage n is

$$\mathbf{X}(s_n) = \{x_n \mid 0 \le x_n \le s_n / a_n \text{ and integer}\},$$

where a_n is the weight of item n. This restriction is necessary so the weight limitation is not violated.

Transition Function: $s_{n+1} = s_n - a_n x_n$.

Decision Return: $f_n(s_n, x_n) = c_n x_n + f^*_{n+1}(s_{n+1})$, where c_n is the benefit of item n.

Recursive Equation: $f^*_n(s_n) = \text{Max}\ [f_n(s_n, x_n) \mid x_n \in \mathbf{X}(s_n)]$.

SOLUTION OF THE KNAPSACK PROBLEM

The recursive equations may now be solved using a tabular approach. At stage 3, the optimum solution is to bring as many of item 3 as allowed by the remaining weight capacity. Thus we obtain the first table below. Note that we have listed together the range for states that have the same solution.

$n = 3$

s_3	$f^*_3(s_3)$	$x^*_3(s_3)$
0–6	0	0
7–10	11	1

To solve the recursive equation for stage 2 we must compute the decision return for each feasible value of the decision variable. We have substituted the transition function for s_3.

$n = 2$

	$f_2 = 8x_2 + f^*_3(s_2 - 5x_2)$				
s_2	$x_2 = 0$	$x_2 = 1$	$x_2 = 2$	$f^*_2(s_2)$	$x^*_2(s_2)$
0–4	0	—	—	0	0
5–6	0	8	—	8	1
7–9	11	8	—	11	0
10	11	8	16	16	2

Every entry in this table requires several computations. For instance for $s_2 = 8$ with $x_2 = 1$, the following computations are required

$$R_2(8, 1) = 8 * 1 = 8,$$
$$s_3 = t_2(8, 1) = 8 - 5 * 1 = 3.$$

From the table for f^*_3 we find $f^*_3(3) = 0$, and finally,

$$f_2(8, 1) = R_2(8, 1) + f^*_3(3) = 8.$$

For stage 1 it is only necessary to compute the optimum solution for the initial state, $s_1 = 10$. We will also solve the recursive equation for 8 and 9 for illustration.

$n = 1$ $\qquad f_1 = 6x_1 + f^*_2(s_1 - 3x_1)$

s_1	$x_1 = 0$	$x_1 = 1$	$x_1 = 2$	$x_1 = 3$	$f^*_1(s_1)$	$x^*_1(s_1)$
8	11	14	12	—	14	1
9	11	14	12	18	18	3
10	16	17	12	18	18	3

The optimum contents of the knapsack can now be determined since the optimum policy is available for every state in every stage. The tabular format below organizes the steps of the algorithm.

n	s_n	$x^*_n(s_n)$	$s_{n+1} = t_n(s_n, x^*_n)$
1	10	3	1
2	1	0	1
3	1	0	1

The solution brings three units of item 3 and none of the others. One unit of weight remains unused.

The solution for a knapsack of size 8 is available from the table for stage 1. Note that it is very little more effort to compute the optimum for various values of s_1.

n	s_n	$x^*_n(s_n)$	$s_{n+1} = t_n(s_n, x^*_n)$
1	8	1	5
2	5	1	0
3	0	0	0

In this case one unit each of items 1 and 2 use up all the weight resource.

E.11.2. 0–1 Knapsack Problem Modify the problem of E11.1 so that the boy can bring only one of each item. This is called the 0–1 knapsack problem. The only change required for the formulation is to change the feasible set of decisions for each stage. Now

$$\mathbf{X}(s_n) = \{x_n \mid 0 \le x_n \le s_n / a_n \text{ and } x_n = 0, 1\}.$$

The format of the computations do not change except that only two values of the decision variables need be enumerated. The table for f_3 does not change but the tables for f_2 and f_1 become,

$n = 2$

$f_2 = 8x_2 + f^*_3(s_2 - 5x_2)$

s_2	$x_2 = 0$	$x_2 = 1$	$f^*_2(s_2)$	$x^*_2(s_2)$
0–4	0	—	0	0
5–6	0	8	8	1
7–10	11	8	11	0

$n = 1$

$f_1 = 6x_1 + f^*_2(s_1 - 3x_1)$

s_1	$x_1 = 0$	$x_1 = 1$	$f^*_1(s_1)$	$x^*_1(s_1)$
8	11	14	14	1
9	11	14	14	1
10	11	17	17	1

The optimum solution becomes

n	s_n	$x^*_n(s_n)$	$s_{n+1} = t_n(s_n, x^*_n)$
1	10	1	7
2	7	0	7
3	7	1	0

E11.3 Take the problem described in E11.1 and let one more item become available with benefit 7 and weight 4. Find the new optimum solution for a weight capacity of 10.

Note that in E.11.1 we have already completely solved the problem for stages 2 and 3, and that we have solved for some of the states of stage 1. We add the new item as stage 0. We could have renumbered the items to maintain our notation, but this approach is simpler. Completing the calculations for stage 1 we obtain.

$n = 1$

$f_1 = 6x_1 + f^*_2(s_1 - 3x_1)$

s_1	$x_1 = 0$	$x_1 = 1$	$x_1 = 2$	$x_1 = 3$	$f^*_1(s_1)$	$x^*_1(s_1)$
0–2	0	—	—	—	0	0
3–4	0	6	—	—	6	1
5	8	6	—	—	8	0
6	8	6	12	—	12	2
7	11	6	12	—	12	2
8	11	14	12	—	14	1
9	11	14	12	18	18	3
10	16	17	12	18	18	3

$n = 0$

$f_0 = 7x_0 + f^*_1(s_0 - 4x_0)$

s_0	$x_0 = 0$	$x_0 = 1$	$x_0 = 2$	$f^*_0(s_0)$	$x^*_0(s_0)$
10	18	19	14	19	1

Now the optimum becomes

n	s_n	$x^*_n(s_n)$	$s_{n+1} = t_n(s_n, x^*_n)$
0	10	1	6
1	6	2	0
2	0	0	0
3	0	0	0

E11.4. Soot Collection This is a dynamic planning model. A polution control device in a smoke stack collects soot (particulate matter from the fire). The amount of soot which is deposited depends on the month as indicated in the table below. The device must be cleaned occasionally to remove the soot. It may be cleaned at the end of any month. The cost of cleaning is a fixed charge of 10.

The stack does not operate as efficiently when there is soot in the device as when it is clean. If at the beginning of any month the amount of soot present is y, the increase in operating cost associated with the soot is 2y. At most 10 units of soot can be in the device at the beginning of any month.

Set up the dynamic programming model that can be used to solve the problem of determining the optimum cleaning times for a 10-month period with the soot generation data given below. Assume at the beginning of the period the device is clean. In addition to other times that might be selected, the device must be cleaned at the end of the tenth month.

Soot Generation by Month

Month	1	2	3	4	5	6	7	8	9	10
Soot	5	3	2	8	6	2	3	6	5	3

FORMULATION OF THE SOOT COLLECTION PROBLEM

Stages: Ten stages or $N = 10$.

State: s_n = The amount of soot accumulated at the beginning of month n . $0 \leq s_n \leq 10$ and integer.

Initial State: $s_1 = 0$. The device is empty at the beginning.

Final State: $s_{N+1} = 0$. The device is to be empty at the end.

Final State Value: $f^*_{N+1} = 0$.

Decision:

$$x_n = \begin{cases} 1 \text{ if soot is to be cleaned at the end of month } n. \\ 0 \text{ if soot is not cleaned.} \end{cases}$$

$$X(s_n) = \{ x_n \mid x_n = 0,1 \text{ if } s_n + a_n \leq 10; \text{ or } x_n = 1 \text{ if } s_n + a_n > 10 \},$$

where a_n is the soot deposited during month n.

Transition Function:

$$s_{n+1} = \begin{cases} 0 & \text{if } x_n = 1 \\ s_n + a_n & \text{if } x_n = 0 \end{cases}$$

Decision Return:

$$f_n(s_n, x_n) = 10x_n + 2 * s_n + f^*_{n+1}(s_{n+1}).$$

Recursive Equation: $f^*_n(s_n) = \text{Min}\,[f_n(s_n, x_n) \mid x_n \in X(s_n)]$.

Solving the recursive equations, starting with $n = 10$ and progressing backwards to $n = 1$, will yield the optimum policy. The value of $f^*_1(0)$ will be the cost of the optimum solution.

E11.5. Path Problem You must travel by car on the road system shown in Fig. 11.2 from node (1,2) to node (5,2). The number shown adjacent to each arc is the time to travel the road represented by the arc. The goal is to travel by the route with the least total travel time. At each node you must make the decision to go up (+45°) direction) or go down (−45° direction). Formulate and solve this problem by

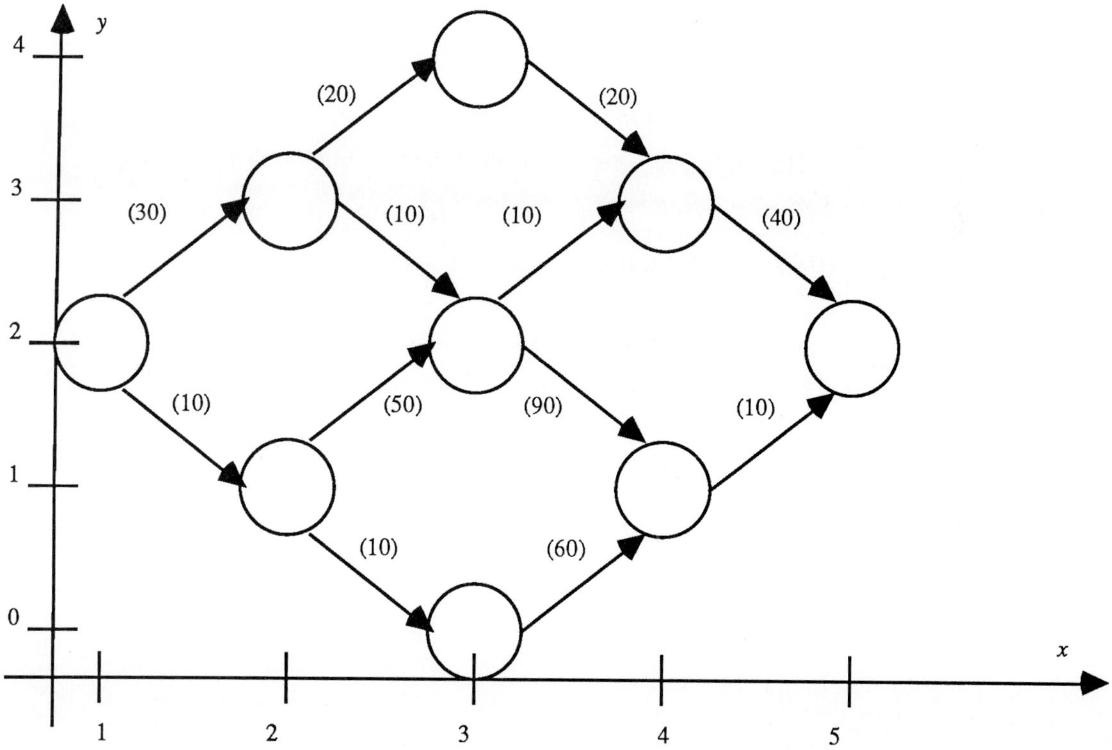

Figure 11.2 **Road Network for Path Problem**

dynamic programming. Note that we have shown coordinates on the road system. Stages are identified on the x-axis. States are identified on the y-axis.

FORMULATION OF THE PATH PROBLEM

Stages: Four stages, or $N = 4$, shown along the x-axis.

State: s_n = The location at stage n as indicated by the y coordinate. The feasible values of s_n depend on the stage.

Initial State: $s_1 = 2$. The location at the start of the trip.

Final State: $s_5 = 2$. The location at the end of the trip.

Final State Value: $f^*_5 = 0$.

Decision:

$$x_n = \begin{cases} +1 & \text{move up} \\ -1 & \text{move down.} \end{cases}$$

$\mathbf{X}(s_n) = \{x_n \mid s_n + x_n$ falls within the boundaries shown in Fig. 11.2$\}$.

We adopt this informal definition of feasible decisions rather attempting a more complicated mathematical statement.

Transition Function:

$$s_{n+1} = s_n + x_n .$$

Decision Return:

$$f_n(s_n , x_n) = a_n(s_n, s_{n+1}) + f^*_{n+1} (s_{n+1}).$$

Here $a_n(s_n, s_{n+1})$ is the length of the road from s_n to s_{n+1} at stage n.

Recursive Equation: $f^*_n(s_n) = \text{Min } [f_n(s_n, x_n) \mid x_n \in \mathbf{X}(s_n)]$.

SOLUTION OF THE PATH PROBLEM

At stage 4, the decisions are fixed because the final state is given.

$n = 4$

s_4	$f^*_4(s_4)$	$x^*_4(s_4)$
1	10	+1
3	40	−1

$n = 3$

s_3	$f_3 = a_3(s_3, s_4) + f^*_4(s_3 + x_3)$: $x_3 = -1$	$x_3 = +1$	$f^*_3(s_3)$	$x^*_3(s_3)$
0	—	70	70	+1
2	100	50	50	+1
4	60	—	60	−1

$n = 2$

$f_2 = a_2(s_2, s_3) + f^*{}_3(s_2 + x_2)$

s_2	$x_2 = -1$	$x_2 = +1$	$f^*{}_2(s_2)$	$x^*{}_2(s_2)$
1	80	100	80	−1
3	60	80	60	−1

$n = 1$

$f_1 = a_1(s_1, s_2) + f^*{}_2(s_1 + x_1)$

s_1	$x_1 = -1$	$x_1 = +1$	$f^*{}_1(s_1)$	$x^*{}_1(s_1)$
2	90	90	90	−1 or +1

Here we have a tie for the optimum solution. We will generate the two optimal paths.

n	s_n	$x^*{}_n(s_n)$	$s_{n+1} = t_n(s_n, x^*{}_n)$
1	2	−1	1
2	1	−1	0
3	0	+1	1
4	1	+1	2

n	s_n	$x^*{}_n(s_n)$	$s_{n+1} = t_n(s_n, x^*{}_n)$
1	2	+1	3
2	3	−1	2
3	2	+1	3
4	3	−1	2

E11.6. Personnel Assignment Problem This problem has two components in the state and decision vectors. A company has two electrical engineers (EE), two mechanical engineers (ME), and an unlimited number of masters of business administration (MBA). The company has four jobs to do in the next week, A, B, C, and D. The chart below shows the costs of doing each of the jobs with various combinations of personnel. The problem is to determine an optimal assignment of workers to the jobs that will minimize the total cost. Formulate the dynamic programming model that when solved will determine an optimum assignment.

Job	*MBA's*	*1 ME*	*2 ME's*	*1 EE*	*2 EE's*	*1 ME & 1 EE*
A	50	49	90	47	51	15
B	X	73	15	X	27	20
C	60	52	24	78	84	X
D	56	22	57	56	80	67

FORMULATION OF THE PERSONNEL ASSIGNMENT PROBLEM

Stages: A stage for each job, or $N = 4$. Let the jobs A, B, C, D be assigned to stages 1, 2, 3, and 4, respectively.

State: $\mathbf{s}_n = (s_{1,n}, s_{2,n})$. Two state variables are required because there are two scarce resources, electrical engineers and mechanical engineers. No state variable is necessary for MBAs since there is an unlimited supply.

Let $s_{1,n}$ = number of MEs remaining. Let $s_{2,n}$ = number of EEs remaining.

Initial State: $\mathbf{s}_1 = (2, 2)$.

Final State: $\mathbf{s}_{N+1} = (s_{1,n+1}, s_{2,n+1})$ where the state values may be 0, 1, or 2. It is not necessary to use all the engineers.

Final State Value: $f^*_{N+1} = 0$. Leftover engineers have no value.

Decision: $\mathbf{x}_n = (x_{1,n}, x_{2,n})$. The decision is a vector with two components because there are two decisions to be made at each stage concerning the number of engineers of each type to use. If no engineers are used, the job is done by MBAs.

Let $x_{1,n}$ = number of MEs assigned. Let $x_{2,n}$ = number of EEs assigned.

$$\mathbf{X}(\mathbf{s}_n) = \{\mathbf{x}_n \mid s_{i,n} - x_{i,n} \geq 0 \text{ for } i = 1, 2\}.$$

Transition Function:

$$\mathbf{s}_{n+1} = \mathbf{s}_n - \mathbf{x}_n .$$

Decision Return:

$$f_n(\mathbf{s}_n, \mathbf{x}_n) = a_n(\mathbf{x}_n) + f^*_{n+1}(\mathbf{s}_{n+1}).$$

Here $a_n(\mathbf{s}_n)$ is the cost of doing job n with assignment $\mathbf{x}_n$.

Recursive Equation: $f^*_n(\mathbf{s}_n) = \text{Min}\,[f_n(\mathbf{s}_n, \mathbf{x}_n) \mid \mathbf{x}_n \in \mathbf{X}(\mathbf{s}_n)]$.

SOLUTION OF THE PERSONNEL ASSIGNMENT PROBLEM

$n = 4$

	$f_4 = a_4(\mathbf{x}_4) + f^*_5(\mathbf{s}_4 + \mathbf{x}_4)$							
$\mathbf{s}_4$	(0, 0)	(1, 0)	(2, 0)	(0, 1)	(0, 2)	(1, 1)	$f^*_4(\mathbf{s}_4)$	$\mathbf{x}^*_4(\mathbf{s}_4)$
(0, 0)	56	—	—	—	—	—	56	(0, 0)
(0, 1)	56	—	—	56	—	—	56	(0, 0) or (0, 1)
(0, 2)	56	—	—	56	80	—	56	(0, 0) or (0, 1)
(1, 0)	56	22	—	—	—	—	22	(1, 0)
(1, 1)	56	22	—	56	—	67	22	(1, 0)
(1, 2)	56	22	—	56	80	67	22	(1, 0)
(2, 0)	56	22	57	—	—	—	22	(1, 0)
(2, 1)	56	22	57	56	—	67	22	(1, 0)
(2, 2)	56	22	57	56	80	67	22	(1, 0)

$n = 3$

s_3	$f_3 = a_3(\mathbf{x}_3) + f^*_4(s_3 + \mathbf{x}_3)$ (0, 0)	(1, 0)	(2, 0)	(0, 1)	(0, 2)	(1, 1)	$f^*_3(s_3)$	$\mathbf{x}^*_3(s_3)$
(0, 0)	116	—	—	—	—	—	116	(0, 0)
(0, 1)	116	—	—	134	—	—	116	(0, 0)
(0, 2)	116	—	—	134	140	—	116	(0, 0)
(1, 0)	88	108	—	—	—	—	88	(0, 0)
(1, 1)	88	108	—	100	—	—	88	(0, 0)
(1, 2)	88	108	—	100	106	—	88	(0, 0)
(2, 0)	88	74	80	—	—	—	74	(1, 0)
(2, 1)	88	74	80	100	—	—	74	(1, 0)
(2, 2)	88	74	80	100	106	—	74	(1, 0)

$n = 2$

s_2	$f_2 = a_2(\mathbf{x}_2) + f^*_3(s_2 + \mathbf{x}_2)$ (0, 0)	(1, 0)	(2, 0)	(0, 1)	(0, 2)	(1, 1)	$f^*_2(s_2)$	$\mathbf{x}^*_2(s_2)$
(0, 0)	—	—	—	—	—	—	M	—
(0, 1)	—	—	—	—	—	—	M	—
(0, 2)	—	—	—	—	143	—	143	(0, 2)
(1, 0)	—	189	—	—	—	—	189	(1, 0)
(1, 1)	—	189	—	—	—	136	136	(1, 1)
(1, 2)	—	189	—	—	115	136	115	(0, 2)
(2, 0)	—	161	131	—	—	—	131	(2, 0)
(2, 1)	—	161	131	—	—	102	102	(1, 1)
(2, 2)	—	161	131	—	101	102	101	(0, 2)

Here M is a large number, indicating that there are no feasible solutions for states (0, 0) and (0, 1). For stage 1 it is only necessary to perform the computations for the initial state.

$n = 1$

s_1	$f_1 = a_1(\mathbf{x}_1) + f^*_2(s_1 + \mathbf{x}_1)$ (0, 0)	(1, 0)	(2, 0)	(0, 1)	(0, 2)	(1, 1)	$f^*_1(s_1)$	$\mathbf{x}^*_1(s_1)$
(2, 2)	161	164	233	149	182	151	149	(0, 1)

To recover the optimum solution

n	s_n	$\mathbf{x}^*_n(s_n)$	$s_{n+1} = t_n(s_n, \mathbf{x}^*_n)$
1	(2, 2)	(0, 1)	(2, 1)
2	(2, 1)	(1, 1)	(1, 0)
3	(1, 0)	(0, 0)	(1, 0)
4	(1, 0)	(1, 0)	(0, 0)

Thus one EE is assigned to job A, one ME and one EE to job B, MBAs to job C, and one ME to job D.

COMPUTATIONAL CONSIDERATIONS

Although all dynamic programming problems have a similar structure, they are usually very different with regard to the computational processes required for solution. For this reason it is difficult to provide a "general" computer code for dynamic programming. It is usually necessary to write one's own computer code to solve a specific problem type. This is one of the reasons that dynamic programming is much less often used than linear programming. Linear programming models can be created independently of the computer program, leaving the coding of algorithms to the professionals.

Dynamic programming is, however, much more general than linear programming with respect to the class of problems to which it is applicable. As these examples suggest, there is no difficulty with the integrality of decision variables. There is no requirement for linearity of the functions. There is also never any question of local optima, as dynamic programming always finds the global optimum.

The computational difficulty associated with solving a discrete problem depends strongly on the number of state variables. Let there be m state variables, each assuming p discrete values for each stage. Let there be N stages and d discrete values for the decision variables. The number of evaluations of the decision return function required to solve the problem is

$$N * d * m^p .$$

This number depends linearly on the number of stages and the number of decision alternatives but exponentially on the number of state variables. For many problems, p is limited for practical computational effort to 2 or 3. Since the number of state variables is usually equal to the number of constraints that link decision variables in different stages, this limitation is quite restrictive with respect to the class of problems that can be practically solved. There has been quite a lot of research on ways to reduce the number of state variables or the number of values for each state variable.

PROBLEMS

P11.1 Formulate and solve the 0-1 knapsack problem below with dynamic programming.

$$\text{Maximize } 4x_1 + 7x_2 + 3x_3 + 10x_4$$

Subject to

$$7x_1 + 5x_2 + 4x_3 + 9x_4 \le 12$$

$$x_j = 0 \text{ or } 1 \text{ for } j = 1, 2, 3, 4$$

P11.2 To the problem in E11.1, add the constraint

$$x_1 + x_2 + x_3 \le 2.$$

Solve the problem with dynamic programming. Another state variable will be required.

P11.3 Find $f^*_5(s_5)$ and $x^*_5(s_5)$ for $s_5 = 4$ and $s_5 = 2$ using the given recursive equation, transition equation, and the information in the tables.

$f^*_5(s_5) = \text{Min } \{R_5(s_5, x_5) + f^*_6(s_6)\}$
$s_6 = s_5 + x_5$ with the restriction that $s_6 \leq 5$.

s_6	0	1	2	3	4	5
$f^*_6(s_6)$	74	89	70	69	103	89

	$R_5(s_5, x_5)$				
s_5	0	1	2	3	4
$x_5 = 0$	12	32	14	17	12
$x_5 = 1$	19	18	13	32	28
$x_5 = 2$	24	26	30	24	19

P11.4 For the road network of Fig. 11.2, assume the number given on each road is the percentage of speeding cars that are caught by the police. You are a speeder and you want to select the route that minimizes your chance of getting caught. The probability of not being caught is the product of the probabilities of not being caught over all the roads selected on the route. Use dynamic programming to find the optimum route.

Probabilistic Dynamic Programming (11.4)

An unfortunate characteristic of many decision problems is that when one makes a decision, there is no certainty about what the outcome will be. This makes the transition function of the last section inappropriate. In this section, we modify the transition function so that the next state depends not only on the current state and decision but also on a random variable with a known distribution. Using probabilistic dynamic programming for this new model, one can find a policy that will minimize or maximize the expected sum of the returns from the stages of the model. This modification of assumptions allows the modeling and solution of a number of new and interesting problems. The computational methods are conceptually only slightly different than for the deterministic case.

GOAL

- Given a problem that has the general characteristics of a dynamic programming model with the added information concerning the probability distribution of a random variable that affects the state transition, be able to formulate and solve the problem using probabilistic dynamic programming.

DEFINITIONS

Here we change the definitions and notation of the introductory section of this chapter to account for the probabilistic nature of state transitions. We show the states and decisions as scalars, but they may be vectors.

Transition Function ($t_n(s_n, x_n, y)$): A function that determines the new state given the current state, the decision, and a random variable, y.

Transition Probability Distribution (p_y): The probability distribution of the random variable y at stage n. The distribution may be a function of the state and decision. Assume y is a discrete random variable with the realizations y_1, y_2, . . . , y_m. Then a requirement of the distribution is

$$\sum_{i=1}^{m} p_y(y_i) = 1.$$

Stage Return Function ($R_n(s_n, x_n, s_{n+1})$): A function determining the immediate return from making decision x_n in state s_n and moving to state s_{n+1}.

Optimum Value Function ($f^*_n(s_n)$): The value associated with starting in state s_n at stage n and always taking the decision that minimizes the sum of the expected returns.

Decision Return ($f_n(s_n, x_n)$): The expected value of making decision x_n from state s_n and then using the optimum policy starting from state s_{n+1}.

$$f_n(s_n, x_n) = \sum_{i=1}^{m} p_y(y_i) \, [\, R_n(s_n, x_n, s_{n+1}) + f^*_{n+1}(s_{n+1}) \,],$$

where

$$s_{n+1} = t_n(s_n, x_n, y_i).$$

Recursive Relationship: The function determining the optimum expected value for state s_n.

$$f^*_n(s_n) = \text{Min} \,\{\, f_n(s_n, x_n) | \, x_n \in \mathbf{X}(s_n)\}.$$

ALGORITHM

The recursive equations for probabilistic dynamic programming are solved in the same fashion as the deterministic case except that the expected decision return must be found for each decision at each state. The expected return comprises a sum of as many as m terms, thus multiplying the computational effort by as much as m.

The optimum solution cannot be recovered as for the deterministic case. Solution of the recursive equations provides a policy for every state. Thus given the initial state s_1, the first decision can found as $x^*_1(s_1)$. The second and subsequent decisions cannot be determined, however, because the transition to the next state is uncertain. After the random variable is realized, the policy function will determine the next decision.

EXAMPLES

E11.7. Path Problem with Uncertainty Consider the path problem described previously in E11.5. You have just discovered that you have a bad steering mechanism so that your auto will not always travel in the direction that you want. When you decide to go up, you will actually go up with a 0.9 probability and go down with a 0.1 probability. If you decide to go down, you will actually go up with a 0.4 probability and go down with a 0.6 probability. These rules do not hold where only one direction of travel is possible (i.e., nodes (3,0), (3,4), (4,1), (4,3)). At these nodes travel in the feasible direction is assured. In this risky situation, you decide to make decisions that will minimize your expected travel time. Formulate and solve the dynamic programming model for this situation.

FORMULATION OF THE PATH PROBLEM WITH UNCERTAINTY

The formulation of this problem remains as in E11.5 except that we replace the transition function with

$$s_{n+1} = s_n + y$$

with y having the discrete probability distribution shown below. The distribution depends on the decision.

	$p_y(y)$	
	$y = 1$	$y = -1$
$x_n = +1$	0.9	0.1
$x_n = -1$	0.4	0.6

The decision return at all nodes except (3,0), (3,4), (4,1), and (4,3) is

$$\begin{aligned} f_n(s_n, +1) &= 0.9\,[\,a_n(s_n, s_n+1) + f^*_{n+1}(s_n+1)] \\ &\quad + 0.1\,[\,a_n(s_n, s_n-1) + f^*_{n+1}(s_n-1)] \\ f_n(s_n, -1) &= 0.4\,[\,a_n(s_n, s_n+1) + f^*_{n+1}(s_n+1)] \\ &\quad + 0.6\,[\,a_n(s_n, s_n-1) + f^*_{n+1}(s_n-1)]. \end{aligned}$$

At nodes (3,0) and (4,1):

$$f_n(s_n, +1) = a_n(s_n, s_n+1) + f^*_{n+1}(s_n+1).$$

At nodes (3,4) and (4,3):

$$f_n(s_n, -1) = a_n(s_n, s_n-1) + f^*_{n+1}(s_n-1).$$

SOLUTION FOR THE PATH PROBLEM WITH UNCERTAINTY

At stage 4 the decisions are fixed and there is no uncertainty.

$n = 4$	s_4	$f^*_4(s_4)$	$x^*_4(s_4)$
	1	10	+1
	3	40	−1

$n = 3$	s_3	$x_3 = -1$	$x_3 = +1$	$f^*_3(s_3)$	$x^*_3(s_3)$
	0	—	70	70	+1
	2	80	55	55	+1
	4	60	—	60	−1

$n = 2$	s_2	$x_2 = -1$	$x_2 = +1$	$f^*_2(s_2)$	$x^*_2(s_2)$
	1	90	102.5	90	−1
	3	71	78.5	71	−1

$n = 1$	s_1	$x_1 = -1$	$x_1 = +1$	$f^*_1(s_1)$	$x^*_1(s_1)$
	2	100.4	100.9	100.4	−1

The optimum policy has been determined for every state, but the optimum route cannot be determined. The initial decision at stage 1 is to go down; however, the next decision depends on the outcome of the random variable.

COMPUTATIONAL CONSIDERATIONS

Conceptually probabilistic dynamic programming is not much different from the deterministic variety. If one assumes the discrete random variable has m realizations, the computational difficulty is a factor of m greater than for a similar deterministic problem. Thus the number of decision return computations is bounded by

$$N * d * m^{p+1},$$

where the factors in this expression were defined in the last section.

PROBLEMS

P11.5 A person plays a game for which his probability of winning is 0.6 and probability of losing is 0.4. The person has \$50 and will play the game twice. At each play, the bet will be either \$10 or the whole amount currently held. If the person wins, the amount bet will be added to his total. If he loses, the amount bet will be deleted from his total. Thus, in the first play the bet can be either \$10 or \$50. If the bet is \$10, the man can end the play with either \$40 or \$60 depending on whether the game is won or lost. If the bet is \$50, the results may be either 0 or \$100. After the first play, the person will bet again using the same rules. After the second play, the person will go home with the amount remaining.

Use dynamic programming to determine the player's optimum strategy to maximize his expected holdings after two plays. Reduce the number of states by considering only those states that can be reached during the play of the game.

Problems

P11.6 A dynamic programming problem has four stages, with one state variable and one decision variable at each stage. The transition equations that relate the state variables at the stages are

$$s_1 = 10,$$
$$s_2 = s_1 - x_1,$$
$$s_3 = s_2 - 2x_2,$$
$$s_4 = s_3 - 3x_3,$$
$$s_5 = s_4 - 4x_4.$$

Most of the computations have already been done, with the results shown below.

s_i	$x^*_4(s_4)$	$x^*_3(s_3)$	$x^*_2(s_2)$	$f^*_2(s_2)$
10	2	1	3	90
9	2	0	2	80
8	2	1	1	72
7	1	0	0	60
6	1	0	3	52
5	1	1	2	45
4	1	1	1	38
3	0	1	0	30
2	0	0	1	22
1	0	0	0	12
0	0	0	0	0

For $s_1 = 10$, solve the recursive equation

$$f^*_1(s_1) = \text{Max}\{R_1(x_1) + f^*_2(s_2)\},$$

where

$$R_1(0) = 0, R_1(1) = 12, R_1(2) = 20.$$

Find all alternative optimum solutions.

P11.7 Use the data of problem P11.6 but assume the transition function at stage 1 depends on the random variable y.

$$s_2 = s_1 - x_1 - y,$$

where $p_y(0) = 0.2$, $p_y(1) = 0.4$, $p_y(2) = 0.1$, and $p_y(3) = 0.3$. The recursive equation for stage 1 is now

$$f^*_1(s_1) = \text{Max }\{\text{Exp }[R_1(x_1) + f^*_2(s_2)]\ \}.$$

Solve this equation to find the optimum decision at stage 1.

P11.8 For the path problem of E11.5, assume there is a penalty for turning left of 20 and a penalty for turning right of 5. Incorporate the penalties into the path problem model (another state variable is required) and find the route that minimizes the sum of travel times plus turn penalties.

P11.9 Consider a knapsack problem in which the item weights are no longer deterministic but are random variables. Three quantities are given for each item in the table below: the cost per unit, the benefit per unit, and the nominal weight per unit.

Item	*1*	*2*	*3*
Cost	1.0	2.5	3.0
Benefit	6.0	8.0	11.0
Nom. weight	3.0	5.0	7.0

The actual weight of item n is

$$a_n + y,$$

where $p_y(-1) = 0.25$, $p_y(0) = 0.5$, and $p_y(+1) = 0.25$. The values of a_n are the nominal weights.

The goal of the problem is to choose the number of each item that maximizes net benefit (total benefit – total cost), while assuring that the knapsack weighs no more than 10 pounds.

The selection of the number of a particular item must take place before its exact weight is known. After the selection, the random variable is realized. If the weight resource is not used up by the selection, the decision process continues. If the decision results in a knapsack requiring more than the allowed weight, a sufficient number of the items must be returned to bring the knapsack weight within the allowed limit. The items returned have the cost given above but do not yield a benefit. At most, three units of each item may be brought.

Use probabilistic dynamic programming to find the policy for the boy scout.

P11.10 Road Repair A repair policy is to be determined for a road for the next 10 years. There are two types of repair that can be done: a long term fix (LT), and a short term fix (ST). Relevant parameters of the two types of repair are shown in the table below. In addition to the actual cost of repair, you must account for an annual maintenance cost that is incurred every year and that depends on the type of repair last done. The current time is 0 and the road must now be repaired in some fashion. The road is to be completely rebuilt after 10 years. The short term fix cannot be done two times in succession. Show the dynamic programming formulation that will determine a policy that minimizes the total cost over the 10 years. All costs are in thousands of dollars. Find the solution when the first repair is at time 0. Find the solution when the first repair can be put off until time 1.

Type of repair	*LT*	*ST*
Cost of repair	1500	400
Annual cost of maintenance	50	100
Time until next repair	5	2

P11.11 An electronic system has n components. The reliability of a component is the probability that it will not fail during a mission. The reliability of component i is given as $r(i)$. The reliability of the system is the probability that none of the system components fail, which is the product of the component reliabilities.

In order to increase the reliability of the system, extra components may be included as backups for the original components. These are called redundant since they are not required for the system unless the original components fail. The probability that a collection of x components of the same type fail is the probability that they all fail. Thus the reliability of a component type with x redundant elements is

$$R(i) = 1 - [1 - r(i)]^{(1+x)}.$$

The reliability of the system is the product of the component type reliabilities.

We want to determine how many redundant components of each type to provide. There is a budget restriction for redundant components. A component of type i has the cost $a(i)$.

a. Formulate this problem using the notation of this section.
b. Explain how you would incorporate additional system constraints such as weight and power limitations.
c. Solve the specific problem with the data below using a dynamic programming approach.

Item	*1*	*2*	*3*	*4*
Reliability	0.9	0.8	0.95	0.75
Cost per item	150	50	100	200

The cost of the redundant components is to be less than or equal to \$500.

P11.12. Capacity Expansion A city expects the following annual growth in electricity demand during the next 10 years.

Year	1	2	3	4	5	6	7	8	9	10
Growth	2	3	1	5	2	3	4	3	2	1

To meet the demand, generation capacity must be installed. The construction cost of capacity as a function of size is shown below.

Size	1	2	3	4	5
Cost	20	38	55	70	80

The discount rate for time value of money calculations is 10%. Capacity can be installed instantaneously. There must always be sufficient capacity to meet demand. Use dynamic programming to find the capacity expansion policy that will minimize the present worth of the construction cost.

CHAPTER 12

Game Theory

Two-Person Zero-Sum Game

This chapter considers the game in which two players each have several strategies from which to select. The selection is to be made without knowledge of the other player's choice. Depending on the strategies chosen, a payoff is made. A gain to one player is a loss to the other, thus providing the zero-sum characteristic. Since we assume that the goal of each player is to minimize the maximum loss, the optimum strategies for the players are called minimax strategies. For this simple type of game, the optimum strategies for both players are easy to determine.

GOALS

- Be able to identify the terms associated with two-person zero-sum games.
- Be able to recognize and eliminate dominated strategies.
- Be able to find the minimax pure strategies when the game is stable.
- Be able to find the optimum mixed strategies for an unstable game with both the graphical and linear programming methods.

DEFINITIONS

Two-Person Game: A competitive situation with two players, designated player I and player II. The game is specified by the sets of strategies available to the two players and the payoff table.

Strategy: An alternative course of action for a player. The set of strategies for player I is indexed from 1 through m. The set of strategies for player II is indexed from 1 through n.

Payoff Table: A table specifying the payoff to player I.

Payoff Table for Player I

		Player II strategy 1	2	n
Player I strategy	1	p_{11}	$p_{12} \cdots$	p_{1n}
	2	p_{21}	$p_{22} \cdots$	p_{2n}
	$\vdots$	$\vdots$	$\vdots$	$\vdots$
	m	p_{m1}	$p_{m2} \cdots$	p_{mn}

The element p_{ij} is the payoff to player I when player I uses strategy i and player II uses strategy j. A positive number is a gain for player I and a negative number is a loss. The payoff table describes the losses of player II since this is a zero-sum game.

Dominated Strategy: A strategy for player I is dominated if all the elements of the strategy's row in the payoff table are less than or equal to the corresponding elements of some other row. For player I, strategy i is dominated by strategy k if

$$p_{ij} \leq p_{kj} \quad \text{for } j = 1, \ldots, n$$

For player II, a strategy is dominated if all the elements of its column are greater than or equal to the corresponding elements of some other column. Strategy j is dominated by strategy k if

$$p_{ij} \geq p_{ik} \quad \text{for } i = 1, \ldots, m.$$

Minimax Criterion: This chapter assumes that each player will select strategies to minimize his or her maximum loss. This criterion is equivalent to the goal of maximizing the minimum gain.

Pure Minimax Strategy: For player I, this is the strategy that maximizes the minimum gain. It is defined as the strategy that obtains the maximum in

$$v_L = \underset{i=1,\ldots,m}{\text{Maximize}} \left(\underset{j=1,\ldots,n}{\text{Minimum}}\, p_{ij} \right).$$

For player II, this is the strategy that minimizes the maximum loss. It is defined as the strategy that obtains the minimum in

$$v_U = \underset{j=1,\ldots,m}{\text{Minimize}} \left(\underset{i=1,\ldots,n}{\text{Maximum}}\, p_{ij} \right).$$

Value of the Game (v): The quantities v_L and v_U defined above are called the lower and upper value of the game, respectively. When these two values are the same, the common result is called the value of the game.

Fair Game: A game for which the value is zero.

Saddle Point: When the same element of the payoff table determines the minimax strategies for both players, the upper and lower values are equal, and that element is called the saddle point.

Stable Game: A game with a saddle point. In this game, both players can adopt the pure minimax strategy and cannot improve their positions by moving to any other strategy.

Unstable Game: A game with no saddle point. In this case upper and lower values are not equal. A player cannot adopt the pure minimax strategy without providing the opportunity for the opponent to gain an improved return.

Mixed Strategy: A procedure for playing the game by which each player chooses the strategy on the basis of a probability distribution. For player I, the probabilities are $(x_1, x_2, \ldots, x_m)$, where x_i is the probability that strategy i will be chosen. For player II, the probabilities are $(y_1, y_2, \ldots, y_n)$, where y_j is the probability that strategy j will be chosen. Both sets of probabilities must sum to 1.

Expected Payoff: The expected value of the payoff of the game when the players use a mixed strategy.

$$\text{Expected payoff} = \sum_{i=1}^{m} \sum_{j=1}^{n} p_{ij} x_i y_j .$$

Minimax Criterion for Mixed Strategies: A player will select the mixed strategy that will minimize the maximum expected loss. In terms of the payoff, player I will adopt a mixed strategy that will maximize the minimum expected payoff, and player II will adopt a mixed strategy that will minimize the maximum expected payoff.

Value of the Game for Minimax Strategies (v): If both players follow their minimax strategies, the value of the game is equal to the expected payoff.

RESULTS

Given the player strategies and the payoff table, the problem is to find the optimum pure or mixed strategies for both players. The solution procedure follows the steps below in the order given.

Eliminate Dominated Strategies Start with player I and eliminate any dominated strategies. Reduce the payoff table by deleting the rows of dominated strategies. For player II, eliminate any dominated strategies and reduce the payoff table by deleting the associated columns. If any strategies are eliminated in this step, return again to player I and check for dominated strategies. If any of the player I strategies are then eliminated, return to player II. The process continues until no dominated strategies remain for either player. If only one strategy remains for both players, these strategies are the solution to the problem.

Find the Pure Minimax Strategy for Each Player If the upper and lower values are equal, the game has a saddle point solution. The associated pure minimax strategies for the players define the optimum solution.

Find the Optimum Mixed Strategy with the Graphical Approach If one of the players has only two strategies remaining, the graphical approach may be used to find the solution. If player I has two strategies, use the payoff table directly. If player II has two strategies, take the negative of all entries in the payoff table and reverse the definitions of player I and player II.

Let x_1 be the probability of strategy 1 for player I and $1 - x_1$ be the probability for strategy 2. For each pure strategy of player II, define the line

$$z_j = p_{1j}\, x_{1x} + p_{2j}(1 - x_1) = p_{2j} + (p_{1j} - p_{2j})x_1 \quad \text{for } j = 1, \ldots, n.$$

Plot the n lines using x_1 as the horizontal axis and the values of z_j on the vertical axis. Identify the lower envelope defined by the lines. At any value of x_1 the line on the lower envelope is the one with the smallest value of z_j. At different values of x_1, different lines may define the lower envelope.

The optimum x_1 is the value that gives the highest point on the lower envelope. Let this value be x^*_1. If the optimum is not at 0 or 1, the case of a pure strategy, at least two lines intersect at the optimum value. If more than two intersect, choose any two. Let the indices of the two lines be j and k . The value of the game is

$$v = p_{2j} + (p_{1j} - p_{2j})x^*_1 = p_{2k} + (p_{1k} - p_{2k})x^*_1.$$

Find the optimum strategy for player II by solving the pair of equations

$$p_{1j}y^*_j + p_{1k}y^*_k = v$$
$$p_{2j}y^*_j + p_{2k}y^*_k = v.$$

The probabilities for all other strategies for player II are zero. If more than two lines intersect at x^*_1, then there are alternative optimum solutions that can be found by selecting different pairs of intersecting strategies.

Find the Optimum Mixed Strategy with the Linear Programming Approach If both players have more than two undominated strategies, the graphical approach can't be used. The optimum can be found by solving a linear programming model. Before proceeding, add a positive amount to all the elements of the payoff table to bring the most negative value up to zero. If there are no negative elements, this step is not necessary. This assures that the value of the game will be positive, but does not change the optimum solution. Set up the following linear programming model for player I.

Objective: Maximize the value of the game

$$\text{Maximize } Z = v.$$

Subject to: The expected payoff must exceed or equal v for any pure strategy of player II.

$$\sum_{i=1}^{m} p_{ij} x_i \geq v \quad \text{for } j = 1, \ldots, n.$$

The probabilities must sum to 1.

$$\sum_{i=1}^{m} x_i = 1.$$

Nonnegativity:

$$v \geq 0 \text{ and } x_i \geq 0 \quad \text{for } i = 1, \ldots, m.$$

Since v is a variable it must be moved to the left side of the constraints for solution by a computer program. The optimum solution to this linear program gives the optimum mixed strategy for player I. The dual solution is the optimal strategy for player II.

An alternative formulation gives the solution for player II directly.

Objective: Minimize the Value of the Game (The value is a loss to player II.)

$$\text{Minimize } Z = v.$$

Subject to: The expected payoff must be less than or equal to v for any pure strategy of player I.

$$\sum_{j=1}^{n} p_{ij} y_j \leq v \quad \text{for } i = 1, \ldots, m.$$

The probabilities must sum to 1.

$$\sum_{j=1}^{n} y_j = 1.$$

Nonnegativity:

$$v \geq 0 \text{ and } y_j \geq 0 \quad \text{for } j = 1, \ldots, n.$$

The optimum solution to this linear program gives the optimum mixed strategy for player II. The dual solution is the optimal strategy for player I. This problem may be more easily solved by a primal approach since it has "less than or equal to" constraints. A little reflection will show that the two formulations are dual problems to each other.

EXAMPLES

E12.1 Given the payoff table below, find the optimum minimax strategy for both players.

Payoff Table for Player I

		Player II strategy			
		1	2	3	4
Player I strategy	1	5	5	1	0
	2	4	0	2	7
	3	3	4	3	4

To solve this problem we first check for dominated rows. Recall that a dominated row has all elements less than or equal to some other row. Comparing all combinations of two rows, we find that none are dominated. Now we check for dominated columns. Recall that a column is dominated if all its elements are greater than or equal to some other column. Comparing columns 1 and 3, we find that column 1 is dominated, so it can be eliminated. The revised matrix is shown below. We have also indicated the minimum in each row and the maximum in each column.

Payoff Table for Player I

		Player II strategy			
		2	3	4	*Min*
Player I strategy	1	5	1	0	0
	2	0	2	7	0
	3	4	3	4	3
	Max	5	3	7	

For player I find the maximum of the minimum gains,

$$v_L = \text{Max } \{0, 0, 3\} = 3,$$

with the maximum obtained for strategy 3. For player II find the minimum of the maximum losses,

$$v_U = \text{Min } \{5, 3, 7\} = 3,$$

with the minimum obtained for strategy 3.

Since $v_L = v_U$, this is a stable strategy with value, $v = 3$. Both players should use strategy 3.

E12.2 Given the payoff table below, find the optimum minimax strategy for both players.

Payoff Table for Player I

		Player II strategy			
		1	2	3	4
Player I strategy	1	3	–1	0	5
	2	4	0	6	–2
	3	3	4	1	7

Reviewing this table for dominated rows or columns, we note that row 1 is dominated by row 3. Eliminating this row, the remaining table with the minimum of each row and the maximum of each column is obtained. We have renumbered the strategies of player I.

Payoff Table for Player I

		Player II strategy				
		1	*2*	*3*	*4*	*Min*
Player I strategy	1	4	0	6	−2	−2
	2	3	4	1	7	1
	Max	4	4	6	7	

For player I find the maximum of the minimum gains,

$$v_L = \text{Max}\ \{-2, 1\} = 1,$$

with the maximum obtained for strategy 2. For player II find the minimum of the maximum losses,

$$v_U = \text{Min}\ \{4, 4, 6, 7\} = 4,$$

with the minimum obtained for strategies 1 and 2.

Since $v_L < v_U$, the pure strategies are not stable and the optimum must be a mixed strategy.

Since only two strategies remain for player I, we will do a graphical analysis to determine the optimum mixed strategy. Let x_1 be the probability of strategy 1 for player I and $(1 - x_1)$ be the probability of strategy 2. The four strategies remaining for player II define four lines in terms of x_1. The general formula is

$$z_j = p_{2j} + (p_{1j} - p_{2j})\, x_1 \quad \text{for } j = 1, 2, 3, 4.$$

Specifically

$$z_1 = 3 + (4 - 3)\, x_1 = 3 + 1x_1$$
$$z_2 = 4 + (0 - 4)\, x_1 = 4 - 4x_1$$
$$z_3 = 1 + (6 - 1)\, x_1 = 1 + 5x_1$$
$$z_4 = 7 + (-2 - 7)\, x_1 = 7 - 9x_1.$$

These lines are plotted in Fig. 12.1. The lower envelope is shown with the heavy line. It describes the payoff for player I as a function of x_1 if the opponent chooses the strategy that minimizes the payoff to player I. The value of x_1 that determines the maximum point on the lower envelope is the optimum value. The maximum occurs at the intersection of the second and third lines. Equating these two lines and solving for the intercept, we have

$$4 - 4\, x_1 = 1 + 5x_1$$
$$x_1 = 1/3.$$

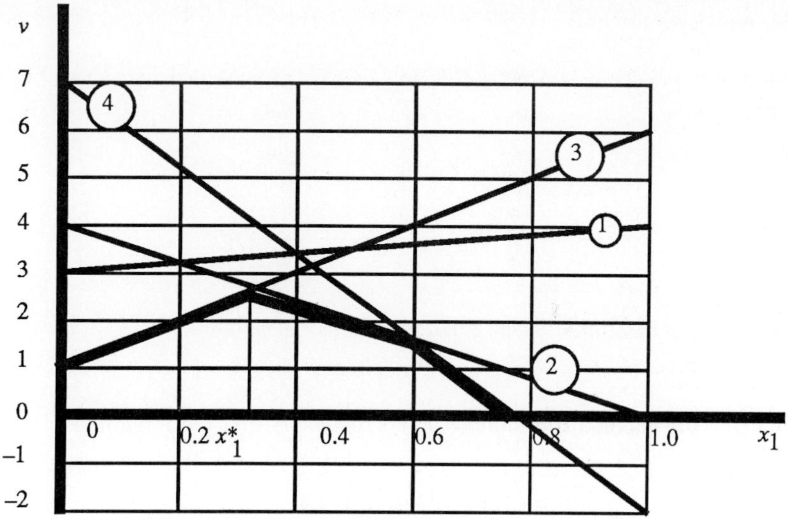

Figure 12.1 **Example of the graphical solution approach**

The optimum solution is to use strategy 1 (originally 2) with probability 1/3, and strategy 2 (originally 3) with probability 2/3.

To find the solution for player II, first solve for the value of the game

$$v = 4 - 4\,(1/3) = 8/3.$$

Only the strategies providing the intersecting lines will be used by player II. These are strategies 2 and 3. Find the optimum strategy for player II by solving the pair of equations

$$p_{12}\, y^*_2 + p_{13}\, y^*_3 = v$$
$$p_{22}\, y^*_2 + p_{23}\, y^*_3 = v$$

or

$$0y^*_2 + 6y^*_3 = 8/3$$
$$4y^*_2 + 1y^*_3 = 8/3.$$

Therefore, the optimum strategy for player II is to play strategy 2 with probability 5/9 and strategy 3 with probability 4/9.

E12.3 Given the following payoff table, find the optimum minimax strategy for both players. The minimums of the rows and maximums of the columns are already computed and shown with the table.

Payoff Table for Player I

		Player II strategy				
		1	*2*	*3*	*4*	*Min*
Player I strategy	1	5	3	6	1	1
	2	4	2	2	4	2
	3	3	4	3	5	3
	Max	5	4	6	5	

For player I find the maximum of the minimum gains,

$$v_L = \text{Max } \{ 1, 2, 3 \} = 3,$$

with the maximum obtained for strategy 3. For player II find the minimum of the maximum losses,

$$v_U = \text{Min } \{ 5, 4, 6, 5 \} = 4,$$

with the minimum obtained for strategy 2. Since $v_L < v_U$, the pure strategies are not stable and the optimum must be a mixed strategy. More than two strategies remain for both players, so we will construct the linear programming model for player I.

Objective: Maximize the value of the game

$$\text{Maximize } Z = v.$$

Subject to: The expected payoff must exceed or equal v for any pure strategy of player II.

Strat. 1: $5x_1 + 4x_2 + 3x_3 - v \geq 0$
Strat. 2: $3x_1 + 2x_2 + 4x_3 - v \geq 0$
Strat. 3: $6x_1 + 2x_2 + 3x_3 - v \geq 0$
Strat. 4: $1x_1 + 4x_2 + 5x_3 - v \geq 0$

The probabilities must sum to 1:

$$x_1 + x_2 + x_3 = 1.$$

Nonnegativity:

$$v \geq 0 \text{ and } x_i \geq 0 \text{ for } i = 1, 2, 3.$$

Solving this model, we find the solution for player I.

$$x_1 = .333, x_2 = 0, x_3 = 0.667, v = 3.667.$$

The dual variables of the linear program give the solution for player II.

$$y_1 = 0.583, y_2 = 0.167, y_3 = 0, y_4 = 0.25.$$

Problems

For P12.1 through P12.4 use the given payoff table for player I to find the optimum minimax strategies for both players.

P12.1

		Player II strategy			
		1	*2*	*3*	*4*
Player I strategy	1	5	4	–3	–2
	2	2	–1	–2	0
	3	2	4	–1	0
	4	1	3	2	1

P12.2

		Player II strategy			
		1	*2*	*3*	*4*
Player I strategy	1	–1	0	4	–1
	2	5	1	3	1
	3	–2	0	–1	4
	4	–3	–2	4	5

P12.3

		Player II strategy			
		1	*2*	*3*	*4*
Player I strategy	1	–2	3	5	2
	2	5	–1	–2	0

P12.4

		Player II strategy				
		1	*2*	*3*	*4*	*5*
Player I strategy	1	–7	–3	0	4	6
	2	1	–5	–2	0	2
	3	5	0	–5	–8	–6
	4	–3	–2	4	0	2
	5	–5	–2	1	5	0

P12.5 Two companies, A and B, are bidding on a contract for the government. Three bids are possible: low, medium, and high. The lowest bid placed by the two companies will be chosen, but if the bids are equal, the government will choose company A over B. Both companies have the same data regarding the cost of the project. If a company wins with the low bid, the costs will equal the income and no profit is made. If a company wins with a medium bid, a profit of 5 is realized. If a company wins with a high bid, a profit of 10 is earned. The table below shows the payoff matrix for company A. If the company losses the bid to its opponent, this is counted as a loss with respect to the relative position of the two companies. The bids are sealed and the companies have no information about each other except that they both use a minimax policy. What is the optimum bidding policy for the two companies? Who will win the contract? What profit will be made?

Payoff Table for Company A

		Company B strategy		
		Low	*Med.*	*High*
Company A strategy	Low	0	0	0
	Med.	0	5	5
	High	0	–5	10

P12.6 At a particular point in a football game, the offensive team and the defensive team must select a strategy for the next play. Both teams have the same statistical information that predicts the expected yardage to be gained for various combinations of offensive and defensive strategies. The information is given in the following table, which shows yards gained for the offensive team for every combination. Determine the minimax policy for both teams. What is the expected gain in yardage?

Payoff Table for Offense (yards gained)

		Defensive strategy				
		1	*2*	*3*	*4*	*5*
Offensive strategy	1	–2	0	2	4	5
	2	–2	–4	0	5	10
	3	10	0	–3	5	10
	4	20	15	5	–5	0
	5	30	20	8	0	–10

P12.7 If in the last problem the offensive team could add 5 to any individual cell in the table, where should the increment be added to most increase the expected payoff? How will the strategies and the value of the game be changed?

P12.8 Set up the linear programming model to determine the optimum strategy for player II in E12.3. Show that the solution determines the same policies for the two players as found in the example.

CHAPTER 13

Integer Programming

Modeling (13.1, 13.2)

Integer programming is concerned with a linear programming model in which some or all of the decisions variables must take on only integer values. In many realistic situations, fractional values are not appropriate. This is particularly true when a variable represents a binary decision, such as the response to a question where only yes or no is allowed. A variable can be defined for which 1 represents yes and 0 represents no; but a linear program may yield the answer 0.5—rather indecisive for a decision. In integer programming, such variables are forced to assume integer values. We will see in this chapter that the models of integer programming are much richer than linear programming in terms of the kinds of restrictions one can place on decision variables. We will also see that integer programming models are much more difficult to solve. Where it is possible to solve linear programs with thousands of decision variables, it is often impossible to solve integer programs with hundreds of decision variables.

GOALS

- Know the special kinds of constraints that are possible with an integer programming model.
- Given a problem situation requiring discrete variables, be able to formulate the appropriate integer programming model.

DEFINITIONS

Integer Program: A model with a linear programming form in which all the variables are required to be integer.

Mixed Integer Program: A model with a linear programming form in which only some of the variables are required to be integer while the others may assume any real values allowed by the constraints.

Binary Integer Program: A model with a linear programming form in which all the variables are required to assume the values 0 or 1.

RESULTS

Since most integer programming models will take the mathematical form of a linear program, all the modeling tools of linear programming are available. There are, however, some special modeling capabilities introduced by the use of integer variables that allow a much greater class of problems to be approached. These will be the subject of this section. We will be primarily concerned with binary integer variables, because the more general integer variables that may assume all nonnegative integer values are usually used in a model in the same way as the continuous variables of linear programming. The binary variables allow the imposition of logical constraints not possible with linear programming, thus justifying this greater interest.

In the following we will use y_j to refer to the jth 0–1 integer variable and x_j to refer to the jth real variable. In models the variables may have arbitrary names, but they must be carefully identified as being either integer or real. If both real and integer variables appear, the model must be a mixed integer program.

Mutually Exclusive Variables If it is required that at most one of the decisions in the set M may be set to 1, this is represented by the constraint

$$\sum_{j \in M} y_j \leq 1$$

Setting any one of the variables to 1 restricts all others to be 0.

Either-or Variables If it is required that one and only one of the decisions in the set M must be set to 1, this is represented by the constraint

$$\sum_{j \in M} y_j = 1$$

Contingent Variables If a variable y_k can be set to 1 only if the variable y_j is set to 1, the decision y_k is said to be contingent upon the decision y_j. This can be represented by the constraint

$$y_k \leq y_j \text{ or } y_k - y_j \leq 0.$$

If y_j is 0, y_k must be 0.

A real variable may also be made contingent on a 0–1 decision variable. If it is required that the real variable x_k must be 0 unless the associated 0–1 variable y_k is 1, this can be represented by the constraint

$$x_k \le u_k\, y_k \ \text{ or } \ x_k - u_k\, y_k \le 0.$$

Here u_k is a given upper bound on x_k. If there is no upper bound stated, use a large number M.

K out of N Constraints Let there be N linear constraints defined for the real variables:

$$f_i(x_1, x_2, \ldots, x_n) \le d_i \qquad \text{for } i = 1, \ldots, N.$$

If only K of these constraints are required to hold for a feasible solution, the constraints should be replaced by

$$\begin{aligned} &f_1(x_1, x_2, \ldots, x_n) \le d_1 + My_1 \\ &f_2(x_1, x_2, \ldots, x_n) \le d_2 + My_2 \\ &\quad\vdots \\ &f_N(x_1, x_2, \ldots, x_n) \le d_N + My_N \\ &\sum_{i=1}^{N} y_i = N - K . \end{aligned}$$

with

$$y_i = 0, 1 \quad \text{for } i = 1, \ldots, N.$$

Here M is a large number. If y_i is set to 1, the corresponding constraint is made ineffective.

Functions with N Possible Values Let there be N values defined for a function of the real variables

$$f(x_1, x_2, \ldots, x_n) \le d_1 \text{ or } d_2 \text{ or} \ldots d_N.$$

This is represented in the integer programming model by the constraints

$$\begin{aligned} &f(x_1, x_2, \ldots, x_n) \le \sum_{i=1}^{N} d_i\, y_i \\ &\sum_{i=1}^{N} y_i = 1 . \end{aligned}$$

with

$$y_i = 0, 1 \text{ for } i = 1, \ldots, N.$$

Fixed Charge Problem It often happens that in order to select a nonzero value for a real decision variable, it is necessary to expend a fixed charge that is independent of the value. For instance, if the real variable represents the amount of use of a facility such as a road or factory, the fixed charge could represent the construction cost of the facility. In this case the objective function (written as a minimization) would include the terms

$$\text{Minimize } Z = \ldots k_j y_j + c_j x_j \ldots,$$

and the constraint set will include the contingent constraint

$$x_j \le u_j y_j,$$

where k_j is the fixed charge for constructing the facility, c_j is the linear unit cost of the facility, u_j is the upper bound on the use, x_j is the real variable representing the amount the facility will be used, and y_j is a binary variable indicating whether the facility will be built.

Concave Cost Function An alternative to the fixed charge is a concave cost function as illustrated in Fig. 13.1. Such a function, $h_j(x_j)$, represents a facility cost that exhibits economies of scale. The figure shows a piecewise linear function that can approximate a function with continuous derivatives with arbitrary accuracy. The approximation identifies p points along the x_j axis, $a_1, a_2, \ldots, a_p$, and p points along the h_j axis, $c_1, c_2, \ldots, c_p$. This defines p pieces representing the objective function term with the first starting at the origin. Let $a_0 = c_0 = 0$. If the function starts at a nonzero cost, that constant can be dropped without changing the optimum solution.

The piecewise linear approximation can be implemented in a mixed integer programming model by defining the variables $x_{j1}, x_{j2}, \ldots, x_{jp}$ to represent the pieces. The slope of the kth piece is

$$s_{jk} = (c_k - c_{k-1}) / (a_k - a_{k-1}).$$

The piecewise linear approximation to the objective function is:

$$\sum_{k=1}^{p} s_{jk} x_{jk} .$$

We must define the equivalence between x_j and its parts by the constraint

$$\sum_{k=1}^{p} x_{jk} - x_j = 0.$$

In order to assure that the pieces of the function are used in the proper order, binary variables must be defined.

$$\text{Define } y_{jk} = \begin{cases} 1 \text{ if piece } k \text{ is included} \\ 0 \text{ if piece } k \text{ is not included.} \end{cases} \qquad k = 1, \ldots, p$$

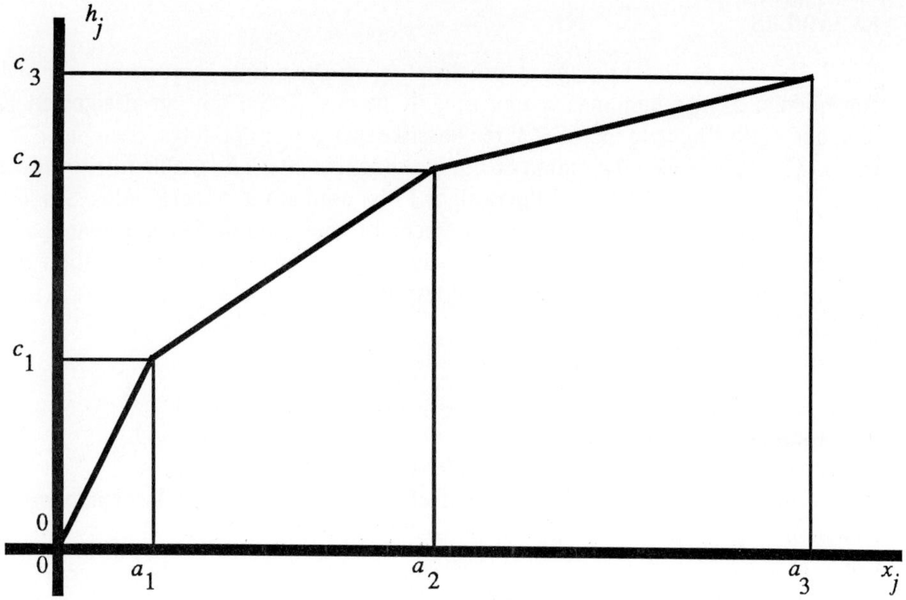

Figure 13.1 **Concave Cost Function Showing Economies of Scale**

We must impose contingent constraints to insure that the real component of piece k is zero if piece k is not selected:

$$x_{jk} / (a_k - a_{k-1}) \leq y_{jk} \text{ for } k = 1, \ldots, p.$$

A second set of contingent constraints requires each real variable to be at its upper bound, if the following piece is selected.

$$y_{j,k+1} \leq x_{jk} / (a_k - a_{k-1}) \text{ for } k = 1, \ldots, p - 1.$$

The model thus modified has p variables replacing one. To obtain a linear model, one pays the price of an expanded problem. The approximation can be made as accurate as required by defining enough pieces, but with a corresponding increase in problem size. Every variable having a nonlinear term in the objective must be expanded in this manner, but the number of pieces in the approximations may vary. The modification adds integer variables that cause a significant computational burden since integer problems are so difficult to solve. A similar procedure can also be used for convex functions in maximization problems.

If the problem includes a convex function for a minimization problem or a concave function for a maximization problem, the piecewise linear approximation can be used without the integer variables, a significant savings. The contingent constraints are replaced with simple upper bound constraints.

$$x_{jk} \leq (a_k - a_{k-1}) \text{ for } k = 1, \ldots, p.$$

This approach is discussed more fully in Chapter 14 as separable programming.

EXAMPLES

E13.1 Consider an investment problem in which a firm is planning for the construction of new buildings at four sites in the city. These sites are designated 1, 2, 3, and 4. At each site there are three possible designs of buildings, designated A, B, and C. There is also the option of not building at a site. The problem is to select the sites on which to build and the designs to be used at the selected sites. Studies have determined the investment requirement of each option and the annual net income of each option. These are shown in the table below with the notation A1 used to identify design A at site 1. Building B3 has been eliminated because it is not feasible.

Option	A1	B1	C1	A2	B2	C2	A3	C3	A4	B4	C4
Investment	12	20	24	30	39	45	10	28	42	50	55
Annual income	2	4	6	5	7	11	5	12	16	19	22

The company has an investment budget of 80 and the objective is to maximize annual income.

To formulate the integer programming model:

$$\text{Let } y_{ij} = \begin{cases} 1 \text{ if design } i \text{ is selected at site } j \\ 0 \text{ if design } i \text{ is not selected at site } j. \end{cases} \qquad i = \text{A, B, C}; \; j = 1, 2, 3, 4; \; ij \neq \text{B3}$$

The objective function is then

$$\text{Maximize } Z = 2y_{A1} + 4y_{B1} + 6y_{C1} + 5y_{A2} + 7y_{B2} + 11y_{C2} + 5y_{A3} + 12y_{C3} + 16y_{A4} + 19y_{B4} + 22y_{C4}.$$

The budget constraint is

$$\text{(B)} \qquad 12y_{A1} + 20y_{B1} + 24y_{C1} + 30y_{A2} + 39y_{B2} + 45y_{C2} + 10y_{A3} + 28y_{C3} + 42y_{A4} + 50y_{B4} + 55y_{C4} \leq 80.$$

Various logical constraints also affect the solution. The most obvious constraint is the requirement that at most one building can be built on each site. Thus the variables defined for each site are mutually exclusive.

$$\text{(M1)} \qquad y_{A1} + y_{B1} + y_{C1} \leq 1$$

$$\text{(M2)} \qquad y_{A2} + y_{B2} + y_{C2} \leq 1$$

$$\text{(M3)} \qquad y_{A3} + y_{C3} \leq 1$$

$$\text{(M4)} \qquad y_{A4} + y_{B4} + y_{C4} \leq 1.$$

Management has decided that for political reasons a building must be built at location 4. Thus the variables for location 4 are either-or variables. Constraint (E4) can replace (M4).

$$\text{(E4)} \qquad y_{A4} + y_{B4} + y_{C4} = 1.$$

The architect specifies that plan A will be available on sites 1, 2, and 3 only if it is selected for site 4. This limitation is imposed with a contingent constraint since buildings A1, A2, and A3 are contingent upon A4.

(C1)
$$y_{A1} + y_{A2} + y_{A3} \le 3y_{A1}, \text{ or}$$
$$y_{A1} + y_{A2} + y_{A3} - 3y_{A1} \le 0$$

Certain combinations of designs are infeasible due to competitive considerations. Specifically, designs B1, B2, and C4 cannot all be built. This is modeled with the constraint

(X1)
$$y_{B1} + y_{B2} + y_{C4} \le 2.$$

This completes the model. Its solution will define an optimum investment plan.

E13.2 Suppose that in addition to the situation described in E13.1, there is an annual cost of maintenance that depends on the number of projects built. For the first two projects built, this cost is 0.2 million per project. If between 3 and 5 projects are built, the cost is 0.15 for each project over 2. If between 6 and 11 projects are built the cost is 0.1 million for all projects over 5. This is a concave cost function that must be subtracted from the objective function defined in E13.1. The cost function is similar to the one of Fig. 13.1. Let x be the number of facilities built. Then we must add a constraint (P) to the model to determine this variable as a function of the decisions.

(P)
$$y_{A1} + y_{B1} + y_{C1} + y_{A2} + y_{B2} + y_{C2} + y_{A3} + y_{C3} + y_{A4} + y_{B4} + y_{C4} - x = 0.$$

Here the piecewise linear function is defined by the breakpoints:

Index	*(k)*	*0*	*1*	*2*	*3*
Breakpoint	(a_k)	0	2	5	11
Cost	(c_k)	0	0.4	0.85	1.45
Slope	(s_k)	—	0.2	0.15	0.1

We define the three variables x_1, x_2, and x_3 to represent the three pieces.

The objective function is changed by adding the following terms. They are negative because the objective is a maximization.

$$\text{Max. } Z = \ldots - 0.2x_1 - 0.15x_2 - 0.1x_3 \ldots$$

We must add an additional constraint to define x in terms of x_1, x_2, and x_3.

$$x_1 + x_2 + x_3 - x = 0.$$

This equation could be used to eliminate x in constraint (P), thus eliminating one constraint and the variable x.

Binary variables and contingent constraints must also be added to assure that the pieces are used in the proper order.

$$\text{Define } z_k = \begin{cases} 1 \text{ if piece } k \text{ is included} \\ 0 \text{ if piece } k \text{ is not included.} \end{cases} \qquad k = 1, \ldots, 3$$

The contingent constraints are:

(CX1) $x_1/2 \leq z_1$

(CX2) $x_2/3 \leq z_2$

(CX3) $x_3/6 \leq z_3$

and

(CZ1) $z_2 \leq x_1/2$

(CZ2) $z_3 \leq x_2/3.$

PROBLEMS

P13.1 A convenience store chain is planning to enter a new market and the locations of new stores are to be determined. The figure shows a map of the major streets in the affected area. Adjacent streets are 1 mile apart. The small x's indicate possible locations of stores. All travel must follow the street network, so distance is measured with a rectilinear metric. For instance the distance between corners A1 and B2 is 2 miles. Set up the integer program that will find the optimum locations of stores. Use the data and restrictions given below.

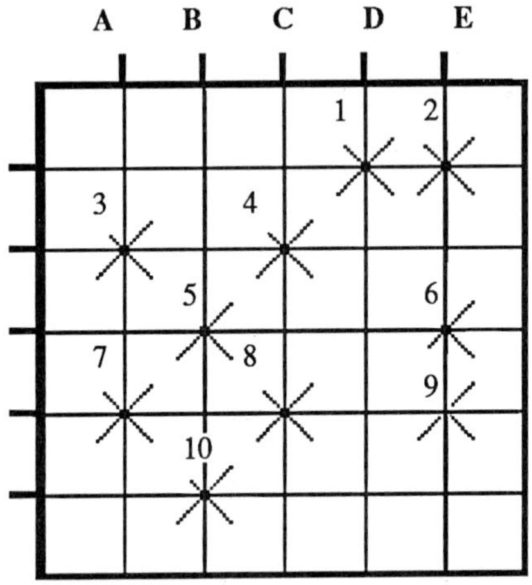

a. The cost to construct a store at the various locations is given in the following table.

Location	1	2	3	4	5	6	7	8	9	10
Cost	100	80	90	50	80	90	100	70	90	80

b. No two stores selected can be on the same street (either north-south or east-west).

c. Stores must be at least 3 miles apart. Stores exactly three miles apart are acceptable, but any less is not allowed.

d. Every grid point (such as A1, B2, etc) must be no more than three miles from a store. Three miles or less is acceptable.

P13.2 Show the equivalent mixed integer programming model for the nonlinear problem given below.

$$\text{Maximize } h_1(x_1) + h_2(x_2) + h_3(x_3)$$

subject to:

$$x_1 + 2x_2 + 3x_3 \leq 13$$
$$2x_1 - x_3 \geq 0$$
$$0 \leq x_1 \leq 5 \text{ and integer,}$$
$$0 \leq x_2 \leq 9,\ 0 \leq x_3 \leq 5.$$

Note that x_2 and x_3 are not required to be integer. The functional forms for h_1, h_2, and h_3 are shown in the figures.

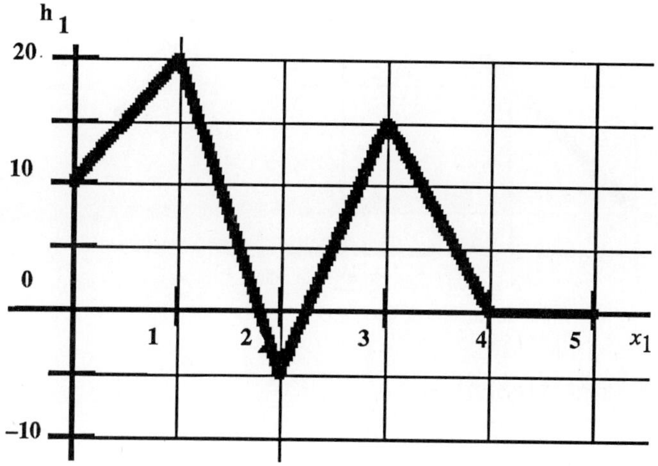

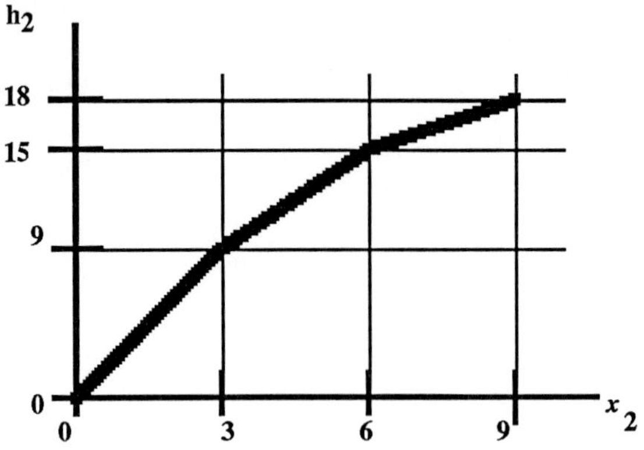

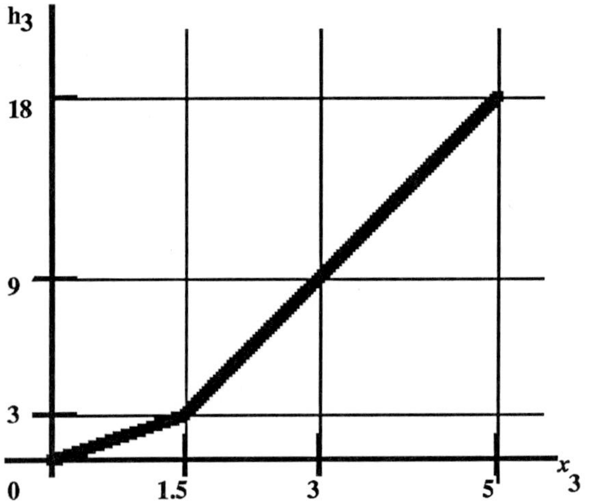

A Branch-and-Bound Algorithm for Binary Integer Programming (13.5)

The method that is used most often to solve integer programs is called branch and bound. This is an enumerative procedure because all possible values of the integer variables are examined, either implicitly or explicitly, in the search for an optimum. Because every bounded integer program has a finite number of solutions, it is conceivable that one could examine every solution with an exhaustive enumeration procedure and choose the optimum feasible solution. The number of solutions may be very large, however, and exhaustive enumeration is impractical except for very small problems. Branch-and-bound procedures include tests to implicitly enumerate (and eliminate) solutions. We call the methods implicit enumeration because individual solutions are not actually reviewed for elimination, but rather reviewed in sets. If a set of solutions has certain characteristics, that will be described later, the whole set may be eliminated. Although this procedure is used in practice to solve problems with perhaps hundreds of integer variables, it is not very effective for very large problems. Problems with only a few integer variables can be solved by hand, but computer programs are necessary to solve practical problems.

This section introduces the basic components of branch-and-bound in the context of the algorithm that solves the binary integer program. The concepts are general, however, and can be adapted to solve a variety of problem types. The solution of the mixed integer program is considered in the next section.

GOALS

- Know the components of the branch-and-bound procedure and the definitions of the various associated terms.
- Be able to perform the procedure described in this chapter to solve small binary integer programs by hand.

DEFINITIONS

Standard Form: For this chapter, we assume that the binary integer program is in the standard form shown below.

$$\text{Minimize } Z = \sum_{j=1}^{n} c_j x_j$$

Subject to

$$\sum_{j=1}^{n} a_{ij} x_j \geq b_i \quad \text{for } i = 1, \ldots, m$$

$$x_j \text{ is binary for } j = 1, \ldots, n.$$

Furthermore, the model is required to have all objective coefficients nonnegative, and the variables must be arranged so that

$$0 \leq c_1 \leq c_2 \leq c_3 \leq \ldots \leq c_n.$$

It is always possible to put an integer program into this form, as will be discussed under the modeling part of this section.

Solution Subset: A subset of the solutions of the integer program defined by setting some of the variables to specific values. To define a solution subset for this algorithm, we will set the first N variables to values as defined by the vector $(x_1, \ldots, x_N)$. For this vector, N may range from 0 to n, and the values of x_j are either 0 or 1. This vector is called a *partial solution*. When $N = 0$ the partial solution vector is empty.

When values are assigned to the remaining variables, $(x_{N+1}, x_{N+2}, \ldots, x_n)$, the result is called a *completion* of the partial solution. The solution subset defined by any partial solution is the set of all completions to the partial solution. Since each variable in the completion may assume two values, the number of solutions in the subset depends on N, as

$$2^{n-N}.$$

When $n = N$ the partial completion vector is empty and there is only one completion. To illustrate, suppose $n = 3$. A solution is defined by the vector (x_1, x_2, x_3). When $N = 0$, the subset of solutions comprises all eight possible binary vectors:

(0,0,0), (0,0,1), (0,1,0), (0,1,1), (1,0,0), (1,0,1), (1,1,0), (1,1,1).

When $N = 1$ and the partial solution is $(x_1) = (1)$, the solution subset is:

(1,0,0), (1,0,1), (1,1,0), (1,1,1).

When $N = 2$, and the partial solution is $(x_1, x_2) = (1,0)$, the solution subset is:

(1,0,0), (1,0,1).

When $N = 3$, and the partial solution is $(x_1, x_2, x_3) = (1,0,1)$, the solution subset is: (1,0,1), with only one member.

Partition: A division of a solution subset into two parts formed by adding one additional variable $(N + 1)$ to the partial solution. The two subsets are defined by first setting x_{N+1} to 0 and then to 1.

To illustrate suppose $n = 3$ and $N = 0$. The solution subset has eight solutions as listed above. We partition the subset into two parts by adding x_1 to the partial solution with its two possible values.

Partial solution: $(x_1) = (1)$. Solution subset: (1,0,0), (1,0,1), (1,1,0), (1,1,1).
Partial solution: $(x_1) = (0)$. Solution subset: (0,0,0), (0,0,1), (0,1,0), (0,1,1).

We have partitioned the set of eight solutions into two subsets of four.

Lower Bound (Z_L): A number less than or equal to the optimum solution of the integer program when allowing only the solutions in a given subset. The lower bound is a function of the partial solution that determines the solution subset. The usual procedure for finding a lower bound is to create a *relaxation* of the integer program. The problem is relaxed by dropping some restrictions, thus ideally making the problem easier to solve. Whenever a restriction is dropped, the optimum objective can only decrease (or stay the same), thus yielding a lower bound.

Upper Bound (Z_U): A number greater than or equal to the objective for the optimum solution of the integer program. An upper bound is the objective function evaluated for any feasible solution of the original problem. The algorithm to be described will find feasible solutions as it progresses. The upper bound will be provided by the *incumbent* solution, the best feasible solution "found so far" by the algorithm.

Fathoming by Bound: If it is discovered that the lower bound (Z_L) for a particular subset of solutions is greater than or equal to the upper bound (Z_U), then that subset cannot contain the optimum and it can be eliminated. The subset is said to be **fathomed.** This is one method for eliminating solutions. The test for fathoming by bound is

$$\text{If } Z_L \geq Z_U \text{, then eliminate the subset.}$$

Fathoming by Infeasibility: If it is discovered that there are no feasible solutions in a particular subset, then that subset cannot contain the optimum and it can be eliminated.

ALGORITHM

The algorithm described here is an enumerative procedure that starts with the set of all solutions and successively partitions the set into smaller and smaller subsets until the individual solutions are obtained. After a subset is created, an attempt will be made to fathom the subset in the hope that it can be eliminated from further consideration. In the following, we first give a general statement of the algorithmic step, and then show the specific implementation for the binary problem.

A0. Initialization Start the process with the subset of all solutions. If a feasible solution can be easily found with a heuristic method, let this solution be the incumbent and let the objective value for this solution be Z_U. Otherwise let $Z_U = M$, where M is a large positive number.

A1. Iterative Step

BRANCH STEP
Use a branch rule to select a subset that has not been previously partitioned or fathomed. Partition the subset.

For the binary integer program we will select the subset with the greatest number of variables in the partial solution (largest N). If two of these exist they will differ only in the value of x_N. If this is the case select the subset with $x_N = 1$. Partition the subset into two new subsets by setting x_{N+1} to 1 and then to 0.

BOUND STEP
Redefine N to include the new variable (N is increased by 1). Compute a lower bound for each new subset.

For the binary integer program the lower bounds will be

$$Z_L = \begin{cases} \sum_{j=1}^{N} c_j x_j & \text{if } x_N = 1 \\ \sum_{j=1}^{N} c_j x_j + c_{N+1} & \text{if } x_N = 0\,. \end{cases}$$

FATHOMING STEP
For each new subset, perform the following tests.

Test 1: If $Z_L \geq Z_U$, fathom the subset and go to A2.

Test 2: If the subset contains no feasible solutions, fathom the subset and go to A2.

We accomplish this for the binary problem by determining for each constraint if

$$\sum_{j=1}^{N} a_{ij}\, x_j + \sum_{j=N+1}^{n} \max\,(0, a_{ij}) < b_i \,.$$

If this result is true for any constraint, there exists no feasible solution and the subset should be fathomed.

Test 3: Try to find the best feasible solution in the subset. If the objective for this solution is less than Z_U, replace Z_U by the objective for the solution and replace the incumbent solution. Perform test 1 on all remaining unfathomed and unpartitioned solutions with the new upper bound.

For the binary problem, we consider the solution:

$$(x_1\,, x_2, \ldots, x_N) \text{ defined by the partial solution,}$$
$$x_{N+1} = 1 - x_N,$$
$$x_j = 0 \text{ for all } j = N+2, \ldots, n.$$

If this solution is feasible, the value of Z_L is the objective value. Replace Z_U by Z_L and replace the incumbent by this solution.

A2. Optimality Test If unfathomed or unpartitioned subsets remain, return to step A1. Otherwise, the algorithm stops. If $Z_U = M$, there is no feasible solution. Otherwise the current incumbent is optimum.

MODELING

If the model is not in the standard form, various transformations are required. If the problem is a maximization, multiply all terms in the objective by –1 to change it to a minimization. "Less than or equal to constraints" are changed to "greater than or equal to" constraints by multiplying both sides by –1. Equality constraints can be changed into two inequalities by

$$f(\mathbf{x}) = b \Leftrightarrow f(\mathbf{x}) \geq b \text{ and } -f(\mathbf{x}) \geq -b \,.$$

If the objective function coefficient is negative for some variable x_j, replace the variable with the equivalent

$$x_j = 1 - x'_j.$$

This transformation will introduce constants into the constraints that must be moved to the right side. Constants in the objective function may be dropped. The variables may have to be rearranged and renumbered so that the objective coefficients are increasing with index.

It is possible to solve problems with nonbinary integer variables if they are transformed into equivalent sums of binary variables. For instance if x_j is an integer variable bounded by 15, it can be replaced by

$$x_j = x_{j1} + 2x_{j2} + 4x_{j3} + 8x_{j4},$$

where the variables x_{j1}, x_{j2}, x_{j3}, and x_{j4} are binary variables.

COMPUTATION

The algorithm described is a simple variation of the Balas additive algorithm. It is called additive because only addition is required in its implementation. Many improvements have been proposed to make this algorithm more efficient through a variety of additional tests and computational procedures.

The branch-and-bound approach has been used in a number of algorithms designed for different classes of problems involving discrete decisions. Thus we have algorithms for the facility location problem, production scheduling problem, partitioning problem, covering problem, fixed charge problem, and many others. The various problems all have special structure that can be used to make the approach more efficient. Although computer programs for the general integer programming problem exist, the most successful algorithms are designed for particular problem classes.

All these algorithms are called "exponential algorithms" because the difficulty of solving a problem is an exponential function of the problem size. Thus although an algorithm may solve a certain problem with fair ease, it is very likely that there will be some not much larger problem that will be impossible to solve with a practical expenditure of computer resources.

EXAMPLES

E13.3 Solve the following problem with the branch-and-bound algorithm.

$$\begin{array}{llllll} \text{Minimize } Z = & 5x_1 & +7x_2 & +10x_3 & +13x_4 & \\ \text{Const. 1:} & -3x_1 & +4x_2 & +2x_3 & +5x_4 & \geq 5 \\ \text{Const. 2:} & +5x_1 & -1x_2 & +5x_3 & +3x_4 & \geq 4 \end{array}$$

$$x_j = 0, 1 \text{ for } j = 1, 2, 3, 4.$$

This problem is already in the form required by the algorithm and needs no transformations. The sequence of algorithm steps taken to solve the problem is shown in Table 13.1. In the table the following notation is used.

The partial solution is $\mathbf{x} = (x_1, x_2, \ldots, x_N)$.

The objective function of the partial solution is

$$C = \sum_{j=1}^{N} c_j x_j .$$

The constraint values for a partial solution is

$$b'_i = \sum_{j=1}^{N} a_{ij}\, x_j \text{ for } i = 1 \ldots m.$$

The constraint values for the set of constraints are shown by the vector

$$\mathbf{b'} = (b'_1, b'_2, \ldots, b'_m).$$

The incumbent solution is the vector $\mathbf{x_U}$.

Each line of the table represents a partial solution and the associated set of complete solutions of the problem. The generation sequence column indicates the order in which the partial solutions were generated. The partition sequence column shows the order in which the partial solutions were partitioned. Lines with dashes indicate partial solutions that are fathomed rather than partitioned. The remainder of each line shows various numerical information about the partial solution, the lower bound for the solution as calculated by the equations shown in the algorithm, the upper bound available when the solution was generated, and the action taken concerning the partial solution. Every partial solution must be either fathomed or partitioned. Note that the incumbent solution remaining when the algorithm terminates is (0,1,1,0). This is the optimal solution to the problem. The student should try to construct this table following the steps of the algorithm.

Figure 13.2 shows a graphical presentation of the enumeration process called the enumeration tree. Each node represents a partial solution. The tree can be divided into levels according to the value of N. Each node is either partitioned to form two new partial solutions or fathomed according to the rules of the algorithm. The nodes are numbered to agree with the generation numbers in the first column of Table 13.1. The solution process is nicely illustrated using both the table and the tree, but

***Table 13.1* Sequence of Partial Solutions Considered**

Gen. seq.	*Part. seq.*	*N*	**x**	*C*	(b'_1, b'_2)	Z_L	Z_U	*Action*
1	1	0	—	0	(0, 0)	0	*M*	Partition into 2 and 3
2	5	1	(0)	0	(0, 0)	7	*M*	Partition into 10 and 11
3	2	1	(1)	5	(–3, 5)	5	*M*	Partition into 4 and 5
4	—	2	(1,0)	5	(–3, 5)	15	*M*	Fathom by test 2 (Const.1)
5	3	2	(1,1)	12	(1, 4)	12	*M*	Partition into 6 and 7
6	—	3	(1,1,0)	12	(1, 4)	25	*M*	Fathom by test 3 $Z_U = 25$, $\mathbf{x_U} = (1,1,0,1)$
7	4	3	(1,1,1)	22	(3, 9)	22	25	Partition into 8 and 9
8	—	4	(1,1,1,0)	22	(3, 9)	22	25	Fathom by test 2 (Const. 1)
9	—	4	(1,1,1,1)	35	(8,12)	35	25	Fathom by test 1
10	—	2	(0,0)	0	(0, 0)	10	25	Fathom by test 1 using Z_U obtained at solution #13
11	6	2	(0,1)	7	(4, –1)	7	25	Partition into 12 and 13
12	—	3	(0,1,0)	7	(4, –1)	20	25	Fathom by test 2 (Const. 1)
13	—	3	(0,1,1)	17	(6, 4)	17	25	Fathom by test 3 $Z_U = 17$, $\mathbf{x_U} = (0,1,1,0)$

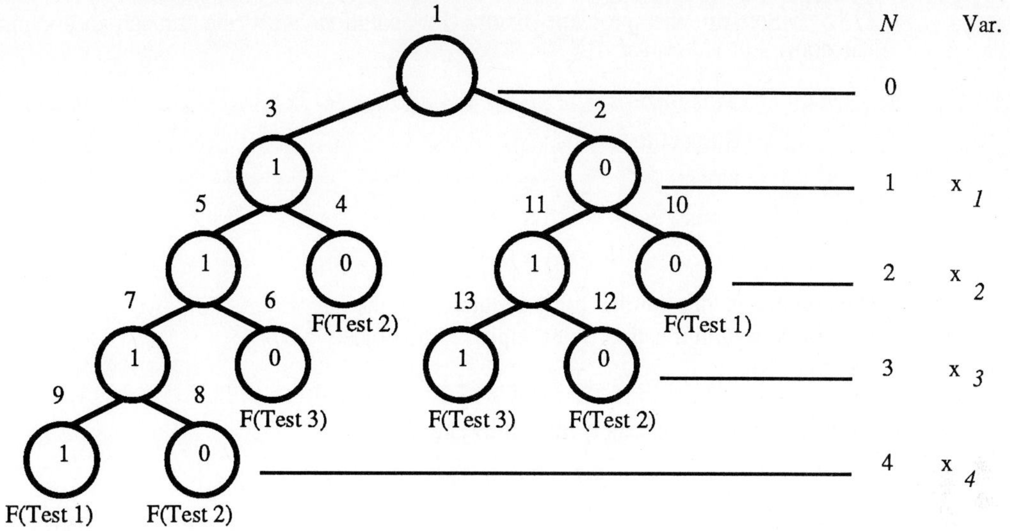

Figure 13.2 **The Enumeration Tree for the Example Problem**

the tree is difficult to draw for problems not much larger than this example. The format given in the table is useful for performing the algorithm by hand although the table can become very long.

E13.4 Answer the following questions concerning the enumeration process followed in E13.3.

a. Which solutions were eliminated when the partial solution #4 was fathomed?
Ans: This partial solution is $\mathbf{x}$ = (1,0). The subset of solutions represented by this partial solution is: (1,0,0,0), (1,0,0,1), (1,0,1,0), (1,0,1,1). Constraint 1 is not satisfied for any of these solutions. This was the conclusion of test 2.

b. Which solutions were eliminated when the partial solution #9 was fathomed?
Ans: This partial solution is $\mathbf{x}$ = (1,1,1,1). The subset represented by this solution has only one member, the solution itself. Only this solution is eliminated. This illustrates why we want strong fathoming tests that eliminate nodes high in the enumeration tree.

c. If the upper bound of 17 had been known before the algorithm began, which partial solutions would not have been generated by the algorithm?
Ans: With this change any solution with a lower bound of at least 17 would have been fathomed and not partitioned. Only solution #7 would have been fathomed in this manner, and solutions #8 and #9 would not have been generated.

E13.5 Set up the problem below for solution with the branch-and-bound algorithm.

$$\begin{aligned}
&\text{Maximize } Z = -5x_1 + 7x_2 - 10x_3 + 13x_4\\
&\text{Subject to}\\
&\text{Const. 1:} \quad +3x_1 + 4x_2 - 2x_3 + 5x_4 \le 4\\
&\text{Const. 2:} \quad +5x_1 + 1x_2 + 5x_3 - 3x_4 \ge 2\\
&\qquad x_j = 0, 1 \text{ for } j = 1, 2, 3, 4.
\end{aligned}$$

This model is not in the form required by the algorithm. First we change the problem to a minimization by multiplying the objective by –1.

$$\text{Minimize } Z = +5x_1 - 7x_2 + 10x_3 - 13x_4$$

We then change constraint 1 by multiplying by –1.

$$\text{Const. 1:} \quad -3x_1 - 4x_2 + 2x_3 - 5x_4 \ge -4.$$

In order to obtain all positive objective coefficients we make the transformations

$$\begin{aligned}
&x'_2 = 1 - x_2 \text{ and } x'_4 = 1 - x_4.\\
&\text{Minimize } Z = +5x_1 - 7(1 - x'_2) + 10x_3 - 13(1 - x'_4)\\
&\text{Subject to}\\
&\text{Const. 1:} \quad -3x_1 - 4(1 - x'_2) + 2x_3 - 5(1 - x'_4) \ge -4\\
&\text{Const. 2:} \quad +5x_1 + 1(1 - x'_2) + 5x_3 - 3(1 - x'_4) \ge 2
\end{aligned}$$

Moving all constants to the right in the constraints and dropping constants from the objective, we finally obtain the proper form.

$$\begin{aligned}
&\text{Minimize } Z = 5x_1 + 7x'_2 + 10x_3 + 13x'_4\\
&\text{Subject to}\\
&\text{Const. 1:} \quad -3x_1 + 4x'_2 + 2x_3 + 5x'_4 \ge 5\\
&\text{Const. 2:} \quad +5x_1 - 1x'_2 + 5x_3 + 3x'_4 \ge 4\\
&\qquad x_j = 0, 1 \text{ for } j = 1, 2, 3, 4.
\end{aligned}$$

Problems

P13.3 For the problem below, do 12 replications of the iterative step of the branch and bound method.

$$\begin{aligned}
&\text{Maximize } 84x_1 + 48x_2 + 25x_3 + 29x_4 + 128x_5\\
&\text{Subject to } 49x_1 + 30x_2 + 19x_3 + 29x_4 + 91x_5 \le 130\\
&\qquad x_j = 0,1 \text{ for } j = 1, \ldots, 5\,.
\end{aligned}$$

P13.4 Solve the problem below with branch and bound.

$$
\begin{array}{lrrrrl}
\text{Minimize} & 3x_1 & +7x_2 & +4x_3 & +5x_4 & \\
\text{Subject to} & 2x_1 & +x_2 & +3x_3 & +4x_4 & \geq 6 \\
 & x_1 & +2x_2 & +4x_3 & +2x_4 & \geq 6 \\
 & 3x_1 & +4x_2 & +x_3 & +x_4 & \geq 6 \\
 & \multicolumn{5}{l}{x_j = 0,1 \text{ for } j = 1, 2, 3, 4.}
\end{array}
$$

P13.5 Solve the 0–1 integer program below.

$$
\begin{array}{lrrrrrl}
\text{Minimize} & +10x_1 & +5x_2 & +7x_3 & +2x_4 & +8x_5 & \\
\text{Subject to} & -3x_1 & +1x_2 & +5x_3 & +3x_4 & -2x_5 & \geq +6 \\
 & +2x_1 & -3x_2 & -1x_3 & +10x_4 & -1x_5 & \geq +9 \\
 & +5x_1 & +4x_2 & +10x_3 & -2x_4 & +2x_5 & \geq +8 \\
 & +3x_1 & -3x_2 & -4x_3 & +5x_4 & -5x_5 & \geq +4 \\
 & \multicolumn{6}{l}{x_j = 0,1 \text{ for } j = 1, \ldots, 8}
\end{array}
$$

Branch-and-Bound Algorithm for Mixed Integer Programming (13.6)

Many integer programming algorithms use a linear programming relaxation to obtain the lower bound required by the branch-and-bound procedure. This relaxation is effected by dropping the integrality constraints on the variables and solving the resultant linear program. Since the new problem is less restricted than the original, the value of the optimum solution to the linear program must provide a lower bound to the original. Mixed integer programming problems are generally solved by this procedure as illustrated in this section, although the method can also be applied to pure integer programs.

The mixed integer programming model is assumed here to be defined by a linear model with some of the variables required to be integer. The objective is a minimization, but there are no further restrictions on the model.

GOAL

- Given an integer program, be able to use the branch-and-bound procedure using a linear programming relaxation.

ALGORITHM

We will use the outline of the branch-and-bound algorithm given in the last section with some changes in the iterative step.

A1. Iterative Step

SELECTION STEP
Here we want to select a subset that was not previously partitioned or fathomed. We will not be definitive about this step because there are a number of valid strategies for this selection, and various algorithms differ in this respect.

BOUND STEP
Solve the linear programming relaxation of the model to obtain Z_L.

FATHOMING STEP
Using the linear programming solution, perform the following tests.

Test 1: If the linear program has a feasible solution and $Z_L \geq Z_U$, fathom the subset. The optimum solution from this subset is not better than the incumbent.

Test 2: If the linear program does not have a feasible solution, fathom the subset. The subset does not include a feasible solution.

Test 3: If the solution to the linear program has all integer values for the variables specified as integer in the original problem, then Z_L is the value of a feasible solution. Replace Z_U by Z_L, replace the incumbent with the solution of the linear program, and fathom the subset.

BRANCH STEP
If the subset was fathomed go to step A2.

If the subset was not fathomed, select a variable that was specified as integer in the original problem but that has a fractional value in the linear programming solution. Say the variable is x_j and lies between the integers k and $k + 1$.

$$k < x_j < k + 1.$$

Partition the subset into two subsets by adding constraints.

For the first subset add $x_j \leq k$, and
for the second subset add $x_j \geq k + 1$.

Together the two subsets formed have the same set of integer solutions as the subset used for the partition. Continue with step A2.

EXAMPLES

E13.6 To illustrate this procedure we use the facility location problem. This is an important application of mixed integer programming and the subject of a great deal of research. Figure 13.3 shows the unit costs of transporting a commodity from each of three proposed warehouse locations to each of five customer locations. The demand for the commodity is also shown in the figure. We must decide which of the three locations should have a warehouse. The capacity of a warehouse, if built, is 30. The cost of building a warehouse at locations 1 or 3 is 200. The cost of building a warehouse at location 2 is 300.

		CUSTOMER 1	2	3	4	5
	1	15	15	16	11	11
WAREHOUSE	2	13	11	15	9	6
	3	8	12	11	7	8
DEMAND		5	10	15	5	10

Figure 13.3 **Trasportation Costs**

The most obvious mixed integer programming formulation of this problem follows the linear programming model of the transportation problem. We show the general formulation. Here m is the number of warehouse locations and n is the number of customers. For this model let

x_{ij} = the amount shipped from warehouse location i to customer j for $i = 1, \ldots, m$ and $j = 1, \ldots, n$.

y_i = the decision whether to build at location i for $i = 1, \ldots, m$.

$y_i = 1 \Rightarrow$ build at location i.

$y_i = 0 \Rightarrow$ do not build at location i.

The shipment amounts will be taken as the real variables and the building decisions will be the integer variables. The model is then

$$\text{Minimize } Z = \sum_{i=1}^{m} \sum_{j=1}^{n} c_{ij}\, x_{ij} + \sum_{i=1}^{m} f_i\, y_i$$

where c_{ij} are transportation costs and f_i are construction costs.
Subject to: All demand must be met.

$$\sum_{i=1}^{m} x_{ij} = d_j \quad \text{for } j = 1, \ldots, n. \quad (d_j \text{ are demands})$$

Shipments can only come from an open warehouse and must not exceed the capacity.

$$\sum_{j=1}^{n} x_{ij} \le u_i\, y_j \quad \text{for } i = 1, \ldots, m. \quad (u_i \text{ is the warehouse capacity})$$

Nonnegativity and integrality:

$$x_{ij} \geq 0 \text{ for all } i \text{ and } j. \; y_i = 0,1 \text{ for all } i.$$

It has been found that this formulation, although correct, is inefficient for branch-and-bound, because the solution of the linear programming relaxation does not give a large enough bound and is ineffective for Test 1 of the algorithm. A more efficient model uses the following variables.

x_{ij} = the fraction of the demand of customer j met from warehouse i for $i = 1, \ldots, m$ and $j = 1, \ldots, n$.

y_i = the decision whether to build at location i for $i = 1, \ldots, m$.

Now the model becomes

$$\text{Minimize } Z = \sum_{i=1}^{m} \sum_{j=1}^{n} (d_j \; c_{ij}) \, x_{ij} + \sum_{i=1}^{m} f_i \, y_i$$

Subject to: All demand must be met.

$$\sum_{i=1}^{m} x_{ij} = 1 \text{ for } j = 1, \ldots, n.$$

Shipments can only come from an open warehouse and must not exceed the capacity.

$$\sum_{j=1}^{n} d_i x_{ij} \leq u_i y_j \quad \text{for } i = 1, \ldots, m.$$

Nonnegativity and integrality.

$$x_{ij} \geq 0 \text{ for all } i \text{ and } j. \; y_i = 0,1 \text{ for all } i.$$

To this point the two models are equivalent, but one additional type of constraint is used that significantly increases the efficiency of the procedure. This constraint specifies that the use of any shipping link is possible only if the corresponding warehouse is open.

$$x_{ij} \leq y_i \text{ for } i = 1, \ldots, m \text{ and for } j = 1, \ldots, n.$$

This set of $m \times n$ constraints is clearly redundant; however, they force the values of the y_i to assume the maximum value of the shipment variables leaving warehouse i. This causes the linear programming relaxation to yield better bounds.

To form the linear programming relaxation, the integrality constraints are replaced by simple bounds

$$0 \leq y_i \leq 1.$$

The enumeration tree of the branch-and-bound procedure is illustrated in Fig. 13.4. In the following, we identify the subsets of solutions with the index shown adjacent

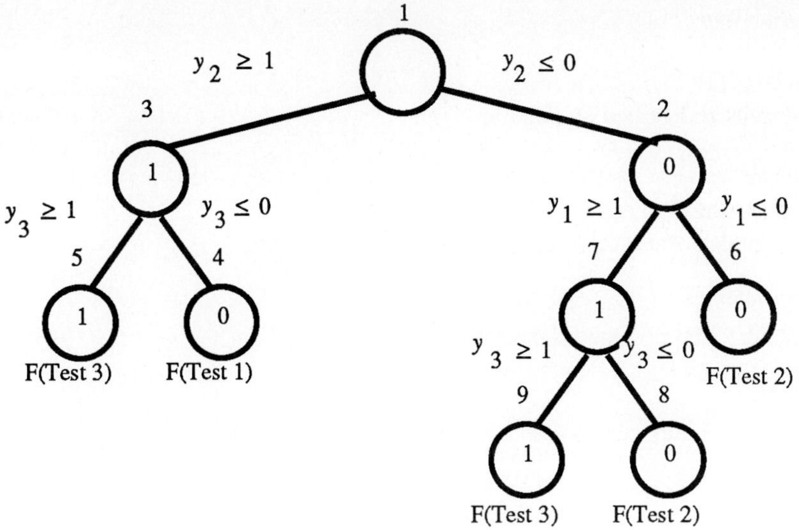

Figure 13.4 **Enumeration Tree for the Example Problem**

to each node. The linear program relaxations are solved with a computer program. The details of the algorithmic steps for the example problem are listed below.

A0. Initialization Set $Z_U = M$. Define the initial subset consisting of all integer solutions, identified by node 1 in Figure 13.4.

A1. Iterative Step

SELECTION STEP
Select the subset identified by node 1.

BOUND STEP
The LP relaxation determines $Z_L = 790$, $y_1 = 0$, $y_2 = 0.5$, $y_3 = 1$.

FATHOMING STEP
Tests 1, 2, and 3 do not fathom the subset.

BRANCH STEP
Partition subset 1 into subsets 2 and 3 with the added constraint

$y_2 \leq 0$ for subset 2, and
$y_2 \geq 1$ for subset 3.

A2. Optimality Step Subsets still remain, so go to step A1.

A1. Iterative Step

SELECTION STEP
Select the subset identified by node 3.

BOUND STEP
The LP relaxation includes $y_2 \geq 1$.
The optimum determines $Z_L = 860$, $y_1 = 0$, $y_2 = 1$, $y_3 = 0.5$.

FATHOMING STEP
Tests 1, 2, and 3 do not fathom the subset.

BRANCH STEP
Partition subset 3 into subsets 4 and 5 with the added constraint

$$y_3 \leq 0 \text{ for subset 4, and}$$
$$y_3 \geq 1 \text{ for subset 5.}$$

A2. Optimality Step Subsets still remain, so go to step A1.

A1. Iterative Step

SELECTION STEP
Select the subset identified by node 5.

BOUND STEP
The LP relaxation includes $y_2 \geq 1$ and $y_3 \geq 1$.
The optimum determines $Z_L = 910$, $y_1 = 0$, $y_2 = 1$, $y_3 = 1$.

FATHOMING STEP
Test 3 determines that this is a feasible solution. Set $Z_U = 910$, with the incumbent $\mathbf{y} = (0, 1, 1)$. Fathom the subset.

A2. Optimality Step Subsets still remain, so go to step A1.

A1. Iterative Step

SELECTION STEP
Select the subset identified by node 4.

BOUND STEP
The LP relaxation includes $y_2 \geq 1$ and $y_3 \leq 0$.
The optimum determines $Z_L = 932.5$, $y_1 = 0.5$, $y_2 = 1$, $y_3 = 0$.

FATHOMING STEP
Test 1 fathoms this subset because $Z_L > Z_U$.

A2. Optimality Step Subsets still remain, so go to step A1.

A1. Iterative Step

SELECTION STEP
Select the subset identified by node 2.

BOUND STEP
The LP relaxation includes $y_2 \leq 0$. The optimum determines $Z_L = 792$, $y_1 = 0.5$, $y_2 = 0$, $y_3 = 1$.

FATHOMING STEP
Tests 1, 2, and 3 do not fathom the subset.

BRANCH STEP
Partition subset 2 into subsets 6 and 7 with the added constraint

$y_1 \leq 0$ for subset 6, and
$y_1 \geq 1$ for subset 7.

A2. Optimality Step Subsets still remain, so go to step A1.

A1. Iterative Step

SELECTION STEP
Select the subset identified by node 7.

BOUND STEP
The LP relaxation includes $y_2 \leq 0$ and $y_1 \geq 1$. The optimum determines $Z_L = 857.5$, $y_1 = 1$, $y_2 = 0$, $y_3 = 0.5$.

FATHOMING STEP
Tests 1, 2, and 3 do not fathom the subset.

BRANCH STEP
Partition subset 7 into subsets 8 and 9 with the added constraint

$y_3 \leq 0$ for subset 8, and
$y_3 \geq 1$ for subset 9.

A2. Optimality Step Subsets still remain, so go to step A1.

A1. Iterative Step

SELECTION STEP
Select the subset identified by node 9.

BOUND STEP

The LP relaxation includes $y_2 \le 0$, $y_1 \ge 1$, and $y_3 \ge 1$. The optimum determines $Z_L = 885$, $y_1 = 1$, $y_2 = 0$, $y_3 = 1$.

FATHOMING STEP

Test 3 determines that this is a feasible solution. Set $Z_U = 885$, with the incumbent $\mathbf{y} = (1, 0, 1)$. Fathom the subset.

A2. Optimality Step Subsets still remain, so go to step A1.

A1. Iterative Step

SELECTION STEP

Select the subset identified by node 8.

BOUND STEP

The LP relaxation includes $y_2 \le 0$, $y_1 \ge 1$, and $y_3 \le 0$. This problem is infeasible.

FATHOMING STEP

Test 2 fathoms this subset because of infeasibility.

A2. Optimality Step Subsets still remain, so go to step A1.

A1. Iterative Step

SELECTION STEP

Select the subset identified by node 6.

BOUND STEP

The LP relaxation includes $y_2 \le 0$, and $y_1 \le 0$. This problem is infeasible.

FATHOMING STEP

Test 2 fathoms this subset because of infeasibility.

A2. Optimality Step No subsets remain, and the enumeration is complete. The optimum is the current incumbent $\mathbf{y} = (1, 0, 1)$.

E13.7 Recognizing that at least two facilities must be included to meet the demand, add this constraint to the mixed integer programming model.

$$y_1 + y_2 + y_3 \ge 2.$$

Now solve the mixed integer program.

When this constraint is added and the linear programming relaxation is solved, the optimum integer solution is obtained: $\mathbf{y} = (1, 0, 1)$ and $Z = 885$, without any additional branching from node 1. (Node 1 is fathomed with test 3.) This illustrates that redundant constraints, when added to an integer or mixed integer program, can markedly affect the efficiency of the solution process.

PROBLEMS

P13.6 The following tableau gives the LP solution to the relaxation of an integer programming (not 0–1) problem. The problem is a maximization.

Row	*Var.*	Z	x_1	x_2	x_3	x_4	x_5	x_6	b
0	Z	1	0.1	0.3	0	0.2	0	0	23.1
1	x_6	0	1.3	–0.3	0	–1.0	0	1	5.3
2	x_3	0	0	1.1	1	0.4	0	0	1.6
3	x_5	0	–0.8	–0.2	0	–0.5	1	0	3.7

a. Add the constraint $x_3 \le 1$ and solve the linear programming problem using the dual simplex method. What subset of feasible solutions is defined by this operation and what upper bound can be placed on the optimum for this subset?

b. Add the constraint $x_3 \ge 2$ and solve the linear programming problem using the dual simplex method. What subset of feasible solutions is defined by this operation and what upper bound can be placed on the optimum for this subset?

P13.7 Solve the facility location problem of this section using the first formulation given. Use a computer program to solve the linear programming relaxations. Show the enumeration tree generated by the procedure.

Computer Program

Microsolve includes a computer code for the pure binary integer program. Although the algorithm used is similar to the one introduced in this chapter it is sufficiently different to warrant a detailed description. The program includes a good number of screen displays that allow the student to follow the course of the algorithm and a certain knowledge of the algorithm will enable the student to understand the displays. Because of space limitations, this description is terse. More detailed expositions are found in the references. *

This algorithm uses an alternative standard form for the model.

* Balas, Egon: "An Additive Algorithm for Solving Linear Programs with Zero – One Variables," *Operations Research*, **13**: 517–546, July–August1965.

Garfinkel, R. S., and G.L. Nemhauser: *Integer Programming*, Wiley, New York, 1972.

$$\begin{aligned} &\text{Maximize} \quad \mathbf{c\,y} \\ &\text{Subject to} \\ &\qquad \mathbf{Ay} \le \mathbf{b} \\ &\qquad y_j = 0,1 \text{ for } j = 1, \ldots, n, \end{aligned}$$

where **y** is a column vector of n binary variables and **c**, **A**, and **b** are integer matrices with the usual linear programming definitions. In addition all the coefficients in **c** must be nonpositive. Models of arbitrary form can be transformed into this standard using the methods described in this chapter. Integer programming models entered into the linear programming generator of *Microsolve* will be automatically transformed by the program.

DEFINITIONS

For purposes of the revised version of the algorithm add the following definitions.

Variables Set to 1 (W^+): This is the set of variables that are set to 1 for a given partial solution.

Variables Set to 0 (W^-): This is the set of variables that are set to 0 for the partial solution.

Free Variables (W^0): This is the set of variables that have not yet been set to 0 or 1 for the partial solution.

Current Objective Value (Z'): The value of the objective function considering only the variables set to 1.

$$Z' = \sum_{j \varepsilon W^+} (c_j).$$

Current Right Sides (r_i): The right sides of the constraints adjusted for the values of the variables set to 1.

$$r_i = b_i - \sum_{j \varepsilon W^+} (a_{ij}).$$

Negative Coefficients of the Free Variables (t_i): The sum of the negative coefficients of the free variables in the constraints.

$$t_i = \sum_{j \varepsilon W^0} \min (a_{ij}, 0)$$

ALGORITHM

Since the standard form is a maximization rather than a minimization the roles of the upper and lower bounds are reversed from those described in this chapter. In addition to the bound and feasibility tests for the solution subsets, we also use tests to determine whether individual variables must be set to 0 or 1 for the feasibility or optimality of a subset.

A0. Initialization Start the process with the subset of all solutions. If a feasible solution can be easily found with a heuristic method, let this solution be the incumbent and let the objective value for this solution be Z_L. Otherwise let $Z_L = -M$, where M is a large positive number.

A1. Iterative Step

BRANCH STEP

Use a branch rule to select a subset that has not been previously partitioned or fathomed.

We will select the unpartitioned and unfathomed subset that was last generated. Find W^+, W^-, and W^0 for this partial solution.

BOUND STEP

Compute an upper bound for the subset.

The upper bound is simply the current objective value Z'.

$$Z_U = Z'.$$

FATHOMING STEP

For the new subset perform the following tests.

Test 1: If $Z_U \leq Z_L$, fathom the subset and go to A2.

Test 2: If the subset contains no feasible solutions fathom the subset and go to A2.

If for some constraint i,

$$t_i > r_i ,$$

there exists no feasible solution and the subset should be fathomed.

Test 3. Try to find the best feasible solution in the subset. If the objective for this solution is greater than Z_L, replace Z_L by the objective for the solution and replace the incumbent solution and go to A2.

If for the subset, the current right sides are all positive, the solution defined by setting all the variables in W^+ to 1, and all variables in W^- and W^0 to 0 is feasible. The value of Z' is the objective value. Replace Z_L by Z' and replace the incumbent by this solution. Formally, the test for feasibility is

$$r_i \geq 0 \text{ for } i = 1, \ldots, m.$$

Test 4: Try to set additional variables to 0 or 1.

For each free variable, $y_j \varepsilon W^0$, make the following tests. If $Z' + c_j \leq Z_L$, then y_j cannot be 1 in the optimum solution, so set y_j to 0.

For any constraint i,

if $a_{ij} > 0$ and $a_{ij} + t_i > r_i$, then set y_j to 0 for feasibility.
if $a_{ij} < 0$ and $-a_{ij} + t_i > r_i$, then set y_j to 1 for feasibility.

If any variables are set to 0 or 1 by this step, perform tests 1, 2, and 3 in an attempt to fathom the subset. If the tests fathom the subset, go to A2.

PARTITIONING STEP

Select a free variable for partitioning. Form two new subsets by first setting the variable equal to 0, and then setting the variable equal to 1.

For each free variable compute

$$I_j = \sum_{i=1}^{m} \text{Min}\ [0, (r_i - a_{ij})]\ .$$

The partitioning variable is the one with the greatest value of I_j. Setting this variable to 1 will move the partial solution closest to feasibility.

A2. Optimality Test If unfathomed or unpartitioned subsets remain, return to step A1. Otherwise, the algorithm stops. If $Z_L = -M$, there is no feasible solution. Otherwise, the current incumbent is optimum.

USING THE PROGRAM

Integer programming models are entered into the computer using the Linear Model Generator of *Microsolve*. Models are limited to 20 binary variables. Selecting option 8 from the menu of this program transforms the model to the required standard form and calls the implicit enumeration program that solves the problem with the algorithm described above.

The menu for the solution program is shown in Fig. 13.5. The problem is solved by selecting option 2. The first data required is a maximum percentage deviation from the optimum. When zero is entered, the program will find the optimum solution. With a number greater than zero is entered, the program may not find the optimum, but the objective function will be within the requested percentage of the maximum value. This is useful for large problems for which the time to obtain the optimum may be excessive. Let p be the percentage. The algorithm uses p in a modified version of test 1.

Test 1: If $Z_U \leq Z_L\ (1 - p\ /100)$, fathom the subset and go to A2.

```
1. SHOW MODEL
2. SOLVE INTEGER PROGRAM
3. REVIEW SOLUTION
4. REVISE MODEL
5. TURN PRINTER ON
6. RETURN TO DISK MENU

PROBLEM 'IP EXAMPLE' IS LOADED
12 VARIABLES AND 8 CONSTRAINTS

ENTER OPTION:
```

Figure 13.5 **Integer Programming Solution Algoritm Menu**

Clearly, if p is greater than zero, it will be easier to fathom subsets; however, the optimum may be discarded by this test.

Several display options are provided for the program. Of course, the minimum output option gives the most rapid solution. Other output options allow the steps of the algorithm to be displayed in a continuous fashion or with a pause after each step. The latter feature is useful for students attempting to learn the details of the procedure. As the algorithm proceeds, the display of Fig. 13.6 appears on the screen. All information refers to the model in the standard form which may be different than that originally entered. In the upper left, the current incumbent solution is shown. This changes as better solutions are discovered. The band on the upper right shows the current partial solution. The numbers refer to the indices of the decision variables. A number preceded by a "+" has been set to 1. A number preceded by a "–" has been set to 0. If the number is white on a black background, the alternative branch of the enumeration tree has already been explored. If it is black on a white background, the alternative branch has not yet been explored. The number in the lower right shows the percentage of solutions remaining to be enumerated. The number starts at 100 and goes to zero. A difficult problem may run several hours, and this will give a rough measure of the time required to finish. The field in the lower left of the screen shows algorithmic details useful for the inquisitive student.

When the solution algorithm is complete, the incumbent solution is transformed to conform to the original definitions of the model. Figure 13.7 shows the results for the investment problem given at the beginning of the chapter.

```
                                                        +12
BEST SOLUTION FOUND TO THIS POINT                       +11
                                                        –10
OBJECTIVE = –91                                         +6
                                                        +5
VARIABLES                                               +4
0          1   2   3   4   5   6   7   8   9            +9
                                                        +3
1–9        0   1   1   1   1   1   1   0   1            –2
10–19      0   1   1                                    +1
                                                        +8
WORKING AT LEVEL 11

RELAXED SOLUTION : Z = –93
Y = (1, 0, 1, 1, 1, 1, 0, 1, 1, 0, 1, 1)

                                                        SOL
                                                        REM
                                                        84%
```

Figure 13.6 **Display of Intermediate Results**

TRANSFORMED RESULTS

A1 = 0	B1 = 0	C1 = 0
A2 = 0	B2 = 0	C2 = 0
A3 = 0	B3 = 0	C3 = 1
A4 = 0	B4 = 1	C4 = 0

OBJECTIVE = 31

Figure 13.7 **Optimum Solution for the Investment Problem**

Problems

P13.8 For the problem:

$$\begin{array}{llllllll} \text{Maximize} & 8x_1 & +5x_2 & +7x_3 & +6x_4 & +4x_5 & \\ \text{Subject to} & 5x_1 & +3x_2 & +7x_3 & +6x_4 & +9x_5 & \leq 14 \\ & x_1 & +x_2 & +x_3 & +x_4 & +x_5 & \leq 2 \\ & x_j = 0,1 \text{ for } j = 1, \ldots, 5. \end{array}$$

a. Solve with the binary branch-and-bound algorithm showing the complete implicit enumeration tree. Solve by hand and do not use the computer.

b. Solve with a linear programming relaxation at each vertex and show the complete enumeration tree. Solve by hand and do not use the computer.

P13.9 For the problem:

$$\begin{array}{llll} \text{Minimize} & 2x_1 & +5x_2 & \\ \text{Subject to} & x_1 & +x_2 & \leq 5 \\ & +x_1 & -x_2 & \leq 2 \\ & x_1 & -x_2 & \geq 2 \\ & x_1 & +x_2 & \geq 3 \\ & x_1, x_2 \geq 0 \text{ and integer.} \end{array}$$

a. Solve this problem with branch–and-bound using a linear programming relaxation. Use a graphical procedure to solve the linear program.

b. Use the procedure for transforming general integer variables to binary variables and solve with the branch-and-bound algorithm.

P13.10 Consider the binary integer programming problem with four constraints.

$$\begin{array}{llllllll} & \text{Minimize} & 2x_1 & +4x_2 & +6x_3 & +8x_4 & +10x_5 & \\ \text{(C1)} & \text{Subject to} & 1x_1 & +3x_2 & +2x_3 & +5x_4 & +1x_5 & \geq 8 \\ \text{(C2)} & & 3x_1 & +2x_2 & +4x_3 & +1x_4 & +2x_5 & \geq 8 \\ \text{(C3)} & & 1x_1 & +5x_2 & +3x_3 & +2x_4 & +1x_5 & \geq 8 \\ \text{(C4)} & & 4x_1 & +2x_2 & +3x_3 & +1x_4 & +2x_5 & \geq 8 \\ & & x_j = 0,1 \text{ for } j = 1, \ldots, 5 \end{array}$$

a. Solve the problem with only the first two constraints.

b. Show on the table constructed for part a the changes in the enumeration when all four constraints are observed.

Comment on the relation between the number of constraints and the effort required to obtain a solution of an integer programming problem.

Computer Problems

If no computer is available these problems can be used as setup exercises.

P13.11 A company is planning production for the next four time periods. The production must meet the demands below.

Period	1	2	3	4
Demand	20	10	30	10

To meet the demand a quantity p_t must be produced in period t, where $t = 1, 2, 3, 4$. Any production above current demand must be placed in inventory. The quantity stored in inventory at the end of period t is I_t. The initial and final inventories are zero. There is a cost of $12 per unit per period to store an item. This cost is charged for inventory remaining at the end of a period.

A production run requires a setup cost of $200. If there is no production in a period, this cost is not expended.

The problem is to determine a production schedule that meets the demand while minimizing total setup and inventory cost.

a. Show the mixed integer programming model that represents this situation. The integer variables represent the decisions whether or not to produce in each period. The real variables represent the production in each period and the inventory at the end of each period.

b. Since the demands are all in units of 10, it is possible to write this problem as a pure binary programming model with no more than 20 variables. Do this, and solve the model with the *Microsolve* program.

P13.12 A company is considering three major research projects labeled A, B, and C. Each of the projects can be selected for any of the next three years or not at all. The years are numbered 1, 2, and 3. The total return for each project based on the year it is selected is shown in the table below. This return includes all relevant cash flows, including investments. It also includes the effects of the time value of money.

		Project	
Year	*A*	*B*	*C*
1	7	6	4
2	5	4	4
3	8	7	5

The investment required for each project occurs entirely within the year for which it is selected and is shown below.

Project	A	B	C
Investment	5	3	5

Select a year for each project that maximizes the total return subject to the following constraints.

No more than two projects can be selected in any year.

Total investment in any year cannot exceed 9.

Project B must be selected after project A.

Project A and B cannot be selected in the same year.

A project can be selected at most once.

P13.13 The space agency is preparing the menu for a mission. The astronauts have given value measures for one unit of each food type. The nutritional content of each food is also given in the table. No more than three units of any one food may be brought.

Food Type	A	B	C	D	E	F	G	H
Utility	9	12	4	8	15	3	6	7
Vitamins	10	2	7	12	4	6	9	15
Fat	8	13	12	6	18	9	17	3
Sugar	16	15	2	14	13	9	8	4

a. Find the menu that will maximize the total utility subject to the following nutritional requirements: the diet must have a minimum of 40 vitamin units, a maximum of 30 fat units, and a maximum of 30 sugar units. Only whole units of food may be brought.

b. Compare the answer of part a with the solution of an L.P. model obtained when the integrality conditions are dropped.

c. An alternative goal is to maximize vitamin intake subject to the other nutritional restrictions. What is the new diet? How does it affect the menu utility as compared to the answer to part a?

P13.14 Table 13.2 shows the shipping costs between five locations. Each of the locations has a weekly demand for some commodity as given in the column on the right. The supplier of the commodity wants to establish warehouses in one or more of the locations. The warehouses have a maximum capacity of 100 units.

The goal is to minimize total shipping costs plus the amortized cost of the warehouses. The fixed and variable construction costs of warehouses at the locations

Table 13.2 Per Unit Shipping Cost

Location	1	2	3	4	5	*Demand*
1	8	21	42	12	37	20
2	21	10	31	24	40	30
3	42	31	4	14	32	40
4	12	24	14	7	12	25
5	37	40	32	12	10	30

Table 13.3 Construction Cost (per Week)

Location	1	2	3	4	5
Fixed cost	1000	1500	1700	1400	1200
Variable cost	20	17	13	25	33

are shown in Table 13.3. The variable costs are construction costs per unit of capacity. The capacity is measured in units shipped per week. The warehouses are to be amortized over 20 years with no interest charge. The numbers in the table show the amortized cost specified on a weekly basis.

Set up this problem as a mixed integer programming problem. If a mixed integer programming code is available, run the problem on a computer code and show the solution obtained. If a mixed integer code is not available, perform the branch and bound procedure manually using a linear programming code to solve the relaxations.

P13.15 A computer service company needs to establish communications between 10 cities. An analysis of various media has determined that the monthly cost of connecting a pair of cities i and j with a link is $c(i, j)$. The connection allows communications in both directions. There is a monthly cost of establishing interconnection facilities at each city that depends on the number of links touching the city.

If one link touches the city the cost is d_1.

The second link touching the city adds the cost d_2.

The third link touching the city adds the cost d_3.

These costs are related as: $d_1 > d_2 > d_3$.

Construct the integer programming model that incorporates the information given below.

- **a.** The objective is to minimize monthly cost.
- **b.** Each city must be touched by at least one connection.
- **c.** The links selected must form a tree.
- **d.** No more than three links can touch a city.

Solve the problem with the cost data given below.

City	*Connection Cost* 1	2	3	4	5
1	—	15	13	19	21
2	15	—	10	9	14
3	13	10	—	14	17
4	19	9	14	—	13
5	21	14	17	13	—

$d_1 = 5, d_2 = 3, d_3 = 1.$

P13.16–13.18 Set up and solve with integer programming the following problems from Chapter 11: E11.6, P11.10, P11.11.

CHAPTER 14

Nonlinear Programming

Introduction

The most basic assumption of the linear programming model is that the objective function and all the constraint functions are of a linear form. This leads to the result that some basic solution is always the optimum solution and ultimately to the very efficient simplex technique for solving linear programs. A natural question is how does one deal with a model that is not linear? Nonlinear models arise in many contexts but are particularly prevalent for engineering problems that deal with the modeling of physical systems. It can be argued that all linear models are really approximations of nonlinear systems.

The solution techniques for nonlinear programming are much more complex and much less successful than those for linear programming. The complexity is partly due to the large variety of functional forms that may appear when nonlinear functions are allowed. Where almost all linear programming algorithms are based on the simplex method, many procedures have been invented to solve nonlinear problems. The success of a particular procedure depends a great deal on the type of model involved. Where one can be confident of obtaining the optimum for a linear program with thousands of variables, there is a reasonable chance that a nonlinear programming algorithm will fail with only a few variables.

Notwithstanding the difficulties, nonlinear programming is a very important subject, because some problems simply cannot be successfully modeled as a linear program. This field is continually evolving with the efforts of many researchers, and good computer codes are becoming available for a variety of problem classes. Generally, however, it is difficult to use nonlinear programming codes. There are parameters to set that affect the speed of convergence to an optimum and the criterion for termination. The algorithms may take a long time to converge, or even converge to a point that is not an optimum solution. There is a risk associated with these codes that the inexperienced user will blindly accept a termination point as the global optimum when it really is a local optimum or not an optimum at all. The user of nonlinear programming codes should be well acquainted with the mathematical characteristics of the model and be very careful about the interpretation of the output of a computer program.

This chapter of the Guide, and also of H & L, is meant to provide an introduction to the topic and not a careful mathematical treatment. Nonlinear programming is a very mathematical subject, as a student who opens any of the source books referenced in H & L will discover.

GOALS

- Know the general statement of the nonlinear programming problem.
- Be able to characterize the objective function and constraints as either convex or concave.
- Be able to determine whether or not the feasible region is convex.
- Know the principal classes of nonlinear programming models and be able to classify a given model.

DEFINITIONS

General Form of the Nonlinear Programming Model:

Maximize $f(\mathbf{x})$

Subject to

$$g_i(\mathbf{x}) \leq b_i, \quad \text{for } i = 1, \ldots, m$$

and

$$\mathbf{x} \geq 0.$$

Here $\mathbf{x}$ is an n-dimensional vector of decision variables, $\mathbf{x} = (x_1, x_2, \ldots, x_n)$. There are m constraints, with the ith constraint defined by the function $g_i(\mathbf{x})$ and the constant b_i. The objective function is specified by the function $f(\mathbf{x})$. All non-linear programming problems can be put in this form with transformations that have already been discussed. The terms "feasible solution", "infeasible solution", "feasible region", and "nonnegativity restrictions" have the same meaning as in linear programming.

Strict Local Maximum: A solution that has an objective function value greater than the values for all other feasible solutions in a suitably small neighborhood of the solution. Deleting the word "strict" allows some points in the neighborhood to have a value equal to the maximum. (Throughout this chapter we refer to maximization problems. Similar definitions are appropriate for minimization problems.)

Strict Global Maximum (x^*): The solution that has an objective function value greater than the values for all other feasible solutions. Dropping the word "strict" allows multiple global maximums.

Concave Function: A function with the characteristic that a straight line drawn between any two points on the function will lie entirely on or below the function.

Convex Function: A function with the characteristic that a straight line drawn between any two points on the function will lie entirely on or above the function.

Convex Set: A set of points such that if a straight line is drawn between any two points in the set, the line lies entirely in the set. Nonlinear programming problems are generally easier if the feasible region forms a convex set.

DEFINITIONS OF PROBLEM CLASSES

Based on the characteristics of the objective and constraint functions, a nonlinear programming problem can be identified as being in one of several classes. This is important because algorithms often only work for members of a particular class. Also, the interpretation of a result at the termination of the algorithm depends on the problem class.

Unconstrained Problem: A problem with no constraints.

Constrained Problem: A problem with at least one constraint.

Linearly Constrained Problem: A problem with a nonlinear objective function but with linear constraints.

Quadratic Program: A problem with a quadratic objective function and linear constraints. When the objective function is concave, a local maximum solution is also global.

Convex Program: A problem with a concave objective function with all constraints defined by convex functions. In this case the feasible region is a convex set and the local maximum solution is also global.

Separable Program: A convex program for which the objective function and constraints are separable functions of the decision variables. A separable function can be expressed as a sum of terms in which each term is a function of only a single decision variable.

Nonconvex Program: A problem that is not a convex program. In this case a local maximum is not necessarily the global maximum. In fact, there may be many local maximums. Algorithms generally find local maximums and cannot guarantee that a particular solution is a global maximum unless the problem is a convex program. This is a difficulty for many practical problems for which there are no simple solutions.

Problem with a Convex Objective and Linear Constraints: This problem exhibits the interesting characteristic that the maximizing solution is a basic solution as in linear programming. Usually there are a number of basic solutions which are local maximums and the test for global optimality used for linear programming does not work.

Geometric Program: A problem in which both objective and constraint functions take the form

$$g(\mathbf{x}) = \sum_{i=1}^{N} c_i P_i(\mathbf{x}),$$

where $P_i(\mathbf{x}) = (x_1{**}a_{i1})\,(x_2{**}a_{i2})\ldots(x_n{**}a_{in})$, for $i = 1, \ldots, N$.

Here we use ** to indicate exponentiation.

Special procedures are available to solve this type of problem, especially when the coefficients of the terms are all positive. In this case the problem is called a *posinomial.*

Fractional Program: A problem in which the objective function is a ratio of two functions.

Complementarity Problem: A problem which arises as part of some solution algorithms. The problem is to find two p-dimensional row vectors, **w** and **z**, to satisfy the conditions

$$\mathbf{w} = \mathrm{F}(\mathbf{z}),\ \mathbf{w} \geq \mathbf{0},\ \mathbf{z} \geq \mathbf{0},\ \mathbf{w}^{\mathrm{T}}\mathbf{z} = 0.$$

The last condition is called the *complementarity* constraint.

RESULTS

To classify a problem it is necessary to identify whether the objective and constraint functions are convex, concave, or neither. The following results provide tests for these properties. Where necessary we assume that the functions involved have both first and second derivatives.

Condition for Convexity in One Dimension A function $f(x)$ is convex in the variable x if and only if the second derivative is nonnegative.

$$\frac{d^2 f(x)}{dx^2} \geq 0, \quad \text{for all } x.$$

If the inequality is strict (>), the function is strictly convex.

Condition for Concavity in One Dimension A function $f(x)$ is concave in the variable x if and only if the second derivative is nonpositive.

$$\frac{d^2f(x)}{dx^2} \leq 0, \quad \text{for all } x.$$

If the inequality is strict (<), the function is strictly concave.

Condition for Strict Convexity in Multiple Dimensions Let $h_{ij}(\mathbf{x})$ be the second partial derivative with respect to x_i and x_j.

$$h_{ij} = \frac{\partial^2 f(\mathbf{x})}{\partial x_i \, \partial x_j}, \text{ for } i = 1, \ldots, n, j = 1, \ldots, n.$$

The Hessian Matrix is the n by n matrix of second derivatives.

$$\mathbf{H} = \begin{bmatrix} h_{11} & h_{12} & \cdots & h_{1n} \\ h_{21} & h_{22} & \cdots & h_{2n} \\ \vdots & \vdots & & \vdots \\ h_{n1} & h_{n2} & \cdots & h_{nn} \end{bmatrix}.$$

The ith principal determinant of $\mathbf{H}$ is the determinant of the matrix formed by taking the intersection of the first i rows and the first i columns. Let H_i be the value of this determinant. Then

$$H_1 = h_{11}$$
$$H_2 = \begin{vmatrix} h_{11} & h_{12} \\ h_{21} & h_{22} \end{vmatrix}$$

and so on until H_n is defined. Note that these determinants may be functions of $\mathbf{x}$. The function $f(\mathbf{x})$ is strictly convex if the values of all the principal determinants are positive for all $\mathbf{x}$.

$$H_i > 0, \quad \text{for } i = 1, \ldots, n, \text{ and for all } \mathbf{x}.$$

A matrix that has this characteristic is called *positive definite.*

Condition for Strict Concavity in Multiple Dimensions A function is strictly concave if $H_1 < 0$, and the remaining principal determinants alternate in sign as the index of the determinant increases.

$$H_2 > 0, H_3 < 0, H_4 > 0, \ldots$$

A matrix that has this characteristic is called *negative definite.*

Condition for Convexity or Concavity for a Sum of Functions If a function $f(\mathbf{x})$ is made up of a sum of other functions, then $f(\mathbf{x})$ is convex if all the functions in the sum are convex. The function $f(\mathbf{x})$ is concave if all the functions in the sum are concave.

Convexity and Concavity for Linear Functions Linear functions are both convex and concave. They are neither strictly convex nor strictly concave.

Convexity and Concavity at a Point An arbitrary function is convex at a given point if the Hessian matrix evaluated at that point is positive definite. The function is concave at the point if the Hessian matrix is negative definite.

The Negative of Convex and Concave Functions The negative of a convex function is concave. The negative of a concave function is convex.

Condition for a Convex Set Let the feasible region be defined by the constraints of the standard form defined above. The feasible region is a convex set if all the constraint functions are convex.

EXAMPLES

Determine whether the following functions are convex, concave, or neither. In the following let $f'(x)$ refer to the first derivative and $f''(x)$ refer to the second derivative.

E14.1

$$\begin{aligned} f(x) &= 4x^2 - 20x + 10 \\ f'(x) &= 8x - 20, \ f''(x) = 8 > 0, \text{ for all } x. \end{aligned}$$

Therefore, the function is strictly convex. Note that the constant and linear term have no effect.

E14.2

$$\begin{aligned} f(x) &= -4x^2 - 20x \\ f'(x) &= -8x - 20, \ f''(x) = -8 < 0, \text{ for all } x. \end{aligned}$$

Therefore, the function is strictly concave.

E14.3

$$\begin{aligned} f(x) &= 8x^3 + 15x^2 + 9x + 6 \\ f'(x) &= 24x^2 + 30x + 9, \ f''(x) = 48x + 30. \end{aligned}$$

The second derivative is negative for $x < -0.625$, zero for $x = -0.625$, and positive for $x > -0.625$. Therefore the function is neither convex nor concave.

E14.4 Suppose the variable in E14.3 is restricted to nonnegative values. What can we now say concerning the function in this region?

Since $f''(x) > 0$ for all $x \geq 0$, the function is strictly convex in the region.

E14.5

$$f(x) = \ln x, \text{ where ln is the natural log, for } x > 0$$
$$f'(x) = 1/x, \; f''(x) = -1/(x^2).$$

Since the second derivative is negative for all feasible x, the function is concave in this region.

E14.6

$$f(\mathbf{x}) = 2(x_1)^2 + 4(x_2)^2.$$

Here let h_i refer to the first partial derivative with respect to x_i , and h_{ij} refer to the second partial derivative with respect to x_i and x_j .

$$h_1 = 4x_1, h_2 = 8x_2, h_{11} = 4, h_{22} = 8, h_{12} = h_{21} = 0.$$

Evaluating the principal determinants of the Hessian matrix, we find

$$H_1 = 4 \text{ and } H_2 = 32.$$

This function is strictly convex. We should also note that $f(\mathbf{x})$ is a separable function and that each term is convex. Because $f(\mathbf{x})$ is a sum of convex functions, it too is convex.

E14.7

$$f(\mathbf{x}) = -2(x_1)^2 + 4x_1 x_2 - 4(x_2)^2 + 4x_1 + 4x_2 + 10$$
$$h_1 = -4x_1 + 4x_2 + 4, h_2 = 4x_1 - 8x_2 + 4,$$
$$h_{11} = -4, h_{22} = -8, h_{12} = h_{21} = 4.$$

Evaluating the principal determinants of the Hessian matrix, we find

$$H_1 = -4 \text{ and } H_2 = 16.$$

This function is strictly concave.

E14.8

$$f(\mathbf{x}) = -0.5(x_1)^2 - 2x_1 x_2 - 2(x_2)^2$$
$$h_1 = -x_1 - 2x_2, h_2 = -2x_1 - 4x_2, h_{11} = -1, h_{22} = -4, h_{12} = h_{21} = -2.$$

Evaluating the principal determinants of the Hessian matrix, we find

$$H_1 = -1 \text{ and } H_2 = 0.$$

This result is not sufficient to either prove or disprove concavity. More analysis, which is beyond the scope of this discussion, must be performed.

PROBLEMS

P14.1 Determine the convexity or concavity of each of the functions below.

$$a(\mathbf{x}) = 2(x_1)^2 - 30x_1 + 10$$

$$b(\mathbf{x}) = -4(x_2)^2 + 20x_2$$
$$c(\mathbf{x}) = \ln(x_1 + 1) + \ln(x_2 + 1)$$
$$d(\mathbf{x}) = 5(x_1)^2 + 3(x_2)^2$$
$$e(\mathbf{x}) = -2(x_1)^2 + x_1 x_2 - 4(x_2)^2$$
$$f(\mathbf{x}) = x_1 + x_2 .$$

P14.2 Classify the following mathematical programming problems, which are defined in terms of the functions of P14.1.

a. Min $\{a(\mathbf{x}) - b(\mathbf{x})\}$, subject to $f(\mathbf{x}) \leq 10$.
b. Max $\{b(\mathbf{x}) + c(\mathbf{x})\}$, subject to $d(\mathbf{x}) \leq 10$, $\mathbf{x} \geq 0$.
c. Max $\{d(\mathbf{x})\}$, subject to $c(\mathbf{x}) \geq 4$, $e(\mathbf{x}) \geq -5$, $f(\mathbf{x}) \leq 10$, $\mathbf{x} \geq 0$.
d. Min $\{d(\mathbf{x})\}$, subject to $c(\mathbf{x}) \geq 4$, $e(\mathbf{x}) \geq -5$, $f(\mathbf{x}) \geq 2$, $a(\mathbf{x}) \geq 8$, $\mathbf{x} \geq 0$.
e. Max $\{d(\mathbf{x})/f(\mathbf{x})\}$, subject to $f(\mathbf{x}) \geq 4$.

Unconstrained Optimization (14.4, 14.5)

When a linear program has no constraints, the problem has no bounded solution. When a nonlinear program has no constraints, the problem may possess a maximizing solution when the objective function is concave. Classical calculus can be used to find stationary points that will include the optimum point we are seeking, but the classical procedures may yield a nonlinear set of equations that is difficult to solve. Furthermore the classical methods are not usually convenient for computer programs. In this section, therefore, we consider both classical and algorithmic methods for finding the unconstrained optimum of a function. In addition to their value for solving unconstrained problems, the methods of this section are frequently used as components of algorithms that solve constrained problems.

GOALS

The following goals assume that mathematically tractable functions are given. The student should be particularly prepared to deal with polynomials.

- Given a concave function in one or more variables, be able to find with classical calculus the unconstrained maximum point of the function.
- Given a concave function in one variable, be able to find the maximum point with a one-dimensional search procedure.
- Given a concave function in multiple variables, be able to find the maximum point with a gradient search procedure.

DEFINITION

Gradient ($\nabla f(\mathbf{x})$): The gradient of a function $f(\mathbf{x})$ is the vector of the first partial derivatives.

$$\nabla f(\mathbf{x}) = \left(\frac{\partial f(\mathbf{x})}{\partial x_1}, \frac{\partial f(\mathbf{x})}{\partial x_2} \cdots \frac{\partial f(\mathbf{x})}{\partial x_n} \right).$$

RESULTS

One Variable Unconstrained Optimization — Global Optimum A necessary and sufficient condition for the global maximum point of a concave function is that the first derivative of the function be zero.

$$\frac{df(x)}{dx} = 0 \text{ at } x = x^* .$$

This is also a necessary and sufficient condition for the minimum of a convex function. The optimum point is determined by setting the derivative function equal to zero and solving for the roots of the function.

One Variable Unconstrained Optimization — Local Optimum A sufficient condition for a local maximum point of an arbitrary function is that the first derivative of the function be zero and the second derivative be negative at the point.

A sufficient condition for a minimum of an arbitrary function is that the first derivative of the function be zero and the second derivative be positive at the point.

Multiple Variable Unconstrained Optimization — Global Optimum A necessary and sufficient condition for the maximum point of a concave function is that all first partial derivatives be zero at the point.

Let $h_i(\mathbf{x})$ be the first partial derivative function with respect to x_i. The condition for optimality is

$$h_i(\mathbf{x}) = 0 \quad \text{for } i = 1, \ldots, n.$$

This defines a set of n equalities in n unknowns. The solution is the maximum point of a concave function. The same procedure determines the minimum of a convex function.

Multiple Variable Unconstrained Optimization — Local Optimum A sufficient condition for a local maximum point of an arbitrary function is that all first partial derivatives be zero and that the Hessian matrix be negative definite at the point.

A sufficient condition for a local minimum point of an arbitrary function is that all first partial derivatives be zero and that the Hessian matrix be positive definite at the point.

ALGORITHMS

The classical conditions for optimality may yield a set of equations that is difficult to solve. The conditions are also inconvenient to implement in a computer program. We here describe algorithms that can be used to find an optimum solution.

One-Dimensional Search Procedure

This algorithm assumes that the function being searched, $f(x)$, is concave, and that one can easily calculate or evaluate the derivative of the function. Let $f'(x)$ be the derivative at point x.

A1. Initialization Step Find a lower bound, x_L, and an upper bound, x_U, to the optimum point. Select ε, a small number, representing the desired accuracy for the optimum point. Compute a trial point:

$$x' = (x_L + x_U)/2.$$

A2. Iterative Step Evaluate the derivative at x', as $f'(x')$.

If $f'(x') \geq 0$, let $x_L = x'$.
If $f'(x') \leq 0$, let $x_U = x'$.
Let $x' = (x_L + x_U)/2$.

A3. Stopping Step If $x_U - x_L < 2\varepsilon$, then stop, the solution is within ε of x'. Otherwise return to step A.2.

An alternative to computing the derivative, sometimes used in computer programs, is to estimate the derivative with the expression

$$f'(x) \approx \frac{f(x + \delta) - f(x)}{\delta},$$

where δ is a small positive number. Since we are only concerned about the sign of the derivative, it unneccessary to actually divide by δ.

The Gradient Search Procedure

This algorithm assumes that the goal is to maximize the function $f(\mathbf{x})$ to find the point $\mathbf{x}^*$. When the function is concave, the procedure converges to the global maximum. If the function is not concave, the procedure will converge to a local maximum. The termination rule is

Stop the procedure if the magnitude of each component of the gradient is less than ε. The current trial solution, $\mathbf{x}'$, is an estimate of the optimum solution, $\mathbf{x}^*$.

If there is no global maximum, the algorithm may terminate, indicating an unbounded solution.

A1. Initialization Step Select a small number, ε, for the termination rule. Select a starting trial point $\mathbf{x}'$. Compute the gradient. Stop if the termination rule is satisfied.

A2. Iterative Step Construct the line that passes through the trial solution and goes in the direction of the gradient.

$$\mathbf{x} = \mathbf{x}' + t\,[\nabla f(\mathbf{x}')].$$

Find the value of t that maximizes $f(\mathbf{x})$ along this line. If no value of t maximizes the function, stop with an unbounded solution. If there is a maximizing value of t, let it be t^*. Let the new trial solution be the point defined by t^*.

$$\mathbf{x}' \Leftarrow \mathbf{x}'\ t^*\,[\nabla f(\mathbf{x}')].\ (\Leftarrow \text{ means "replaced by".})$$

A3. Termination Step Compute the gradient at the trial point. Test the trial point to see if it satisfies the termination rule. If so, then stop. If not, go to step A2.

Gradient Search on a Quadratic in Two Dimensions

For purposes of solving example and homework problems, it is convenient to specialize the gradient search procedure to a quadratic function. This material is not included in H & L.

A two-dimensional quadratic function can be written in algebraic form as

$$\begin{aligned} f(\mathbf{x}) &= +\,c_1x_1 + c_2x_2 - (1/2)[\,q_{11}\,x_1^2 + q_{22}\,x_2^2 + 2q_{12}\,x_1\,x_2\,] \\ &= \mathbf{cx} - (1/2)\mathbf{x}^T\mathbf{Qx}. \end{aligned}$$

where

$$\mathbf{Q} = \begin{bmatrix} q_{11} & q_{12} \\ q_{12} & q_{22} \end{bmatrix}.$$

The gradient of $f(\mathbf{x})$ can be written

$$\nabla f(\mathbf{x}) = \mathbf{c} - \mathbf{x}^T\,\mathbf{Q}.$$

The gradient will be

$$\nabla f(\mathbf{x}) = [\,(c_1 - q_{11}\,x_1 - q_{12}\,x_2),\,(c_2 - q_{12}\,x_1 - q_{22}\,x_2)] = [\,\nabla_1, \nabla_2].$$

We must search in the direction of the gradient. Thus starting from a trial point $\mathbf{x}'$, the new point is on the line

$$\mathbf{x} = \mathbf{x}' + t[\nabla f(\mathbf{x}')] = (x'_1, x'_2) + t\,[\,\nabla_1, \nabla_2].$$

The optimum step size is determined by plugging this function into the $f(\mathbf{x})$ and finding the t that maximizes the function.

$$f(\mathbf{x}) = f((x'_1, x'_2) + t[\,\nabla_1, \nabla_2]).$$

It can be shown that the optimum step size is

$$t^* = \frac{-\,\nabla_1[q_{11}x'_1 + q_{12}x'_2 - c_1\,] - \nabla_2[q_{22}x'_2 + q_{12}x'_1 - c_2\,]}{q_{11}(\nabla_1)^2 + q_{22}(\nabla_2)^2 + 2q_{12}\,\nabla_1\,\nabla_2}$$

EXAMPLES

These examples consider the functions given in E14.1 through E 14.8. The convexity or concavity of the functions have been established in the last section.

E14.9 $f(x) = 4x^2 - 20x + 10$. This function is convex. The first derivative is: $f'(x) = 8x - 20$. Solving for the root of this equation, we find: $x^* = 2.5$. Since the function is convex, this is a minimum point.

E14.10 $f(x) = -4x^2 - 20x$. The function is concave. The first derivative is: $f'(x) = -8x - 20$. Solving for the root of this equation, we find: $x^* = -2.5$. Since the function is concave, this is a maximum point.

E14.11 $f(x) = 8x^3 + 15x^2 + 9x + 6$. Although the function is neither convex nor concave, we will continue to find the roots of its first derivative. The first derivative is: $f'(x) = 24x^2 + 30x + 9 = (6x + 3)(4x + 3)$. The roots of the function are at $x = -0.5$ and $x = -0.75$. From the second derivative we compute: $f''(-0.5) = 6$, and $f''(-0.75) = -6$. Since the second derivative is positive at $x = -0.5$, this is a local minimum. Since the second derivative is negative at $x = -0.75$, this is a local maximum. The points are not global optima because the function is actually unbounded from both above and below.

E14.12 $f(x) = \ln x$, where ln is the natural log, for $x > 0$. The function is concave. The first derivative is: $f'(x) = 1/x$. The function has no finite root, so it has no maximum.

E14.13 $f(\mathbf{x}) = 2(x_1)^2 + 4(x_2)^2$. The function is convex. The first partial derivatives are: $h_1 = 4x_1$ and $h_2 = 8x_2$. These are simulateously zero at $\mathbf{x}^* = (0,0)$, so this is the minimum point.

E14.14 $f(\mathbf{x}) = -2(x_1)^2 + 4x_1 x_2 - 4(x_2)^2 + 4x_1 + 4x_2 + 10$. The function is concave. The first partial derivatives are: $h_1 = -4x_1 + 4x_2 + 4$, $h_2 = 4x_1 - 8x_2 + 4$. Setting the partial derivatives equal to zero:

$$-4x_1 + 4x_2 + 4 = 0$$
$$4x_1 - 8x_2 + 4 = 0.$$

Solving the set of linear equations yields the maximum point: $\mathbf{x}^* = (3, 2)$.

E14.15 Using the one-dimensional search algorithm to find the maximum of

$$f(x) = -4x^2 - 20x.$$

The first derivative is: $f'(x) = -8x - 20$. We start the algorithm by selecting $\varepsilon = 0.1$, and $x_L = -10$, $x_U = 12$. It is not obvious how to choose an initial range that brackets the optimum; however, a successful selection will have $f'(x_L) > 0$ and $f'(x_U) < 0$. This is satisfied by our selection. The following table shows the sequence of trial points and upper and lower bounds on the search range.

Iteration	Lower bound	Upper bound	Trial point	Derivative
1	−10	12	1.0	− 28
2	−10	1	− 4.5	16
3	− 4.5	1	− 1.75	− 6
4	− 4.5	− 1.75	− 3.125	5
5	− 3.125	− 1.75	− 2.4375	− 0.5
6	− 3.125	− 2.4375	− 2.78125	2.25
7	− 2.78125	− 2.4375	− 2.609375	0.875
8	− 2.609375	− 2.4375	− 2.5234375	

The termination criterion is satisfied at iteration 8 and the solution $x' = -2.5234375$ is accepted as an estimate of the optimum.

E14.16 Perform a gradient search on the following function, starting at the point (0,0).

$$f(\mathbf{x}) = -(x_1 - 4)^2 - 4(x_2 - 2)^2 = -(x_1)^2 - 4(x_2)^2 + 8x_1 + 16x_2 + 32.$$

We have purposely chosen a rather simple function to make the procedure apparent. Obviously the solution is at $\mathbf{x}^* = (4, 2)$.

From this form we identify the coefficient values:

$$c_1 = 8, c_2 = 16, q_{11} = 2, q_{22} = 8, q_{12} = 0.$$

The gradient will be

$$\nabla f(\mathbf{x}) = [\,(c_1 - q_{11}\,x_1 - q_{12}\,x_2), (c_2 - q_{12}\,x_1 - q_{22}\,x_2)]$$
$$\nabla f(\mathbf{x}) = [\,\nabla_1, \nabla_2] = [\,8 - 2x_1\,, 16 - 8x_2].$$

Starting from a trial point $\mathbf{x}'$, the new point is on the line

$$\mathbf{x} = \mathbf{x}' + t[\nabla f(\mathbf{x}')] = (x'_1, x'_2) + t[\,8 - 2x'_1, 16 - 8x'_2\,].$$

The value of t that maximizes this expression is

$$t^* = \frac{-\nabla_1[2x'_1 - 8\,] - \nabla_2[8x'_2 - 16\,]}{2(\nabla_1)^2 + 8(\nabla_2)^2}.$$

The gradient search starting from the point (0,0) is shown in the following table and illustrated in part in Fig. 14.1.

Gradient Search

Iteration	Trial point	Value	Gradient	Step size (t^*)
1	(0.00, 0.00)	0.000	(8.0000, 16.0000)	0.147
2	(1.18, 2.35)	23.529	(5.6471, −2.8235)	0.312
3	(2.94,1.47)	29.758	(2.1176, 4.2353)	0.147
4	(3.25, 2.09)	31.406	(1.4948, −0.7474)	0.313
5	(3.72,1.86)	31.843	(0.5606, 1.1211)	0.147
6	(3.80, 2.02)	31.958	(0.3957, −0.1978)	0.312
7	(3.93, 1.96)	31.989	(0.1484, 0.2968)	0.147
8	(3.95, 2.01)	31.997	(0.1047, −0.0524)	0.313
9	(3.98,1.99)	31.999	(0.0393, 0.0786)	0.147
10	(3.99, 2.00)	32.000		

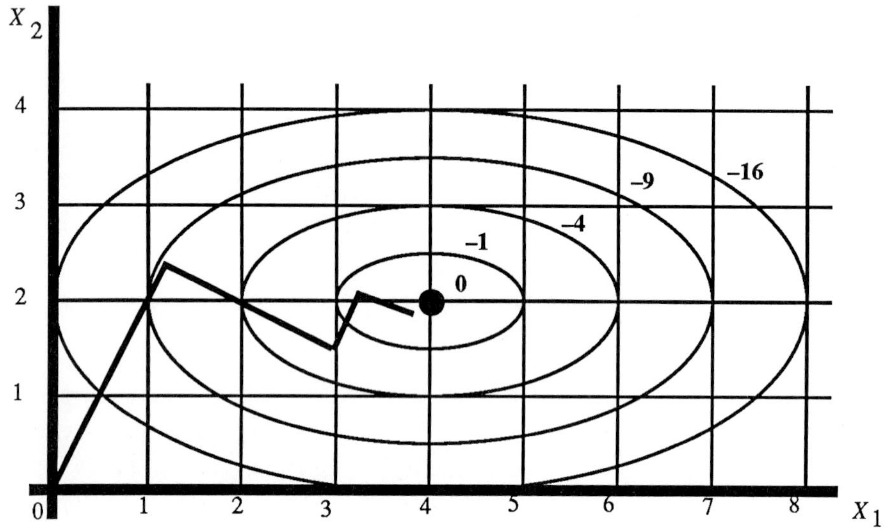

Figure 14.1 **Example of a Gradient Search Procedure**

The example illustrates that the gradient method often oscillates in the neigborhood of the optimum, but it does converge toward the optimum for a concave function. Much more efficient search methods are available, particularly for a quadratic function.

E14.17 Five oil wells have the coordinates (a_i, b_i) in the x,y-plane given by:

$$(a_1, b_1) = (5,0), \quad (a_2, b_2) = (0,10), \quad (a_3, b_3) = (10,10),$$
$$(a_4, b_4) = (50,50), \quad (a_5, b_5) = (-10,50).$$

It is desired to connect all the wells to a single collection point using the minimum total amount of pipe. Each pipe is placed in a straight line from the well to the collection point. Where should the collection point be?

This is a variety of the Steiner-Weber problem. It has also been called the Euclidean distance location problem. The decision variables are the coordinates of the collection point (x, y). The general problem having m wells with the objective function written as a maximization is:

$$\text{Maximize } Z = -\sum_{i=1}^{m} D_i$$

where D_i is the distance from the ith well to the collection point.

$$D_i = \text{SQR}[(x - a_i)^2 + (y - b_i)^2] \qquad \text{(SQR stands for the square root)}.$$

It can be shown that this function is strictly concave. The gradient of the function with respect to the decision variables is determined by

$$\frac{\partial Z}{\partial x} = \sum_{i=1}^{m} \frac{(a_i - x)}{D_i}$$

$$\frac{\partial Z}{\partial y} = \sum_{i=1}^{m} \frac{(b_i - y)}{D_i}$$

These partial derivatives can be used in a gradient search routine to find the optimum. There is the problem that the partial derivatives are not defined for solutions on any of the well locations, where one of the distances is zero. This problem can be handled, with a small approximation, by adding a small number to every distance.

$$D_i = \text{SQR}[\,(x - a_i)^2 + (y - b_i)^2 + \varepsilon\,]\,.$$

We have solved this problem with the computer program. Because no closed form solution is available, a one-dimensional search procedure is used to find the optimum step size. The results are shown in the following table. The approximate optimal solution is to place the collection point at (7.34, 11.32).

Gradient Search

Iteration	*Trial point*	*Value*	*Gradient*	*Step size*
1	(20.00, 20.00)	–146.36	(–2.2015, –0.5401)	6.560
2	(5.56, 16.46)	–125.48	(0.2579, –1.0716)	4.776
3	(6.79, 11.34)	–122.01	(0.1328, 0.0179)	2.870
4	(7.17, 11.39)	–121.97	(0.0649, –0.0304)	0.667
5	(7.21, 11.37)	–121.97	(0.0589, –0.0258)	0.651
6	(7.25, 11.35)	–121.97	(0.0535, –0.0223)	1.638
7	(7.34, 11.32)	–121.96	(0.0411, –0.0152)	0.036
8	(7.34, 11.32)	–121.96		

PROBLEMS

For P14.3 to P14.6, find the stationary points by setting the first partial derivatives to zero and solving the resulting equations. Determine, if possible, whether the points obtained are local or global maximums or minimums.

P14.3

$$f(\mathbf{x}) = -\,2(x_1)^3 + 3(x_1)^2 + 72x_1 + 30.$$

P14.4

$$f(\mathbf{x}) = 3(x_1)^2 + 4(x_2)^2 - 1x_1x_2 - 5x_1 - 8x_2.$$

P14.5

$$f(\mathbf{x}) = -\,2(x_1)^2 - (x_2)^2 - 4(x_3)^2 - 3x_1x_3 + 3x_2x_3 - x_1 - 2x_2 - 3x_3.$$

P14.6

$$f(\mathbf{x}) = -2(x_1)^2 - (x_2)^2 - 4(x_3)^2 - 8x_1x_3 + 4x_2x_3 - x_1 - 2x_2 - 3x_3.$$

P14.7 Use the one-dimensional search procedure to find the maximum of the function given in P14.3 in the range $1 \le x_1 \le 20$.

P14.8 Use a gradient search procedure to find the maximum of the function

$$f(\mathbf{x}) = -3(x_1)^2 - 4(x_2)^2 + 1x_1x_2 + 5x_1 + 8x_2.$$

Start at the point (0,0) and do four iterations. Determine the value of t^* at each iteration with the special procedure described for quadratic functions.

P14.9 Use a gradient search procedure to find the maximum of the function given in P14.5. Start at the point (1,1,1) and do two iterations. Use the step size that maximizes the function in the search direction.

P14.10 Repeat P14.9, but instead of using the closed form solution for t^*, use a one-dimensional search procedure to find the optimum step size. Use an initial range of 0 to 1 and $\varepsilon = 0.1$ for the one-dimensional search for t.

Constrained Optimization (14.6)

Most practical problems involve the optimization of an objective function subject to constraints. When nonlinear functions are involved, this field of study is called nonlinear programming. A great deal of research has gone into this area and a number of computational techniques have been suggested. This section describes the general conditions for optimality, and the following several sections describe computational techniques.

GOALS

- Given a nonlinear objective function with nonnegativity restrictions on the decision variables, be able to write the necessary conditions for an optimum and know when they are sufficient.
- Given a general nonlinear programming problem, be able to write the necessary conditions for an optimum and know when they are sufficient.
- Be able to determine if the necessary conditions are satisfied for a given point.

DEFINITION

General Form of the Nonlinear Programming Model We repeat this definition for easy reference.

Maximize $f(\mathbf{x})$
Subject to

$$g_i(\mathbf{x}) \leq b_i\,, \quad \text{for } i = 1, \ldots, m.$$

and

$$\mathbf{x} \geq \mathbf{0}.$$

RESULTS

Conditions for a Maximum with Only Nonnegativity Constraints When m is zero, the necessary conditions for a particular point $\mathbf{x}^*$ to be a maximum are

$$\frac{\partial f}{\partial x_j} \leq 0 \qquad x^*_j \frac{\partial f}{\partial x_j} = 0, \quad \text{for } j = 1, \ldots, n,$$

where the partial derivatives are evaluated at $\mathbf{x}^*$. The conditions are sufficient if $f(\mathbf{x})$ is concave.

General Conditions for a Maximum (The Karuth-Kuhn-Tucker Conditions) Let the Lagrangian function be defined by

$$L(\mathbf{x}) = f(\mathbf{x}) - \sum_{i=1}^{m} u_i(g_i(\mathbf{x}) - b_i),$$

where $\mathbf{u} = (u_1, u_2, \ldots, u_m)$ are variables called the Lagrange multipliers. For a particular point $\mathbf{x}^*$ to be a maximum, there must exist values of the Lagrange multipliers such that the following conditions are satisfied. All partial derivatives are evaluated at $\mathbf{x}^*$. When $f(\mathbf{x})$ is concave and all constraint functions are convex, the conditions are also sufficient for a maximum.

(1) and (2) $\quad \dfrac{\partial L}{\partial x_j} \leq 0, \quad$ and $x^*_j \dfrac{\partial L}{\partial x_j} = 0, \quad$ for $j = 1, \ldots, n.$

(3) $\quad g_i(\mathbf{x}^*) - b_i \leq 0 \quad$ for $i = 1, \ldots, m.$

(4) $\quad u_i(g_i(\mathbf{x}^*) - b_i) = 0 \quad$ for $i = 1, \ldots, m.$

(5) $\quad \mathbf{x} \geq \mathbf{0}$

(6) $\quad \mathbf{u} \geq \mathbf{0}.$

(*Note:* The H & L text suggests that certain regularity conditions must also be satisified for these conditions to be valid. The regularity conditions usually hold for practical problems, but the reader should consult the source references for a specific description.)

An alternative way to write (3) and (4) which may be easier to remember is

(3) and (4). $\quad \dfrac{\partial L}{\partial u_i} \leq 0, \quad$ and $u_i \dfrac{\partial L}{\partial u_i} = 0, \quad$ for $i = 1, \ldots, m.$

Conditions (5) and (6) are simple nonnegativity conditions. Condition (3) describes the original constraints. The variables of **u** can be interpreted as the dual variables of the problem. Conditions (2) and (4) then correspond to the complementary slackness conditions discussed in Chapter 6.

EXAMPLES

The KKT conditions are not much use for solving problems directly, but they are important for the theoretical development of algorithms.

E14.18 Solve the problem

$$\text{Maximize } f(x) = -(x_1)^2 - 4(x_2)^2 + 8x_1 + 16x_2 - 32$$
$$\text{Subject to } x_1 + x_2 \le 5, \text{ and } x_1 \ge 0, x_2 \ge 0$$

First writing the Lagrangian function

$$L(\mathbf{x}, \mathbf{u}) = -(x_1)^2 - 4(x_2)^2 + 8x_1 + 16x_2 - 32 - u_1(x_1 + x_2 - 5).$$

The KKT conditions are

(1) $$-2x_1 + 8 - u_1 \le 0$$
$$-8x_2 + 16 - u_1 \le 0$$

(2) $$x_1(-2x_1 + 8 - u_1) = 0$$
$$x_2(-8x_2 + 16 - u_1) = 0$$

(3) $$x_1 + x_2 - 5 \le 0$$

(4) $$u_1(x_1 + x_2 - 5) = 0$$

(5) and (6) $$x_1 \ge 0, x_2 \ge 0, u_1 \ge 0.$$

Try the unconstrained optimum: $\mathbf{x} = (4,2)$. Since the variables are not zero, Eqs. (2) require that $u_1 = 0$. Now this solution statisfies all the conditions except (3), because the solution is not feasible.

Try the solution: $\mathbf{x} = (3.2, 1.8)$. From Eqs. (2) we compute $u_1 = 1.6$. This solution satisfies all the conditions. Since $f(\mathbf{x})$ is concave, this is the optimum (maximizing) solution.

PROBLEM

P14.11 Consider each objective function given below with the constraints

$$x_1 + x_2 \le 4$$
$$-x_1 + x_2 \le 1$$
$$x_1 \ge 0, x_2 \ge 0.$$

For each case test the KKT conditions for the points (1.5, 2.5), (4,0), and (3, 0.5). If none of these points maximize the function, try to find the point that does. Prove that the point is the optimum with the KKT conditions.

a. $f(\mathbf{x}) = -(x_1 - 3)^2 - (x_2 - 5)^2$.
b. $f(\mathbf{x}) = -(x_1 - 3)^2 - (x_2 - 2.5)^2$.
c. $f(\mathbf{x}) = -(x_1 - 3)^2 - (x_2 - 0.5)^2$.

Quadratic Programming (14.7)

When the objective function is a quadratic function and all constraints are linear, the model has the form of this special case. The KKT conditions are used to derive the optimality conditions for this problem, which turn out to be a set of linear equations subject to the complementarity conditions. These can be solved by a modified simplex method.

GOALS

- Given a quadratic programming problem, be able to write the set of equations that may be solved to find the optimum solution.
- Be able to solve the set of equations using a modified form of the simplex method.

DEFINITION

Quadratic Programming Problem: The general form we will use is

$$\text{Maximize } f(\mathbf{x}) = \mathbf{cx} - (1/2)\mathbf{x}^T\mathbf{Qx},$$
$$\text{Subject to} \quad \mathbf{Ax} \leq \mathbf{b}, \text{ and } \mathbf{x} \geq \mathbf{0}.$$

Here $\mathbf{c}$ is an n-dimensional row vector defining the linear terms and $\mathbf{Q}$ is an $(n \times n)$ symmetric matrix defining the quadratic terms of the objective function. Any constant term is dropped. The decision variables are defined by $\mathbf{x}$, an n-dimensional column vector. $\mathbf{A}$ is the $(m \times n)$ matrix of constraint coefficients and $\mathbf{b}$ is an m-dimensional column vector.

It is assumed here that the objective function is strictly concave. A sufficient condition for this is that $\mathbf{Q}$ be positive definite for all points in the feasible region.

RESULT

KKT Conditions for Quadratic Programming The conditions are numbered below to correspond to the general definition of the KKT conditions given in the last section.

(1)	$\mathbf{Qx} + \mathbf{A}^T\mathbf{u} - \mathbf{y} = \mathbf{c}^T$
(3)	$\mathbf{Ax} + \mathbf{v} = \mathbf{b}$
(5) and (6)	$\mathbf{x} \geq \mathbf{0}, \mathbf{u} \geq \mathbf{0}, \mathbf{y} \geq \mathbf{0}, \mathbf{v} \geq \mathbf{0}$
(2) and (4)	$\mathbf{x}^T\mathbf{y} + \mathbf{u}^T\mathbf{v} = 0.$

In these expressions, $\mathbf{u}$ is an m-dimensional column vector defining the Lagrange multipliers or dual variables, $\mathbf{y}$ is the n-dimensional column vector of surplus variables for the inequalities defined by condition (1), and $\mathbf{v}$ is the m-dimensional column vector of slack variables for the inequalities defined by condition (3).

ALGORITHM

Set up a linear programming model with the following procedure

1. Let the constraints be the equations specified by (1) and (3).
2. If any of the right sides are negative, multiply through the equation by –1.
3. Add an artificial variable for each equation.
4. Let the objective function be the sum of the artificial variables added in step 3.

Find the solution to this linear program that minimizes the sum of the artificial variables, subject to the added complementarity constraint shown above as (2) and (4).

To solve the problem, the rule for selecting the entering variable for the simplex algorithm will be modified. In the model above we note the following complementary variables:

x_j and y_j are complementary for $j = 1, \ldots, n$.
u_i and v_i are complementary for $i = 1, \ldots, m$.

Use the usual "most negative value" rule for selecting the entering variable, except:

if x_j is basic do not allow y_j to enter the basis,
if y_j is basic do not allow x_j to enter the basis,
if u_i is basic do not allow v_i to enter the basis,
if v_i is basic do not allow u_i to enter the basis.

At the conclusion of the simplex algorithm, the vector $\mathbf{x}$ defines the optimum solution, and the vector $\mathbf{u}$ defines the optimum dual variables.

EXAMPLE

E14.19 Solve the problem

Maximize $f(\mathbf{x}) = -(x_1)^2 - 4(x_2)^2 + 8x_1 + 16x_2$
Subject to $x_1 + x_2 \leq 5$, $x_1 \leq 3$, and $x_1 \geq 0$, $x_2 \geq 0$.

From the problem statement we define the following matrices.

$$\mathbf{c} = (8, 16) \qquad \mathbf{Q} = \begin{bmatrix} 2 & 0 \\ 0 & 8 \end{bmatrix}$$

$$\mathbf{x} = (x_1, x_2)^T, \qquad \mathbf{A} = \begin{bmatrix} 1 & 1 \\ 1 & 0 \end{bmatrix} \qquad \mathbf{b} = \begin{bmatrix} 5 \\ 3 \end{bmatrix}$$

$$\mathbf{u} = (u_1, u_2)^T, \quad \mathbf{y} = (y_1, y_2)^T, \quad \mathbf{v} = (v_1, v_2)^T.$$

The equations that describe the KKT conditions are:

$$\begin{array}{llllllllll}
(1) & 2x_1 & & +u_1 & +u_2 & -y_1 & & & & = 8 \\
(2) & & 8x_2 & +u_1 & & & -y_2 & & & = 16 \\
(3) & x_1 & +x_2 & & & & & +v_1 & & = 5 \\
(4) & x_1 & & & & & & & +v_2 & = 3
\end{array}$$

and nonnegativity and complementarity constraints.

We add artificial variables to constraints (1) and (2) and obtain the following linear program.

$$\text{Minimize } x_{a1} + x_{a2} + x_{a3} + x_{a4}$$

$$\begin{array}{lllllllllll}
(1) & 2x_1 & & +u_1 & +u_2 & -y_1 & & & & +x_{a1} & = 8 \\
(2) & & 8x_2 & +u_1 & & & -y_2 & & & +x_{a2} & = 16 \\
(3) & x_1 & +x_2 & & & & & +v_1 & & +x_{a3} & = 5 \\
(4) & x_1 & & & & & & & +v_2 & +x_{a4} & = 3
\end{array}$$

and nonnegativity and complementarity contraints.

Applying the modified simplex technique to this example, yields the following sequence of iterations.

Iteration	*Basic variables*	*Solution*	*Objective value*	*Entering variable*	*Leaving variable*
1	$(x_{a1}, x_{a2}, x_{a3}, x_{a4})$	(8, 16, 5, 3)	32	x_2	x_{a2}
2	$(x_{a1}, x_2, x_{a3}, x_{a4})$	(8, 2, 3, 3)	14	x_1	x_{a3}
3	$(x_{a1}, x_2, x_1, x_{a4})$	(2, 2, 3, 0)	2	u_1	x_{a4}
4	(x_{a1}, x_2, x_1, u_1)	(2, 2, 3, 0)	2	u_2	x_{a1}
5	(u_2, x_2, x_1, u_1)	(2, 2, 3, 0)	0		

The optimum solution to the original problem has $(x_1, x_2) = (3, 2)$.

PROBLEM

P14.12 Set up the linear programming model that solves the following problem.

$$\text{Max } -2(x_1)^2 - 4(x_2)^2 - 3(x_3)^2 + 4x_1x_2 + 2x_1x_3 - 2x_2x_3 + 10x_1 + 15x_2 + 20x_3.$$

$$\begin{array}{llllll}
\text{Subject to} & x_1 & +x_2 & +x_3 & \le 15 \\
& 2x_1 & +4x_2 & & \le 26 \\
& & x_2 & +3x_3 & \le 20 \\
& x_j \ge 0, & \text{for } j = 1, 2, 3. & &
\end{array}$$

Separable Programming

If each term of the objective function and constraints is a function of only one decision variable, the problem is called a separable program. Under certain conditions the nonlinear functions can be replaced with piecewise linear approximations and the problem solved with linear programming.

GOALS

- Given a model with linear constraints and a separable nonlinear objective function, be able to create an approximate linear model.
- Be able to differentiate between cases that may be solved with a linear programming algorithm and those that must be solved with an integer programming algorithm.

DEFINITIONS

Separable Objective Function: An objective function for which each term depends on only one decision variable.

$$Z = f_1(x_1) + f_2(x_2) + \ldots f_n(x_n).$$

Piecewise Linear Function: A function in the form of Fig. 14.2. Such a function may arise naturally in a model. An example is the revenue from a product whose unit price decreases with total sales. The function may also be an approximation for a continuous nonlinear function. The approximation can be made as accurate as desired by using a sufficiently large number of pieces. There are p points specified along the x_j axis, $a_1, a_2, \ldots, a_p$, and p points along the f_j axis,

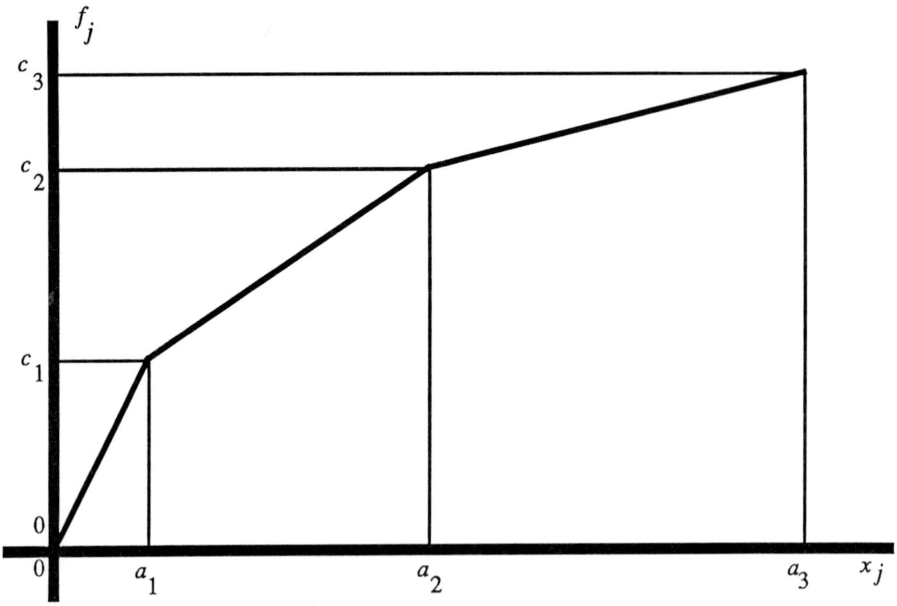

Figure 14.2 **Concave Piecewise Linear Function**

$c_1, c_2, \ldots, c_p$. Since the function begins at the origin we take $c_0 = a_0 = 0$. If $f_j(0)$ is not zero, f_j can be replaced by $f_j - f_j(0)$ without affecting the optimum solution.

An important characteristic of the function is its concavity or convexity. The slope of the kth piece is

$$s_{jk} = (c_k - c_{k-1}) / (a_k - a_{k-1}).$$

If the function is concave, the relative values of the slopes are

$$s_{j1} > s_{j2} > \cdots > s_{jp} .$$

If the function is convex, the relative values of the slopes are

$$s_{j1} < s_{j2} < \cdots < s_{jp} .$$

RESULTS

Representation of a Piecewise Linear Function in a Linear Model The piecewise linear approximation can be described in a linear model by defining the variables $x_{j1}, x_{j2}, \ldots, x_{jp}$ to represent the pieces. Each nonlinear term in the objective function is replaced by

$$f_j(x_j) = \sum_{k=1}^{p} s_{jk} x_{jk} \quad \text{for } j = 1, \ldots, n.$$

The following constraint defines the equivalence between x_j and its parts. The contraint may used to eliminate x_j from the model.

$$\sum_{k=1}^{p} x_{jk} - x_j = 0 \quad \text{for } j = 1, \ldots, n.$$

Nonnegativity and simple upper bound constraints limit the values of the parts.

$$0 \le x_{jk} \le (a_k - a_{k-1}) \text{ for } j = 1, \ldots, n \text{ and } k = 1, \ldots, p.$$

Solution of the Linear Model Under certain conditions, the model can be solved directly with linear programming while if these conditions do not hold, integer programming must be used. Since integer programming is so much more difficult than linear programming, this is a very important practical distinction. Linear programming can be used when it is optimum to select the pieces in the proper order. Thus, x_{j1} must be at its upper bound before x_{j2} can increase above zero.

Linear Programming should be used if:

The objective is to maximize and all objective function terms are concave.
The objective is to minimize and all objective function terms are convex.

Integer Programming should be used if:

The objective is to maximize and some objective function terms are convex.
The objective is to minimize and some objective function terms are concave.

When integer programming is used, integer variables and other constraints must be added. These are described in Chapter 13.

MODELING

When maximizing profit, revenue terms in the objective function have a positive sign and cost terms have a negative sign. Thus in order to use linear programming to find a solution, all revenue terms must be concave functions and all cost terms must be convex functions (the negative of a convex function is concave). There are important practical instances when this is appropriate. The revenue, or benefit, from most commodities has a concave shape because of the principle of decreasing marginal returns. There are many examples of price discounts to gain additional sales, as illustrated by airline ticket discount plans. In many natural situations, cost will be a convex function of quantity produced. For instance, to increase short run production, it may be necessary to pay overtime or use less efficient means of production. These circumstances promise an easy solution because the model can be approximated with piecewise linear terms and solved with a linear programming algorithm.

Unfortunately, there are also many practical instances when linear programming cannot be used. These most often arise in problems involving capacity expansion of facilities. The cost of a facility sometimes exhibits economies of scale; the larger the facility, the smaller the marginal cost. This is a concave cost function, and linear programming will give the wrong answer. The solution can be obtained with integer programming as discussed in Chapter 13, but with significantly greater computational effort.

EXAMPLE

E14.20 Use a piecewise linear approximation for the nonlinear terms of the problem introduced in E14.19 and show the linear programming model. The problem is

$$\text{Maximize } f(\mathbf{x}) = -(x_1)^2 - 4(x_2)^2 + 8x_1 + 16x_2$$

$$\text{Subject to} \quad x_1 + x_2 \le 5$$

$$x_1 \le 3$$

$$x_1 \ge 0,\; x_2 \ge 0.$$

The nonlinear terms of the objective are:

$$f_1(x_1) = -(x_1)^2 + 8x_1$$

$$f_2(x_2) = -4(x_2)^2 + 16x_2\,.$$

We choose to use a piecewise approximation with the integers as breakpoints. Since x_1 is limited by 3, we define the following breakpoints:

k	0	1	2	3
a_k	0	1	2	3
c_k	0	7	12	15
s_{1k}		7	5	3

Since x_2 is limited by 5, we define the following breakpoints:

k	0	1	2	3	4	5
a_k	0	1	2	3	4	5
c_k	0	12	16	12	0	–20
s_{2k}		12	4	–4	–12	–20

The linear program is then

$$\text{Maximize } Z = 7x_{11} + 5x_{12} + 3x_{13} + 12x_{21} + 4x_{22} - 4x_{23} - 12x_{24} - 20x_{25}$$
$$x_{11} + x_{12} + x_{13} + x_{21} + x_{22} + x_{23} + x_{24} + x_{25} \le 5$$
$$x_{11} + x_{12} + x_{13} \le 3$$
$$0 \le x_{ik} \le 1 \text{ all } i \text{ and } k.$$

Since all the terms are concave and the objective is to maximize, the solution may be obtained with a linear programming algorithm. In general, the solution will only be approximate, but in this case the optimum is obtained.

PROBLEMS

P14.13 Set up the linear program for the problem of E14.20 using the breakpoints:

for x_1: 0, 2, 3.
for x_2: 0, 2, 4, 5.

P14.14 Decide for each of the objective functions listed below whether a piecewise linear approximation solved with a linear programming algorithm will yield an acceptable solution. In all cases the variables are nonnegative.

a. Maximize $f(\mathbf{x}) = -2(x_1)^2 + 4x_1x_2 - 4(x_2)^2 + 4x_1 + 4x_2$.
b. Maximize $f(\mathbf{x}) = \ln(x_1 + 1) + \ln(x_2 + 1)$
c. Maximize $f(\mathbf{x}) = (x_1)^2 + 4(x_2)^2 - 10x_1 + 20x_2$.
d. Minimize $f(\mathbf{x}) = (x_1)^2 + 4(x_2)^2 - 10x_1 + 20x_2$.
e. Minimize cost:

$$f(\mathbf{x}) = \sum_{j=1}^{n} f_j(x_j)$$

where $f_j(x_j) = a_j\, x_j^{-b}$, with $a_j > 0$ and $0 < b < 1$.

f. Maximize profit = revenue – cost:

$$f(\mathbf{x}) = \sum_{j=1}^{n} r_j(x_j) - \sum_{j=1}^{n} c(x_j)$$

where $r_j = a_j[1 - \exp(-b_j x_j)]$, with $a_j > 0$ and $b_j > 0$
$c_j = d_j[\, x_j\,]^b$ with $d_j > 0$ and $b > 1$.

Sequential Unconstrained Minimization Technique (14.10)

A number of algorithms have been suggested for the general convex and nonconvex nonlinear programming problem. The algorithm of this section transforms the constrained problem into an unconstrained problem by adding a term to the objective function called a barrier function. A series of unconstrained problems are solved with the solutions converging to the solution of the constrained problem. Thus, we have "sequential unconstrained minimization (or maximization) technique," abbreviated SUMT. We will describe the algorithm as a maximization procedure to agree with the conventions of this chapter.

GOALS

- Given a general nonlinear programming problem, be able to set up the SUMT unconstrained problem.
- Be able to use a gradient search procedure to solve a series of SUMT problems to obtain an approximate solution to the nonlinear programming problem.
- Know how to deal with the problem of local optimum solutions for nonconvex models.

DEFINITION

Barrier Function ($B(\mathbf{x})$): A function that exhibits the following properties:

1. the function is small when $\mathbf{x}$ is far from the boundaries of the feasible region.
2. the function is large when $\mathbf{x}$ is close to a boundary of the feasible region.
3. the function goes to infinity as the distance from $\mathbf{x}$ to the nearest boundary goes to zero.

The barrier function used for SUMT when all the constraints are inequalities is

$$B(\mathbf{x}) = \sum_{i=1}^{m} \frac{1}{b_i - g_i(\mathbf{x})} + \sum_{j=1}^{n} \frac{1}{x_j} .$$

The first set of terms provides the barrier for the constraints, and the second set of terms provides the barrier for the nonnegativity conditions.

The SUMT Problem: The unconstrained optimization solved for SUMT is

$$\text{Maximize } P(\mathbf{x}; r) = f(\mathbf{x}) - rB(\mathbf{x}),$$

where r is a positive parameter that will be used to vary the importance of the barrier term. It is important that the maximization only consider solutions in the interior of the feasible region, so the barrier function terms remain positive.

RESULTS

Solution to the SUMT Problem Solving the SUMT problem with an unconstrained search procedure, such as the gradient method, one obtains a solution **x'** that is feasible for the constrained problem. If a series of SUMT problems with successively smaller values of r is solved, the solutions will converge to a local maximum of the constrained problem.

Solution Bounds Let **x'** be a solution to the SUMT problem and let **x*** be the optimal solution to the constrained problem. For a convex programming problem, upper and lower bounds on the objective function value of the optimal solution are

$$f(\mathbf{x}') \le f(\mathbf{x}^*) \le f(\mathbf{x}') + rB(\mathbf{x}').$$

ALGORITHM

A1. Initialization Step Find a feasible solution to the constrained problem, $\mathbf{x}^0$. Select an initial value of r. Select $q < 1$. Let $k = 1$.

A2. Iterative Step Starting from $\mathbf{x}^{k-1}$, use a gradient search technique to solve the SUMT problem. Let this solution be $\mathbf{x}^k$.

A3. Stopping Rule If the change from $\mathbf{x}^{k-1}$ to $\mathbf{x}^k$ or the difference between the bounds on the objective value is smaller than some previously set criterion, stop with $\mathbf{x}^k$ an estimate of the optimum solution. Otherwise replace r with qr, replace k with $k + 1$, and return to A2.

With a convex programming problem, the solutions of the SUMT problems will approach a global optimum. When the problem is nonconvex, the solutions will approach a local optimum. One way to search for the global optimum is to perform the algorithm a number of times with different starting points. If more than one solution is obtained, the one with the greatest objective value should be chosen. This does not guarantee that the result obtained is the global maximum, but it should always be done when convexity cannot be assured.

EXAMPLES

E14.21 Solve the problem given in E14.19 with SUMT. Repeating the model

$$\text{Maximize } f(\mathbf{x}) = -(x_1)^2 - 4(x_2)^2 + 8x_1 + 16x_2$$

$$\text{Subject to: } \quad x_1 + x_2 \le 5,\ x_1 \le 3, \text{ and } x_1 \ge 0,\ x_2 \ge 0.$$

The unconstrained problem including thc barrier function is

$$\text{Maximize } f(\mathbf{x}) = -(x_1)^2 - 4(x_2)^2 + 8x_1 + 16x_2 - rB(\mathbf{x})$$

where

$$B(\mathbf{x}) = \frac{1}{5 - x_1 - x_2} + \frac{1}{3 - x_1} + \frac{1}{x_1} + \frac{1}{x_2}.$$

The procedure must start in the interior of the feasible region and remain within the feasible region throughout the search. We choose (1,1) as the starting point and show the results of the first gradient search in Table 14.1.

The sequence of gradient searches taken during the process is shown in Table 14.2 as it converges on the optimum solution of (3,2). The columns show in order: the value of the parameter r, the solution at the end of the gradient search procedure, the value of the objective for the solution including the barrier function, the lower bound on the objective value, and the upper bound.

PROBLEM

P14.15 Consider the location problem described in E14.17 but add the constraint that the coordinates of the collection point must be positive and must sum to no more than 11. Show the unconstrained objective function that will be used by SUMT.

Computer Program

The linear programming code in *Microsolve* can be used to solve small quadratic programming problems. The equality form of the KKT conditions must be entered into the linear model generator as below.

$$\mathbf{Qx} + \mathbf{A}^T\mathbf{u} - \mathbf{y} = \mathbf{c}^T$$
$$\mathbf{Ax} + \mathbf{v} = \mathbf{b}.$$

Table 14.1 **First Gradient Search in SUMT Procedure. Gradient Search $r = 1$**

Iter.	*Trial point*	*Value*	*Gradient*	*Step size*
1	(1.00, 1.00)	16.18	(6.6395, 8.8844)	0.130
2	(1. 86, 2.15)	24.44	(2.7542, –2.0561)	0.157
3	(2. 30, 1.83)	25.43	(0.2689, 0.3395)	0.069
4	(2. 31, 1.85)	25.44	(–0.0153, 0.0114)	0.018

Table 14.2 **Solutions to the Sequence of Unconstrained Problems**

r	*Solution* (x*)	*Value*	*Lower bound*	*Upper bound*
1.0	(2.31, 1.85)	25.44	29.07	32.70
.1	(2.75, 1.90)	29.62	30.41	31.19
.01	(2.92, 1.94)	30.61	30.82	31.03
.001	(2.97, 1.96)	30.89	30.94	31.00
.0001	(2.99, 1.96)	30.96	30.98	31.00
.00001	(3.00, 1.97)	30.99	30.99	31.00
.000001	(3.00, 1.97)	30.99	30.99	31.00

The nonnegativity restrictions and artificial variables are automatically created by the program. When the program is solved, one must choose the "watch algorithm and help make decisions" display option. Here one can control the variables that enter the basis so that the complementarity conditions can be satisfied.

Problems

P14.16 In each part below, state the range of values of the parameters a and b for which the function $c(x)$ is convex in the range $0 < x \le 1$.

a. $c(x) = ax + b$.
b. $c(x) = ax^b$.
c. $c(x) = a^{bx}$.
d. $c(x) = a \ln (bx)$.
e. $c(x) = 1 + ae^{-x} + bx^2$.

P14.17 Let a quadratic function be described with the matrix form

$$f(x) = \mathbf{cx} - (1/2)\mathbf{x}^T\mathbf{Qx}$$

where **c** is an n-dimensional row vector, **x** is an n-dimensional column vector, and **Q** is an n x n matrix. Determine whether $f(\mathbf{x})$ is concave, convex, or neither for the following specifications of **Q**.

a. $\begin{bmatrix} 1 & -1 & -1 \\ -1 & 2 & 4 \\ -1 & 4 & 6 \end{bmatrix}$ **b.** $\begin{bmatrix} 4 & 2 & -2 \\ 2 & 4 & 2 \\ -2 & 2 & 5 \end{bmatrix}$

P14.18 Determine whether the following are convex, concave, or neither.

a. $f(x) = x_1^2 + x_1x_2 + x_2^2$.
b. $f(x) = x_1^2 + 2x_1x_2 + x_2^2$.
c. $f(x) = x_1^2 + 4x_1x_2 + x_2^2$.
d. $f(x) = x_1^2 + 2x_1x_2 + 2x_2^2$.
e. $f(x) = 2x_1^2 + 3x_1x_3 + x_2^2 + 3x_2x_3 + 4x_3^2 + x_1 + 2x_2 + 3x_3$.
f. $f(x) = 2x_1^2 + 2x_1x_3 + x_2^2 - 2x_2x_3 + x_3^2 + x_1 + 2x_2 + 3x_3$.

P14.19 Determine whether or not the following constraint sets define convex regions.

a. $0 \le x \le 12$.
b. $|x| \ge 6$.
c. $|x| \le 6$.
d. $4x^2 - 20x \ge 0$.
e. $\ln x \ge 1$.
f. $x_1 + 2x_2 + x_3 \le 10$
$x_1 - 2x_3 \le 9$
$x_1 \ge 2, x_2 \ge 0, x_3 \ge 0$.

g. $x_1^2 + x_2^2 + x_3^2 \le 9$
$1.5x_1 + x_3 \ge 4.$

h. $-2x_1^2 + 4x_1x_2 - 4x_2^2 + 4x_1 + 4x_2 \le 0.$

P14.20 For the functions below, find the points at which the gradient is zero and determine whether these points are maximum or minimum points.

a. $f(x) = 2x_1^2 + 20x_2^2 + 43x_3^2 + 12x_1x_2 - 16x_1x_3 - 56x_2x_3 + 8x_1 + 20x_2 + 6x_3.$

b. $f(x) = 100x_1^4 + 100x_2^2 - 200x_1^2x_2 + x_1^2 - 2x_1.$

P14.21 Find the minimum of the function in part a of P14.20 using a gradient search procedure.

P14.22 For each of the objective functions given below solve the problem

$$\text{Maximize } f(\mathbf{x}), \text{ subject to } \mathbf{x} \ge \mathbf{0}.$$

Find the optimum **x** by observation and prove that it is optimum with the necessary and sufficient conditions.

a. $f(x) = -(x_1 - 5)^2 - (x_2 - 3)^2.$
b. $f(x) = -(x_1 + 5)^2 - (x_2 - 3)^2.$
c. $f(x) = -(x_1 - 5)^2 - (x_2 + 3)^2.$
d. $f(x) = -(x_1 + 5)^2 - (x_2 + 3)^2.$

P14.23 Consider the problem

$$\begin{aligned} \text{Maximize } Z = \; & -(x_1 - 5)^2 - x_2^2 - x_3^2 \\ \text{Subject to } \; & x_1^2 + x_2^2 + x_3^2 \le 9 \\ & (2 - 5^{1/2})x_1 + 2x_3 \ge 4 \\ & x_1 \ge 0, x_2 \ge 0, x_3 \ge 0. \end{aligned}$$

Note: Read $5^{1/2}$ as the square root of 5.

Test the KKT conditions for each of the points below and determine which is the global maximum.

a. $\mathbf{x} = (0, 5^{1/2}, 2).$
b. $\mathbf{x} = (0, 0, 2).$
c. $\mathbf{x} = (2, 0, 5^{1/2}).$
d. $\mathbf{x} = (0, 3, 0).$
e. $\mathbf{x} = (3, 0, 0).$

P14.24 Consider the problem

$$\begin{aligned} \text{Maximize } Z = \; & -(x_1 - 4)^2 - (x_2 - 4)^2 - (x_3 - 4)^2 \\ \text{Subject to } \; & x_1 + x_2 + x_3 \ge 1 \\ & x_1 + x_2 + x_3 \le 6 \\ & x_1 \ge 0, \quad x_2 \ge 0, \quad x_3 \ge 0. \end{aligned}$$

Using the KKT conditions, investigate the solutions (1,0,0), (1,1,1), (0,0,6), and (2,2,2). Determine which solution is a maximum.

P14.25 Set up and solve the problem given in P14.24 with quadratic programming.

P14.26 Solve the problem given in P14.24 using quadratic programming with the following objective functions.

a. Maximize $Z = -(x_1 - 1)^2 - (x_2 - 1)^2 - (x_3 - 1)^2$
b. Maximize $Z = -(x_1 + 4)^2 - (x_2 - 4)^2 - (x_3 - 4)^2$

P14.27 Three products X, Y, and Z are to be made with with three raw materials, A, B, and C. The following information is given.

Each unit of product X requires 2, 1, and 3, units of A, B, and C, respectively. The per unit revenue for product X is $200 if no more than 80 units are sold, $95 for every unit above 80 but no more than 120, and $175 for every unit above 120 but less than 150. No more than 150 can be sold.

Each unit of product Y requires 3, 0, and 2 units of A, B, and C, respectively. The per unit revenue for product Y is $130 if no more than 50 units are sold, $100 for every unit above 50 but no more than 70, and $87 for every unit above 70 but less than 100. No more than 100 can be sold.

Each unit of product Z requires 1, 3, and 1, units of A, B, and C, respectively. The per unit revenue for product Z is $100 if no more than 130 units are sold, $90 for every unit above 130 but no more than 160, and $75 for every unit above 160 but less than 200. No more than 200 can be sold.

Currently 150 units of raw material A are available, but more may be purchased. The per unit cost is $10 if no more than 200 additional units are purchased. The price goes up to $13 per unit for any additional amount up to a maximum of 400.

Currently 20 units of raw material B are available, but more may be purchased. The per unit cost is $25 if no more than 240 additional units are purchased. The price goes up to $30 per unit for any additional amount up to a maximum of 380.

Currently 90 units of raw material C are available, but more may be purchased. The per unit cost is $17 if no more than 160 additional units are purchased. The price goes up to $21 per unit for any additional amount up to a maximum of 460.

Set up the linear programming model to maximize profit.

Computer Problems

P14.28 Set up and solve the following problem using quadratic programming.

$$\text{Minimize } Z = 2x_1^2 + 20x_2^2 + 43x_3^2 + 12x_1x_2 - 16x_1x_3 - 56x_2x_3 + 8x_1 + 20x_2 + 6x_3.$$

Subject to

$$\begin{aligned} 3x_1 &+ 2x_2 &+ 5x_3 &\le 35 \\ x_1 &+ 2x_2 &+ 3x_3 &\ge 5 \\ -x_1 &+ 2x_2 &- 5x_3 &\le 3 \\ 5x_1 &- 3x_2 &+ 2x_3 &\le 30 \end{aligned}$$

$$x_1 \ge 0,\ x_2 \ge 0,\ x_3 \ge 0\,.$$

P14.29 Solve the problem described in P14.27 with a linear programming code.

P14.30 Approximate the problem given in P14.24 using separable programming and solve with linear programming. Use the integer values as breakpoints.

P14.31 Use a computerized nonlinear programming algorithm to solve the problems given in P14.23, P14.24, and P14.28.

P14.32 Use a computerized program to solve P14.28, this time finding the global maximum solution. Since this problem may have local maxima, use multiple starting points.

P14.33 Use a computer program to perform the gradient search procedure to find the maximum of the function below. Start the search at the origin.

$$\begin{aligned} f(\mathbf{x}) = \ & -100\{x_3 - [(x_1 + x_2)/2]^2\}^2 - 25\,\{x_1 - x_2^2 + x_3^2\}^2 \\ & - \{10 - x_1 + x_2 - x_3\}^2 - \{x_1 x_2 x_3\}^2\,. \end{aligned}$$

P14.34 Use a computer program to solve the location problem described in E14.17 with the added restriction that the length of each pipe connecting a well to the collection point should be less than 40.

CHAPTER 15

Stochastic Processes

Many situations studied by operations researchers involve variables that change over time. For instance, the analyst may be observing the line of customers that forms before the service windows at a post office. The variable of interest is the number of customers in line. Casual observation reveals that this number varies over time, sometimes growing and sometimes declining. The number at any given time cannot be predicted with certainty so it must be a random variable. We are not however, concerned about a single time, but rather about characterizing the random variable over a range of times, perhaps all time. A process that involves a random variable that changes over time is called a stochastic process. We will be considering several kinds of stochastic processes in the sections to follow; however, this section begins study of a special type called the Markov chain.

Markov Chains (15.3)

The Markov chain is a stochastic process in which the random variable is observed at discrete points in time. Thus the random variable can be described with the notation X_t, where t represents time, taking on the values 0, 1, 2, ... Time can be measured in any appropriate unit such as seconds, minutes, or weeks. The general time interval is called the period. The random variable itself is a discrete random variable representing the state of the system under study. The goal of an analysis is to make probability statements about the state of the system at various points in time. This section and others that follow provide formulas and techniques for computing a variety of results. The Markov chain model for a given problem has two principal components: the state definition and the specification of the probability transition matrix. These are defined below with examples following.

GOALS

- For a given system appropriate to the Markov chain model, be able to identify the system states and the transition matrix.
- For a given transition matrix, be able to find the probability distribution of the system state at any time.
- For a given one-step transition matrix, be able to compute the n-step transition matrix.

DEFINITIONS

State: One of $M + 1$ mutually exclusive possible conditions for a given system. The states are numbered 0, 1, . . . , M. The set of states must identify all possible conditions for the system.

Transition Probability (pij): The probability that the system will be in state j at some period, given that it was in state i in the previous period.

$$p_{ij} = P\{X_{t+1} = j \mid X_t = i\}.$$

For the Markov model to be applicable, the probability p_{ij} cannot depend on the path by which the system has reached state i. This is called the Markovian property. The transition probability also does not depend on the time t. This is called the stationarity property.

Transition Matrix (P): A matrix that gives the transition probability from each state to every other state.

$$\mathbf{P} = \begin{bmatrix} p_{00} & p_{01} & \cdots & p_{0M} \\ p_{10} & p_{11} & \cdots & p_{1M} \\ \vdots & \vdots & & \vdots \\ p_{M0} & p_{M1} & \cdots & p_{MM} \end{bmatrix}$$

Note that since the $M + 1$ states represent all possible states of the system the sum of the probabilities in any row of this matrix must equal 1.

***n*-Step Transition Probability** ($p_{ij}^{(n)}$): The probability that the system will be in state j, given that the system was in state i n time periods earlier.

***n*-Step Transition Matrix** ($\mathbf{P}^{(n)}$): A matrix that gives the n-step transition probability from each state to every other state.

State Probability ($Q_t(i)$): The probability that the system is in state i at time t.

$$Q_t(i) = P\{X_t = i\}.$$

State Probability Vector ($\mathbf{Q}_t$): A vector that gives the probability of each state at time *t*.

$$\mathbf{Q}_t = [Q_t(0), Q_t(1), \ldots, Q_t(M)].$$

$\mathbf{Q}_0$ is the initial state probability vector that must be given for a complete specification of the stochastic process.

RESULTS

Computing the n-Step Transition Matrix

$$\mathbf{P}^{(n)} = \mathbf{P} \cdot \mathbf{P}^{(n-1)}$$

Matrix multiplication is implied here. For the (i, j) element this has the algebraic expression:

$$p_{ij}^{(n)} = \sum_{k=0}^{M} p_{ik} p_{kj}^{(n-1)}.$$

That is, the element (i, j) of $\mathbf{P}^{(n)}$ is the dot product of the *i*th row of $\mathbf{P}$ and the *j*th column of $\mathbf{P}^{(n-1)}$.

Computing the State Probability Vector

$$\mathbf{Q}_t = \mathbf{Q}_{t-1} \cdot \mathbf{P}.$$

Algebraically the probability of state *j* at time *t* is:

$$Q_t(j) = \sum_{k=0}^{M} Q_{t-1}(k) \cdot p_{kj},$$

or the *jth* component of $\mathbf{Q}_t$ is the dot product of $\mathbf{Q}_{t-1}$ and the *j*th column of $\mathbf{P}$.

EXAMPLES

E15.1 A markov chain has two states labeled 0 and 1. The transition matrix is shown below. Find the 4-step transition matrix.

$$\mathbf{P} = \begin{bmatrix} 0.2 & 0.8 \\ 0.7 & 0.3 \end{bmatrix}.$$

There are a number of ways to do this.

$$\mathbf{P}^{(4)} = \mathbf{P} \cdot \mathbf{P} \cdot \mathbf{P} \cdot \mathbf{P}.$$

Alternatively, first find $\mathbf{P}^{(2)} = \mathbf{P} \cdot \mathbf{P}$. Then find $\mathbf{P}^{(4)} \cdot = \mathbf{P}^{(2)} \cdot \mathbf{P}^{(2)}$. The latter approach requires fewer matrix multiplications.

$$\mathbf{P}^{(2)} = \begin{bmatrix} 0.2 & 0.8 \\ 0.7 & 0.3 \end{bmatrix} \begin{bmatrix} 0.2 & 0.8 \\ 0.7 & 0.3 \end{bmatrix}$$

$$= \begin{bmatrix} 0.6 & 0.4 \\ 0.35 & 0.65 \end{bmatrix}$$

$$\mathbf{P}^{(4)} = \begin{bmatrix} 0.6 & 0.4 \\ 0.35 & 0.65 \end{bmatrix} \begin{bmatrix} 0.6 & 0.4 \\ 0.35 & 0.65 \end{bmatrix}$$

$$= \begin{bmatrix} 0.5 & 0.5 \\ 0.4375 & 0.5625 \end{bmatrix}.$$

Several probability statements can be made from this information.

$$P\{X_4 = 0 \mid X_0 = 0\} = 0.5$$
$$P\{X_4 = 1 \mid X_0 = 0\} = 0.5$$
$$P\{X_4 = 0 \mid X_0 = 1\} = 0.4375$$
$$P\{X_4 = 1 \mid X_0 = 1\} = 0.5625.$$

E15.2 For the transition matrix given in the last example, find the state probability vector after four steps. The process starts in state 1.

Here the given information provides that

$$\mathbf{Q}_0 = [0, 1].$$

We want to compute $\mathbf{Q}_4$.

$$\mathbf{Q}_1 = \mathbf{Q}_0 \cdot \mathbf{P} = [0, 1] \begin{bmatrix} 0.2 & 0.8 \\ 0.7 & 0.3 \end{bmatrix} = [0.7 \;\; 0.3].$$

$$\mathbf{Q}_2 = \mathbf{Q}_1 \cdot \mathbf{P} = [0.7 \; 0.3] \begin{bmatrix} 0.2 & 0.8 \\ 0.7 & 0.3 \end{bmatrix} = [0.35 \; 0.65].$$

$$\mathbf{Q}_3 = \mathbf{Q}_2 \cdot \mathbf{P} = [0.35 \; 0.65] \begin{bmatrix} 0.2 & 0.8 \\ 0.7 & 0.3 \end{bmatrix} = [0.525 \; 0.475].$$

$$\mathbf{Q}_4 = \mathbf{Q}_3 \cdot \mathbf{P} = [0.525 \; 0.475] \begin{bmatrix} 0.2 & 0.8 \\ 0.7 & 0.3 \end{bmatrix} = [0.4375 \; 0.5625].$$

These computations are somewhat simpler than the matrix calculations required to compute the four-step transition matrix. The vector $\mathbf{Q}_4$ corresponds to the bottom row of $\mathbf{P}^{(4)}$ because the initial state of the system was state 1. If the system had started in state 0 (i.e., $\mathbf{Q}_0$ = [1,0]), we would have obtained the top row of $\mathbf{P}^{(4)}$. The components of $\mathbf{Q}_t$ should always sum to 1, as in this example.

E15.3 An office has two typewriters, and there has been some trouble with failures. It has been observed that when both are working in the morning, there is a 30% chance that one will fail by evening and a 10% chance that both will fail. If it happens that only one typewriter is working in the morning, there is a 20% chance that it will fail by evening. If it happens that neither machine is working in the morning, the office sends all work to a typing service. Of course no machines will fail in this instance. If a typewriter fails during the day, a repairman picks it up the next morning. One day is required to repair a failed typewriter.

This situation can be modeled as a Markov chain with the state of the system being the number of failed typewriters observed in the morning after the repairman has returned any repaired machines but before any failures have occurred. Thus, the system has three states: 0, 1, and 2. To determine the transition matrix we must analyze the system in each of the three possible states.

State 0: No machines failed. Here the transition probabilities are obvious from the problem statement. The system will remain in state 0 on the next day if no machines fail, go to state 1 if one machine fails, or go to state 2 if they both fail. Thus

$$p_{00} = 0.6, \ p_{01} = 0.3, \ p_{02} = 0.1.$$

State 1: One machine failed (and one working). If one machine is failed in the morning, it must go to the repairman. It will be returned the next morning. Thus the system will be in state 0 on the next morning if the remaining working machine does not fail. From the problem statement we determine that p_{10} = 0.8. If the remaining machine does fail, although the repairman returns one machine, he will pick up the other, and the system remains in state 1. Thus p_{11} = 0.2. There is no way the system can go into state 2, so $p_{12} = 0$.

State 2: In this situation, no additional machines can fail and the system will return to state 0 on the following morning. Thus

$$p_{20} = 1, p_{21} = 0, \text{ and } p_{22} = 0.$$

The complete transition matrix is

$$\mathbf{P} = \begin{bmatrix} 0.6 & 0.3 & 0.1 \\ 0.8 & 0.2 & 0.0 \\ 1.0 & 0.0 & 0.0 \end{bmatrix}.$$

The transition matrix can be used to answer probability questions. For instance, what is the probability distribution of the number of failed machines after three days if it is assumed that all machines are working on the morning of the first day? Note that since $\mathbf{Q}_0$ is the state probability vector at the beginning of the first day, $\mathbf{Q}_3$ gives the probabilities at the beginning of the fourth day (after three days). The easiest way to find $\mathbf{Q}_3$ is to compute sequentially $\mathbf{Q}_1$, $\mathbf{Q}_2$, and then $\mathbf{Q}_3$, or

$$\begin{aligned}
\mathbf{Q}_0 &= [1\ 0\ 0] \\
\mathbf{Q}_1 &= \mathbf{Q}_0 \cdot \mathbf{P} = [0.6\ \ 0.3\ \ 0.1] \\
\mathbf{Q}_2 &= \mathbf{Q}_1 \cdot \mathbf{P} = [0.7\ \ 0.24\ \ 0.06] \\
\mathbf{Q}_3 &= \mathbf{Q}_2 \cdot \mathbf{P} = [0.672\ \ 0.258\ \ 0.07]\ .
\end{aligned}$$

The expected number of failed typewriters after three days is

$$\begin{aligned}
E\{X_t\} &= \sum_{k=1}^{M} k\, P\{X_t = k\} \\
&= 0(0.672) + 1(0.258) + 2(0.07) = 0.398.
\end{aligned}$$

E15.4 Change E15.3 so that the repairman can only work on one machine at a time. If two are at the shop, the second must wait until the first is completed. The analysis of states 0 and 1 are the same. If the system is in state 2, however, it will surely return to state 1 at the next step since only one machine can be fixed. The third row of the transition matrix will change to: $p_{20} = 0$, $p_{21} = 1$, $p_{22} = 0$.

E15.5 Change E15.4 so that the repair operation takes two days. It is no longer possible to allow the number of failed machines to identify the states. If one machine is failed it is impossible to determine the transition probabilities without additional information on how long the machine has been in repair. Similar information must be available when both machines are failed. Now five states are required:

State 0: No machines are failed.

State 1: One machine is failed and has just gone to repair.

State 2: One machine is failed and has been in repair for one day.

State 3: Two machines are failed and both have just gone to the shop.

State 4: Two machines are failed and one has been in repair for one day.

Note that each state represents a relatively complex situation with more information than simply the number of failed machines. The information provided is necessary to determine the transition matrix.

$$\mathbf{P} = \begin{bmatrix}
0.6 & 0.3 & 0.0 & 0.1 & 0.0 \\
0.0 & 0.0 & 0.8 & 0.0 & 0.2 \\
0.8 & 0.2 & 0.0 & 0.0 & 0.0 \\
0.0 & 0.0 & 0.0 & 0.0 & 1.0 \\
0.0 & 1.0 & 0.0 & 0.0 & 0.0
\end{bmatrix}.$$

E15.6 We will continue the assumptions of E15.5, except that we drop the previous assumptions about the probabilities of failures during the day. Rather we assume that the two typewriters fail independently. The probability of failure of each typewriter (assuming it is working at the beginning of the day) is 0.2. The probability that is does not fail is 0.8. With this assumption, if both typewriters are working at the beginning of the day, the number that fail is a random variable with a binomial distribution. Let Y be the number of failures in a day.

$$P\{Y = k\} = \frac{2!}{k!\,(2-k)!}(0.2)^k (0.8)^{2-k}$$

$$P(0) = 0.64,\ P(1) = 0.32,\ P(2) = 0.04.$$

These can be used to replace the three nonzero elements for state 0. The other rows of the transition matrix do not change because either one or no typewriters are working for the other states. Now

$$\mathbf{P} = \begin{bmatrix} 0.64 & 0.32 & 0.0 & 0.04 & 0.0 \\ 0.0 & 0.0 & 0.8 & 0.0 & 0.2 \\ 0.8 & 0.2 & 0.0 & 0.0 & 0.0 \\ 0.0 & 0.0 & 0.0 & 0.0 & 1.0 \\ 0.0 & 1.0 & 0.0 & 0.0 & 0.0 \end{bmatrix}.$$

This illustrates that the individual elements of the transition matrix may be determined by one of the special case discrete probability distributions.

E15.7 A submarine commander is resupplied only once every year. An important component on the submarine fails at random with an average time between failures of 1/2 year. To protect against losing the component the ship has 2 extras on board (3 in all). Two replacements are delivered each year. If the delivery results in more than 3 working components, the excess is returned.

The number of working components remaining at the end of the year can range from 0 through 3. These numbers represent the states of the system. After the delivery, the number of working components at the beginning of the year will be either 2 or 3 (the excess above 3 is returned). The number of components remaining at the end of the year is equal to the number at the beginning less the number of failures.

The assumption of random failures leads us to use the Poisson distribution to determine the transition probabilities. Let Y be the number of failures that arrive during the year. The average number of failures is 2. Thus the probability distribution on Y is

$$P\{Y = k\} = \frac{2^k e^{-2}}{k!} \quad k \geq 0.$$

$$P\{Y=0\} = 0.135 \qquad F(0) = 0.135$$
$$P\{Y=1\} = 0.271 \qquad F(1) = 0.406$$
$$P\{Y=2\} = 0.271 \qquad F(2) = 0.677$$
$$P\{Y=3\} = 0.180 \qquad F(3) = 0.857\,.$$

To determine the transition probabilities, consider each state in turn.

State 0: If the system has no working components at the end of the year, the two deliveries will bring that number to 2 at the beginning of the next. The number of working components will be 2 less the number of failures. Of course the number of failures cannot exceed 2. Thus

$$p_{00} = P\{Y \geq 2\} = 1 - F(1) = 0.594$$
$$p_{01} = P\{Y = 1\} = 0.271$$
$$p_{02} = P\{Y = 0\} = 0.135$$
$$p_{03} = 0\,.$$

State 1–3: If the system has 1 or more working component at the end of the year, the delivery will bring that number to 3 (the excess will be discarded). Thus for k =1, 2, and 3,

$$p_{k0} = P\{Y \geq 3\} = 1 - F(2) = 0.323$$
$$p_{k1} = P\{Y = 2\} = 0.271$$
$$p_{k2} = P\{Y = 1\} = 0.271$$
$$p_{k3} = P\{Y = 0\} = 0.135\,.$$

PROBLEMS

P15.1 Use the one-step Markov chain transition probability matrix shown below. The states are 0, 1, and 2.

$$\mathbf{P} = \begin{bmatrix} 0 & 0.3 & 0.7 \\ 0.9 & 0.1 & 0.0 \\ 0.2 & 0 & 0.8 \end{bmatrix}$$

a. Find the state probabilities after two steps, assuming the system begins in state 2.

b. Find the four-step transition matrix.

P15.2 For the Markov chain transition matrix below,

State	0	1	2	3
0	0.2	0.8	0	0
1	0	0.9	0.1	0
2	0.3	0	0.2	0.5
3	0	0	0.1	0.9

a. Let the initial state probability matrix be $Q_0 = [0, 0.4, 0.5, 0.1]$. Find the state probability matrix after five steps.
b. Find the two-step transition matrix.

P15.3 A dealer in high priced cars expects the following weekly demand distribution.

Demand	0	1	2
Probability	0.1	0.5	0.4

He adopts the policy of placing an order for 3 cars whenever his inventory level plus amount on order reaches 2 or less at the end of a week. If a demand for a car occurs and there is no inventory, the sale is lost. Show the transition matrix for the Markov process that describes his inventory level at the end of each week under the following conditions.

a. The order takes 1 week to arrive.
b. The order takes 2 weeks to arrive.

P15.4 Do both parts of problem P15.3 when the demand is assumed to follow a Poisson distribution with a mean demand of 1.5 cars per week.

P15.5 A military maintenance depot overhauls army tanks. There is room for 3 tanks in the maintenance facility and 1 tank in an overflow area outside. At most 4 tanks can be at the depot at one time.

Every morning a tank arrives at the depot for overhaul unless the depot is full. When it is full the entire overhaul schedule is delayed 1 day. The effect is simply that the arrival does not occur when the depot is full.

In any given day, the depot can complete the overhaul of tanks with the following probabilities.

Number of tanks completed	0	1	2	3
Probability	0.2	0.4	0.3	0.1

These probabilities are independent of the number in the depot, except that the depot can complete no more tanks than are available at the start of the day.

a. Define the Markov chain matrix when the state is the number in the depot at the *start* of each day (after the scheduled arrival).
b. Define the Markov chain matrix when the state is the number in the depot at the *end* of each day.

First Passage Times (15.5)

Assume we are in some arbitrary system state i, and for some reason we are concerned about the number of steps (time intervals) before we reach state j for the *first* time. This number is called the first passage time from state i to state j. Since the state transitions for a Markov chain are governed by probabilities, the first passage time is a discrete random variable taking on the values 1, 2, 3, ... The lower range is 1 because it will take at least one step to make the passage, and the upper range goes to infinity because it is conceivable that the system will never pass from state i to state j. This section is concerned with computing the probability distribution of the first passage time and also the mean of the distribution.

GOALS

- Given a Markov chain transition matrix, be able to compute the first several values for the probability distribution of the first passage time between any two states of the system.
- Given a Markov chain transition matrix, be able to compute the average value of the first passage time between any two states of the system.
- Be able to classify the states of a Markov chain as recurrent, absorbing, or transient.

DEFINITIONS

First Passage Time: The number of steps (time intervals) of the Markov process required for the first passage from some given state i to some other given state j.

Probability Distribution of the First Passage Time ($f_{ij}^{(n)}$): The probability that the first passage from i to j will take n steps, where n ranges from 1 to infinity.

Expected First Passage Time (μ_{ij}): The expected value of the first passage time from state i to state j.

Recurrent State: A state of a Markov process that has the characteristic that if the system ever enters the state, it will eventually return to the state. For a recurrent state:

$$\sum_{n=1}^{\infty} f_{ii}^{(n)} = 1 \quad \text{and} \quad \mu_{ii} < \infty.$$

Absorbing State: A state that has the characteristic that once the process enters the state it never leaves. An absorbing state is also recurrent. If state i is an absorbing state, $p_{ii} = 1$.

Transient State: A state that has the characteristic that once the process enters the state, there is a finite probability that it will never return. Note that a state will be either recurrent or transient. For a transient state:

$$\sum_{n=1}^{\infty} f_{ii}^{(n)} < 1 \quad \text{and} \quad \mu_{ii} = \infty.$$

RESULTS

Set of Equations Defining the First Passage Time Distribution
Consider any two states i and j. The probabilities for the first passage time from i to j are determined by evaluating the equations:

$$\begin{aligned}
f_{ij}^{(1)} &= p_{ij} \\
f_{ij}^{(2)} &= p_{ij}^{(2)} - f_{ij}^{(1)} * p_{jj} \\
f_{ij}^{(3)} &= p_{ij}^{(3)} - f_{ij}^{(1)} * p_{jj}^{(2)} - f_{ij}^{(2)} * p_{jj} \\
f_{ij}^{(4)} &= p_{ij}^{(4)} - f_{ij}^{(1)} * p_{jj}^{(3)} - f_{ij}^{(2)} * p_{jj}^{(2)} - f_{ij}^{(3)} * p_{jj} \\
&\vdots \\
f_{ij}^{(n)} &= p_{ij}^{(n)} - f_{ij}^{(1)} * p_{jj}^{(n-1)} - f_{ij}^{(2)} * p_{jj}^{(n-2)} - \cdots - f_{ij}^{(n-1)} * p_{jj} .
\end{aligned}$$

Note that in these equations $p_{ij}^{(n)}$ represents an n-step transition probability. To use these equations to evaluate the probabilities from 1 to n, all the multistep transition matices from 1 to n must be available. The equations are evaluated recursively, first finding $f_{ij}^{(1)}$, then finding $f_{ij}^{(2)}$, and so on.

Set of Equations Defining the Expected First Passage Times
When all the states are recurrent, there is a set of equations that when solved will yield the expected first passage times from each state into some given state j. The set of equations is:

$$\mu_{ij} = 1 + \sum_{k \neq j} p_{ik}\, \mu_{kj} \qquad \text{for } i = 0, 1, 2, \ldots, M.$$

Note that this is a set of $M + 1$ linear equations in $M + 1$ unknowns, μ_{ij} for i ranging from 0 to M. The coefficients in the equations are from the one-step transition matrix. The equations can be solved using any convenient technique for solving linear equations.

EXAMPLES

E15.8 Consider the n-step transition matrices:

$$\mathbf{P} = \begin{bmatrix} 0.2 & 0.8 \\ 0.7 & 0.3 \end{bmatrix} \qquad \mathbf{P}^{(2)} = \begin{bmatrix} 0.6 & 0.4 \\ 0.35 & 0.65 \end{bmatrix}$$

$$\mathbf{P}^{(3)} = \begin{bmatrix} 0.4 & 0.6 \\ 0.525 & 0.475 \end{bmatrix} \qquad \mathbf{P}^{(4)} = \begin{bmatrix} 0.5 & 0.5 \\ 0.4375 & 0.5625 \end{bmatrix}$$

Find the first four probabilities in the distribution of the first passage time from state 0 to state 0. The first passage time from a state to itself is called the recurrence time. From the general equations above we obtain:

$$
\begin{aligned}
f_{00}^{(1)} &= p_{00} = 0.2 \\
f_{00}^{(2)} &= p_{00}^{(2)} - f_{00}^{(1)} p_{00} = 0.6 - (0.2)(0.2) = 0.56 \\
f_{00}^{(3)} &= p_{00}^{(3)} - f_{00}^{(1)} p_{00}^{(2)} - f_{00}^{(2)} p_{00} \\
&= 0.4 - (0.2)(0.6) - (0.56)(0.2) \\
&= 0.168 \\
f_{00}^{(4)} &= p_{00}^{(4)} - f_{00}^{(1)} p_{00}^{(3)} - f_{00}^{(2)} p_{00}^{(2)} - f_{00}^{(3)} p_{00} \\
&= 0.5 - (0.2)(0.4) - (0.56)(0.6) - (0.168)(0.2) \\
&= 0.0504 \, .
\end{aligned}
$$

If we call Y the first recurrence time for state 0. The probability distribution of Y is:

k	1	2	3	4	$k > 4$
$P_Y(k)$	0.2	0.56	0.168	0.0504	0.0216

The expected value of the recurrence time for state 0 can be found by constructing the set of equations:

$$\mu_{i0} = 1 + \sum_{k \neq 0} p_{ik} \, \mu_{k0} \qquad \text{for } i = 0, 1$$

$$\mu_{00} = 1 + p_{01}\mu_{10} \qquad \text{or} \qquad \mu_{00} = 1 + (0.8)\,\mu_{10} \qquad (1)$$

$$\mu_{10} = 1 + p_{11}\mu_{10} \qquad \text{or} \qquad \mu_{10} = 1 + (0.3)\,\mu_{10}\,. \qquad (2)$$

Solving Eq. (2) for μ_{10} yields μ_{10} = 1.429 (steps). Using this value in Eq. (1) yields μ_{00} = 2.142 (steps).

PROBLEMS

P15.6 For the Markov chain in E15.8 compute $f_{00}^{(5)}$ and $f_{00}^{(6)}$.

P15.7 For the Markov chain in E15.8, find the first four values for the first passage probabilities and the expected first passage time for:

- **a.** transition from state 0 to state 1.
- **b.** transition from state 1 to state 0.
- **c.** transition from state 1 to state 1.

Classification of States (15.6)

Some useful properties of the Markov chain hold only if the states can be identified as belonging to a certain class. This section provides a number of definitions and provides rules by which states can be classified.

GOAL

- Given a Markov chain, be able to classify the states according the definitions listed below.

DEFINITIONS

Accessible: One state j is said to be accessible from another state i if it is possible to go from state i to state j. Alternatively if $p_{ij}^{(n)} > 0$ for some n, then state j is accessible from state i

Communicate: Two states i and j are said to communicate if i is accessible from j, and j is accessible from i. Every state communicates with itself.

Irreducible Markov Chain: A Markov chain is irreducible if all states communicate with each other. The states in an irreducible Markov chain are always recurrent states.

Class: A set of states such that all states in the set communicate with each other. A class is either all recurrent or all transient.

Periodic State: A state that can only be observed periodically where the period is greater than 1. Alternatively if $p_{ii}^{(n)} = 0$ whenever n is not n divisible by t and $p_{ii}^{(n)} > 0$ whenever n is divisible by t, state i is said to be periodic with period t.

Aperiodic State: A state that is not periodic.

Ergodic State: An aperiodic recurrent state.

Irreducible Ergodic Markov Chain: A Markov chain in which all states communicate and all states are aperiodic.

RESULTS

Characteristics of States

Recurrent is opposite to transient. Every state is either recurrent or transient.

Periodic is opposite to aperiodic. Every state is either periodic or aperiodic.

An absorbing state is a type of recurrent state.

A state may be both recurrent and periodic.

A state may be both transient and periodic.

Once a process leaves a transient class, it will never return.

Once a process enters a recurrent class, it will never leave.

A Method for Classification

To help in the classification of states, we will draw a directed network with each state represented by a node. Each nonzero transition probability p_{ij} will be represented by an arc from node i to node j. If there exists a path of one or more arcs from some node k to another node m, we can say that state m is accessible from state k. If no path exists from k to m, then state m is not accessible from state k. With the accessibility information, the states can be classified. The method is illustrated with the examples.

EXAMPLES

Only the nonzero entries of the transition matrix are of importance in classifying the states of the Markov chain. These are shown as X's in the examples. The problem is to classify each of the states and also the Markov chain.

E15.9

State	0	1	2	3
0	0	X	X	0
1	X	0	0	0
2	0	0	0	X
3	X	0	0	X

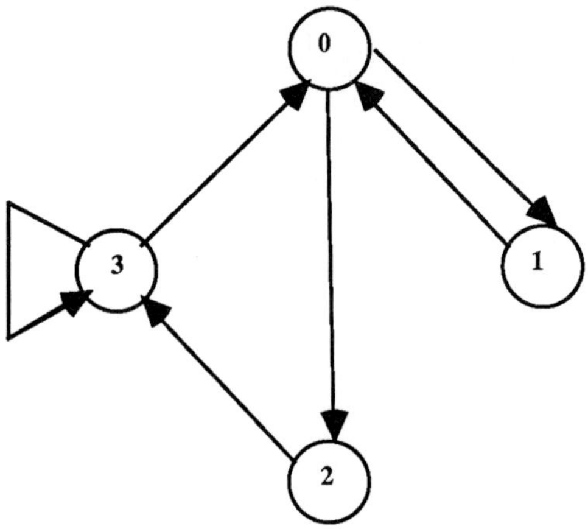

Considering each state in turn, a path can be traced on the network from each state to every other state. Thus every pair of states communicate, and the states form a single class of recurrent states. The states are not periodic, so this is an irreducible Markov chain.

E15.10

State	0	1	2	3	4
0	X	X	0	0	0
1	X	X	0	0	0
2	0	0	X	0	0
3	0	0	X	X	0
4	X	0	0	0	0

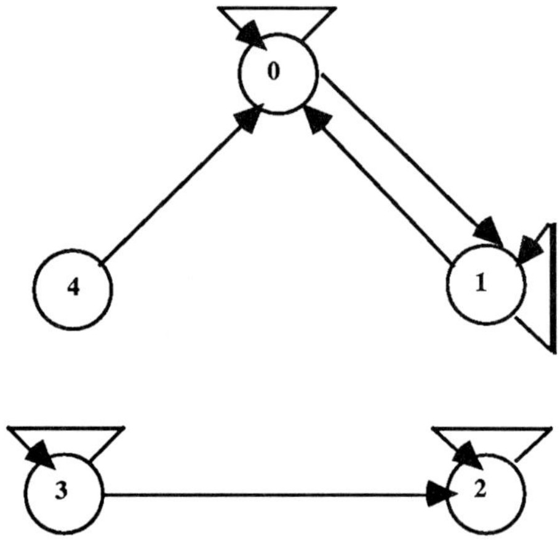

From the network, note that states 0 and 1 communicate. No arcs leave the set, so states 0 and 1 comprise a recurrent class. State 2 communicates only with itself. Since no arcs leave the state it must be a recurrent class by itself. State 2 is an absorbing state. Since an arc leaves state 3 but no arcs enter, it must be a transient class. State 4 communicates only with itself. Since an arc leaves state 4, it must comprise by itself a transient class. In this example four classes of states are defined.

E15.11

State	0	1	2	3
0	0	X	X	0
1	0	0	0	X
2	0	0	0	X
3	X	0	0	0

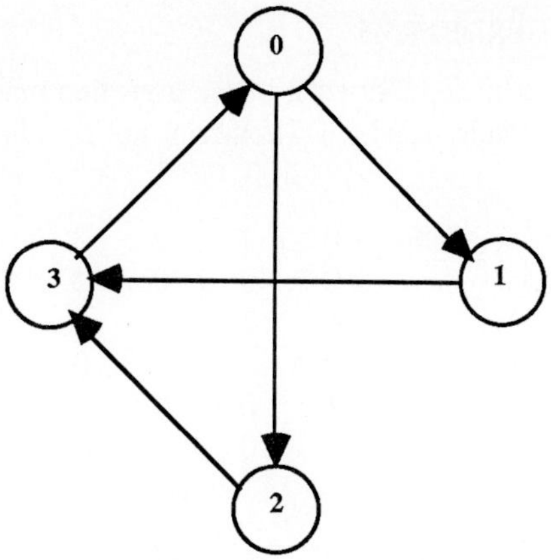

Review of this figure reveals that every state communicates with every other state, so this must be an irreducible Markov chain. More careful review will show that every path from a state back to itself must pass through a multiple of three arcs. For instance, starting at state 0, there are two possible paths that return to state 0: (0, 1, 3, 0) and (0, 2, 3, 0). Thus state 0 is a periodic state with period 3. Starting from state 1, paths returning to the state are: (1, 3, 0, 1), (1, 3, 0, 2, 3, 0, 1), and others that repeat the cycle (0, 2, 3, 0) more than once. Although the system may not return to state 1 every 3 steps, all paths are a multiple of three steps. State 1, therefore, is periodic with a period of 3. States 2 and 3 are also periodic with a period of 3. The Markov chain is irreducible but not ergodic.

E15.12

State	0	1	2	3
0	0	X	0	X
1	0	X	0	0
2	0	0	X	0
3	X	0	X	0

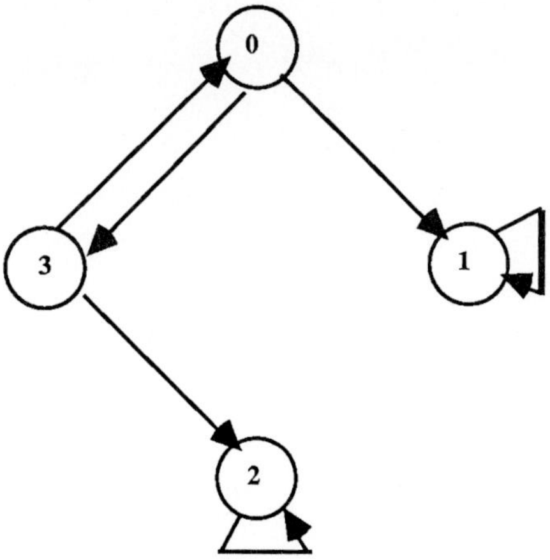

States 0 and 3 communicate, but since arcs leave the set, the two states form a transient class. State 1 communicates only with itself, so it forms a recurrent class. It must be an absorbing state. State 2 communicates only with itself, so it is also a recurrent class and an absorbing state. This example has three classes of states, one transient and two recurrent.

PROBLEMS

P15.8 For each of the transition matrices below, classify the states of the Markov chain. Also tell whether or not the chain is irreducible and whether it is ergodic.

a.

State	0	1	2	3	4
0	0	0	0	X	X
1	0	X	X	0	0
2	0	X	X	0	0
3	X	0	0	0	0
4	X	0	0	0	0

b.

State	0	1	2	3
0	X	0	0	0
1	0	X	X	0
2	0	X	X	0
3	X	0	0	X

c.

State	0	1	2	3
0	X	X	X	0
1	0	X	0	X
2	0	0	X	0
3	0	X	0	0

d.

State	0	1	2	3
0	0	0	X	X
1	0	0	X	0
2	0	X	0	0
3	X	X	0	0

e.

State	0	1	2	3
0	0	0	X	X
1	0	X	X	0
2	X	X	0	0
3	X	0	0	0

f.

State	0	1	2	3
0	0	X	0	0
1	0	0	X	0
2	0	0	0	X
3	X	0	0	0

Long-Run Properties (15.7)

As we let n, the number of periods or steps, of a Markov process increase indefinitely, certain quantities become independent of the initial state of the process. Among these are the n-step transition matrix and the state probability vector. The expected recurrence times and the expected average cost per unit time are also long run properties of interest. All these results hold for the irreducible, ergodic Markov chain. Some of them hold for less restricted Markov chains. This section tells how to compute the long-run results.

GOALS

- Given the transition matrix of an irreducible ergodic Markov chain, be able to calculate the steady-state probabilities, the long run n-step transition matrix, and the expected recurrence time.
- Given cost information concerning the states of a Markov chain, be able to calculate the expected average cost per unit time.

DEFINITIONS

Steady-State Probabilities (π_j): For irreducible ergodic Markov chains, the state probabilities approach a constant value, independent of the initial state as n gets large. The vector of steady-state probabilities is

$$\Pi = [\pi_0, \pi_1, \pi_2 \ldots \pi_M]$$

$$\pi_j = \lim_{n \to \infty} p_{ij}^{(n)} = \lim_{t \to \infty} Q_t\,(j) \qquad \text{for } j = 0, 1, 2, \ldots, M.$$

Expected Recurrence Time: The expected time of first passage from a state back to itself.

RESULTS

Finding the Steady-State Probabilities The steady-state probabilities can be found by solving the following set of linear equations.

$$\pi_j = \sum_{i=0}^{M} \pi_i\, p_{ij}, \qquad \text{for } j = 0, 1, 2, \ldots, M$$

$$\sum_{j=0}^{M} \pi_j = 1.$$

There are $M + 2$ equations in $M + 1$ unknowns. Any one of the first $M + 1$ equations must be dropped in order to solve the set of equations. In matrix format, the first set of equations may be written

$$\Pi = \Pi\,\mathbf{P}.$$

Finding the Expected Recurrence Time The expected first time of passage from a state back to itself is the reciprocal of the steady-state probability for the state.

$$\mu_{jj} = 1/\pi_j \quad \text{for } j = 0, 1, 2, \ldots, M.$$

n-Step Transition Matrix As n gets large, all the rows of the n-step transition matrix approach the steady-state probability vector. Thus all the rows are identical and equal to Π.

Expected Average Cost per Unit Time When the cost of $C(j)$ is expended when the process is in state j. The expected average cost per unit time is

$$\sum_{j=0}^{M} C(j)\, \pi_j.$$

When the cost depends on the state, j, and also a random variable D_t, which is independent and identically distributed in each period (or step), then the per period cost is $C(j, D_t)$. The expected average cost per unit time is

$$\sum_{j=0}^{M} K(j)\, \pi_j,$$

where $K(j)$ is the expected cost in state j:

$$K(j) = E[C(j, D_t)].$$

The expected value is taken over the random variable and computed using the standard methods of probability theory.

EXAMPLES

E15.13 Find the long-run properties for the Markov chain:

$$\mathbf{P} = \begin{bmatrix} 0.2 & 0.8 \\ 0.7 & 0.3 \end{bmatrix}.$$

Set up the equations

(1)	$\pi_0 = 0.2\, p_0 + 0.7\, \pi_1$
(2)	$\pi_1 = 0.8\, p_0 + 0.3\, \pi_1$
(3)	$1 = \pi_0 + \pi_1.$

We have three equations in the two unknowns π_0 and π_1.

From Eq. (3):	$\pi_1 = 1 - \pi_0$
Substituting in Eq. (1):	$\pi_0 = 0.2\, \pi_0 + 0.7(1 - \pi_0)$
Grouping terms:	$\pi_0(1 - 0.2 + 0.7) = 0.7$
Solving:	$\pi_0 = 0.7/1.5 = 0.46667$
From (3):	$\pi_1 = 1 - \pi_0 = 0.53333.$

The same result would have been obtained if (3) had been used to eliminate π_0 in equation (2).

The steady-state probabilities can also be found by computing $\mathbf{Q}_t$ for large t. Let $\mathbf{Q}_0 = (1, 0)$. Using the expression $\mathbf{Q}_{t+1} = \mathbf{Q}_t\mathbf{P}$:

Period	$Q_t(0)$	$Q_t(1)$	*Period*	$Q_t(0)$	$Q_t(1)$
1	0.2	0.8	8	0.4687	0.5313
2	0.6	0.4	9	0.4657	0.5343
3	0.4	0.6	10	0.4672	0.5328
4	0.5	0.5	11	0.4665	0.5335
5	0.45	0.55	12	0.4668	0.5332
6	0.475	0.525	13	0.4667	0.5333
7	0.4625	0.5375			

Note that the state probabilities converge to the steady-state values. The same result would have been noted if $\mathbf{Q}_0 = (0, 1)$.

All rows of the n-step transition matrix converge to the steady-state probabilities. For the example:

$$\mathbf{P}^{(2)} = \begin{bmatrix} 0.6 & 0.4 \\ 0.35 & 0.65 \end{bmatrix} \qquad \mathbf{P}^{(4)} = \begin{bmatrix} 0.5 & 0.5 \\ 0.4375 & 0.5625 \end{bmatrix}$$

$$\mathbf{P}^{(8)} = \begin{bmatrix} 0.4687 & 0.5313 \\ 0.4649 & 0.5351 \end{bmatrix} \qquad \mathbf{P}^{(\infty)} = \begin{bmatrix} 0.4667 & 0.5333 \\ 0.4667 & 0.5333 \end{bmatrix}$$

E15.14 Find the long-run properties for the Markov chain:

$$\mathbf{P} = \begin{bmatrix} 0 & 0.3 & 0.7 \\ 1 & 0 & 0 \\ 1 & 0 & 0 \end{bmatrix}.$$

To find the steady-state probabilities, set up the equations

(1) $\pi_0 = \pi_1 + \pi_2$

(2) $\pi_1 = 0.3\,\pi_0$

(3) $\pi_2 = 0.7\,\pi_0$

(4) $1 = \pi_0 + \pi_1 + \pi_2.$

Dropping Eq. (1) and using Eq. (2) and (3) to substitute for π_1 and π_2 in Eq. (4) we find that

$$1 = \pi_0 + 0.3\,\pi_0 + 0.7\,\pi_0 \quad \text{or} \quad \pi_0 = 0.5.$$

Substituting this result into (2) and (3) yields

$$\pi_1 = 0.15 \quad \text{and} \quad \pi_2 = 0.35.$$

Computing the state probability vector for several time periods we observe with

$$Q_0 = (1, 0, 0)$$

the following state probabilities as a function of time.

Period	$Q_t(0)$	$Q_t(1)$	$Q_t(2)$
1	0	0.3	0.7
2	1	0	0
3	0	0.3	0.7
4	1	0	0
5	0	0.3	0.7
6	1	0	0
7	0	0.3	0.7

Clearly, the state probability vector is not converging to any steady state. The difference between this example and E15.13 is that the Markov chain has periodic states. In general if the Markov chain is irreducible (all states are recurrent and communicate) but not ergodic (the states are periodic), the equations defining the steady state can be solved, but the results are not the long-run state probabilities. These do not converge. The vector Π is not without meaning in this case, however. The value of π_j is the probability that the system will be found in state j if the system is observed at a random point in time (for n some large value). It is also the long-run proportion of the time the system will be in state j. These alternative interpretations of π_j are also appropriate for the ergodic case. For a periodic Markov chain, the n-step transition matrix also fails to approach a limit as n increases indefinitely.

E15.15 Find the long-run properties for the Markov chain:

$$\mathbf{P} = \begin{bmatrix} 1 & 0 & 0 \\ 0.1 & 0.7 & 0.2 \\ 0 & 0 & 1 \end{bmatrix}.$$

To find the steady-state probabilities, set up the equations

(1) $\pi_0 = \pi_0 + 0.1\,\pi_1$

(2) $\pi_1 = 0.7\,\pi_1$

(3) $\pi_2 = 0.2\,\pi_1 + \pi_2$

(4) $1 = \pi_0 + \pi_1 + \pi_2.$

Rewriting the first three equations we obtain

(1) $0 = 0.1\,\pi_1$

(2) $0 = -0.3\,\pi_1$

(3) $0 = 0.2\,\pi_1$

(4) $1 = \pi_0 + \pi_2.$

The equations ascertain that π_1 is zero, but do not provide sufficient information to determine π_0 and π_2. This example illustrates a Markov chain with more than one absorbing state. In this case there is no steady state because the long-run state of the system depends on the initial state. When the system begins in state 0

$$Q_0 = (1, 0, 0),$$

the system will remain in state 0 for all t. When the system begins in state 2

$$Q_0 = (0, 0, 1),$$

the system will remain in state 2. State 1 is a transient state, and when the system begins in state 1

$$Q_0 = (0, 1, 0),$$

the following is observed.

Period	$Q_t(0)$	$Q_t(1)$	$Q_t(2)$
1	0.1	0.7	0.2
4	0.2533	0.2401	0.5066
8	0.3141	0.0576	0.6282
12	0.3287	0.0138	0.6574
16	0.3322	0.003	0.6644
20	0.3330	0.0007	0.6661

The probabilities are approaching limiting values with

$$Q_\infty(0) = 1/3,\ Q_\infty(1) = 0, \text{ and } Q_\infty(2) = 2/3.$$

The value $Q_\infty(j)$ should be interpreted as the probability that the system will eventually go to state j, given that the system begins in state 1. If the system has a single absorbing state with all the other states transient, the steady-state probability will be 1 for the absorbing state. If the system has more than one absorbing state, there is no steady state; however, the state probabilities will approach a limit that depends on the initial state.

E15.16 Consider the typewriter example of E15.3. The transition matrix for this example is

$$\mathbf{P} = \begin{bmatrix} 0.6 & 0.3 & 0.1 \\ 0.8 & 0.2 & 0.0 \\ 1.0 & 0.0 & 0.0 \end{bmatrix}.$$

State 0 represents the condition of no typewriters failed at the beginning of the day, state 1 indicates that one typewriter is failed, and state 2 indicates that two typewriters are failed. This is an irreducible ergodic Markov chain that has a steady state. The steady-state equations are

(1) $$\pi_0 = 0.6\,\pi_0 + 0.8\,\pi_1 + \pi_2$$

(2) $$\pi_1 = 0.3\,\pi_0 + 0.2\,\pi_1$$

(3) $\pi_2 = 0.1\,\pi_0$

(4) $1 = \pi_0 + \pi_1 + \pi_2.$

Using (2) and (3) to solve for π_1 and π_2 in terms of π_0, and substituting into Eq. (4)

$$1 = \pi_0 + 0.375\,\pi_0 + 0.1\,\pi_0 \quad \text{or} \quad \pi_0 = 0.678.$$

Using (2) and (3) determines

$$\pi_1 = 0.254 \qquad \text{and} \qquad \pi_2 = 0.068.$$

Let us add the information that whenever one typewriter is failed, some office work must be sent to a typing service at a cost of \$20 per day. Whenever both typewriters are failed, the cost of the typing service increases to \$100 per day. The repairman charges \$40 for repairing a typewriter. The cost of operation depends on the state of the system, according to

$$C(0) = 0,\ \ C(1) = 20 + 40 = \$60,\ \ C(2) = \$100 + 80 = \$180.$$

With this information the expected cost of operating the system is

$$\begin{aligned} E[\text{cost per day}] &= C(0)\,\pi_0 + C(1)\,\pi_1 + C(2)\,\pi_2 \\ &= (0)(0.678) + (60)(0.254) + (180)(0.068) = \$27.48. \end{aligned}$$

PROBLEMS

P15.9 The manager running the office referred to in the example above has the option of buying an additional typewriter which will be kept as a spare in case of failure. It will not be used in normal operation, but will be placed into service when a typewriter fails. The effect will be to reduce the cost of the typing service. The spare machine will not fail when it is not in use, but will fail with the same probabilities as the original machines when it is in service. The cost of ownership of the spare typewriter is \$5 per day. Should the manager buy the spare typewriter?

P15.10 Find the steady-state probabilities associated with the submarine component of E15.7. The loss of the component is a very serious event with respect to the submarine's operation. With every additional failure after the spares are exhausted, a replacement must be flown to the submarine at a cost of \$20,000. The spares that are obtained in this fashion can not be used for the next year's operation, thus the transition matrix obtained in E15.7 is still appropriate. What is the expected annual cost of flying in spares?

P15.11 Considering the situation described in P15.10, would it be economic to allow another spare to the ships complement? Two are delivered each year, but four may be retained. The cost of ownership of the additional spare is \$5000 per year.

Computer Program

This chapter describes a number of numerical techniques that can be used to answer important questions about Markov chains. Since most of the techniques involve

1. DEFINE STATES
2. SHOW STATES
3. ENTER OR CHANGE TRANSITION MATRIX
4. SHOW TRANSITION MATRIX
5. COMPUTE TRANSIENT STATE PROBABILITIES
6. SIMULATE PROCESS
7. READ DATA FROM DISK
8. SAVE DATA ON DISK
9. TURN PRINTER ON
10. RUN NEW PROBLEM
11. LOAD SAMPLE PROBLEM
12. RETURN TO DISK MENU

Figure 15.1 **Menu for Markov Chain Program**

matrix operations, they are generally difficult to use if hand calculations are required and there are more than two or three states. Most practical problems have a much larger number of states. The computer program provided with the *Microsolve* package can help with certain computations for problems with as many as 16 states.

The menu for the program is shown in Fig. 15.1. The first selection for a new problem is option 1, which defines the states of the model. States should be given names representative of their purpose. Option 3 should then be selected to enter the transition matrix. The program provides a convenient matrix display, which allows easy entry or modification of transition probabilities. Only nonzero values need be entered. Options 2 and 4 allow for review of the model.

Option 5, the most useful part of the program, computes transient state probabilities. It computes the state probability vector, with a given initial state, for any number of steps. By computing the probabilities for a large number of steps the long-run characteristics can be observed. The significance of this output depends on the classification of the Markov matrix as listed below.

- Irreducible ergodic matrix: Here the state probability vector converges to the steady-state probabilities independent of the initial state.
- Reducible matrix: Transient state probabilities will go to zero.
- Periodic matrix: Here the state probability vector does not converge, but will illustrate the periodic nature of the state probabilities.
- Matrix with more than one absorbing state: The convergence of the long-run state probabilities will depend on the initial state. The state probability of an absorbing state will converge to the probability of terminating the process in that state.

Option 6 simulates the Markov process. This is primarily an instructional tool to illustrate the dynamic nature of the process. The system may start in any state and operate for any number of steps. Statistics are maintained on the relative frequencies of the states. One will note the large number of observations required to obtain an accurate estimate of the state probabilities. Other characteristics, such as the distribution of first passage times, can be estimated by directly observing the sequence of states generated by the simulation.

Problems

P15.12 Use the Markov chain transition probability matrix shown below. The states are 0, 1, and 2.

$$\mathbf{P} = \begin{bmatrix} 0 & 0.3 & 0.7 \\ 0.9 & 0.1 & 0 \\ 0.2 & 0 & 0.8 \end{bmatrix}.$$

a. Find the state probability vector for the first five steps, assuming the system begins in state 2.
b. Given that the system begins in state 2, find the probability that the first passage to state 0 will require one step, two steps, three steps.
c. Find is the expected first passage time from state 2 to state 0.
d. Find the steady-state probability vector for this Markov chain.

P15.13 Use the Markov chain transition matrix below. The time step represented by the matrix is 1 week.

State	0	1	2	3
0	0.2	0.8	0	0
1	0	0.9	0.1	0
2	0.3	0	0.2	0.5
3	0	0	0.1	0.9

a. Find the expected first passage time from state 3 to state 0.
b. Find the expected first passage time from state 0 to state 3.
c. Find the expected recurrence time for state 0.
d. Find the steady-state probabilities.

P15.14 Classify the states for the markov chains given below.

a.
$$\begin{bmatrix} 0 & 0 & 0 & 0.5 & 0.5 & 0 \\ 0 & 0 & 0 & 0 & 0 & 1 \\ 0 & 0 & 0 & 0.1 & 0.9 & 0 \\ 0.1 & 0.01 & 0.89 & 0 & 0 & 0 \\ 0.8 & 0 & 0.2 & 0 & 0 & 0 \\ 0 & 1 & 0 & 0 & 0 & 0 \end{bmatrix}$$

b.
$$\begin{bmatrix} 0 & 0 & 0 & 0.5 & 0.5 & 0 \\ 0 & 0 & 0 & 0 & 0 & 1 \\ 0 & 0 & 0 & 0.1 & 0.9 & 0 \\ 0.1 & 0.01 & 0.89 & 0 & 0 & 0 \\ 0.8 & 0 & 0.2 & 0 & 0 & 0 \\ 0.1 & 0.9 & 0 & 0 & 0 & 0 \end{bmatrix}$$

c.
$$\begin{bmatrix} 0 & 1 & 0 & 0 \\ 0 & 0 & 1 & 0 \\ 0.3 & 0 & 0 & 0.7 \\ 0 & 1 & 0 & 0 \end{bmatrix}$$

d.
$$\begin{bmatrix} 0.2 & 0.8 & 0 & 0 \\ 0 & 0.9 & 0.1 & 0 \\ 0 & 0 & 1 & 0 \\ 0 & 0 & 0.1 & 0.9 \end{bmatrix}$$

e.
$$\begin{bmatrix} 0.2 & 0.8 & 0 & 0 \\ 0 & 0.9 & 0.1 & 0 \\ 0.3 & 0 & 0.2 & 0.5 \\ 0 & 0 & 0.1 & 0.9 \end{bmatrix}$$

f.
$$\begin{bmatrix} 0.2 & 0 & 0.8 & 0 \\ 0 & 0.9 & 0.1 & 0 \\ 0.3 & 0 & 0.7 & 0 \\ 0 & 0 & 0.1 & 0.9 \end{bmatrix}$$

P15.15 The enrollment in the Engineering College ranges between 4500 and 6000 students. The lower bound represents a pool of students who will always go to engineering school no matter what the economic climate. The upper bound triggers enrollment control measures that will always bring enrollment down. The Dean's office has originated a study that estimates the Fall semester enrollment in each year. The statistical study has determined that enrollment change is primarily determined by the "economic climate" which has been determined to have two states, *good* and *bad.*

Student enrollment has been discretized into steps of 500 students ranging from 4500 to 6000. The enrollment in any one year will either increase by 500 students, stay the same, or decrease by 500 students. In a year with *good* economic climate, enrollment will go up with probability 0.5, stay the same with probability 0.2, or go down by 500 with probability 0.3. In a year with *bad* economic climate, enrollment will go up with probability 0.2, stay the same with probability 0.4, or go down with probability 0.4. These probabilities are based on the economic condition at the beginning of the year. One exception to this rule occurs when the enrollment reaches 6000 students. The enrollment control measures will always reduce enrollment to 5500 at the beginning of the next year. When the enrollment is 4500 at the beginning of one year, it may not decrease further. In this case the probability of decrease is included with the probability that the enrollment doesn't change.

The Bureau of Business Research has determined that if the climate is good at the beginning of one year, there is a 0.7 chance that it will be good again at the beginning of the next. If the climate is bad at the beginning of one year, there is a 0.6 chance that it will be bad again at the beginning of the next.

Show the Markov chain transition matrix for this problem. Be sure to define appropriate states. Find the steady-state probability distribution for the number of students in the school.

P15.16 Consider a barber shop with one barber (with a barber chair) and two waiting chairs. In any given minute of the day only one of three things may happen:

1. A customer can arrive at the shop.
2. A customer can leave the shop.
3. There are no arrivals or departures.

The probability that a customer arrives in a particular minute is 0.01. If he arrives and finds both waiting chairs full he will not stay. A customer may depart from the shop only if there is a customer in the shop. Then the probability that a customer departs in a particular minute is 0.02. Assume that during a 1-minute interval, two or more events will not occur.

a. Construct the transition matrix that describes a 1-minute interval. The states are the number of people in the shop (not counting the barber).
b. Compute steady-state probabilities and use them to answer the questions below.
c. If the barber earns \$5 each time someone leaves the shop, what is his expected daily earnings? Assume an 8-hour day.
d. What percentage of the time would you expect the shop to be full?
e. What percentage of the time would you expect to shop to have no customers?

Computer Problems

P15.17 Enter the transition matrix described in P15.16 into the *Microsolve* program. Starting with the system empty, observe how many steps it takes before the transient state probabilities approximate the steady-state probabilities with two decimal place accuracy. Using the simulation option of the program, observe how many minutes must be simulated before the states' frequencies estimate the steady-state probabilities with two decimal point accuracy.

P15.18 Enter each of the transition matrices of P15.14. Comment on the long-run state probability vector for each case. Let the initial state be 0 for each run.

P15.19 A seller of diamonds determines the following probability distribution on the number of customers arriving each day.

Number of Customers	0	1	2	3	4
Probability	0.2	0.3	0.3	0.1	0.1

Assume that each customer will buy a diamond if it is available. Otherwise the sale is lost.

Each morning the seller looks at his inventory. If there are 3 or fewer diamonds (and no diamonds on order), he orders 3 more diamonds from his supplier. They arrive 2 days later (on the second morning after the order). For problem c through g, use steady-state probabilities.

a. Show the transition matrix that models this inventory situation.
b. If the store has 3 diamonds on Monday morning, what is the probability distribution for the number of diamonds on hand 5 days later? What is the probability that some diamonds are on order?
c. What is the steady-state probability that the store will have no diamonds in the morning?
d. If the cost of holding diamonds in inventory is \$10 per day per diamond, what is the expected annual inventory cost? Assume 260 workdays per year.
e. What is the expected number of orders that must be placed in each year? If the cost of placing an order is \$50, what is the expected annual ordering cost?
f. What is the expected annual cost of lost sales if the per unit cost is \$200?
g. Based on the results of (d), (e), and (f), experiment on different ordering policies for the seller to find some policy that minimizes total inventory holding cost, ordering cost, plus lost sales cost.

P15.20 For the situation described in P15.5a, use the computer to answer the following questions.

a. Assume that on Monday morning (after the arrival of a tank) the system has three tanks in the maintenance facility while the overflow area is empty. Show the state probabilities for the next 5 days.
b. Compute the state probabilities after a number of periods to estimate the steady-state probabilities. Use these probabilities to estimate the number of days in the year (assume 200 working days) on which a delay in the schedule is necessary.
c. From the steady-state probabilities, estimate the percent utilization of the depot in terms of percentage of the capacity that is used. Assume the maintenance capacity is three tanks.

CHAPTER 16

Queueing Theory

A stochastic process that has received considerable attention from the operations research community is the waiting line or queue. An example is the line of customers that forms in front of the service windows at a post office. The number of customers in the line grows and declines with time, and as any potential customer can attest, the number in the line at any given time is highly unpredictable. This number is a random variable that is a function of time; thus it is a stochastic process. With reasonable assumptions a great deal can be learned about the characteristics of the line, such as the average number in the line, the average waiting time for a customer, and the percentage of time the servers are busy. These questions are answered using the results of queueing theory, which is the subject of this chapter. The principal topics of the chapter are the notation of queueing theory, the important cases of the exponential and Poisson distributions, the computational procedures of the general birth-death process, the special cases of various single- and multiple-channel queueing systems, and a discussion of networks of queues.

Basic Structure of Queueing Models (16.2)

The basic queueing process is illustrated in Fig. 16.1. Customers arrive to the queueing system from some input source. If the service mechanism is busy, the customers must wait in a queue until a server is available. Some time is required for service, after which the customer departs. The details of this procedure depend on various assumptions and parameters adopted for the components of the system.

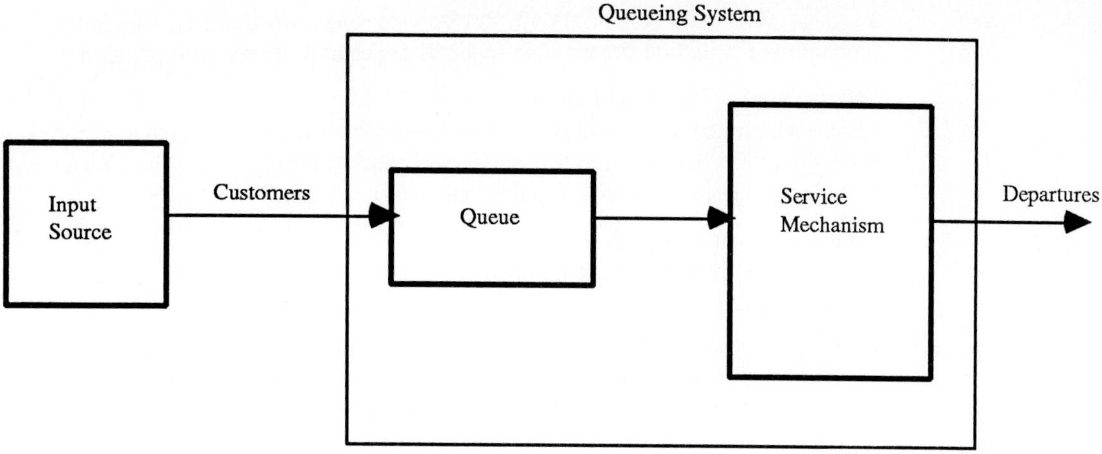

Figure 16.1 **Schematic of the Queueing System**

GOALS

- For a given situation appropriate for a queueing model, be able to identify and characterize the input source, the queue, and the service process.
- Know the meaning of the mathematical notation used to quantify queueing systems.
- Be able to use the basic relationships between the steady state measures describing average number in the system or queue and average time in the system or queue.

DEFINITIONS

Input Source: This is also called the calling population. It is the collection of customers providing inputs to the queueing system. Characteristics are the size and interarrival distribution. The size is the number of potential customers. This is either infinite or finite. In the latter case some number must be specified. The interarrival time is the time between successive arrivals to the queue. The time is usually a random variable with some given probability distribution called the interarrival distribution.

Queue: The place where customers reside while waiting for service. A queue discipline defines the rules by which customers are selected for service. A common discipline is first-come-first-served.

Service Mechanism: A description of the process by which the customers are served. The assumption of this chapter is that the service is provided by one or more identical servers (or channels) operating in parallel. The characteristics of such a system are number of servers and service time distribution. The latter is a probability distribution for the time required to perform the service operation.

Steady State: The condition reached in the long-run operation of a queueing system where various measures of system operation become independent of the time since operation began. Not all systems will reach a steady state. The chapter will provide conditions for which a steady state will be obtained.

Characteristics of the System

State of the system: Total number of customers in the system, including the number in the queue and in service.

K: The maximum number in the system. When the maximum number in the system is finite and the number in the system has reached this limit, an arriving customer "balks" and does not enter.

$P_n(t)$: The probability of n customers in the system at time t.

P_n: Probability of n customers in the system at steady state.

L: Average number in the system at steady state.

W: Average customer time in the system at steady state.

Characteristics of the Arrival Process

N: The size of the input source.

λ_n: The arrival rate or the expected number of arrivals per unit time when n customers are in the system.

λ: The arrival rate when the state of the system does not affect the rate of customer arrivals. The expected time between arrivals is $1/\lambda$.

Characteristics of the Queue

Maximum number in the queue: The maximum number in the system less the number of servers.

L_q: The expected number in the queue at steady state.

W_q: The expected customer waiting time in the queue at steady state.

Queue discipline: The rule by which customers are chosen from the queue to receive service. Possible rules are first-come-first-served, last come first served, or selection by some priority rule. This chapter assumes that customers form a single queue even if there are multiple service channels.

Characteristics of the Service Process

s: Number of service channels. All are assumed equally capable.

L_s: Expected number in service at steady state.

μ_n: Mean service rate for the system when there are n customers in the system.

μ: The mean service rate for a single busy server when the number in the system does not affect the service rate. The expected time for a single service action is $1/\mu$.

ρ: The utilization factor for the service system. The fraction of the time the servers will be busy.

Specification of System Characteristics

We use the three part notation shown below to identify some of the important characteristics of the queueing system.

arrival distribution/service distribution/number of servers.

The first and second terms identify the probability distributions of the interarrival times and the service times, respectively. The following symbols are used to identify important distributions:

M = exponential distribution,

D = constant time,

E_k = Erlang distribution with parameter k,

G = general or arbitrary distribution.

The last term is a number specifying the number of servers. When a finite number is given as the maximum number in the system, that number is used as a fourth term of the notation.

RESULTS

The following relations hold at steady state.

Relation Between Average Number and Average Time When λ is independent of the state of the system,

$$\text{In system: } L = \lambda W.$$

$$\text{In queue: } L_q = \lambda W_q.$$

Relation Between Average Times in Queue and System When μ is independent of the state of the system,

$$W = W_q + 1/\mu .$$

Expected Number in the System

$$L = \sum_{n=1}^{\infty} n P_n.$$

Expected Number in the Queue When s is independent of the state of the system,

$$L_q = \sum_{n=s}^{\infty} (n-s) P_n.$$

Expected Number in the Service

$$L_s = L - L_q = \sum_{n=1}^{s-1} nP_n + s\,[1 - \sum_{n=0}^{s-1} P_n\,]$$

System Utilization When s is independent of the state of the system,

$$\rho = L_s / s\,.$$

When μ, λ, and s are independent of the state of the system,

$$\rho = \lambda / s\mu\,.$$

EXAMPLES

In the following examples we will identify the characteristics of the queueing models and, if appropriate, use the relationships above to compute quantitative measures describing the system.

E16.1 A post office has three windows staffed with clerks. Customers arrive with an average time between arrivals of 30 seconds. Postal clerks work at a steady pace, with the average time for serving a customer equal to 1.25 minutes. Say as much as you can about the queueing system.

Arrival process: Infinite calling population because no reasonably small finite limit can be placed on the number of potential customers.

The arrival rate is independent of the number of customers and equal to

$$\lambda = 1/0.5 = 2 \text{ per minute.}$$

Note that the arrival rate has the dimension [1/time]. The specific time dimension chosen (seconds, minutes, hours) is not critical, but the same dimension should be chosen for all problem characteristics. Usually the time dimension is chosen to give reasonably sized numbers.

Queue: The maximum queue size is infinite. Although this probably is not exactly true, there is no limit stated in the problem. For most situations the maximum queue size can be assumed to be infinite if the actual limit is fairly large. The queue discipline is first-come-first-served.

Service process: The service process has three clerks, so $s = 3$. The service rate per channel is

$$\mu = 1/1.25 = 0.8 \text{ per minute.}$$

System: G/G/3 (No distributions are identified.)

Utilization: $\rho = \lambda / s\,\mu = 2/(3 * 0.8) = 0.8333$. This implies that 83% of the system's capacity is utilized. If the work is divided evenly among the clerks, each clerk is idle around 17% of the time.

Average time in the system: $W = 3$ minutes. (This is given.)

Average number in the system: $L = \lambda W = 2 * 3 = 6$ customers.

Average time in the queue: $W_q = W - 1/\mu = 3 - 1.25 = 1.75$ minutes.

Average number in the queue: $L_q = \lambda W_q = 2 * 1.75 = 3.5$ customers.

This example illustrates the problems facing the designers of the queueing system. Although the workers of the system are idle a good portion of the time, the number in the queue will average 3.5 customers. This apparently contradictory state of events is due to the stochastic nature of the process. Sometimes the number in the system will be smaller than three and some workers will be idle, and sometimes the line will be very long and individual customers will have to wait a long time.

E16.2 In an effort to provide better service to customers, an additional clerk is added. The expected time in the system for a customer is now measured as 1.52 minutes. How have the system measures changed?

System: G/G/4

Utilization: $\rho = 2/4 * (0.8) = 0.625$.

Number in system: $L = (2) * (1.52) = 3.04$ customers.

Time in queue: $W_q = 1.52 - 1.25 = 0.27$ minutes.

Number in queue: $L_q = 2 * (0.27) = 0.54$ customers.

Service is much improved, but the utilization of the system has been reduced.

E16.3 A machine shop has 10 machines. Each machine while working will fail with the average time between breakdowns of 100 hours. The time between failures has an exponential distribution. Failed machines are sent to a repair shop where one machine is fixed at a time. It takes on the average 20 hours to fix a machine. The time for repair has an Erlang distribution with $k = 3$. What can we say about this situation?

This is a queueing model with a finite calling source. There are only 10 potential customers, the 10 machines. The service mechanism has a single channel since only one machine can be repaired at a time. The queue comprises the machines waiting for repair. The arrival rate of customers into the system depends on the number of customers already in the system because it is assumed that a machine cannot fail again while awaiting or undergoing repair. The failure rate of a single machine is 1/100 or 0.01 per hour. When all 10 machines are operating and none are in the queueing system, the arrival rate into the system is $10 * (0.01) = 0.1$ per hour. When only 9 are operating and 1 is in the system, the arrival rate becomes $9 * (0.01) = 0.09$ per hour. In general,

$$\lambda_n = (10 - n) * (0.01) \text{ per hour} \quad \text{for } n = 0, 1, 2, \ldots, 10.$$

This equation recognizes that when all 10 are in the system, the arrival rate is zero, because no additional failures can occur.

The queue is infinite. Although clearly the maximum queue size is limited to 10, the limit is due to the size of the calling population and is not a characteristic of the queue.

The service rate for the single channel is 1/20 or 0.05 per hour, which is independent of the number in the system. The service rate of the system does depend on the number in the system as follows:

$\mu_0 = 0$ there can be no service when the system is empty.

$\mu_n = \mu = 0.05$ for $n = 1, 2, \ldots, 10$.

The general expressions for ρ, L, L_q, W, and W_q are not appropriate for this situation since the arrival rate is a function of the number in the system. The system would be specified as a $M/E_3/1$ system with a finite input source.

E16.4 A downtown gas station has two pumps and a single space for a waiting car. If a customer arrives when both pumps and the waiting space are full, he or she will not remain but will seek gas elsewhere. The service rate per pump is 0.7 customers per minute. The arrival rate of customers is 1.2 customers per minute. Both interarrival time and service time have exponential distributions.

This situation represents a finite queue model. The maximum queue size is 1, and the maximum number in the system is 3. The calling population is infinite with $\lambda = 1.2$; however, the arrival rate into the system is affected by the finite queue as follows

$$\lambda_n = 1.2 \quad \text{for } n = 0, 1, 2$$
$$\lambda_3 = 0$$

The general expressions for ρ, L, L_q, W, and W_q are not appropriate for this situation. The system would be specified as a M/M/2/3.

E16.5 A system has 2 servers and the maximum number in the system is 5. The following steady-state probabilities are observed.

n	0	1	2	3	4	5
P_n	0.05	0.15	0.25	0.25	0.2	0.1

Because no distributions are specified, the system is G/G/2/5. From this data, we can calculate

$$L = 0(0.05) + 1(0.15) + 2(0.25) + 3(0.25) + 4(0.2) + 5(0.1) = 2.7$$
$$L_q = 0(0.25) + 1(0.25) + 2(0.2) + 3(0.1) = 0.95$$
$$L_s = 2.7 - 0.95 = 1.75$$
$$\rho = L_s / s = 1.75/2 = 0.875.$$

PROBLEMS

For each situation below, identify the characteristics of the components of the queueing system. Use the relationships given above to compute measures of system performance.

P16.1 The time between the arrivals of patients to a medical clinic has a normal distribution with a mean of 12 minutes and a standard deviation of 5 minutes. Three doctors treat the patients. The treatment time has an exponential distribution with a mean time of 30 minutes. The secretary who has been taking data has found that the average time a patient must wait before being seen by a doctor is 20 minutes.

P16.2 Cars arrive at a stop sign on a two-lane road at an average rate of 110 per hour. The arrival process is Poisson (meaning the time between arrivals has an exponential distribution). The time it takes a car to clear the stop sign once the car reaches the front of one of the lanes also has an exponential distribution with a mean time of 1 minute. The average number of cars at the stop sign (either waiting in the queue or preparing to cross) is 11.4.

P16.3 The same as P16.2 except that whenever there are 6 cars at the corner, any additional arriving cars take a convenient side street and bypass the stop sign.

P16.4 A supermarket has five checkout stands. The average time to check out a customer is 8 minutes. That time has a normal distribution with a standard deviation of 2 minutes. The time between arrivals has an exponential distribution with a mean rate of 1 2/3 customers per minute. The average number of customers in the queueing system is 13.

P16.5 Four robots have been installed for manufacturing some part. The time to make one part is constant at 4 minutes. The demand for the part averages 50 per hour. The time between calls for the part has an exponential distribution. The average number of calls in the queue is 4.1.

P16.6 Three bank teller drive-in windows have been installed. Besides the spaces adjacent to the windows, there is room for three waiting cars. Cars arriving when there is no waiting space balk and do not join the queue. Work sampling has established the following percentages

Number of busy windows	0	1	2	3
Percent of the time	10	15	20	55
Number of waiting cars	0	1	2	3
Percent of the time	60	20	15	5

What can you compute concerning this system?

Exponential Distributions (16.4)

The exponential continuous probability distribution and the associated Poisson discrete probability distribution have special importance to the study of queues. Many of the useful results of queueing theory are derived using the assumptions that the time between arrivals and the time for service are both random variables having exponential distributions. These assumptions are reasonably appropriate for some practical applications, but perhaps more importantly they lead to a mathematical tractability that is otherwise very difficult to obtain. The approximation associated with these assumptions must be justified for each specific application.

GOALS

- List the five properties of an exponential distribution.
- Use the exponential distribution to make probability statements concerning the time between arrivals or departures.
- Use the Poisson distribution to make probability statements about the number of arrivals and departures in some interval of time.

DEFINITIONS

State of the Queueing System: The number of customers in the system, ranging from 0 to the maximum number in the system. We use n for the general state.

Poisson Arrival Process: An input source of a queueing system that generates arrivals such that the time to the next arrival has an exponential distribution. The arrival rate is λ_n when the system is in state n.

Poisson Departure Process: A service mechanism for which the time until the next departure from the system has an exponential distribution. The departure rate is μ_n when the system is in state n.

RESULTS

The Exponential Distribution The random variable, T, is the time to the next occurrence of some event. The exponential distribution is

$$f_T(t) = \begin{cases} \alpha e^{-\alpha t}, & \text{for } t \geq 0 \\ 0, & \text{for } t < 0. \end{cases}$$

The parameter α is greater than 0 and is the mean rate of occurrences of the event per unit time. The dimension of α is [1/time]. The expected time between occurrences of the event is $1/\alpha$ with dimension [time]. The cumulative distribution is

$$F_T(t) = 1 - e^{-\alpha t} \quad \text{for } t \geq 0.$$

Properties of the Exponential Distribution

1. $f_T(t)$ is a strictly decreasing function of t ($t \geq 0$).
2. The exponential distribution has no memory.
3. The minimum of several independent exponential random variables has an exponential distribution. If α_i is the parameter of the ith distribution, then the parameter of the minimum of k random variables is

$$\alpha = \sum_{i=1}^{k} \alpha_i.$$

4. If the time between occurrences has an exponential distribution with parameter a, then the number of occurrences of the event in an interval of time t has a Poisson distribution with parameter $\alpha\, t$.

$$P\{k \text{ occurrences in time } t\} = \frac{(\alpha\, t)^k\, e^{-\alpha t}}{k\,!}.$$

Here $\alpha\, t$ can be interpreted as the expected number of occurrences of the event in the interval t. The parameter of the Poisson distribution ($\alpha\, t$) is dimensionless.

5. The probability of the occurrence in the next small interval of time Δt is proportional to the length of the interval.

$$P\{T \le t + \Delta t \mid T > t\} = \alpha\, \Delta t.$$

EXAMPLES

E16.6 For the following examples consider a queueing system with an infinite calling population. The input source is a Poisson process with an average time between arrivals of 2 minutes. The queue is infinite (is not limited in size). The service mechanism has three parallel servers (channels). The time for service is a random variable with an exponential distribution. The average time for service is 5 minutes.

It is traditional that we use λ to represent the parameter α when dealing with arrivals and μ to represent α when dealing with services. With this information we determine that the time between arrivals has an exponential distribution with

$$\lambda = 1/2 = 0.5 \text{ (arrivals per minute)}.$$

The time for service has an exponential distribution with

$$\mu = 1/5 = 0.2 \text{ (services per minute)}.$$

To distinguish between them we will call the time between arrivals T_a and the time for service T_s.

a. What is the probability that the next arrival will occur within the next 3 minutes? This question can be answered from the cumulative distribution of T_a.

$$P\{T_a < 3\} = F_T(3) = 1 - e^{-0.5(3)} = 1 - 0.223 = 0.777.$$

b. Given that the last arrival occurred 10 minutes ago, what is the probability that the next arrival will occur within the next 3 minutes? Because the exponential distribution has no memory, the answer is still the same, 0.777.

c. Compare the probability that the next arrival will occur during the next 3 minutes to the probability that the next arrival will occur between 9 and 12 minutes from now.

$$
\begin{aligned}
P\{0 < T_a < 3\} &= 0.777 \\
P\{9 < T_a < 12\} &= (1 - e^{-(0.5)(12)}) - (1 - e^{-(0.5)(9)}) \\
&= 0.9975 - 0.9889 = 0.0086.
\end{aligned}
$$

This illustrates property 1.

d. If it is given that the next arrival does not occur during the next 9 minutes, what is the probability that it will occur between times 9 and 12?

$$P\{9 < T_a < 12 \mid T_a > 9\} = \frac{P\{9 < T_a < 12\}}{1 - P\{T_a < 9\}} = \frac{0.0086}{0.0111} = 0.777.$$

This illustrates property 2.

e. What is the probability that two arrivals will occur during the next 3 minutes? Based on property 4, the Poisson distribution can be used here with the time interval of 3. The parameter of the Poisson is

$$\lambda t = (0.5)(3) = 1.5.$$

This is the expected number of arrivals during the period. Using the Poisson with X_a the number of arrivals,

$$P\{X_a = 2\} = [(1.5)^2 e^{-(1.5)}]/2! = 0.251.$$

f. What is the probability that no arrivals occur during the next 3 minutes? Again using the Poisson,

$$P\{X_a = 0\} = [(1.5)^2 e^{-(1.5)}]/0! = 0.223.$$

g. There is one customer in the system, so one server is busy while the other two are idle. What is the probability that the service operation will be completed within the next 2 minutes. Using the cumulative of the exponential distribution with $\mu = 0.2$,

$$P\{T_s < 2\} = 1 - e^{-(0.2)(2)} = 0.330.$$

h. There are two customers in the system, so two servers are busy. What is the probability that the next service operation will be completed in 2 minutes? The time of the next service completion is the minimum of the completion times of the two in process. According to property 3, this minimum has an exponential distribution with parameter equal to the sum of the parameters of the two service operations in process. Thus

$$\alpha = \mu + \mu = 0.2 + 0.2 = 0.4.$$

Calling T' the time to the next service, the desired probability is

$$P\{T' < 2\} = 1 - e^{-(0.4)(2)} = 0.551.$$

Note: In general, if n servers are busy, the probability distribution for the time to the next service completion is exponential, with parameter

$$\alpha = n\mu,$$

where μ is the service rate for a single server.

i. There are currently two customers in the system. What is the probability that three customers will complete service within the next 10 minutes? Such a situation is possible because additional customers may enter the system during the period. One might be tempted to use the Poisson distribution to answer this question; however, it is not appropriate. The service rate may not be constant over the 10-minute interval. The rate at a particular time depends on the number of busy servers, and the number of busy servers may vary over the interval. This question cannot be answered easily.

j. It is given that over a particular 10-minute interval all three servers are busy all the time. What is the probability distribution of the number of customers served over that period? Here the Poisson may be used with parameter

$$\alpha t = 3\mu t = 3(0.2)(10) = 6.$$

The Poisson is appropriate because the number of busy servers and hence the average rate of service are constant in the interval.

k. A new class of customers now begins to use the queueing system. These customers arrive at an average rate of one every 10 minutes. The new customers receive the same service as the original ones. How does this change affect the analysis? The time between arrivals is now the minimum of two random variables with exponential distributions, one with a rate of 0.5 per minute and one with a rate of 0.1 per minute. By property 3, the combined time between arrivals is also an exponential distribution with a parameter equal to the sum of the two contributing rates. Analysis of the new situation will proceed with the parameter

$$\lambda = 0.5 + 0.1 = 0.6.$$

MODELING

The assumption of an exponential distribution for time between arrivals is quite appropriate for many applications. If customers arrive "independently" or "at random," the use of the exponential distribution is theoretically justified. The main requirement is that the arrival of a customer not be affected in any way by the arrival of any other. A classic example is the arrival of calls at a telephone switchboard. Clearly the arrivals cannot influence each other. The time between failures of electronic devices is often assumed to have an exponential distribution.

The exponential assumption is not justified when arrivals occur in groups. Examples include couples arriving at a movie theatre, and orders for a product that may arrive at random but in multiples of more than one unit.

Justifying that the service time has an exponential distribution is perhaps more difficult. If all customers receive approximately the same service, the assumption is unlikely to hold. For instance the time to get a haircut probably does not have an exponential distribution. The time required to check out at a grocery store may be exponentially distributed if the numbers of items in the shopping baskets are approximately exponentially distributed (making allowances for the discrete nature of this random variable). Note that the lack of memory property need not hold for the individual customer. Clearly a grocery store customer with many items can expect a long service time. The exponential distribution is a property of the service times for the population of customers.

The following sections assume that the exponential distribution is an appropriate approximation for both interarrival and service times. This is necessary to derive analytical results. If the assumptions are seriously violated for an application, the results are probably not useful. Simulation is an alternative method of analysis, which will yield results under a variety of assumptions but at a much greater computational cost. Simulation is discussed in Chapter 23.

PROBLEMS

P16.7 Cars pass an intersection at an average rate of 20 per minute. The time between successive cars has an exponential distribution. You are standing on the corner watching the cars.

a. What is the expected time to the next arrival?
b. What is the probability that you will have to wait more than 10 seconds for the next arrival?
c. What is the probability that the next arrival will occur in less than 3 seconds?
d. What is the probability of four cars passing in 6 seconds?
e. What is the probability of fewer than four cars passing in 6 seconds?
f. You haven't seen a car pass for the last minute. What is the expected time to the next arrival?

P16.8 Customers arrive at a queueing system with a Poisson arrival process with an average arrival rate of three per hour. The system has an infinite queue and four servers. The service time has an exponential distribution with the mean service time of one hour.

a. What is the mean time between arrivals?
b. What is the rate of departures from the system when one server is busy, two servers are busy, all four servers are busy?
c. What is the probability that more than one customer arrives in a two-hour interval?
d. What is the probability that a particular customer will require more than eight hours for the service operation?

Birth-Death Processes (16.5)

The queueing models to be considered in the next few sections can all be considered to be special cases of the birth-death process. A population of some type is observed over time. Increases in the population occur with births while decreases occur with deaths. Since we will most often be dealing with a population consisting of customers in a queue, we will equate a birth with an arrival and a death with a service completion or departure. The state of the system at any time is the number in the population. Since arrivals and departures occur according to some random mechanism, this number is a stochastic process. This section describes the general analytical techniques with which quantitative questions about the birth-death process can be answered.

GOALS

- Given a situation that can be analyzed as a birth-death process, construct the rate diagram for the process.
- From the arrival and departure rates given on the rate diagram, compute the factor C_n for each state.
- From the C_n factors, compute the steady-state quantities $P_0, P_1, \ldots, P_n$, L, L_q, W, and W_q.

DEFINITIONS

Birth-Death Process: A model characterized by a population that takes on integer values 0, 1, 2, ... The population is called the state of the system. Assuming the system is in some state k at a given time, the system will move to state $k + 1$ if an arrival (birth) occurs, move to state $k - 1$ if a service (death) occurs, or stay in state k.

Arrival (Birth) Rate (λ_n): The parameter of the exponential distribution for the time to the next arrival when the system is in state n. The expected time to the next arrival is $1/\lambda_n$.

Service (Death) Rate (μ_n): The parameter of the exponential distribution for the time to the next service completion when the system is in state n. The expected time to the next service is $1/\mu_n$.

Rate Diagram: A diagram as illustrated in Fig. 16.2. The states are shown as numbered circles. Possible transitions between the states are shown as arcs. For the birth-death process, the only possible transitions from the general state n are to state $n + 1$, when an arrival occurs, or to state $n - 1$, when a service is completed. The numbers adjacent to an arc are the rates associated with the transition. On the arc from state n to $n + 1$ is the arrival rate, λ_n, and on the arc from n to $n - 1$ is the service rate, μ_n. Note that except for state 0, two arcs enter each state and two leave each state. Since there is no state -1, state 0 originates a single arc to state 1 and terminates a single arc from state 1. It is possible to have a finite birth-death

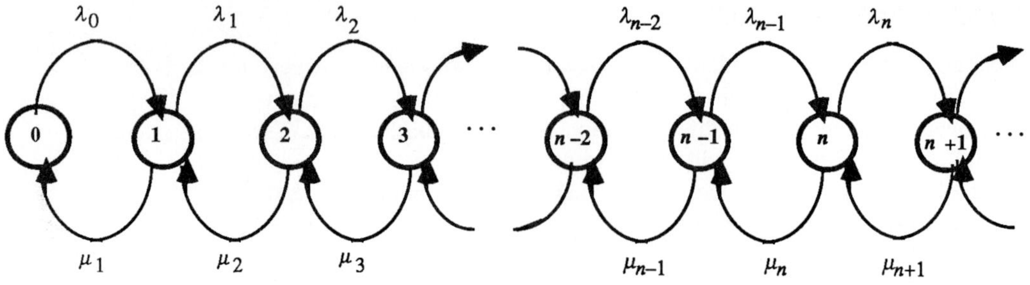

Figure 16.2 **The General Rate Diagram**

process with a maximum population of K. In this case state K will originate a single arc to state $K-1$ and terminate a single arc from state $K-1$.

RESULTS

Computing State Factors Using the rates identified on the rate diagram, one can compute a factor associated with each state, C_n. These factors are useful for computing steady-state measures.

$$C_n = \frac{\lambda_{n-1}\lambda_{n-2}\cdots\lambda_0}{\mu_n\mu_{n-1}\cdots\mu_1} \quad \text{for } n = 1, 2, \ldots.$$

If there is a finite number of states, K, $C_n = 0$ for $n > K$. To simplify computations on a calculator, note that the factors can be computed sequentially starting with C_1.

$$C_1 = \lambda_0/\mu_1,\ C_2 = C_1(\lambda_1/\mu_2), \ldots,\ C_n = C_{n-1}(\lambda_{n-1}/\mu_n).$$

Steady-State Probabilities The steady-state probabilities are computed from the state factors by

$$P_0 = 1/[\,1 + \sum_{n=1}^{\infty} C_n\,].$$

$$P_n = C_n P_0.$$

The Average Arrival Rate

$$\lambda_b = \sum_{n=0}^{\infty} \lambda_n P_n.$$

The Average Number and Time in the System

$$L = \sum_{n=0}^{\infty} nP_n \qquad W = L/\lambda_b.$$

The Average Number and Time in the Queue

$$L_q = \sum_{n=s}^{\infty} (n - s) P_n \qquad W_q = L_q / \lambda_b.$$

EXAMPLES

The examples and problems for this section will be restricted to models that have a finite number of states. This makes it possible to evaluate the sums in the equations above. Later sections will deal with situations that have an unlimited number of states.

E16.7 A single barber operates a shop with a service chair, on which customers sit while having their hair cut, and two waiting chairs. Customers arrive at the shop independently at an average rate of 4 per hour. The time for the barber to complete a cut is exponentially distributed with an average of 10 minutes. This assumes that most customers have very little hair while there are a very few with a great deal of hair. When a customer arrives and finds both chairs filled, he balks and goes somewhere else for a cut. Find the probability distribution of the number of customers in the shop.

Here the state of the system ranges from 0, when the barber is alone, to 3, when the service chair and both waiting chairs are full. The arrival rate is constant at 4 (per hour), except for state 3 when it is 0. The zero arrival rate models the balking of customers. They arrive at the shop but do not enter the system. The service rate is a constant of 6 (per hour) except for state 0, when it is 0. Note that all rates must be stated in the same units. This situation is shown on the following rate diagram.

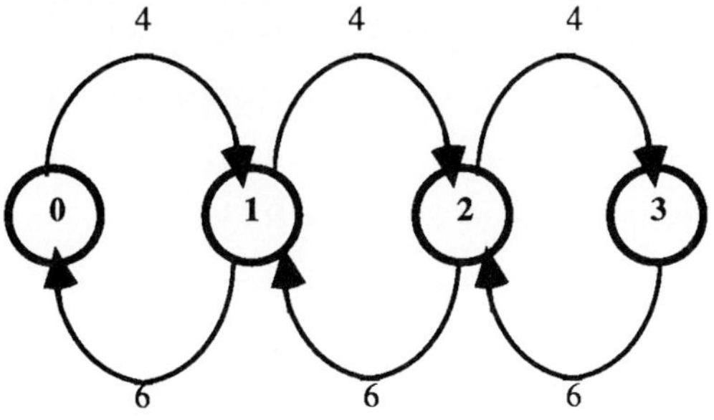

Using these rates we compute

$$C_1 = \lambda_0 / \mu_1 = 4/6 = 0.667$$
$$C_2 = \lambda_1 \lambda_0 / \mu_2 \mu_1 = 4^2/6^2 = 0.444$$
$$C_3 = \lambda_2 \lambda_1 \lambda_0 / \mu_3 \mu_2 \mu_1 = 4^3/6^3 = 0.296.$$

Now

$$P_0 = 1/[1 + 0.667 + 0.444 + 0.296] = 0.415$$
$$P_1 = (0.415)(0.667) = 0.277$$
$$P_2 = (0.415)(0.444) = 0.185$$
$$P_3 = (0.415)(0.296) = 0.123.$$

As a check, the probabilities must sum to 1.

Using these probabilities we note that the barber is idle about 41% of the time. The shop is full 12% of the time. A randomly arriving customer has a 0.123 probability of finding the shop full; therefore, we can state that 12.3% of the potential customers arriving at the shop will balk. Even though the barber is idle almost half the time, he is losing 12% of his business because he is too busy. This seemingly contradictory result is common when dealing with queueing questions. It illustrates the difficulty one experiences when trying to manage a stochastic process.

Other interesting measures that can be computed are

Average arrival rate: $\lambda_b = \lambda_0 P_0 + \lambda_1 P_1 + \lambda_2 P_2 + \lambda_3 P_3$
$= (4)(0.415) + (4)(0.277) + (4)(0.185) + (0)(0.123)$
$= 3.508$ customers/hour.

This is the rate of the customers actually coming into the shop.

Average number in the shop: $L = (1)P_1 + (2)P_2 + (3)P_3$
$= (1)(0.277) + (2)(0.185) + (3)(0.123)$
$= 1.016$ customers.

Average time in the shop: $W = L / \lambda_b = 1.016/3.508$
$= 0.289$ hours (17.37 minutes).

Average number in the queue ($s = 1$): $L_q = (1)P_2 + (2)P_3$
$= (1)(0.185) + (2)(0.123)$
$= 0.431$ customers.

Average time in the queue: $W_q = L_q / \lambda_b = 0.431/3.508$
$= 0.123$ hours (7.37 minutes).

Average number in service: $L_s = L - L_q$
$= 1.016 - 0.431 = 0.585.$

Utilization: $\rho = L_s / s = 0.585/1 = 0.585.$

E16.8 The barber is considering various ways to increase business and reduce his idle time. In each case below show the state diagram, compute the percentage of idle time, the percentage of customers lost, and the average time in the queue.

a. Add another waiting chair.

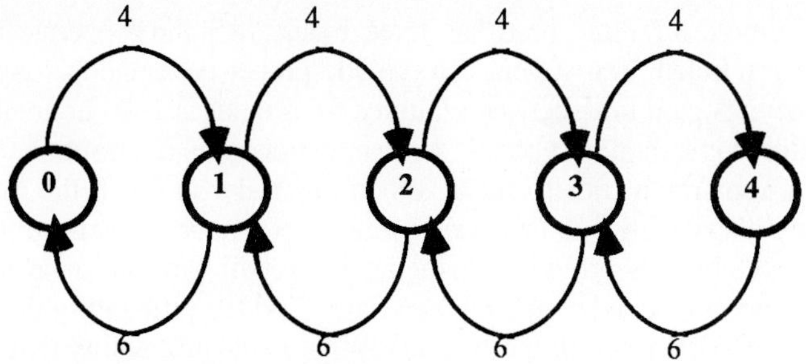

Percentage of idle time: 38.4%
Percentage of customers lost: 7.6%
Average time in queue: 0.169 hours (10.14 minutes).

b. Change one of the waiting chairs to a service chair and add another barber.

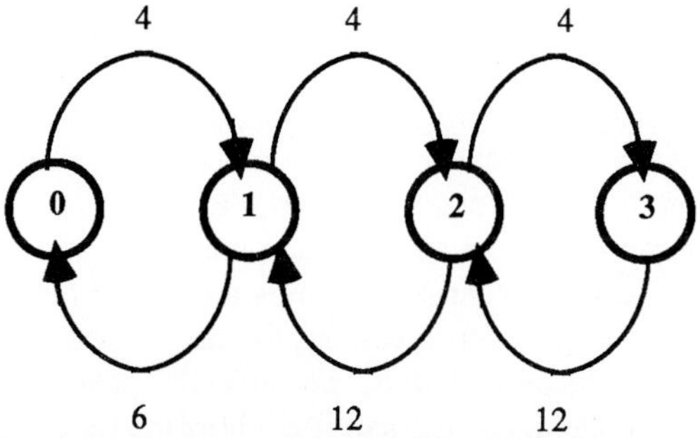

Percentage of time both barbers are idle: 50.9%
Percentage of time one barber is idle: 33.9%
Percentage of customers lost: 3.8%
Average time in queue: 0.0098 hours (0.58 minutes).

c. Work faster by reducing the average cut time to 6 minutes when both waiting chairs are full.

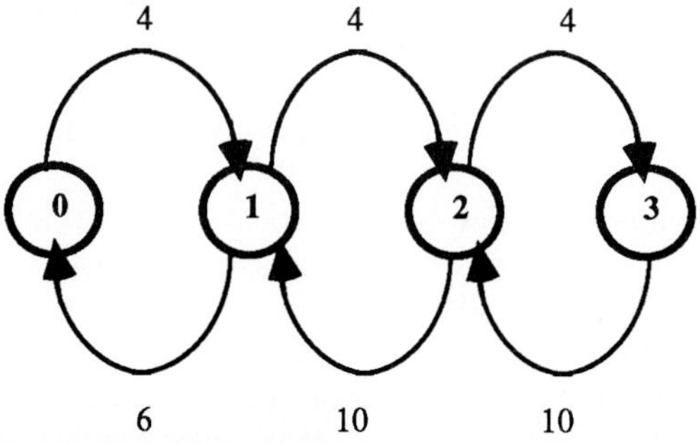

Percentage of idle time: 43.7%
Percentage of customers lost: 7.8%
Average time in queue: 0.095 hours (5.68 minutes).

PROBLEMS

P16.9 A remote air force base has three radars. All three operate all the time unless some are failed. The system can provide proper coverage as long as two are working. The expected time between failures for a radar is 1000 hours and the time between failures is a random variable with an exponential distribution. Whenever a radar fails, a repairman tries to fix it. When one radar is failed the repair time is exponentially distributed with an average time of 500 hours. Whenever two or more are failed, extra help is provided, reducing the repair time to an average of 200 hours. Only one radar can be repaired at a time. Find the probability that the system is operating with either two or three radars. What is the probability that no radars at all are available? What is the proportion of the time the repair shop is idle? What is the expected time a radar will spend in the shop (either waiting or in repair)? Show the rate diagram with your solution. Note that in this case the arrival rate of failed radars to the shop depends on the number operating. A single radar fails at a rate of 1/1000 = 0.001 per hour. When three radars are working the arrival rate is (3)(0.001) = 0.003. The arrival rate is proportional to the number operating.

P16.10 A service station has two self-service pumps. The time for a customer to pump his gas has an exponential distribution with an average time of three minutes. In addition to the space at the pumps, there is room for two more waiting cars. Cars arrive at random at the station with an average rate of 60 per hour when there is room at the pumps. When both pumps are in use the arrival rate drops to 40 per hour. When one customer is waiting the arrival rate drops to 20 per hour. When both waiting spaces are full, no arrivals occur. Compute the state probabilities at steady-state, L, W, L_q, and W_q. Show the rate diagram.

P16.11 Show the effects on the situation of problem P16.10 of adding another pump. The number of waiting spaces remains at two. Show the rate diagram, steady-state probabilities, L, W, L_q, and W_q.

Queueing Models with Infinite Queue and Input Source (16.6)

Certain special cases of the birth-death process allow easy determination of the steady-state relations and convenient formulas for evaluating system properties. These are queueing models that are used frequently in operations research to model simple systems. In this section we deal with the M/M/s model shown schematically in Fig. 16.3. The system consists of an infinite input source developing a constant rate of arrivals into the system λ. The service process has s parallel servers, alternatively called channels, each with a constant service rate (when busy) of μ. Both the input source and the service operation are Poisson processes. Customers arriving at the system will immediately enter service if the number in the system is less than s. If more than one server is available, the customer is assigned randomly to one of them. If all servers are busy, the customer goes to the end of the single queue. Queue discipline is first-come-first-served, and

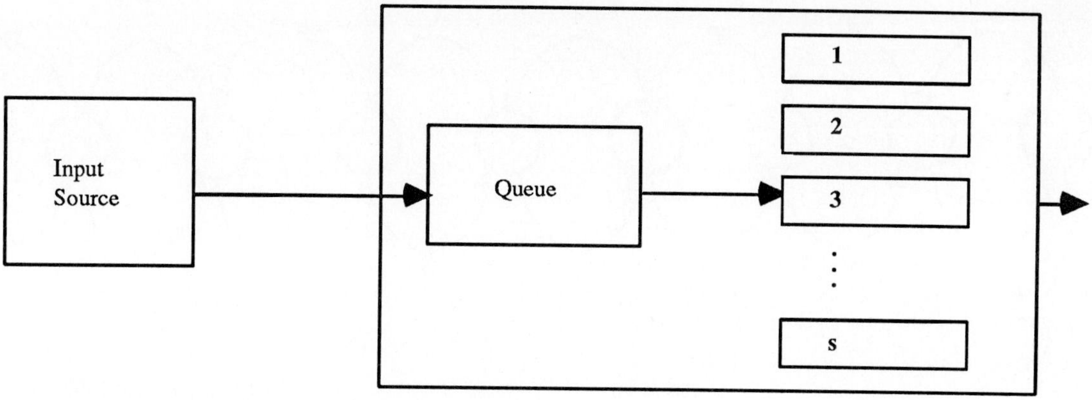

Figure 16.3 **The M/M/s Multichannel Queueing System**

there is no limit to the allowable queue length. When a service is completed, the first customer in the queue (if it is not empty) immediately enters the vacated channel. Only steady-state operation of the system is considered in this unit. An important parameter of this system is the utilization

$$\rho = \lambda / s\mu.$$

A system has a steady state if $\rho < 1$. If $\rho \geq 1$, the system is unstable and cannot reach steady state.

GOAL

- Be able to use the equations for the infinite input source, infinite queue case to calculate steady-state properties of applicable queueing systems.

RESULTS FOR THE MULTIPLE-CHANNEL CASE (M/M/s)

With these assumptions, the rate diagram of the birth death process is shown in Fig. 16.4. Note that the arrival rate is independent of the state of the system. The departure rate is proportional to the number in the system if the state of the system is less than s. When all servers are busy $(n \geq s)$ the departure rate is $s\mu$.

State Probabilities Using the methods described in section 16.5 the following equations can be derived.

$$P_0 = 1 / \left[\left(\sum_{k=0}^{s-1} \frac{(\lambda/\mu)^k}{k\,!} \right) + \left(\frac{(\lambda/\mu)^s}{s\,!\,[1 - (\lambda/s\mu)]} \right) \right]$$

$$C_n = \left[\frac{(\lambda/\mu)^n}{n\,!} \right] \quad \text{for } n = 1, 2, \ldots, s$$

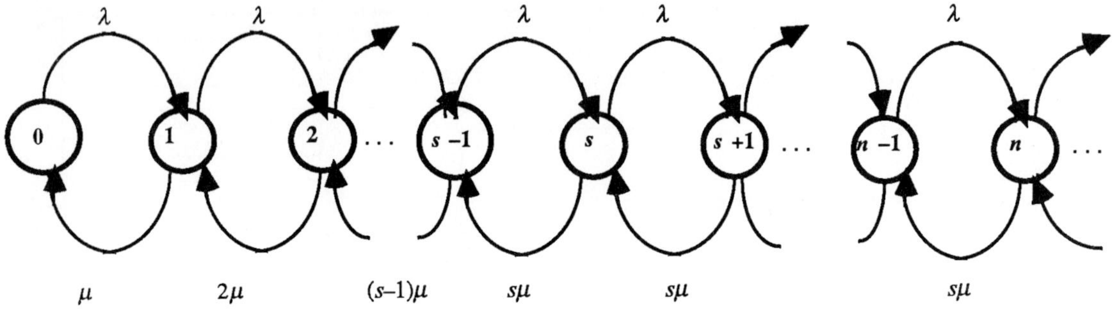

Figure 16.4 **Rate Diagram for the M/M/s System**

$$C_n = \left[\frac{(\lambda/\mu)^n}{s!(s^{n-s})} \right] \quad \text{for } n = s+1, s+2, \ldots$$

$$P_n = C_n P_0.$$

Note that there are $s + 1$ terms in the denominator of the expression for P_0. The first term is 1 (for $k = 0$).

Average Number and Time in the Queue

$$L_q = \frac{P_0(\lambda/\mu)^s \rho}{s!(1-\rho)^2} \qquad W_q = L_q / \lambda.$$

Average Number and Time in the System

$$L = L_q + \lambda/\mu \qquad W = L/\lambda = W_q + 1/\mu.$$

Percent Utilization

$$100\,\rho.$$

Probabilities Concerning the Time a Customer Is in the System Let T_s be the time in the system.

$$P\{T_s > t\} = e^{-\mu t} \left[1 + \frac{P_0(\lambda/\mu)^s}{s!(1-\rho)} \left(\frac{1 - e^{-\mu t(s-1-\lambda/\mu)}}{s-1-\lambda/\mu} \right) \right] \quad \text{for } t \geq 0$$

When $s - \lambda/\mu = 1$, the terms in the inner bracket are replaced by μt.

Probabilities Concerning the Time a Customer Is in the Queue Let T_q be the time in the queue.

$$P\{T_q = 0\} = \sum_{n=0}^{s-1} P_n$$

$$P\{T_q > t\} = [1 - P\{T_q = 0\}]e^{-s\mu(1-\rho)t} \qquad \text{for } t \geq 0.$$

RESULTS FOR THE SINGLE-CHANNEL CASE (M/M/1)

These equations simplify considerably when there is only one channel ($s = 1$). Here the utilization is $\rho = \lambda / \mu$.

State Probabilities

$$P_0 = 1 - \rho$$
$$C_n = \rho^n \qquad \text{for } n = 1, 2, \ldots$$
$$P_n = C_n P_0 \qquad \text{for } n = 1, 2, \ldots.$$

Average Number and Time in System

$$L = \rho / (1 - \rho) = \lambda / (\mu - \lambda),$$
$$W = L / \lambda = 1/[\mu (1 - \rho)] = 1/(\mu - \lambda).$$

Average Number and Time in Queue

$$L_q = L - \rho = \lambda^2/[\mu (\mu - \lambda)],$$
$$W_q = L_q / \lambda = W - 1/\mu = \lambda / [\mu (\mu - \lambda)].$$

Probabilities Concerning the Time a Customer Is in the System

$$P\{T_s > t\} = e^{-\mu(1-\rho)t}, \quad \text{for } t \geq 0.$$

Probabilities Concerning the Time a Customer Is in the Queue

$$P\{T_q = 0\} = 1 - \rho,$$
$$P\{T_q > t\} = \rho\, e^{-\mu(1-\rho)t}, \quad \text{for } t \geq 0.$$

MODELING

Rarely are all the assumptions that justify these queueing models satisfied exactly. The use of the models is an abstraction or simplification that yields information that otherwise would be impossible to obtain.

Steady-state results may not be appropriate for some systems. For instance, a restaurant may be very busy only during a short period and probably will not reach steady-state before the busy time passes. One might analyze the restaurant using peak hour arrival and service rates. The steady-state results for this "worst case" will overestimate average number and time in the system but may provide useful performance information. This approach certainly would not be appropriate if the arrival rate is greater than the service rate, a possibility during a short time period. If steady-state results are not useful, it will be necessary to do a transient analysis, which is discussed in more advanced books, or a simulation analysis.

EXAMPLES

E16.9 Between 5 P.M. and 6 P.M., the bank has a single open drive-in window. The mean time for a teller transaction is 30 seconds. Customers arrive at the window with an average time between arrivals of 40 seconds. There seems to be plenty of time for the teller to meet the demand for service, but frequently there is a long line of waiting cars, sometimes stretching into the street. There is room for three cars in the queue on bank property. Customers are also complaining about the long wait. Analyze the current situation and propose a solution. As a goal, the management has stated that the queue must remain on bank property 90% of the time and that no more than 10% of the customers spend more than 1 minute in the queue.

For analysis purposes we assume the arrivals occur independently, a reasonable assumption in this instance. We also assume an exponential distribution for service time. Because of the variety of services offered at the window and the fact that many customers are simply requesting cash, requiring a short service time, this also seems to be reasonable. These assumptions justify the use of the models for Poisson input and service processes. Although the queue is practically limited in length, we assume an unlimited queue to do the analysis. With all these assumptions the single-channel queue model with the formulas listed above is appropriate.

We compute the following steady-state measures of performance.

System:	M/M/1
Arrival rate:	$\lambda = 1/40 = 0.025/\text{sec} = 1.5/\text{min}$
Service rate:	$\mu = 1/30 = 0.333/\text{sec} = 2/\text{min}$
Utilization:	$\rho = \lambda/\mu = 0.75$
State probabilities:	$P_0 = 1 - \rho = 0.25$
	$P_1 = \rho(1 - \rho) = 0.1875$
	$P_2 = \rho^2(1 - \rho) = 0.1406$
	$P_3 = \rho^3(1 - \rho) = 0.1055$
	$P_4 = \rho^4(1 - \rho) = 0.0791$
	$P\{n > 4\} = 0.2373$
Average number in system:	$L = \rho/(1 - \rho) = 3.0$
Average time in system:	$W = L/\lambda = 2$ min
Average number in queue:	$L_q = L - \rho = 2.25$
Average time in queue:	$W_q = W - 1/\mu = 1.5$ min
Proportion waiting too long:	$P\{T_q > 1 \text{ min}\} = \rho\, e^{-\mu(1-\rho)*1} = 0.545.$

Clearly the present arrangement does not reach the goals. The line will go into the street ($n > 4$) almost one quarter of the time, and over half of the customers must wait more than 1 minute. In an attempt to meet the goals we propose to open another window. The second server will have the same rate as the first. Cars waiting will continue to form a single line with room for three cars on bank property. To analyze the new situation we must use the formulas for the multichannel queue with $s = 2$.

System: M/M/2

Utilization: $\rho = \lambda / s\mu = 0.375$

State probabilities:

$$P_0 = 1 / \left[\sum_{k=0}^{1} \frac{(\lambda/\mu)^k}{k!} + \frac{(\lambda/\mu)^2}{2![1 - (\lambda/2\mu)]} \right]$$

$$= 1/[\,1 + 0.75 + 0.45\,] = 0.4545$$

$C_1 = 0.75,\quad P_1 = C_1 P_0 = 0.3409$

$C_2 = 0.2813,\quad P_2 = C_2 P_0 = 0.1278$

$C_3 = 0.1055,\quad P_3 = C_3 P_0 = 0.0479$

$C_4 = 0.0392,\quad P_4 = C_4 P_0 = 0.0180$

$C_5 = 0.0147,\quad P_5 = C_5 P_0 = 0.0067$

$P\{n > 5\} = 0.0042$

Average number in queue: $L_q = [P_0(\lambda/\mu)^s \rho\,]/[s\,!(1-\rho)^2] = 0.1227$

Average time in queue: $W_q = L_q/\lambda = 0.0818$ min

Average number in system: $L = L_q + \lambda/\mu = 0.8727$

Average time in system: $W = L/\lambda = 0.5818$ min

Proportion with no wait: $P\{T_q = 0\} = P_0 + P_1 = 0.7954$

Proportion waiting too long: $P\{T_q > 1\} = [1 - P\{T_q = 0\}]e^{-s\mu(1-\rho)t} = (0.2046)(0.0821) = 0.0167.$

Clearly this solution meets the goals of management, with the cars reaching the street less than 1% of the time and fewer than 2% of the customers waiting more than 1 minute. Use the following problems to investigate other solutions to the problem.

PROBLEMS

In each case below calculate the system performance measures as above for the following situations. All start from the base case given for the example above.

P16.12 Open three windows rather than one. Each server has the same performance. Reduce the space allowed for the queue to one.

P16.13 Open only one window but increase the bank-owned space for the queue to five cars.

P16.14 Open only one window, but add a computer terminal for the teller. This decreases average service time to 25 seconds. Keep the queue space at three cars.

P16.15 Open a second window whenever the number in the system reaches four. Close the window when the number drops to three. Note that the multichannel queue equations do not work for this problem. You will have to derive new equations using the general birth-death model. Do not try to compute the probabilities associated with time in the queue and system.

Queueing Models with a Finite Queue (16.6)

In this section we consider a special case of the birth-death queueing model, the case of an infinite input source and a finite queue. For this model we assume that customers arrive at the system according to a Poisson process with constant arrival rate λ. The system, however, has only a finite number of spaces allowed in the queue. The maximum number in the system is K, so the maximum number in the queue is $K - s$. When all the spaces in the queue are full (the system is said to be full), an arriving customer will not enter the system. Rather the customer will "balk" and go away. The system has s identical servers, each with a service rate of μ. The system is identified as M/M/s/K, with the last number indicating the maximum number in the system.

With these assumptions the rate diagram of the birth death process is shown in Fig. 16.5. Note that the arrival rate is constant for all states except K, at which it is zero. The departure rate is proportional to the number in the system if the state of the system is less than s. When all servers are busy ($n \geq s$) the departure rate is $s\mu$. The factor $\rho = (\lambda / s\mu)$ need not be less than 1 for this model, since the queue cannot grow indefinitely. This factor no longer represents the utilization of the servers. Equations derived from this diagram using the general birth-death model follow.

GOAL

- Be able to use the equations provided for the finite queue case to calculate steady-state properties of applicable queueing systems.

RESULTS FOR THE MULTIPLE-CHANNEL CASE (M/M/s/K)

State Probabilities

$$P_0 = 1 \Big/ \left[\left(\sum_{k=0}^{s-1} \frac{(\lambda/\mu)^k}{k!} \right) + \left(\frac{(\lambda/\mu)^s}{s!} \sum_{k=s}^{K} \left(\frac{\lambda}{s\mu} \right)^{k-s} \right) \right]$$

$$C_n = \left[\frac{(\lambda/\mu)^n}{n!} \right] \qquad \text{for } n = 1, 2, \ldots, s$$

$$C_n = \left[\frac{(\lambda/\mu)^n}{s!(s^{n-s})} \right] \qquad \text{for } n = s+1, s+2, \ldots, K$$

$$P_n = C_n P_0.$$

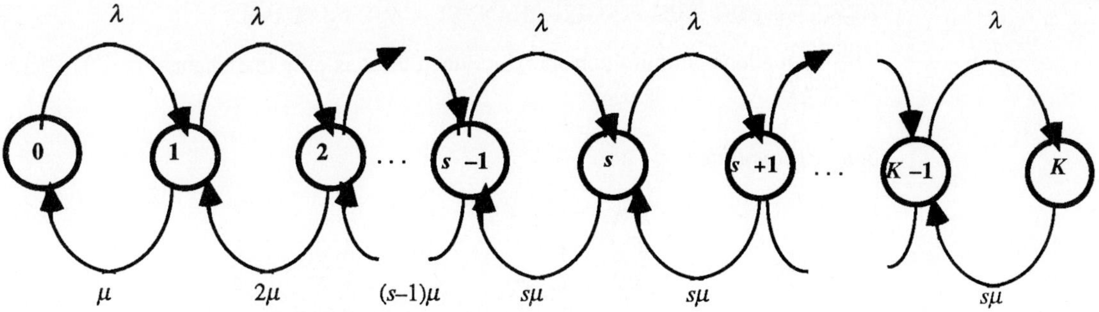

Figure 16.5 **Rate Diagram for M/M/s/K System**

Average Arrival Rate This is a newly defined quantity necessary for cases in which not all customers who arrive at the system enter the system. It is the average arrival rate of customers *into* the system.

$$\lambda_b = \lambda(1 - P_K).$$

Average Number and Time in the Queue

$$L_q = \frac{P_0 \, (\lambda/\mu)^s \rho}{s!(1-\rho)^2} \, [1 - \rho^{K-s} - (K-s)\, \rho^{K-s} (1-\rho)].$$

This is the formula for the infinite queue case with the bracketed factor added to account for customers lost through balking.

$$W_q = L_q / \lambda_b.$$

Average Number and Time in Service

$$L_s = \sum_{n=0}^{s-1} nP_n + s \left(1 - \sum_{n=0}^{s-1} P_n \right).$$

The average time in service is $1/\mu$.

Average Number and Time in the System

$$L = L_q + L_s$$
$$W = L / \lambda_b.$$

Percent Utilization $100 * L_s/s$.

Probability that the System Is Busy P_K

This is the probability that all queue spaces are filled. It is also the proportion of customers lost due to balking.

Probabilities Concerning the Time Spent in the System or Queue There are no simple formulas for calculating these probabilities.

RESULTS FOR THE SINGLE-CHANNEL CASE (M/M/1/K)

These equations simplify considerably when there is only one channel ($s = 1$). Here $\rho = \lambda/\mu$.

State Probabilities

$$P_0 = (1-\rho)/(1-\rho^{K+1})$$
$$C_n = \rho^n \qquad \text{for } n = 1, 2, \ldots, K$$
$$P_n = C_n P_0 \qquad \text{for } n = 1, 2, \ldots, K.$$

Average Number and Time in System

$$L = \frac{\rho}{(1-\rho)} - \frac{(K+1)\rho^{K+1}}{1-\rho^{K+1}}$$
$$W = L/\lambda_b.$$

Average Number and Time in Service

$$L_s = (1 - P_0).$$

The average time in service is $1/\mu$.

Average Number and Time in Queue

$$L_q = L - (1 - P_0),$$
$$W_q = L_q/\lambda_b.$$

EXAMPLES

E16.10 Consider again the bank problem of the last section. Recall that during the time interval of interest the mean time between arrivals was 40 seconds and that the mean time for service was 30 seconds. However, in this example assume that cars are not allowed to wait in the street. When the number in the queue reaches 3, no more waiting customers can be accommodated. Although in reality customers who cannot enter the system because of the line limitation will probably return later, for approximation purposes we assume they balk. This may be reasonable because unsatisfied customers will probably return at a less busy time. With this limitation, customers will always remain on bank property. We adopt the design goal that no more than 5% of arriving customers must be turned away because of the limited queue.

For a single open window, the model has $s = 1$ and $K = 4$. Note that K is the maximum number in the system (including service).

System:	M/M/1/4
Arrival rate:	$\lambda = 1/40 = 0.025/\text{sec} = 1.5/\text{min}$
Service rate:	$\mu = 1/30 = 0.333/\text{sec} = 2/\text{min}$
Utilization factor:	$\rho = \lambda/\mu = 0.75$

State probabilities: $P_0 = (1-\rho)/(1-\rho^{K+1}) = 0.3278$

$P_1 = \rho P_0 = 0.2458$

$P_2 = \rho^2 P_0 = 0.1844$

$P_3 = \rho^3 P_0 = 0.1383$

$P_4 = \rho^4 P_0 = 0.1037.$

It is interesting to compare these results with those of the infinite queue: (P_0 = 0.25, P_1 = 0.1875, P_2 = 0.1406, P_3 = 0.1055, P_4 = 0.0791). All the probabilities are higher for the finite case because there is no possibility that the number in the system will exceed 4.

Average number in system: $L = \rho/(1-\rho) - [(K+1)\rho^{K+1}/(1-\rho^{K+1})]$
$= 3.0 - 1.556 = 1.444.$

This compares to the value of 3 for the infinite queue case.

Average arrival rate: $\lambda_b = \lambda(1 - P_K) = 1.5(1 - 0.1037) = 1.344$

Average time in system: $W = L/\lambda_b = 1.074$ min.

This compares to an average time of 2 minutes for the infinite case.

Average number in service: $L_s = 1 - P_0 = 0.6722$

Average number in queue: $L_q = L - L_s = 0.7720$

Average time in queue: $W_q = L_q/\lambda_b = 0.5743$ min.

Comparing to the infinite queue case (L_q = 2.25 and W_q = 1.5 min), the finite queue looks more efficient. But this is at the cost of lost customers.

Probability that the system is full and the proportion of customers lost is: $P_K = 0.1037$

Utilization percentage: $100 * L_s/s = 67.22\%$.

Clearly this solution does not meet the design goal, with over 10% of the customers balking. We now propose to open another window. The second server will have the same rate as the first. We assume that the new window does not reduce the space for waiting cars. There is still room for 3. Cars waiting will continue to form a single line. To analyze the new situation we must use the formulas for the finite multichannel queue with $s = 2$ and $K = 5$.

System: M/M/2/5

Utilization factor: $\rho = \lambda/s\mu = 0.375$

State probabilities:

$$P_0 = 1/\left[\sum_{k=0}^{1} \frac{(\lambda/\mu)^k}{k!} + \frac{(\lambda/\mu)}{2!}\sum_{k=s}^{5} \rho^{k-2}\right]$$

$= 1/[1 + 0.75 + 0.281 + 0.1054 + 0.0396 + 0.0148]$

$= 0.4564$

C_1	$= 0.75$,	P_1	$= C_1P_0$	$= 0.3423$
C_2	$= 0.281$,	P_2	$= C_2P_0$	$= 0.1284$
C_3	$= 0.105$,	P_3	$= C_3P_0$	$= 0.0481$
C_4	$= 0.0396$,	P_4	$= C_4P_0$	$= 0.0181$
C_5	$= 0.0148$,	P_5	$= C_5P_0$	$= 0.0068$

Average number in queue: $L_q = L_q' * [1 - \rho^{K-s} - (K-s)\,\rho^{K-s}(1-\rho)]$,
where L_q' is the average number in the queue for the infinite queue.

$L_q = 0.1227 * (0.8484) = 0.104$

Average arrival rate: $\lambda_b = \lambda\,(1 - P_K) = 1.5(0.9932) = 1.49$

Average time in queue: $W_q = L_q/\lambda_b = 0.0702$ min.

Average number in service: $L_s = 1P_1 + 2P_2 + 2P_3 + 2P_4 + 2P_5 = 0.745$

Average number in system: $L = L_q + L_s = 0.8495$

Average time in system: $W = L/\lambda_b = 0.5702$ min

Percent utilization $100 * L_s/s = 37.2\%$

Proportion of the time the system is full and the proportion of balks:

$$P_K = 0.0068.$$

Clearly this solution meets the goals of management, with the percentage of customers not receiving service less than 1%. Note that the finite queue results are much closer to the infinite results calculated earlier. Of course the two approach identity as K gets larger and larger. In the following problems we investigate other solutions to the problem.

PROBLEMS

For P16.16 to P16.18, calculate the system performance measures as above for the following situations. All start from the base case given for the example above. The changes in the base case are not cumulative. In each case assume the queue must remain entirely on bank property. Customers arriving when the queue is full will balk and not enter the system.

P16.16 Open three windows rather than one. Each server has the same performance. Reduce the space allowed for the queue to one.

P16.17 Open only one window but increase the bank-owned space for the queue to five cars.

P16.18 Open a second window whenever the number in the system reaches four. Close the window when the number returns to three. There are three spaces for the queue on bank property. Note that the multichannel queue equations do not work for this problem. You will have to derive new equations using the general birth-death model.

P16.19 A company plans to advertise a new product with orders to be taken by phone. Currently the company has two phone lines. Using data taken during a dry run of the system, it is determined that the average time to take a customer's order is 1.5 minutes. If the advertisement has the desired effect, orders will arrive on the average rate of two a minute. If the customer receives a busy signal the order is assumed lost. Assume arrival and service processes are Poisson. For each case below, compute the average time in the system, the percentage utilization of the phones, and the proportion of customers lost.

- **a.** Leave the phone system as it is.
- **b.** Install an additional phone with an operator.
- **c.** Have three phones with operators and add a call holding facility that can hold one waiting customer.
- **d.** Have three phones but add a call holding facility that can handle any number of waiting customers.
- **e.** Have four phones but add a call holding facility that can handle any number of waiting customers.

Queueing Models with a Finite Input Source (16.6)

In this section we consider another special case of the birth-death queueing model, the case of a finite input source. As before, the service process consists of s identical servers, each with a service rate μ. The time for service has an exponential distribution with mean $1/\mu$. For this model we identify N individual customers that have access to the queueing system. Each customer alternates between being in the system and being out of the system. When the customer leaves the system, the time until he next enters the system has an exponential distribution with the mean time $1/\lambda$. (The assumption of exponential distribution is not necessary for the results to hold.) When the customer enters the system he will either enter service if some channel is available or he will enter a queue if all servers are busy. The number in the system can never exceed N ; however, otherwise there is no limit to the number in the queue.

With these assumptions the rate diagram of the birth death process is shown in Fig. 16.6. The principal difference between this model and the others previously

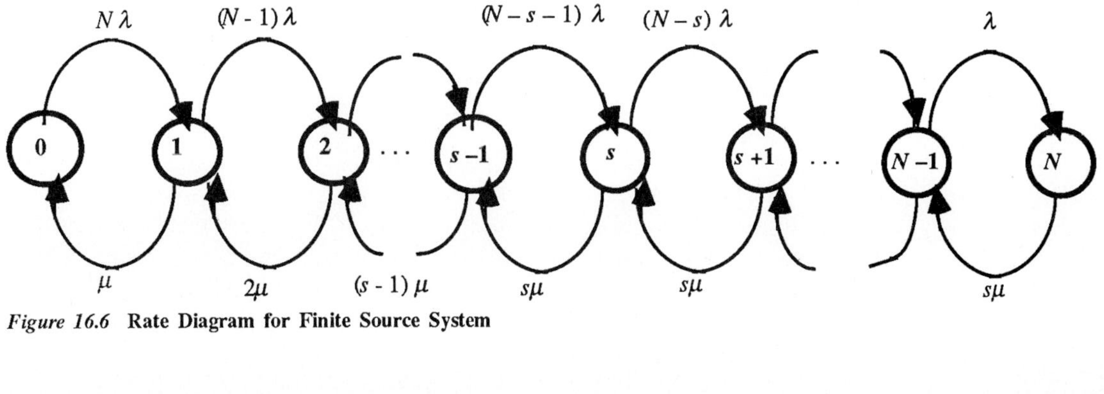

Figure 16.6 **Rate Diagram for Finite Source System**

considered concerns the arrival process. Previously λ was the arrival rate generated by the entire input source (or calling population). Now λ is the arrival rate of *each* member of the calling population when the member is not already in the system. With n customers already in the system, only $N - n$ customers remain to generate arrivals. The arrival rate at state n is $(N - n)\lambda$. The departure rate is proportional to the number in the system if the state of the system is less than s. When all servers are busy $(n \geq s)$ the departure rate is $s\mu$. There is no reason for s, the number of servers, to be greater than N, the number of customers.

GOAL

- Be able to use the equations provided for the finite input source case to calculate the steady-state properties of applicable queueing systems.

RESULTS FOR THE MULTIPLE-CHANNEL CASE (M/M/s)

State Probabilities

$$P_0 = 1/D$$

where D is the denominator of the expression as given below.

$$D = \sum_{k=0}^{s-1} \frac{N!}{(N-k)!k!}\left(\frac{\lambda}{\mu}\right)^k + \sum_{k=s}^{N} \frac{N!}{(N-k)!s!s^{k-s}}\left(\frac{\lambda}{\mu}\right)^k$$

There are $N + 1$ terms in the expression for D.

$$C_n = \left[\frac{N!}{(N-n)!n!}\left(\frac{\lambda}{\mu}\right)^n\right] \qquad \text{for } n = 1, 2, \ldots, s$$

$$C_n = \left[\frac{N!}{(N-n)!s!s^{n-s}}\left(\frac{\lambda}{\mu}\right)^n\right] \qquad \text{for } n = s + 1, s + 2, \ldots, N$$

$$P_n = C_n P_0.$$

Average Arrival Rate

$$\lambda_b = \sum_{n=0}^{N} (N - n)\lambda P_n.$$

Average Number and Time in the Queue

$$L_q = \sum_{n=s}^{N} (n-s)\, P_n$$

$$W_q = L_q / \lambda_b.$$

Average Number and Time in Service

$$L_s = \sum_{n=0}^{s-1} nP_n + s\left(1 - \sum_{n=0}^{s-1} P_n\right).$$

The average time in service is $1/\mu$.

Average Number and Time in the System

$$L = L_q + L_s$$

$$W = L / \lambda_b.$$

Percent Utilization $100 * L_s / s$.

RESULTS FOR THE SINGLE-CHANNEL CASE (M/M/1)

Using $s = 1$ in the formulas above results in some simplification.

State Probabilities

$$P_0 = 1/\left(\sum_{n=0} \frac{N!}{(N-n)!}\left(\frac{\lambda}{\mu}\right)^n\right)$$

$$C_n = \left[\frac{N!}{(N-n)!}\left(\frac{\lambda}{\mu}\right)^n\right] \qquad \text{for } n = 1, 2, \ldots, N$$

$$P_n = C_n P_0 \qquad \text{for } n = 1, 2, \ldots, N.$$

Average Number and Time in the Queue

$$L_q = N - \frac{\lambda + \mu}{\lambda}(1 - P_0)$$

$W_q = L_q/\lambda_b$, with λ_b calculated as above.

Average Number and Time in Service

$$L_s = (1 - P_0).$$

The average time in service is $1/\mu$.

Average Number and Time in the System

$$L = L_q + L_s,$$
$$W = L/\lambda_b.$$

EXAMPLES

E16.11 The classic example of this situation is a repair shop that handles all the repair work for the machines of an organization. Consider an example that has five machines and a single repairman. Each machine when working has an average time to failure of 50 hours. A common assumption is that the time to failure has an exponential distribution. The time required to repair a machine also has an exponential distribution with an average time of 20 hours. All the machines are operating when they are not in the repair shop. For this case $N = 5$ and $s = 1$.

Arrival rate per machine:	$\lambda = 1/50 = 0.02$/hour
Service rate:	$\mu = 1/20 = 0.05$/hour
Utilization factor:	$\rho = \lambda/\mu = 0.4$
State probabilities:	

$$P_0 = 1/[1 + 5 * \rho^1 + 5 * 4 * \rho^2 + 5 * 4 * 3 * \rho^3 + 5 * 4 * 3 * 2 * \rho^4 + 5 * 4 * 3 * 2 * 1 * \rho^5]$$
$$= 1/14.34 = 0.0697.$$

The terms in the denominator are the state factors C_n, which are easily calculated cumulatively with a calculator.

$$C_1 = 5\rho, \qquad P_1 = C_1 P_0 = 0.1395$$
$$C_2 = C_1 * 4\rho \qquad P_2 = C_2 P_0 = 0.2231$$
$$C_3 = C_2 * 3\rho \qquad P_3 = C_3 P_0 = 0.2678$$
$$C_4 = C_3 * 2\rho \qquad P_4 = C_4 P_0 = 0.2142$$
$$C_5 = C_4 * 1\rho \qquad P_5 = C_5 P_0 = 0.0857.$$

Average number in queue:	$L_q = 0P_1 + 1P_2 + 2P_3 + 3P_4 + 4P_5 = 1.744.$
Average arrival rate:	$\lambda_b = 0.1P_0 + 0.08P_1 + 0.06P_2 + 0.04P_3 + 0.02P_4 + 0P_5 = 0.0465$/hour.
Average time in queue:	$W_q = L_q/\lambda_b = 37.50$ hours.
Average number in service:	$L_s = 1 - P_0 = 0.9303.$
Average number in the system:	$L = L_q + L_s = 2.674.$

This number has special significance here as it indicates that, on the average, over half of the five machines are in the repair shop.

Average number in operation:	$N - L = 2.336$
Average time in the system:	$W = L/\lambda_b = 57.5$ hours
Percentage utilization:	$100 * L_s/s = 93\%.$

This solution may not be acceptable for the company, because so many machines are in the repair shop. There is an 8.6% chance that no machines are operating at all. To obtain a better solution, we investigate adding another repairman. Now N = 5 and s = 2.

Utilization factor: $\rho = \lambda / \mu = 0.4$

State probabilities:

$$P_0 = 1/[\,1 + C_1 + C_2 + C_3 + C_4 + C_5\,]$$
$$C_1 = 5(0.4) = 2$$
$$C_2 = C_1 * 4 * (0.4)/2 = 1.6$$
$$C_3 = C_2 * 3 * (0.4)/2 = 0.96$$
$$C_4 = C_3 * 2 * (0.4)/2 = 0.384$$
$$C_5 = C_4 * 1 * (0.4)/2 = 0.0768$$

Summing the terms and adding 1, we find the denominator 6.0208. From which

$$P_0 = 0.1661$$
$$P_1 = C_1 P_0 = 0.3322$$
$$P_2 = C_2 P_0 = 0.2657$$
$$P_3 = C_3 P_0 = 0.1594$$
$$P_4 = C_4 P_0 = 0.0638$$
$$P_5 = C_5 P_0 = 0.0128.$$

Average arrival rate:

$$\lambda_b = \lambda\,(5P_0 + 4P_1 + 3P_2 + 2P_3 + 1P_4 + 0P_5) = 0.06678/\text{hour}.$$

Average number and time in the queue:

$$L_q = 0P_2 + 1P_3 + 2P_4 + 3P_5 = 0.3253$$
$$W_q = L_q / \lambda_b = 4.871 \text{ hours.}$$

Average number in service: $L_s = 0P_0 + 1P_1 + 2[1 - (P_0 + P_1)] = 1.3356.$

Average time in service: $1/\mu = 20$ hours.

Average number and time in the system: $L = L_q + L_s = 1.6609$

$$W = L/\lambda_b = 24.87 \text{ hours.}$$

Percent utilization: $100 * L_s / s = 66.78\%.$

The system with two servers has reduced the average number of machines in the repair shop to 1.33, leaving 3.66 in operation. All of the machines are in the repair shop a little over 1% of the time. This improvement has been at the cost of an additional repairman. On the average the repairmen are idle about one-third of the time.

PROBLEMS

P16.20 Analyze the system above if three repairmen are used.

P16.21 The company proposes to add another machine. The purpose is to increase the average number of machines in operation and thus increase the production capacity of the company. All machines operate if not in the repair shop. If one repairman is used, how much does the added machine improve the operation of the system?

P16.22 A radar installation requires three working radars to effectively observe the entire horizon. When three or more radars are working, the system is in the "operational" mode. The system works in a "reduced effectiveness" mode if only two radars are working. With fewer than two working radars, the system is said to be in the "failed" mode. In order to maintain the effectiveness five radars are installed. The extra two radars are called backup radars.

Both working and backup radars fail at the same average rate, once every 500 hours. Radars fail randomly. Failed radars are sent to a repair shop where only one radar is fixed at a time. If more than one has failed, the others must wait their turn. The repair operation takes an average time of 40 hours, but the actual repair time has an exponential distribution. Compute the proportion of the time the system will be in each of the modes noted above.

P16.23 Repeat Prob. P16.22 with the new assumption that at most three radars are operated at a time. Backup radars not in operation do not fail. With this assumption, the formula for P_0 used in this section is not appropriate. Derive a new formula and compute the mode probabilities.

P16.24 Repeat Prob. P16.23 with the assumption that backup radars do fail when not in operation, but at a rate of once every 1000 hours, rather than once every 500 hours.

Queueing Models with Nonexponential Service Times (16.7)

The last few sections assumed that both the interarrival time and service times had exponential distributions. The assumption regarding interarrival times is not too bad since it is implied by "random" or "independent" arrivals. The service time, however, will often not have an exponential distribution. For the case of a single server with an infinite queue, some simple steady-state results are available. These are particularly useful for observing the effects of the exponential assumption in comparison to other assumptions regarding the service time distribution. The system considered is M/G/1.

GOALS

- Know and be able to apply the formulas available for the single-channel, infinite queue, Poisson arrival process, nonexponential service time queueing model.

- Know the variances for several possible service time distributions.

RESULTS

Given λ the constant arrival rate, $1/\mu$ the average service time, and σ the standard deviation of the service time, the following steady-state results are available for a single server and with $\rho = \lambda/\mu < 1$. These formulas work for *any* service time distribution.

Probability That the System Is Empty

$$P_0 = 1 - \rho.$$

Average Number and Time in the Queue

$$L_q = \frac{\lambda^2\sigma^2 + \rho^2}{2(1-\rho)},$$

$$W_q = L_q/\lambda.$$

Average Number and Time in the System

$$L = L_q + \rho,$$

$$W = L/\lambda = W_q + 1/\mu.$$

Percent Utilization $\quad 100 * \rho.$

Standard Deviations of Distributions Several important service time distributions have the following standard deviations. We use m_s for the mean service time and σ for the standard deviation.

Exponential distribution:	$m_s = 1/\mu$ and $\sigma = 1/\mu$.
Constant service time:	$m_s = 1/\mu$ and $\sigma = 0$.
Normal distribution:	$m_s = 1/\mu$
	σ must be given.

Erlang distribution: This distribution models a service that consists of a sequence of k activities, each of which has an exponential distribution with mean $1/k\,\mu$. For the Erlang distribution,

$$m_s = 1/\mu \text{ and}$$

$$\sigma = (1/k^{1/2})(1/\mu).$$

The standard deviation varies inversely as the square root of the number of activities.

EXAMPLES

E16.12 A single-channel queue has random arrivals with a mean arrival rate of 8 per hour. The mean service rate is 10 per hour. Compute steady-state results for each of the following service time distributions. In each case the arrival rate is λ =

8/hour, the average service rate is μ =10/hour, the utilization factor is $\lambda / \mu = 0.8$, and the mean service time is $m_S = 0.1$ hours. The different distributions differ in standard deviation.

Exponential Service Time: $\sigma = 1/m_S = 0.1$

Probability of empty system: $P_0 = 1 - \rho = 0.2$

Average number and time in the queue:

$$L_q = \frac{8^2 0.1^2 + 0.8^2}{2(1-0.8)} = 3.2, \qquad W_q = 3.2/8 = 0.4 \text{ hours}$$

Average number and time in the system:

$$L = L_q + \rho = 4, \qquad W = 4/8 = 0.5 \text{ hours}$$

Percent utilization: $100 * \rho = 80\%$.

Constant Service Time: $\sigma = 0$

Probability of empty system: $P_0 = 1 - \rho = 0.2$

Average number and time in the queue:

$$L_q = \frac{8^2 0^2 + 0.8^2}{2(1-0.8)} = 1.6, \qquad W_q = 1.6/8 = 0.2 \text{ hours}$$

Average number and time in the system:

$$L = L_q + \rho = 2.4, \qquad W = 2.4/8 = .3 \text{ hours}$$

Percent utilization: $100 * \rho = 80\%$.

Erlang Service Time: $k = 4$: $\sigma = (1/4^{1/2})(1/\mu) = 0.05$

Probability of empty system: $P_0 = 1 - \rho = 0.2$

Average number and time in the queue:

$$L_q = \frac{8^2 0.05^2 + 0.8^2}{2(1-0.8)} = 2, \qquad W_q = 2/8 = 0.25 \text{ hours}$$

Average number and time in the system:

$$L = L_q + \rho = 2.8, \qquad W = 2.8/8 = 0.35 \text{ hours}$$

Percent utilization: $100 * \rho = 80\%$.

These examples illustrate that the variability of the service process affects the efficiency of the queueing system. As the standard deviation decreases, the average customer time in the system and queue goes down. The constant service time case is the most efficient. The times cannot be reduced below these levels without reducing the variability of the arrival process.

PROBLEMS

P16.25 An assembly line has five stations through which every unit of production must pass. The arrival of units at the line is random with an exponential distribution for time between arrivals. The stations operate independently and queues are allowed to gather between stages. The mean time between arrivals is 20 minutes. All stations along the line have the same mean processing time of 15 minutes. For analysis purposes assume that the arrival process is Poisson for all stations. This assumption is correct for part **a** below, but not for part **b**. Determine the total average number of units in the five queues with the following design possibilities.

a. The processing time at each station has an exponential distribution.
b. The processing time at each station is a constant value of 15.

P16.26 An alternative to the assembly line of P16.25 is a single machine that performs all five operations. Each operation performed by the machine has an exponential distribution with a mean time of 3 minutes. Only one unit can be processed by the machine at a time so all five operations must be complete on a unit before the machine can accept the next unit. What is the average queue with this alternative?

P16.27 Analyze the situation described in P16.26 if the processing time for each operation of the machine is a constant 3 minutes.

Queueing Networks (16.9)

In many applications, rather than passing through a single queue, the customer will pass though a series of queues. An example is the registration procedure at a college where students must visit a number of stations in their quest for an academic program. Each station involves one or more servers and a queue of waiting students. Another example is a job shop consisting of a number of machines. Each job entering the shop must be processed by one or more machines before it is complete. An example case is illustrated by Fig. 16.7. Each rectangle is a queueing system, which we will call a station. There are one or more classes of customers each entering at one station, passing through a fixed series of stations, and leaving at another station. The collection of stations is called a network of queues.

The study of queueing networks is of great practical importance in operations research because so many systems can be described by such a model. Very often analysis is accomplished by simulation on a digital computer. Commercial simulation languages such as SLAM, SIMSCRIPT, GPSS, and others are widely used. Simulation, although very useful, is expensive and may yield unreliable results. There are some analytical procedures based on the results of this chapter that are appropriate in certain instances. They are very easy to apply and may yield insights important to the design of a system. These are the subject of this section.

GOALS

- Know the equivalence property and know when it is applicable.

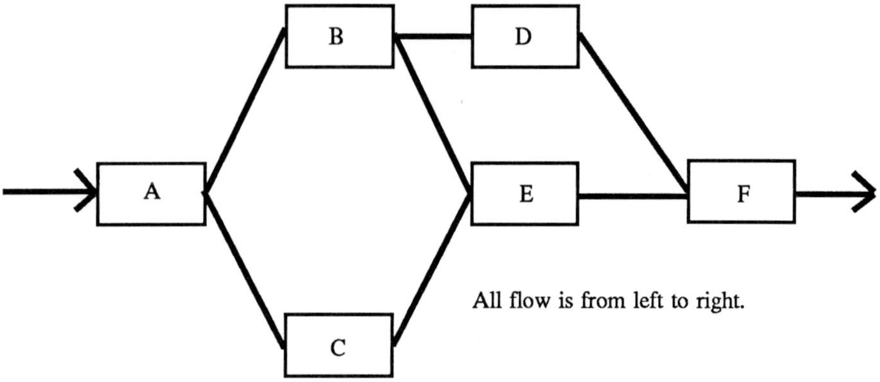

Figure 16.7 **An Example Queueing Network**

- When the equivalence property is applicable for a network of queues, be able to calculate steady-state results for the stations in the network, and the various classes of customers using the network.

RESULTS

Equivalence Property An M/M/s queueing system has a Poisson input with parameter λ. The system has an infinite queue and s parallel servers, each with the same exponential service time distribution with mean $1/\mu$, where $s\mu > \lambda$. The steady-state *output* of this queueing system is also a Poisson process with parameter λ.

Significance of the Result Because of the equivalence property, when a number of queueing systems of this type (stations) are arranged in a network, the input process for each station is a Poisson process, and the steady-state results for each station can be determined independently. These results can be used to answer a number of important questions about the network.

Limitations of the Result Each station must have a Poisson service process and an infinite queue. At each station, each customer has the same service time distribution. A given customer class must pass through the stations in a fixed order with no cycles. Queue discipline is not important to the results.

Addition of Input Sources If a station has more than one Poisson input source with rates $\lambda_1, \lambda_2, \ldots, \lambda_m,$ the input to the station can be considered as a single Poisson process with rate

$$\lambda = \lambda_1 + \lambda_2 + \ldots + \lambda_m.$$

This follows from property 3 of Sec. 16.3.

EXAMPLES

E16.13 Batch jobs submitted to a computer center may pass through three steps: an input processor, the central processor, and an output printer. All jobs must go through the input processor. Because of errors, only 80% of the jobs will go through the central processor. Only 40% of the jobs passing through the central processor will go to the output printer.

Jobs arrive to the computer center at random at a rate of 10 per minute. To handle the load of jobs submitted, the computer center may have more than one of the three types of processors operating in parallel. The times for the three steps have exponential distributions for each processor with means as follows: input processor 10 seconds, central processor 5 seconds, and printer 70 seconds. When processors are not immediately available for a job, the job will be placed in a queue. There is a queue for each processor.

Find the minimum number of each processor and compute the average time required for a job to pass through the system. This is a queueing network with three stations in series: input processor (I), central processor (C), and printer (P). First compute the rates into each processor and the minimum number of processors.

Input processor: Input rate $\lambda_I = 10$/minute.
Service rate $\mu_I = 6$/minute.

Minimum number required:

$$s_I > \lambda_I / \mu_I = 1.67, \text{ so use } s_I = 2.$$

Central processor: Input rate $\lambda_C = 10\ (0.8) = 8$/minute.
Service rate $\mu_C = 20$/minute.

Minimum number required:

$$s_C > \lambda_C / \mu_C = 0.4, \text{ so use } s_C = 1.$$

Printer: Input rate $\lambda_P = 8\ (0.4) = 3.2$/minute.
Service rate $\mu_P = 0.857$/minute.

Minimum number required:

$$s_P > \lambda_P / \mu_P = 3.73, \text{ so use } s_P = 4.$$

Assuming an infinite queue can form before each processor, processors can be analyzed independently to determine steady-state characteristics. Using the equations for the infinite queue case, we construct the table below.

	Input processor	*Central processor*	*Printer*
λ(per min.)	10	8	3.2
μ (per min)	6	20	0.857
s	2	1	4
L	5.45	0.667	15.63
W (min)	0.545	0.833	4.891
L_q	3.79	0.267	11.90
W_q (min)	0.379	0.033	3.723
ρ	0.833	0.40	0.933

The total average time required for a job to pass through all three stations is the sum of the average station times, 6.269 minutes. A total of 4.135 minutes, or about two-thirds of the time, is spent in queues. The times for jobs that do not pass through all three stations are found by adding the relevant station times. One must remember that these are only average (or expected) times. Individual times are random variables, which may be much smaller or larger than the average. The table shows that the printer is clearly the bottleneck in this system. Measures to improve this portion of the system by obtaining another printer, increasing printing speed, or reducing the input rate would improve the system performance.

E16.14 Assume that Fig. 16.7, shown at the beginning of this unit, represents a job shop manufacturing system. The rectangles identify machine types. There are three classes of products, which take different routes through the shop. The order rate for the classes along with the routing information is shown in the table below.

Product	*Order rate*	*Route*
1	30/month	A B D F
2	10/month	A B E F
3	20/month	A C E F

The table below shows the number and the average production rate of each type of machine. The production time has an exponential distribution. Also shown in the table are the arrival rates of products at each machine and information computed using the multichannel, infinite queue formulas. Note that the arrival rates are computed by simply summing the arrival rates of the products passing through the machines. Using the equivalence property, the inputs to each machine are Poisson processes.

Machine	*A*	*B*	*C*	*D*	*E*	*F*
λ (/mo.)	60	40	20	30	30	60
μ (/mo.)	25	22	29	11	23	20
s	3	2	1	3	2	5
L	4.99	10.47	2.22	11.05	2.27	3.35
W (mo.)	0.083	0.261	0.111	0.368	0.076	0.056
L_q	2.59	8.65	1.53	8.32	0.965	0.354
W_q (mo.)	0.043	0.216	0.077	0.277	0.032	0.006
ρ	0.80	0.909	0.689	0.909	0.652	0.60

For problems of this type the number of units in the system comprises the *in-process inventory*. It is the goal of most companies to reduce this quantity since it represents a significant capital cost. When evaluating these results it is most revealing to look at the "average number in the queue" row. The "average number in the system" includes the number in service, which cannot be affected by changing the number of channels in a queueing station. (The number in service is $L_S = \lambda / \mu$, and is unaffected by s.) It is apparent that the stations with the largest average queue are B and D. This is also indicated by the high utilization factor for these stations. Although both stations have the same value of ρ, they are not of equal importance; B has a larger queue than D. Thus if the products are equally valuable, station B is the most critical in this network.

It is also interesting to look at the average time through the system for each product, as this quantity represents the manufacturing lead time. Information for the individual products is shown in the table below. The times were determined by adding the time for each station visited by the product. The inventory was determined by multiplying the system time by the order rate.

Product	*Order rate (per mo.)*	*Route*	*System time (mo.)*	*Queue time (mo.)*	*Inventory (units)*
1	30/mo.	A B D F	0.768	0.542	23.04
2	10/mo.	A B E F	0.476	0.297	4.76
3	20/mo.	A C E F	0.326	0.158	6.52

This total shows a marked difference between the products in terms of lead time and in-process inventory.

PROBLEMS

P16.28 For E16.13, determine the system with the minimum number of channels in each station if the arrival rate is increased to 15. Show the results for this situation with a table similar to the one used in E16.13. Add a channel to the station that would most reduce the total system time summed over all users. Show the results for the revised system.

P16.29 Starting from the system in E16.14, show the effect of adding an additional channel for station B. Repeat the tables for the revised system.

P16.30 Starting from the system in E16.14, change the order rate of product 2 to 20 per month. If necessary add additional channels to the stations to allow a steady-state solution. Compute the steady-state solutions and show tables similar to those used in E16.14. Identify the most critical station.

Computer Program

Although the steady-state equations used in this chapter are simple in concept, they are difficult to evaluate by hand if the number of channels exceeds two or three. This makes it hard to perform design studies, which frequently require the evaluation of several system alternatives. The results of this chapter are also limited by the assumption of Poisson arrival and service processes.

The *Microsolve* package has two computer programs to partially resolve these difficulties. The first is called Birth-Death Processes and the second is called Queueing Simulation. The birth-death program has two principal parts. The first part allows the user to enter data for a general birth-death process. This consists of the arrival and departure rates for all the states of the system (up to 100). The program then evaluates the state probabilities for the system and the various steady-state properties. The second part of the program solves the finite or infinite multichannel queue with Poisson arrival and service processes. The maximum number in a finite system may be as large as 100 and the number of channels may be as large as the maximum number in the system. An infinite queue case may be analyzed by pressing ENTER in response to the request for the "maximum number in the system" data.

Steady-state probabilities and other system properties are computed. Figure 16.8 shows the birth-death model and the steady-state probabilities for a three-channel queue with an arrival rate of 0.1 per hour and a service rate for each channel of 0.05 per hour. This is a finite queue with the maximum number in the system equal to 10. Figure 16.9 shows the various measures describing the system performance computed by the general birth-death analytical formulas.

The second program allows the simulation of a multichannel queue with arrival and service processes that are not Poisson. Chapter 23 discusses how a simulation is carried out. Three alternative interarrival and service time distributions are provided: exponential, constant, and normal. The number of channels can be as many as five, and the maximum number in the queue may range from 0 to 100. The program simulates the operation of the queueing system for some fixed length of time and computes statistics that allow the estimation of the steady-state properties. Figure 16.10 shows the simulation results for the the system analyzed above as a birth-death process.

It should not be surprising that the results obtained by the two programs are not the same. The birth-death answers come from an analytical model which accurately computes the steady-state measures. The simulation represents one realization of the stochastic process for a given amount of time. The results obtained are averages of the quantities over the period of the simulation. Thus the simulation provides a statistical estimate of the analytical results. For a system with Poisson input and service processes, the birth-death analysis is always

STATE	ARRIVAL RATE PER HOUR	SERVICE RATE PER HOUR	PROB.
0	.1	0	.1130719
1	.1	.05	.2261439
2	.1	.1	.2261439
3	.1	.15	.1507626
4	.1	.15	.1005084
5	.1	.15	.0670056
6	.1	.15	.0446704
7	.1	.15	.0297802
8	.1	.15	.0198535
9	.1	.15	.0132356
10	0	.15	8.82E–03

Figure 16.8 **Definition and Steady-State Probabilities of the Birth-Death Process**

AVERAGE ARRIVAL RATE	=.099117 PER HOUR
AVERAGE NUMBER IN SYSTEM	= 2.71045
AVERAGE NUMBER IN QUEUE	=.728099
AVERAGE TIME IN SYSTEM	= 27.3458 HOURS
AVERAGE TIME IN QUEUE	= 7.34581 HOURS
PROPORTION OF THE TIME THE SYSTEM IS EMPTY	=.113071
PROPORTION OF THE TIME THE SYSTEM IS FULL	= 8.8E–03
PROPORTION OF THE TIME ALL CHANNELS ARE BUSY	=.434640
PERCENT UTILIZATION	= 66.0784
EXPECTED NUMBER OF BUSY CHANNELS	= 1.98235
EXPECTED NUMBER OF IDLE CHANNELS	= 1.01764

Figure 16.9 **Steady-State Expected Values Determined by the Analytical Solution**

preferred because it is accurate and easy. The advantage of the simulation model is that it can handle processes that are not Poisson. Commercial simulation packages can also handle far more complex structures than the multichannel queue model considered here.

The results of a simulation run depend to some extent on the "random number seed." This is a quantity that determines the sequence of random numbers generated by the computer and subsequently the sequence of events in the simulation. Choosing a different random number seed, which is an input to the program, will result in a different realization of the stochastic process. The student should run a given simulation several times with different seeds to get some idea of the statistical variability of the simulation results.

Another parameter affecting the results is the "initial number in the system." This is the number of customers in the system when the simulation begins. To

ARRIVAL INFORMATION	
TOTAL SIMULATION TIME	= 264
NUMBER OF ARRIVALS	= 38
NUMBER OF BALKS	= 0
MAXIMUM QUEUE LENGTH	= 10
AVERAGE TIME BETWEEN ARRIVALS OR BALKS	= 5.168221

AVERAGES DETERMINED BY SIMULATION	
AVERAGE NUMBER IN QUEUE	= 3.781825
AVERAGE NUMBER IN SERVICE	= 2.673071
AVERAGE NUMBER IN SYSTEM	= 6.454897
AVERAGE TIME IN QUEUE	= 18.39430
AVERAGE SERVICE TIME	= 14.89059
AVERAGE TIME IN SYSTEM	= 33.28489
PERCENT UTILIZATION	= 89.10238

Figure 16.10 **Simulation Results**

minimize the effect of this parameter on the steady-state results, the initial number should be set to the long-run average number in the system. The latter can be estimated by making a trial run of the simulation.

The "simulation time" determines the importance of the seed and the initial number in the system. If the simulation is run for a long enough time, the averages will not be significantly affected by the two parameters. The seed, initial number, and time are required inputs to the computer program and are under the control of the user. Although we are dealing here with a simple system, these parameters are typical of those that must be supplied for more complicated simulations. The problem of statistical variability is present with all simulations of stochastic processes.

Problems

P16.31 A finite queue has three servers and two spaces in the queue. There is an infinite input source, and the arrival rate to the system is 50/hour. When arrivals find the queue full, they balk. The following probabilities have been determined for the number in the system:

$$P_0 = 0.05, P_1 = 0.12, P_2 = 0.23, P_3 = 0.25, P_4 = 0.20, P_5 = 0.15.$$

Find:

- **a.** the expected number in the queue.
- **b.** the expected time in the queue.
- **c.** the expected number in the system.
- **d.** the expected time in the system.
- **e.** the expected number in service.
- **f.** the expected time in service.
- **g.** the proportion of customers who balk.
- **h.** the percent utilization of the servers.
- **i.** the probability that there will be fewer than two in the system.
- **j.** the probability that there will be four or more in the system.
- **k.** the probability that an arriving customer will obtain immediate service (rather than waiting in a queue).

P16.32 In the following problems, let P_1, P_2, P_3, . . . stand for the steady-state probabilities associated with the queueing system. In general P_n is the probability that the system is in state n. In each case below answer the problems in terms of these probabilities.

- **a.** The system has an infinite queue with three servers. What is the probability that an arriving customer will spend no time in the queue?
- **b.** The system has a finite queue with two servers and three spaces in the queue. Customers finding the queue full will balk. The arrival rate to the system is 20 per hour. What is the average time spent in the queue?

c. The queueing system represents a repair shop for a taxi cab company. The shop repairs only the five cabs owned by the company. There is a single repairman. The state of the system represents the number of cabs in the shop. What is the average number of cabs not in the repair shop?

P16.33 A multichannel queueing system has four servers. The arrival rate from the infinite input source is 3 per hour. The mean time required to complete a service is 1 hour. Both arrival and service processes are Poisson. There is no limit to the number in the queue.

a. What is the probability that more than one customer will arrive in a 15 minute period?
b. Assuming all servers remain busy, what is the probability that the next service operation will require less than1 hour?
c. Assuming all servers remain busy, what is the probability that each of the next two service operations will require more than 30 minutes?
d. Say you are a customer in this system. You waited for 1 hour in the queue and you have been in service for 25 minutes. How long should you expect to remain in the system before completing service?
e. What is the expected number of arrivals in an 8-hour period?
f. An individual customer arrives into the system and finds one other person in the queue. If the queue discipline is first- come- first- served, how long should the customer expect to spend in the system?
g. Assuming that all servers remain busy, what is the probability that exactly four customers will complete service in the next hour?
h. Assuming that all servers remain busy, what is the expected number of customers served in a 4-hour period?

P16.34 For this rate diagram show the system parameters and the computed values listed below.

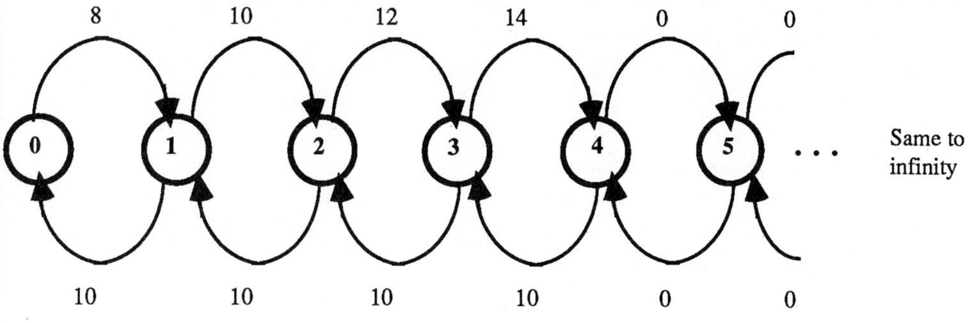

a. Give the maximum number in the system.
b. Give the arrival or birth rate for each state.
c. Give the service or death rate for each state.
d. Compute the steady-state probabilities for the states of the system.

e. Compute the average arrival rate.
f. Compute the average number in the system.
g. Compute the average time in the system.
h. Assume there are two servers. Compute the average number in the queue.
i. Compute the average time in the queue.
j. Find the probability that both servers are idle.

P16.35 Show the rate diagrams for the following queueing systems. All arrival and service processes are Poisson. From each diagram compute the steady-state probabilities for states 0 through 4.

a. A system has two servers and a finite input source. Four customers use the system, each with an arrival rate of 2 per day. The mean service time is 5 hours. Assume an 8-hour day.
b. A system with an infinite queue has two servers. The first server has a service rate of 4 per hour and the second server has a service rate of 3 per hour. Whenever there is only one customer in the system, the first server is used. The arrival rate is 5 per hour.
c. A finite queue with an arrival rate of 5 per hour. Whenever there are four customers in the system, all arrivals balk. Whenever there are three customers in the system, half the arrivals balk. If there are two or fewer in the system, none of the arrivals balk. There is one server with a rate of 4 per hour.
d. A system with an infinite queue has two classes of customers. The mean time between arrivals for customers of class A is 2 hours. The mean time between arrivals for customers of class B is 3 hours. Both times are exponentially distributed. There is a single server, with the average service time of 1 hour.

P16.36 A multichannel queueing system has four servers. The arrival rate from the infinite input source is 3 per hour. The mean time required to complete a service is 1 hour. Both arrival and service processes are Poisson. There is no limit to the number in the queue.
Find:

a. the expected number in the queue.
b. the expected time in the queue.
c. the expected number in the system.
d. the expected time in the system.
e. the expected number in service.
f. the expected time in service.
g. the proportion of customers that balk.
h. the percent utilization of the servers.
i. the probability that there will be fewer than two in the system.
j. the probability that there will be four or more in the system.
k. the probability that an arriving customer will obtain immediate service (rather than waiting in a queue).

P16.37 A microcomputer laboratory has six microcomputers for use by students. During the busy time of the day, students arrive at the computer room at random at an average rate of 12 per hour. Unfortunately many times the student will find all the computers busy. When all the computers are busy, an arriving student will not wait but will rush off to one of the other computer labs on campus. The average time a student will spend on the computer is 1/2 hour, but the time is actually exponentially distributed.

a. Sketch the rate diagram for this situation.
b. What is the average number in the queue of this system?
c. What proportion of the arriving students will be served by this computer lab?
d. What is the utilization percentage (the proportion of the time the computers are in use) for the computers in the lab?

P16.38 A family has four children and a single bathroom. Each morning during a 1 hour period before school, there is a congestion problem related to the bathroom. The parents minimize the problem by remaining in bed. While lying in bed, the mother, who is studying queueing theory, makes the following observations. The requirement to use the bathroom seems to be a random process. The time between the moment when one child leaves the bathroom and the moment when the same child desires to return averages 15 minutes, but actually the time is a random variable with an exponential distribution. The time spent in the bathroom in any one instance is also exponentially distributed with a mean time of 5 minutes. A child arriving at the bathroom and finding it busy will wait in a queue, making loud noises to the person occupying the bathroom and thus disturbing the parents.

a. Although clearly this is a transient situation, make an analysis to determine the steady-state probabilities associated with the number in this system.
b. It is relatively quiet while there is no queue. For how many minutes in the 1 hour period should the parents expect to have quiet rest?

P16.39 Every year each faculty member must submit an annual report showing his or her accomplishments during the previous year. These are usually prepared in handwritten form and must be retyped by a secretary in the format required by the dean. During the late spring these arrive at the chairman's office at an average rate of one per day; however, the actual arrival process is Poisson. The time required to retype the information is highly variable due to the professors' bad writing and different levels of accomplishment. The average time to type a report is 1.5 days. For analysis purposes assume this time is exponentially distributed. In order to finish the reports promptly, two secretaries are assigned full time for this purpose.

The associate chairman of the department is proposing a different procedure. All professors must enter their data on printed forms. The secretary will then enter the data into a personal computer. It is estimated that this procedure will not change the arrival process, but the time to enter the data into the computer and print out the report will now be normally distributed with a mean time of 2/3 day with a standard deviation of 1/3 day. Under this proposal only one secretary will be required.

Compare the present method with the proposed method in terms of the utilization of the secretaries and the mean interval between when the professor submits the report and the time when the secretary finishes it.

P16.40 Two operations are required to repair a roof: first the old roof must be removed and then the new roof must be installed. The time between the beginning of the removal of the old roof and the completion of the installation of the new is important because the house may be ruined if it rains during this period.

Customers call at random to a roofing contractor at an average rate of 12 per month (4 weeks). An average time of 0.5 weeks is required to remove a roof and 1 week to install a new one. Both times are exponentially distributed. The contractor has two kinds of worker crews, a removal crew and an installation crew. When a customer order arrives, the customer must wait until a removal crew is available. After the roof is removed, the customer enters a queue to wait for an installation crew to become available.

- **a.** Draw a diagram showing this queueing network. Show relevant arrival and service rates for each station. Compute the minimum number of crews required for the two operations.
- **b.** Compute the average danger period using the minimum number of crews. The danger period is the time between the moment when the removal crew begins to remove the roof and the moment when the installation crew completes the installation of the new roof.

Computer Problems

16.41 Arrivals at a self-service gasoline station are random with a mean rate of 12 per hour. The station has a single pump. The time spent by a motorist at the pump has an exponential distribution with a mean of 3 minutes. In the following, assume there is no limit to the number of cars waiting.

- **a.** What proportion of the time is the pump (or pumps) busy?
- **b.** How much room must be left on the station property for the waiting line if the space is to be sufficient 85% of the time?
- **c.** What is the average time required for the customer to get gas?
- **d.** If the arrival rate changes to 50 per hour, what is the minimum number of pumps required to handle the load? Answer parts (a), (b), and (c) using this number of pumps. Also do the three parts with one more than this minimum.
- **e.** Analyze this system if the arrival rate is 45 per hour and 4 pumps are used. The queue size is limited to 4 cars. How many customers will be lost because of this limit?
- **f.** Analyze the system of part (c) if the service time could be made more uniform with an attendant. Specifically, the average time will still be 3

minutes, but the standard deviation will be 1 minute. The time has a normal distribution.

P16.42 An airline reservation office receives telephone calls at the rate of one every 10 seconds. Calls require an average of 3 minutes to complete. Calls are taken either immediately by an operator if one is available or placed on hold if a holding line is available. Both arrival and service processes are Poisson.

Design the system by determining the number of operators and number of hold lines if it is required that the average time on hold be no more than 1 minute and that no more than 1% of the customers be lost.

P16.43 A blood bank has two kinds of customer, those that donate their blood and those that sell their blood. Donors arrive at the blood bank at an average rate of 6 per hour. Sellers arrive at the blood bank at an average rate of 10 per hour. Both kinds of arrivals are random and independent. There are two receptionists for the two types of customers. This is necessary because different forms must be filled out depending on the type of customer. The "donation" receptionist can handle an average of 10 customers per hour, and the "selling" receptionist can handle an average of 15 customers per hour. The service times for both receptionists are exponentially distributed.

After filling out the forms both types of customers go to the blood-donation room and lie on tables where the required amount of blood is removed. Because of the different reactions of patients to this process, the time a patient spends on the table is a random variable with a mean of 10 minutes and an exponential distribution. the number of tables used is the minimum that will handle the total load of the two types of givers.

a. Draw a diagram describing this situation showing all relevant queueing system parameters.
b. What is the average time required for persons to finish the blood-donation process?
c. The customers share a single waiting room for all three operations in this system. What is the average number of persons using the waiting room?
d. What is the probability that the waiting room will be empty?

CHAPTER 17

The Application of Queueing Theory

Decision Models (17.1–17.4)

The previous two chapters provide tools for analyzing stochastic systems. Thus, given the model structure and values for the various parameters, one can compute measures of effectiveness such as average number and time in a queueing system. This is in contrast to the optimization methods of the first 14 chapters, which, given the model structure and parameters, determine optimum solutions. The analysis procedures do not determine a solution; they only evaluate a given solution. This chapter introduces some typical decision problems involving queueing systems and provides guidance for modeling the problems. Powerful techniques for optimizing general models involving stochastic systems are not known. The primary mechanism by which one finds solutions is exhaustive enumeration.

GOALS

- Know the alternative models for evaluating expected waiting cost for a queueing system.
- Given a decision problem involving a queueing system, be able to formulate a model that determines the total cost, including expected service and waiting costs, as a function of the decision variables.

- For the various kinds of decision problems, know how to use the total cost model to find optimum decisions.

DEFINITIONS

Decision Variables: In the design of a queueing system, the principal decision variables are:

Number of servers at a service facility (s)

Efficiency of the servers (μ)

Number of service facilities

Location of service facilities (to be considered in the next section).

Expected Service Cost ($E(SC)$): The expected value of the cost of providing the service facilities in a queueing system. This is a cost rate so its dimensions are dollars per unit time. ($/time).

Expected Waiting Cost ($E(WC)$): The expected value of the cost associated with the customers who are in the queueing system. ($/time).

Expected Total Cost ($E(TC)$): The sum of expected service and waiting costs. ($/time).

$$E(TC) = E(SC) + E(WC).$$

RESULTS

Waiting Cost as a Function of the Number in the System Here we assume that the waiting cost at any particular time depends on how many customers are in the system. The cost rate with n customers in the system is $g(n)$. The expected waiting cost is then

$$E(WC) = \sum_{n=1}^{\infty} g(n)P_n,$$

where the P_n are the steady-state probabilities.

When $g(n)$ is a linear function of the number in the system, the expected waiting cost is proportional to the average number in the system. Let C_w be the cost rate per individual in the system measured in ($/time). Then

$$g(n) = C_w\, n,$$
$$E(WC) = C_w\, L\,.$$

Waiting Cost as a Function of the Time in the System Here we assume that waiting cost for an individual is a function of the time spent in the system. If we denote T as the random variable which is time in the system, the cost for a customer is given by the function $h(T)$. With $f_T(w)$ given as the probability density function of the time, the expected value of the waiting cost per customer is

$$E\{h(T)\} = \int_0^{\infty} h(w) f_T(w) dw .$$

This expected value is a cost rather than a cost rate, so to obtain a rate we must multiply the expression by the arrival rate λ.

$$E(WC) = \lambda E\{h(T)\}.$$

In this text, the only density function for waiting time that has been shown is for the M/M/s system. The integration required above is only tractable for $s = 1$ and for simple forms of $h(w)$.

When the waiting cost is a linear function of time spent in the system, the expected waiting cost is again proportional to the average number in the system. Let C_w be the rate for an individual in the system measured in (\$/time). Then

$$h(T) = C_w T,$$
$$E(WC) = \lambda E\{h(T)\} = \lambda C_w W = C_w L .$$

When waiting cost is either linearly related to the number in the system or time in the system, the expected waiting cost has the same formula.

MODELING

In the following we investigate decision problems that might arise in the design of a queueing system, propose a specific model for each, and suggest how the model might be solved.

Determining the Number of Servers Here we consider a system in which the arrival and service rates per channel are constant and investigate the problem of finding an optimum number of servers. From previous discussions, it is clear that as the number of servers increases, the average number and time in the system decrease. Since the cost of a service facility will increase with number of servers there is a tradeoff between the cost of waiting and the cost of service. Assume that each server has a cost of C_s; then the cost model for this case is

$$E(TC) = sC_s + E(WC).$$

For this expression to be dimensionally consistent, C_s must be specified in cost per unit time (\$/time).

The decision variable, s, is an integer. For a system with an infinite population and queue, the minimum value of s is equal to the smallest integer greater than λ/μ . (For a finite system the minimum of s is 1.) The optimum s can be found by starting from this minimum value and evaluating $E(TC)$ for increasing values of s. When the total cost stops decreasing with s and begins to increase, the optimum is indicated. This approach is valid if $E(WC)$ is a convex function of s, as is usually the case.

Determining the Number of Servers and the Service Efficiency Say there are several alternative types of servers with different efficiencies as measured by the service rate μ. We want to choose the type of server and the number of servers s. The cost for each server is a function of μ, $f(\mu)$. The cost model is then

$$E(TC) = sf(\mu) + E(WC).$$

The solution is found by determining the optimum value of s for each alternative and then selecting the alternative with the least total cost.

When the alternatives for μ are continuous, $f(\mu)$ is a linear or concave function of μ, and it is feasible to use a single channel. It is always optimum to use a single channel rather than multiple channels for a queueing system. Where it is applicable, this is a useful result, because the optimum can be found without an exhaustive search over alternative values of s.

Determining the Number of Service Facilities For this case there is a specified arrival rate into the system and we are considering dividing the arriving customers between two or more service facilities. If λ_p is the arrival rate for the population and n is the number of facilities, the arrival rate into any one of them is

$$\lambda = \lambda_p/n .$$

Assume that there is a fixed cost C_f of establishing a facility and a variable cost C_s per server. Both costs have the dimensions (\$/time). The total cost of the system of facilities is

$$E(TC) = n[C_f + sC_s + E(WC)]$$

where $E(WC)$ is the expected waiting cost at each facility.

The solution to this model will always result in a single facility ($n = 1$). It is for this reason that many "real world" queueing systems have multiple servers but only a single queue. This is evident in United States post offices, banks, and large amusement parks, where ropes or metal bars organize waiting customers into long snake-like queue patterns.

In the next section we will investigate a model in which the locations of facilities are also decision variables. Here the time spent in travel is relevant, and the optimum solution is not necessarily a single facility.

EXAMPLES

E17.1 Customers arrive at random at a rate of 110 per hour. There is no limit to the size of the queue. One channel in a service facility operates at a rate of 30 per hour. The waiting cost depends linearly on the number in the system with a cost of $20 per hour per customer. The cost of providing a service channel is $50 per hour. What is the optimum number of channels?

Solution From the data provided, $\lambda = 110$ and $\mu = 30$. The minimum number of channels is the smallest integer greater than 110/30 or 4. The waiting cost function is

$$g(n) = 20n \,.$$

Since this function is linear, $E(WC) = 20L$. The service cost is $E(SC) = 50s$. The total cost as a function of the number of channels is

$$E(TC) = 50s + 20L \,.$$

Recall that the average number in the system is a function of s. Using the steady-state formulas for the M/M/s queue we find the following results.

(s)	(L)	$E(SC)$	$E(WC)$	$E(TC)$
4	12.69	200	454	654
5	4.86	250	97	347
6	3.99	300	80	380

The optimum number of channels is five.

E17.2 Use the same situation as E17.1 except assume that there is no waiting cost if a customer is in service, but the cost is \$60 per hour for each customer in the queue.

Solution The waiting cost depends on the number in the system as follows.

$$g(n) = 0 \qquad \text{if } n < s$$
$$g(n) = 60\,(n - s) \qquad \text{if } n \geq s$$

The expected waiting cost is then

$$E(WC) = \sum_{n=s}^{\infty} 60\,(n - s)\, P_n = 60L_q \,.$$

Again we use enumeration to find the optimum solution.

s	L_q	$E(SC)$	$E(WC)$	$E(TC)$
4	9.02	200	541	741
5	1.19	250	71	321
6	0.33	300	20	320
7	0.108	350	7	357

The optimum number of channels is six.

E17.3 Use the same situation as E17.1 except assume that waiting cost is given by

$$g(n) = 10n^2.$$

Find the optimum number of channels.

Solution The expected waiting cost is

$$E(WC) = \sum_{n=0}^{\infty} n^2 P_n.$$

This expression must be numerically evaluated for each alternative using the steady-state probabilities. Again the optimum is determined by enumeration. We omit the details here.

E17.4 Assume that two separate service facilities are created to handle the demand described in E17.1. Each will have an arrival rate of 55. Waiting and service costs are as described in E17.1. Find the optimum number of channels for each facility and compare the resulting system cost to the cost of the optimum facility determined in E17.1.

Solution The minimum number of channels for each facility is 2. The optimum number is found from the computations below.

s	L	$E(SC)$	$E(WC)$	$E(TC)$
2	11.46	100	229	329
3	2.41	150	48	198
4	1.94	200	39	239

The optimum number of channels for each facility is three, with a cost of 198. The total cost of the system is 396. As one would expect, this system is less efficient than the single facility.

E17.5 An alternative mechanism is available for providing the service desired in E17.1. This mechanism has a service rate of 40 per hour but costs \$60 per hour to operate. Is this alternative better?

Solution Using the procedure described in E17.1, this situation results in an optimum design using four channels with a cost of 313. This is superior to the service facility suggested in E17.1, and the alternative should be used.

E17.6 Consider again the situation described in E17.1 but assume the service rate is continuously adjustable. The rate can be increased but with additional cost. The formula for cost is

$$f(\mu) = 25 + 0.30\mu .$$

Find the optimum design by specifying μ and s.

Solution Since the cost function is linear with μ, the optimum is to use a single channel. For this queueing system the average number in the system is

$$L = \lambda /(\mu - \lambda).$$

The total cost function is then

$$E(TC) = 25 + 30\mu + 20[\lambda /(\mu - \lambda)].$$

Taking the derivative of this function with respect to μ and solving for the optimum μ, one obtains the expression

$$\mu^* = ((20/0.3)\lambda)^{1/2} + \lambda = 195.$$

PROBLEMS

P17.1 Consider the bank example described in E16.9. The average time between arrivals for drive-in banking is 40 seconds. The service operation requires an average time of 30 seconds. Currently there is one bank teller window. On bank property, there is room for one car in service and three cars in the queue. Additional waiting cars will spill over into the street. Bank managers are concerned about this because of the traffic congestion it causes. There is also concern about the waiting time for customers. Rather than set criteria for a successful system as was done in Chapter 16, we would like to design the system using a total cost approach. The cost of providing a teller window is $100 per hour. New teller windows use up space formerly used for waiting cars. Evaluate independently the various design ideas presented below.

- **a.** Assign a cost of $20 per customer hour spent in the system. Find the optimum number of windows without concern for the queue problem.
- **b.** Assign a cost of $100 per minute for cars forced to queue in the street. Neglecting the customer waiting time, find the optimum number of windows.
- **c.** Combine the costs of parts (a) and (b) and find the optimum number of windows.
- **d.** Assume that the police restrict cars from queueing in the street. Rather customers must balk if they find the space on the bank property insufficient. The bank assigns a cost of $50 per balking customer. Find the optimum number of windows. In addition to the balking cost, include the waiting cost for customers and the cost of the teller windows in the total cost function.

P17.2 Consider the production system defined by the queueing network of E16.14. Let the products described have equal value so that the in-process inventory cost of each is $200 per unit per year. Assume the marginal cost of the machines at each of the stations is equal to $500 per year. Find the optimum number of each type of machine.

Queueing Systems with Travel Times (17.5)

As established in the last section, it is rarely wise to divide the resources of a service facility into several facilities. When the facilities are to be located some distance apart, however, the travel time of customers may be important, and it may be advisable to provide separate facilities. Here not only the number of facilities but also the location of facilities is a decision variable. There are many examples of this including fire stations in a city, rest rooms in an office complex, and tool cribs in a manufacturing plant.

GOALS

- Be able to formulate the model that measures the total cost for multiple service facilities located in different places.
- Be able to compute the travel cost component of total cost when travel is rectilinear and customers are distributed uniformly over a rectangular area.
- Be able to find the optimum queueing system design when the decision variables are the number of facilities, the location of facilities, and the number of servers at each facility.

DEFINITIONS

Rectilinear Travel Distance: Let locations be defined on a two-dimensional plane with the orthogonal axes x and y. If a route from one place to another follows paths that are always parallel to the axes, the travel is said to be rectilinear. This assumption is appropriate for manufacturing plants or office complexes where aisles form a rectangular array, or for cities with streets arranged in a rectangular pattern. The rectilinear distance between two points (x_1, y_1) and (x_2, y_2) is

$$D = |x_1 - x_2| + |y_1 - y_2|.$$

Besides being practically justified in many instances, this metric simplifies the mathematics of some procedures.

In the following we will define the coordinate system so that the service facility is at the origin as in Fig. 17.1. Then the distance from point (x,y) to the facility is

$$D = |x| + |y|.$$

Travel Velocity (v): The speed of travel for a customer going to and from a service facility.

Expected Travel Time ($E(T)$): The time it takes to travel between two points depends on the velocity of travel and the distance

$$T = D/v\ .$$

The expected travel time is the travel time averaged over all customers spread over some region. The dimension of this quantity is time.

Expected Travel Cost ($E(TV)$): The expected value of the cost associated with the customers who are traveling to or from the service facility. ($/time).

RESULTS

Computation of Expected Travel Time Assume a facility is located at the origin of a rectangular region as shown in Fig. 17.1, and that customers are located uniformly throughout the region. Note that a and b are positive numbers with point $(-a, -b)$ identifying the lower left corner of the region. The point (c, d) identifies the

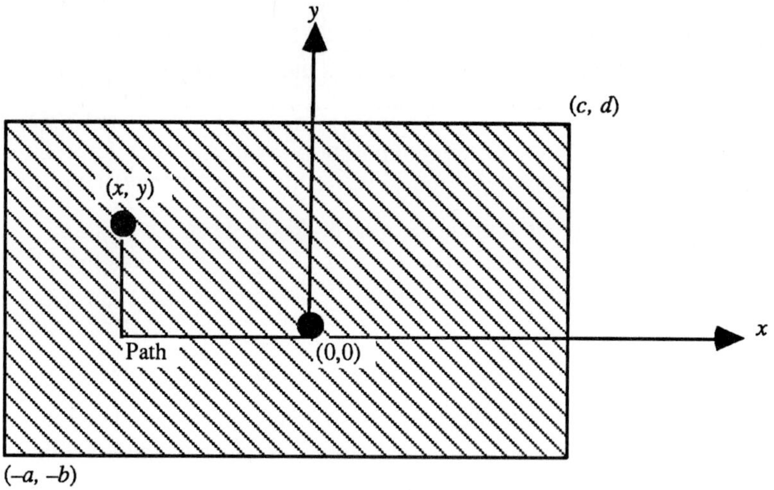

Figure 17.1 **Rectangular Region with Facility at the Origin**

upper right corner. The expected travel time for a customer traveling both to and from the facility (two-way) is

$$E(T) = \frac{1}{v}\left(\frac{a^2 + c^2}{a + c} + \frac{b^2 + d^2}{b + d}\right).$$

Computation of Expected Travel Cost Let C_t be the cost per unit time for customers traveling to and from the service facility. The cost per trip is then

$$C_t E(T).$$

The cost per unit time (or the cost rate) for travel is then

$$E(TV) = \lambda C_t E(T),$$

where λ is the arrival rate to the facility.

MODELING

We will use the results of this section to solve problems regarding the dispersion of service facilities. If there are n facilities each having the same number of servers, serving regions with the same size and populations, and in the same relative locations within the regions, the total cost function is

$$E(TC) = n[(C_f + sC_s) + E(WC) + \lambda C_t E(T)],$$

where $\lambda = \lambda_p / n$ and λ_p is the total arrival rate.

If the facilities are in some sense different from each other we will subscript the variable parameters with the index i and sum over the facilities.

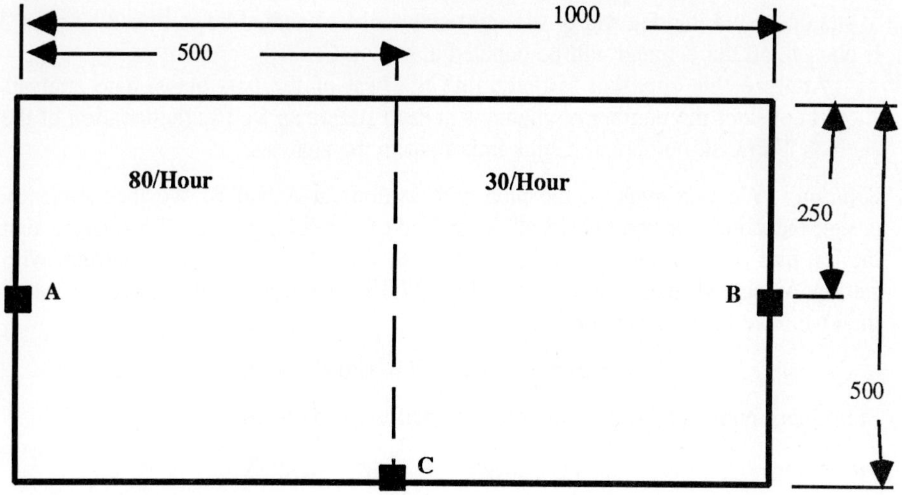

Figure 17.2 **Plant with Nonuniform Demand**

$$E(TC) = \sum_{i=1}^{n} [(C_f + s_i C_s) + E(WC_i) + \lambda_i C_t E(T_i)],$$

where $\lambda_p = \lambda_1 + \lambda_2 + \ldots + \lambda_n$.

EXAMPLE

E17.2 A plant has the shape shown in Fig. 17.2. All dimensions are in feet. To provide a particular service to the employees, management will install service stations within the plant. Two plans are available:

1. Install stations at locations A and B.
2. Install a single station at C.

Demand for the service occurs nonuniformly in the plant with the demand of 80 per hour in the left half and 30 per hour in the right half. The demand is uniformly distributed within each half. The demand is a Poisson process. Each service facility will have one or more channels. Each channel has a service rate of 40 per hour. The service time has an exponential distribution.

There is a cost associated with employees who are waiting or being serviced in the service facility or who are traveling to or from the facility. The cost is \$20/hour. Travel to a facility is rectilinear. A two-way trip is required for each visit to the facility. Employees travel at a rate of 10,000 feet per hour. There are 2000 work hours in 1 year.

The cost of establishing a station at any location is \$20,000 per year independent of the number of channels, with an added cost of \$15,000 per year per channel. If plan 1 is chosen, the demand of the left side of the plant will be handled at station A and the demand of the right side will be handled by station B. If plan 2 is chosen, all the demand will be handled at station C.

Analyze this situation to determine the best of the two plans. The analysis should consider the number of channels at each station as well as the location of the stations. Show all numerical results important to the analysis.

Solution We first evaluate the plan with stations at A and B. We independently design the stations at the two locations and add the resulting costs. Considering first the left half of the region served by station A, we define a coordinate system with station A located at the origin as in Fig. 17.3. For purposes of estimating travel time we have from this figure

$$a = 0,\ b = 250,\ c = 500, \text{ and } d = 250.$$

From these numbers we compute the expected two-way travel time.

$$E(T) = \frac{1}{10000}\left(\frac{0^2 + 500^2}{0 + 500} + \frac{250^2 + 250^2}{250 + 250}\right) = 0.075 \text{ hours.}$$

Since most of the data is given in hours, we will express the fixed and variable facility cost in per hour equivalents.

$$C_f = 20{,}000/2000 = \$10/\text{hour}$$
$$C_s = 15{,}000/2000 = \$7.50/\text{hour.}$$

The service cost is then

$$E(SC) = 10 + 7.5s \quad (\$/\text{hour}).$$

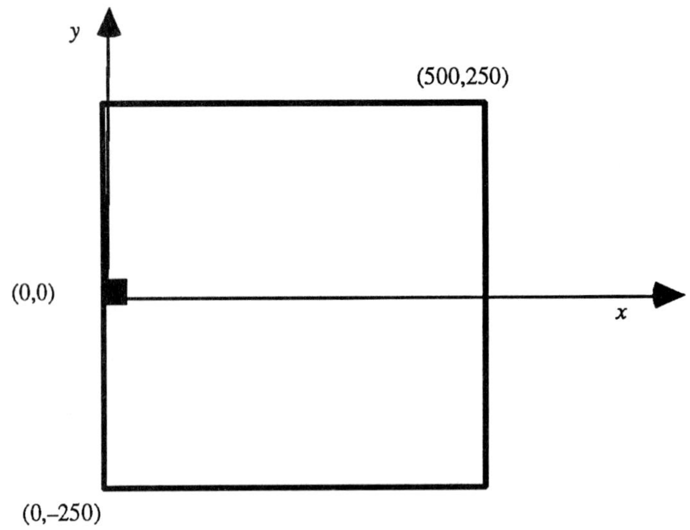

Figure 17.3 **Coordinate System for Station A**

The waiting cost is linear with number in the system, therefore,

$$E(WC) = 20L \quad (\$/\text{hour}).$$

The travel cost is

$$E(TV) = \lambda 20E(T) \quad (\$/\text{hour}).$$

For station A this is

$$(80)(20)(0.075) = \$120/\text{hour}.$$

The expected total hourly cost of the facility at A is

$$E(TC_A) = 10 + 7.5s + 20L + 120.$$

To design the station at A we must use enumeration to find the optimum number of channels as in the table below. The table is constructed for $\lambda = 80$ and $\mu = 40$.

(*s*)	(*L*)	*E*(*SC*)	*E*(*WC*)	*E*(*TC*)
3	2.888	32.5	57.76	210.26
4	2.174	40.0	43.48	203.48
5	2.040	47.5	40.80	208.30

The optimum number of channels is four and the cost of the optimum system at A is \$203.48.

Station B is similar to station A with respect to travel time but it has an arrival rate of 30 per hour. The total cost function for station B is

$$E(TC_B) = 10 + 7.5s + 20L + 45.$$

The table below is constructed for $\lambda = 30$ and $\mu = 40$.

(*s*)	(*L*)	*E*(*SC*)	*E*(*WC*)	*E*(*TC*)
1	30.0	17.5	60.0	122.50
2	0.873	25.0	17.45	87.45
3	0.765	32.5	15.29	92.79

The optimum number of channels at B is two with a total cost of \$87.45. Therefore, the optimum design for the system consisting of stations at A and B is \$290.93 per hour.

To design the single station at C, note that this station handles all the arrivals. The arrival rate for the station is the sum of the rates for the two parts or 110 per hour. We must determine the travel distance independently for the two parts. Relative to the right side with the location of C at (0,0) we have

$$a = 0, b = 0, c = 500, d = 500.$$

From these results we call calculate the average two-way travel distance as 1000 feet. The two-way travel time is then 0.1 hour. Because of symmetry, the same time is appropriate for the left side of the region. The expected travel cost is the sum from the two sides or

$$E(TV) = (80)(20)(0.1) + (30)(20)(0.1) = \$220/\text{hour}.$$

The expected total cost for C is

$$E(TC_C) = 10 + 7.5s + 20L + 220.$$

To find the optimum design we construct the table below with $\lambda = 110$ and $\mu = 40$.

(s)	(L)	$E(SC)$	$E(WC)$	$E(TC)$
3	12.04	32.5	240.1	492.6
4	3.65	40.0	73.02	333.02
5	2.97	47.5	59.37	326.87
6	2.81	55.0	56.19	331.19

The optimum number of channels is five with a cost of \$326.87. This is greater than the system with stations at A and B, which must be the selected alternative.

PROBLEM

P17.3 Find the cost of a single facility placed at the center of the region.

Computer Program

Since the steady-state equations for more than one channel are not very convenient for hand computations, computer programs can be of great help for evaluating alternative designs. If the input and service processes are Poisson, the Birth-Death program in *Microsolve* will generate the accurate steady-state results required for the cost equations. The program can be easily run with alternative parameters.

If input and service processes are not Poisson, the Queue Simulation program can be used to estimate steady-state results. Here, however, great care should be exercised with regard to the statistical variability of the simulation results. It is very possible that this variability will entirely mask substantial differences between alternative systems resulting in the wrong selection.

Problems

P17.4 Two alternative designs are being considered for the service facility of a finite queueing system. Alternative A has a single server and alternative B has two servers. The cost of the service facility has two parts: a fixed cost of \$50,000 per year, which is independent of the number of servers, and a variable cost, which is proportional to the number of servers. The variable cost is \$30,000 per server per year. Simulation analysis has determined the following probability distributions for the number of customers in the system.

Design A

n	0	1	2	3	4
P_n	0.12	0.25	0.38	0.15	0.10

Design B

n	0	1	2	3	4
P_n	0.38	0.30	0.21	0.06	0.05

In addition the simulation has determined that 10% of the customers balk with design A, while 5% of the customers balk with design B. The arrival rate to the system (including balks) is 1500 customers customers per year.

Management has determined that a customer who balks costs the company $100 in lost profits. The cost of persons waiting in the system is $20 per hour (for each customer in the system).

Determine the system that minimizes total cost. Assume that a year has 2000 hours.

P17.5 A pizza parlor is initiating a delivery service in a small city. For simplicity assume the city has a square shape, as indicated in Fig. 17.4. Two alternatives are being considered for location of the delivery depots: either a single depot is to be located at site A, or four depots are to be located at sites B, C, D, and E. In the latter case, the city will be divided into quadrants with each customer served by the closest depot.

Calls for pizza arrive from the entire city at random with an average rate of 20 per hour. The calls are distributed uniformly throughout the city. When a call is received, the pizza is prepared and a driver delivers the pizza to the customer. Here we are only concerned about the delivery process, so we neglect the preparation time. The time for delivery is the round-trip time from the depot to the customer. Assume all travel is rectilinear with respect to the orientation of the city boundaries. The average speed of travel is 20 miles per hour. For analysis purposes,

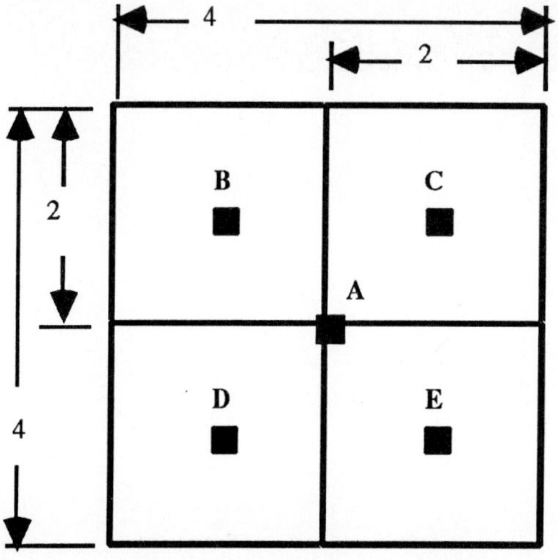

Figure 17.4 **Layout for Pizza Delivery Problem**

compute the average travel time from the geometry given, but assume the delivery time has an exponential distribution. The delivery process is a queueing system because orders must wait for the availability of a driver.

There is a fixed cost of $15,000 per year of establishing a depot. The cost of hiring a driver and providing a delivery vehicle is also $15,000 per year. You are to determine the best delivery depot plan. The plan must specify the location of the depots and the number of drivers to provide at each depot. To provide a measure of service quality, you are to use a cost of $20 per hour for the time required for a customer to receive his pizza (the time between when the order is placed and when it is delivered). Assume that there are 2000 hours in a year.

CHAPTER 18

Inventory Theory

Inventories are products stored for later use. They are ubiquitous in modern business. Observation of almost any company balance sheet reveals that a very significant part of its assets comprise inventories of raw materials, products within the production process, and finished products. Most businessmen don't like inventories, because they are, after all, like money placed in a drawer, assets tied up in investments that are not earning money. They also incur costs for the care of the stored material and are subject to spoilage and obsolescence. The main purpose of programs such as "just-in-time" delivery is to reduce inventory levels.

In spite of all these bad features, inventories do have purposes. Raw material inventories provide a stable source of the means of production. A large inventory requires fewer replenishments and may reduce ordering costs because of economies of scale. In-process inventories reduce the impacts of the variability of the production rates in a plant and protect against failures in the processes. Final goods inventories provide for better customer service. The variety and easy availability of the product is an important marketing consideration.

There are other kinds of inventories, including spare parts inventories for maintenance, excess capacity built into facilities to take advantage of the economies of scale of construction, and water stored in reservoirs to reduce the effects of the vagaries of nature.

Because of their practical and economic importance, the subject of inventory control has become a major consideration in many situations. Questions must be constantly answered as to when and how much raw material should be ordered, when a production order should be released to the plant, what level of safety stock should be maintained at a retail outlet, how much bank (in-process inventory) is to be maintained in a production process, or how much water should be released from a reservoir. These questions are amenable to quantitative analysis through the subject of inventory theory.

Components of Inventory Models (18.2)

This section lists the factors that are important in making decisions related to inventories and establishes some of the notation that will be used throughout the chapter. Dimensional analysis is sometimes useful for modeling inventory systems, so we provide the dimensions of each factor. Additional model-dependent notation will be introduced later.

GOAL

- Be able to list the factors that are important to the quantitative analysis of a single product inventory.

DEFINITIONS

Ordering Cost ($c(z)$)**:** This is the cost of placing an order to an outside supplier or releasing a production order to the shop. The amount ordered is z. $c(z)$ is often a nonlinear function. The dimension of ordering cost is ($).

Setup Cost (K)**:** A common assumption is that the ordering cost consists of a fixed cost, which is independent of the amount ordered, and a variable cost which depends on the amount ordered. The fixed cost is called the setup cost. The dimension of K is ($).

Product Cost (c)**:** This is the unit cost of purchasing the product as part of an order. If the cost is independent of the amount ordered, the total cost is cz, where c is the unit cost and z is the amount ordered. The product cost may be a decreasing function of the amount ordered. The dimension of c is ($/unit).

Holding Cost (h)**:** This is the cost of holding an item in inventory for some given unit of time. It usually includes the lost investment income caused by having the asset tied up in inventory. This is not a real cash flow, but it is an important component of the cost of inventory. If c is the unit cost of the product, this component of the cost is $c\alpha$, where α is the discount or interest rate. The holding cost may also include the cost of storage, insurance, and other factors that are proportional to the amount stored in inventory. The units of h are ($/unit-time).

Shortage Cost (p)**:** When a customer seeks the product and finds the inventory empty, the demand can either go unfulfilled or be satisfied later when the product becomes available. The former case is called a lost sale, and the latter is called a backorder. Although lost sales are often important in inventory analysis, they are not considered in this text, so no notation is assigned to it. The total backorder cost is assumed to be proportional to the number of units backordered and the time the customer must wait. The constant of proportionality is p, the per unit backorder cost. The dimensions of p are (\$/unit-time).

Discount Rate (α): As mentioned earlier, the holding cost consists primarily of the lost opportunity cost of having cash tied up in inventory. This cost is proportional to the value of the product and time value of money. The time value of money has various names, including interest rate, discount rate, and minimum acceptable rate of return. The dimensions of α are (1/time).

Deterministic - Continuous Review - Uniform Demand (18.3)

For every quantitative analysis it is necessary to abstract or simplify the system under study to obtain a mathematical model. The abstraction is usually identified by listing a set of "assumptions." It is not true that the analyst actually believes that the system obeys these assumptions; they are simplifications made for purposes of analysis. Whether the results obtained from a model that incorporates such assumptions will be useful is a subject that certainly deserves attention, but it is clear that an analysis is impossible without them.

This section describes the most abstract and hence simplest of the inventory control models. Although it is doubtful that any real inventory system actually operates as the model proposes, the results obtained are simple and easily implemented. Perhaps because of this, the results are widely known and used. This class of models is called the lot size model.

The assumptions of the model are described in part by Fig. 18.1, which shows a plot of inventory level as a function of time. The inventory level ranges between 0 and the amount Q (units). The fact that it never goes below 0 indicates that no shortages are allowed. Periodically an order is placed for replenishment of the inventory. The order quantity is Q. The arrival of the order is assumed to occur instantaneously, causing the inventory level to shoot from 0 to the amount Q. Between orders the inventory decreases constantly at a rate a. This assumes that the demand for the product is at a constant rate a (units/time). The time between orders is called the cycle and is the time required to use up the amount of the order quantity or Q/a. The dimension of the cycle time is (time).

A second lot size model considered in this section allows shortages to be backordered. This situation is illustrated in Fig. 18.2. In this model the inventory level decreases below the 0 level. This implies that a portion of the demand is backlogged. The maximum inventory level is S and occurs when the order arrives. The maximum backorder level is $Q–S$. A backorder is represented in the figure by negative inventory.

The third lot size model considered incorporates quantity discount prices that depend on the amount ordered. For this model no shortages are allowed, so the inventory pattern appears as in Fig. 18.1. The discounts will affect the optimum order quantity.

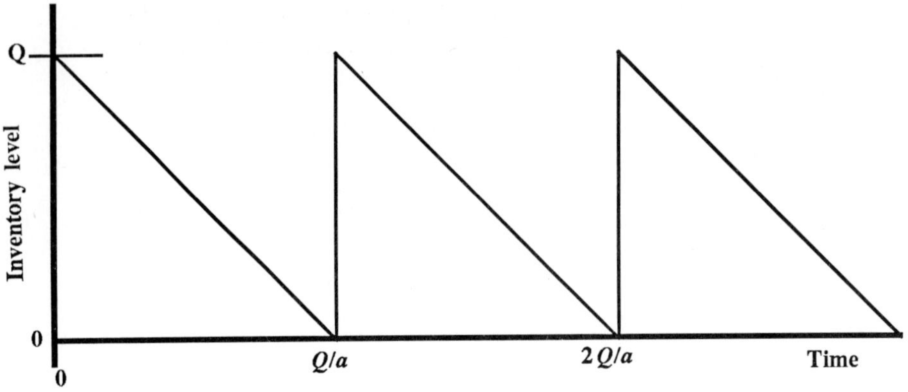

Figure 18.1 **Lot Size Model with No Shortages**

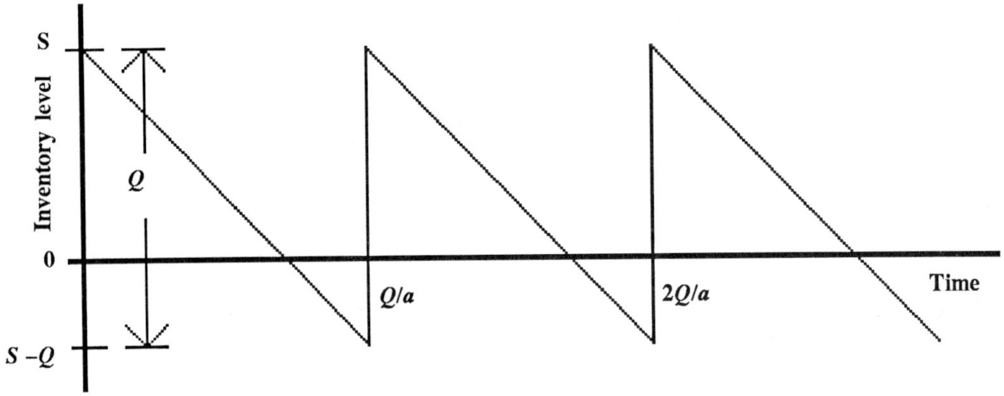

Figure 18.2 **Lot-Size Model with Shortages Allowed**

GOALS

- Know and be able to use the quantitative results for the lot size models that describe the optimum order quantity, the optimum cycle time, and, if appropriate, the optimum maximum backorder level.
- Be able to compute the costs of alternative policies.

DEFINITIONS

Demand Rate (a)**:** The rate at which the product is withdrawn from inventory (units/time).

Lot Size (Q)**:** The quantity received at each inventory replenishment (units).

Order Level (S): The maximum inventory level (units). When shortages are not allowed, this quantity is the same as Q. When shortages are allowed, it is less than Q.

Cycle Time (t): The time between consecutive inventory replenishments (time). For the models of this section $t = Q/a$.

Cost per Time (T): The total of all costs related to the inventory system that are affected by the decision under consideration ($/time).

Optimum Quantities (Q^*, S^*, t^*, T^*): The quantities defined above for the optimum solution.

The following definitions are for the model with quantity discounts. Here the price of the product depends on the quantity ordered.

Number of Different Prices (N)

The Order Quantity at Which the kth Price Becomes Effective (q_k) Note that this is a lower limit on the quantity ordered at the k th price level.

$$q_1 = 0 \text{ and } q_{N+1} = \infty.$$

Price at the k th Level (c_k) The price is in effect for orders $q_k \leq Q \leq q_{k+1}$.

RESULTS

These results are for the model in which shortages are not permitted as in Fig. 18.1.

Total Cost Model

$$T = \underbrace{[aK/Q]}_{\text{Setup cost}} + \underbrace{ac}_{\text{Product cost}} + \underbrace{[hQ/2].}_{\text{Holding cost}} \qquad (1)$$

Optimum Solution Setting to zero the derivative of T with respect to Q

$$Q^* = (2aK/h)^{1/2} \qquad (2)$$

$$t^* = Q^*/a. \qquad (3)$$

Note: the exponent 1/2 indicates that the square root is taken.

These results are for the model in which shortages are permitted as in Fig. 18.2.

Total Cost Model

$$T = \underbrace{[aK/Q]}_{\text{Setup cost}} + \underbrace{ac}_{\text{Product cost}} + \underbrace{[hS^2/2Q]}_{\text{Holding cost}} + \underbrace{[p(Q-S)/2Q].}_{\text{Backorder cost}} \qquad (4)$$

Optimum Solution Setting to zero the partial derivatives of T with respect to Q and S yields

$$S^* = [2aK/h]^{1/2}\ [p/(p+h)]^{1/2} \qquad (5)$$

$$Q^* = [\,2aK/h\,]^{1/2}\,[\,(p+h)/p\,]^{1/2} \qquad (6)$$

$$t^* = Q^* / a. \qquad (7)$$

These results are for the model with quantity discounts. No shortages are permitted. In this model the price of the product changes with the amount ordered.

Optimum Order Quantity at Level k (Q_k) Since the optimum order quantity determined by Eq. (2) is not affected by c, the value of Q_k would be the same for all price levels if not for the ranges of order size over which the prices are effective. Therefore compute Q^* with Eq. (2). Find for each k the value of Q_k such that

$$\text{if } q_{k+1} < Q^* \text{ then } Q_k = q_{k+1}, \qquad (8)$$

$$\text{if } q_k > Q^* \text{ then } Q_k = q_k, \qquad (9)$$

$$\text{if } q_k \le Q^* < q_{k+1} \text{ then } Q_k = Q^*. \qquad (10)$$

Optimum Order Quantity (Q^{**})

a. Find the level for which relation (10) is true. Let this be level n^*. Compute the total cost for this lot size with Eq. (1). Let this be T_{n^*}.
b. For each level $k > n^*$, compute the total cost T_k for the lot size Q_k.
c. Let k^* be the level that has the smallest value of T_k. The optimum lot size Q^{**} is the value of Q_{k^*}.

EXAMPLES

E18.1 A product has a constant demand of 100 units per week. The cost to place an order for inventory replenishment is $1000. The holding cost for a unit in inventory is $0.40 per week. No shortages are allowed. Find the optimum lot size and the corresponding cost of maintaining the inventory. Using Eq. (2), the optimum lot size is

$$Q^* = [\,(2 * 100 * 1000)/\,0.4\,]^{1/2} = 707.$$

Using (1) compute the value

$$T^* = \$282.84.$$

From Q* compute the cycle time,

$$t^* = 7.07 \text{ weeks}.$$

The unit cost of the product was not given in this problem because it is irrelevant to the determination of the optimum lot size. The product cost is, therefore, not included in T^*.

Although these results are easy to apply, a frequent mistake is to use inconsistent time dimensions for the various factors. Demand may be measured in units per week while holding cost may be measured in dollars per year. The results do not depend on the time dimension that is used; however, it is necessary that demand be translated to an annual basis or holding cost translated to a weekly basis.

E18.2 Suppose now that shortages are allowed. They are backordered at a cost of \$1 per unit-week. From Eqs. (5), (6), and (7) we find

$$S^* = [(2 * 100 * 1000)/0.4]^{1/2}\ [1/(1 + 0.4)]^{1/2} = 597.61$$
$$Q^* = [(2 * 100 * 1000)/0.4]^{1/2}\ [(1 + 0.4)/1]^{1/2} = 836.66$$
$$t^* = 836.66/100 = 8.36 \text{ weeks.}$$

From (1), using $c = 0$, we find

$$T^* = \$239.04.$$

The cost of operation has decreased since we have removed the constraint that no shortages are allowed. There is a shortage of 239 during each cycle.

E18.3 The company from which the inventory is purchased hopes to increase sales by offering a break on the price of the product for larger orders. For an amount purchased from 0 to 500 units the unit price is \$100. For orders at or above 500 but less than 1000, the unit price is \$90. Note that this price applies to all units purchased. For orders at or greater than 1000 units, the unit price is \$85. Find the optimum lot size.

From this data we establish that $N = 3$. Also

$$q_1 = 0 \text{ and } p_1 = 100,$$
$$q_2 = 500 \text{ and } p_2 = 90,$$
$$q_3 = 1000 \text{ and } p_3 = 85,$$
$$q_4 = \infty.$$

Neglecting the quantity ranges, the lot size is 707 regardless of price. We note that this quantity falls in the second price range. All lower ranges are then excluded. We must then compare the cost at $Q = 707$ and $p = 90$, with the cost at $Q = 1000$ and $p = 85$. We find, using Eq. (1) for these two cases,

$$T_2 = \$9{,}282 \text{ (for } Q = 707 \text{ and } p = 90)$$
$$T_3 = \$8{,}800 \text{ (for } Q = 1000 \text{ and } p = 85).$$

The optimum policy is to order 1000 for each replenishment. The cycle time associated with this policy is 10 weeks.

E18.4 A gift shop operator has a relatively constant demand for a certain type of wall hanging. She can order a case that holds 12 units for a cost of \$1200 or a gross that holds 144 units for \$13,000. These costs include delivery and product costs. The demand for the product is 12 units per month, so the alternatives represent ordering a 1-month or 1-year supply. As an approximation assume that demand is at a constant rate and no shortages are allowed. A principal concern for this business woman is the cost of capital, which is 20% per year. Which plan should she adopt?

In this case it is unnecessary to determine an optimum lot size, since only two alternatives are available. One must decide on the basis of the total cost formula.

Since the delivery cost is included in the product price, the analysis is to be made for unit prices, c_1 =1200/12 and c_2 =13000/144. The value of the holding cost depends on the amount invested in each unit of the product, $h_j = \alpha c_j$, where α =0.2. The demand is expressed on an annual basis of 144 units per year. The total cost considers only the terms for product and holding cost.

$$T_j = c_j a + h_j Q_j/2.$$

The two cases with the corresponding total costs are shown below.

$Q_1 = 12$	$Q_2 = 144$
$c_1 = 1200/12 = \$100$	$c_2 = 13000/144 = \$90.28$
$h_1 = 0.20 * 100 = \$20$	$h_2 = 0.20 * 90.28 = \$18.06$
$T_1 = 100 * 144 + 20 * 12/2 = \$14{,}520$	$T_2 = 90.28 * 144 + 18.06 * 144/2 = \$14{,}300.$

The case having the larger lot size and lower unit cost has a slight cost advantage. Practical considerations such as the risk of obsolescence of the inventory and financing might favor the smaller lot size.

MODELING

The inventory modeler has three principal tasks: constructing the mathematical model, specifying the values of the model parameters, and finding the optimum solution. This section has presented only the simplest cases, with the model specified as the total cost function. This model can be varied in a number of important aspects. For instance some texts consider noninstantaneous replenishment rate (see P18.2), multiple products, and constraints on maximum inventory.

Models will most often describe a nonlinear total cost function with only a few variables. Thus the classical optimization procedures of calculus sometimes can be used. Some assumptions, however, lead to complex optimization problems requiring nonlinear programming or other numerical methods.

The classical lot size formulas involve a number of assumptions that are not exactly satisfied in practice. Certainly the requirement of constant withdrawals from inventory is rarely met. To use the formulas for cases of random demand, the average demand rate can be estimated using the forecasting procedures of Chapter 19. Later sections of this chapter give procedures by which randomness may be handled explicitly. We leave the often difficult determination of the cost factors such as holding and backorder costs to the accountants. With the admitted difficulties of parameter estimation, one might question whether the lot size formulas should be used at all. That certainly is a valid question. Note, however, that whether or not the formulas are used, the lot size must be determined (it is done thousands of times every day). The formulas at least make apparent important relationships between the various cost factors and the lot size.

PROBLEMS

P18.1 It is now January 1. A hardware distributor is reviewing his inventory policy for hammers, which have a relatively constant demand of 2000 units per month. The distributor buys the hammers from his supplier for \$5 each and sells them for \$7. Every time he places an order for replenishment a shipping and paper preparation cost of \$500 is charged. The distributor's holding cost is 15% (annual) of his average investment in inventory. (Note that the holding cost is specified as $h = \alpha c$, so it is a function of the unit cost and does not include the delivery cost. This is the assumption required in order to use the lot size formulas in this unit.)

Answer each of the following independently (one part does not depend on another). Assume 20 working days per month.

a. The current inventory policy is to replenish the inventory every month. What is the total annual cost of this policy?
b. What is the optimum lot size when no shortages are allowed?
c. The distributor wants to order only at the beginning of the month, so the cycle time must be in whole months. What is the optimum lot size in this case?
d. An O.R. analyst suggests that money might be saved if the customers would accept backorders. If the distributor offers a discount of 1% of the purchase price for every day the customer has to wait for delivery, what is the optimum policy?
e. The supplier, in an effort to get larger orders, offers a \$0.10 discount on the price of hammers for an order of at least 10,000 units. Should the distributor take advantage of this deal? Assume no shortages are allowed.
f. It is now January 1, and the current inventory is 3500 units. There is a lead time (time between when the order is placed and when it is delivered) of 1 month. When should the next order be placed for the solutions of parts (b), (c), (d), and (e) of this problem?
g. Compute the monthly profit on hammers for parts (a), (b), (c), (d), and (e).

P18.2 Rather than an instantaneous replenishment of inventory as assumed in this unit, the inventory is replaced by a production process that can add units to the inventory at a constant rate $r (r > a)$. Of course the process cannot be operated continually but must be started and stopped. Each time the process is begun a setup cost K is expended. Otherwise the inventory problem is the same as previously stated. Derive a formula for the optimum lot size when no shortages are allowed.

P18.3 A meat market advertises that its' hamburger is the freshest in town. In order to get rid of old stock, the price of the hamburger is reduced by \$0.10 per pound for every hour it remains unsold after it is ground (for simplicity assume this reduction is linear in time). The demand for hamburger is 250 pounds per hour. No shortages are allowed. The cost to set up and run the hamburger grinder is \$100, independent of the amount processed. How much should be ground at each setup?

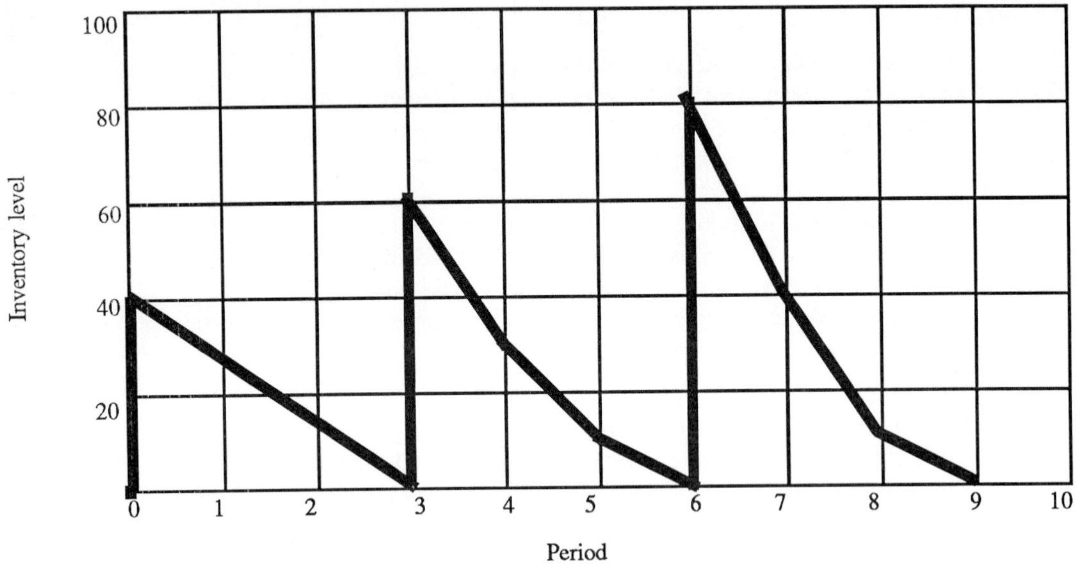

Figure 18.3 **Optimum Solution for the Example Problem**

Deterministic - Periodic Review - Production Planning (18.3)

In this unit we consider the situation in which inventory is reviewed and replenished at periodic points in time, perhaps every day, week, or month. The demand is no longer assumed to be constant but varies from period to period over a fixed time horizon. The demand is assumed to be deterministic. We are to find the optimum periods in which to replenish the inventory. This is a classic production scheduling problem for a single product. It is sometimes suggested as a way to determine a master production schedule for an MRP system (Materials Requirements Planning). H & L present three methods for solving the problem: dynamic programming, "an algorithm," and integer programming. We review the middle of the three because it is far more efficient that the other two. The method is really a type of dynamic programming algorithm and is called the Wagner-Whitin approach. Fig. 18.3 shows a typical inventory pattern.

GOAL

- Be able to solve the deterministic, periodic review, production planning problem with the Wagner-Whitin approach.

DEFINITIONS

The Planning Horizon (n)**:** The number of periods in the problem.

Period Demand (r_i)**:** The demand in period i, $1 \le i \le n$.

Holding Cost per Period (*h*)**:** The amount charged per unit of product remaining in the inventory at the end of a period. ($/unit-period).

Setup Cost (*K*)**:** The cost to set up for a production run, assumed independent of production quantity. Delivery of a production quantity occurs at the beginning of the period.

Cost of a Production Run (C_{ij})**:** The cost of making a production run at the beginning of period i which meets the demand for periods $i, i+1, \ldots, j$.

Unit Cost: We will not use the unit product cost in this section, since for constant unit cost the optimal policy is not affected.

RESULTS

Times for Production For the optimum solution in the situation described, production will take place only when the inventory reaches zero. Then the amount produced will equal the total demand for an integer number of periods.

Amount Produced The amount produced to meet the demand for periods i through j is

$$r_i + r_{i+1} + \ldots + r_j.$$

Cost of a Production Run The cost of a production run is the setup cost plus the total inventory cost until the next production run.

$$C_{ij} = K + h * (r_{i+1} + 2r_{i+2} + \ldots (j-i)\, r_j) \quad \text{for } j > i \qquad (11)$$
$$C_{ij} = K \quad \text{for } j = i.$$

Finding the Optimum Solution The optimum solution is found by solving the recursive equations

$$C(i,j) = C_{ij} + f_{j+1} \qquad \text{for } 1 \le i \le n, j \ge i. \qquad (12)$$
$$f_i = \min_{i \le j \le n} \{C(i, j)\} \qquad \text{for } 1 \le i \le n.$$
$$f_{n+1} = 0$$

The equations are solved in a backward order: $n, n-1, \ldots, 1$. Here f_i is the cost of the optimum production schedule starting at period i. $C(i,j)$ is the cost of producing to meet the demand from period i to period j and then following the optimum policy from period $j + 1$. The optimum policy, $x^*(i)$ is defined by the index that obtains the minimum for f_i.

EXAMPLE

E18.5 For this example assume that $K = 100$ and $h = 1$. Table 18.1 shows the period demands and the quantities C_{ij} for every $j \ge i$. Table 18.2 shows the computations of the dynamic programming approach together with the optimum policy.

Table 18.1. **The Values of C_{ij}**

Per.	1	2	3	4	5	6	7	8	9
r_i	10	20	10	30	20	10	40	30	10
9									100
8								100	110
7							100	130	150
6						100	140	200	230
5					100	110	190	280	320
4				100	120	140	260	380	430
3			100	130	170	200	360	510	570
2		100	110	170	230	270	470	650	720
1	100	120	140	230	310	360	600	810	890

Table 18.2. **The Values of $C(i,j)$, f_i, and x^*_i.**

Per.	1	2	3	4	5	6	7	8	9		
r_i	10	20	10	30	20	10	40	30	10	f_i	x^*_i
9									100	100	9
8								200	110	110	9
7							210	230	150	150	9
6						250	250	300	230	230	9
5					330	260	300	380	320	260	6
4				360	350	290	370	480	430	290	6
3			390	390	400	350	470	610	570	350	6
2		450	400	430	460	420	580	750	720	400	3
1	500	470	430	490	540	510	710	910	890	430	3

Recovering the optimum solution from Table 18.2 results in the following conclusions.

- The optimum solution in period 1 is $x^*_1 = 3$, implying that the production is for periods 1, 2, and 3 for a quantity of 40.
- The next production is in period 4. From $x^*_4 = 6$, we discover that the next quantity is the sum of the demands from periods 4 through 6 or 60.
- The next production is in period 7. From $x^*_7 = 9$, we discover that the next quantity is the sum of the demands from periods 7 through 9 or 80.
- The cost of the optimum is $f_1 = 430$.

The inventory pattern of the solution is shown in Fig. 18.3. The number of computations required for this procedure is proportional to $n(n + 1) / 2$. They can easily be accomplished using a spreadsheet program on a microcomputer.

PROBLEMS

P18.4 Solve E18.5 when $K = 50$ and then with $K = 200$. Compare the solutions to that obtained for $K = 100$.

P18.5 Estimate the demand rate per period as the average of the period demands given in E18.5. Using the values of K and h given in the example and the lot size formulas of the last unit (no shortages allowed), find the optimum order quantity Q. Use this lot size on the example problem with the rule that production must be performed at the beginning of a period if otherwise a shortage would occur. Compare the costs of this solution with the cost of the solution determined with the Wagner-Whitin algorithm.

P18.6 Use $K = 100$, $h = 1$, and $n = 10$. The following is the sequence of period demands: 40, 20, 10, 50, 40, 20, 10, 20, 10, 30. Find the optimum production policy.

Stochastic Models (18.4)

There is no question that uncertainty plays a role in most inventory management situations. The retail merchant wants enough supply to satisfy customer demands, but ordering too much increases holding costs and the risk of losses through obsolescence or spoilage. An order too small increases the risk of lost sales and unsatisfied customers. The water resources manager must set the amount of water stored in a reservoir at a level that balances the risk of flooding and the risk of shortages. The production manager sets a master production schedule considering the imprecise nature of forecasts of future demands, the lead times of the production process which themselves are uncertain, and the fact that completed final products bear more inventory costs than raw materials. These situations are common, and the answers one gets from a deterministic analysis very often are not satisfactory when uncertainty is present. The decision maker faced with uncertainty does not act in the same way as the one who operates with perfect knowledge of the future.

In this and the next four sections we deal with inventory models in which the stochastic nature of demand is explicitly recognized. Several models are presented which again are only abstractions of the real world, but whose answers can provide guidance and insight to the inventory manager. A number of interesting questions have been considered by researchers, and several are described in this chapter of H & L. In this guide, however, we restrict consideration to those results that can be easily applied to find numeric answers. The following goals relate to all the sections on stochastic models.

GOALS

- Given a practical problem, be able to determine which of the four models listed below is most appropriate or whether none is appropriate.

  Single period with no setup cost
  Single period with setup cost
  Multiperiod with no setup cost and an infinite horizon
  Continuous review with fixed delivery lag time

- Know the quantitative results for each of the models and be able to apply them given specific numerical information.

DEFINITIONS

Random Variable for Demand (D): A random variable which is the demand for a given period of time. Care must be taken to recognize the period for which the random variable is defined because it differs among the models considered.

Discrete Demand Probability Distribution ($P(d)$): When demand is assumed to be a discrete random variable this gives the probability that the demand equals d. It is defined over all feasible values of d. (*Note:* The distribution should have a subscript D to indicate that demand is the random variable. Since demand is the only random variable considered, however, we delete the subscript here and for the other distributions listed below.)

Continuous Demand Probability Density Function ($\phi(\xi)$): When demand is assumed to be continuous, this is its density function. The variable ξ is a variable of integration, because the function always appears as part of an integral.

$$P(a \le D \le b) = \int_a^b \phi(\xi)\, d\xi$$

Discrete Cumulative Distribution Function ($F(b)$): The probability that demand is less than or equal to b when demand is discrete.

$$F(b) = \sum_{d=0}^{b} P(d). \tag{13}$$

Continuous Cumulative Distribution Function ($\Phi(b)$): The probability that demand is less than or equal to b when demand is continuous.

$$\Phi(b) = \int_0^b \phi(\xi)\, d\xi . \tag{14}$$

Parameters will be defined separately for each of the models. Take care that definitions are followed carefully, because parameters with similar notation take various meanings in the different models.

MODELING

An important modeling decision concerns which distribution to use for demand. A common assumption of queueing theory is that individual demand events occur independently. This assumption leads to the Poisson distribution when the expected demand in a time interval is small and the normal distribution when the expected demand is large. Let a be the average demand rate. Then for an interval of time t the expected demand is at. The Poisson distribution is then

$$P(d) = \frac{e^{-(at)}(at)^d}{d!} \tag{15}$$

This can be evaluated with a calculator or with a Poisson table.

When at is large the Poisson distribution can be approximated with a normal distribution with mean and standard deviation

$$\mu = at \qquad \sigma = (at)^{1/2}. \qquad (16)$$

Values of $\Phi(b)$ can be evaluated for a normal distribution using the standard normal deviant

$$z = (b - at)/(at)^{1/2}.$$

Of course other distributions can be assumed for demand. Common assumptions are the normal distribution with other values of the mean and standard deviation, the uniform distribution, and the exponential distribution. The latter two are useful for their analytical simplicity. Formulas for these are given below.
Uniform distribution ranging from A to B :

$$\phi(\xi) = 1/(B-A) \text{ for } A \le \xi \le B \qquad (17)$$
$$= 0 \text{ otherwise}$$
$$\Phi(b) = (b-A)/(B-A) \text{ for } A \le b \le B \qquad (18)$$
$$= 0 \text{ for } b \le A$$
$$= 1 \text{ for } b \ge B.$$

Exponential Distribution with mean demand equal to λ :

$$\phi(\xi) = (1/\lambda)\, e^{-(\xi/\lambda)} \text{ for } \xi \ge 0 \qquad (19)$$
$$\Phi(b) = 1 - e^{-(b/\lambda)} \text{ for } b \ge 0. \qquad (20)$$

Stochastic - Single-Period - No Setup Cost (18.4)

This model is for an inventory situation in which the current order for the replenishment of inventory can be evaluated independently of future decisions. Such cases occur when inventory cannot be added later (e.g., spares for a space trip, stocks for the Christmas season), or when inventory spoils or becomes obsolete (e.g., fresh fruit, current newspapers). The problem may have multiple periods, but the current inventory decision must be independent of future periods.

GOAL

- Be able to identify when this model is appropriate, extract parameter values from a problem description, find the optimum operating policy, and compute the expected cost for this policy.

DEFINITIONS

Purchase Cost per Unit (c): The cost of obtaining the inventory is assumed to be a linear function of the amount ordered (\$/unit).

Holding Cost (h): The cost of storage less the salvage value charged to the amount of inventory remaining at the end of the period. The value of h may be negative if the revenue received from remaining items is greater than the cost of storage (\$/unit).

Cost per Unit of Unsatisfied Demand (p)**:** When inventory is not sufficient to meet demand, sales are lost (not backordered). This cost includes "loss of good will" and the income lost because of the shortage. If the demand is actually met by some extraordinary means such as buying the stock from a different supplier, this cost is also included ($/unit).

Initial Inventory Level (x)**:** The amount of inventory available before the order is placed (units).

Order Level (y)**:** This is the decision variable to be determined by the analysis. It is the desired inventory at the beginning of the period after the order is placed. When an order is made, the order quantity is $y - x$. (units).

RESULTS

These are the results when the demand is a discrete random variable.

Total Expected Cost

$$C(y) = cy + \sum_{d=y}^{\infty} p(d-y)P(d) + \sum_{d=0}^{y-1} h(y-d)P(d). \tag{21}$$

Product cost — Shortage cost — Holding cost

Optimal Solution (y°) The optimal order level is the smallest integer such that

$$F(y^\circ) \geq \frac{p-c}{p+h}. \tag{22}$$

These are the results when the demand is a continuous random variable.

Total Expected Cost

$$C(y) = cy + \int_y^{\infty} p(\xi - y)\,\phi(\xi)\,d\xi + \int_0^{y} h(y-\xi)\,\phi(\xi)\,d\xi. \tag{23}$$

Product cost — Shortage cost — Holding cost

Optimal Solution (y°) The optimal order level is the value such that

$$\Phi(y^\circ) = \frac{p-c}{p+h}. \tag{24}$$

Optimal Order Policy In both discrete and continuous cases, the optimum policy is

$$\text{If } x < y^\circ, \text{ then order } y^\circ - x \tag{25}$$

$$\text{If } x > y^\circ, \text{ then order none.}$$

EXAMPLES

E18.6 The classic illustration of this problem involves a newsboy who must purchase a quantity of newspapers for the day's sale. The purchase price of the papers is $0.10 and they can be sold to customers for a price of $0.25. Papers unsold at the end of the day can be returned to the publisher for \$0.02. The boy does not like to disappoint his customers (who might turn elsewhere for supply), so he estimates a "good will" cost of \$0.15 for each customer who will not be satisfied if the supply of papers runs out. The boy has kept a record of sales and shortages, and estimates that the mean demand during the day is 250 and the standard deviation is 50. A normal distribution is assumed. How many papers should he purchase?

This is a single-period problem because today's newspapers will be obsolete tomorrow. The factors required by the analysis are

c = 0.10, the purchase price of each paper.
h = –0.02, the net cost of excess inventory at the end of the day. It is negative because the 2 cents is an income.
p = 0.40, the lost income of an unsold paper plus the "good will" cost.

Since we have assumed a continuous distribution, Eq. (24) can be used to find the optimum order level.

$$\Phi(y^\circ) = \frac{0.40 - 0.10}{0.40 - 0.02} = 0.789.$$

From the cumulative normal distribution table we find that

$$P(z < 0.80) = 0.788.$$

Since $z = (y^\circ - \mu)/\sigma$, solve for y°,

$$y^\circ = \sigma z + \mu = (50)(0.8) + 250 = 290.$$

Notice that the risk of a shortage during a day is

$$1 - \Phi(y^\circ) = 0.212.$$

E18.7 A submarine has a very critical component that has a reliability problem. The submarine is beginning a 1-year cruise, and the supply officer must determine how many spares of the component to stock. Analysis shows that the time between failures of the component is 6 months. A failed component cannot be repaired but must be replaced from the spares stock. Only the component actually in operation may fail; components in the spares stock do not fail. If the stock is exhausted an expensive resupply will be accomplished with a cost of \$75,000 per component. The component has a unit cost of \$10,000 if stocked at the beginning of the cruise. Component spares also use up space and other scarce resources. To reflect these factors a cost of \$25,000 is added for every component remaining unused at the end of the trip. There is essentially no value to spares remaining at the end of the trip because of technical obsolescence.

This is a single-period problem because the decision is to be made only for the current trip. Failures occur at random, with an average rate of 2 per year. Thus the expected number of failures during the cruise is 2. The number of failures has a Poisson distribution. The parameters required for the analysis are

$c =$ 10,000, the purchase cost of each component.
$h =$ 25,000, the implied cost of a component remaining unused at the end of the trip.
$p =$ 75,000, the resupply cost after the spares are exhausted.

Since the number of failures has a discrete distribution, Eq. (22) is relevant.

$$F(y^\circ) \geq \frac{75{,}000 - 10{,}000}{75{,}000 + 25{,}000} = 0.65.$$

From a cumulative Poisson distribution table using a mean of 2, or from Eqs. (15) and (13), we find

$$F(0) = 0.135$$
$$F(1) = 0.406$$
$$F(2) = 0.677$$
$$F(3) = 0.857.$$

The smallest value that exceeds 0.65 occurs for $y^\circ = 2$. Thus we have the surprising result that only two spares should be brought. This is in addition to the component initially installed so that only on the third failure will a resupply be required. The probability of one or more resupply is

$$1 - F(2) = 0.323.$$

The resupply operation is an aspect of the situation that makes this model appropriate. If the system simply stopped after the spares were exhausted and a single cost of failure were expended, then the assumption of the linear cost of lost sales would be violated. The model might be used in such a situation, however, recognizing that some approximation is involved.

PROBLEM

P18.7 A garden nursery has a short selling season of 20 days for a certain kind of tree. The nursery currently has 20 such trees in stock and has one last opportunity to order more. The expected demand for trees is 3 per day, but the actual demand has a Poisson distribution. The nursery purchases the trees for \$75 and sells them for \$175. Trees remaining at the end of the season must be cared for until the next year. The cost of such care per tree is \$20 and the holding cost on investment is \$2. If demand occurs after the inventory is exhausted, the sales are lost. Find the number of trees that should be ordered and the probability that this inventory will be sufficient to meet all demand. (Note that since leftover trees will actually be kept after the season and eventually sold, the purchase cost is not relevant. Only the shortage cost and holding cost should be used.)

Stochastic - Single Period - Setup Cost (18.4)

In this section we add a setup cost to the single-period model. With no setup cost it is always advisable to place a replenishment order unless the initial inventory is already greater than the optimum order level. With a setup cost there will be some amount smaller than the order level, called the reorder point. If the initial inventory is below the reorder point, it will be advisable to place an order, but if it is above the reorder point, no order should be placed. In this and the following sections we deal with only continuous demand distributions.

GOAL

- Be able to identify when this model is appropriate, extract parameter values from a problem description, find the optimum operating policy, and compute the expected cost for this policy.

DEFINITIONS

Setup Cost (K): The fixed cost required to order any nonzero amount.

(s, S) Inventory Policy: A policy in which an order is placed when the inventory level x is below s. The amount ordered is $S - x$. The reorder point is s and the order level is S.

RESULTS

Expected Shortage Plus Holding Cost When the initial inventory level is y, the expected shortage plus inventory cost is

$$L(y) = \int_y^{\infty} p[\xi - y]\, \phi(\xi)\, d\xi + \int_0^{y} h[y - \xi]\, \phi(\xi)\, d\xi. \qquad (26)$$

Optimum Order Level The value of S that statisfies the equation

$$\Phi(S) = \frac{p - c}{p + h}. \qquad (27)$$

Optimum Reorder Point The value of s that satisfies the equation

$$cs + L(s) = K + cS + L(S). \qquad (28)$$

Optimum Policy

If $x < s$, order up to S, an amount $(S - x)$ (29)

If $x \geq s$, do not order.

EXAMPLES

E18.8 For a single-period model the current level of inventory is 100 units. The demand for the next period is a random variable with a uniform distribution ranging from 50 to 250 units. The purchase cost of an item is \$100. The selling price is \$150. Items unsold at the end of the period go "on sale" for \$20. All will be disposed of at this price. If the inventory is not sufficient, sales are lost, with a penalty equal to the selling price of the item. Additional items may be ordered at this time; however, a delivery fee will consist of a fixed charge of \$500 plus \$10 per item ordered. How many items should be ordered?

To analyze this problem first determine the parameters of the model.

c = \$110, the purchase cost plus the variable portion of the delivery fee
K = \$500, the fixed portion of the delivery fee
p = \$150, the lost income associated with a lost sale
h = –\$20, the negative of the salvage value of the product.

From (27), the reorder level is S such that

$$\Phi(S) = \frac{150 - 110}{150 - 20} = 0.31.$$

Setting the cumulative distribution for the uniform distribution (Eq. (17)) equal to this value and solving for S,

$$\Phi(S) = (S - 50)/(250 - 50) = 0.31.$$
$$S = 112.$$

To obtain a general equation for $L(y)$ for the uniform distribution, substitute the density function into Eq. (26).

$$L(y) = \int_y^B p\,[(\xi - y)/(B - A)]\,d\xi + \int_A^y h[(y - \xi)/(B - A)]\,d\xi.$$

$$L(y) = \frac{p(B - y)^2 + h(y - A)^2}{2(B - A)} \qquad (30)$$

$$= [150(250 - y)^2 + (-20)(y - 50)^2]/400.$$

Evaluating this equation at $y = S = 112$,

$$L(112) = 6949.$$

Inserting the parameters into Eq. (28)

$$110s + [150\,(250 - s)^2 + (-20)\,(s - 50)^2]\,/\,400 = 500 + 12320 + 6949.$$

Solving for s to the nearest integer

$$s = 72.$$

The current inventory level falls above the reorder point, so no additional inventory should be purchased. If there were no fixed charge for delivery, the order would be for 12 units.

Note: The solution to the quadratic $ax^2 + bx + c = 0$ is

$$x = (-b \pm [b^2 - 4ac]^{1/2})/2a.).$$

E18.9 Answer E18.8 if demand has an exponential distribution with a mean value of 150. Using Eq. (20) for the exponential distribution with $\lambda = 150$,

$$\Phi(S) = 1 - e^{-(S/150)} = 0.31.$$

Solving for S,

$$S = -150 \ \ln\ (1 - 0.31) = 56.$$

In this section, H & L show that the difference between s and S for the exponential distribution is approximately

$$\Delta = S - s = [(2\lambda K/(c + h)]^{1/2} = [(2(150)(500)/(110 - 20)]^{1/2} = 41$$
$$s = 56 - 41 = 15.$$

For this distribution of demand, the current inventory is considerably above both the order point and the order level. Certainly an order should not be placed.

PROBLEM

P18.8 With the parameters given in E18.8 the probability of a shortage is almost 70%. Management has determined that this is too high. A level of 10% is considered an acceptable probability of shortage. If all other parameters remain the same, what penalty is implicitly being charged for a shortage? For this value find the policy for the uniform distribution of E18.8 and the exponential distribution of E18.9.

Stochastic - Multiperiod - No Setup Cost (18.4)

Most inventories are ongoing in time with the inventory level increasing when a replenishment is received and decreasing as demand causes items to be withdrawn. We previously considered this case for deterministic demand and obtained the lot size models of section 18.3. When demand is stochastic the economic lot size policies are not appropriate, or at least must be modified. In this unit we consider a multiperiod model in which periodic inventory replenishment decisions must be made. Sometimes this is called a periodic review model. At the moment of review, the current inventory level is observed and a decision is made on how much to order. We could also consider the question whether or not an order should be placed, but since we are here considering the case of "no setup cost," this question is not relevant.

In this section we are making the assumption of an infinite time horizon and a demand probability distribution that does not vary over time. In this case the solution is simple. Alternative assumptions that allow a nonzero setup cost, a finite time horizon, or a time variable demand distribution can conceivably be solved by dynamic programming; however, there are significant computational difficulties.

GOAL

- Be able to identify when this model is appropriate, extract parameter values from a problem description, and find the optimum operating policy.

DEFINITIONS

Period: The interval of time between consecutive reviews of the inventory level.

Random Variable for Demand (D): In this section the random variable is the demand for one period.

Discount Factor (α): This is the factor that represents the current value of $1 received or spent one time period in the future. If r is the interest rate for one period then

$$\alpha = 1/(1 + r).$$

Holding Cost (h): This is the holding cost of having one unit in inventory at the end of a period ($/unit). The quantity may sometimes be estimated as cr, where r is the interest rate defined above.

Backorder Cost (p): This model assumes shortages are backordered. The cost should be the penalty associated with the backorder and not the lost income, as sometimes assumed in the single-period case ($/unit).

Unit Product Cost (c): The cost of purchasing one unit for the inventory. ($/unit).

RESULTS

Optimum Order Level (y°) Find y° such that

$$\Phi(y^\circ) = \frac{p - c(1-\alpha)}{p + h} \tag{31}$$

Optimum Policy Order in every period the amount $(y^\circ - x)$, where x is the inventory level at the beginning of the period.

EXAMPLES

E18.10 Consider an inventory system in which the inventory is reviewed every month. The monthly demand for the product is assumed to have a normal distribution with a mean of 100 and a standard deviation of 20. The interest rate used for time value of money calculations is 12% per year. The purchase cost of the product is $1000 and it is sold for $1600. When it is necessary to backorder a customer request, the cost of paperwork and good will is estimated to be $200. Holding cost is estimated using the interest cost of the money invested in a unit of inventory. Find the optimum inventory policy.

The parameters of the model are

r = 0.12/12 = 0.01, the interest rate per month
h = 1000 (0.01) = $10, the cost of holding one unit for one month
p = 200, the cost of backordering one unit
$\alpha = 1/(1 + r) = 0.990$, the current value of $1 received in one month

With these values the optimal policy can be determined.

$$\Phi(y^\circ) = \frac{200 - 1000(1 - 0.990)}{200 + 10} = 0.957.$$

Using a normal table, we find that the cumulative distribution has the value 0.905 for $z = 1.31$. Thus the value order level is

$$y^\circ = 100 + 20(1.31) = 126.$$

The optimum policy is to order a quantity $(126 - x)$ each month. The probability of a shortage during the month is

$$1 - \Phi(y^\circ) = 0.097.$$

E18.11 Analyze the situation of E18.10 if the review period were every 2 months. The revised parameters are

r = 0.12/6 = 0.02, the interest rate for the 2-month period
h = 1000 (0.02) = \$20, the cost of holding one unit for one period
p = 200, the cost of backordering one unit
α = $1/(1 + r)$ = 0.980, the current value of \$1 received in 2 months.
(This assumes a simple interest computation.)

The distribution of demand must now be found for the 2-month period. Assuming monthly demands are independent,

$$\mu = 100 + 100 = 200, \quad \sigma = [2(20^2)]^{1/2} = 28.28.$$

Now the optimal policy can be determined.

$$\Phi(y^\circ) = \frac{200 - 1000(1 - 0.980)}{200 + 20} = 0.820.$$

Using a normal table, we find the value $z = 0.91$. Thus the order level is

$$y^\circ = 200 + 28.28(0.91) = 226.$$

The optimum policy is to order a quantity $(226 - x)$ each period.

PROBLEM

P18.9 Find the optimum order level for an inventory system for which orders are placed every 2 weeks. The weekly demand has a normal distribution with a mean of 25 and a standard deviation 5. The cost of the item is \$20. Interest per year is 20%. Assume a 50-week year. The backorder cost is \$5 per unit.

Stochastic - Continuous Review - Fixed Delivery Lag (18.4)

This model assumes continuous review of the inventory level (the last section assumed periodic review). When the level reaches some specified reorder point, s, an order is placed for a lot of size Q. This is called a (Q, s) policy. After the order is placed, it arrives to replenish the inventory after a fixed lead time λ. The random demand during the lead time gives rise to the possibility of a shortage before the inventory is replenished. Shortages are backordered. The problem is to choose the reorder point and lot size to minimize expected total cost, which includes setup cost, inventory holding cost, and backorder cost.

GOAL

- Be able to identify when this model is appropriate, extract parameter values from a problem description, find the optimum operating policy, and compute the expected cost for this policy.

DEFINITIONS

Lead Time (λ): The time between the placing of an order and the replenishment of the inventory.

Random Variable for Demand (D): The demand during the lead time.

Probability Density for Demand ($\phi(\xi)$): A continuous probability density for the demand during the lead time. With the average demand rate equal to a, the expected value is $a\lambda$.

Setup Cost (K): The fixed cost associated with placing an order. ($).

Holding Cost (h): The cost of holding an item for one unit of time. This is multiplied by average inventory level to obtain total cost. ($/unit-time).

Shortage Cost (p): The cost incurred for each unit of demand not met during the lead time. Shortages are backordered. ($/unit).

Unit Cost (c): The unit purchase cost of inventory items. ($/unit).

Reorder Point (s): The inventory level that triggers an order. (units).

Order Quantity (Q): The size of the order. (units).

Total Cost (E(Q, s)): The expected total cost as a function of Q and s. ($/time).

RESULTS

Expected Ordering Cost ($/time)

$$\mathrm{E(OC)} = (a/Q)(K + cQ) = (aK/Q) + ac. \tag{32}$$

Expected Holding Cost ($/time)

$$\mathrm{E(HC)} = h\,(Q/2 + s - a\lambda). \tag{33}$$

Expected Shortage Cost (\$/time)

$$E(SC) = (ap/Q)\left[\int_s^{\infty} (\xi - s)\,\phi(\xi)\,d\xi\right] \tag{34}$$

Expected Total Cost (\$/time)

$$E(Q, s) = E(OC) + E(HC) + E(SC). \tag{35}$$

Optimum Order Quantity (units)

$$Q^* = [\{2a\,[K + p\int_{s^*}^{\infty} (\xi - s^*)\,\phi(\xi)\,d\xi\,]\}/h]^{1/2}. \tag{36}$$

Optimum Reorder Point (units) Find s^* so that

$$\int_{s^*}^{\infty} \phi(\xi)\,d\xi = h\,Q^*/p\,a. \tag{37}$$

Q^* and s^* are functions of each other, so they cannot be determined independently. Given any s, however, the optimum order quantity can be found by substituting s for s^* in Eq. (36). Similarly, given a value for Q, the associated optimum reorder point is found by substituting Q for Q^* in Eq. (37). If the optimums for both quantities are desired, they can be found by a successive approximation procedure.

EXAMPLES

E18.12 In E18.10 a multiperiod problem is described in which orders are placed every month. An alternative is to adopt a continuous review policy in which the order quantity is the average demand for 1 month. The lead time for this situation is 1 week. The fixed order cost is \$800. Analyze this alternative using the data of E18.10.

We must first adopt a time dimension for those data items related to time. Here we use 1 year to contrast with E18.10, which, because of the period, used 1 month. For this selection,

a = 1200 units/year, the average monthly demand multiplied by 12.
h = 1000(0.12) = \$120/unit-year, the unit cost multiplied by the interest rate.
p = \$200, the backorder cost, which is independent in time.
K = \$800, given in the problem statement.

We must also describe the distribution of demand during the lead time. E18.10 specified the demand per month as normally distributed with mean 100 and standard deviation 20. For convenience we assume that 1 month has 4 weeks and that the demands in the weeks are independent and identically distributed normal variates. With these assumptions the weekly demand has

$$\mu = 100/4 = 25 \qquad \sigma^2 = 20^2/4 = 100 \text{ or } \sigma = 10.$$

The problem specifies the value of Q as 1 month's demand; thus $Q = 100$. Using this value in (37) we can find the associated optimum reorder point.

$$\int_{s^*}^{\infty} \phi(\xi)\,d\xi = (120)(100)/(200)(1200) = 0.05.$$

Note that this is the right-hand tail of the normal distribution. From a normal table we find that this is associated with a standard normal deviant of $z = 1.64$. The reorder point is then

$$s^* = \mu + (1.64)\sigma = 25 + 1.64\ (10) = 41.4 \approx 42 \text{ (conservatively rounded up).}$$

This is the optimum for the given value of Q. The quantity computed with Eq. (37) is the risk of shortage during the lead time. We find that value to be 5%.

E18.13 If the reorder point is fixed at 50 for E18.12, what is the optimum order quantity?

For a normal distribution we find that the expected shortage is

$$\int_s^\infty (\xi - s)\,\phi(\xi)\,d\xi = \sigma G_u(z)$$

where $z = (s - \mu)/\sigma$. We compute* for $s = 50$, $z = 2.5$,

$$G_u(2.5) = 0.002004.$$

and the expected shortage per period is

$$\sigma G_u(2.5) = 0.02004$$

Now from Eq. (36)

$$Q^* = [2(1200)[\,800 + 200(0.02004)]/120]^{1/2} = 126.6 \approx 127.$$

E18.14 Find the optimum, Q^* and s^* for the data of E18.12. First assume $p = 0$ and solve (36) for $Q = 126.5$. Using this value in (37), with $p = 200$, we find the associated reorder point

$$s = 40.3 \text{ with } z = 1.53.$$

The expected shortage per period with this reorder point is

$$\sigma G_u(1.53) = (10)(0.02736) = 0.2736$$

From Eq. (36)

$$Q = [2(1200)[800 + 200(0.2736)]/120]^{1/2} = 130.7.$$

From Eq. (37) we find the reorder point corresponding to this lot size.

$$s = 40.1 \text{ with } z = 1.51.$$

Using Eq. (36) with the value of $G_u(1.51) = 0.2865$, we find

$$Q = 130.9.$$

It appears that the values are converging, so we adopt the policy

$$Q^* = 131 \text{ and } s^* = 40.$$

* $G_u(z) = \phi_u(z) - z(1 - \Phi_u(z))$, where ϕ_u and Φ_u are the density function and cumulative distribution of the standard (or unit) normal. For a derivation of these results and tables of $G_u(z)$ see Silver, E. A., and R. Peterson, *Decision Systems for Inventory Management and Production Planning*, John Wiley and Sons, 1985.

PROBLEMS

P18.10 Using the data of E18.12 compute the optimum (Q, s) policy when the following changes are made. The changes are not cumulative.

- **a.** The average demand doubles but the standard deviation remains the same.
- **b.** The standard deviation of demand per week doubles.
- **c.** The fixed setup cost doubles.
- **d.** The holding cost doubles.
- **e.** The backorder cost doubles.
- **f.** The lead time doubles.

P18.11 Use the data of P18.9 and add the information that the setup cost is $200 and the lead time is 1 week. Find the optimum continuous review policy when:

- **a.** the order quantity is set to the average demand for 1 month.
- **b.** the reorder point is set at the average demand over the lead time.
- **c.** neither the reorder point nor the order quantity is specified.

Problems

P18.12 Light bulbs come in cases of 144 bulbs. A case of bulbs costs $200. An office building uses bulbs at an average rate of 1000 bulbs per month. The company that sells the bulbs charges $50 per delivery, regardless of the number of cases delivered. The management of the building uses a 15% annual carrying cost rate for inventory. No shortages are allowed.

- **a.** Assuming the usage rate for bulbs is constant, how many cases of bulbs should be ordered in each delivery? Only whole cases can be ordered.
- **b.** With this order quantity, how often will bulbs be delivered?
- **c.** A long-standing policy has been to receive 10 cases per delivery. What is the annual cost penalty of this nonoptimum policy over the cost of the optimum policy?

P18.13 Find the optimum policy for P18.12 if backorders are allowed. A failed bulb is simply not replaced until the beginning of the next month if the supply is exhausted. The management assumes a "loss of good will" charge of $10 per bulb per month for backorders.

P18.14 The demand for some product is shown below for the next 10-months. The setup cost for producing the product is $1000. The inventory cost is $15 per unit per month (charged on inventory remaining at the end of any month). Determine the optimum production schedule using the Wagner-Whitin method.

Week	1	2	3	4	5	6	7	8	9	10
Demand	20	30	50	10	5	10	20	30	40	20

P18.15 A supplier of rebuilt engines expects an average of three engine customers every 2 months. Customers arrive as a Poisson process. She obtains her engines from a manufacturer who delivers with a lead time of 2 months.

a. What should be the supplier's reorder point if she wants a 60% chance of not having a shortage during the lead time?
b. What should be the reorder point if the lead time were 1 month?

P18.16 A dishonest developer wants to make quick money building a condominium. He sets a 1-year time table for his activities, after which he will leave town for places unknown. His problem is to determine how many units to build. He estimates the following probabilities for the demand for his units. In the table below, x is the number of units demanded and $p(x)$ is the probability of that demand.

x	1	2	3	4	5	6	7	8
$p(x)$	0.02	0.03	0.09	0.14	0.19	0.14	0.10	0.05
x	9	10	11	12	13	14	15	
$p(x)$	0.05	0.05	0.04	0.04	0.03	0.02	0.01	

The selling price for a condo unit is \$100,000, while it will cost only \$40,000 to build it. If the year passes and he has not sold all his units, he will have to dump them for \$20,000 each. How many units should he build to maximize his expected profit?

P18.17 A military commander faces a dangerous mission which requires the use of helicopters. The commander wants to determine how many to bring on the mission. The helicopters cost \$1 million each. At least five are required for mission success. Any number less than five is judged a serious detriment to the mission. In order to quantify the situation, the commander has attached a cost of \$10 million for every unit less than five that finishes the mission. Any units that remain at the end of the mission are destroyed.

Failure-causing events are assumed to occur at random on the average of once every hour. The number of events is independent of the number of helicopters active. Each event will destroy one helicopter. The mission lasts 15 hours.

How many helicopters should the commander bring?

P18.18 Consider a problem with the following parameters: c = \$10, h = \$1, p = \$100, and K = \$200. Find the optimum (s, S) policy when:

a. demand has a uniform distribution with $A = 20$ and $B = 60$.
b. demand is exponential with $\lambda = 40$.

P18.19 Consider the situation of P18.12 except that demand is stochastic rather than deterministic. The weekly demand for light bulbs is a random variable with a normal distribution that has a mean of 250 bulbs and a standard deviation of 50 bulbs. An order for bulbs is placed once a month (on the first of the month) and the order is delivered right away. If the supply of bulbs runs out and a bulb fails, the tenant simply must wait until the beginning of the next month. For purposes of analysis, this event is assumed to have a cost of \$1. Assume for simplicity that months are 4 weeks long and that there are 48 weeks in a year. What specific numerical rule should the management use to determine how much to order each month?

P18.20 The average demand for a product at a warehouse is 1200 units per year. Customers arrive at random (a Poisson process) so the exact demand for any given period of time cannot be computed. The warehouse manager replenishes the inventory by a monthly order to the factory. The size of the order equals the previous month's sales.

a. What kind of inventory system is this?
b. What order level will provide a 95% chance that the inventory will not run out during an order cycle?

P18.21 The manager in P18.20 installs computerized inventory control so that continuous review is possible. He adopts a (Q, s) policy. A lead time of 1 week passes between when an order is placed and when the inventory is replenished. A lot size of 100 is selected. Assume a month is 4 weeks.

a. What reorder point will provide a 95% chance that the inventory will not run out during an order cycle?
b. What is the average cycle time for this plan?

P18.22 A gasoline distributor has a weekly demand that is highly variable. The average demand is 10,000 gallons per week; however, the standard deviation is 3000 gallons. His demand per week is approximately normally distributed. His supply is replenished every 6 weeks. He must pay \$0.75 per gallon. His cost of capital is 0.5% per week. He recovers this cost in the price he charges for gasoline, but if any remains in inventory when the next order arrives he charges a holding cost based on this interest rate and the value of the inventory. If the distributor runs out of supply during the period, he "borrows" gas from other distributors, paying an extra \$0.10 per gallon for the privilege. The borrowed gas must be returned when his supply is replenished. What is the optimum inventory policy for the distributor?

P18.23 One of the disadvantages of using large order quantities in a production process is of course large holding costs. Another disadvantage is the inflexibility associated with having a large inventory. If a design change is to be incorporated into the product or some custom feature is to be added for particular customers, the modification must await the next production cycle while the entire inventory is depleted. The average length of the cycle is Q/a, so as Q grows so does the length of the cycle. This might be called the lead time of the production process. The reason for a large order quantity is a large setup cost, so reducing setup cost results in reduced holding cost, decreased production lead time, and increased flexibility. Analyze the following production systems, which are characterized by different setup costs, K, and different annual costs to implement the production process, B.

a. $K = \$10{,}000$, $B = \$10{,}000$
b. $K = \$5{,}000$, $B = \$30{,}000$
c. $K = \$1{,}000$, $B = \$110{,}000$

In each case weekly demand has a normal distribution with mean 50 and standard deviation 10. Use a 50-week year. Use a (Q, s) inventory policy. Other parameters are $p = \$100$/unit, $h = \$200$/unit-year, lead time when a reorder is placed is 1 week. Compute the optimum values of Q and s for each case and compare their total costs (including B) and production lead times. Choose the least cost system.

CHAPTER 19

Forecasting

Forecasting Techniques (19.4 – 19.5)

Although this book has emphasized models and mathematical techniques for analyzing, optimizing and otherwise manipulating the models, a critical aspect of an operations research study involves determining the coefficients and constants that define the model. Linear programming has matrices of numbers **c**, **b**, and **A**, queueing theory requires arrival and service rate parameters, and inventory theory uses holding, order, and shortage cost estimates along with demand information. Statistics plays a major role in estimating parameters for models; however, when the quantity of interest is a future value of a time-varying series, the estimation process is called forecasting or time series analysis.

GOAL

- Given a series of historical data representing a realization of a stochastic process, be able to use the forecasting techniques listed below to estimate future values of the process.

DEFINITIONS

Stochastic Process: A sequence of random variables $X_1, X_2, \ldots, X_t$. The subscript will generally represent time.

Expected Value of the Random Variable ($E(X_t)$): The expected value of the probability distribution of X_t.

Realization of the Stochastic Process: A series of observations of the random variables of the stochastic process, $x_1, x_2, \ldots, x_t$.

Estimate of Expected Value ($E'(X_t)$): An estimation of the expected value of X_t based on the data from the realization of the stochastic process. *Note:* H & L use an E covered with a hat symbol for the estimate.

Forecast ($F(X_{t+T})$): An estimate of the expected value of the stochastic process for T time periods in the future. An estimate of $E(X_{t+T})$.

Residual: The difference between the forecast and the observed value.

$$F(X_t) - x_t.$$

A measure of the effectiveness of a forecasting method is the mean absolute residual, the sum of the absolute values of the residuals for some number of periods divided by the number of periods.

RESULTS

Several common methods for providing a forecast are listed below. All assume the data from previous periods, $x_1, x_2, \ldots, x_t$, is available and will be used to provide the forecast.

Moving Average The average of the last n observations.

$$E'(X_t) = \sum_{i=m}^{t} x_i / n,$$

where $m = t - n + 1$.

The quantity n can be called the time range and is the parameter of the method. The forecast is the same as the estimate:

$$F(X_{t+T}) = E'(X_t).$$

Exponential Smoothing The weighted average of the last observation and the last estimate.

$$E'(X_t) = \alpha x_t + (1 - \alpha)E'(X_{t-1}),$$

where α is a parameter of the method. The forecast is the same as the estimate.

$$F(X_{t+T}) = E'(X_t).$$

Exponential Smoothing Adjusted for Trend This method attempts to estimate the means of two stochastic processes, $E(X_t)$ and $E(S_t)$. The first of these has already been defined. The second is the expected value of the linear trend of the process. The assumption is that $E(X_t)$ changes by an amount $E(S_t)$ during period t. The estimates of the two quantities are

$$E'(X_t) = \alpha x_t + (1-\alpha)[E'(X_{t-1}) + E'(S_{t-1})]$$
$$E'(S_t) = \beta[E'(X_t) - E'(X_{t-1})] + (1-\beta)E'(S_{t-1}).$$

The forecast for the $(t+T)$th period is

$$F(X_{t+T}) = E'(X_t) + TE'(S_t).$$

α and β are parameters for this method.

Box-Jenkins Method A procedure from modern time series analysis that estimates both the model form and coefficients from the data. Detailed consideration of this method is beyond the scope of this text.

Regression Analysis This is a general procedure for deriving an equation which predicts some dependent variable, Y, as a function of some number of independent variables, $X_1, X_2, \ldots, X_m$. The simplest, and most often used, function is linear with the general form

$$Y = a + b_1X_1 + b_2X_2 + \ldots + b_nX_m,$$

where a is a constant term and $b_1, b_2, \ldots, b_m$ are coefficients that are to be estimated from historical data. Here we are not necessarily working with a time series and the X_i have different definitions than used for the previous results. Computer programs are readily available for both mainframe and microcomputers to compute the linear regression coefficients.

In this chapter we are only concerned with simple linear regression where there is only one independent variable. In this case the regression equation is

$$Y = a + bX.$$

Estimating the Coefficients for Simple Linear Regression To estimate the constant term, a, and coefficient, b, for simple linear regression, assume n data pairs are available $(x_1, y_1), (x_2, y_2), \ldots, (x_n, y_n)$. A data pair is obtained by setting the independent variable to the value x_i and observing the resulting value of the dependent variable, y_i. The easiest way to calculate the desired results with a calculator or computer is with the procedure below.
Define the following notation:

$$(X) = \sum_{i=1}^{n} x_i \qquad (Y) = \sum_{i=1}^{n} y_i$$

$$(X^2) = \sum_{i=1}^{n} (x_i)^2 \qquad (XY) = \sum_{i=1}^{n} x_i\, y_i\,.$$

Then

$$b = \frac{(XY) - (X)\,(Y)/n}{(X^2) - (X)^2/n} \qquad a = (Y)/n - b\,(X)/n.$$

These coefficients provide what is called the least squared estimate because they are the coefficients which obtain the minimum of the sum of the squared deviations of the observed values less the estimated values of the independent variable.

$$\text{Min} \sum_{i=1}^{n} [y_i - (a - bx_i)]^2.$$

Using Simple Regression for Forecasting a Time Series Regression can be used in much the same way as the moving average to forecast the future observations of a time series. In this case the dependent variable is the random observation at time t, Y_t, and the independent variable is time, t. The regression equation is now

$$Y_t = a + bt.$$

(We are using Y_t here to represent the random variable to forestall the confusion that results when X_t is used as for the other forecasting methods.) The data pairs are now $(1, y_1), (2, y_2), \ldots, (n, y_n)$.

The factors in the estimating equations become somewhat simpler:

$$(X) = \sum_{i=1}^{n} i = \frac{(n+1)(n)}{2} \qquad (Y) = \sum_{i=1}^{n} y_i$$

$$(X^2) = \sum_{i=1}^{n} (i)^2 \qquad (XY) = \sum_{i=1}^{n} iy_i \,.$$

To obtain a forecast, simply evaluate the regression equation at the desired time.

$$F(Y_t) = a + b(t).$$

For forecasting, it is unlikely that one will include the data for all time periods. Rather, as in the moving average method, only the last n observations will be used. Time 1 for the regression model will then correspond to the real time, $t - n + 1$. The value of n can be called the time range of the regression and is a parameter of the method.

MODELING

Selection of a forecasting method with its parameters is a difficult task, which must be conditioned by knowledge concerning the quantity being forecast. We can, however, point out some simple characteristics of the methods that have been described. With forecasting procedures we are generally trying to recognize a change in the underlying process of a time series while remaining insensitive to variations caused by purely random effects. Planning is to respond to fundamental changes, not to spurious effects.

With a method based on purely historical data, it is impossible to have both results simultaneously. The problem is to set parameters that find an acceptable tradeoff between them. If the process is changing very slowly, both the moving average and the regression approach can use a large time range with much data. The exponential smoothing method will use a small value of α. Stochastic variations will be entirely filtered out.

If the process is changing rapidly with a linear trend, the moving average and the exponential smoothing methods are at a disadvantage because they are not designed to recognize trends. Since the process is changing rapidly, the time range of the moving average method must be set small and the α of the exponential smoothing method must be set to a larger value so that the forecasts will respond to the change. Nevertheless, these two methods will always fall behind a linear trend. The forecasts will never converge to a trend line even if there is no random variation. Of course with the adjustment of parameters to allow a response to a process change, the forecasts become more sensitive to random effects.

The exponential smoothing method with a trend adjustment and the regression method are designed to respond to a linear trend and will eventually converge to a trend line. Thus in the absence of a change in trend, the time range of the regression data can be large, and the α and β values of the exponential smoothing method can be small, thus reducing the random effects.

If the process is changing rapidly with rapid changes in the linear trend, every method will have trouble, because it is difficult to separate changes in the process from random changes. The time ranges must be set small for the moving average and regression methods resulting in sensitivity to random effects. Similarly the α and β parameters for exponential smoothing must be set to larger values with a corresponding increase in sensitivity to randomness.

Both the moving average and regression methods have the disadvantage that they are most accurate with respect to forecasts in the middle of the time range. Unfortunately all interesting forecasts are in the future, outside the range of the data. Of course for all methods, the uncertainty must increase with the distance into the future one wishes to forecast.

EXAMPLES

E19.1 To illustrate the characteristics of the forecasting methods described in this chapter, we first consider a very simple time series labeled as "model" in Fig. 19.1. The model begins at 20 and remains at that level until time 10. For times 11 through 30, the function rises linearly with a slope of +2. For times 31 through 50 the function decreases linearly with a slope of –2. For each time, we have used the four forecasting techniques to predict the next observation based on the observations that have previously occurred. More specifically, at time t, the data set $x_1, x_2, \ldots, x_t$, is available. Based on this information we make the forecast $F(x_{t+1})$. We will show this value and compare it to the actual observation x_{t+1} on the figures that follow.

Figure 19.1 shows the moving average and regression forecasts. Both are based on a time range of 10. Clearly, the moving average forecasts lag the time series during the periods when there is a trend. When the trend is constant, the forecast predicts the correct response five periods late. The regression forecast, however, does

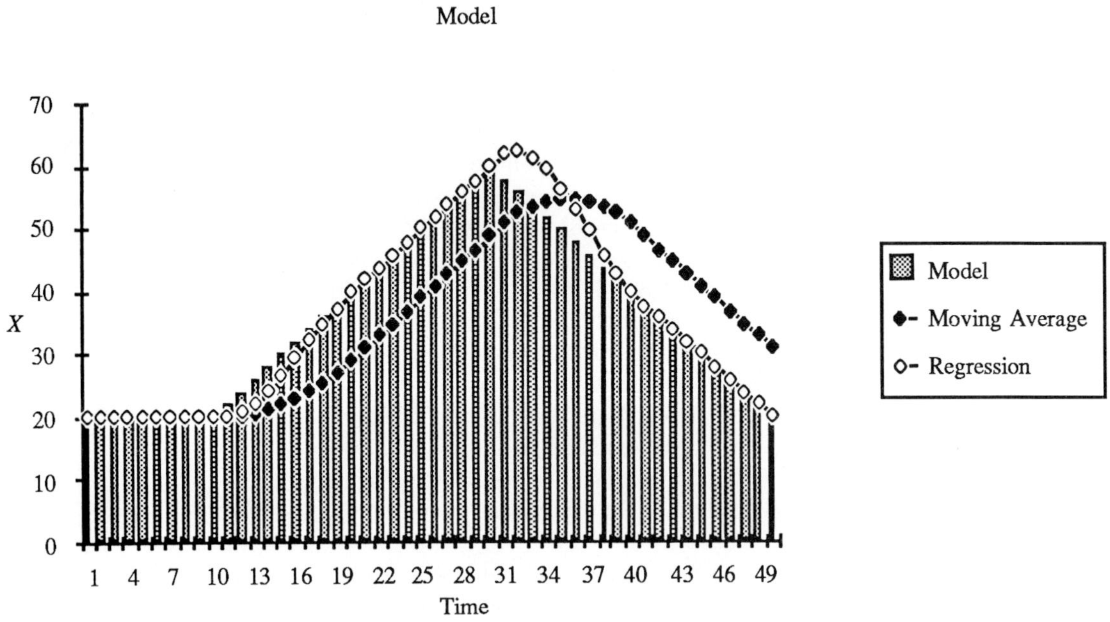

Figure 19.1 **Moving Average and Regression Forecasts with the Model**

eventually recognize the trend and, after a period of adjustment following a trend change, converges to the model.

Figure 19.2 shows the same model with the forecasts based on the exponential smoothing and exponential smoothing with trend adjustment methods. For both methods α is set to 0.3. For the latter method β is set equal to 0.2. As expected, the exponential smoothing method also lags the time series, while the trend adjustment allows the forecast to converge to the model. It is not meaningful to compare the results of the exponential smoothing methods with moving average and regression methods since the results depend on the values of the parameters selected.

E19.2 Now we compare the four methods using more typical data. Table 19.1 shows 50 observations simulated by applying a random deviation to the model shown in Figs. 19.1 and 19.2. For each time an approximately normal observation was generated with a mean equal to the model value and a standard deviation of 5. The results of the four forecasting methods are shown along with the data in Figs. 19.3 and 19.4.

It is important to remember that the methods are not really attempting to forecast the actual observations. These cannot be precisely predicted because of the random component of the observation. The purpose of the methods is to predict the mean of the distributions from which the observations are drawn. For this example, this mean is actually the model shown in the earlier figures, and it can be compared

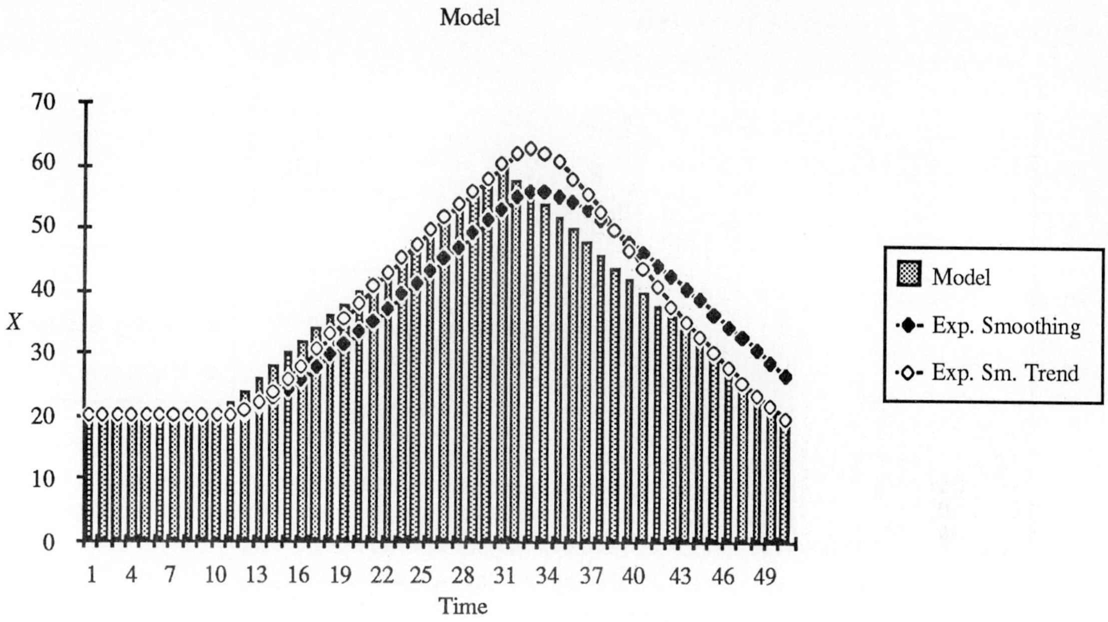

Figure 19.2 **Exponential Smoothing Forecasts with the Model Data**

Table 19.1 **Random Data**

Time	*Observations*									
1 – 10	21	24	16	21	24	25	24	25	21	20
11 – 20	22	25	30	28	27	27	40	44	42	43
21 – 30	39	53	45	50	56	52	54	48	64	69
31 – 40	56	67	58	60	53	55	44	41	48	42
41 – 50	33	38	26	23	35	30	23	18	23	20

with the forecast values. This is done for the regression and exponential smoothing with trend adjustment methods in Fig. 19.5. The forecasts track the true mean more accurately than the observations.

We can also evaluate the forecasting methods using the mean absolute residuals, as shown in Table 19.2. The "model vs. model forecast" column is derived from the plots shown in Figs. 19.1 and 19.2. The "random data vs. data forecast" column comes from the plots shown in Figs. 19.3 and 19.4. Fig. 19.5 shows the source of the "model vs. data forecast" column for two of the methods. The smaller the mean absolute residual, the better the forecast.

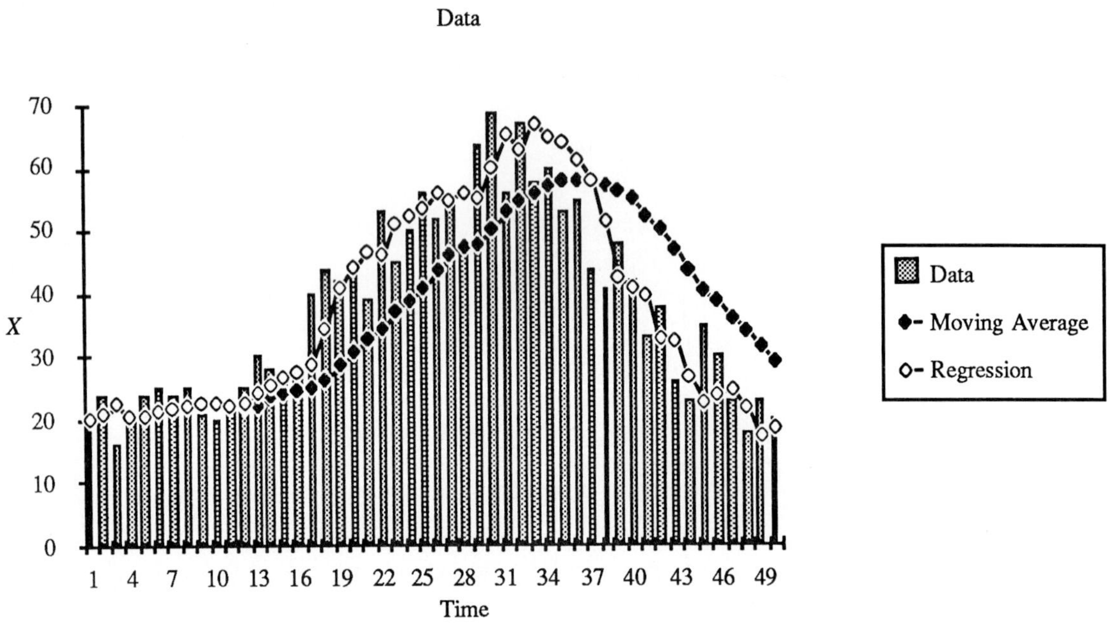

Figure 19.3 **The Moving Average and Regression Forcasts Applied to Random Data**

Table 19.2 **Mean Absolute Residuals**

Method	*Model vs. model forecast*	*Random data vs. data forecast*	*Model vs. data forecast*
Moving average	7.2	8.6	7.3
Regression	1.3	5	3.9
Exponential smoothing	4.5	5.9	4.6
Exp. smoothing with trend	1.7	5.2	4.2

E19.3 To illustrate the computational processes involved with the forecasting methods, we will use observations for times 25 through 44 taken from Table 19.1.

x_{25}–x_{34}	56	52	54	48	64	69	56	67	58	60
x_{35}–x_{44}	53	55	44	41	48	42	33	38	26	23

Assume in the following that the observation of 60 for time 34 has just been observed. Make the forecast for times 35, 36, and 37, with the four methods.

MOVING AVERAGE

Using a time range of 10, we take the average of the observations from 25 to 34. The result is 58.4. Since this method assumes no trend, the forecasts for the three times are the same.

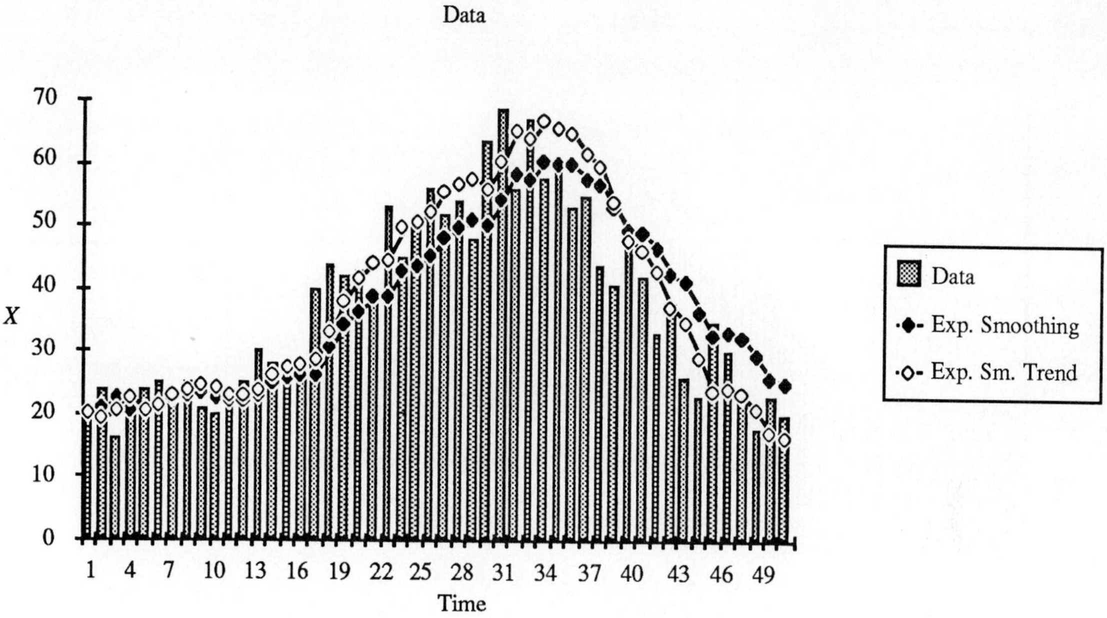

Figure 19.4 **The Exponential Smoothing Forecasts Applied to Random Data**

$F(X_{35}) = 58.4,$ $\quad F(X_{36}) = 58.4,$ $\quad F(X_{37}) = 58.4.$

REGRESSION

Again with a time range of 10, we renumber the last 10 observations 1 through 10. Thus we have the data pairs (x_t, y_t):

(1,56) (2,52) (3,54) (4,48) (5,64) (6,69) (7,56) (8,67) (9,58) (10,60).

Using the formulas introduced earlier for estimating regression coefficients.

$$(X) = 55 \qquad (Y) = 584 \qquad (X^2) = 385 \qquad (XY) = 3298$$

$$b = \frac{(3298) - (55)(584)/10}{385 - (55)^2/10} = \frac{86}{82.5} = 1.0424$$

$$a = 584/10 - (1.0424)(55)/10 = 52.667.$$

The forecast is therefore

$$F(Y_t) = 52.667 + 1.0424\ (t).$$

Note that we have adjusted the time index for the calculations, so to find a forecast for times 35,36, and 37 we have, respectively,

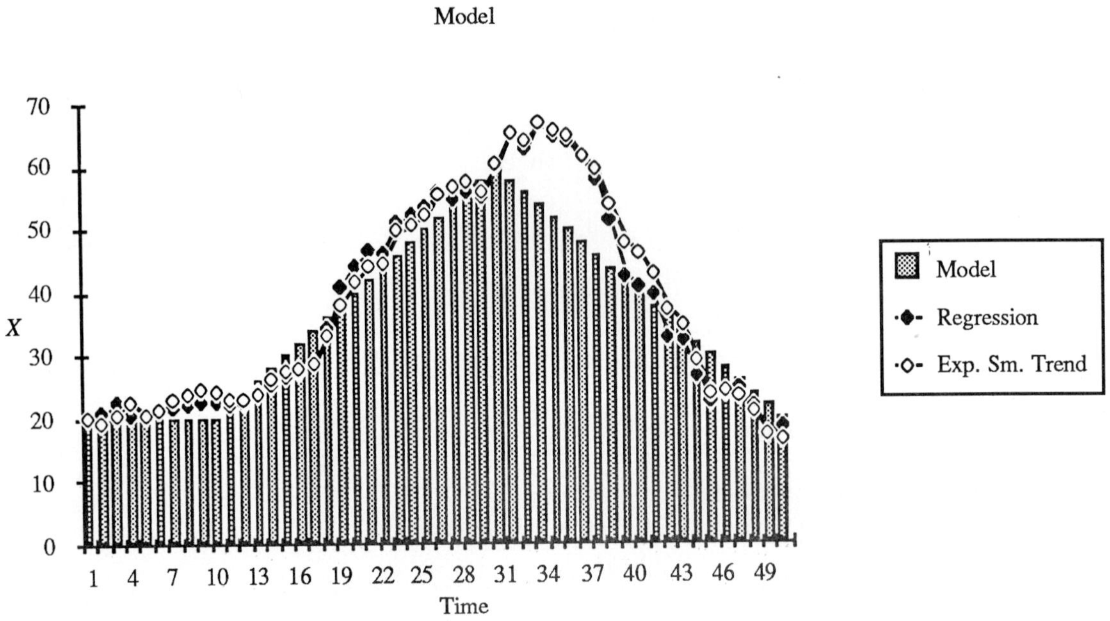

Figure 19.5 **Comparison of the Regression and Exponential Smoothing with Trend Adjustment Forcasts with The Mean Value**

$$F(Y_{35}) = 52.667 + 1.0424\ (11) = 64.13$$
$$F(Y_{36}) = 52.667 + 1.0424\ (12) = 65.18$$
$$F(Y_{37}) = 52.667 + 1.0424\ (13) = 66.22.$$

Note that we are using the Y random variable to agree with the notation used with regression.

EXPONENTIAL SMOOTHING

This method requires only the last data point and the last estimate of the expected value. Given that $\alpha = 0.3$ and $E'(X_{33}) = 59.828$, the next estimate is

$$E\ (X_{34}) = \alpha x_{34} + (1 - \alpha)E'(X_{33}) = (0.3)(60) + (0.7)(59.828) = 59.88.$$

Since there is no inclusion of trend, the forecasts for the three times are

$$F(X_{35}) = 59.88, \qquad F(X_{36}) = 59.88, \qquad F(X_{37}) = 59.88.$$

EXPONENTIAL SMOOTHING WITH TREND ADJUSTMENT

This method requires the last data point, the last estimate of the expected value, and the last estimate of the trend. Given that $\alpha = 0.3$, $\beta = 0.2$, $E'(X_{33}) = 64.342$, and $E'(S_{33}) = 1.392$, the next estimates of expected value and slope are

$$E'(X_t) = \alpha x_t + (1 - \alpha)[E'(X_{t-1}) + E'(S_{t-1})]$$
$$E'(X_{34}) = (0.3)(60) + (0.7)[64.342 + 1.392]$$
$$= 64.014.$$
$$E'(S_t) = \beta\,[E'(X_t) - E'(X_{t-1})] + (1 - \beta)E'(S_{t-1})$$
$$E'(S_{34}) = (0.2)[64.014 - 64.342] + (0.8)(1.392)$$
$$= 1.048.$$

The forecast for the $(t + T)$th period is

$$F(X_{t+T}) = E'(X_t) + TE'(S_t)$$
$$F(X_{35}) = 64.014 + (1)(1.048) = 65.06$$
$$F(X_{36}) = 64.014 + (2)(1.048) = 66.11$$
$$F(X_{37}) = 64.014 + (3)(1.048) = 67.16.$$

E19.4 Now assume the datum of 53 is observed for time 35. Update the forecasts for time 36.

MOVING AVERAGE

This estimate is easily updated by dropping the oldest data point from the sum and adding the new.

$$E'(X_{35}) = F(X_{36}) = (584 - 56 + 53)/10 = 58.1.$$

REGRESSION

Notice that the values of (X) and (X^2) remain the same since we always use the time indices 1 though 10. The other sums are easily adjusted. Designating the new values with a prime and the latest observation as x,

$$(Y)' = (Y) - x_1 + x$$
$$(XY)' = (XY) - (Y) + nx.$$

Using the formulas introduced earlier for estimating regression coefficients.

$$(X) = 55 \qquad (Y) = 584 - 56 + 53 = 581$$
$$(X^2) = 385 \qquad (XY) = 3298 - 584 + (10)(53) = 3244$$
$$b = \frac{(3244) - (55)(581)/10}{82.5} = \frac{48.5}{82.5} = 0.588$$
$$a = 581/10 - (0.588)(55)/10 = 54.866.$$

The forecast is therefore

$$F(Y_{36}) = 54.866 + (0.588)(11) = 61.33.$$

EXPONENTIAL SMOOTHING

Given that $\alpha = 0.3$, and $E'(X_{34}) = 59.88$,

$$E'(X_{35}) = F(X_{36}) = (0.3)(53) + (0.7)(59.88) = 57.816.$$

EXPONENTIAL SMOOTHING WITH TREND ADJUSTMENT

Given that $\alpha = 0.3$, $\beta = 0.2$, $E'(X_{34}) = 64.014$, and $E'(S_{34}) = 1.048$, the next estimates of expected value and slope are

$$E'(X_{35}) = (0.3)(53) + (0.7)[64.014 + 1.048] = 61.443$$
$$E'(S_{35}) = (0.2)[61.443 - 64.014] + (0.8)(1.048) = 0.3242$$
$$F(X_{36}) = 61.443 + (1)(0.3242) = 61.77.$$

Notice that all the methods can be easily updated with an additional data point.

Problems

P19.1 Continuing the series described in E19.3 and E19.4, let the next data point in the series, $x_{36} = 55$. Update each of the forecasts for time 37.

P19.2 Use the data provided for times 35 through 44. Forecast the observations for times 45 through 50. For purposes of exponential smoothing use

$$\alpha = 0.3 \text{ and } E'(X_{43}) = 35.54.$$

For exponential smoothing with the trend adjustment use

$$\alpha = 0.3, \beta = 0.2, E'(X_{43}) = 39.36, E'(S_{43}) = 0.37.$$

P19.3 The table below shows an additional data series.

Time	*Observations*									
1 – 10	99	104	112	85	95	98	91	87	112	103
11 – 20	106	96	109	69	78	98	74	79	65	93
21 – 30	58	76	70	61	75	58	63	32	43	41
31 – 40	25	44	25	54	44	49	39	35	49	56
41 – 50	49	45	38	45	44	50	62	51	55	58
51 – 60	58	49	61	65	50	71	77	87	70	68

Using the data provided for times 1 through 10, generate a forecast for time 11. Then sequentially observe x_{11} through x_{20} (as given in the table). After each observation, x_t, forecast the mean of the next observation, $F(x_{t+1})$. Compare the forecasts with the actual data and compute the mean absolute residual of the 10 observations. Do this for the following cases.

- **a.** Moving average with $n = 5$.
- **b.** Moving average with $n = 10$.
- **c.** Regression with $n = 5$.
- **d.** Regression with $n = 10$.
- **e.** Exponential smoothing with $\alpha = 0.2$ and $E'(X_9) = 100$.
- **f.** Exponential smoothing with $\alpha = 0.1$ and $E'(X_9) = 100$.
- **g.** Exponential smoothing and trend adjustment with $\alpha = 0.2, \beta = 0.2, E'(X_9) = 100, E'(S_9) = 0$.
- **h.** Exponential smoothing and trend adjustment with $\alpha = 0.1, \beta = 0.1, E'(X_9) = 100, E'(S_9) = 0$.

Table 19.3 **Random Variations**

Time	*Variations*									
1 – 10	+1	+4	–4	+1	+4	+5	+4	+5	+1	0
11 – 20	0	+1	+4	0	–3	–5	+6	+8	+4	+3
21 – 30	–3	+9	–1	+2	+6	0	0	–8	+6	+9
31 – 40	–2	+11	+4	+8	+3	+7	–2	–3	+6	+2
41 – 50	–5	+2	–8	–9	+5	0	–3	–6	+1	0

Note: The estimates given for the exponential smoothing cases are not computed from the data, but are the model values for this point.

Computer Problems

It is quite easy to implement the forecasting equations using a spreadsheet program for a microcomputer. It is also easy to code a small program in BASIC for this purpose. This is especially true if the computation simplifications illustrated in E19.4 are used. Use either of these approaches to investigate the following problems.

P19.4 Table 19.3 shows the random variations added to the model of E19.1 to obtain the data of Table 19.1. Double the values of these deviations and add them to the model to obtain a new set of data. Repeat the computations performed in E19.2 and compare the mean residuals for the four forecasting methods. In each case, use the first ten observations to initialize the model and forecast the remaining 40 observations. Compute the residual with ABS[$F(t+1) - X(t)$].

P19.5 The data below is simulated from a model that has a constant value of 20 for times 1 through 15. At times 16 through 30, the model jumps to 40. For times 31 through 50, the model goes back to 20. Experiment with the parameters of the forecasting methods to find the one that best forecasts this time series with jumps.

Time	*Observations*									
1 – 10	21	24	16	21	24	25	24	25	21	20
11 – 20	20	21	24	20	17	35	46	48	44	43
21 – 30	37	49	39	42	46	40	40	32	46	49
31 – 40	18	31	24	28	23	27	18	17	26	22
41 – 50	15	22	12	11	25	22	17	14	21	20

CHAPTER 20

Markovian Decision Processes

Linear Programming Formulation (20.2 – 20.3)

Chapter 15 introduced a stochastic process called the Markov chain. This model has $M + 1$ states, numbered from 0 to M, and a transition matrix that specifies the probabilities of transition from each state to every other state. The procedures described in that chapter allow one to analyze the system by computing such measures as the long-run state probabilities. This chapter adds the dimension of decision making to the Markov chain. Now, at every step of the process, before the transition to the next state is determined, a decision must be made that affects the transition probabilities. This section explains how the problem can be stated and solved as a linear program. There are number of interesting applications of this model and the associated solution procedures.

GOALS

- Be able to describe a Markov decision process in terms of the notation defined in this chapter.
- Be able to set up and solve a Markov decision process as a linear program.

DEFINITIONS

States: The states of the Markov process numbered 0 through M.

Decision (d_i)**:** A number representing the decision to be made if the system is in state i. Possible decisions are indexed with integer numbers and numbered 1 through K.

Policy (R): A rule for making decisions at each step of the process. The rule specifies a decision for each state as represented by the decision vector

$$\{d_0(R), d_1(R), \ldots, d_M(R)\},$$

where $d_i(R)$ is a number representing the decision made in state i.

Transition Probability ($p_{ij}(k)$)**:** Given that the system is in state i, this is the probability of a transition to state j, when the decision is k. For policy R,

$$k = d_i(R).$$

Decision Cost (C_{ik})**:** The cost incurred during the next step if the system is in state i and decision k is made.

Steady-State Distribution (π_i)**:** The steady-state probability for state i. Since the transition matrix depends on the policy R, the steady-state distribution also depends on R.

Expected Average Cost ($E(C)$)**:** The long-run expected cost per unit time of operating the system with policy R.

$$E(C) = \sum_{i=0}^{M} C_{ik}\, \pi_i \,.$$

The goal is to find the policy that minimizes the expected average cost.

Decision Matrix (D): An $M + 1$ by K matrix with component D_{ik}, defined as the probability that the decision k will be taken, given that the system is in state i.

$$D_{ik} = P\{\text{decision} = k \mid \text{state} = i\} \quad \text{for } i = 0, \ldots, M,\ k = 1, \ldots, K.$$

The decision matrix completely defines a decision policy. This matrix can have probabilities between 0 and 1, thus allowing a mixed policy (as defined relative to Game Theory in Chapter 12). It turns out that the optimal solution will always have components that are either 0 or 1. The optimum solution will be a pure policy.

RESULTS

Linear Programming Model for the Markov Decision Problem Decision variables:

$$y_{ik} = P\{\text{state is } i \text{ and the decision is } k\} \quad \text{for } i = 0, \ldots, M,\ k = 1, \ldots, K.$$

Objective function: Minimize expected average cost

$$\text{Minimize } Z = \sum_{i=0}^{M} \sum_{k=1}^{K} C_{ik} y_{ik}.$$

Constraints: The steady-state probabilities must sum to 1:

$$\sum_{i=0}^{M} \sum_{k=1}^{K} y_{ik} = 1.$$

Equations defining the steady-state probabilities:

$$\sum_{k=1}^{K} y_{jk} - \sum_{i=0}^{M} \sum_{k=1}^{K} y_{ik} p_{ij}(k) = 0 \quad \text{for } j = 0, 1, \ldots, M.$$

Nonnegativity:

$$y_{ik} \geq 0 \quad \text{for } i = 0, 1, \ldots, M \text{ and } k = 1, 2, \ldots, K.$$

After the linear program is solved, the results in more usable form can be obtained by computing the steady-state distribution and the decision probabilities.

$$\pi_i = \sum_{k=1}^{K} y_{ik}, \quad \text{for } i = 0, 1, \ldots, M$$

$$D_{ik} = y_{ik} / \pi_i \quad i = 0, 1, \ldots, M \text{ and } k = 1, 2, \ldots, K.$$

EXAMPLE

E20.1 Consider again the typewriter repair problem that was described in E15.3 and E15.16. An office has two typewriters. It has been observed that when both are working in the morning, there is a 30% chance that one will be failed by evening and a 10% chance that both will be failed. If it happens that only one typewriter is working in the morning, there is a 20% chance that it will be failed by evening.

With one typewriter failed, some of the office work must be sent to a typing service at a cost of \$20 per day. With both machines failed, the cost of the service increases to \$100 per day.

The repairman charges \$40 to fix a typewriter and it takes 1 day for the repair. When he is called in the morning he picks up the failed machines immediately and will guarantee their return by the next morning. The man also charges a fixed fee of \$50 to pick up the machines. This fee is independent of how many need repair. This last condition has been added to the previous examples concerning this situation.

The office manager must decide when to call the repairman. Should he be called after the first machine fails or after both have failed? Which policy yields the smallest average cost?

Solution There are really only two possible decisions at any state:

1. Do not call the repairman.
2. Call the repairman.

Thus we have $K = 2$ with the alternatives numbered as above.

The state of the system is the number of failed typewriters observed after the repairman has returned repaired machines. There are three states for this problem:

0. No typewriters failed.
1. One typewriter failed.
2. Two typewriters failed.

The obvious decision for state 0 is not to call the repairman. Thus $d_0 = 1$. When the system is in state 2, the optimum plan is to call the repairman (the machines must eventually be repaired so there is no point delaying). Thus $d_2 = 2$. State 1 involves the only question with both alternatives as reasonable possibilities.

We will use the linear programming model described in the results section to solve this problem. Since there are two decisions and three states, there are potentially six decision variables.

$$y_{01} = P\{\text{no typewriters are failed and repairman is not called}\}$$
$$y_{02} = P\{\text{no typewriters are failed and repairman is called}\}$$
$$y_{11} = P\{\text{one typewriter is failed and repairman is not called}\}$$
$$y_{12} = P\{\text{one typewriter is failed and repairman is called}\}$$
$$y_{21} = P\{\text{two typewriters are failed and repairman is not called}\}$$
$$y_{22} = P\{\text{two typewriters are failed and repairman is called}\}$$

We delete y_{02} and y_{21} as impractical alternatives.

If we define $\mathbf{P}_i(k)$ as row i of the transition matrix when decision k is selected, we have for the remaining decisions

$$\mathbf{P}_0(1) = [\,0.6 \quad 0.3 \quad 0.1\,]$$
$$\mathbf{P}_1(1) = [\,0 \quad 0.8 \quad 0.2\,]$$
$$\mathbf{P}_1(2) = [\,0.8 \quad 0.2 \quad 0\,]$$
$$\mathbf{P}_2(2) = [\,1 \quad 0 \quad 0\,].$$

One can also compute the cost of operation given the state and decision.

$C_{01} =$ 0, there is no cost if no typewriters are failed.

$C_{11} =$ 20, this is the cost of the typing service with one failed.

$C_{12} =$ 110, this is the cost of the typing service plus the cost of repairing the machine.

$C_{22} =$ 230, this is the cost of the typing service plus the cost of repairing two machines.

Using notation we have the following linear programming model.

Minimize $Z = C_{01}y_{01} + C_{11}y_{11} + C_{12}y_{12} + C_{22}y_{22}$

Subject to:

$$y_{01} + y_{11} + y_{12} + y_{22} = 1$$
$$y_{01} - [p_{00}(1)y_{01} + p_{10}(1)y_{11} + p_{10}(2)y_{12} + p_{20}(2)y_{22}] = 0$$
$$y_{11} + y_{12} - [p_{01}(1)y_{01} + p_{11}(1)y_{11} + p_{11}(2)y_{12} + p_{21}(2)y_{22}] = 0$$
$$y_{22} - [p_{02}(1)y_{01} + p_{12}(1)y_{11} + p_{12}(2)y_{12} + p_{22}(2)y_{22}] = 0$$
$$y_{01} \ge 0 \quad y_{11} \ge 0 \quad y_{12} \ge 0 \quad y_{22} \ge 0.$$

Plugging in the probabilities and costs computed above we have the following linear programming model.

Minimize $Z = 0y_{01} + 20y_{11} + 110y_{12} + 230y_{22}$

Subject to:

$$y_{01} + y_{11} + y_{12} + y_{22} = 1$$
$$0.4y_{01} - 0.8y_{12} - y_{22} = 0$$
$$-0.3y_{01} + 0.2y_{11} + 0.8y_{12} = 0$$
$$-0.1y_{01} - 0.2y_{11} + y_{22} = 0$$
$$y_{01} \ge 0 \quad y_{11} \ge 0 \quad y_{12} \ge 0 \quad y_{22} \ge 0.$$

The optimum solution to this linear program has

$$Z = 43.56, \; y_{01} = 0.678, y_{11} = 0, y_{12} = 0.254, y_{22} = 0.068.$$

From this result we can compute the steady state probabilities

$$\pi_0 = 0.678, \pi_1 = 0.254, \pi_2 = 0.068,$$

and the optimum decision matrix

$$D_{01} = 1, D_{11} = 0, D_{12} = 1, D_{22} = 1.$$

The optimum decision is to call the repairman if there are either one or two machines failed. The expected cost per day is \$43.56.

Problems

P20.1 Consider the example of E20.1 but assume the company buys another typewriter, for a total of three machines. When all three machines are working in the morning there is a probability of 32% that one will be failed by evening, a probability of 10% that two will be failed, and a probability of 3% that all three will be failed. As before, when two are working in the morning, there is a 30% chance that one will be failed by evening and a 10% chance that both will be failed. If it happens that only one typewriter is working in the morning, there is a 20% chance that it will be failed by evening.

With one typewriter failed, some of the office work must be sent to a typing service at a cost of \$10 per day. With two machines failed the cost will be \$25, and with all three machines failed the cost of the service increases to \$100 per day.

The repairman charges $40 to fix a typewriter and it takes 1 day for the repair. When he is called in the morning he picks up the failed machines immediately and will guarantee their return by the next morning. The man also charges a fixed fee of $50 to pick up the machines. This fee is independent of how many need repair. With a minimum cost policy, how many machines must be failed before the office manager calls the repairman?

P20.2 This is an abstract problem in which there are three states. In each state, one of three decisions must be made. The matrices below show the transition probabilities, assuming the same decision is made in every state. This is not a limitation, however, since the policy may use a different decision for each state. Also shown below is the decision cost matrix. Set up and solve a linear program to determine the optimum decision in each state. Also find the steady-state probabilities. The goal is to minimize long-run average cost.

$$P(1) = \begin{bmatrix} 0 & 0.3 & 0.7 \\ 0.9 & 0.1 & 0 \\ 0.2 & 0 & 0.8 \end{bmatrix}$$

$$P(2) = \begin{bmatrix} 0.1 & 0.6 & 0.3 \\ 0.7 & 0.2 & 0.1 \\ 0.1 & 0.3 & 0.6 \end{bmatrix}$$

$$P(3) = \begin{bmatrix} 0.3 & 0.5 & 0.2 \\ 0.6 & 0.1 & 0.3 \\ 0.2 & 0.4 & 0.4 \end{bmatrix}$$

$$C = \begin{bmatrix} 10 & 15 & 20 \\ 15 & 20 & 25 \\ 20 & 25 & 30 \end{bmatrix}$$

P20.3 A dealer in high priced cars expects the following weekly demand distribution.

Demand	0	1	2
Probability	0.1	0.5	0.4

The dealer looks at the inventory at the end of each week and must determine if an order should be placed and how many cars to order. The cars arrive 1 week after the order is placed. There may be a total of no more than five cars either in inventory or on order. The cost of placing an order is $600, independent of how many cars are ordered. If there is a demand for a car and there is no inventory, the sale is lost with a lost profit of $2000. The cost associated with an unsold car in inventory at the end of a week is $200. Set up this problem as a Markov decision process and find the optimum policy.

Computer Problem

P20.4 A queueing system has three service channels. Using a 5-minute study period, the following probabilities have been determined for the number of arrivals during the period.

Arrivals	0	1	2	3
Probability	0.1	0.3	0.4	0.2

For simplicity assume that the arrivals occur at the beginning of the period. These arrivals will enter the system until the number in the system is 10. When this occurs the arrivals will balk. The cost of a balking customer is \$100.

The number of customers who leave the system during a period depends on the number of channels open and the number in the system at the beginning of the period. The probability distribution for the number of service completions given that there are sufficient customers in the system is given below for the various numbers of channels.

Completions	0	1	2	3	4
One channel open	0.3	0.5	0.2	0	0
Two channels open	0.1	0.2	0.4	0.3	0
Three channels open	0	0.1	0.2	0.5	0.2

If there aren't enough customers in the system to utilize the full capacity of a particular channel configuration, the probabilities for the excess capacities are combined with the probability for the specific number of customers in the system. For instance if there are only two customers in the system at some period, the service probability distributions appear as below.

Completions	0	1	2	3	4
One channel open	0.3	0.5	0.2	0	0
Two channels open	0.1	0.2	0.7	0	0
Three channels open	0	0.1	0.9	0	0

Let the charge for an open channel be \$7 per period. Let the waiting cost for a customer be \$2 for each whole period spent in the system.

You must determine a policy for how many channels to open as a function of the number of customers in the system. Describe this problem as a Markov decision problem and solve it with a linear programming algorithm.

CHAPTER 21

Reliability

Although the technological achievements of the 20th century can hardly be disputed, there is clearly one weakness in all mankind's devices. That is the possibility of failure. What citizen has not experienced the frustration of an automobile that fails to start or a breakdown in a household appliance. The introduction of every new device must be accompanied by provision for maintenance, repair parts, and protection against failure. This is certainly apparent to the military, where the life cycle maintenance costs of systems far exceed the original purchase costs. The problem pervades modern society, from the homeowner and the annoyance caused by appliance failures, to the electric utility faced with the potentially disastrous results of nuclear reactor failure. The insurance industry would not exist without the possibility of one type of failure or another.

A subject that is so important to many decisions in this world could hardly escape quantitative analysis. The name *reliability* is given to the field of study that attempts to assign numbers to the propensity of systems to fail. In a more restrictive sense, the term "reliability" is defined to be the probability that a system performs its mission. Since mission is often specified in terms of time, reliability is often defined as the probability that a system will operate satisfactorily for a given time. Thus reliability may be a function of time.

This chapter is an introduction to the estimation of the reliability of a complex system given the reliability of its component parts. Since reliability is a probability, the developments of the chapter rest on the theory of probability.

Structure Function of a System (21.2)

Usually a device or system can be described as a collection of parts or components. The system operates satisfactorily if all its components operate satisfactorily (do not fail), but it may also operate if some subset of components is failed. The structure function provides a means to determine the status of the system, given the status of its components.

GOAL

- Given a system divided into components, be able to determine the structure function if the system is: a series system, a parallel system, a k out of n system, or a more complex system.

DEFINITIONS

System: A physical system consisting of n identifiable components.

Success: The system performs its function satisfactorily for a given period of time, where the criterion for success is clearly defined.

Failure: The system fails to perform its function satisfactorily.

Reliability: The probability that a system performs its function satisfactorily (i.e., the probability of success).

Success Indicator: A binary random variable X_i that indicates the status of component i.

$$X_i = 1 \text{ implies component } i \text{ is successful}$$
$$X_i = 0 \text{ implies component } i \text{ is failed.}$$

Status Vector: The vector of component status indicators,

$$\mathbf{X} = (X_1, X_2, \ldots, X_n).$$

There are 2^n possible realizations of this vector.

Structure Function: A binary function that indicates the status of the system (success or failure) given the status of each component.

$$\phi(X_1, X_2, \ldots, X_n) \quad \text{or} \quad \phi(\mathbf{X})$$

is the structure function, which has a value for each of the 2^n possible vectors $\mathbf{X}$.

Series System: A system in which all components must be successful for the system to be successful. Alternatively, the failure of any one component will cause the system to fail.

Parallel System: A system in which if any one component is successful the system is successful. Alternatively, all the components must fail before the system will fail.

***k* out of *n* System:** A system that is successful if any k out of the n components are successful.

Coherent System: A system with the property that when the system is successful for some status vector **X** it will continue to be successful if some components of **X** change from 0 to 1. More formally, a coherent system has the property that when **X** and **Y** are two status vectors such that $\mathbf{Y} \geq \mathbf{X}$,

$$\phi(\mathbf{Y}) \geq \phi(\mathbf{X}).$$

RESULTS

Series System Structure Function

$$\phi(X_1, X_2, \ldots, X_n) = X_1 X_2 \ldots X_n,$$

where n is the number of components.

Parallel System Structure Function

$$\phi(X_1, X_2, \ldots, X_n) = 1 - (1 - X_1)(1 - X_2) \ldots (1 - X_n),$$

where n is the number of components.

k out of n System Structure Function

$$\phi(X_1, X_2, \ldots, X_n) = \begin{cases} 1, & \text{if } \sum_{i=1}^{n} X_i \geq k \\ 0, & \text{if } \sum_{i=1}^{n} X_i < k. \end{cases}$$

EXAMPLES

E21.1 A stereo system has a turntable, an amplifier, and two speakers (A and B). If successful operation requires all four components to work, show the structure function of the system.

Associate the indicator variables X_1, X_2, X_3, and X_4 with the turntable, amplifier, speaker A, and speaker B, respectively. This is a series system, so the structural function is

$$\phi(\mathbf{X}) = X_1 X_2 X_3 X_4.$$

E21.2 Consider the system of E21.1 with a revised criterion for success. For successful operation the turntable, amplifier and at least one of the speakers must work. To construct the function first note that the two speakers comprise a parallel system. Thus the structure function for the speaker combination is

$$\phi_S = 1 - (1 - X_3)(1 - X_4).$$

The speaker combination forms a series system with the turntable and amplifier, so the complete structural function is

$$\phi(\mathbf{X}) = X_1X_2\phi_s = X_1X_2[1 - (1 - X_3)(1 - X_4)].$$

E21.3 A space vehicle has three identical computers operating simultaneously and solving the same problems. The outputs of the three computers are compared, and if two or three of them are identical, that result is used. This is called a majority vote system, and in this mode one of the three computers can fail without causing the system to fail. To construct the structure function, note that this is a two out of three system. Identifying the success or failure of each of the computers with the variables X_1, X_2, and X_3, the function may be written:

$$\phi(\mathbf{X}) = \begin{cases} 1, & \text{if } X_1 + X_2 + X_3 \geq 2 \\ 0, & \text{if } X_1 + X_2 + X_3 < 2. \end{cases}$$

Alternatively, the structure function may be written

$$\phi(\mathbf{X}) = 1 - [(1 - X_1X_2)(1 - X_1X_3)(1 - X_2X_3)].$$

Any combination of two or more X_i set equal to 1 will cause this function to assume the value 1, while fewer than two will result in a 0 value.

E21.4 If all three of the computers of E21.3 must work for successful operation, construct the structure function. This is a series system, so

$$\phi(\mathbf{X}) = X_1X_2X_3.$$

E21.5 If only one of the computers of E21.3 must work for successful operation, construct the structure function. This is a parallel system, so

$$\phi(\mathbf{X}) = 1 - [(1 - X_1)(1 - X_2)(1 - X_3)].$$

MODELING

For some problems the system may be viewed as a combination of simple structures. Thus the system of E21.2 comprised a parallel arrangement of the speakers in series with the other two components. In this fashion the structure function of a complex system may be constructed using only the simple systems described in this section.

PROBLEMS

P21.1 A missile complex has four subsystems: the radar subsystem, the missile, the computer control devices, and the human operators. Four radars are provided, of which three are required for successful operation. The complex has only a single missile. There are three computers operating in a majority vote arrangement. There are two human operators, one of whom must be capable of firing the missile. Write the structure function for this system consisting of 10 components.

P21.2 A student drives to school each day over the same route. She prides herself on her ability to control the speed of her car so she never has to stop at a traffic signal. She calls her day successful if she can accomplish that feat. If there are six traffic signals on her route, show the structure function for the system of traffic signals for this particular driver. How would the structure function change if the student were willing to change her criterion of success to allow a pause at no more than one signal?

P21.3 In order to assure the discovery of a vaccine for a disease, the government awards independent study contracts to four drug firms. Surely, they say, one of the companies will make the discovery. If success is defined as the discovery of the vaccine, what is the structure function for this system?

System Reliability (21.3)

Given the structure function of the system, one can compute a measure of system quality called the reliability. This section defines reliability and shows how to compute it for the simple (series, parallel, and k out of n) systems.

GOAL

- Be able to compute system reliabilities for simple system structures.

DEFINITIONS

Component Reliability (p_i)**:** The probability that a component is successful.

$$p_i = P\{X_i = 1\}.$$

Component Failure Probability (q_i)**:**The probability that a component fails.

$$q_i = P\{X_i = 0\} = 1 - p_i.$$

System Reliability (R)**:** The probability that the system is successful.

Independence of Component Failures: When the probability of success or failure of a component does not depend on the status of some other component, the components are said to be independent. The assumption of this section is that all components are independent.

RESULTS

System Reliability The probability that the structure function is 1,

$$R = P\{\phi(\mathbf{X}) = 1\}.$$

Reliability of a Series System

$$R = p_1 p_2 \cdots p_n,$$

where n is the number of components.

Reliability of a Parallel System

$$R = 1 - [(1-p_1)(1-p_2)\dots(1-p_n)]$$
$$= 1 - [q_1 q_2 \dots q_n].$$

Reliability of a k out of n System Assume that all components have the same reliability, $p_i = p$ for $i = 1 \dots n$. Then

$$R = \sum_{i=k}^{n} \binom{n}{i} p^i (1-p)^{n-i}, \text{ where } \binom{n}{i} = \frac{n!}{(n-i)!\, i!}$$

This reliability is derived from the binomial distribution.

EXAMPLES

E21.6 A stereo system has a turntable, an amplifier, and two speakers (A and B). Successful operation requires all four components to work. The reliabilities of the components are turntable ($p_1 = 0.97$), amplifier ($p_2 = 0.99$), each speaker ($p_3 = p_4 = 0.98$). Find the reliability of the system.

Since this is a series system the reliability is the product of the component reliabilities:

$$R = p_1 p_2 p_3 p_4 = 0.9222.$$

E21.7 Consider the system of E21.6 with a revised criterion for success. For successful operation the turntable, amplifier, and at least one of the speakers must work. Find the reliability of this case.

First consider the two speakers as a parallel system since only one must work for successful operation.

$$R_s = 1 - (1-p_3)(1-p_4) = 1 - (0.02)(0.02) = 0.9996.$$

The speaker combination forms a series system with the turntable and amplifier, so the total reliability is

$$R = p_1 p_2 R_s = (0.97)(0.99)(0.9996) = 0.9599.$$

The revised criterion for success has increased significantly the reliability of the system. When reliabilities get close to 1, it is more meaningful to compare the probabilities of failure of the system. For E21.6, the probability of failure is

$(1 - R) = 1 - 0.9222 = 0.0778$, about an 8% chance of failure.

For E21.7, the probability of failure is

$(1 - R) = 1 - 0.9599 = 0.0401$, about a 4% chance of failure.

The chance of failure has been almost cut in half. Of course the quality of performance has been also been reduced.

E21.8 A space vehicle has three identical computers operating simultaneously and solving the same problems. The outputs of the three computers are compared, and if two or three of them are identical, that result is used. The reliability of each computer is 0.9. The system is successful if two out of three of the computers are successful. Compute the reliability of the system.

Using the formula for the two out of three system:

$$R = \sum_{j=2}^{3} \binom{3}{i} (0.9)^i (0.1)^{3-i}$$

$$= 3(0.9)^2(0.1) + (0.9)^3 = 0.972.$$

The reliability of the combination of three computers is much greater than that of an individual. This is an example of the use of redundancy to increase reliability. Since only one computer is required to perform the function, the other two are redundant from a functional point of view. They do play an important role, however, in increasing the reliability of the system.

The independence of failures is important here. If some failure mechanism causes all three computers to fail simultaneously, the reliability improvement will not be realized. For instance if all three computers used the same program and the program had an error, the combination of results will certainly be no better than any one of the individuals. The use of redundancy is frequently found in systems for which failure has particularly severe consequences, such as in the space program or for very complex systems with many components.

E21.9 If all three of the computers of E21.8 must work for successful operation, determine the system reliability. Since this is a series system the reliability is

$$R = p_1 p_2 p_3 = p^3 = (0.9)^3 = 0.729.$$

E21.10 If only one of the computers of E21.8 must work for successful operation, determine the system reliability. This is a parallel system, so

$$R = 1 - [(1-p_1)(1-p_2)(1-p_3)] = 1 - q^3 = 1 - (0.1)^3 = 0.999.$$

MODELING

In order to compute the reliability of systems that are not simple series, parallel or k out of n, it may be necessary to decompose the system into subsystems, that can first be analyzed independently. Each of the subsystems can then be replaced by a single component with the subsystem reliability. The resultant reduced system may be of one of the simple structures.

Often the reliabilities of components are given as functions of time. For instance, a common assumption is that components have an exponential distribution for time to failure. In this case the component reliability is

$$p(t) = 1 - P\{\text{failure time} < t\} = e^{-\lambda t}.$$

The parameter λ is called the failure rate of the component and given as failures per unit time. λ must use the same time dimension as t. This distribution for failure time implies that the component fails at random. This is typical when the propensity for failure does not depend on the component's age. This assumption is often adopted for electronic components. It is also appropriate when the component is itself a complex system of many parts. After the system has been in operation for some time many of the parts will have failed and been replaced. Thus the system has a mixture of old and new parts and the failure rate will approach a constant.

One of the advantages of the constant failure rate assumption is obtained with a series system. In this case the system reliability is

$$R(t) = p_1 p_2 \ldots p_n = (e^{-\lambda_1 t})(e^{-\lambda_2 t}) \ldots (e^{-\lambda_n t}) = \exp\left(-\sum_{i=1}^{n} \lambda_i t\right).$$

From this expression we note that the system failure rate is the sum of the component failure rates.

Other failure distributions are appropriate for other classes of components. A common one is the Wiebold distribution, which allows one to model components that age. The variation of system reliability with time is computed by evaluating the reliability function using the time-varying component reliabilities.

PROBLEMS

P21.4 Compute the reliability of the system of 21.1 when the reliabilities of the various components are given in the table below.

Component	Radar	Missile	Computer	Human
Reliability	0.9	0.96	0.98	0.95

P21.5 The Defense Department would like to increase the reliability of the missile system of P21.4. Evaluate the system reliabilities for the system changes proposed below. The changes are not cumulative.

a. Add another radar with the same reliability. Three radars are required for successful operation.
b. Add a third human operator. Only one is required.
c. Add an entire duplicate missile system at a nearby location. Only one of the two systems must work for mission success.

P21.6 Consider again the computers of E21.8 but now find the reliability of the two out of three system as a function of time. Assume the time for failure of each of the computers has an exponential distribution with a mean time between failures of 50 hours. The failure rate (λ) to be used in the equation is the reciprocal of the mean time between failures. Plot a curve of the reliability as a function of time over the range 0 to 100. Plot the curves for the system and for a single computer. Comment on the effects of this arrangement of redundancy over time.

P21.7 Assume that all three computers must work successfully for system success. With the failure rates used in P21.6 plot system reliability over the range in time of 0 to 100. What is the failure rate of the system?

P21.8 Assume that the three computers are arranged in parallel and that only one must work successfully for system success. With the failure rates used in P21.6 plot system reliability over the range in time of 0 to 100.

Exact System Reliability (21.4)

If the system structure is not one of the simple systems, it becomes difficult to compute the exact system reliability. This section presents several methods based on a graphical description of the system.

GOAL

- Given a flow network describing a system, be able to compute the exact system reliability using either the minimum cuts or the minimum paths of the network.

DEFINITIONS

Flow Network: A directed network consisting of nodes and arcs, as illustrated in Fig. 21.1. One node is defined as the source (node A in the example), and a second node is defined as a sink (node D). Each component of the network is identified as an arc passing from one node to another. The arcs are numbered for identification. A failure of a component is equivalent to an arc being removed or cut from the network. The system is successful if there exists a path from the source to the sink. The system is failed if there exists no such path. The reliability of the system is the probability that there exist one or more paths from the source to the sink.

Minimal Path: A set of components such that if all the components in the set are successful while all other components of the system are failed, the system is successful; however, if any one component is removed from the minimal path, the system will fail. A minimum path corresponds to a simple path from the source to the sink in the flow network. In the example the sets {1,4}, {1,3,5}, {2,5} define the minimal paths.

Minimal Cut: A set of components such that if all the components in the set fail while all other components in the system are successful, the system will fail; however, if any one component is removed from the minimal cut, the system will be successful. In the flow network a minimal cut breaks all simple paths from the source to the sink. From Fig. 21.1 we note that the minimal cuts are: {1,2}, {1,5}, {2,3,4}, and {4,5}.

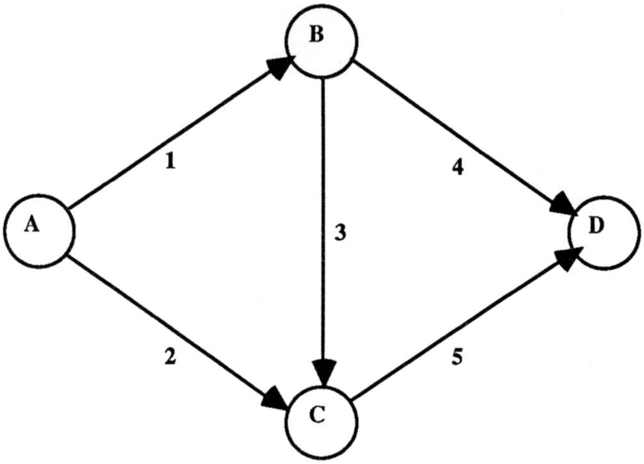

Figure 21.1 **Flow Network Describing a System of Five Components**

RESULTS

System Reliability The probability that the system structure function is 1.

$$R = P\{\phi(\mathbf{X}) = 1\}.$$

The Structure Function in Terms of Minimal Paths Let $\boldsymbol{P}$ be a set of components comprising a minimal path. Using X_i as an indicator of the success of component i, the event of a successful path is

$$\prod_{i \varepsilon P}(X_i), \qquad (\Pi \text{ means product}).$$

The event of a failed path is

$$1 - \prod_{i \varepsilon P}(X_i).$$

The system is successful if all the minimal paths do not fail:

$$\phi(\mathbf{X}) = 1 - [1 - \prod_{i \varepsilon P_1}(X_i)][1 - \prod_{i \varepsilon P_2}(X_i)] \ldots [1 - \prod_{i \varepsilon P_k}(X_i)], \qquad (1)$$

where $\boldsymbol{P}_1, \boldsymbol{P}_2, \ldots, \boldsymbol{P}_k$ are the minimal paths of the system.

The Structure Function in Terms of Minimal Cuts Let $\boldsymbol{C}$ be a set of components comprising a minimal cut. Using X_i as an indicator of the success of component i, the event that all components in the cut fail is

$$\prod_{i \varepsilon C}(1 - X_i),$$

The event that all the cut components do not fail is

$$1 - \prod_{i \varepsilon C}(1 - X_i).$$

The system is successful if none of the minimal cuts fail:

$$\phi(\mathbf{X}) = [1 - \prod_{i \varepsilon C_1}(1 - X_i)][1 - \prod_{i \varepsilon C_2}(1 - X_i)] \ldots [1 - \prod_{i \varepsilon C_k}(1 - X_i)], \tag{2}$$

where $C_1, C_2, \ldots, C_k$ are the minimal cuts of the system.

Computing Exact Reliability Starting from either of the structure functions defined above, one can multiply through the factors until one obtains a sum of terms such that each term is a product of factors having the form X_i or $(1 - X_i)$. Substituting in this expression p_i for X_i and q_i for $(1 - X_i)$ one obtains an exact expression for the system reliability.

EXAMPLES

E21.11 A system has four components in series with reliabilities

$$p_1 = 0.97, p_2 = 0.99, p_3 = p_4 = 0.98.$$

Find the system reliability with both the cut and path approaches.

The network for the series system is shown in the figure. The source is A and the sink is E. The component reliabilities are shown in the figure.

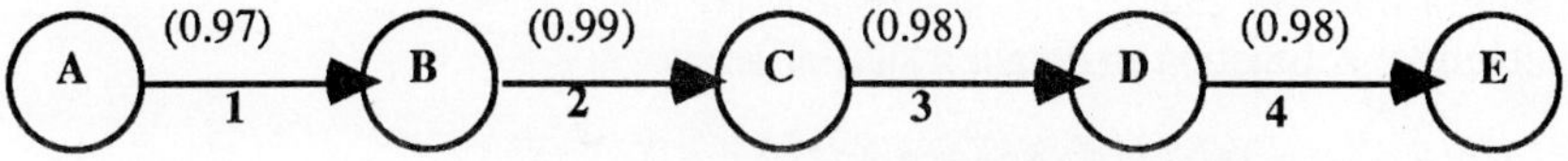

By observation we note that the system has a single minimal path:

$$P_1 = \{1, 2, 3, 4\}.$$

Using this path, the structure function can be written according to Eq. (1):

$$\phi(\mathbf{X}) = 1 - [\ 1 - X_1X_2X_3X_4\ ] = X_1X_2X_3X_4.$$

The reliability of the system is obtained by substituting p_i for X_i in this expression.

$$R = p_1p_2p_3p_4 = 0.9222.$$

Alternatively we can derive the reliability from the cuts of the system. Again by observation we note that there are four minimal cuts:

$$C_1 = \{1\}, C_2 = \{2\}, C_3 = \{3\}, C_4 = \{4\}.$$

Using Eq. (2), the system structure function is:

$$\begin{aligned}\phi(\mathbf{X}) &= [1 - (1 - X_1)]\ [1 - (1 - X_2)]\ [1 - (1 - X_3)]\ [1 - (1 - X_4)] \\ &= X_1X_2X_3X_4.\end{aligned}$$

As expected, the same structure function is obtained. There is really no need to use this analysis for the series system, because we have noted these results in earlier units, but it does illustrate the approach to more complex systems.

E21.12 Consider the system of E21.11 except that now we only require that components 1, 2, and *either* component 3 or 4 must work for system success. The flow network for this case is shown in the figure. The network graphically illustrates that components 3 and 4 are now in parallel and the pair is in series with components 1 and 2. Node A is the source and node D is the sink.

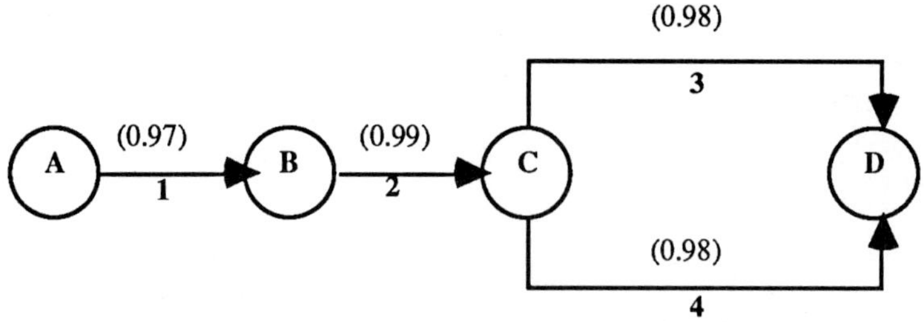

To derive the structure function we note that the minimal paths are

$$\boldsymbol{P}_1 = \{1, 2, 3\}, \text{ and } \boldsymbol{P}_2 = \{1, 2, 4\}.$$

Using Eq. (1), the structure function is

$$\phi(\mathbf{X}) = [1 - (1 - X_1X_2X_3)]\,[1 - (1 - X_1X_2X_4)].$$

Manipulating this function to obtain a sum of terms,

$$\phi(\mathbf{X}) = X_1X_2X_3 + X_1X_2X_4 - X_1X_2X_3X_4.$$

For this result we have used the fact that since X_i is a binary variable,

$$X_i^2 = X_i.$$

Since the structure function is now in the form of a sum of terms, the reliability is easily determined by substituting p_i for X_i.

$$\begin{aligned} R &= p_1p_2p_3 + p_1p_2p_4 - p_1p_2p_3p_4. \\ &= (0.97)(0.99)(0.98) + (0.97)(0.99)(0.98) - (0.97)(0.99)(0.98)(0.98) \\ &= 0.9599 \end{aligned}$$

which is the same as the answer obtained in E21.7.

The results can also be found using the minimal cuts. The cuts are

$$\boldsymbol{C}_1 = \{1\}, \boldsymbol{C}_2 = \{2\}, \boldsymbol{C}_3 = \{3,4\}.$$

Using Eq. (2),

$$\phi(\mathbf{X}) = [1 - (1 - X_1)]\,[1 - (1 - X_2)]\,[1 - (1 - X_3)(1 - X_4)].$$

Manipulating this expression to obtain a sum of terms we obtain

$$\begin{aligned}\phi(\mathbf{X}) = 1 &- (1 - X_1) - (1 - X_2) - (1 - X_3)(1 - X_4) + (1 - X_1)(1 - X_2) \\ &+ (1 - X_1)(1 - X_3)(1 - X_4) + (1 - X_2)(1 - X_3)(1 - X_4) \\ &- (1 - X_1)(1 - X_2)(1 - X_3)(1 - X_4).\end{aligned}$$

Although it does not happen in the example, we will use the identity

$$(1 - X_i)^2 = (1 - X_i)$$

if a factor is squared during the manipulation.

The reliability function is obtained by replacing $(1 - X_i)$ with q_i,

$$\begin{aligned}\phi(\mathbf{X}) &= 1 - q_1 - q_2 - q_3q_4 + q_1q_2 + q_1q_3q_4 + q_2q_3q_4 - q_1q_2q_3q_4 \\ &= 1 - 0.03 - 0.01 - (0.02)(0.02) + (0.03)(0.01) + (0.03)(0.02)(0.02) \\ &\quad + (0.01)(0.02)(0.02) - (0.03)(0.01)(0.02)(0.02) \\ &= 1 - 0.04008388 = 0.9599.\end{aligned}$$

E21.13 A system has three computers of which at least two must work for successful operation. The reliability of each computer is 0.9. Find the reliability of the system.

We identify the components of the system with the indices 1, 2, and 3. This is a two out of three system previously analyzed in E21.8. There is no way to draw a flow diagram for this system in which each component appears only once. It is possible to enumerate the minimal cuts and paths using simple logic. The minimal requirement for system operation is that two of three computers must work, so the minimal paths are

$$\boldsymbol{P}_1 = \{1, 2\}, \boldsymbol{P}_2 = \{1, 3\}, \text{ and } \boldsymbol{P}_3 = \{2, 3\}.$$

The minimum requirement for system failure is that two components fail, so the minimum cuts are

$$\boldsymbol{C}_1 = \{1, 2\}, \boldsymbol{C}_2 = \{1, 3\}, \text{ and } \boldsymbol{C}_3 = \{2, 3\}.$$

In this interesting case, the sets defining the minimum cuts and the minimum paths are the same.

Using Eq. (1) we derive the structure function

$$\phi(\mathbf{X}) = 1 - (1 - X_1X_2)\,(1 - X_1X_3)\,(1 - X_2X_3).$$

From this expression we obtain

$$\begin{aligned}\phi\,(\mathbf{X}) &= X_1X_2 + X_1X_3 + X_2X_3 - 2X_1X_2X_3 \\ R &= p_1p_2 + p_1p_3 + p_2p_3 - 2p_1p_2p_3.\end{aligned}$$

When all three components have the same reliability, p,

$$R = 3p^2 - 2p^3.$$

This expression is equivalent to the one obtained earlier for the two out of three system. A different but equivalent expression can be derived using the minimal cut approach.

COMPUTATIONAL CONSIDERATIONS

This procedure can be used to derive the structure function and associated reliability function for any system that can be defined by a flow network. There are two difficulties with this approach. The first is determining the set of minimum paths or cuts. In general the system with many components will have very many cuts and paths, and it is a difficult computational problem to determine the complete set. In our examples we have simply used observation; however, that procedure will hardly be satisfactory for a network of reasonable size. The second problem is to construct and evaluate the structure and reliability functions. In general if there are k cuts or paths, the corresponding reliability equation will have $2^k - 1$ terms. Because of these difficulties it is common to approximate the reliability function of complicated systems. This is the subject of the next unit.

MODELING

For a complicated network it is often beneficial to look for subsystems of components that form simple structures such as the series, parallel, or k of n structures. The reliabilities of these subsystems can be determined first and the subsystem replaced with a single equivalent component. Even subsystems not having a simple structure can be analyzed with the methods of this unit with the subsystem replaced by a single equivalent component whose reliability is the reliability of the subsystem. When as many subsystems as possible have been reduced in this fashion, the resultant network will be much smaller and will perhaps have a simple structure or be amenable to further reduction. This decomposition approach is often effective in significantly reducing computational effort.

Complex structures will have different numbers of minimal cuts and paths. Since an exact analysis can be done using either, it is best to use the method with the smallest number. For instance a series system with n components has n cuts but only one path. A parallel system with n components has n paths but only one cut.

PROBLEMS

P21.9 The figure below represents a series-parallel system. The components in each parallel set all have the same reliability as shown on the figure. Find the system reliability by:

- **a.** constructing the reliability function by enumerating the minimal paths.
- **b.** constructing the reliability function by enumerating the minimal cuts.
- **c.** first evaluating the parallel structures and then combining the parallel results as a series system.

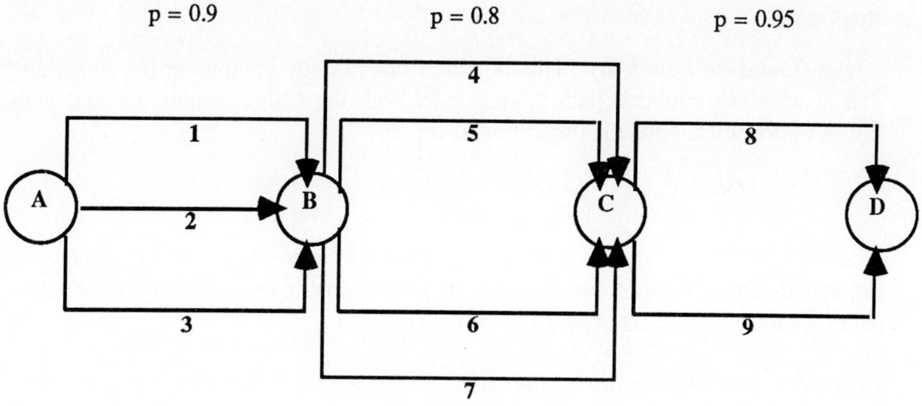

P21.10 Find the system reliability for the flow network with both the cut and path methods.

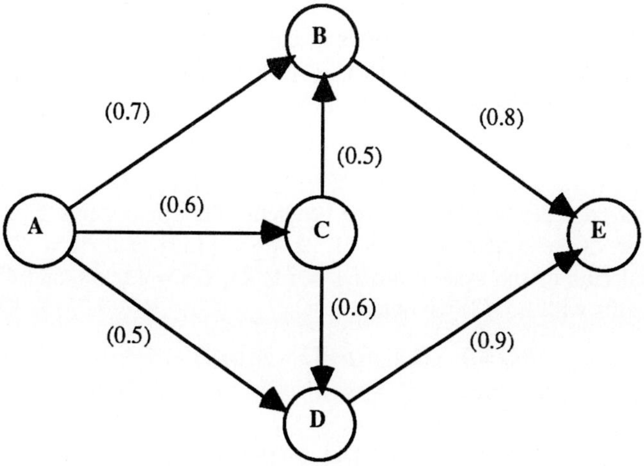

Bounds on System Reliability (21.5)

One of the reasons it is difficult to compute the exact reliability of a complex system is the difficulty in manipulating the structure function to obtain the proper form. The minimum paths and cuts defined in the last section can be used to obtain upper and lower bounds on the exact reliability in a fashion that makes it unnecessary to do these manipulations.

GOAL

- Given a flow diagram representing a system, be able to compute upper and lower bounds on the exact reliability using the minimal paths and cuts of the network.

RESULTS

Upper Bound on Reliability This bound is obtained by computing the probability that at least one minimal path is successful with the added assumption that paths fail independently. Thus the upper bound is

$$R_U = 1 - [1 - \prod_{i \varepsilon P_1} p_i]\,[1 - \prod_{i \varepsilon P_2} p_i] \cdots [1 - \prod_{i \varepsilon P_k} p_i], \tag{3}$$

where $P_1, P_2, \ldots, P_k$ are the minimal paths of the network. The inaccuracy in the equation results from the fact that, in general, paths are not independent since some components are common to more than one path.

Lower Bound on Reliability This bound is obtained by computing the probability that every minimal cut is successful, with the added assumption that cuts fail independently. Thus the lower bound is

$$R_L = [1 - \prod_{i \varepsilon C_1} q_i]\,[1 - \prod_{i \varepsilon C_2} q_i] \cdots [1 - \prod_{i \varepsilon C_k} q_i], \tag{4}$$

where $C_1, C_2, \ldots, C_k$ are the minimal cuts of the network. The inaccuracy in the equation results from the fact that, in general, cuts are not independent since some components are common to more than one cut.

EXAMPLE

E21.14 Consider the two out of three problem with components 1, 2, and 3. The minimal paths of the system are $P_1 = \{1, 2\}$, $P_2 = \{1, 3\}$, and $P_3 = \{2, 3\}$. The minimal cuts of the system are $C_1 = \{1, 2\}$, $C_2 = \{1, 3\}$, and $C_3 = \{2, 3\}$. Using the paths with Eq. (3) we obtain

$$R_U = 1 - [1 - p_1p_2][1 - p_1p_3][1 - p_2p_3].$$

Using the cuts with Eq. (4) we obtain

$$R_L = [1 - q_1q_2][1 - q_1q_3][1 - q_2q_3].$$

Assuming all components have equal reliabilities of 0.9 ($p = 0.9$, $q = 0.1$), the bounds become

$$R_U = 1 - (1 - p^2)^3 = 1 - (.19)^3 = 0.993141$$
$$R_L = (1 - q^2)^3 = (0.99)^3 = 0.9702991.$$

This compares to the exact reliability calculated earlier:

$$R = 0.972.$$

MODELING

In the previous example, the lower bound appears to be closer to the exact reliability than the upper bound. The lower bound will usually be a better approximation than the upper bound when component reliabilities are high (>0.9).

With high component reliabilities it is more likely that a single cut will cause failure rather than a collection of two or more. The assumption of independence of cuts will cause less inaccuracy in this case. The cut approximation converges to the true reliability as the component reliability approaches 1. The upper bound approximation will usually be a better approximation when the reliability is very low. Since for most reliability studies component reliabilities are high and a lower bound is a conservative measure of reliability, the minimal cut approximation is practically the more important of the two.

PROBLEMS

P21.11 Compute the upper and lower bound approximations for the network of P21.9 and compare them with the exact reliability.

P21.12 Compute the upper and lower bound approximations for the network of P21.10 and compare them with the exact reliability.

P21.13 For the two out of three system considered in E21.14, compute the upper and lower bound approximations as a function of time. Assume each component has an exponential distribution for time to failure with a failure rate of 0.02/hour. Plot a curve showing the upper and lower bound approximations together with the exact reliability curve over the time range from 0 to 100 hours.

P21.14 Repeat P21.13 if the system is a three out of five system.

P21.15 Repeat P21.12 if the system is a four out of seven system.

Problems

P21.16 The figure shows a system with nine components with reliabilities given. Components 3, 4, and 5 form a two out of three system. Write the structure function for this system. Compute the accurate probability that a successful path will exist from A to B. Compute the minimal cut and minimal path approximations.

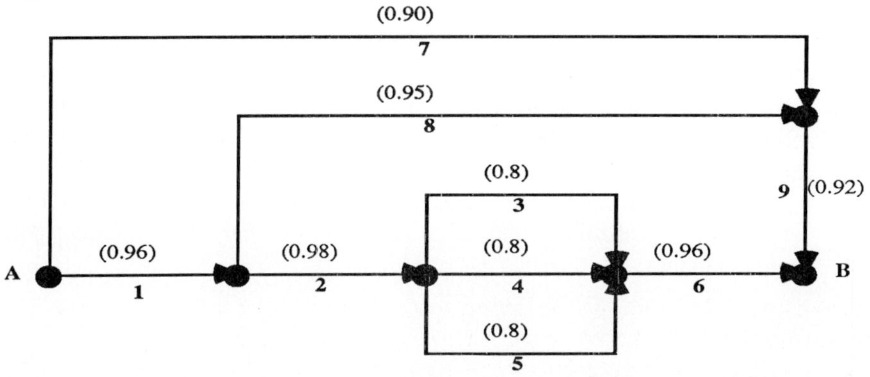

P21.17 A fuse is used to protect an electrical circuit from overload. The fuse can fail in two modes, short and open. If it fails in the short mode, the fuse will not interrupt the circuit when necessary. If it fails in the open mode, the circuit will be interrupted by the fuse itself. Assume a single fuse has probabilities of open and short of q_O and q_S, respectively. The events of open and short are independent. Define success in two ways: the system does not fail because of shorts, and the system does not fail because of opens. Write structure functions for both definitions for each arrangement shown in the figure. Let the reliability be the probability that the system does not fail in either mode. Compute accurate reliabilities for each definition for success using $q_O = 0.05$ and $q_S = 0.1$.

a.

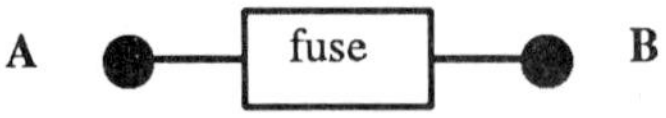

b.

c.

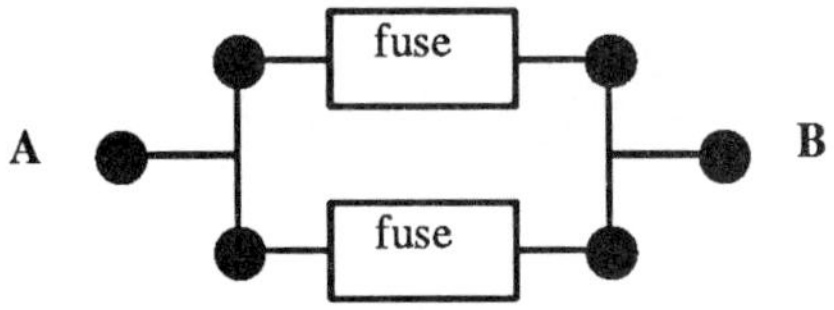

d.

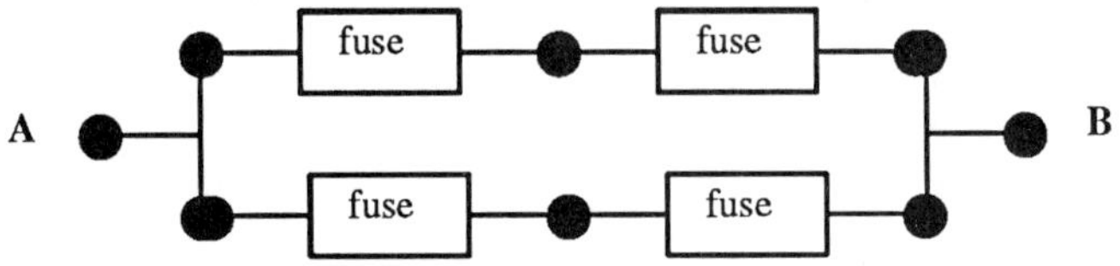

e.

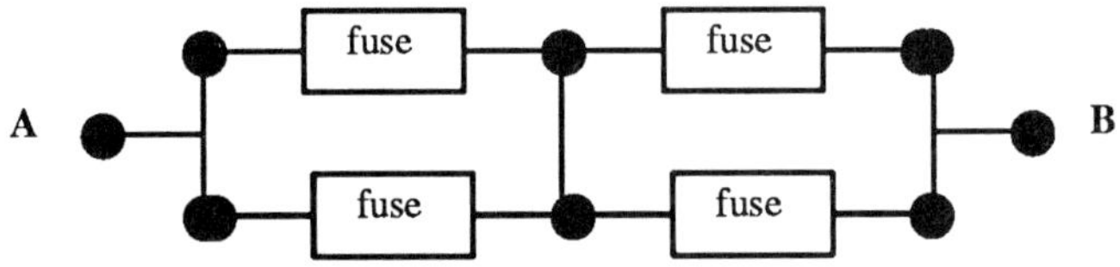

P21.18 The figure shows roads between two towns, A and B, in a mountainous area. During the winter, travel is difficult because of the threat of snow. The probability that any given road will be impassable is 0.6. The conditions on the roads are independent. Find the probability that there will be a passable route from A to B. Roads can be traveled in either direction. Find the accurate probability and also the minimal cut and minimal path approximations.

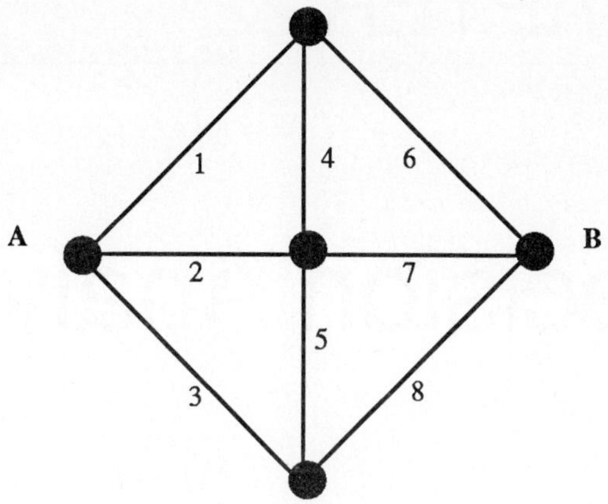

P21.19 The figure shows the pipe layout in a lawn sprinkler system. Sprayers are located at every intersection of the pipe and also at the corners of the system. Thus there are 16 sprayers. Two things can happen to a sprayer: it can break off or it can get clogged. If any one of the sprayers breaks off, a great stream of water will pour forth and the system will have failed. If one of the sprayers clogs, it will fail to water the lawn in the immediate vicinity; however, adjacent sprayers can reach the affected areas. The system is judged to be failed if any two adjacent sprayers are both clogged. For one sprayer, let the probability of breakage be 0.01 and the probability of clogging be 0.05. Find the reliability of the system (the probability that it does not fail in either mode) using the minimal cut approximation.

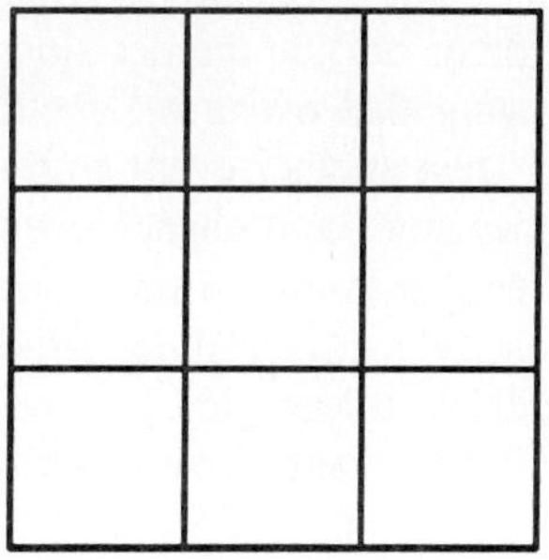

CHAPTER 22

Decision Analysis

Decision Trees (22.4)

Consider a decision problem of the following nature. Some decision must initially be made involving the commitment of resources. After that decision an event will occur that is influenced by forces outside the decision maker's control and whose outcome is uncertain. Following that event yet another decision must be made, again committing resources. Then another event with uncertain results will occur. This process of alternating decisions and chance events will continue until some final result occurs and the effectiveness of the entire decision process can be judged. This decision problem is easily recognized in activities such as chess games, development of properties, and battle strategies. It makes some difference whether or not the forces affecting the chance events are competitive. In the competitive case, the procedures of game theory are appropriate. If the forces are benign, then the methods of decision analysis, as discussed in this chapter, are appropriate. Here we will call the forces "nature" and assume that nature does not operate in a competitive fashion, but rather according to probabilistic laws that can be estimated by experimentation or expert judgment. Given enough data, decision analysis allows one to determine an optimum policy.

GOALS

- Given an appropriate decision problem, be able to construct a decision tree representing the sequence of decisions and chance events.

- Given prior and conditional probabilities of events, be able to compute posterior probabilities.
- Given a decision tree with all relevant parameters, be able to determine an optimum policy according to Bayes' criterion.

DEFINITIONS

To illustrate these definitions we use the oil-drilling example from H & L. The problem involves two decisions; first, whether to perform seismic tests on the well site; then, after observing the results of the test, if performed, what method should be used to bring the well into production. Various details of the problem will be presented with the definitions and results that follow.

Decision Tree: A graphical description of a sequential process, as illustrated in Fig. 22.1. The tree is made up of decision nodes, shown in the figure as squares, chance nodes, shown as white circles, and terminal nodes, shown as black circles. Branches, the lines connecting the nodes, represent specific decisions and outcomes of chance events. We will draw the tree from left to right. Branches leave nodes going to the right and enter nodes coming from the left. We have also numbered the nodes so that every node has an unique index which is smaller than any of its successor nodes. Node 1, which precedes all other nodes, is called the root node. (To increase clarity, we have not numbered the terminal nodes. They are indexed 23 through 82. Because of size limitations, some nodes at the bottom of the figure are not shown.)

Decision Node: A node shown as a square. The node represents some decision that must be made in the sequential process. The capital letter in bold italics within the square is the name of the set of possible decisions. The branches that leave the node describe the individual decisions in the set. On the figure the branches are numbered, 1, 2, ... The associated decision will be identified with a lowercase letter with the number used as an index. For instance the decision nodes in the example problem with the corresponding decision sets are

$$\boldsymbol{S} = \{s_1, s_2\}$$
$$\boldsymbol{A} = \{a_1, a_2, a_3\}.$$

$\boldsymbol{S}$ is the decision regarding seismic testing, where s_1 is the decision not to do seismic testing and s_2 is the decision to do seismic testing. The decision set A includes the possible actions regarding the well; a_1, a_2, and a_3 are, respectively, drill for oil, unconditionally lease the well, and conditionally lease the well.

A number in parentheses adjacent to the branch shows a cost particularly associated with the decision. The cost adjacent to the s_2 branch is the cost of testing. In general we use $C(j)$ as the cost associated with decision j.

Chance Node: A node represented by a circle. The node represents some chance event that occurs during the sequential process. The capital letter in bold italics within the circle is the name of the set of possible outcomes of the event. The

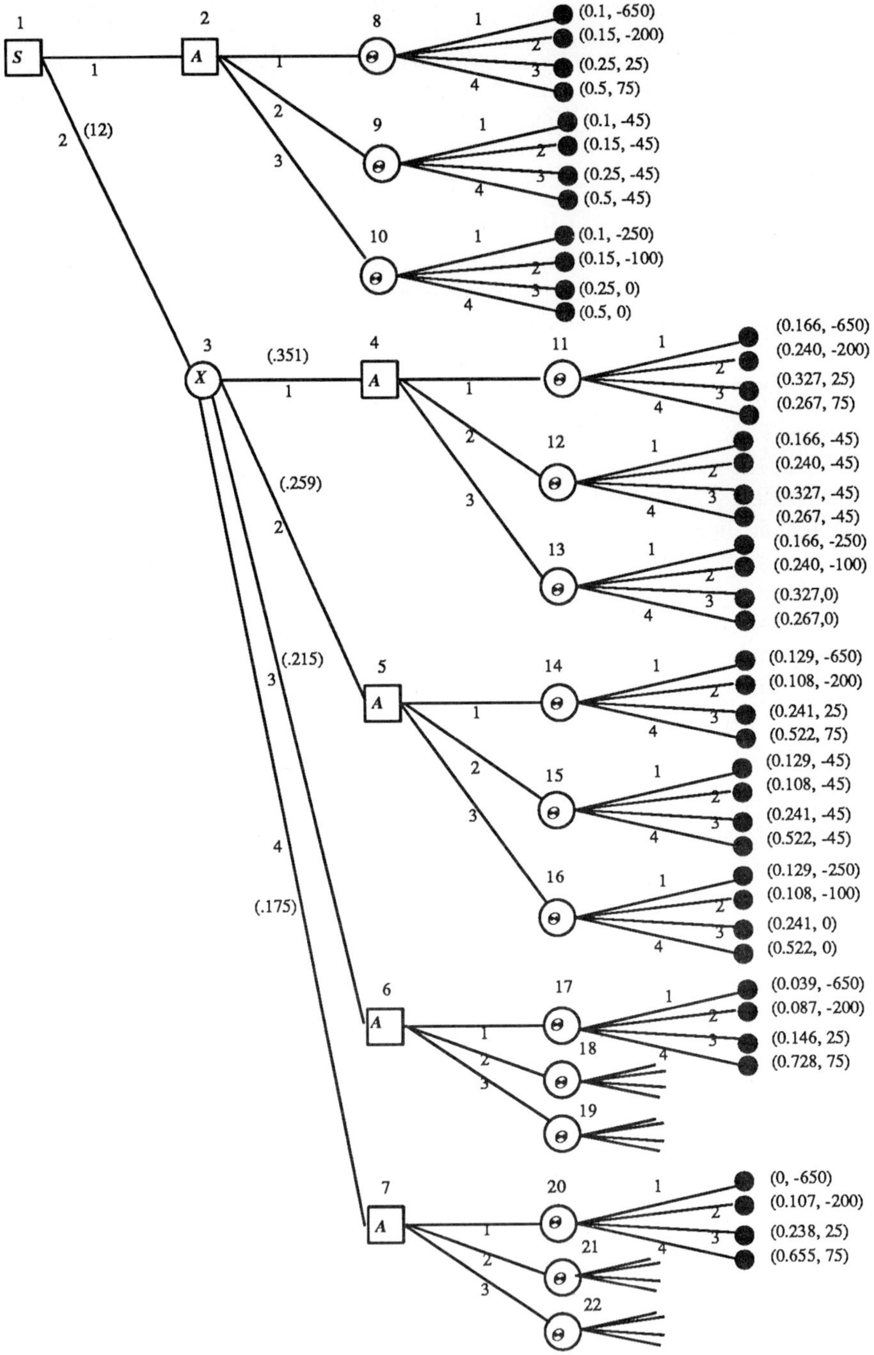

Figure 22.1 **Decision Tree**

branches that leave the node describe the individual outcomes in the set. The outcome associated with a branch will be identified with a lowercase letter with the number adjacent to the branch used as an index. For instance the chance nodes in the figure with the corresponding outcome sets are

$$X = \{x_1, x_2, x_3, x_4\}$$
$$\Theta = \{\theta_1, \theta_2, \theta_3, \theta_4\}.$$

In the example, X is the set of possible outcomes of the seismic test, with the four outcomes in order: closed geological structure, probably a closed structure, nonclosed structure, and no structure. The set Θ is the set of outcomes regarding the success of the well with the four outcomes in order: 500,000 barrel well, 200,000 barrel well, 50,000 barrel well, and dry well.

A number must be associated with each branch leaving a chance node, which gives the conditional probability of that particular outcome, given all the decisions and chance outcomes on the path from the root node to the chance node. In general we show these probabilities in parentheses adjacent to the outcome branch. Because of space limitations in Fig. 22.1, the probabilities are shown to the right of the terminal nodes.

A number can also be associated with a branch leaving a chance node showing the cost associated with that outcome. Again we use the notation $C(j)$ to specify this cost for outcome j. If this number is not zero, it appears as the second number in the parentheses adjacent to an outcome branch.

For the example, only the outcomes leading to terminal nodes have these costs. They are shown in the parentheses to the right of the terminal nodes. The costs are based on the table below, which shows the income as a function of well success and the method selected for bringing the well into production. A positive return is shown as a negative number on the decision tree because that figure shows cost or loss as a positive number.

		Revenue			
Well success		q_1	q_2	q_3	q_4
Decision =	a_1	650	200	–25	–75
	a_2	45	45	45	45
	a_3	250	100	0	0

Conditional Probabilities ($P\{j \mid \text{Path}\}$)**:** Every branch leaving a chance node must be assigned a number which is the conditional probability of that particular outcome given all the decisions and chance outcomes on the path from the root node to the chance node. In the example, the decisions do not affect the probabilities of the chance events. The probabilities leaving the chance node X are the unconditional probabilities of the various test outcomes since no other chance events precede X. In the lower part of the diagram, where testing is done, the probabilities leaving the nodes marked Θ are the conditional probabilities of well success, given the results of the test. In the upper part of the diagram, where no testing is performed, they are simply the unconditional probabilities of well success.

We use the notation above to indicate this probability with "Path" designating the intersection (the symbol $\cap$ means intersection) of all decisions and chance outcomes on the path from the root node. For instance for outcome x_1 leaving node 3, we can write the conditional probability as

$$P\{x_1 \mid s_2\} = P\{x_1\}.$$

The second form is appropriate in this case since the decision to perform the test does not affect the basic structure of the well site.

The outcome θ_1 leaving node 11 will have conditional probability

$$P\{\theta_1 \mid s_2 \cap x_1 \cap a_1\} = P\{\theta_1 \mid x_1\}.$$

Again, the second form is preferred because the decisions do not affect the probabilities of the outcome θ_1. The probability is affected by the results of the test. In general, we include in the conditional statement only decisions and outcomes that have an effect on the probability. If the outcomes θ_1 and x_1 were statistically independent we could remove the x_1 from this probability statement.

Since all possible outcomes are included in the set of branches leaving a chance node, the sum of the conditional probabilities leaving the node must equal 1.

Decision Function (*d*): A function that specifies a decision for each decision node. In Fig. 22.1, the decision nodes are identified by the indices 1, 2, 4, 5, 6, and 7. A decision function must specify a decision for each of these nodes. The optimum decisions will be identified as $d^*(i)$, where i is the index of a decision node.

Expected Loss ($f(i)$): The expected loss (or cost) associated with node i obtained by following a given decision function.

Bayes Criterion: A criterion for optimality that specifies that all decisions should be made to minimize the expected loss at every decision node.

RESULTS

Computing Conditional Probabilities The probability for a branch on the decision tree is the conditional probability of the outcome, given the decisions and outcomes on the path from the root node to the branch. Unfortunately, probability data for an outcome may be provided as a conditional probability of the outcome, given the outcomes leading from the branch to a terminal node. For instance in the example problem the prior probabilities of well success are provided as

$$P\{\theta_1\} = 0.1, P\{\theta_2\} = 0.15, P\{\theta_3\} = 0.25, P\{\theta_4\} = 0.5.$$

The probabilities of the results of the seismic test are provided as probabilities conditioned by the characteristic of well success, $P\{x_i \mid \theta_j\}$. These probabilities are given in the table below.

Well success		$P\{x_i \mid \theta_j\}$ θ_1	θ_2	θ_3	θ_4
Test results =	x_1	0.583	0.563	0.458	0.188
	x_2	0.333	0.188	0.250	0.271
	x_3	0.083	0.125	0.125	0.313
	x_4	0.000	0.125	0.167	0.229

The analysis requires the marginal probabilities, $P\{x_i\}$, and the posterior probabilities, $P\{\theta_j \mid x_i\}$. These can be determined by applying Bayes' law:

$$P\{x_i\} = \sum_{j=1}^{4} P\{x_i \mid \theta_j\}\, P\{\theta_j\}$$

$$P\{\theta_j \mid x_i\} = \frac{P\{x_i \mid q_j\}\, P\{\theta_j\}}{P\{x_i\}}\ .$$

The results of these calculations are displayed below.

$$P\{x_1\} = 0.351, P\{x_2\} = 0.259, P\{x_3\} = 0.215, P\{x_4\} = 0.175.$$

Well success		$P\{\theta_i \mid x_j\}$ θ_1	θ_2	θ_3	θ_4
Test results =	x_1	0.166	0.240	0.327	0.267
	x_2	0.129	0.108	0.241	0.522
	x_3	0.039	0.087	0.146	0.728
	x_4	0.000	0.107	0.238	0.655

Computing Expected Loss at a Chance Node Let M represent a general chance node with index i. There are K outcomes leaving the node $(m_1, m_2, \ldots, m_K)$. Let $t(m_k)$ be the index of the node terminating the branch representing outcome m_k, $C(m_k)$ be the cost for the outcome, and $P\{m_k \mid \text{Path to } M\}$ be the conditional probability associated with the outcome. Then the expected loss at the chance node is

$$f(i) = E(\text{loss at } M)$$

$$= \sum_{k=1}^{K} P\{m_k \mid \text{Path to } M\}\ [C(m_k) + f(t_k)]. \qquad (1)$$

Computing Minimum Expected Loss at a Decision Node Let M represent a general decision node with index i. There are K decisions leaving the node $(m_1, m_2, \ldots, m_K)$. Let $t(m_k)$ be the index of the node terminating the branch representing decision m_k and $C(m_k)$ be the cost for the decision. Then the minimum expected loss at the decision node is

$$f(i) = \text{Minimum } E(\text{loss at } M)$$

$$f(i) = \underset{m_k \varepsilon M}{\text{Minimum}}\ [C(m_k) + f(t_k)]. \qquad (2)$$

The optimum decision is the index that obtains the minimum. We call this

$$d^*(i) = (k^* \mid C(m_{k^*}) + f(t_{k^*}) = \underset{m_k \varepsilon M}{\text{Minimum}} [C(m_k) + f(t_k)]).$$

ALGORITHM

The results described in Eqs. (1) and (2) suggest a simple algorithm to solve the decision tree for the optimum decision function. It is similar to a dynamic programming algorithm since it starts at the end of the tree and works backwards toward the root. It is a one-pass algorithm since it only visits each node once.

A1. Choose the node with the largest index. Let this be node *i*. (Recall that the nodes are numbered so that every node has an index smaller than any of its successor nodes.)

A2. If node *i* is a terminal node go to step A3.

If node *i* is a chance node, use Eq. (1) to evaluate its expected loss and go to step A3.

If node *i* is a decision node, use Eq. (2) to evaluate its expected loss. Record the optimum decision as part of the optimum decision function. Go to step A3.

A3. Decrease *i* by 1. If *i* is greater than 0, go to step A2. Otherwise, stop with the optimum decision function.

EXAMPLE

The algorithm has been applied to the decision tree in Fig. 22.1, and the results are shown in the table below. Only decision and chance nodes are shown because no action is required for terminal nodes.

Node	*Name*	*Type*	*Expected loss*	*Optimum decision*
22	θ	Chance	–10.7	—
21	θ	Chance	–45.0	—
20	θ	Chance	+33.675	—
19	θ	Chance	–18.45	—
18	θ	Chance	–45.0	—
17	θ	Chance	+15.5	—
16	θ	Chance	–43.05	—
15	θ	Chance	–45.0	—
14	θ	Chance	–60.275	—
13	θ	Chance	–65.5	—
12	θ	Chance	–45.0	—
11	θ	Chance	–127.7	—
10	θ	Chance	–40.0	—
9	θ	Chance	–45.0	—
8	θ	Chance	–51.25	—
7	A	Decision	–45.0	2
6	A	Decision	–45.0	2
5	A	Decision	–60.275	1
4	A	Decision	–127.7	1
3	X	Chance	–78.01	
2	A	Decision	–51.25	1
1	S	Decision	–66.01	2

The optimum decision function is

$d^*(1) = 2$ Do seismic testing.
$d^*(2) = 1$ If seismic testing is not done, drill.
$d^*(4) = 1$ If seismic testing shows x_1, drill.
$d^*(5) = 1$ If seismic testing shows x_2, drill.
$d^*(6) = 2$ If seismic testing shows x_3, unconditionally lease.
$d^*(7) = 2$ If seismic testing shows x_4, unconditionally lease.

The decision function shows the optimum decision for every decision node.

Problems

P22.1 Consider again the example of this chapter but assume the effectiveness of the seismic test has been reevaluated with the results shown below. Find the optimum policy with this new data.

		$P\{x_i \mid \theta_j\}$			
Well success		θ_1	θ_2	θ_3	θ_4
Test results =	x_1	0.484	0.418	0.258	0.188
	x_2	0.233	0.242	0.250	0.271
	x_3	0.183	0.170	0.225	0.313
	x_4	0.100	0.170	0.267	0.228

P22.2 A new oil field has been discovered with different prior probabilities of well success. Using the original conditional probabilities for the results of the seismic test, find the optimum policy.

$$P\{\theta_1\} = 0.25, P\{\theta_2\} = 0.35, P\{\theta_3\} = 0.15, P\{\theta_4\} = 0.25.$$

P22.3 Use the original statement of the example but let the conditional leasing arrangement change. The returns for conditional lease are \$450,000 for a 500,000 barrel well, 175,000 for a 200,000 barrel well, and no return for 50,000 barrel or a dry well. Find the optimum policy.

P22.4 A bank manager wants to develop a decision policy to assist the bank's credit officers. We use a \$20,000 loan for a case study. The following information has been gathered from historical records regarding the percentage of customers in various income classes who seek such a loan.

Customer type	*Income (x 1000)*	*Percentage*
A	> 100	10%
B	80 – 100	20
C	60 – 80	40
D	< 60	30

There are several steps in the decision process for each customer. The officer first decides whether to reject the loan application, accept the application, or call for a credit check. Whenever a customer is rejected there is a loss of good will, which can be reflected as a cost that depends on the class of customer. When the application is accepted, there is a probability that the customer will default and the loan principal will be lost. If the customer does not default, the gain will be the interest income from the loan. All this information is shown in the table below.

Customer type	*Loss from rejection*	*Probability of default*	*Loss on default*	*Income from loan*	*Probability of good credit check*
A	1000	0.05	20000	2000	.95
B	500	0.10	20000	2200	.90
C	200	0.10	20000	2500	.80
D	0	0.15	20000	3000	.70

The cost of a credit check is $300. The results of the check are "good risk" or "bad risk." The good risk customer has a probability of default .05 less than the entries in the table above. The bad risk customer has a probability of default .05 more than the entries in the table above. After the credit check, the officer must accept or reject the loan application.

When a customer is rejected, assume that the alternative investment for the $20,000 has a $1500 return.

Show the decision tree for this situation and find the optimum decision policy.

P22.5 A microcomputer repairgirl has just been given a failed machine by a good customer. She would like to fix it with the least expenditure of money. One of four parts is probably failed. They are A, B, C, and D, with the cost of replacement $100, $200, $30, and $80, respectively. Let E be the event that something else is wrong. Three tests, X, Y, and Z, are available to help locate the failed part. The tests cost $50, $70, and $80, respectively. If E is discovered or the repairgirl decides to abandon testing, the motherboard can be replaced at a cost of $500. The prior probabilities for the components are

$$P\{A\} = 0.15, P\{B\} = 0.2, P\{C\} = 0.3, P\{D\} = 0.25, P\{E\} = 0.1.$$

a. When the repair girl first gets the machine she can repair the machine by replacing the motherboard at a cost of $500 or use test X to get a better idea what's wrong.

b. Test X can come up with three indications: 1. probably A or B failed, 2. probably C or D failed, 3. replace the motherboard. Conditional probabilities are

				$P\{x_j \mid F\}$		
Component (F)		*A*	*B*	*C*	*D*	*E*
Test results =	x_1	0.6	0.7	0.15	0.05	0.1
	x_2	0.2	0.2	0.55	0.85	0.3
	x_3	0.2	0.1	0.3	0.1	0.6

If Test X shows indication 1, the repairgirl can either use test Y or replace the motherboard. If the test shows indication 2, she can use test Z or replace the motherboard. If the test shows indication 3 she must replace the motherboard.

c. Test Y can come up with three indications: 1. A is failed, 2. B is failed, 3. replace the motherboard. The latter result occurs if the real problem is C, D, or E.

d. Test Z can come up with three indications: 1. C is failed, 2. D is failed, 3. replace the motherboard. The latter result occurs if the real problem is A, B, or E.

Show the decision tree for this problem and find the minimum expected cost policy.

CHAPTER 23

Simulation

Simulation Model for a Queueing System

Simulation, as it is used in Operations Research, is a mathematical modeling and solution technique quite different from the mathematical programming and stochastic process models described in the first 22 chapters of this book. With simulation, the analyst creates a model of each component of a complex system; we call this a module. The modules try to reproduce, with some approximation, the actual operation of the real components. They have time-varying inputs and time-varying outputs usually affected by random processes. The modules of the simulation are interconnected, with the outputs of one providing the inputs to others. A controller provides the logic that controls the flow among the several modules of the system.

Since the model is actually a computer program, which operates as a facsimile of its real world counterpart, it is much less restricted than analytical models. A skilled programmer can duplicate, within the limitations of the input and output interfaces of the computer, most operations that can be observed and understood. Because of this capacity for detail, simulation has become a very popular method of analysis. Particularly appealing is its capacity to model random variables with arbitrary distributions and systems that have a number of interacting random processes. Modern simulation languages, implemented on both mainframe and microcomputers, are very powerful modeling tools, allowing even a beginner to create representations of complex systems.

The method does have its costs, however. Because it attempts to reproduce a great deal of detail, a simulation model may require a large programming effort, its accuracy may be difficult to verify, and it probably will consume significant computer resources while running. Like queueing analysis, simulation is a tool that requires the enumeration of alternatives to determine an optimum design. Unlike queueing analysis, simulation does not yield expected values. Rather, a simulation run is like making an observation in the real world. The simulation provides statistics observed from the simulation run. Since statistics are themselves random variables, the interpretation of the results must be done carefully, with procedures based on statistical theory. This latter requirement is often neglected in practice, giving rise to the possibility of the misinterpretation of results.

In this chapter we adopt the limited goals of learning how to generate random variables, how to simulate a multichannel queue, and how to collect statistics from a simulation output. These simple skills are a good introduction to the much more complicated simulation programs encountered in practice.

GOALS

- Be able to simulate the realization of random variables with given distributions.
- Given the parameters of a multichannel queue, be able to simulate the operations of the system by hand using next-event incrementing.
- From the simulation of the multichannel queue, be able to compute statistics that measure the performance of the system.

DEFINITIONS

Event: Some occurrence that has significance to the system being modeled, such as an arrival of a customer at a queueing system or the completion of a service operation.

Fixed Time Incrementing: A procedure for performing a simulation in which time is advanced in discrete steps with equal intervals. At each time step the events that occurred during the interval are determined, and statistics concerning the system operation are gathered.

Next Event Incrementing: A procedure for performing a simulation in which time is advanced in discrete steps with unequal intervals. The system is observed and statistics gathered only at times when events occur.

Random Number: A number consisting of a specified number of random digits. A random digit is a realization of a random variable which takes on the integer values from 0 to 9. The probability distribution of the random variable is the discrete uniform distribution.

RESULTS

Generating Random Observations from a Probability Distribution This procedure is general for any distribution; however, for many distributions there are preferred alternative procedures. Say we have a random variable X, with a known probability density function $f_X(y)$. The cumulative distribution of the random variable is

$$F_X(x) = P(X \leq x) = \int_{-\infty}^{x} f_X(y)dy.$$

A random observation from the distribution is simulated with the following process.

- **a.** Select a random number and place a decimal point in front of it. Let the resulting number be called r. In this way we get a random number drawn from a uniform distribution with the range 0 to 1. The number of digits in the random number determines the accuracy of this procedure.
- **b.** Set the random number equal to the cumulative distribution expressed as a function of x.

$$r = F_X(x).$$

- **c.** The desired random observation is the value of x that solves this equation.

$$x = F_X^{-1}(r).$$

Generating Random Observations from an Exponential Distribution The exponential distribution with expected value $1/\alpha$ has the cumulative distribution

$$F_X(x) = 1 - e^{-\alpha x}, \text{ for } x \geq 0.$$

Applying the general procedure above to this specific distribution, one can solve in closed form for the value of the random observation.

$$x = -(1/\alpha) \ln (1 - r).$$

Alternatively, since $(1 - r)$ also comes from a uniform distribution, the following equation provides a random observation from the exponential distribution. We will use this equation for the examples and problems.

$$x = -(1/\alpha) \ln (r).$$

Generating Random Observations from an Erlang Distribution This is the distribution of a sum of k random variables, each having an exponential distribution with expected value $1/k\alpha$. An observation is simulated by drawing k random numbers between 0 and 1, $r_1, r_2, \ldots, r_k$. The simulated value is

$$x = -(1/k\alpha) \ln \{ \prod_{i=1}^{k} r_i \} = -(1/ka) \{ \sum_{i=1}^{k} \ln r_i \}.$$

Generating Random Observations from a Normal Distribution A number which is approximately normally distributed can be obtained by adding several random variables taken from uniform distributions. Thus if we draw n random numbers between 0 and 1, $r_1, r_2, \ldots, r_n$. The simulated value is

$$x = \frac{\sigma}{(n/12)^{1/2}} \sum_{i=1}^{n} r_i + \{\mu - \frac{n\sigma}{2(n/12)^{1/2}}\},$$

where μ and σ are the mean and standard deviation of the normal distribution. The value of n determines the accuracy of the simulated distribution. A reasonable approximation is obtained with $n = 5$.

ALGORITHM

In the following we will describe an algorithm for simulating a multichannel finite queue. There are two modules to this program, one to simulate the interarrival times and one to simulate the service times. The algorithm will control the operation of the simulation and gather statistics.

The two driving events for this simulation are

- Arrival event — A customer will arrive and attempt to enter the system. The customer will balk if the system is full.
- Service event — A customer will complete service and leave the system.

The reaction of the system to these events depends on its current status, as indicated by these three numbers: number in service, number in the queue, and number in the system. Fig. 23.1 shows a chart of the three numbers obtained from a typical simulation of a single-channel queue. The number in service is shown as the black area on the bottom. The number in the queue is the dotted area above. The number in the system is the sum of the other two quantities and is shown by the envelope of the two curves. The numbers vary up and down in a random fashion as determined by the stochastic arrival and service processes. We describe the computational process by listing the logical rules that govern the effects of arrivals and services on these three numbers. The number of channels in the system is s and the maximum number in the system is N.

- If an arrival occurs when the system is full (the number in the system is N), the customer balks and the numbers do not change.
- If an arrival occurs when all servers are busy but the system is not full, the number in the queue and the number in the system increase by 1.
- If an arrival occurs when a server is idle, then the customer goes directly to a service channel; the number in the system and the number in service increase by 1, while the number in the queue remains at zero.
- If a service occurs when the queue is empty, the number in the system and the number in service decrease by 1, while the number in the queue remains at zero.
- If a service occurs when the queue is not empty, the number in the system and the number in the queue decrease by 1, while the number in service remains at s.

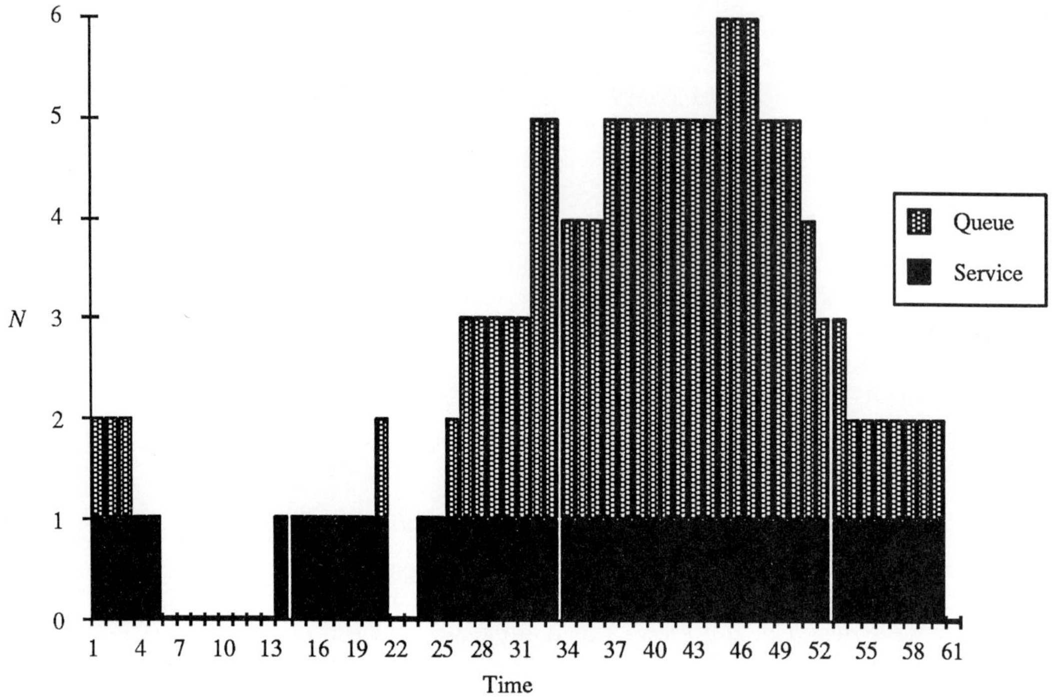

Figure 23.1 **Chart Showing the Results of a Typical Simulation Run**

- A service cannot occur when the system is empty.

We describe below how the multichannel queue simulation is implemented by the *Microsolve* program. The program uses randomly generated arrival and service times and a next-event simulation. Imminent events, such as the time to the next arrival and the time to service completion at each of the busy channels, drive the simulation. The simulated time advances in jumps to each event time in the order in which they occur. At each event time, the variations in the system numbers are computed using the logical rules above, and summary statistics are accumulated. When the simulated time reaches a specified maximum, the arrivals stop and the system is allowed to service the queue. When the queue is finally empty, the simulation terminates and average results are computed. This process will be illustrated in the examples.

In order to formalize the collection of statistics and the computation of average results, we will use the following notation.

System parameters:

s = number of channels
N = maximum number in the system
T = simulation time
n_0 = initial number in the system.

Statistics from the simulation:

T_f = Time when the last customer leaves the system (finish time)
n_a = Number of arrivals to the system, not including the initial number
n_b = Number of balks
A_s = Area under the number in service curve up to the simulation time
A_q = Area under the number in the queue curve up to the simulation time
F_s = Area under the number in service curve up to the finish time
F_q = Area under the number in the queue curve up to the finish time.

From the statistics we can compute the following estimates of the steady-state system characteristics. We use a prime to indicate that they are estimates. The computations for the average numbers in service and in the queue are based on the result that the average of a time-varying function over some time interval is the area under the function divided by the length of the interval. We use the simulation time for these computations to reduce the effects of the events at the end of the simulation. Thus we have

Average number in service: $L'_s = A_s/T.$
Average number in the queue: $L'_q = A_q/T.$
Average number in the system: $L' = L'_s + L'_q.$
Utilization: $\rho' = L'_s/s.$

The computations for the average times are based on the result that the average time is simply the total time divided by the number of individuals using the system. We use the finish time in these computations so that the full times for all arrivals are included. Thus we have

Average time in service: $W'_s = F_s/(n_a - n_b + n_o)$
Average time in the queue: $W'_q = F_q/(n_a - n_b + n_o)$
Average time in the system: $W = W'_s + W'_q.$

EXAMPLE

E23.1 To illustrate the procedure we simulate a single-channel queue for a time of 50 minutes. The input and service processes are Poisson. The mean time between arrivals is 5 minutes, and the mean time for service is 4 minutes. We assume that two customers are initially in the system. The maximum number in the system is 10.

The first step is to generate a number of customers, each with a simulated interarrival time and a time for service. The number of customers that will arrive during the interval is not strictly determined; however, the given average time between arrivals suggests that there will be 10 arrivals in the 50-minute simulation. The results of this activity are shown in Table 23.1.

Except for the first two, each customer has been assigned two random numbers to simulate the interarrival and service times. The first two customers are assumed to arrive at time zero, so they need only one random number. Since the interarrival

Table 23.1 **Simulated Interarrival and Service Times**

Customer number	*Random number*	*Interarrival time*	*Random number*	*Time for service*
1	—		0.525	2.58
2	—		0.544	2.44
3	0.068	13.44	0.149	7.62
4	0.292	6.15	0.978	0.09
5	0.483	3.64	0.094	9.45
6	0.642	2.21	0.842	0.69
7	0.967	0.17	0.034	13.58
8	0.367	5.01	0.482	2.92
9	0.976	0.12	0.813	0.83
10	0.700	1.78	0.605	2.01
11	0.487	3.60	0.172	7.04
12	0.224	7.47	0.903	0.41

times are exponentially distributed, they are generated using the formula given previously. The parameter α is the arrival rate, in this case 0.2. For instance, the interarrival time for the third customer is

$$x = -(1/\alpha) \ln (r) = -(5) \ln (0.068) = 13.44.$$

This is the simulated time interval between the arrival of the second customer (time 0) and the arrival of the third customer. The service time for the third customer is simulated in a similar fashion using the service rate (0.25) as α.

$$x = -(1/\alpha) \ln (r) = -(4) \ln (0.149) = 7.62.$$

The remainder of the customer data is simulated with the random numbers provided. We have selected three-digit random numbers rather arbitrarily. This allows 1000 different values of the simulated observations. One should add (.0005) to each of the random numbers to assure that the number 0 does not appear in the natural log function.

Once the simulated times are available, the next-event simulation can proceed. Table 23.2 provides a tabular format for keeping track of the important numbers. Each row shows the complete information requirement for the single-channel queue simulation at a given time. The first column is a sequence number. The second and third show the event times and the type of event that has occurred. Using the logical rules listed above, the numbers in the queue and service are computed and shown in the fourth and fifth columns. Finally, the last two columns list the next arrival time and next service completion time, respectively.

Whenever an arrival event occurs, the next arrival column changes. For instance consider line 4, which indicates that customer 3 has arrived at time 13.44. The next arrival time is found by adding the interarrival time of customer 4 to the current time (13.44 + 6.15 = 19.59). When the next arrival would occur beyond the simulation time, we put a large number as the next arrival time so that no additional arrivals will occur. If the service channel is empty when an arrival occurs

Table 23.2 **Steps in the Next-Event Simulation**

Number	*Time*	*Event*	*No. in service*	*No. in queue*	*Next arrival*	*Next service*
1	0	Initial (1, 2)	1	1	13.44	2.58
2	2.58	Service 1	1	0	13.44	5.02
3	5.02	Service 2	0	0	13.44	99999.00
4	13.44	Arrival 3	1	0	19.59	21.06
5	19.59	Arrival 4	1	1	23.23	21.06
6	21.06	Service 3	1	0	23.23	21.15
7	21.15	Service 4	0	0	23.23	99999.00
8	23.23	Arrival 5	1	0	25.44	32.68
9	25.44	Arrival 6	1	1	25.61	32.68
10	25.61	Arrival 7	1	2	30.62	32.68
11	30.62	Arrival 8	1	3	30.74	32.68
12	30.74	Arrival 9	1	4	32.53	32.68
13	32.53	Arrival 10	1	5	36.13	32.68
14	32.68	Service 5	1	4	36.13	33.37
15	33.37	Service 6	1	3	36.13	46.95
16	36.13	Arrival 11	1	4	43.60	46.95
17	43.6	Arrival 12	1	5	99999.00	46.95
18	46.95	Service 7	1	4	99999.00	49.87
19	49.87	Service 8	1	3	99999.00	50.70
20	50	End Sim.	1	3		
21	50.07	Service 9	1	2	99999.00	52.71
22	52.71	Service 10	1	1	99999.00	59.75
23	59.75	Service 11	1	0	99999.00	60.16
24	60.16	Service 12	0	0	99999.00	99999.00

(next service time is 99999), the time for the next service becomes the current time plus the service time for the arriving customer. The case is illustrated by line 8.

Whenever a service event occurs, the next service column changes. For instance in line 6 we have customer 3 completing service at time 21.06. Customer 4, who is in the queue, will then enter service. The next service time is found by adding the service time for customer 4 to the current time (21.06 + 0.09 = 21.15). If no customers are in the queue, as in lines 3 and 7, a large number appears as the next service time to show that no service is imminent.

For each line, the next event in the sequence is found by choosing the minimum of the next arrival time and the next service time. This determines the time and event for the next line of the table (this is the source of the name "next-event simulation").

The simulation results can be used to compute the averages that measure the performance of the system. The computations of the areas under the numbers in service and in the queue are shown in Table 23.3. The numbers in the last two columns are the incremental contributions to the areas since the last event. Thus the interval of time from line 10 to line 11 is (30.62 − 25.61)5.01. During this interval, the number in service is 1 and the number in the queue is 2. Thus we see

Table 23.3 **Computation of Areas**

Number	*Time*	*Event*	*No. in service*	*No. in queue*	*Service area*	*Queue area*
1	0	Initial	1	1		
2	2.58	Service	1	0	2.58	2.58
3	5.02	Service	0	0	2.44	0.00
4	13.44	Arrival	1	0	0.00	0.00
5	19.59	Arrival	1	1	6.15	0.00
6	21.06	Service	1	0	1.47	1.47
7	21.15	Service	0	0	0.09	0.00
8	23.23	Arrival	1	0	0.00	0.00
9	25.44	Arrival	1	1	2.21	0.00
10	25.61	Arrival	1	2	0.17	0.17
11	30.62	Arrival	1	3	5.01	10.02
12	30.74	Arrival	1	4	0.12	0.36
13	32.53	Arrival	1	5	1.79	7.16
14	32.68	Service	1	4	0.15	0.75
15	33.37	Service	1	3	0.69	2.76
16	36.13	Arrival	1	4	2.76	8.28
17	43.6	Arrival	1	5	7.47	29.88
18	46.95	Service	1	4	3.35	16.75
19	49.87	Service	1	3	2.92	11.68
20	50	End Sim.	1	3	0.13	0.39
21	50.07	Service	1	2	0.07	0.21
22	52.71	Service	1	1	2.64	5.28
23	59.75	Service	1	0	7.04	7.04
24	60.16	Service	0	0	0.41	0.00
Total area to simulation time (A_s and A_q)					39.50	92.25
Total area to end time (F_s and F_q)					49.66	104.78

in line 11 the incremental amounts of 5.01 and 10.02 added to the service area and queue area, respectively. The total areas are shown at the bottom of the chart.

The simulation statistics are calculated from the total areas under the curves.

Average number in service: $L'_s = A_s / T = 39.5/50 = 0.79$
Average number in the queue: $L'_q = A_q / T = 92.25/50 = 1.845$
Average number in the system: $L' = L'_s + L'_q = 0.79 + 1.845 = 2.635$
Utilization: $\rho' = L'_s / s = 0.79$
Average time in service: $W'_s = F_s/(n_a - n_b + n_o) = 49.66/12 = 4.14$
Average time in the queue: $W'_q = F_q/(n_a - n_b + n_o) = 104.78/12 = 8.73$
Average time in the system: $W' = W'_s + W'_q = 12.87.$

The average time between arrivals is the time of the last arrival divided by the number of arrivals in the interval, not including the initial number.

Average time between arrivals: 43.6 /10 = 4.36.

These are statistics with which the system can be evaluated. Remember that the simulation will yield different results with a different set of random numbers determining the interarrival and service times.

E23.2 Using the interarrival and service times of E23.1, simulate the system with two service channels.

Here we will modify Table 23.2 to add an extra column for the second service channel. The simulation is shown in Table 23.4. The arrivals and services are not identified by customer in this table, because this is not really necessary and it is sometimes difficult to keep track of which customers are in service at any particular time.

E23.3 Simulate the one-channel queue of E23.1, except let the maximum number in the system be two. An arrival will balk if two customers are already in the system.

The simulation table for this example is shown in Table 23.5. Arrivals 7, 8, 9, and 10 balk when they find the system full. The service times for these customers are not used since they never enter the system. An interesting statistic from a finite queue simulation is the proportion of customers who balk. For this case the proportion is (4/10) 0.4.

Table 23.4 **Simulation with Two Service Channels**

Number	*Time*	*Event*	*No. in service*	*No. in queue*	*Next arrival*	*Next serv. 1*	*Next serv. 2*
1	0	Initial (1, 2)	2	0	13.44	2.58	2.44
2	2.44	Service	1	0	13.44	2.58	99999.00
3	2.58	Service	0	0	13.44	99999.00	99999.00
4	13.44	Arrival	1	0	19.59	21.06	99999.00
5	19.59	Arrival	2	0	23.23	21.06	19.63
6	19.63	Service	1	0	23.23	21.15	99999.00
7	21.15	Service	0	0	23.23	99999.00	99999.00
8	23.23	Arrival	1	0	25.44	32.68	99999.00
9	25.44	Arrival	2	0	25.61	32.68	26.13
10	25.61	Arrival	2	1	30.62	32.68	26.13
11	26.13	Service	2	0	30.62	32.68	39.71
12	30.62	Arrival	2	1	30.74	32.68	39.71
13	30.74	Arrival	2	2	32.53	32.68	39.71
14	32.53	Arrival	2	3	36.13	32.68	39.71
15	32.68	Service	2	2	36.13	35.60	39.71
16	35.60	Service	2	1	36.13	36.43	39.71
17	36.13	Arrival	2	2	43.60	36.43	39.71
18	36.43	Service	2	1	43.60	38.44	39.71
19	38.44	Service	2	0	43.60	45.48	39.71
20	39.71	Service	1	0	43.60	45.48	99999.00
21	43.6	Arrival	2	0	99999.00	45.48	44.01
22	44.01	Service	1	0	99999.00	45.48	99999.00
23	45.48	Service	0	0	99999.00	99999.00	99999.00
24	50	End sim.	0	0			

Table 23.5 **Simulation with Balking**

Number	Time	Event	No. in service	No. in queue	Next arrival	Next service
1	0	Initial (1, 2)	1	1	13.44	2.58
2	2.58	Service 1	1	0	13.44	5.02
3	5.02	Service 2	0	0	13.44	99999.00
4	13.44	Arrival 3	1	0	19.59	21.06
5	19.59	Arrival 4	1	1	23.23	21.06
6	21.06	Service 3	1	0	23.23	21.15
7	21.15	Service 4	0	0	23.23	99999.00
8	23.23	Arrival 5	1	0	25.44	32.68
9	25.44	Arrival 6	1	1	25.61	32.68
10	25.61	Arrival 7-Balk	1	1	30.62	32.68
11	30.62	Arrival 8-Balk	1	1	30.74	32.68
12	30.74	Arrival 9-Balk	1	1	32.53	32.68
13	32.53	Arrival 10-Balk	1	1	36.13	32.68
14	32.68	Service 5	1	0	36.13	99999.00
15	33.37	Service 6	0	0	36.13	99999.00
16	36.13	Arrival 11	1	0	43.60	43.17
17	43.17	Service 11	0	0	43.60	99999.00
18	43.6	Arrival 12	1	0	99999.00	44.01
19	44.01	Service 12	0	0	99999.00	99999.00
20	50	End sim.	0	0		

E23.4 Using the five random numbers (0.068, 0.292, 0.483, 0.642, 0.967) simulate an observation from an approximately normal distribution with mean 20 and standard deviation 6. Using the formula given earlier, the simulated observation is

$$x = \frac{6}{(5/12)^{1/2}} \sum_{i=1}^{5} r_i + \{20 - \frac{(5)(6)}{2(5/12)^{1/2}}\} = 19.55.$$

Computer Programs

The Queue Simulation program in *Microsolve* implements the procedures described in this chapter for systems with as many as five channels. The maximum number in the system may range from the number of channels to 100. The simulation time should be less than 9000. The distributions of interarrival and service times may be specified as exponential, normal, or constant (not a random variable). All distribution parameters should be given in the same time dimensions. Since a counter shows integer time values, all distribution parameters should be normalized so that they are moderately sized numbers between 2 and 30. This will make a better display. Figures showing the output of the simulation program are provided in the "computer program" section of Chapter 16.

Random numbers used for the simulation come from the computer's built-in random number generator. The generator requires a "seed," which determines the sequence of random numbers obtained. The program asks for a seed as part of the simulation data. Any negative integer number may be entered; however, different seeds should be used for different replications of the simulation model.

The program generates random observations as they are needed rather than all at one time as shown in the examples. Thus two simulations with the same seed but with different system configurations will not have the same interarrival time or service time sequence. This makes it impossible to compare alternative systems with the same interarrival time and service time sequence.

For a given system, the program will give different results depending on the initial number in the system, the random number seed, and the simulation time. For the best estimation of steady-state measures, the initial number in the system should be set to the integer closest to long-run average value. Unfortunately this cannot be known prior to the simulation, but sample runs will provide some guidance. A long simulation time will reduce to some extent the effects of the initial conditions and also the approximation introduced by the procedures used at the end of the simulation run. Several independent runs with moderate simulation times are probably better than very long runs, because the former gives a better idea of the statistical variability of the results and allows the use of standard statistical methods. For proper interpretation, it is necessary to treat the output of a simulation run as a single observation from a population of possible results. Standard statistical techniques such as confidence limits and tests of hypotheses should be used to analyze multiple runs for a given model.

Problems

Some of the following problems require random numbers. When a random number is called for, use one of the three-digit groups from the list below.

005	192	941	720	596	206	233	711	909	994
624	684	748	187	069	399	527	291	388	965
599	081	086	757	758	345	845	664	775	645
914	326	213	101	662	263	784	995	347	006
344	986	776	312	512	435	160	014	255	349
799	812	863	992	680	589	143	858	958	662

P23.1 Simulate 12 service times from a population that is normally distributed with a mean of 4 minutes and a standard deviation of 1 minute. Use the first 48 random numbers given above with 4 random numbers for each simulation. If the simulated time is less than zero, replace it with zero.

P23.2 Compute the mean and standard deviation of the sample of service times simulated in P23.1. Compare them to the population mean and standard deviation ($\mu = 4$ and $\sigma = 1$).

P23.3 Using the same random numbers used in P23.1, simulate 12 observations

P23.4 Use the service times found in P23.1 to replace those in Table 23.1. With these numbers, simulate the single-channel queue described in E23.1. Compute the various statistics for this modified problem. Is the system better or worse when the service times have less variability? (The standard deviation of the exponential distribution is equal to its mean.)

P23.5 From the information shown in Table 23.4 for the two-channel queue, compute the areas under the number in service and number in queue charts as was done for the single-channel queue case in Table 23.3. From this information compute the evaluation statistics and compare the single-channel and two-channel systems.

P23.6 From the information shown in Table 23.5 for the single-channel finite queue, compute the areas under the number in service and number in queue charts as was done for the single-channel queue case in Table 23.3. From this information compute the evaluation statistics and observe the effect of limiting the queue size to one.

P23.7 Consider a network of two queueing systems in series. The two-channel system described in E23.2 is followed by a single-channel system with a mean service time of 3 minutes. The service times have an exponential distribution. The second system receives its inputs from the first system. Simulate the operation of the second system using the information from Table 23.4 to determine the inputs to this system. Use the last 12 random numbers from the table above to generate the simulated service times. Compute evaluation statistics for this network of queues.

P23.8 Simulate a two-channel queueing system, given the information below. The system has a finite queue. The maximum number of spaces in the queue is two. Customers arriving when the queue is full will balk. Of course the time for service given is irrelevant for a balking customer. Queue discipline is first-come-first-served. The first customer arrives at time zero. Compute queue statistics from the simulation.

Customer	*Time between arrivals*	*Time for service*
1	—	12
2	5	8
3	2	13
4	7	7
5	1	8
6	8	10
7	2	11
8	5	10
9	3	5
10	7	9

P23.9 Simulate a finite input source model as described in Sect. 16.6. The situation under consideration involves a machine shop with five machines. The failure rate of each machine while in operation is 0.1 per hour. When a machine fails, it is sent to the repair shop. The shop has a single-service channel with a repair rate of 0.3 per hour. The arrival rate to the shop is $0.1n$, where n is the number of machines currently operating. Simulate this system for 30 hours, starting with one machine already in the repair shop. Arrival and service processes are Poisson.

Computer Problems

P23.10 Use a computer program to simulate the single-channel queue of E23.1. Make 10 simulation runs, each using a simulation time of 200. Let the initial number in the system be 3 for each run. Record the average number in the system and the average time in the system for each run. For each statistic compute the mean and standard deviation over the sample of 10 observations. Assuming the statistics come from normal populations, use the t distribution to find confidence intervals for the true steady-state values of the mean number in the system and the mean time in the system. Compare the values found with the analytic steady-state solution found with queueing analysis. *Note:* The birth-death program of *Microsolve* computes analytic results.

P23.11 Repeat P23.10 with simulation times of 1000.

Problems P23.12 through P23.16 are design problems. Use the simulation program to analyze the situations and arrive at some answer. There are no "right" answers to these problems since there are several measures of effectiveness for the queueing systems. Show curves of the measures of performance against values of the decision variables. Run the programs several times for each parameter setting to determine the variability of the simulation results.

P23.12 A restaurant is open from 12 noon to 2 P.M. During this time customer groups arrive at random at an average rate of 6 per hour. Each group uses one table and spends an average of 0.5 hour at the table, with a standard deviation of 10 minutes (use a normal distribution). Seated customers may remain after 2 P.M. How many tables should be provided? If a waiter spends an average of 10 minutes with a customer (the time has an exponential distribution), how many waiters should be hired?

P23.13 A bank wants to determine how many drive-in windows to install and how much room to allow for waiting cars. If waiting cars exceed the space allowed, the police force them to move on. The average time between arrivals is 1 minute, and customers arrive at random. The average service time is 2.5 minutes with a standard deviation of 1 minute. This time has a normal distribution. Determine a policy for the bank.

P23.14 A shop currently has a machine with a highly variable processing time. The time has an exponential distribution with a mean time of 20 minutes. Jobs arrive to the machine irregularly at the rate of 2.5 per hour (the time between arrivals has an exponential distribution). Long queues have been noted at the machine. Management has been considering installing a second machine with the same characteristics to reduce the queue. An engineer has proposed that rather than purchase the second machine, a robot be installed with much less variability. In fact, the robot will require exactly 20 minutes for each processing operation. Analyze the two alternatives.

P23.15 A doctor can partially control the rate of arrivals at the office by keeping an appointment book. The average time required to treat a patient is 15 minutes. This time has an exponential distribution. The doctor can schedule the average time between arrivals, but whatever the choice, the standard deviation will be 5 minutes. Assume the interarrival time has a normal distribution. Discuss how the doctor should schedule arrivals. The doctor has four office hours each day and always makes sure that there are two patients available at the beginning of the period. The doctor must remain in the office until all scheduled arrivals are treated.

P23.16 A private airport has two busy periods in a day, 1 hour in the morning and 1 hour in the evening. During these times, the arrival rate is 12 per hour. Arrivals occur at random. A runway must be dedicated to an arriving plane for 10 minutes with a standard deviation of 3 minutes. How many runways should be provided?